Inspiration for Every Celebration!

Dear Friend,

As the new President of Wilton Enterprises, it's my pleasure to welcome you to the 2009 Wilton Yearbook. While the Yearbook has reflected many changes in cake decorating style since I joined the company 30 years ago, our dedication to making celebrations more fun will never change. As you will see in this edition, we are more committed than ever to bringing you exciting decorating ideas for unforgettable parties.

A great cake captures your guests' attention the moment they enter the room. That is what our Yearbook special section, *Desserts in 3-D!* is all about. The sensational animal party scene on our cover is a perfect example of a cake that is a spectacular dessert and becomes part of the fun. It's a bigger-than-life cupcake made in our Dimensions® pan, which bakes 2 layers that stack together to create that terrific 3-D shape. With a fondant bear popping from the top and stand-up animal cupcakes all around, it's a can't-miss birthday treat kids will never forget.

Many more incredible dimensional cakes are waiting for you in *Desserts in 3-D!* From the towering rocket ship on a launching pad to the dream doll house filled with fondant furniture, you'll be amazed at the exciting 3-dimensional cakes that will make your celebration the perfect party.

3-D cakes are just the start of the thrills in this 2009 Yearbook. Look for wonderful seasonal designs like the coconut and candy bird nests for spring and a snowman made entirely of spritz cookies. Find great theme birthday ideas with golf designs and popular new characters like Disney/Pixar's *WALL•E*. Or host a cupcake decorating party for kids, with easy designs that are fun for everyone to make.

Great wedding cakes are part of the Yearbook excitement as well. Look for the chocolate stairstep cake, with a richly-textured fondant carpet made with our new Imprint Mat. And don't miss our quilling flower cake, with looped pastel petals that bring lively color and a lighter-than-air look to the reception.

It's time to start a new year of decorating fun. Turn to the 2009 Yearbook to create your best celebrations for any occasion.

Marvin Oakes

Marvin Oakes
President
Wilton Enterprises

Cake Decorating

2009 WILTON YEARBOOK

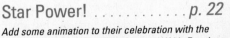

Wild Birthdays! . . . . p. 4

The best way to handle one more candle is to put it on an amazing cake! Find them here: A barrelful of fun monkeys, a fleet of pirate ships, a round of golf designs and so many more great party theme ideas.

Star Power! . . . . p. 22

Add some animation to their celebration with the characters kids love! New favorites WALL•E and Abby Cadabby join a great cast, including SpongeBob SquarePants as a cool cowpoke and Strawberry Shortcake playing a sweet guitar solo.

Holiday Heroes! . . . . p. 36

Your calendar is full of thrilling desserts. Dig our pretzel graveyard, bake cookies with the Clauses for Christmas and sew the Stars & Stripes with Betsy Ross for the perfect patriotic party cake.

Life's Landmarks . . . . p. 62

Cakes that deserve a great reception, including a torrent of umbrella designs for the baby shower, a fondant Christening carriage and an openwork Bar Mitzvah candy plaque.

Love Becomes Legend . . . p. 72

You're settling down, but you won't settle for an ordinary cake. Choose a design rich in detail—imprinted flowers in fondant, shimmering diamonds and pearls, looped pastel petals and more.

SPECIAL SECTION

Desserts in 3-D! . . . . p. 90

No special glasses required for these eye-popping cakes! They practically jump off the table to welcome your guests. See a 3-D pirate chest loaded with a trove of treats, a cupcake barn and circus tent, plus an enchanting tea table with graceful fondant chairs and umbrella.

Decorating Guide . . . . . . p. 110

It's easy to find the help you need! Our biggest guide ever includes step-by-step techniques, luscious recipes, construction guides and cutting charts, cookie and candy tips.

Product Shops . . . . p. 127

Everything you need to create the exciting ideas in this Yearbook! From decorating tips to famous Wilton bakeware, from character candles to elegant wedding ornaments, find it all here.

The Wilton School . . . . . . p. 238

The world's leading experts on cake decorating are waiting to teach you! Get class descriptions and schedules for courses throughout the year.

Index . . . . p. 239

CREATIVE DIRECTOR
Daniel Masini

ART DIRECTOR/CAKE DESIGNER
Steve Rocco

DECORATING ROOM SUPERVISOR
Cheryl Brown

SENIOR CAKE DECORATORS
Mary Gavenda
Susan Matusiak

CAKE DECORATORS
Jenny Jurewicz
Diane Knowlton
Mark Malak
Tracey Wurzinger
Debbie Friedman
Michele Poto

EDITOR/WRITER
Jeff Shankman

WRITER/COPY EDITOR
Jane Mikis

WRITERS
Mary Enochs
Marita Seiler

PRODUCTION MANAGER
Challis Yeager

ASSOCIATE PRODUCTION MANAGER
Mary Stahulak

GRAPHIC DESIGN/PRODUCTION
Deborah Casciato
RNB Graphics
Courtney Kieras

PHOTOGRAPHY
DeBolt Photography
Black Box Studios
Image Craft Chicago, Inc.
Alter

PHOTO STYLIST
Carey Thornton

CREATIVE SERVICES ASSISTANT
Sharon Gaeta

PRODUCT DEVELOPMENT/PUBLICATIONS
Tina Celeste

For photography purposes, many cakes in this book were decorated (by right- and left-handed decorators) with royal icing. Printed in U.S.A.

IN U.S.A.
Wilton Industries, Inc.
2240 West 75th Street, Woodridge, IL 60517
www.wilton.com

Retail Customer Orders:
Phone: 800-794-5866 • Fax: 888-824-9520
Online: www.wilton.com

Class Locations:
Phone: 800-942-8881
Online: www.wilton.com/classes/classlocator.cfm

IN CANADA
Wilton Industries Canada Company
98 Carrier Drive, Etobicoke, Ontario M9W5R1 Canada
Phone: 416-679-0790

Class Locations:
Phone: 416-679-0790, ext. 200
E-mail: classprograms@wilton.ca

¡SE HABLA ESPAÑOL!
Para mas informacion, marque 800-436-5778
In Mexico: www.wiltonmexico.com.mx

TINA

Wild Birthdays!

Let kids be kids! Throw a birthday bash filled with goodies that play to their imaginations. Take a pirate voyage with a cake carrying a boatload of swashbuckling skeletons, then land on an island of cupcakes bordered by a sea of candy-filled ships. Fulfill your princess' every wish, with a fairy tale cake topped by a candy plaque castle and surrounded by a court of colorful candy maidens. Or let the chimps do their tricks with cupcake gifts, swinging cookie pops and a dancing monkey cake. It's birthday fun the way nature intended!

Monkey Shines!

Pans: Monkey, p. 160; 14 x 2 in. Round, p. 153; Non-Stick Cookie Sheet, p. 150

Tips: 1, 3, 6, 12, p. 144

Colors:* Brown, Red-Red, Black, p. 134

Candy: Light Cocoa (4 pks.), White (2 pks.) Candy Melts®†, Primary and Garden Candy Color Sets, p. 166; Candy Melting Plate, p. 168; 8 in. Lollipop Sticks, p. 169

Recipe: Buttercream Icing, p. 116

Also: 2009 Pattern Book (Hat), p. 128; 101 Cookie Cutters Set, p. 164; Flowerful Medley Sprinkles, p. 136; 16 in. Tall Tier Cake Plate, Bottom Bolt, 7¾ in. Columns (2), Glue-On Plate Legs (6), Cake Corer Tube, p. 229; Cake Boards, p. 232; Parchment Triangles, p. 143; Cake Dividing Set, p. 137; curling ribbon, glue for plastic, waxed paper, ruler, toothpicks

In advance: Mold monkey candy plaque, candy monkey faces, name and balloons (p. 126). **Also:** Attach lollipop sticks to back of balloons and letters using melted candy. **And:** Glue 6 legs onto bottom of 16 in. plate.

Prepare 2-layer round cake for Center Column Construction (p. 115). Ice smooth; position on 16 in. plate. Insert plastic dowel rods in cake where candy plaque will rest. Pipe details using buttercream icing. Use tip 6 to pipe highlights on balloons, top and bottom bead borders and pull-out dot fringe on hat brim and top. Attach confetti from Flowerful Medley assortment to hat. Divide cake into 12ths. Attach monkey heads to cake sides with icing. Pipe tip 12 bodies (pat smooth with finger dipped in cornstarch). Use tip 3 to pipe muzzle, ears and belly (pat smooth), arms, fingers, legs, feet and tail. Use tip 1 to pipe facial features and hat fringe. Attach confetti to cake sides. Assemble candy pieces using melted candy. Attach monkey plaque to center columns; hold until set. Attach balloons to back of monkey. Attach 18 in. lengths of ribbon from back of balloons to hand. Insert letters. Serves 63.

*Combine Brown with Red-Red and a little Black for brown icing shown.

Chipper Chimp

Pans: Mini Ball, p. 161; Cookie Sheet, Cooling Grid, p. 154

Tips: 2, 3, 5, p. 144

Colors:* Brown, Red-Red, Black, Lemon Yellow, Leaf Green, p. 134

Recipes: Buttercream Icing, Roll-Out Cookies, p. 116

Also: 2009 Pattern Book (Hat, Ears), p. 128; Flowerful Medley Sprinkles, p.136; knife, cornstarch

In advance: Make cookies. Prepare dough and roll out. Use patterns to cut 2 hats and 2 ears for each treat. Bake and cool cookies.

Bake and cool mini ball cake; ice smooth. Use tip 5 to outline and fill in muzzle (pat smooth with finger dipped in cornstarch). Use tip 3 to pipe dot eyes and nose; pipe tip 2 outline mouth. Sandwich hat cookies together with icing; ice top cookie smooth. Ice ears smooth; outline and pipe in inner ears using tip 5 (pat smooth). Attach ears and hat to head with icing. Attach confetti to hat with dots of icing. Pipe tip 3 pull-out dot fringe on hat brim and tip. Each serves 1.

*Combine Brown with Red-Red for brown shown.

Monkeys Get Funky!

Pan: Standard Muffin, p. 154

Tips: 1, 2, 2A, p. 144

Colors:* Brown, Red-Red, Black, Leaf Green, Lemon Yellow, Rose, p. 134

Fondant: White Ready-To-Use Rolled Fondant, Brush Set, p. 130; Rolling Pin, Roll & Cut Mat, Gum-Tex™, p. 133

Candy: White Candy Melts®†, Primary Candy Color Set, p. 166; Candy Melting Plate, p. 168; Party Time Lollipop Mold, p. 167; 4 in. Lollipop Sticks, p. 169

Recipes: Buttercream, Royal Icings, p. 116

Also: Dazzling Dots Standard Baking Cups, p. 189; Flowerful Medley Sprinkles, p. 136; Meringue Powder, p. 135; Decorator Brush Set, p. 168 or Parchment Triangles, p. 143; Cake Boards, p. 232; waxed paper

In advance: Mold package candies in candy mold using painting or piping method (p. 125). **Also:** Make fondant monkeys (p. 121).

Spatula ice cupcakes. Sprinkle with confetti. Insert monkeys. Each serves 1.

*Combine Brown with Red-Red for brown shown. Combine Leaf Green with Lemon Yellow for green shown.

In the Birthday Swing!

Pans: Round Cookie Treat, p. 163; Cookie Sheet, Cooling Grid, p. 154

Tips: 2, 2A, 3, 5, 352, p. 144-145

Colors:* Brown, Red-Red, Leaf Green, Lemon Yellow, Rose, Royal Blue, Black, p. 134

Recipes: Royal Icing, Roll-Out Cookies, p. 116

Also: Mini Geometric Crinkle Cutter Set, p. 165; 6 in. Cookie Treat Sticks, p. 163; Party Time Icing Decorations, p. 184; Cake Board, p. 232; Meringue Powder, p. 135; waxed paper, green curling ribbon, double-stick tape, cornstarch

In advance: Make monkey's head and gift bows on waxed paper-covered cake board (p. 121). **Also:** Make cookies. Prepare dough and roll out. Cut gifts using square crinkle cutter. Press remaining dough into cookie treat pan with cookie stick. Bake and cool cookies. **And:** Decorate cookies. Position round cookie on cooling grid over cookie sheet; cover with thinned royal icing (p. 124) and let dry. Ice gift cookie smooth with royal icing; pipe tip 3 outline ribbon. Let dry.

Use tip 3 to pipe outline vine on round cookie; attach head. Pipe tip 2A ball body (flatten and smooth) and tip 5 outline arm and legs; attach gift. Pipe tip 2 fingers and toes. Pipe tip 3 tail. Wind curling ribbon around cookie stick; tape to secure. Pipe tip 352 leaves on vine and stick; let dry. Each serves 1.

*Combine Brown with Red-Red for brown shown.

†Brand confectionery coating.

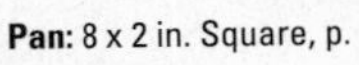

◀ Party in a Package!

Pan: 8 x 2 in. Square, p. 153

Tip: 2, p. 144

Colors:* Violet, Rose, Lemon Yellow, Golden Yellow, p. 134

Fondant: White Ready-To-Use Rolled Fondant (48 oz.), Neon Colors Fondant Multi Pack, White Pearl Dust™, Fine Tip FoodWriter Edible™ Color Markers, Brush Set, p. 130; Easy-Glide Fondant Smoother, Gum-Tex™, p. 131; Rolling Pin; Roll & Cut Mat, p. 133

Recipe: Buttercream Icing, p. 116

Also: 2009 Pattern Book (Bow), p. 128; Flowerful Medley Sprinkles, p. 136; 6 in. Cookie Treat Sticks, p. 163; Cake Board, Fanci-Foil Wrap, p. 232

2 days in advance: Make fondant bow. Tint 6 oz. fondant yellow; add ½ teaspoon Gum-Tex. Roll out fondant ⅛ in. thick. Using pattern, cut out entire bow, additional center bow loop and knot. Attach additional center loop to bow with damp brush. Cut ¼ in. wide strips for bow overlay trim and attach in a loop shape. Attach knot; let dry. Brush bow with Pearl Dust. Reserve remaining yellow fondant.

Bake and cool 2-layer cake (bake two 1½ in. layers for a 3 in. high cake); prepare for rolled fondant (p. 117). Tint fondant violet and cover cake; smooth with Fondant Smoother. Roll out remaining yellow fondant ⅛ in. thick. Cut a 14 x 1 in. wide ribbon strip; attach to center of cake with damp brush and brush with Pearl Dust. Roll out neon fondant ⅛ in. thick. Cut balloons using wide end of tip 2; roll very thin logs for strings. Cut ¾ in. triangles for hats; roll small balls for pompoms and ⅛ in. logs for fringe. Attach balloons and hats to cake with damp brush. Attach confetti sprinkles from Flowerful Medley assortment with dots of icing. For tag, roll out white fondant ⅛ in. thick. Cut 2 x 3 in. rectangle; write message using FoodWriter. Position on cake; attach ⅛ in. wide strip for tie. Serves 20.

*Combine Violet with Rose for violet shown. Combine Lemon Yellow with Golden Yellow for yellow shown.

▼ A Piece of Perfection

Pan: 14 x 2 in. Round, p. 153

Tips: 4, 5, 7, 12, 18, 21, 32, 789, p. 144-145

Colors: Lemon Yellow, Golden Yellow, Royal Blue, Rose, Violet, Leaf Green, p. 134

Fondant: White Ready-To-Use Rolled Fondant (18 oz.), p. 130; Cutter/Embosser, Brush Set, p. 131; Rolling Pin, Roll & Cut Mat, p. 133

Recipes: Buttercream, Chocolate Buttercream Icings, p. 116

Also: Cake Dividing Set, p. 137; Plastic, Wooden Dowel Rods, p. 231; 12 in. Cake Circles, Cake Boards, Fanci-Foil Wrap, p. 232; Piping Gel, p. 135; Jumbo Confetti Sprinkles, p. 136; paper towels, waxed paper, ruler, knife, black shoestring licorice, cornstarch

In advance: Prepare board. Tape 2 cake circles together; wrap with foil and cover with fondant (p. 124). **Also:** Prepare candle. Cut plastic dowel rod to 8 in. high. Tint 1 oz. fondant rose; roll out ⅛ in. thick. Cut a ¼ x 10 in. long strip. Attach around top 4½ in. of dowel rod with damp brush for spiral stripe. Position small amount of white fondant over top and shape to form side drips. Tint small amount of fondant Golden Yellow; roll out ¼ in. thick. Cut 1 in. high flame. Cut a small piece of licorice for wick; insert wick in flame and flame in candle.

Bake and cool 1-layer cake. Divide and cut into 6ths (2 sections will not be used). Fill and stack 4 sections into two 2-layer cakes; prepare for Stacked Construction (p. 114). Place each 2-layer cake on a cut-to-fit cake board; fill and stack for a single cake 8 in. high. Sharpen wooden dowel rod and push through all layers.

Use tip 789 and Chocolate Buttercream to ice 2 straight sides. Sponge on texture (p. 120). Use tip 12 to pipe center filling (pat smooth with finger dipped in cornstarch). Ice cake top and rounded side with a thick layer of icing; smooth. Position cake on prepared board. Pipe tip 7 icing drips along top of straight sides (pat smooth). Decorate rounded side with tip 4, tip 5 and tip 18 zigzag garlands, 1½, 3¼ and 4½ in. deep. Pipe tip 21 shell top border and tip 32 shell bottom border on curved side. Insert candle; pipe tip 21 ring around base. Position confetti. Serves 22.

▲ His Star is Rising!

Pans: Cookie Sheet, Cooling Grid, p. 154

Tip: 2, p. 144

Colors:* Royal Blue, Leaf Green, Red-Red, Christmas Red, Orange, Violet, Rose, Lemon Yellow, Golden Yellow, p. 134

Fondant: White Ready-To-Use Rolled Fondant (24 oz.), p. 130; Gum-Tex™, Rolling Pin, Roll & Cut Mat, p. 133

Recipes: Buttercream Icing, Roll-Out Cookies, p. 116

Also: Pastel Silicone Baking Cups (2 sets), p. 210; 19 Count Cupcakes 'N More® Dessert Stand, p. 147; Stars Plastic Nesting Cutter Set, p. 164; Yellow Cake Sparkles™, Jumbo Confetti Sprinkles, p. 136; Wooden Dowel Rods, p. 231; knife

In advance: Make fondant curliques (p. 124). Add 2 teaspoons of Gum-Tex to fondant. Tint 4 oz. fondant each: blue, green, red, violet and orange. Roll out ⅛ in. thick. Make 19 curliques in each color, cutting 6 x ⅛ in. wide strips. Make extras to allow for breakage and let dry. **Also:** Make cookie stars. Prepare dough and roll out. Cut 18 stars using 2nd smallest star cutter and 1 star using 4th largest star cutter. Bake and cool. Bake and cool cupcakes in silicone cups supported by cookie sheet. Ice cookies and cupcake smooth in buttercream. Sprinkle cookies with Cake Sparkles. Using tip 2, print name on largest cookie. Position cupcakes on stand. Position confetti sprinkles; insert curliques and cookies. Each serves 1.

*Combine Red-Red with Christmas Red for red shown. Combine Violet with Rose for violet shown. Combine Lemon Yellow with Golden Yellow for yellow shown.

▶ It's Fun Being #1!

Pans: Oval Pan Set (2 largest pans used), p. 153; #1, p. 159

Tips: 2, 3, 6, 8, 12, 13, 101, p. 144-145

Colors:* Sky Blue, Leaf Green, Orange, Violet, Rose, Lemon Yellow, Red-Red, Black, p. 134

Candy: White Candy Melts®† (3 pks.), Primary Candy Color Set, p. 166; Candy Melting Plate, 4 in. Lollipop Sticks, p. 169

Recipes: Buttercream, Royal Icings, p. 116

Also: Cake Boards, Fanci-Foil Wrap, p. 232; Wooden, Plastic Dowel Rods, p. 231; Meringue Powder, p. 135; Jumbo Confetti Sprinkles, p. 136; waxed paper, toothpicks, ruler, bubble wrap, cornstarch

Several days in advance: Make clown heads. Tint portion of melted candy using orange candy color. Mold heads in candy melting plate; refrigerate until firm then unmold. Attach lollipop sticks to backs with melted candy. **Also:** Mold candy plaque in #1 cake pan using 2 pks. melted white candy (p. 126). Attach confetti to border using melted candy dots. **And:** Pipe royal icing clowns (p. 121). Let dry for 2 days. **Later:** Set plaque face down on board cushioned with bubble wrap. Use melted candy to attach 2 plastic dowel rods to candy plaque, 1 in. from narrow side edges with 2 in. exposed at the bottom. Reinforce back of clowns with tip 6 and royal icing. Let set several hours.

Bake and cool 1-layer cakes using 2 largest ovals from set. Ice smooth and prepare for Stacked Construction (p. 114). Beginning in back, mark cake edge for garlands 3 in. apart on top cake, 3¾ in. apart on bottom cake. Pipe tip 3 double drop strings, ¾ and 1 in. deep, between marks. Pipe tip 12 balls for balloons (smooth with finger dipped in cornstarch). Pipe tip 8 bead bottom borders. Pipe name with tip 6. Lightly mark where plaque dowel rods will go into cake. Sharpen 2 wooden dowel rods and push through both cakes at marks. Position plaque by sliding plastic dowel rods over wooden rods and through top cake. Serves 37.

*Combine Violet with Rose for violet shown.

†Brand confectionery coating.

▲ One for My Baby ▶

Pans: #1, p. 159; Cookie Sheet, Cooling Grid, p. 154

Tips: 2, 3, 21, p. 144-145

Colors: Royal Blue, Rose, Violet, Brown, Copper (for skin tone shown), Black, Lemon Yellow, p. 134

Fondant: White Ready-To-Use Rolled Fondant (24 oz. for each cake), Brush Set, p. 130; Rolling Pin, Roll & Cut Mat, p. 133; Cutter/Embosser, p. 131; Square, Alphabet/Numbers Cut-Outs™, p. 132

Recipes: Buttercream, Royal Icings, Roll-Out Cookies, p. 116

Also: 101 Cookie Cutters Set, p. 164; Cake Boards, Fanci-Foil Wrap, p. 232; Meringue Powder, p. 135; tape, knife, cornstarch, waxed paper

In advance: Make cookies. Prepare dough and tint a portion light copper; roll out. Cut smallest bear using plain dough and largest boy or girl using tinted dough. Bake and cool cookies. **Also:** Tint 5 oz. fondant rose or blue. Roll out a small amount ⅛ in. thick. Cut a 1 x ¾ in. wide triangle for bear's hat; let dry on cornstarch-dusted board. Reserve remaining fondant.

Decorate cookies using royal icing. Set cookies on waxed paper-covered board. **For bear:** Outline and pipe-in bear (pat smooth with finger dipped in cornstarch). Use tip 3 to pipe dot muzzle (pat smooth); outline and fill in bib. Use tip 2 to pipe dot eyes, outline mouth and bib outline, string and scallops. Use tip 2 to fill in ears, pipe number, attach hat and pipe pull-out dot fringe. **For boy:** Use tip 3 to outline and fill in shirt, overalls and hat (pat smooth). Use tip 2 to pipe facial features, hat outlines, dot buttons and zigzag cuffs. **For girl:** Use tip 3 to outline and fill in shirt, jumper and collar. Use tip 2 to pipe facial features, curly hair, shirt collar and dots on skirt (pat smooth). Pipe tip 3 shoes (pat smooth) and bow in hair.

Ice cake smooth with buttercream. Pipe tip 21 shell bottom border. Roll out white and reserved tinted fondant ⅛ in. thick. Cut squares using smallest Cut-Out. Attach to edge of cake top with dots of icing, alternating colors and trimming as needed to fit curves. Cut name using alphabet cutters; position on cake. Position cookies. Cake serves 12; each cookie serves 1.

BRITTANY

▶ Long on Birthday Fun

Pans: Sports Ball Set, First and Ten Football, Mini Ball, p. 161; Cooling Grid, p. 154

Tips: 3, 16, p. 144-145

Colors:* Lemon Yellow, Golden Yellow, Red-Red, Christmas Red, Sky Blue, Violet, Rose, Leaf Green, p. 134

Fondant: White Ready-To-Use Rolled Fondant, p. 130; Rolling Pin, Roll & Cut Mat, p. 133; Cutter/Embosser, p. 131

Candy: White Candy Melts®†, p. 166; Decorator Brush Set, p. 168; 4 in. Lollipop Sticks, p. 169

Recipes: Buttercream Icing, Roll Out Cookies, p. 116

Also: 2009 Pattern Book (Giraffe Neck, Feet, Ears), p. 128; Cake Board, Fanci-Foil Wrap, p. 232; Piping Gel, p. 135; 8 in. Angled Spatula, p. 138; sugar ice cream cone, blue candy-coated chocolate dots, knife, foamcore board (½ in. thick)

In advance: Prepare base board using ½ sports ball and football pans with neck and leg patterns for size. Cut to fit and wrap with foil.

Bake and cool ½ sports ball cake, football cake, mini ball cake. Trim ½ in. off bottom of mini ball cake where neck will attach, 1½ in. off each pointed side of football cake to round for body. Prepare cookie dough and roll out. Using patterns, cut 3 necks, 4 legs and 2 ears; bake and cool. Attach lollipop sticks to upper back side of 2 legs and to backs of ears with melted candy. Sandwich 3 neck cookies together with melted candy. On base board, assemble giraffe by arranging football cake body, cookie neck, ½ sports ball cake head, mini ball cake muzzle and 2 cookie legs (without sticks). Attach pieces together with icing.

Using tip 3, pipe in nose and mouth. Using spatula, ice inner ears smooth. Cover spots, muzzle, hooves and giraffe's body and head with tip 16 stars. Cover cookie legs on sticks and edge of ear cookies with tip 16 stars; insert into cake. Tint fondant violet, blue, orange and green. For hat, cut ice cream cone to 4½ in. Brush cone lightly with piping gel. Roll out violet fondant ⅛ in. thick and cut a 4½ x 6 in. strip; wrap around cone, trim to fit. For fringe, roll out green fondant ⅛ in. thick. Cut a 2½ x ¾ in. wide strip; cut slits on one long edge and roll up. Attach to tip of hat with melted candy. Cut fringe for bottom of hat as above, using a 5½ x ¾ in. wide strip; attach. Add 2-3 rows of fringe as needed. Cut number for age; attach to hat with damp brush. For 2 horns, roll out sky blue fondant ⅛ in. thick; wrap around 1½ in. of lollipop stick. Roll ¾ in. ball and insert on stick.

Attach hat and candy-coated chocolate dot eyes with icing. Insert horns. For tail, roll a rope of fondant ½ x 5½ in. long; attach. Roll out orange fondant ⅛ in. thick. Cut fringe same as for top of hat. Attach with damp brush. Cakes serve 18; each cookie serves 1.

*Combine Red-Red with Christmas Red for red shown. Combine Leaf Green with Lemon Yellow for green shown. Combine Violet with Rose for violet shown.

†Brand confectionery coating.

▶ Mane Attraction

Pans: Dancing Daisy, p. 157; Soccer Ball, p. 161; Mini Loaf, Cookie Sheet, Cooling Grid, p. 154

Tips: 4, 5, 12, p. 144

Colors:* Golden Yellow, Orange, Royal Blue, Violet, Rose, Brown, Red-Red, p. 134

Recipes: Buttercream Icing, Roll-Out Cookies, p. 116

Also: 2009 Pattern Book (Hat), p. 128; Orange Candy Melts®†, p. 166; Cake Circles, Fanci-Foil Wrap, p. 132; Large Cake Leveler, p. 141; cornstarch, solid vegetable shortening, cheese plane or potato peeler, ruler, knife

In advance: Make candy curls (p. 125). **Also:** Make cookie hat. Prepare dough and roll out. Use pattern to cut out hat. Bake and cool. **And:** Cut a cake board 2 in. larger than Daisy Pan. Wrap with foil (p. 110).

Bake and cool Daisy cake and Soccer Ball. Use Cake Leveler to trim bottom off Soccer Ball cake to make round face 2½ in. deep. Stack cakes on prepared board. Ice smooth face and ear areas with yellow; ice remainder of cake orange. Use tip 12 to outline ears and build up nose (pat smooth with finger dipped in cornstarch). Using tip 5, outline and fill in nose section; pipe dot eyes and outline mouth. Position candy curls. Ice cookie hat smooth; position on cake. Use tip 4 to pipe age; add pull-out dot fringe on brim and tip. Serves 24.

*Combine Violet with Rose for violet shown.
Combine Brown with Red-Red for brown shown.

◀ A Birthday to Roar For!

Pans: Animal Crackers, p. 160; Cookie Sheet, Cooling Grid, p. 154

Tips: 4, 5, 14, 16, p. 144-145

Colors:* Orange, Sky Blue, Violet, Rose, Black, p. 134

Recipes: Buttercream Icing, Roll-Out Cookies, p. 116

Also: 2009 Pattern Book (Hat), p. 128; 6 in. Cookie Treat Sticks, p. 163; Cake Board, Fanci-Foil Wrap, p. 232, knife

In advance: Make cookie hat. Prepare dough and roll out. Use pattern to cut hat; position on cookie sheet over cookie stick, leaving 3 in. of stick exposed. Bake and cool.

Bake and cool cake. Ice inside mouth and ears smooth. Use tip 5 to outline mouth and pipe in eyes and nose (smooth with finger dipped in cornstarch). Cover cake with tip 16 stars. Ice hat cookie smooth and print tip 4 numeral. Insert cookie on top of head. Pipe tip 14 pull-out pompom and hat fringe. Serves 12.

*Combine Violet and Rose for violet shown.

▲ Raptorous Reception

Pans: Dinosaur, p. 160; Cookie Sheet, Cooling Grid, p. 154
Tips: 1, 3, 6, 16, 20, p. 144-145
Colors:* Orange, Lemon Yellow, Golden Yellow, Violet, Rose, Leaf Green, Black, Royal Blue, p. 134
Recipes: Buttercream Icing, Roll-Out Cookies, p. 116
Also: 2009 Pattern Book (Party Hat, Horn, Gift, Message Burst), p. 128; 6 in. Cookie Treat Sticks, p. 163; White Candy Melts®†, p. 166; Rolling Pin, p. 133; Flowerful Medley Sprinkles, p. 136; Cake Board, Fanci-Foil Wrap, p. 232; white cardstock, black fine-tip marker

In advance: Prepare cookie dough and roll out. Cut hat, horn and gift using patterns; bake and cool. Ice cookies smooth. Pipe tip 6 stripes on horn and gift. Using pattern, cut message burst from cardstock; print message with marker.

Bake and cool cake. Ice sides and background areas smooth. Use tip 3 to outline dinosaur and features (front arm will be added later); pipe in eye, pupil, nostrils, mouth and teeth (smooth all with finger dipped in cornstarch). Cover dinosaur and spikes with tip 16 stars. Attach cookie sticks to the backs of hat and horn with melted candy; let set. Insert hat into cake; pipe tip 6 dots, pull-out fringe and pompom. Attach message burst to lollipop stick on back of horn with dots of melted candy; insert. Position gift cookie on cake, outline arm and pipe in claw with tip 3; fill in arm with tip 16 stars (overpipe for dimension). Use tip 3 to pipe in gift tag; print tip 1 message. Pipe tip 20 shell bottom border; attach confetti from Flowerful Medley assortment to cake sides with dots of icing. Serves 12.

*Combine Lemon Yellow and Golden Yellow for yellow shown. Combine Violet and Rose for violet shown.

†Brand confectionery coating.

NICHOLAS

▶ Volcanic, Jurassic Treats

Pans: Mini Wonder Mold, p. 156; Standard Muffin, p. 154
Tips: 5, 233, p. 144-145
Color: Leaf Green, p. 134
Recipes: Buttercream Icing, p. 116; favorite cocoa-flavored crisped rice cereal treats
Also: 2009 Pattern Book (Cloud), p. 128; Dinosaur Party Set (5 sets), p. 192; 19 Count Standard Cupcakes 'N More® Dessert Stand, p. 147; White Candy Melts®†, p. 166; White Standard Baking Cups, p. 189; 6 in. Cookie Treat Sticks, p. 163; Flower Forming Cups, p. 131; Flowerful Medley Sprinkles, p. 136; Red, Orange Tube Decorating Gels, p. 134; Parchment Triangles, p. 143; card stock, black marker, granulated sugar, spearmint leaves, pretzel sticks, knife, scissors, tape

In advance: Make 18 palm trees (p. 122). **Also:** Use pattern to cut out cloud. Print message. Attach cookie stick to back with tape. **And:** Prepare cereal treats for volcano. Press into greased Mini Wonder Mold cavities; remove immediately. Insert cookie stick into top where message will go; remove.

Bake and cool cupcakes; ice smooth. Pipe tip 233 pull-out grass; sprinkle on confetti from Flowerful Medley assortment. Use tip 5 to pipe icing lava onto volcano top; overpipe with Decorating Gels. At party, position cupcakes and volcano on stand. Insert message; position trees and toppers. Each serves 1.

Instructions at bottom right.

◀ Dinosaur Spotted!

Pans: 18 x 3 in. Half Round, p. 152; Non-Stick Cookie Sheet, Cooling Grid, p. 154
Tips: 4, 9, 18, 21, p. 144-145
Colors:* Violet, Rose, Leaf Green, Black, p. 134
Candy: White Candy Melts®† (1 pk.), Garden Candy Colors Set, p. 166; 8 in. Lollipop Sticks, p. 169
Recipes: Buttercream Icing, Roll-Out Cookies, p. 116
Also: 2009 Pattern Book (Dinosaur Head, Neck, Legs, Foot, Tail and Diagram), p. 128; Round Cut-Outs™, p. 132; Fanci-Foil Wrap, p. 232; 24 x 18 x ¼ in. foamcore board, knife, ruler, large marshmallows, toothpicks, cornstarch

In advance: Make cookies. Prepare dough and roll out. Use patterns to cut out head, neck, front and back legs, feet (2) and tail. Bake and cool cookies. **Also:** Make candy spikes. Melt and tint candy. Mold rounds by placing Cut-Outs™ on cookie sheet and filling ¼ in. deep with melted candy. Refrigerate until firm; unmold. Make 10 using large round, 4 using medium round from set.

Bake and cool 1-layer cake. Refer to diagram in Pattern Book; position cake on board allowing room to add cookie pieces. Ice sides smooth; pipe tip 21 star bottom border. Use icing to attach head to cake, 2 bottom feet to board. Use melted candy to attach lollipop sticks to backs of remaining cookies, leaving 2 to 3 in. exposed to insert into cake (refer to diagram). Attach cookie pieces, propping up with marshmallows as needed. Use toothpick to mark spots. Outline body and other details with tip 4; fill in toenails and nostrils. Use tip 9 to fill in eyes (pat smooth with finger dipped in cornstarch); pipe tip 4 dot pupils. Cover cake and cookies with tip 18 stars. Use warm knife to cut spikes to fit curve of cake, beginning at tail. Attach a lollipop stick to backs with melted candy; insert into cake, trimming sticks if needed. Pipe tip 9 name. Serves 55.

*Combine Violet with Rose for violet shown.

▼ T-Rex Team

Pans: Cookie Sheet, Cooling Grid, p. 154
Tips: 2, 14, 352, p. 144-145
Colors: Rose, Royal Blue, Golden Yellow, Black, p. 134
Recipes: Buttercream Icing, Roll-Out Cookies, p. 116
Also: 2009 Pattern Book (Head, Tail), p. 128; Silly-Critters! Silicone Baking Cups, p. 148; Rolling Pin, p. 133, cornstarch

In advance: Prepare dough and roll out. Use patterns to cut one head and tail for each cupcake. Bake and cool cookies.

Bake and cool cupcakes in silicone cups supported by cookie sheet. Insert head and tail cookies into cupcakes. Outline mouth with tip 2. Pipe tip 14 stars on body, head and tail. Pipe tip 352 pull-out spikes. Pipe tip 2 dot eyes (smooth with finger dipped in cornstarch), pupils and nostrils. Each serves 1.

▲ A Royal Rainbow

Pans: Enchanted Castle, p. 157; Oval Set (2 largest pans used), p. 153; Jumbo Muffin, p. 154

Tips: 2, 3, 224, 233, p. 144-145

Colors: Kelly Green, Rose, p. 134

Candy: White (9 pks.), Light Cocoa (1 pk.) Candy Melts®†, Primary and Garden Candy Color Sets, p. 166; Wedding Shower Lollipop and Fairy Tale Large Lollipop Molds, p. 167

Recipes: Buttercream, Royal Icings, p. 116

Also: Meringue Powder, p. 135; Plastic Dowel Rods, p. 231; Decorator Brush Set, p. 168 or Parchment Triangles, p. 143; Cake Boards, p. 232; 18½ x 14½ x ½ in. foamcore board, waxed paper

In advance: Make 45 royal icing drop flowers using tip 224; add tip 3 dot centers. Let dry. **Also:** Make candy plaque (p. 126) using Enchanted Castle Pan and 18 oz. white candy and 10 oz. candy tinted violet. Make oval candy plaque, ¼ in. thick, using 2nd largest oval pan and 2 pkgs. melted white candy tinted green. Refrigerate until firm; unmold. Mold 5 birds using Wedding Shower mold and painting or piping method (p. 125). Attach birds to candy castle using melted candy. Using royal icing, pipe tip 3 dots around door and tip 2 dots around windows; pipe tip 3 outline window sills. **And:** Make 15 princesses in Fairy Tale mold without sticks using painting or piping method and 3 pkgs. of melted candy in various tinted colors. Mold ¼ in. thick bases in muffin pan with 2 pkgs. melted white candy tinted green. Later, attach each princess to a base using melted candy.

Bake and cool 1-layer cake using largest oval pan. Position on foil-wrapped foamcore board. Ice smooth. Cut and insert dowel rods where candy base will sit. Use warm knife to level bottom of candy castle. Cut 3 dowel rods to fit behind 3 tallest turrets; attach with melted candy and refrigerate until firm. Divide cake into 12ths. Pipe tip 3 double drop strings, ¾ and 1 in. deep, between marks. Attach drop flowers at points. Pipe tip 233 pull-out grass bottom border. Position candy oval on cake; attach candy castle with melted candy (hold upright until set). Attach drop flowers at castle base with icing. Position princesses. Cake serves 22; each princess serves 1.

▶ Accessorize the Princess

Pans: Oval Set (2 largest pans used), p. 153; Crown, p. 157
Tips: 2, 7, p. 144
Color: Rose, p. 134
Fondant: White Ready-To-Use Rolled Fondant (96 oz.), Brush Set, White Pearl Dust™, p. 130; Easy-Glide Fondant Smoother, Cutter/Embosser, p. 131; Letters & Numbers Gum Paste & Fondant Mold Set, Heart Cut-Outs™, p. 132; Rolling Pin, Roll & Cut Mat, p. 133
Candy: White Candy Melts®† (3 pks.), Garden Candy Color Set (pink), p. 166; Roses in Bloom Candy Mold, p. 167; Roses Candy Mold, p. 168; Hearts Candy Mold, p. 208
Recipes: Buttercream, Color Flow Icings, p. 116
Also: 2009 Pattern Book (Slipper), p. 128; Color Flow Mix, Piping Gel, p. 135; Plastic Dowel Rods, p. 231; Fanci-Foil Wrap, p. 232; 19 x ¼ in. thick foamcore board, ruler, knife

Several days in advance: Prepare candy plaque crown and color flow slipper (p. 126). **Also:** Prepare foamcore base cut 2 in. larger than largest oval pan. Tint fondant rose and roll out a portion ⅛ in. thick (reserve remaining rose fondant). Wrap board with foil and cover with fondant (p. 124).

Bake and cool 1-layer cakes using 2 largest pans from oval set. Reserve a 2 in. ball of rose fondant. Cover cakes with remaining fondant and prepare for Stacked Construction (p. 114). Position on wrapped board. Add 45° quilting marks, 1 in. apart, on sides of both cakes using Cutter/Embosser fitted with ridged wheel. Roll out ball of rose fondant 1⁄16 in. thick. Cut 55 hearts using smallest Cut-Out. Brush hearts with Pearl Dust; brush backs with damp brush and attach to cake sides where lines intersect. Use buttercream to pipe tip 7 bead bottom borders.

Lightly mark where dowel rods of crown will go into cake. Sharpen 2 wooden dowel rods, 8 in. long, and push through both cakes at marks. At party, position crown by sliding plastic dowel rods over wooden rods and through top cake (for a tighter fit, line plastic dowel rods with a bit of fondant). Attach slipper with icing. Serves 37.

†Brand confectionery coating.

◀ Her Majesty's Carriage

Pan: Princess Carriage, p. 157
Tips: 2, 3, 4, 6, 12, 14, 16, 224, p. 144-145
Colors:* Rose, Violet, Golden Yellow, p. 134
Fondant: White Ready-To-Use Rolled Fondant (24 oz.), Brush Set, p. 130; Rolling Pin, Roll & Cut Mat, Gum-Tex™, p. 133
Recipes: Buttercream, Royal Icings, Roll-Out Cookies, p. 116
Also: 2009 Pattern Book (Pony), p. 128; Cake Boards, Fanci-Foil Wrap, p. 232; Meringue Powder, p. 135; cornstarch, waxed paper, knife, sugar cubes, toothpicks

Several days in advance: Make horses. Add 1 teaspoon Gum-Tex to 12 oz. fondant. Roll out ⅛ in. thick. Use pattern to cut 4 horses. Set on waxed paper-covered boards dusted with cornstarch. Follow pattern to lightly mark details. Decorate with royal icing. Pipe tip 4 outlines for side and neck straps. Use tip 2 to pipe outline bridle, nostril and dot strap details. Outline and fill in hooves and diamond (smooth with finger dipped in cornstarch). Roll small teardrop shapes of fondant for ears and attach using damp brush. Pipe tip 14 elongated shells for plume on head. Use tip 2 to pipe random curls for mane and tail. Let dry at least 2 days. **Also:** Make 50 tip 224 royal icing drop flowers; add tip 2 dot centers. Let dry.

Bake and cool cake. Ice sides, windows, wheels and background areas smooth. Outline wheels with tip 12; outline other details with tip 4. Use tip 4 to pipe top beads and fleurs-de-lis above windows; pipe tip 3 lines for drapes. Cover carriage with tip 16 stars. Use tip 4 to pipe scrolls above and under windows and on wheels. Attach drop flowers with dots of icing. Pipe tip 6 bead bottom border. Position ponies in front of carriage, using sugar cubes to raise the 2 in the foreground. Cake serves 12; each cookie serves 1.

*Combine Violet with Rose for violet shown.

▲ Birthday Buccaneers

Pans: Cookie Sheet, Cooling Grid, p. 154

Tips: 1, 2, 3, 6, 12, p. 144

Colors:* Kelly Green, Christmas Red, Red-Red, Golden Yellow, Copper, (for skin tone shown), Black, p. 134

Recipe: Buttercream Icing (stiff consistency), p. 116

Also: Silly-Feet! Silicone Baking Cups, p. 148; White Ready-To-Use Rolled Fondant (2 oz. per treat), p. 130; 4 in. Lollipop Sticks, p. 169; cornstarch, scissors, ruler, knife

In advance: Prepare fondant pieces. Tint a ¾ in. ball of fondant for each scarf tail. Shape into 2 flat teardrops, ¾ in. long, and pinch together. Let set. Tint a 2 in. ball of fondant for each pair of arms. Roll a ⅜ x 1½ in. long log; insert lollipop stick about 1 in. deep. Flatten and shape for hand; cut slits for fingers. Let set.

Bake and cool cupcakes in silicone cups supported by cookie sheet. Use tip 12 to build up and mound icing; smooth with spatula. Use tip 6 to outline and fill in bandana (pat smooth with finger dipped in cornstarch). Pipe tip 3 eye patch and ear (overpipe for dimension). Use tip 2 to pipe dot eye, pupil, nose and bandana dots; outline mouth and earring. Pipe tip 1 eye patch string. Insert arms, trimming sticks as needed. Attach scarf tails; pipe a tip 6 dot knot. Each serves 1.

*Combine Christmas Red with Red-Red for red shown.

▼ Avast Me, Party!

Pans: Pirate Ship, p. 158; Mini Loaf, p. 154; Cookie Sheet, Cooling Grid, p. 154

Tips: 1, 3, 4, 5, 12, 21, p. 144-145

Colors:* Royal Blue, Black, Brown, Red-Red, Christmas Red, Leaf Green, Violet, Golden Yellow, p. 134

Fondant: White Ready-To-Use Rolled Fondant (24 oz.), Sapphire Blue Pearl Dust™, p. 130; Gum-Tex™, Rolling Pin, Roll & Cut Mat, p. 133

Recipes: Buttercream Icing, Roll-Out Cookies, p. 116; Thinned Fondant Adhesive, p. 117

Also: 2009 Pattern Book (Waves), p. 128; Mini Noah's Ark Metal Cutter Set, p. 165; Cake Boards, Fanci-Foil Wrap, p. 232; Decorator Brush Set, p. 168; 16 x 15 x ½ in. foamcore board, paring knife, sugar cubes, cornstarch

In advance: Make fondant waves. Tint fondant Royal Blue and mix in 2 teaspoons Gum-Tex; roll out ⅛ in. thick. Using pattern and knife, cut out 7 waves, each 17 in. long. Let dry on cornstarch-dusted cake board. When dry, brush with Pearl Dust. **Also:** Make cookies. Prepare and roll out dough. For standing skeletons, cut out 5 cookies using bear cutter; cut off ears. Bake and cool. Ice cookies smooth; pipe tip 1 outline skeletons and bandanas, dot facial features.

Bake and cool ship cake and 3 mini loaf cakes. On foil-wrapped board position ship cake and 3 mini cakes at bottom edge, end to end. Ice sides, deck, portholes, background areas of ship and wave section smooth. Using tip 4, outline deck. Using tip 12, outline mast, boomlines and portholes. Outline and pipe in sails with tip 5 (pat smooth with finger dipped in cornstarch). Ice crow's nest smooth; outline with tip 5. Outline and pipe in tip 3 small flag and tip 4 large flag. Using tip 3 add skulls and crossbones; pipe tip 1 facial features. Cover ship with tip 21 stripes. Using tip 1, pipe skeletons with bandanas in portholes. Pipe tip 5 bead bottom border.

Starting from ship and working outward, position waves, cutting to fit as necessary. Separate with sugar cubes and secure with fondant adhesive. Position cookies on cake. Cake serves 15; each cookie serves 1.

*Combine Brown with Black and Red-Red for light and dark brown shades shown.

▶ Pirate Treat Fleet

Pans: Standard Muffin, p. 154; Cookie Sheet, Cooling Grid, p. 163

Tips: 1, 2, p. 144

Colors: Ivory, Red-Red, Kelly Green, Orange, Royal Blue, Violet, Black, Lemon Yellow, Copper (for skin tone shown), p. 134

Recipes: Buttercream, Royal Icings, Roll-Out Cookies, p. 116; favorite crisped rice cereal treats

Also: 2009 Pattern Book (Pirate Flag), p. 128; 23 Count Standard Cupcakes 'N More® Dessert Stand, p. 147; Diamond Silicone Baking Cups, p. 148; Mini Noah's Ark Metal Cutter Set, p. 165; Rolling Pin, p. 133; Flower Forming Cups, p. 131; Green Candy Melts®†, p. 166; 4 in. Lollipop Sticks, p. 169; Flowerful Medley Sprinkles, p. 136; Parchment Triangles, p. 143; White Standard Baking Cups, p. 189; Meringue Powder, p. 135; pretzel sticks, jelly spearmint leaves, spice drops, caramel squares, assorted candies, white and brown granulated sugars, colored markers, knife, ruler, scissors, skewer, cornstarch, blue plastic wrap

In advance: Make pirates. Prepare dough and roll out. Cut 22 pirates using Bear cutter from mini set. Cut off ears. Bake and cool cookies. Outline and pipe in with light copper royal icing using tip 2 (pat smooth with finger dipped in cornstarch). Pipe on clothes and features using royal icing and tip 1. **Also:** Use pattern, markers and parchment paper to draw flags. Cut with scissors. Poke holes using skewer. Thread onto lollipop stick. Attach spice drop to top. **And:** Make palm trees (p. 122) and treasure chest. For chest, partially cut caramel square about ⅓ from top; lift for lid. Position small yellow confetti from Flowerful Medley assortment inside for gold.

For boats: Press prepared cereal treat mixture into silicone baking cups, filling about halfway. Insert flag; let cool. Add assorted candies. For cupcakes: Bake and cool. Ice smooth then sprinkle tops with granulated brown sugar. Insert palm tree; attach pirate in front with dot of icing or melted candy. At party, arrange scene using blue plastic wrap as water. Position cupcakes on stand and boats around base. Each serves 1.

†Brand confectionery coating.

◀ High Seas Adventurers

Pans: Cookie Sheet, Cooling Grid, p. 154

Tips: 3, 6, 21, 352, 789, p. 144-145

Colors: Red-Red, Orange, Royal Blue, Kelly Green, Black, Copper (for skin tone shown), p. 134

Recipes: Buttercream, Chocolate Buttercream Icings, p. 116

Also: 2009 Pattern Book (Diagram for Ship Cupcake Placement), p. 128; Transportation Puzzle Cakes! Set, p. 146; Alphabet/Numerals Icing Decorations, p. 189; Cake Board, Fanci-Foil Wrap, p. 232; Spatula, p. 138; candy stick, candy-coated chocolates, cornstarch

Follow diagram in Pattern Book for positioning of silicone cups from Puzzle Cakes! Set on cookie sheet (place round cups apart from each other). Bake and cool cupcakes. Position on foil-wrapped cake board. Use tip 789 to cover sail and boat with icing. Use spatula to smooth and score horizontal lines on boat and vertical line on sail. Pipe tip 21 zigzags on top edge of boat; position candy-coated chocolates. Pipe tip 6 outline and fill in portholes, 1½ in. diameter (smooth with finger dipped in cornstarch). Position yellow candy-coated chocolates. Attach candy stick to board between sail and boat with dots of icing. Ice round face cupcakes smooth. Pipe in tip 6 bandanas (smooth with finger dipped in cornstarch). Using tip 3, pipe dot eyes, pupils, nose; pipe in eyepatch and add outline string, mouth and dot cheeks. Pipe tip 352 pull-out tails on bandanas. Position icing decoration name. Each cupcake serves 1.

▲ Bite-Size Buds

Pan: Mini Muffin, p. 154
Recipe: Buttercream Icing, p. 116
Also: Jumbo Confetti Sprinkles, p. 136; White Mini Baking Cups, p. 154; Spatula, p. 138

Bake and cool cupcakes. Spatula ice. Arrange 5 sprinkles for petals. Attach 1 sprinkle to center with icing dot. Each serves 1.

▲ Take Me to Your Party!

Pans: Mini Muffin, p. 154; Cookie Sheet, Cooling Grid, p. 163
Tips: 2, 3, 10, p. 144
Colors:* Leaf Green, Lemon Yellow, Sky Blue, Black, p. 134
Recipe: Buttercream Icing, p. 116
Also: Square Silicone Baking Cups, p. 148; White Mini Baking Cups, p. 189; 101 Cookie Cutters Set, p. 164; 4 in. Lollipop Sticks, p. 169; mini and regular-size candy-coated chocolates, assorted color licorice twists, spice drops

Prepare dough and roll out. Using smallest round cutter from set, cut 1 cookie head for each treat. Bake and cool. Bake and cool square cupcakes in silicone cups supported by cookie sheet. Bake and cool mini muffins.

For each treat, cut one 3 ½ in. long licorice twist for arms and two 2¼ in. long licorice twists for legs. Trim both ends of 3½ in. twist and one end of each 2¼ in. twist on an angle. Trim spice drops for hands and feet, cut a notch for thumb. Use lollipop stick to make holes in the ends of hands and feet. Insert hands and feet on ends of twists. Cut slit horizontally through square cupcake to accommodate arms. Insert arms in slit; insert 2¼ in. legs at bottom. Use tip 10 to cover square cupcake with icing; smooth with spatula. Position mini and regular size candy-coated chocolates on cupcake. Ice smooth round cookie and mini cupcake; position cookie on cupcake. Pipe tip 3 dot eyes, tip 2 dot nose, pupils and outline mouth. Pipe tip 3 dot nose and cheeks. For bolts, cut spice drops in half and attach to sides of head with dots of icing. For antenna, cut lollipop stick to 3 in.; insert in head and attach regular-size candy-coated chocolate with icing. Position mini cupcake head. Each serves 1.

▼ Snug as a Bug

Pans: Cookie Sheet, Cooling Grid, p. 154
Tips: 1, 3, 12, p. 144
Colors: Black, Lemon Yellow, p. 134
Recipe: Buttercream Icing, p. 116
Also: Flower Silicone Baking Cups, p. 148; Truffles Candy Mold, p. 168; Orange Candy Melts®†, p. 166; Yellow Colored Sugar, p. 136; Disposable Decorating Bags, p. 143

In advance: Make ladybug. Mold body in truffle mold using orange candy. Refrigerate until firm; unmold. Using buttercream, pipe tip 12 ball head, tip 3 outline stripe, dot spots and eyes. Pipe tip 1 outline smile and dot pupils.

Bake and cool cupcakes in silicone cups supported by cookie sheet. Ice smooth and sprinkle with yellow sugar. Position ladybug. Each serves 1.

▼ Treasure Cruise

Pan: Mini Loaf, p. 154
Color: Royal Blue, p. 134
Candy: Light Cocoa, White, Red, Blue, Green Candy Melts®†, p. 166; Transportation Candy Mold, p. 167; 4 in. Lollipop Sticks, p. 169
Recipe: Buttercream Icing, p. 116
Also: Petite Loaf Baking Cups, p. 189; Decorator Brush Set, p. 168 or Parchment Triangles, p. 143; Piping Gel, p. 135; Flowerful Medley Sprinkles, p. 136; jelly spearmint leaves, caramel squares, pretzel sticks, granulated brown sugar, knife

In advance: Mold candy boats using painting or piping method (p. 125). Refrigerate until firm; unmold. Attach 4 in. lollipop stick to back with melted candy. **Also:** Make palm trees (p. 122). Make treasure chest. Partially cut caramel square about ⅓ from top; lift for lid. Position small yellow confetti inside for gold.

Ice cakes smooth; sprinkle shore with granulated brown sugar sand. Tint piping gel blue and pipe in water section. Insert palm trees and boat; position treasure chest. Each serves 1.

†Brand confectionery coating.

▲ Queen of Hearts

Pan: Mini Muffin, p. 154
Tip: 3, p. 144
Colors:* Lemon Yellow, Golden Yellow, Brown, Red-Red, Copper (for skin shade shown), p. 134
Recipe: Buttercream Icing, p. 116
Also: Jumbo Hearts Sprinkles, p. 136; White Mini Baking Cups, p. 189

Bake and cool cupcakes. Ice smooth. Use tip 3 to pipe swirl hair, outline mouth and dot nose and eyes. Position sprinkles for crown. Each serves 1.

*Combine Lemon Yellow with Golden Yellow for yellow shown. Combine Brown with Red-Red for brown shown.

▲ Cupcake Capsules

Pans: Standard Muffin, Cookie Sheet, Cooling Grid, p. 154
Tips: 2A, 3, 5, p. 144
Colors: Violet, Rose, Black, p. 134
Recipe: Buttercream Icing, p. 116
Also: Silly-Critters! Silicone Baking Cups, p. 148; White Standard Baking Cups, p. 189; cornstarch

Bake and cool cupcakes in silicone cups supported by cookie sheet. Bake and cool an equal number of standard cupcakes. Ice tops of cupcakes in silicone cups; position an upside-down standard cupcake on top (remove baking cup). Pipe a tip 2A spiral around cupcake; smooth into cone shape. Ice door area smooth with white. Pipe tip 5 outline around door, windows and tip (flatten and smooth with finger dipped in cornstarch). Add tip 3 dot center to windows; flatten. Each serves 1.

et the Kids Decorate!
)ur adorable stand-up baker bear is the perfect
ost for a cupcake decorating party! Give every
id a cupcake and the supplies they need to
nake a work of edible art, then let the fun begin.
We're starting you out with a few easy designs,
ut feel free to check cupcakefun.com for more
reat ideas, or let the kids go wild with their own
upcake conceptions!
Wilton
prinkles
NET WT 3.25 OZ (92g)
Jumbo Confetti
Wilton
sprinkles
NET WT 3 OZ (85g)
bow Nonpare
BOB
Green Decorating Gel
Gel

▲ Piper Cub

Pans: Stand-Up Cuddly Bear Set, p. 160; Cookie Sheet, Cooling Grid, p. 163

Tips: 3, 6, 12, 16, 352, p. 144-145

Colors: Black, Red-Red, Royal Blue, Rose, Kelly Green, Golden Yellow, p. 134

Recipes: Buttercream, Chocolate Buttercream Icings, p. 116

Also: Pastel Silicone Baking Cups, p. 210; Jumbo Confetti Sprinkles, Rainbow Nonpareils, p. 136; Pink, Yellow Sparkle Gels, p. 135; 12 in. Disposable Decorating Bag, Icing Bag Ties, Standard Coupler, p. 143; White Ready-To-Use Rolled Fondant (8 oz.), p. 130; 4 in. Lollipop Sticks, p. 169; Green Tube Decorating Gel, p. 134; marshmallows, knife, ruler, cornstarch

Bake and cool cupcakes in silicone cups supported by cookie sheet. Ice some smooth and decorate. Pipe Sparkle Gel single flower. For bouquet, position jumbo confetti petals, pipe tip 3 vine and tip 352 leaves. For name cupcake, outline edge with tip 6 and immediately cover with nonpareils, print tip 3 name. Bake and cool bear cake. Trim off left arm. Ice smooth inner ears and soles of feet. Using tip 3, outline mouth; outline and fill in eyes and nose (smooth with finger dipped in cornstarch). Cover bear with tip 16 stars. Cut a 4½ x 3 in. fondant apron with ½ in. wide straps; position on bear. Cut 1 in. shaped pocket; attach to apron with damp brush. Cut ¼ in. wide ties; attach. For hat base, shape a 2 x 1½ x 1 in. deep fondant oval; position on cake. Wrap 3 marshmallows in fondant and shape into hat top. Insert 4 in. lollipop stick, extending 2½ in. at bottom. Position hat top by pushing stick through hat base and into cake. For bear's decorating bag, cut 3 in. off wide end of a decorating bag. Attach tip and coupler; add icing and tie closed with bag tie. Bend 1 in. tip of lollipop stick to form a 90° angle; attach to decorating bag at tie. Position bear's bag by inserting stick into cake. Use tip 12 to pipe arm and hand over bag; cover with tip 16 stars. **At party:** Position Bear, cupcakes and decorating supplies. Cake serves 12; each cupcake serves 1.

▶ Par Car

Pan: Mini Loaf, p. 154

Tips: 1M, 2, 3, p. 144-145

Colors: Kelly Green, Black, p. 134

Fondant: White Ready-To-Use Rolled Fondant (2 oz. for each cart), Natural Colors Fondant Multi Pack, Brush Set, p. 130; Rolling Pin, Roll & Cut Mat, p. 133

Recipes: Buttercream Icing, p. 116; Thinned Fondant Adhesive, p. 1

Also: White Ready-To-Use Decorator Icing, Piping Gel, p. 135; 4 in. Lollipop Sticks, p. 169; Cake Circles, Fanci-Foil Wrap, p. 232; scissors, cornstarch, waxed paper, ruler, knife

In advance: Prepare fondant pieces. Cut cake board to 2¼ x 3¼ in. for roof. Brush with piping gel and cover with fondant rolled ⅛ in. thick. Roll out black fondant from Multi Pack ¼ in. thick; cut 4 whee using wide end of tip 1M. Roll out small amount 1/16 in. thick; cut steering wheel using wide end of tip 1M. Let all dry on waxed paper covered board lightly dusted with cornstarch.

Bake and cool cake using firm-textured batter such as pound cake. Cut away angled seating area 1½ in. wide, 1 in. deep. Use tip 6 to pi icing on seating area; smooth with spatula. Ice cart smooth. Pipe ti outline trim around seats. Roll ¼ in. balls of fondant (flatten slightly) and attach to top end of lollipop sticks. Position sticks into cake; attach roof with fondant adhesive. Attach wheels to cake sides wit dots of icing; outline tip 2 wheel centers. Pipe tip 3 outline at base o sticks. Each serves 1.

▲ Glee on the Green! ▶

Pan: Teddy Bear, p. 159

Tips: 3, 4, 5, 16, 18, 47, p. 144-145

Colors: Rose (for her), Royal Blue (for him), Christmas Red, Brown, Black, Copper (for skin tone shown), p. 134

Fondant: White Ready-To-Use Rolled Fondant (12 oz. each cake), Silver Pearl Dust™, Brush Set, p. 130; Rolling Pin, Roll & Cut Mat, Gum-Tex™, p. 133

Recipes: Buttercream Icing, p. 116; Thinned Fondant Adhesive, p. 117

Also: 2009 Pattern Book (Golf Shoe, Putter Head, Hand, Visor Brim), p. 128; Cake Boards, Fanci-Foil Wrap, p. 232; 6 in. Cookie Treat Sticks, p. 163; Wooden Dowel Rods, p. 231; round plastic container (5½-6 in. diameter), ruler, cornstarch, knife, toothpicks

At least 2 days in advance: Prepare fondant hands, shoes, visor/hat brim and putter (p. 122).

Bake and cool cake. Trim off ears, eyes and muzzle; use icing to build up leg area to level of tummy. Ice smooth sleeve openings and mouth; outline mouth with tip 4. Pipe tip 5 dot eyes (flatten with finger dipped in cornstarch); pipe tip 4 dot pupils. Using tip 5, outline waist, her pant cuffs and his cap; outline and fill in shirt collar (pat smooth). Pipe tip 18 zigzag trim on her shorts. Cover face, shirt, pants, her legs, his cap and his ears with tip 16 stars; overpipe noses and his ears for dimension. For her, outline ears with tip 16 C-motion and pipe tip 16 reverse shell hair. For him, outline tip 4 hair. Cut and attach a 10 x ½ x ⅛ in. thick white fondant strip for her visor base. Pipe tip 3 bead tongue, outline eyebrows and dot buttons on his shirt. Pipe tip 47 (smooth side up) belt; overpipe tip 5 belt loops and buckle. Insert hands and feet. Pipe tip 18 line for socks; pipe tip 3 outline laces and pull-out dot spikes. Position visor/hat brim. Each cake serves 12.

▶ Driving Through the Woods

Pan: Standard Muffin, p. 154

Tips: 3, 14, 233, p. 144-145

Color: Kelly Green, p. 134

Recipes: Buttercream, Royal Icings, p. 116

Also: 38 Count Cupcakes 'N More® Dessert Stand, p. 147; Golf Topper Set, p. 188; White Standard Baking Cups, p. 189; 4 in. Lollipop Sticks, p. 169; Meringue Powder, p. 135; Circle Metal Cutter, p. 165; Spatula, p. 138; sugar ice cream cones, construction paper, black marker, glue, ruler, scissors, waxed paper, pencil

In advance: Make royal icing trees. Trim ½ in. off 6 cones, 1 in. off 6 and 1½ in. off 7. Cover with tip 14 pull-out leaves, working from bottom to top. Let dry. **Also:** Make construction paper flags. Cut 1⅜ x 2 in. long triangles; add hole numbers 1 to 18 with marker. Glue flags to top of lollipop sticks. **And:** Make base for topper. Use circle cutter to draw pattern on waxed paper-covered board. Outline circle with tip 3 and royal icing; fill in with thinned royal icing. Let dry.

Bake and cool 37 cupcakes. Spatula ice with buttercream. Position trees on cupcakes. Decorate remaining cupcakes with tip 233 pull-out grass; insert flags. Attach topper to base with icing; let set. **At party:** Position cupcakes and attach topper to stand with royal icing. Each serves 1.

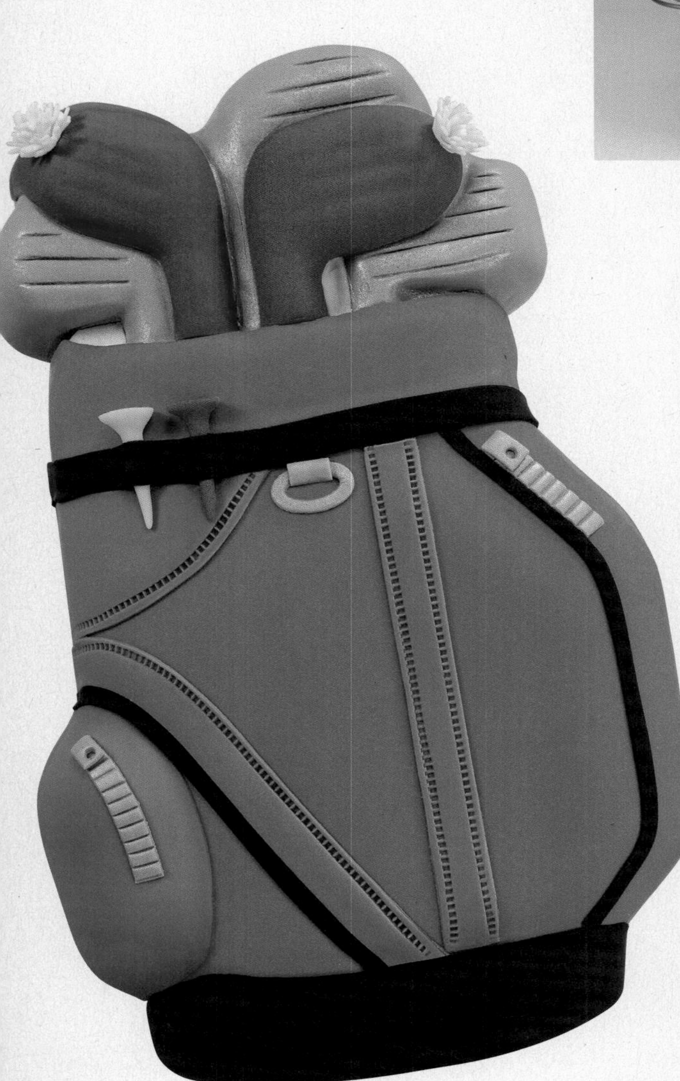

◀ Full Course Selection

Pan: Golf Bag, p. 161

Tip: 5, p. 144

Colors:* Royal Blue, Black, Red-Red, Christmas Red, Kelly Green, Lemon Yellow, Violet, p. 134

Fondant: White Ready-To-Use Rolled Fondant (48 oz.), Silver Pearl Dust™, Brush Set, p. 130; Cutter/Embosser, p. 131; Rolling Pin, Roll & Cut Mat, p. 133

Recipe: Buttercream Icing, p. 116

Also: Cake Board, Fanci-Foil Wrap, p. 232

Bake and cool cake; prepare for rolled fondant (p. 117). Tint 24 oz. fondant blue, 6 oz. gray, 4 oz. each violet, green, red, black and 1 in. ball yellow. Cover three back club heads with gray fondant. Score lines on heads with straight edge wheel of Cutter/Embosser. Roll out red and green fondant ⅛ in. thick; cover 2 front club heads. Roll out blue fondant ⅛ in. thick and cover upper portion of bag. Roll out fondant for trims 1⁄16 in. thick and attach the following with damp brush. Cut and attach violet ball storage area, bag trim below tees and vertical strip 6½ in. x ¾ in. wide; immediately emboss all with ridged wheel of Cutter/Embosser. Shape 2 tees from yellow and red fondant; attach. Cut black base of bag to fit cake, ¼ in. wide strips for right and left side trim, ½ in. wide strip across tee area; attach. For zippers, cut a 2 x ⅜ in. wide gray strip. Score zipper lines with straight wheel; attach. For zipper pulls, cut ½ in. x ⅜ in. gray rectangles; make holes with narrow end of tip 5 and attach. For towel ring, roll a small strip of gray fondant ⅛ in. wide; attach. For pompom on club covers, cut a 2½ x ¼ in. wide strip. Cut slits close together; roll up and trim bottom edge even; attach. Add small pieces of white fondant in void areas between clubs. Brush all gray fondant with silver pearl dust. Serves 12.

*Combine Red-Red with Christmas Red for red shade shown.

▶ Tee and Cookies

Pans: Round Cookie Treat, Cookie Sheet, Cooling Grid, p. 163

Tip: 2, p. 144

Fondant: Primary Colors Fondant Multi Pack, Brush Set, p. 130

Recipes: Color Flow Icing, Roll-Out Cookies, p. 116

Also: Color Flow Mix, p. 135; 8 in. Cookie Treat Sticks, p. 163

Prepare dough and press into treat pan with stick; bake and cool. Cover cookies with thinned color flow (p. 124); let dry completely. Use full-strength color flow and tip 2 to pipe "C" shaped dimples on ball. Shape tee over stick using red fondant; securing with damp brush. Each serves 1.

Disney · PIXAR
WALL·E

STAR POWER!

The characters kids love best are happy to share the spotlight with your birthday boy or girl. Ariel looks more enchanting than ever in an undersea display featuring bright icing coral and cookie fish. Abby Cadabby makes magic with a colorful cake surrounded by sparkling star cookies. Here, WALL•E stars in a galaxy of fun treats, featuring his shaped cake served on a colorful board covered with fondant planets.

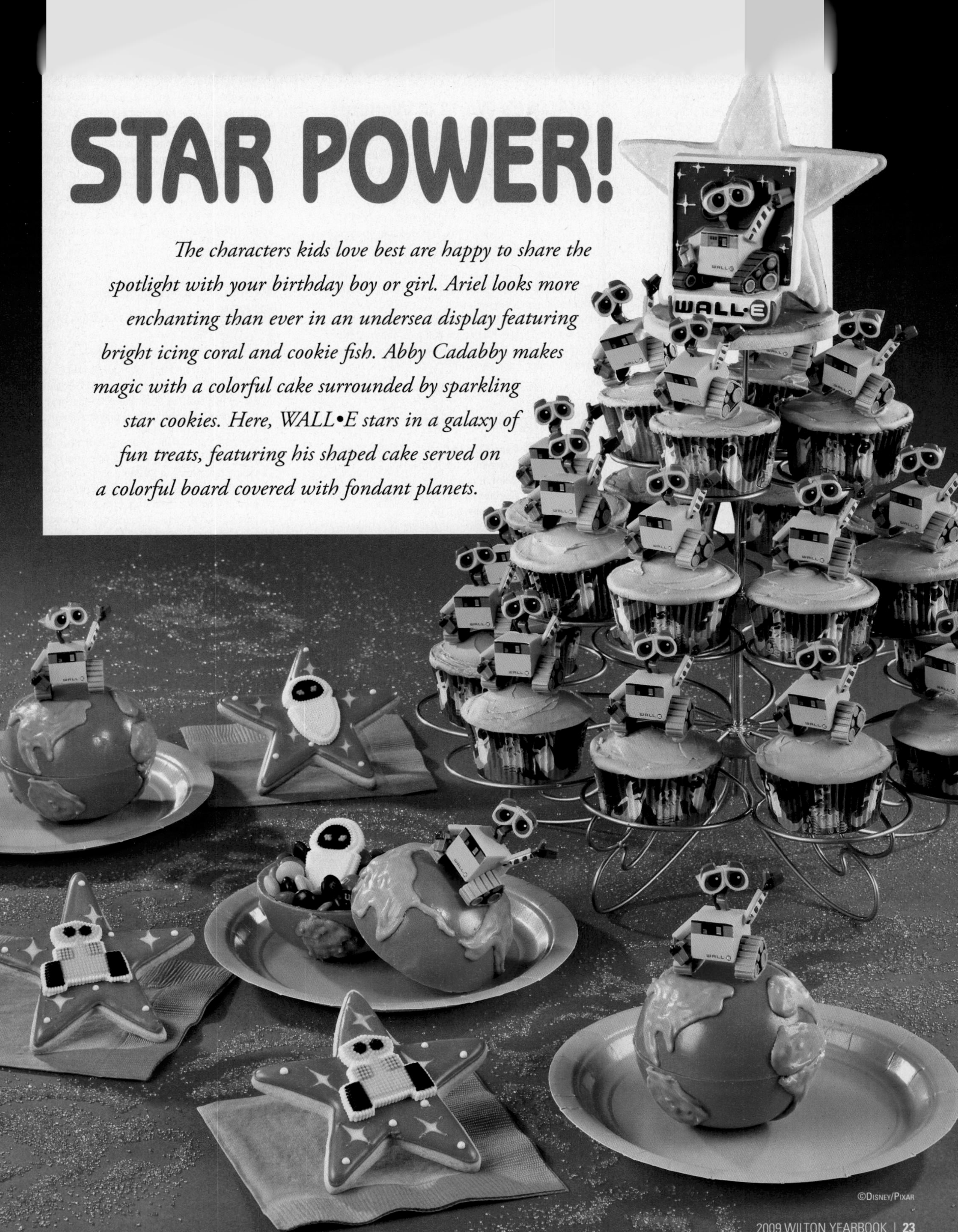

A Wave from *WALL•E!*

Pan: *WALL•E*, p. 171
Tips: 1, 2, 3, 4, 5, 6, 8, 16, 21, p. 144-145
Colors: *WALL•E* Icing Color Set (black, red, yellow), p. 171; Royal Blue, p. 134
Fondant: White Ready-To-Use Rolled Fondant (96 oz.), Primary Colors Fondant Multi Pack, Brush Set, p. 130; Easy-Glide Fondant Smoother, p. 131; Star Cut-Outs™, p. 132; Rolling Pin, Roll & Cut Mat, p. 133
Recipe: Buttercream Icing, p. 116
Also: 101 Cookie Cutters Set, p. 164; Cake Boards, Fanci-Foil Wrap, p. 232; Violet Color Mist™ Food Color Spray, p. 134; Piping Gel, p. 135; 18 x 25 x ½ in. foamcore board, cornstarch, knife, ruler

In advance: Cover base board with fondant (p. 124) using 72 oz. of blue-tinted fondant. Let dry then spray with Color Mist for cloud effect.

Ice smooth *WALL•E* cake sides and background areas. Use tip 3 to outline and fill in gray eye sockets. Use tip 4 to outline and fill in pupil (smooth with finger dipped in cornstarch). Add tip 3 dot highlight. Use tip 8 to outline tire treads in black; fill in with dark gray (smooth with finger). Outline and fill in tire gears with tip 5 (smooth with finger). Outline and fill in smooth area of control box with tip 4 (smooth with finger). Outline remaining details with tip 4; cover with tip 16 stars. For vent, pipe tip 1 lines and tip 3 dot. For smooth control box area, add tip 1 lines and tip 16 star. Pipe tip 8 connector cord. Pipe "*WALL•*" with tip 2; outline and fill in circle then overpipe tip 1 "E." Add tip 21 star bottom border. Position cake on covered board.

Knead together 1 pk. red fondant from Multi Pack with 2 oz. white fondant and a little red color from *WALL•E* Icing Color Set; roll out 1⁄16 in. thick. Cut message using letters from 101 Cutters Set. Brush backs with damp brush and attach to board. Roll out white fondant ⅛ in. thick. Use small and medium Cut-Outs to cut stars; attach to board. Use narrow end of tip 6 to cut small dots, narrow and wide end of tip 8 to cut medium and large dots; attach to cake and board. Serves 12.

WALL•E's World of Wonder!

Pans: Mini Ball, p. 161; Cookie Sheet, p. 154
Candy: White Candy Melts®† (2 pks. makes 4-5 treats), Garden and Primary Candy Color* Sets, p. 166
Also: 2009 Pattern Book (Top, Bottom of World), p. 128; *WALL•E* Party Toppers, Icing Decorations, p. 171; Parchment Triangles, p. 143; waxed paper, toothpicks, candy-coated chocolates

In advance: Tint ¼ cup of candy green; tint remainder blue. Mold candy shells in Mini Ball Pan (p. 125). Use patterns to mark continents around candy shells with a toothpick. Use melted candy in cut parchment bag to outline and pipe in continents. Let set. Fill bottom half with chocolates and icing decoration. Use melted candy to attach top half; attach topper. Each serves 1.

*Combine Green with Yellow for green shown.

Serving Humanity

Pans: Standard Muffin, Cookie Sheet, Cooling Grid, p. 154
Color: Royal Blue, p. 134
Recipes: Buttercream Icing, Roll-Out Cookies, p. 116
Also: *WALL•E* Candle, Party Toppers (4 pks.), Baking Cups, p. 171; 23 Count Standard Cupcakes 'N More® Dessert Stand, p. 147; 101 Cookie Cutters Set , p. 164; Nesting Stars Metal Cutter Set, p. 165; White Candy Melts®†, p. 166; White Sparkling Sugar, p. 136

In advance: Prepare and roll out cookie dough. Cut top star using largest cutter from Nesting set. Cut base using largest round from 101 Cutters Set. For easel back, cut a 2½ x 1 in. rectangle. Bake and cool cookies. Ice star and sprinkle with Sparkling Sugar; ice round cookie. Use melted candy to attach easel to back of star, attach star to round base and attach candle in front of star.

Bake and cool cupcakes. Ice with buttercream. Position on stand. Add Party Toppers. Position cookie star with candle. Each serves 1.

WALL•E Cook-EEs

Pans: Cookie Sheet, Cooling Grid, p. 154
Tip: 2, p. 144
Color: Royal Blue, p. 134
Recipes: Color Flow Icing, Roll-Out Cookies, p. 116
Also: *WALL•E* Icing Decorations, p. 171; Color Flow Mix, p. 135; Nesting Stars Metal Cutter Set, p. 165; Parchment Triangles, p. 143; long straight pin, damp cloth

Prepare and roll out cookie dough. Cut stars using 2nd largest cutter from set. Bake and cool cookies. Use full-strength color flow and tip 2 to outline cookies. Working with 1 cookie at a time, flow-in (p. 126) with thinned blue color flow. For starbursts, pipe a tip 2 dot of white thinned color flow; use pin to pull edges for starburst effect, cleaning pin after each pull. Repeat for additional starbursts. Let dry overnight. Attach icing decorations with full-strength color flow; pipe tip 2 dots. Each serves 1.

▶ *Lightning* Laps the Field

Pan: *Cars*, p. 178
Tips: 2, 3, 5, 16, p. 144-145
Colors:* *Cars* Icing Color Set (red, blue, yellow, black), p. 178; Orange, Violet, Royal Blue, Kelly Green, Black, p. 134
Fondant: White Ready-To-Use Rolled Fondant (90 oz.), Brush Set, p. 130; Easy-Glide Fondant Smoother, p. 131; Square Cut-Outs™, p. 132; Rolling Pin, Roll & Cut Mat, p. 133
Recipe: Buttercream Icing, p. 116
Also: 2009 Pattern Book (Race Track), p. 128; Cake Boards, Fanci-Foil Wrap, p. 232; Piping Gel, p. 135; Jumbo Confetti Sprinkles, p. 136; 20½ x 17½ x ½ in. foamcore board, knife, ruler, cornstarch

One day in advance: Tint fondant as follows: 30 oz. light gray, 12 oz. royal blue, 10 oz. violet, 5 oz. green and 4 oz. black. Prepare race track board (p. 121).

Bake and cool *Cars* cake. Ice cake sides, background areas, headlights, mouth, front windshield, side windows and blue lightning bolt smooth. Using tip 3, outline car details and number; pipe in eyes (smooth with finger dipped in cornstarch); add dot pupils and rivets on hood. Cover tires with tip 16 lines. Cover car, yellow lightning bolt and number with tip 16 stars. Add tip 3 outline muffler. Pipe tip 5 bead bottom border. Position cake on fondant-covered board. Serves 12.

*Combine Royal Blue with Black for light gray track. Combine Violet with Royal Blue for violet track border.

▶ Bronco-Bustin' *Bob*

Pans: *SpongeBob SquarePants™*, p. 179; Cookie Sheet, Cooling Grid, p. 154
Tips: 2, 3, 4, 5, 14, 16, 18, p. 144-145
Colors:* *SpongeBob SquarePants™* Icing Color Set (yellow, red, blue, brown), p. 179; Golden Yellow, Lemon Yellow, Leaf Green, Sky Blue, Black, p. 134
Fondant: White Ready-To-Use Rolled Fondant (6 oz.), p. 130; Rolling Pin, Roll & Cut Mat, p. 133
Recipes: Buttercream Icing, Roll-Out Cookies, p. 116
Also: 2009 Pattern Book (Hat, Message Area), p. 128; Cake Boards, Fanci-Foil Wrap, p. 232; cornstarch, knife, ruler

In advance: Make cookies. Prepare and roll out dough. Use patterns to cut out hat and message area. Bake and cool cookies. Use icing to attach cookies to cut-to-fit, foil-covered cake boards (use 2 boards for message area).

Bake and cool cake. Trim off sleeves and pant legs. Ice smooth message cookie, cake sides and background areas, *SpongeBob* spots and inside mouth. Outline and fill in tongue and whites of eyes with tip 5 (smooth with finger dipped in cornstarch), irises, pupils and teeth with tip 4 (smooth with finger), shirt collar with tip 2. Use tip 4 to outline remaining areas of cake and hat cookie; use tip 2 to pipe plaid lines on shirt. Cover shirt with tip 14 stars; cover remaining areas of cake and hat with tip 16 stars. Pipe tip 3 lines for belt and tip 2 lines for pant leg stitches. Tint 6 oz. fondant golden yellow. Roll out a small amount ⅛ in. thick for belt buckle; cut circle using open end of any standard decorating tip. Roll lightly into 1 in. wide oval. Position on belt; pipe tip 2 initials. Pipe tip 18 shell bottom border. Position message area. Print tip 4 message. Roll remaining yellow fondant into 2 long 3⁄16 in. diameter logs. Cut matching lengths and twist together to form rope sections 4, 12, 15 and 18 in. long plus 2 sections 2 in. long for knot. Attach rope sections and knot with dots of icing. Gently press hat into cake side to position. Cake serves 12; cookie serves 1.

*Combine Leaf Green with Lemon Yellow for green shell border. Combine *SpongeBob SquarePants* yellow, blue and brown from set to make green outlines shown on *SpongeBob*.

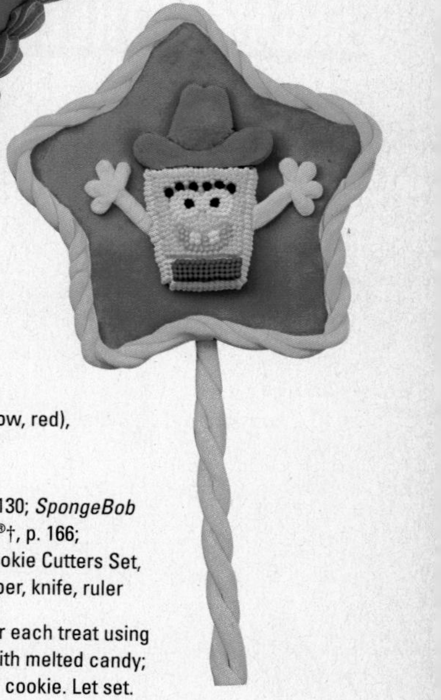

▲ Pace-Setting Pops

Pans: Cookie Sheet, Cooling Grid, p. 154
Tip: 18, p. 145
Color: Black, p. 134
Recipes: Royal Icing, Roll-Out Cookies, p. 116
Also: *Cars* Icing Decorations, Treat Bags, p. 178; White Candy Melts®†, p. 166; 6 in. Cookie Treat Sticks, p. 163; 101 Cookie Cutters Set, p. 164; Rolling Pin, p. 133; Meringue Powder, p. 135; Parchment Triangles, p. 143; knife

Prepare and roll out cookie dough. Cut flags using flag cutter from set; cut off pole top and bottom. Bake and cool cookies. Use royal icing to pipe on tip 18 stars, alternating colors in checkerboard pattern; attach icing decoration. Attach cookie to stick using melted candy in cut parchment bag; refrigerate until firm. Place in treat bags. Each serves 1.

†Brand confectionery coating.

▶ Cowpoke Cookie

Pans: Cookie Sheet, Cooling Grid, p. 154
Tips: 2, 4, 5, p. 144
Colors: *SpongeBob SquarePants™* Icing Color Set (brown, yellow, red), p. 179; Golden Yellow, Sky Blue, p. 134
Recipes: Royal Icing, Roll-Out Cookies, p. 116
Also: White Ready-To-Use Rolled Fondant (3 oz.), Brush Set, p. 130; *SpongeBob SquarePants™* Icing Decorations, p. 179; White Candy Melts®†, p. 166; Merinque Powder, p. 135; Parchment Triangles, p. 143; 101 Cookie Cutters Set, p. 164; 8 in. Cookie Treat Sticks, p. 163; cornstarch, waxed paper, knife, ruler

In advance: Prepare and roll out cookie dough. Cut 2 cookies for each treat using largest star cutter from set; bake and cool. Ice bottom cookie with melted candy; position treat stick, leaving 6 in. exposed at bottom, and add top cookie. Let set. Ice top cookie smooth; let dry.

Tint fondant yellow. Roll 2 thin ropes, 15 x 3⁄16 in. diameter; twist together for rope. Use tip 4 to outline cookie with royal icing; position rope in icing. Attach icing decoration to center with royal icing. Use tip 4 to pipe outline arms and fingers; outline and fill in hat with tip 5, hatband with tip 2 (pat smooth with finger dipped in cornstarch). Roll 2 more thin ropes, 7½ x 3⁄16 in. diameter; twist together and trim to 6 in. Attach to cookie stick using melted candy; let set. Each serves 1.

▶ *Abby* Makes You a Star!

Pans: *Abby Cadabby*, p. 170; Cookie Sheet, Cooling Grid, p. 154
Tips: 2, 3, 7, 12, 13, 16, 21, p. 144-145
Colors: *Abby Cadabby* Icing Colors Set (pink, yellow, blue, violet), p. 170; Black, p. 134
Recipes: Buttercream, Royal Icings, Roll-Out Cookies, p. 116
Also: Nesting Stars Metal Cutter Set, p. 165; Pink, White Cake Sparkles™, p. 136; Meringue Powder, p. 135; Cake Boards, Fanci-Foil Wrap, p. 232; Parchment Triangles, p. 143; waxed paper, cornstarch

In advance: Make cookies. Prepare and roll out dough. Use 2nd largest cutter from set to cut stars for name; cut additional stars with smallest cutter. Bake and cool cookies. Mix pink and white Cake Sparkles together. Use full-strength royal icing and tip 2 to outline cookies. Flow in center with thinned royal icing; immediately sprinkle on mixed Cake Sparkles. Let dry. **Also:** Make tiny stars. Use full strength royal icing to pipe tip 21 stars on waxed paper-covered board. Let dry.

Decorate cake with buttercream. Ice cake sides and background areas smooth. Using tip 3, outline and fill in whites of eyes, eyelashes and eyelids (smooth with finger dipped in cornstarch). Using tip 3, overpipe iris then pupil; add dot highlight. Using tip 3, outline and fill in mouth (smooth with finger); pipe bead tongue. Outline wand with tip 3; fill in with tip 12 (smooth with finger). Outline Abby and dress with tip 3; cover with tip 16 stars. Outline tip 3 hair barrettes. Pipe tip 13 pull out star hair. Pipe tip 3 pull out string pompom. Pipe tip 21 shell bottom border. Print tip 7 letters on large cookies. Arrange cookies and stars around cake. Cake serves 12; each cookie serves 1.

◀ *Abby's* Enchanting Cookies

Pan: Star Cookie Treat, p. 163; Cookie Sheet, Cooling Grid, p. 154
Tip: 3, p. 144
Colors: Rose, Violet, p. 134
Recipes: Royal Icing, Roll-Out Cookies, p. 116
Also: *Abby Cadabby* Icing Decorations, Treat Bags, p. 170; Pink, Purple Cake Sparkles™, p. 136; Meringue Powder, p. 135; 8 in. Cookie Treat Sticks, p. 163

Prepare cookie dough. Press into Cookie Treat Pan; insert Cookie Sticks. Bake and cool treats. Cover cookies with Thinned Royal Icing (p. 124); sprinkle on Cake Sparkles. Let set. Use full-strength icing to pipe tip 3 outline around edge of cookie; immediately sprinkle on Cake Sparkles. Attach Icing Decorations with icing dots. Let set. Place in Treat Bags. Each serves 1.

▼ *Abby* Conjures a Cupcake!

Pan: Standard Muffin, p. 154
Colors: *Abby Cadabby* Icing Color Set, p. 170
Fondant: White Ready-To-Use Rolled Fondant, Brush Set, p. 130; Quick Ease Roller, p. 131; Star Cut-Outs™, p. 132; Roll & Cut Mat, Gum-Tex™, p. 133
Recipe: Buttercream Icing, p. 116
Also: *Abby Cadabby* Party Toppers, Baking Cups, p. 170; White Candy Melts®†, p. 166; 4 in. Lollipop Sticks, p. 169; White Cake Sparkles™, p. 136; Cake Board, p. 232; cornstarch

In advance: Make stars. Tint 2 oz. of fondant for each color; add ¼ teaspoon Gum-Tex and roll out ⅛ in. thick. Cut using small and medium Star Cut-Outs. Set on cornstarch-dusted board. Brush stars with damp brush and sprinkle with Cake Sparkles. Let dry overnight.

Attach 2 small stars per cupcake to lollipop sticks using melted candy; let set. Bake and cool cupcakes; ice smooth. Position topper and stars; insert lollipop sticks. Each serves 1.

†Brand confectionery coating.

▲ *Elmo's* Colorful Cookies

Pans: Cookie Sheet, Cooling Grid, p. 154
Tips: 1, 2, 3, p. 144
Colors: Lemon Yellow, Royal Blue, Kelly Green, Christmas Red, Black, p. 134
Recipes: Royal Icing, Shortbread Cookies, p. 116
Also: Push 'N Print™ Cutter Set, p. 162; *Elmo* Icing Decorations, Treat Bags, p. 181; 8 in. Cookie Treat Sticks, p. 163; Parchment Triangles, p. 143; Meringue Powder, p. 135

Prepare and roll out dough. Bake and cool cookies following cutter set instructions. Attach icing decoration with royal icing; let set. Pipe tip 3 dot fingers. Pipe in tip 2 imprinted message and scallops around cookie. Pipe tip 2 pull-out crayon; add tip 1 lines. Attach stick to back of cookie with royal icing. Let set. Place cookies in treat bags. Each serves 1.

SESAME STREET

▼ *Elmo's* the Birthday Baker

Pans: *Elmo*, p. 181; 11 x 15 x 2 in. Sheet, p. 153; Cookie Sheet, Cooling Grid, Standard Muffin, p. 154
Tips: 2, 3, 16, p. 144-145
Colors: Christmas Red, Orange, Black, Lemon Yellow, Kelly Green, Royal Blue, p. 134
Fondant: White Ready-To-Use Rolled Fondant (80 oz.), Brush Set, p. 130; Easy-Glide Fondant Smoother, p. 131; Rolling Pin, Roll & Cut Mat, p. 133;
Recipes: Buttercream, Royal Icings, Shortbread Cookies, p. 116
Also: 2009 Pattern Book (*Elmo's* Hands, Hat Top and Base), p. 128; *Elmo* Baking Cups, Icing Decorations, p. 181; Disposable Decorating Bags, Standard Decorating Coupler, p. 143; Meringue Powder, p. 135; Cake Boards, Fanci-Foil Wrap, p. 232; Push 'N Print™ Cutter Set, p. 162; knife, cornstarch, waxed paper, rubber band, foamcore board (¼ in. thick), ruler

In advance: Prepare foamcore base board. Use *Elmo* pan and hat pattern as guides for top portion; bottom will be a 10 x 17 in. rectangle. Cut then wrap with foil.
Also: Make cookies. Prepare and roll out cookie dough. Use Push 'N Print Set to cut 7 "Happy Birthday" cookies. Use patterns to cut 2 hands. Bake and cool cookies; decorate with royal icing. Place hand cookies on waxed paper-covered board; cover top and sides with tip 16 stars. For "Happy Birthday" cookies, use tip 2 to fill in letters and outline edges (leave 3 undecorated).

Bake and cool cupcakes. Ice smooth with buttercream. Use tip 3 to add scalloped border. Position icing decoration in center. Bake and cool *Elmo* cake and 1-layer 11 x 15 in. sheet cake. Pipe in mouth, nose, eyes and pupils with tip 3 (smooth with finger dipped in cornstarch); add tip 3 smile lines. Cover face with tip 16 stars. Position cake on prepared board. Cut sheet cake to 8 x 15 in.; prepare and cover with fondant (p. 117). Position sheet cake on board below *Elmo* cake. Roll ¾ in. diameter fondant balls for bottom border on sheet cake; attach with dots of icing. Pipe a tip 3 spiral in buttercream icing on each ball. Roll out a small amount of fondant ¼ in. thick; use pattern to cut hat base. Position against top of *Elmo's* head. Roll out a portion of fondant ½ in. thick; use pattern to cut hat top. Shape and position on board. Prepare *Elmo's* decorating bag with icing, tip and coupler; twist top closed and secure with a rubber band. Position bag, hands and cookies; attach to cake top with icing. Cakes serve 40; each cookie and cupcake serves 1.

◀ A-*Dora*-ble Mermaid!

Pan: *Dora the Explorer*, p. 175

Tips: 1, 2, 2A, 3, 4, 13, 16, p. 144-145

Colors:* *Dora the Explorer* Icing Color Set (pink, brown, *Dora* skin tone), p. 175; Sky Blue, Teal, Black, Kelly Green, Lemon Yellow, Creamy Peach, p. 134

Fondant: White Ready-To-Use Rolled Fondant (24 oz.), White and Orchid Pink Pearl Dust™, Brush Set, p. 130; Star, Round Cut-Outs™, p. 132; Rolling Pin, Roll & Cut Mat, Gum-Tex®, p. 133

Recipes: Buttercream Icing, p. 116; Thinned Fondant Adhesive, p. 117

Also: 2009 Pattern Book (Crown, Shirt, Lower Torso, Fin), p. 128; Seashells Candy Mold, p. 167; 8 in. Lollipop Sticks, p. 169; Cake Boards, Fanci-Foil Wrap, p. 232; non-toxic chalk (green, blue, purple), fine mesh tea strainer, granulated brown sugar, knife, ruler, marshmallows, lemon extract, cornstarch

Several days in advance: Prepare board. Use pan as a pattern; cut board 1½ in. wider than pan on all sides; wrap with foil. **Also:** Make 22 fondant seashells in candy mold. Marbleize 3 oz. white fondant (p. 124) with 1 oz. each of fondant tinted yellow, peach or pink. Dust cavities with cornstarch. Press in fondant and immediately unmold. **And:** Make fondant fins and crown. Tint 4 oz. blue, 4 oz. yellow; mix ½ teaspoon Gum-Tex into each color. Roll out ⅛ in. thick. Use patterns to cut fins and crown. Let dry 48 hours on cornstarch-dusted board. Attach lollipop sticks to backs with fondant adhesive; leaving 3 in. extended to insert into cake.

Bake and cool cake. Trim off shoes, socks and backpack. Ice sides and background areas smooth. Using tip 3, outline arms, hair, face and features; outline and pipe in tongue and whites of eyes (smooth with finger dipped in cornstarch). Use tip 4 to fill in mouth and irises, tip 3 to pipe dot pupils. Using tip 2, add dot highlights to eyes; outline bracelet and pipe dot pearls. Cover arms, face and hair with tip 16 stars. Insert fins, supporting tips with marshmallows, if necessary. Tint 4 oz. fondant green, 1 oz. dark pink, 1 oz. light pink; roll out ⅛ in. thick. Use patterns to cut tail and shirt; attach to cake over thin layer of icing. Use wide end of tip 2A to imprint semicircle scales on torso. Cover neck and belly with tip 13 stars. Cut ¾ in. wide fondant strips for ruffles: 2 in. long for sleeves, 7 in. long for waistband. Gather into pleats and attach with damp brush, trimming as needed to fit. Outline shirt and ruffle edges with tip 3; paint ruffle edges with pink Pearl Dust mixed with extract. Grate colored chalk through tea strainer to a fine powder. Dust torso iwith green chalk dust, fins with purple and blue. Outline torso, fins and add detail lines with tip 3. Outline crown with tip 3. Using white fondant, cut 3 circles and 2 stars with smallest Cut-Outs; outline with tip 1. Attach fondant trims to crown; position crown on cake.

Pipe tip 4 bead bottom border. Spatula ice to edge of board; sprinkle on brown sugar. Pipe tip 3 outline seaweed on cake sides. Position seashells on board. Serves 12.

*Combine Kelly Green with Teal for green shown. Combine Sky Blue with Teal for light blue shown. Combine Brown with Black for hair.

▶ Pearl-Diving *Dora*

Pans: Cookie Sheet, Cooling Grid, p. 163

Colors:* Lemon Yellow, Kelly Green, Teal, p. 134

Fondant: White Ready-To-Use Rolled Fondant (1 oz. for each treat), Brush Set, p. 130; Quick Ease Roller, p. 131; Gum-Tex™, Roll & Cut Mat, p. 133

Candy: White Candy Melts®† (1 pk. makes 6 treats), Primary and Garden Candy Color Sets, p. 166

Recipe: Roll-Out Cookies, p. 116

Also: 2009 Pattern Book (Crown), p. 128; *Dora the Explorer* Party Toppers, p. 175; Daisy Metal Cutter, p. 165; Parchment Triangles, p. 143; Cake Boards, p. 232; waxed paper, cornstarch, scissors, craft knife

In advance: Make cookies. Prepare and roll out dough. Cut 2 cookies per treat using Daisy Cutter. Leave 6 scallops across top; trim sides and straighten bottom edge to make shell shape. Bake and cool cookies. **Also:** Cover cookies with melted candy (p. 124). **And:** Make crown and tail. Tint fondant yellow and green (½ oz. each per treat); add ⅛ teaspoon Gum-Tex. Roll out a 1 in. ball of yellow ⅛ in. thick. Use pattern to cut out crown; let dry on waxed paper-covered board dusted with cornstarch. Press a ¾ in. ball of green fondant onto topper for curved, tapered tail; flatten end, then trim with scissors for fins. Decorate and assemble treats using melted, tinted candy in cut parchment bags. After piping each step, refrigerate until firm. With pink candy, pipe groups of random lines on waxed paper for coral. Trim waist of topper and pipe dots on crown. Attach crown to topper. Cover all grass areas on topper with blue candy for water. Attach topper to bottom cookie. Attach coral pieces behind topper. Attach back cookie using melted candy at base. Each serves 1.

*Combine Kelly Green with Teal for green shown.

†Brand confectionery coating.

▶ Soaring with a Dinosaur!

Pans: *Go, Diego, Go!*, p. 174, Standard Muffin, p. 154
Tips: 3, 16, 21, p. 144-145
Colors: *Go, Diego, Go!* Icing Color Set (brown, blue, black, *Diego* skin tone), p. 174; Royal Blue, Terra Cotta, Golden Yellow, Leaf Green, Orange, p. 134
Fondant: White Ready-To-Use Rolled Fondant (96 oz.), Brush Set, p. 130; Easy-Glide Fondant Smoother, p. 131; Rolling Pin, Roll & Cut Mat, p. 133
Recipes: Buttercream Icing, p. 116
Also: 2009 Pattern Book (Dinosaur, *Diego* Leg and Foot), p. 128; White Standard Baking Cups, p. 188; Piping Gel, p. 135; 24 x 36 x¼ in. foamcore board, cornstarch, knife, ruler, tape, toothpicks

In advance: Prepare board. Divide pattern into 4 sections and copy to 400%; tape sections together. Use pattern to cut foamcore board. Reserve 1 oz. white fondant; tint 1 oz. terra cotta for tongue; tint remainder royal blue. Cover board (p. 117) and smooth with Fondant Smoother. Roll out blue, white and terra cotta fondant ⅛ in. thick. Use pattern to cut out body, arms and wing details; cut tongue, eye and highlight. Brush backs with damp brush and attach to wrapped board. Use knife to score details on face and legs. **Also:** Bake and cool 8 cupcakes. Ice smooth.

Bake and cool *Diego* cake. Position on foil-wrapped cake board. Trim legs and feet flat where board will rest. Ice cake sides and background areas smooth. Pipe tip 21 shell bottom border. Using tip 3, outline all details. Outline and pipe in mouth, tongue, eyes and irises (smooth with finger dipped in cornstarch). Add dot pupils and highlights. Outline and pipe in watch, vest patch and strap. Cover all remaining visible areas with tip 16 stars. Use tip 3 to overpipe outline eyebrows; outline and pipe in blue edging on vest (smooth with finger). Position prepared board over *Diego* cake, using cupcakes to support wings, head and feet. Shape and attach fondant at point of dinosaur head, positioning behind *Diego*; smooth seam. Use pattern to lightly mark *Diego* foot and leg; mound icing for dimension. Outline details with tip 3. Pipe in sole of shoe (smooth with finger). Cover foot and leg with tip 16 stars. Cake serves 12; each cupcake serves 1.

◀ Hi-Ho, *Diego!*

Pans: Cookie Sheet, Cooling Grid, p. 154
Tips: 1, 2, 3, 4, 6, 8, p. 144
Colors: *Go Diego Go!* Icing Color Set (blue, black, brown, *Diego* skin tone), p. 174; Lemon Yellow, Leaf Green, p. 134
Recipes: Royal Icing, Roll-Out Cookies, p. 116
Also: Dinosaur Plastic Cutter, p. 164; *Go Diego Go!* Icing Decorations, p. 174; Meringue Powder, p. 135; Cake Boards, p. 232; Parchment Triangles, p. 143; cornstarch, waxed paper

In advance: Prepare cookie dough and roll out. Cut dinosaurs with cutter; bake and cool cookies. **Also:** Outline cookie with tip 3; fill in with thinned royal icing in a cut parchment bag. Let dry 24 hours. **And:** Add dot and outline facial features with tip 1; let dry.

Secure cookies to waxed paper-covered board with dots of icing. Pipe body with royal icing. Pipe tip 8 pants, tip 6 shirt and tip 3 vest. Add tip 4 arms, leg and sock; pipe tip 3 shoe. Add tip 2 hands, watchband, strap, pocket piping and patch; add tip 1 patch accent. Pipe neck, about 1 in. long; position *Diego* icing decoration on top. Let dry 24 hours. Each serves 1.

◀ *Strawberry* Strums Along

Pan: *Strawberry Shortcake*™, p. 173

Tips: 2, 3, 7, 13, 16, 352, p. 144-145

Colors:* *Strawberry Shortcake* Icing Color Set (red, pink, green, Strawberry Shortcake skin tone), p. 173; Kelly Green, Brown, Black, p. 134

Fondant: White Ready-To-Use Rolled Fondant (12 oz.), Brush Set, p. 130; Rolling Pin, Roll & Cut Mat, Gum-Tex™, p. 133

Recipes: Buttercream Icing, p. 116; Thinned Fondant Adhesive, p. 117

Also: 2009 Pattern Book (Guitar), p. 128; Fine Tip Primary Colors FoodWriter™ Edible Color Markers, p. 130; Cake Boards, Fanci-Foil Wrap, p. 232; craft knife, waxed paper, cornstarch, ruler

Two days in advance: Mix 1 teaspoon Gum-Tex into 12 oz. white fondant. Tint fondant as follows: 4 oz. red, 2 oz. green, ½ oz. dark red. Use pattern to make guitar (p. 122).

Bake and cool cake; trim to level area where guitar will sit. Ice cake sides and background areas smooth. Using tip 3, outline hat, ribbon, bow, face, shirt and top of arm; pipe in ribbon, bow, mouth and bands on shirt (smooth with finger dipped in cornstarch). Using tip 3, outline eyes and pipe smile; pipe in whites of eyes, irises and pupils (smooth with finger dipped in cornstarch); add tip 2 dot eye highlights. Cover hat, shirt and berries with tip 16 stars, cover face with tip 13 stars. Pipe tip 2 eyelashes and berry seeds; pipe tip 352 leaves on berries. Pipe tip 16 pull-out star hair. Position guitar. Using tip 3, pipe nose; outline arms and fingers then cover with tip 16 stars (overpipe as needed to build up arms to meet guitar). Pipe tip 7 bead bottom border and tip 3 musical notes on cake sides. Serves 12.

*Combine Black with Brown for black on face. Combine Icing Color Set Green with Kelly Green for green on guitar.

▼ Pint-Sized Berries

Pans: Mini Heart, p. 206; Cookie Sheet, Cooling Grid, p. 154

Candy: Red and White Candy Melts®†, Primary and Garden Candy Color Sets p. 166

Recipes: Buttercream Icing, Roll-Out Cookies, p. 116

Also: *Strawberry Shortcake*™ Icing Decorations, p. 173; Red Colored Sugar, p. 136; Daisy Cut-Outs™, p. 132; Heart Plastic Nesting Cutter Set, p. 164; Parchment Triangles, p. 143; Quick Ease Roller, p. 131; jelly spearmint leaves, knife, waxed paper, granulated sugar

In advance: Make cookies. Prepare and roll out dough. Use smallest cutter from set to cut about 12 hearts for each treat. Sprinkle with red sugar. Bake and cool. **Also:** Mold candy boxes. Use Mini Heart Pan and Red Candy Melts® to mold 2 candy shells, ⅛ to ¼ in. thick (p. 125), for each box. Refrigerate until firm. If edges are uneven, rub over warmed cookie sheet.

Tint small amounts of candy pink and green (add a touch of yellow for green shown). Using melted pink candy in cut parchment bag, pipe bead seeds on cookies and box lid. Using melted green candy in cut parchment bag, pipe pull-out dot tops and upright stem on cookies. Roll out spearmint leaves between sheets of waxed paper sprinkled with granulated sugar. Cut strawberry top for box lid using medium daisy cutter. Roll ½ in. long log for stem. Using melted candy, attach strawberry top and icing decoration to box lid; attach upright stem to center of top. Arrange cookies in box. Each serves 1.

▶ Berry-Go-Round

Pan: 6 x 2 in. Round, p. 153

Tips: 2, 16, p. 144-145

Colors: *Strawberry Shortcake* Icing Color Set (red used), p. 173

Fondant: White Ready-To-Use Rolled Fondant, Primary Colors Fondant Multi Pack, Brush Set, p. 130; Fondant Shaping Foam, Fondant/Gum Paste Tool Set, p. 131; Alphabet/Numbers, Daisy Cut-Outs™, p. 132; 9 in. Rolling Pin, Roll & Cut Mat, p. 133

Recipes: Buttercream Icing, p. 116

Also: *Strawberry Shortcake* Candle, p. 173; Heart Plastic Nesting Cutter Set, p. 164; Cake Boards, Fanci-Foil Wrap, p. 232; waxed paper, cornstarch, knife, ruler

Bake and cool 2-layer cake; ice smooth. Roll out red fondant from Multi Pack ⅛ in. thick. Cut 11 hearts using 2nd smallest cutter from set. Attach around cake sides with icing dots. Pipe tip 2 bead seeds. Make strawberry top (p. 122). Pipe tip 16 rope border. Roll out additional red fondant ⅛ in. thick. Use Alphabet Cut-Outs to cut fondant letters; attach to cake top. Position candle. Serves 12.

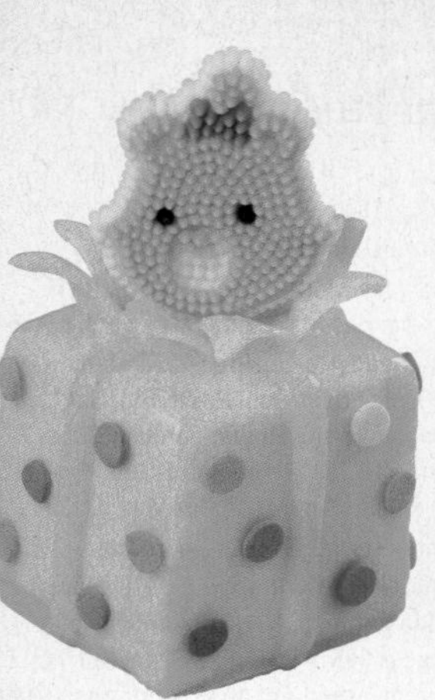

◄ Cakes Wrapped with Care!

Pans: 9 x 13 x 2 in. Sheet, p. 153; Cookie Sheet, Cooling Grid, p. 154

Candy: White Candy Melts®† (1 pk. makes 5 to 6 treats), Primary Candy Color Set, p. 166

Also: *Care Bears™* Icing Decorations, p. 172; Flowerful Medley Sprinkles (confetti), p. 136; Parchment Triangles, p. 143; Plastic Dowel Rods, p. 231; waxed paper, tape, ruler, knife

In advance: Bake and cool sheet cake using firm-textured batter, such as pound cake. Cut into 1½ in. squares. Cover with melted, tinted candy (p. 124); let set.

Make candy tear pieces. Cover dowel rod with waxed paper. Using melted candy in cut parchment bag, pipe triangles in assorted sizes, ¾ in. long. Refrigerate until firm; peel off paper. Tint a portion of melted candy a darker yellow; use a cut parchment bag to pipe ribbon lines over cake top and sides. Using dots of melted candy, attach confetti to sides, icing decoration to top and tear pieces around. Each serves 1.

†Brand confectionery coating.

► *Cheer Bear™* Leads the Team!

Pan: Cookie Sheet, p. 154

Colors: Royal Blue, Lemon Yellow, Golden Yellow, Rose, Kelly Green, p. 134

Fondant: White Ready-To-Use Rolled Fondant (12 oz.), Brush Set, p. 130; Rolling Pin, Roll & Cut Mat, Gum-Tex™, p. 133

Recipes: Buttercream Icing, p. 116

Also: *Care Bears™* Candle, Icing Decorations (2 pks.), p. 172; 13 Count Standard Cupcakes 'N More® Dessert Stand, p. 147; Pastel Silicone Baking Cups, p. 210; Cake Boards, p. 232; Parchment Triangles, p. 143; knife, ruler, cornstarch

In advance: Make fondant bows (p. 121). Let dry 24 hours.

Bake and cool cupcakes in silicone cups supported by baking sheet. Ice smooth. Position 6 loops to form bow. Using cut parchment bag, pipe an icing dot in center; position icing decoration. Position cupcakes and candle on stand. Each serves 1.

*Combine Lemon Yellow with Golden Yellow for yellow shown.

◄ Care Package

Pans: *Care Bears™*, p. 172; Cookie Sheet, Cooling Grid, p. 154

Tips: 2, 3, 6, 16, p. 144-145

Colors: *Care Bears™* Icing Color Set (pink, black, yellow, blue), p. 172; Orange, Leaf Green, Violet, p. 134

Fondant: White Ready-To-Use Rolled Fondant (24 oz.), Brush Set, Fine Tip FoodWriter™ Edible Color Markers (black), p. 130; Heart and Star Cut-Outs™, p. 132; Rolling Pin, Roll & Cut Mat, Gum-Tex™, p. 133

Recipes: Buttercream, Color Flow Icings, Roll-Out Cookies, p. 116; Thinned Fondant Adhesive, p. 117

Also: 2009 Pattern Book (Box, Hat), p. 128; 4 in. Lollipop Sticks, p. 169; 6 in. Cookie Treat Sticks, p. 163; Cake Boards, Fanci-Foil Wrap, p. 232; Parchment Triangles, p. 143; Flowerful Medley Sprinkles, p. 136; knife, ruler, cornstarch

Two days in advance: Make cookies. Prepare and roll out dough. Cut hearts and stars using medium and large Cut-Outs. Bake and cool cookies. Outline with tip 3 and flow in with Color Flow (p. 126); let dry. **Also:** Tint 12 oz. fondant yellow, 2 oz. violet and 1 oz. pink; reserve 2 oz. white. Add 1 teaspoon Gum-Tex to yellow and ¼ teaspoon to all others. Roll out ⅛ in. thick as needed. Prepare fondant box, trims, hat and ribbons (p. 121).

Bake and cool cake. Ice cake sides, tummy, inside ears and background areas smooth. Using tip 3, outline body, eyes, muzzle, mouth and bow; fill in whites of eyes, pupils, inside mouth, tongue, striped bow, rainbow, heart palms and nose (smooth with finger dipped in cornstarch). Cover remainder with tip 16 stars. Add tip 2 outline eyelashes and eyebrows, dot eye highlights. Add tip 6 bead bottom border. Insert hat; pipe tip 3 stripes and tip 16 pull-out star pompom. Position box pieces; outline with tip 3. Position ribbon curls, streamers and gift tag. Cut a ⅛ x 2 in. fondant strip for ribbon on gift tag; turn both ends under and attach from gift tag to box. Cake serves 12; each cookie serves 1.

▼ Floral Fairies

Pans: 10.5 x 15.5 x 1 in. Large Cookie/Jelly Roll, Cooling Grid, p. 154

Colors: Leaf Green, Violet, p. 134

Candy: White Candy Melts®† (1 pk. makes 10-12 treats), Primary, Garden Candy Color Sets, p. 166

Fondant: White Ready-to-Use Rolled Fondant (24 oz.), p. 130; Fondant/Gum Paste Tool Set, Fondant Shaping Foam, Flower Forming Cups, Flower Former Set, p. 131; Leaf Cut-Outs™, p. 132, Gum-Tex™, Rolling Pin, Roll & Cut Mat, p. 133

Recipe: Favorite crisped rice cereal treats

Also: *Disney Fairies* Party Toppers, p. 176; Flower Plastic Cookie Cutter, p. 164; 3 in. Circle Metal Cookie Cutter, p. 165; 8 in. Cookie Treat Sticks, p. 163; 1 in. wide green ribbon (9 in. for each treat), knife, ruler, cornstarch

In advance: Make fondant flowers and leaves. Tint 2 in. balls of fondant violet and green; add ¼ teaspoon Gum-Tex to each and roll out ⅛ in. thick. Cut flowers using plastic cutter; let dry in Flower Forming Cup dusted with cornstarch. Cut leaves with medium Cut-Out. Set on thin foam and imprint veins with veining tool from set. Let dry on medium Flower Formers dusted with cornstarch. **Also:** Prepare stems. Cut Cookie Sticks to 4 in. long. Wrap with ribbon, securing ends with dab of melted candy. Let set. Roll a 1 in. ball of green fondant around 1 end of stick; press fondant into a cone shape, wide end up. Let dry.

Prepare crisped rice cereal treats (1 recipe makes about 15 treats). Press recipe into lightly buttered jelly roll pan; shape remainder into 1¼ in. diameter balls (1 ball makes 2 centers). For bases, use 3 in. metal cutter to cut circles; for flower centers, cut balls in half. Place bases and half balls (flat side down) on cooling grid. Cover with melted candy (p. 124) tinted green and yellow; let set. Make a small hole in center of base; insert stem. Attach leaf to flower stem with melted candy; let set. Using melted candy, attach flower to cone top; let set. Attach flower center and topper with melted candy. Each serves 1.

▲ Treetop *Tink*

Pans: 14 x 3 in. Round, p. 152; 8 x 2 in. Round, p. 153; Sports Ball Set, p. 161

Tips: 1, 3, p. 144

Colors*: Leaf Green, Royal Blue, Lemon Yellow, Violet, Rose, Brown, Red-Red, p. 134

Fondant: White Ready-To-Use Rolled Fondant (72 oz.), Brush Set, White Pearl Dust™ p. 130; Easy-Glide Fondant Smoother, Fondant Shaping Foam, Fondant/Gum Paste Tool Set, Flower Forming Cups, Flower Former Set, p. 131; Flower and Leaf Cut-Outs™, p. 132; Rolling Pin, Roll & Cut Mat, Gum-Tex™, p. 133,

Recipe: Buttercream Icing, p. 116

Also: *Disney Fairies* Candle, p. 176; Tall Tier Cake Stand (10, 16 in. Plates, 2 6½ in. Columns, Top Nut and Bottom Column Bolt), 6 Glue-On Plate Legs, Cake Corer Tube, p. 229; Flower Spikes, p. 231; Light Cocoa, Green Candy Melts®†, p. 166; 6 in. Lollipop Sticks, p. 169; Piping Gel, p. 135; Blue, Violet Color Mist™ Food Color Spray, p. 134; Cake Boards, p. 232; 20-gauge green florist wire (12 9 in. lengths), tea strainer, non-toxic chalks (yellow, light and dark green), plastic glue, knife, ruler, cornstarch

Two days in advance: Make fondant leaves and flowers (p. 122). **Also:** Glue plastic legs onto bottom of 16 in. plate.

Bake and cool 1-layer (2 in. high) 8 in. cake, 1-layer (3 in. high) 14 in. cake and ½ Sports Ball cake. Prepare 14 in. cake for Center Column Construction (p. 115). Position 8 in. cake on 10 in. board with center hole cut out. Ice 14 in. cake blue. Spray with Violet and Blue Color Mist™ for random cloud effect. Position on base plate. Attach 10 in. plate to columns and secure with top nut. Make fondant tree trunk (p. 122). Place 8 in. cake on prepared cake circle; top with ½ Sports Ball cake. Position on 10 in. plate. Ice smooth using extra icing at the bottom to create a smooth mound going all the way to edge of prepared cake circle. Position candle on top. Use icing to attach medium leaves and medium flowers to cover tree top and hide plate edge. (Note: If cake will be transported, you will need to complete decorating at the party, after plate with 10 in. prepared board and cakes are positioned on tree trunk. In this case, keep plate edge exposed and add extra flowers and leaves at the party.) Use icing to attach leaves and flowers to 14 in. cake top and bottom border. Pipe tip 3 name; add tip 1 dots and outline stars. Cut wire into 7 in. and 9 in. lengths. Shape into curls and spirals, leaving 1 end straight; insert straight end into Flower Spikes and secure with fondant. Randomly insert spikes into 14 in. cake top and sides. Attach flowers and leaves, curls and spirals with melted candy. Serves 46.

*Combine Violet with Rose for violet shown. Combine Brown with Red-Red for brown shown.

▶ *Ariel's* Splashy Celebration

Pans: *Disney Princess*, p. 177; 14 x 2 in. Round, p. 153; Cookie Sheet, Cooling Grid, p. 154

Tips: 1, 2, 3, 6, 16, 112, p. 144-145

Colors:* *Disney Princess* Icing Color Set (red, teal, *Ariel* skin tone), p. 177; Lemon Yellow, Orange, Violet, Rose, Royal Blue, Brown, Black, p. 134

Candy: White and Red Candy Melts®† (2 pks. each), Primary and Garden Candy Color Sets, p. 166; Seashells Candy Mold, p. 167; 11¾ in. Lollipop Sticks, p. 169

Recipes: Buttercream, Royal Icings, Roll-Out Cookies, p. 116

Also: Tall Tier Cake Stand Set (18 in. Footed Base, 6½ in. Columns (2), Bottom Column Bolt), Cake Corer Tube, p. 229; Fish Metal Cutter, p. 165; Sapphire Blue Pearl Dust™, p. 130; Blue Color Mist™, p. 134; Meringue Powder, p. 135; Cake Boards, p. 232; Parchment Triangles, p. 143; Plastic Dowel Rods, p. 231; granulated brown sugar, waxed paper, light blue curling ribbon (80 in.), glue

Several days in advance: Make cookies. Prepare and roll out dough. Cut 5 fish using cutter. Bake and cool cookies. Decorate with royal icing on waxed paper-covered board. Ice smooth. Pipe tip 3 dot eye; add tip 3 dot pupil. Pipe tip 6 bead fins and lips. Let dry. **Also:** Use royal icing to pipe seascape details on waxed paper-covered boards. For coral, pipe tip 16 branches, 10 each violet and rose. Pipe 12 pieces of green seaweed, 3½ to 14 in. high, using tip 112. Let dry. Use Thinned Royal Icing in cut parchment bag to pipe bubble groups (½, ¾ and 1 in. dots); let dry overnight then dust edges with Pearl Dust. **And:** Attach seaweed, 6 coral pieces, fish and bubble groups to lollipop sticks with icing. Trim lollipop sticks as needed; for tallest, tape 2 sticks together for extra height. Let dry. **And:** Mold candy pieces. Tint portions of candy orange, pink and yellow using candy colors. Mold 4 solid starfish and 8 marbleized seashells (p. 124). Mold *Ariel* candy plaque (p. 126).

Bake and cool 2-layer cake; prepare for Center Column Construction (p. 115). Ice smooth and spray with Color Mist. Position on 18 in. base plate. Ice outer edge of plate and sprinkle on brown sugar. Pipe tip 6 bead bottom border. Pipe tip 3 message. Insert 2 plastic dowel rods where candy plaque will sit. Attach candy plaque to center column with melted candy. Use icing to attach coral and candy shells around bottom of cake; position remaining pieces of seascape. Tie curling ribbon around exposed lollipop sticks; secure with melted candy. Serves 63.

*Combine Violet with Rose for violet shown.

†Brand confectionery coating.

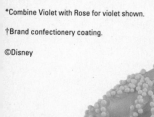

◀ Wish Upon a Starfish

Pan: Mini Star, p. 156; Cookie Sheet, Cooling Grid, p. 154

Candy: White Candy Melts®† (1 pk. covers 6 treats), Primary Candy Color Set, p. 166

Also: *Disney Princess* Party Toppers, p. 177; White Nonpareils Sprinkles, p. 136; Parchment Triangles, p. 143; waxed paper

Bake and cool cakes. Tint white candy light orange using candy color. Cover cakes with melted candy (p. 124), reserving some candy for decorating. Refrigerate until set. Use reserved candy in cut parchment bag to pipe random lines over cake immediately; sprinkle with nonpareils. Attach topper with melted candy. Each serves 1.

THE AMAZING SPIDER-MAN

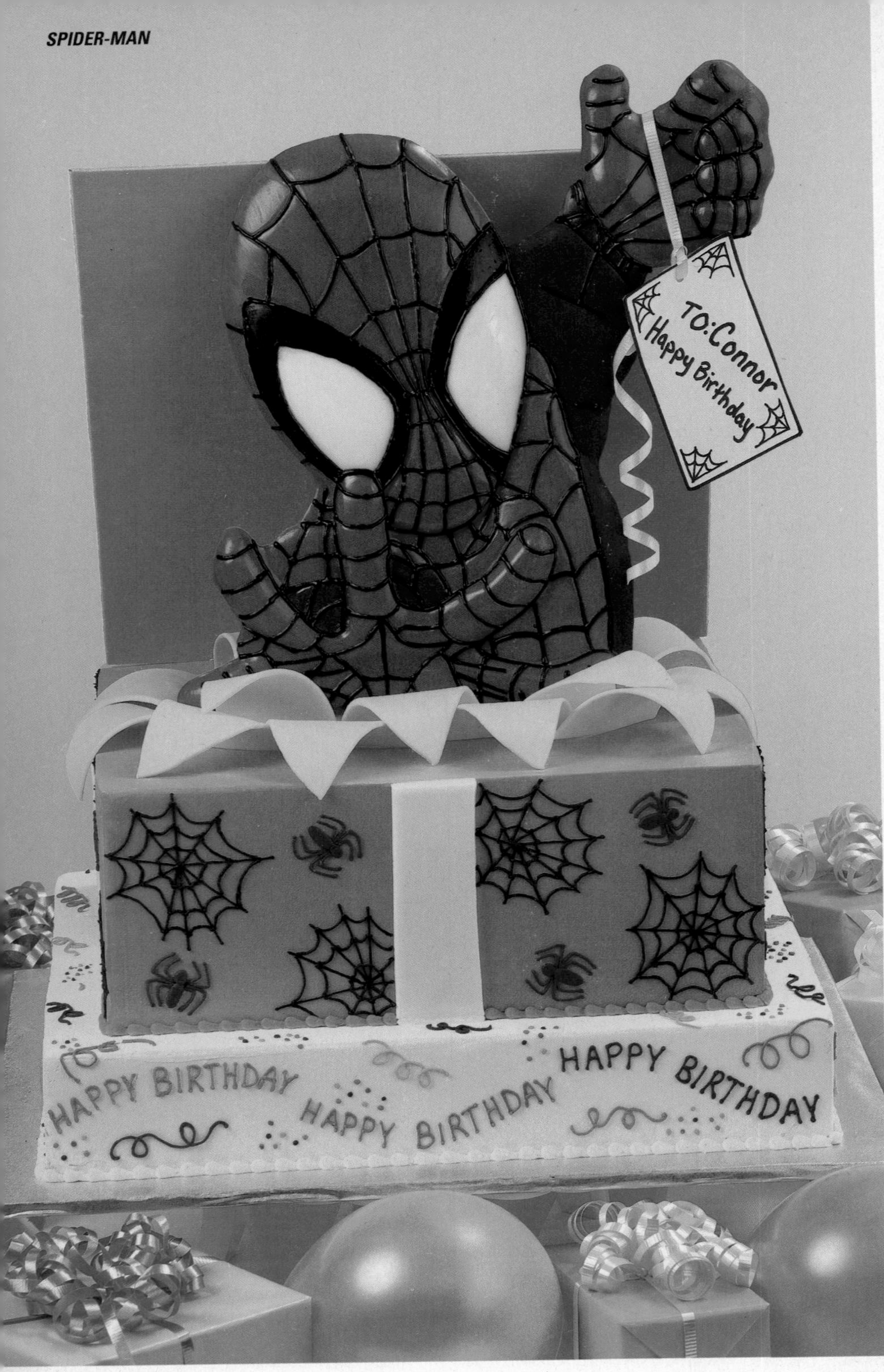

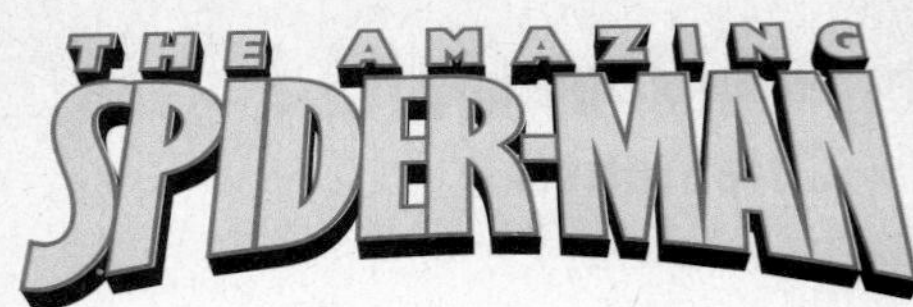

◀ Take His Gift for a Spin!

Pans: *Spider-Man*, p. 180; 10, 12 x 2 in. Squares, p. 153

Tips: 1, 5, p. 144

Colors:* Royal Blue, Black, Lemon Yellow, Golden Yellow, Red-Red, Leaf Green, Orange, p. 134

Fondant: White Ready-To-Use Rolled Fondant (24 oz.), p. 130; Flower Former Set, p. 137; Rolling Pin, Roll & Cut Mat, Gum-Tex™, p. 133

Candy: Red (2 pks.) and White (1 pk.) Candy Melts®†, Primary and Garden Candy Color Sets, p. 166

Recipe: Buttercream Icing, p. 116

Also: 2009 Pattern Book (Paper Tear), p. 128; Tall Tier Cake Stand (14 in. plate, two 7¾ in. columns, bottom bolt), Glue-On Plate Legs (6), Cake Corer Tube, p. 229; Plastic Dowel Rods, p. 231; Cake Boards, Fanci-Foil Wrap, p. 232; Parchment Triangles, p. 143; 14 x 14 x ¼ in. foamcore board, 20 in. yellow curling ribbon, card stock, blue and black markers, ruler, knife, cornstarch, glue for plastic, waxed paper, hole punch

Two or more days in advance: Make candy plaque (p. 126). **Also:** Make fondant pieces. Tint 18 oz. fondant light blue; add 1½ teaspoons. Gum-Tex. Roll out ⅛ in. thick. For paper tears, use pattern to cut 14 pieces. Let dry on medium and large flower formers dusted with cornstarch. For box lid, tint remaining fondant darker blue; roll out ⅛ in. thick. Cut a 10 in. square. Let dry on waxed paper-covered board. **And:** Prepare base plate. Glue 6 legs onto bottom of 14 in. plate from tier set. Cut hole in center of foamcore board for column and wrap with foil (p. 110).

Bake and cool 2-layer 10 in. and 1-layer 12 in. cakes. Prepare bottom board, cakes on cake boards plus 2 extra 10 in. cake circles for Center Column and Stacked Construction (p. 114-115). Ice cakes smooth and stack, placing 10 in. cake circles first on 14 in. plate to fill depression. Tint 6 oz. fondant yellow; roll out ⅛ in. thick. Cut four 1¼ x 4 in. strips for ribbon; attach to 10 in. cake sides with icing. Pipe tip 5 bead bottom borders; pipe tip 1 spiders, webs, letters, confetti and streamers. Position 2 dowel rods in cake where candy plaque will rest. Attach candy plaque to center column with melted candy; hold until set. Arrange paper tear pieces around *Spider-Man*. Lean box lid from back cake edge onto center column; secure with icing. Cut 2 x 4 in. card; decorate and print message with marker. Punch hole and tie onto 20 in. ribbon. Secure one end of ribbon to plaque with melted candy; curl other end. Serves 54.

*Combine Lemon Yellow with Golden Yellow for yellow shown.

▶ Web Walker

Pans: Jumbo Muffin, p. 146; Cookie Sheet, Cooling Grid, p. 154

Candy: White, Red, Dark Cocoa Candy Melts®†, Garden Candy Color Set, p. 166

Also: *Spider-Man* Party Toppers, p. 180; 101 Cookie Cutters Set, p. 164; Parchment Triangles, p. 143; Cake Boards, p. 232; ruler, waxed paper, toothpicks

In advance: Make candy bases using largest round cutter from set. Place cutter on waxed paper-covered board; fill with melted candy to ¼ in. deep. Refrigerate until firm; unmold.

Bake and cool muffins, trim to 1½ in. high. Cover with melted candy (p. 124); let set. Divide into 8ths and lightly mark division points on top and sides. Using melted candy in cut parchment bag, pipe vertical lines over marks and curved lines between. Attach candy base and topper with melted candy. Each serves 1.

MARVEL

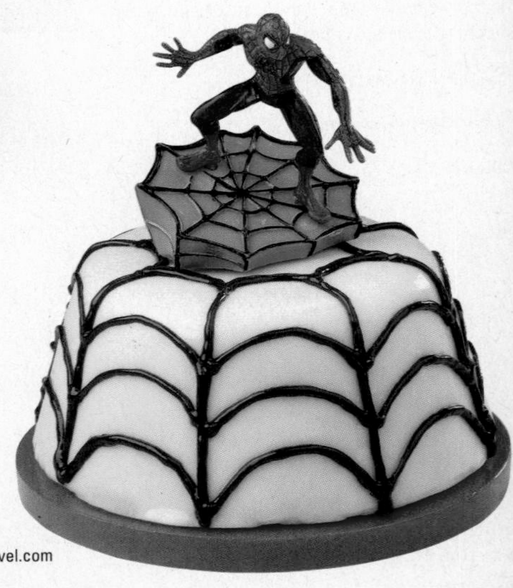

▶ *Scooby's* Sitting on a Secret

Pan: Dimensions® Multi-Cavity Mini Cupcake, p. 151

Candy: White Candy Melts®†, Primary and Garden Candy Color Sets, p. 166

Also: *Scooby-Doo!* Party Toppers, p. 181; Flowerful Medley Sprinkles, p. 136; Parchment Triangles, p. 143; waxed paper, candy-coated chocolates

Melt and tint portions of candy pink, blue and yellow using candy colors; reserve some white. Mold ¼ in. thick candy shells (p. 125) for bottom and lid in pan cavities. Let set; unmold. Attach confetti from Flowerful Medley assortment and topper to lid with melted candy in cut parchment bag. Fill bottom with candy-coated chocolates. Each serves 1.

†Brand confectionery coating.

◀ A *Scooby*-Sized Treat

Pan: *Scooby-Doo!*, p. 181

Tips: 3, 12, 16, 20, p. 144-145

Colors:* *Scooby-Doo!* Icing Color Set (brown, yellow, black, teal), p. 181; Red-Red, Leaf Green, Violet, Rose, p. 134

Fondant: White Ready-To-Use Rolled Fondant (3 oz.), Brush Set, p. 130; Rolling Pin, Roll & Cut Mat, p. 133

Recipes: Buttercream Icing, p. 116; Thinned Fondant Adhesive, p. 117

Also: Jumbo Confetti Sprinkles, Flowerful Medley Sprinkles, p. 136; 6 in. Lollipop Sticks, p. 169; Cake Boards, Fanci-Foil 232; knife, ruler, toothpicks

In advance: Make candle. Tint 1 oz. fondant in each color: light green, dark green, yellow. Roll out light green ¼ in. thick. Cut a ¾ x 2½ in. rectangle for candle base; attach to lollipop stick using thinned fondant adhesive, leaving 1 in. of stick extended at top and bottom. Roll out dark green and yellow fondant ⅛ in. thick. Cut ¼ in. wide green stripes; brush back with damp brush and attach, trimming as needed. Cut 1 in. high yellow flame; attach to top of stick with adhesive. Let dry.

Bake and cool cake. Trim off hamburger and top hand. Ice sides and background areas smooth. Use tip 3 to outline all and pipe in inside ears, eyes, tongue, dog tag and ring, plus eyebrows, nose, mouth and spots (smooth with finger dipped in cornstarch). Pipe tip 3 dot pupils; flatten slightly. Cover Scooby and collar with tip 16 stars. Using tip 12, outline and pipe in baking cup in alternating colors; pipe swirls for cupcake top. Pipe tip 3 name and position confetti from Flowerful Medley assortment; insert candle. Pipe tip 20 rosette bottom border; attach Jumbo Confetti to centers. Serves 12.

MATT

*Combine Violet with Rose for light and dark violet shades shown.

Scary
Boo

Holiday Heroes!

If your cakes and treats make someone smile this season, you deserve a round of applause! Here are the desserts that will make your name: A North Pole Christmas party with gift cookies, stand-up elf cupcakes and 3-D Santa and Mrs. Claus cakes. Easter chicks in chocolate-covered coconut nests, perched high in our cupcake stand with candy leaves all around. For Halloween, a frightful feast of spider sandwiches, ghost cupcakes and a terrifying tier cake with 3-D spiders and jack-o-lantern. With our ideas, it's easy to conquer the calendar!

Spin a Scary Tale

Pans: Dimensions® Large Pumpkin, p. 151; 10, 14 x 2 in. Rounds, p. 153
Tips: 1, 3, 5, 16, p. 144-145
Colors:* Black, Violet, Rose, Orange, Red-Red, Lemon Yellow, Golden Yellow, Leaf Green, p. 134
Fondant: White Ready-To-Use Rolled Fondant (158 oz.), p. 130; Easy-Glide Fondant Smoother, Brush Set, p. 131; Round Cut-Outs™, p. 132; Rolling Pin, Roll & Cut Mat, Gum-Tex™, p. 133
Recipes: Buttercream Icing, p. 116; Chocolate Fondant, Thinned Fondant Adhesive, p. 117
Also: Dark Cocoa Candy Melts®† (63 oz.), p. 166; Pumpkins Nesting Cutter Set, p. 197; 2½ in. Globe Pillar and Base Set, p. 228; 12 in. Decorator Preferred® Smooth Edge Plate, p. 230; Dowel Rod, p. 231; 16 in. Round Silver Cake Base, Cake Boards, p. 232; Piping Gel, p. 135; marshmallows, light corn syrup, cornstarch, ruler, knife

In advance: Prepare 108 oz. of Chocolate Fondant; tint black. Tint white fondant as follows: 36 oz. violet; 12 oz. orange; 1 oz. green (reserve 1 oz. white). **Also:** Make spider legs. (p. 122). **And:** Cover Cake Base (p. 124) with 24 oz. violet fondant.

Bake and cool 2-pc. pumpkin and 2-layer round cakes. Prepare cakes for Stacked (p. 114) and Globe Pillar Construction (p. 115). Prepare and cover both cakes with black fondant (p. 117). Make fondant pumpkins, attach to cake sides and decorate (p. 122). Pipe tip 1 words and swirls on sides of both cakes. Pipe tip 5 bead border on 10 in. cake. For small spiders, pipe tip 5 body and pat smooth. With tip 1, outline and pipe in hats (pat smooth); add outline hat band and stripes, legs, hanging string, dot and string facial features.

Decorate pumpkin. Trim off stem and leaves; position on cut-to-fit cake board. Ice eyes, nose and mouth areas smooth; outline features using tip 3. Cover with tip 16 stars. Attach marshmallow to top for stem; cover with tip 16 lines. Make globe spiders (p. 122). **At party:** Assemble cakes. Serves 113.

*Combine Orange with a little Red-Red for orange shown. Combine Violet with Rose for violet shown. Combine Lemon Yellow with Golden Yellow for yellow shown.

Spiders Step Lively

Pans: Mini Jack-O-Lantern Silicone Mold, p. 194; Cookie Sheet, Cooling Grid, p. 154
Candy: White, Orange Candy Melts®†, Primary, Garden Candy Color Sets, p. 166; Cordial Cups Candy Mold, p. 168
Also: Parchment Triangles, p. 143; pretzel sticks, purple spice drops, knife, scissors, paper, waxed paper, granulated sugar

In advance: Make candy hats and 6 pretzel spider legs per treat (p. 125).

Bake and cool mini cakes; trim off stem and facial features. Lay flat on cooling grid set over drip pan. Use melted candy in cut parchment bag to cover top; let set. Turn cakes over and cover bottom and sides with melted candy (p. 124); let set. Set cakes flat and pipe dot eyes, pupils and nose with melted candy; let set. Use warm knife to cut small holes near bottom for legs; insert legs, adjusting angles so spider will stand. Attach hat with melted candy. Each serves 1.

Spiderwich

Pan: Mini Ball, p. 161
Tips: 2A, 4, 9, p. 144
Also: Ham salad or chicken salad, hot roll mix, cream cheese, black and green olives, whole carrots, carrot sticks, cucumbers, knife, potato peeler

Bake rolls in pan cavities; let cool. Trim carrot sticks to ¼ x 1½ in. long; use peeler to round edges. Cut cucumber slice for hat brim; cut whole carrot piece for hat top. For 6 legs, remove pimiento from green olives and cut hole in side; insert 2 carrot sticks for leg sections. Cut a hole in top of roll; using tip 2A, fill with finely chopped ham or chicken salad. Cut holes in side of roll; insert legs. Cut a black olive half for mouth. Pipe tip 4 dot eyes in cream cheese. Using narrow end of tip 9, cut black olive pupils. Position pupils and hat; attach mouth with cream cheese. Each serves 1.

Ghostly Goodies

Pan: Standard Muffin, p. 154
Recipe: Chocolate Buttercream Icing, p. 116
Also: Boo! Scary! Fun Pix®, Baking Cups, p. 195; Jumbo Ghost Sprinkles, p. 196

Bake and cool cupcakes. Ice with spatula. Insert pick; position ghost sprinkles. Each serves 1.

Creepy Candies

Candy: Happy Haunters Lollipop Mold, White, Orange, Light Cocoa Candy Melts®†, p. 196; Primary, Garden Candy Color Sets, p. 166; Parchment Triangles, p. 143

Mold candies using piping method (p. 125).

▼ Damsels of the Darkside

Pans: Mini Wonder Mold, p. 156; Cookie Sheet, Cooling Grid, p. 154
Tips: 1, 2, 3, 4, 6, 10, p. 144
Colors:* Black, Orange, Leaf Green, Lemon Yellow, Violet, Golden Yellow, p. 134
Cookie: 18 Pc. Halloween Cutter Set, 6 Pc. Halloween Mini Cutter Set, p. 197; 6 in. Cookie Treat Sticks, p. 163
Recipes: Buttercream, Chocolate Buttercream, Royal Icings, Roll-Out Cookies, p. 116
Also: Meringue Powder, p. 135; spearmint leaves, hard stick candy, cornstarch, knife, waxed paper, granulated sugar

In advance: Prepare and roll out cookie dough. Cut heads using Witch and Frankenstein cutters from 18 Pc. Set. Cut cat using cutter from Mini Set. Bake and cool cookies. **Also:** Decorate cookies with royal icing. Ice face areas smooth. Pipe tip 4 dots for whites of eyes. Use tip 3 to overpipe eyelids, add outline ears and pipe dot nose and cheeks. Use tip 2 to pipe dot pupils, zigzag mouth and eyebrows. Finish bride with tip 4 zigzag hair. For witch's hat, outline and pipe in brim and top with tip 6 (smooth with finger dipped in cornstarch). Pipe tip 4 outline band and tip 3 buckle. Finish with tip 3 outline hair and tip 2 tooth. For cat, ice smooth then outline with tip 2; pipe tip 1 line and dot features. Let cookies dry. **And:** Attach cookie sticks to back of heads with royal icing. Let dry.

Bake and cool mini cake bodies. Spatula ice cakes. Cut stick candy to 4 in. long; insert into cake sides for arms, leaving 2 in. exposed. Pipe on icing for sleeves with tip 10; smooth with spatula to cover. Cut spearmint leaves to shape hands; dip in granulated sugar to seal cut edges. Attach with icing. Pipe tip 3 zigzag cuffs. Insert cookie heads; trim cookie sticks as needed. Attach cat to witch. Each serves 1.

*Combine Leaf Green with Lemon Yellow for green shown. For Black, begin with chocolate icing so less color is required.

▲ Ice Scream Sandwiches

Pans: Cookie Sheet, Cooling Grid, p. 154
Tips: 2, 3, p. 144
Colors:* Orange, Leaf Green, Lemon Yellow, Golden Yellow, Black, p. 134
Recipes: Buttercream Icing, Shortbread Cookies, p. 116
Also: Halloween Push 'N Print™ Cutter Set, p. 197; Halloween Confetti, Nonpareils, Ghost Mix Sprinkles, p. 196; Boo! Scary Party Bags, p. 195; ice cream, plastic wrap, cornstarch

In advance: Prepare dough; tint portions green and orange. Roll out and cut cookies using cutter set (2 cookies for each sandwich). Bake and cool. Decorate top cookies and assemble ice cream sandwiches (p. 121). Place sandwiches in Party Bags. Freeze until ready to serve. Each serves 1.

*Combine Leaf Green with Lemon Yellow for green shown.

◀ Quick as a Cat

Pans: Iridescents! Jack-O-Lantern, p. 194; Cookie Sheet, Cooling Grid, p. 154

Tips: 2A, 5, p. 144

Colors:* Christmas Red, Orange, p. 134

Recipes: Buttercream Icing, Roll-Out Cookies, p. 116

Also: 2009 Pattern Book (Ears, Eyes, Nose, Mouth), p. 128; Chocolate Ready-To-Use Decorator Icing, p. 135; White Candy Melts®† (1 pk.), p. 166; 6 in. Lollipop Sticks, p. 169; Cake Boards, Fanci-Foil Wrap, p. 232; Parchment Triangles, p. 143; Quick-Ease Roller, Brush Set, p. 131; large spice drops, black licorice twists, green taffy, waxed paper, granulated sugar, knife, toothpicks, cornstarch, ruler

In advance: Prepare and roll out cookie dough. Use pattern to cut 2 ears (flip pattern for left ear). Bake and cool. Attach lollipop sticks to backs using melted candy.

On 1-layer cake, cut off stem and leaves. Spatula ice cake and cookies. Use tip 5 to outline and fill in inside of ears (smooth with finger dipped in cornstarch). Insert sticks into cake sides to position ears. Using pattern, mark eyes with toothpick; pipe in with tip 2A (flatten with finger dipped in cornstarch). Cut jumbo spice drop in half; attach for pupils. Use pattern and green taffy to shape nose; attach with icing. Cut licorice twists to 3 in. long; attach for whiskers. Using pattern, mark mouth; outline with tip 5. Serves 12.

*Combine Orange with Christmas Red for Orange shown.

▶ The Season's Starlet

Pan: Star, p. 161

Tips: 1, 3, 12, 16, 21, p. 144-145

Colors:* Violet, Rose, Orange, Leaf Green, Lemon Yellow, Black, Red-Red, p. 134

Recipe: Buttercream Icing, p. 116

Also: 2009 Pattern Book (Witch Face, Witch Hat), p. 128; 16 in. Cake Circles, Fanci-Foil Wrap, p. 232; toothpicks, cornstarch

Bake and cool cake. Position on foil-wrapped cake board cut ¾ in. larger than pan. Ice sides smooth. Use patterns to mark face and hat. Use tip 3 to pipe mouth, tongue and teeth (pat smooth with finger dipped in cornstarch). Build up areas for nose, cheeks and whites of eyes using tip 12; pat smooth. Outline and fill in pupils; pat smooth. Pipe tip 1 outline veins. Outline face with tip 3; cover with tip 16 stars. Add tip 3 dot wart on nose. Outline and fill in hat band and buckle with tip 12; pat smooth. Outline hat with tip 3; cover with tip 16 stars then overpipe with more tip 16 stars. Pipe tip 16 lines for hair. Finish with tip 21 star bottom border. Serves 12.

*Combine Violet with Rose for violet shown. Combine Leaf Green with Lemon Yellow for green shown.

◀ Graveyard Wave

Candy: White Candy Melts®† (3 pks.), Primary and Garden Candy Color Sets, p. 166; Tombstones Candy Mold, Mummies, Haunted Halloween, Halloween Pretzel Molds, p. 196; Pumpkin Harvest Pretzel Mold, p. 198

Also: Parchment Triangles, p. 143; Decorator Brush Set, p. 168; Fanci-Foil Wrap, 13 x 19 in. Cake Board, p. 232; pretzel rods, green curling ribbon, craft block, hot glue gun, knife, ruler, plastic wrap

In advance: Cut cake board to 10½x10½ in. and wrap with foil (p. 110). Cut craft block to 7½ x 7½ x 2 in. and wrap with foil.

Melt candy and tint 1 pk. gray (using black candy color) and other portions green (combine yellow and green candy color), light green, yellow, orange, purple and black. Reserve a portion white. Use Tombstone Mold to mold 12 grass bases and 12 tombstones. Refrigerate until firm; unmold. Mold 13 pretzel candies using painting or piping method (p. 125). Refrigerate until firm; unmold.

Attach craft block to cake board using hot glue gun. Use knife to cut tight-fitting holes in block for pretzels, staggering holes. Wrap bottom ends of pretzels with plastic wrap and insert into base. Cut ribbon into various lengths and curl. Arrange around pretzels. Secure grass bases and attach tombstones with melted candy. Each candy serves 1.

†Brand confectionery coating.

▲ He's Counting on You!

Pans: Mini Ball, p. 161; Cooling Grid, p. 154

Candy: *White, Dark Cocoa, Red Candy Melts®†, Primary, Garden Candy Color Sets, p. 166

Also: White Jumbo Baking Cups, p. 148; Parchment Triangles, p. 143; Cake Boards, p. 232; ruler, pencil, waxed paper

In advance: Make candy cowl (p. 125).

Bake and cool mini ball cakes. Trim ¼ in. from bottom for a ¾ in. high cake. Tint portions of melted candy green and black using candy colors. Cover cakes with melted green candy (p. 124); let set. Pipe facial features and hair using melted candy in cut parchment bags; let set. Position cake on candy cowl. Each serves 1.

*Combine green with yellow candy colors for green shown.

▼ Lunar Landing

Pans: Cookie Sheet, Cooling Grid, p. 154

Tip: 3, p. 144

Color: Golden Yellow, p. 134

Recipes: Buttercream Icing, Roll-Out Cookies, p. 116

Also: 18 Pc. Halloween Cutter Set, p. 197; Spiders & Bats Icing Decorations, p. 195; Yellow Sparkle Gel, p. 135

Prepare and roll out cookie dough. Cut cookies using moon cutter from set. Bake and cool. Outline using buttercream and tip 3. Fill in with Sparkle Gel; attach bat before gel sets. Each serves 1.

▲ Hanging Out on Halloween

Pans: 10½ x 15½ x 1 in. Jelly Roll/ Cookie, Cooling Grid, p. 154

Candy: Light Cocoa, White Candy Melts®†, p. 166; 4 in. Lollipop Sticks, p. 169

Also: 18 Pc. Halloween Cutter Set, p. 197; Spiders & Bats Icing Decorations, p. 195; Parchment Triangles, p. 143

Bake and cool 1-in. high cake using firm-textured batter such as pound cake. Cut cakes using spider web cutter from set. Place on cooling grid placed over drip pan. Cover with melted candy (p. 124); let set. Pipe web lines using melted candy in cut parchment bag. Trim lollipop sticks to 3 in. long. Insert into side of cake. Attach icing decorations to stick and to web with melted candy. Each serves 1.

◀ He Owns the Night!

Pans: Teddy Bear, p. 159; Cookie Sheet, Cooling Grid, p. 154

Tips: 3, 16, p. 144-145

Colors:* Black, Red-Red, Christmas Red, Leaf Green, Lemon Yellow, Violet, Rose, p. 134

Fondant: White Ready-To-Use Rolled Fondant (24 oz.), Brush Set, p. 130; Easy-Glide Fondant Smoother, p. 131; Rolling Pin, Roll & Cut Mat, p. 133

Recipes: Buttercream Icing, Roll-Out Cookies, p. 116

Also: 2009 Pattern Book (Cape, Lapels, Foot, Hand), p. 128; Piping Gel, p. 135; Fanci-Foil Wrap, p. 232; ½ in. thick foamcore board, knife, ruler, cornstarch

In advance: Prepare base board. Enlarge cape pattern to double size (approx. 14 in. long) and use to cut out foamcore board. Tint 18 oz. fondant red and 6 oz. black. Cover board with red fondant (p. 124). Roll out black ⅛ in. thick and cut 1 in. wide strips to trim cape and cover board edges; attach with damp brush.

Prepare and roll out cookie dough. Use patterns to cut 3 each right and left feet and hands (reverse patterns for left foot and hand). Bake and cool cookies.

Bake and cool cake. Trim off ears and facial features. Position on covered board. Stack hands and feet cookies (3 each for right and left) with icing and position next to cake. Use tip 3 to outline and fill in whites of eyes, pupils, mouth and shirt (smooth with finger dipped in cornstarch). Outline details with tip 3. Pipe tip 16 pull-out stars for hair. Cover remainder of cake and cookies with tip 16 stars; overpipe nose for dimension. Pipe tip 3 dot for medallion; flatten and edge with tip 3 dots. Outline eyebrows with tip 3. Outline and fill-in teeth (smooth with finger). Cake serves 12; each cookie serves 1.

*Combine Red-Red with Christmas Red for red shown. Combine Leaf Green with Lemon Yellow for green shown. Combine Violet with Rose for violet shown.

▶ Business is in the Red

Pans: Stand-Up House, p. 157; Mini Loaf, p. 154
Tips: 2, 3, 5, 7, 18, p. 144-145
Colors:*: Violet, Rose, Black, Red-Red, Copper (for skin tone shown), Brown, Golden Yellow, Leaf Green, p. 134
Candy:* White, Dark Cocoa, Orange, Red Candy Melts®†, Garden, Primary Candy Color Sets, p. 166; Monsters Candy Mold, p. 196
Recipe: Buttercream Icing, p. 116
Also: Smiling Pumpkins Icing Decorations, p. 195; Parchment Triangles, p. 143; Cake Boards, Fanci-Foil Wrap, p. 232; shredded coconut, cornstarch, tape, ruler, knife

In advance: Make 3 vampire candies without sticks using painting or piping method (p. 125). Refrigerate until firm; unmold. Cut to shorten vampire for coffin. **Also:** Make bases for 2 standing vampires. In Mini Loaf Pan, mold a ¼ in. thick green candy plaque (p. 126). Refrigerate until firm; unmold, bring to room temperature. Cut two 1 x 2 in. rectangles and attach to bottom of vampires with melted candy; let set. **And:** Prepare base board: Cut 3 boards to 8 x 16 in.; tape and wrap with foil.

Bake and cool house and 1 mini loaf. Trim windows off house. Ice smooth 1¾ x 4 in. high door, 1 x 1½ in. high front windows and 1½ x 2 in. high side windows. Outline all with tip 5. Pipe in tip 5 head in window (smooth with finger dipped in cornstarch). Using tip 2, pipe dot eyes, pupils, nose, mouth and pull-out hair. Pipe tip 7 band bricks on house. Overpipe window and door trim with tip 5. Pipe tip 3 outline door handle. Print "FIRST NATIONAL" with tip 3 and other messages with tip 2. Spatula ice roof, creating scalloped look; add tip 18 zigzag eaves.

For coffin, ice mini loaf smooth; mound brown icing on foot half of top for lid. Ice remainder of top smooth in white. Using tip 5, outline top and pipe in pillow. Position half vampire on coffin. Pipe tip 5 outline handles and hinges on coffin. Position standing vampires and coffin on base board. Tint coconut green (p. 120); ice areas on base board and sprinkle with coconut. Position pumpkin icing decorations. Cakes serve 13; each candy serves 1.

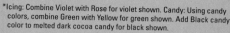

*Icing: Combine Violet with Rose for violet shown. Candy: Using candy colors, combine Green with Yellow for green shown. Add Black candy color to melted dark cocoa candy for black shown.

†Brand confectionery coating.

▲ Creature Reachers

Pan: Cookie Sheet, p. 154
Tips: 2, 2A, 3, 16, p. 144-145
Colors:* Leaf Green, Lemon Yellow, Black, Orange, p. 134
Fondant: White Ready-To-Use Rolled Fondant, Brush Set, p. 130; Cutter/Embosser, p. 131; Rolling Pin, Roll & Cut Mat, p. 133
Recipe: Buttercream Icing (stiff consistency), p. 116
Also: Silly-Feet! Silicone Baking Cups, p. 148; 4 in. Lollipop Sticks, p. 169; Cordial Cups Candy Mold, p. 168; 101 Cookie Cutters Set, p. 164; scissors, cornstarch, ruler, knife

In advance: Make fondant hat and arms. Tint fondant (about 2 oz. black and 2 oz. green plus small amounts of orange. For hat, dust inside of cordial cup mold with cornstarch. Press in black fondant and unmold. Roll out black and orange fondant ⅛ in. thick. Cut brim using smallest round cutter from set. Cut ¼ in. strip for hat band. Assemble hat using damp brush; let dry on cornstarch-dusted surface. For arms, cut lollipop sticks to 3 in. Tint fondant to match icing; roll into logs, ⅜ x 2 in. long. Insert stick, leaving 1½ in. exposed. Taper for wrist and flatten for hand; cut slits for fingers. Set aside to dry.

Bake and cool cupcakes in silicone cups supported by cookie sheet. Cover top with tip 2A icing mound; smooth with spatula. Insert arms. Starting at bottom, pipe tip 16 pull-out hair. Position hat. Use tip 3 to pipe dot nose, cheeks (flatten with fingertip), whites of eyes; outline and fill in mouth. Use tip 2 to pipe dot pupils, square tooth, outline eyebrows and pull-out nails. Each serves 1.

*Combine Leaf Green with Lemon Yellow for green shown.

▲ Sweet Dreams

Pan: 7 x 11 in. Non-Stick Biscuit/Brownie, p. 150
Candy: Monsters Candy Mold, p. 196; White, Dark Cocoa Candy Melts®†, Garden and Primary Candy Color Sets, p. 166
Also: 2009 Pattern Book (Coffin), p. 128; Parchment Triangles, p. 143; 10 x 14 in. Cake Boards, p. 232; knife, ruler, waxed paper, warming tray

In advance: Make coffin (p. 125). Tint portions of melted white candy red, violet, black, gray and yellow using candy colors. Mold monsters using painting method; refrigerate until firm. Pipe coffin handles using melted yellow candy. Position monsters and coffin lids. Each serves 1.

◀ A Season to Crow About!

Pans: Cookie Sheet, Cooling Grid p. 154

Tips: 1, 2, 3, 4, 16, 102, 124, p. 144-145

Colors:* Kelly Green, Golden Yellow, Orange, Red-Red, Christmas Red, Black, Ivory, Royal Blue, p. 134

Recipes: Buttercream, Royal Icings, p. 116

Also: Silly-Feet! Silicone Baking Cups, p. 148; 101 Cookie Cutters Set, p. 164; Meringue Powder, p. 135; Parchment Triangles, p. 143; 4 in. Lollipop Sticks, p. 169; Cake Boards, p. 232; waxed paper, knife, ruler

In advance: Make cookies. Prepare and roll out cookie dough. Cut heads using smallest round cutter from set. Cut ½ x 1¼ in. rectangles for arms. Bake and cool cookies. Decorate cookies on waxed paper-covered board with royal icing. Ice heads smooth. Pipe tip 3 dot eyes and cheeks; flatten slightly. Use tip 2 to outline and fill in nose, pipe mouth and add dot pupils. Pipe tip 1 outline stitches over mouth. Use tip 4 to outline and fill in hat, extending a bit beyond edge of cookie. Pipe tip 102 ruffle hat brim and tip 3 pull-out dot straw hair. For arms, pipe tip 16 stars in checkerboard pattern. Use tip 4 to outline and fill in gloves, extending a bit beyond edge of cookie. Add tip 3 pull-out dot straw. Let dry overnight. Attach lollipop sticks to backs using royal icing. Let dry.

Bake and cool cupcakes in silicone cups supported by cookie sheet. Use spatula to build up and mound icing; smooth. Cover with tip 16 stars in checkerboard pattern. Use tip 4 to outline and fill in suspenders and buttons; smooth with finger. Add tip 124 ruffle at neck. Insert head and arms. Each serves 1.

*Combine Red-Red with Christmas Red for red shown.

▲ Harvest Time Hat

Candy: Light Cocoa, Orange Candy Melts®†, p. 166; Cordial Cups Candy Mold, p. 168

Also: Round Cut-Outs™, p. 132; Quick-Ease Roller, p. 131; Parchment Triangles, p. 143; yellow spice drop, knife, granulated sugar, waxed paper

For hat top, pour melted candy into Cordial Cups mold (can be solid or a candy shell, p. 125). Refrigerate until firm; unmold. For brim, set largest circle cutter on a waxed paper covered surface. Pour in melted candy to ⅛ in. thick. Refrigerate until firm; unmold. Attach hat top to brim with melted candy. Pipe hat band using melted candy in cut parchment bag. Flatten spice drop on waxed paper dusted with sugar. Cut out square for buckle; attach with melted candy. Each serves 1.

▶ Fall for Fudge!

Pans: 11 x 7 x 1½ in. Non-Stick Biscuit/Brownie, p. 150; Cooling Grid, p. 154

Candy: Orange, Yellow, Dark Cocoa Candy Melts®†, p. 166

Recipe: Ready-In-Minutes Cocoa Fudge, p. 126

Also: Leaves and Acorns Nesting Cutter Set, p. 199; Red, Orange Colored Sugars, Chocolate Jimmies, p. 136; Parchment Triangles, p. 143

In advance: Prepare fudge in pan; refrigerate until firm.

Use smallest acorn and medium maple leaf from set to cut fudge. Place treats on cooling grid set over drip pan. Cover fudge with melted candy (p. 124). Let set. Using melted candy in cut parchment bag, pipe candy over top of acorn; immediately sprinkle on jimmies. Using melted candy in cut parchment bag, pipe candy veins on leaves; immediately sprinkle with colored sugar. Let set. Each serves 1.

◀ Leave Me Some Cheesecake

Pan: 9 in. Non-Stick Springform, p. 150

Fondant: Primary and Neon Fondant Multi Packs, Bronze Pearl Dust™, Brush Set, p. 130; Fondant/GumPaste Tool Set, Fondant Shaping Foam, p. 131; Flower Former Set, p. 137; Rolling Pin, Roll & Cut Mat, p. 133

Recipe: Creamy Cheesecake, p. 116

Also: Harvest Mini Metal Cutter Set, p. 199; cornstarch

In advance: Make fondant leaves. Roll out red, orange and yellow fondant 1/16 in. thick. Using 3 leaf cutters from set, cut approximately 50 leaves in various shapes and colors. Place on thin foam and score vein lines using small end of veining tool from set. Let dry in small flower formers dusted with cornstarch. When dry, brush with Pearl Dust.

Bake and cool cheesecake. Position on serving plate and position leaves. Serves 10-12.

◀ Harvest Sweets

Pan: Dimensions® Multi-Cavity Mini Pumpkin, p. 198

Candy: Orange, Green Candy Melts®† (1 pk. each), p. 166

Also: Petite Leaves Icing Decorations, p. 198; Parchment Triangles, p. 143 or Decorator Brush Set, p. 168; candy-coated chocolates

Mold candy shell in pan halves using painting or piping method (p. 125) and melted candy. Refrigerate until firm; unmold. If necessary, even edges by rubbing shell over a warm cookie sheet or plate. Fill with candy and icing decorations. Each serves 1.

▶ Prize-Winning Pumpkin

Pans: Dimensions® Large Pumpkin, p. 198; 12 x 2 in. Round, p. 153; Cookie Sheet, Cooling Grid, p. 154

Tips: 1, 2, 4, 5, 14, 16, 352, p. 144-145

Colors: Golden Yellow, Orange, Red-Red, Brown, Kelly Green, Black, p. 134

Candy:* Pumpkins Candy Mold, Scarecrow Lollipop Mold, p. 198; White, Light Cocoa, Orange, Green, Yellow, Red Candy Melts®†, p. 166; 6 in. Lollipop Sticks, p. 169

Recipes: Buttercream Icing, Roll-Out Cookies, p. 116

Also: Turkey Cutter, p. 199; Round Comfort Grip™ Cutter, p. 165; 5 in. Curved Pillars, 8 in. Decorator Preferred® Smooth Edge Plates (2), p. 230; Dowel Rods, p. 231; Cake Circles, Gold Fanci-Foil Wrap, p. 232; Cake Dividing Set, p. 137; Parchment Triangles, p. 143 or Decorator Brush Set, p. 168; card stock, curling ribbon (18 in. per favor), mini marshmallows, toasted coconut, fine-tip marker, hole punch, scissors, ruler, knife, toothpick, cellophane tape

In advance: Mold candies using painting or piping method (p. 125) and melted candy. Mold 4 each pumpkin candies and scarecrow lollipops (mold extra lollipops for personalized favors shown). Pipe dot eyes after unmolding. For favor name tags, cut 1 x 2½ in. rectangles in card stock; print names. Punch hole in corner; tie onto lollipop sticks with ribbon. **Also:** Make cookies. Prepare and roll out dough. Cut 16 turkeys using turkey cutter; cut off tail, leaving just body and head. Bake and cool cookies.

Bake and cool pumpkin and 2-layer round cakes. Prepare for Separator Plate and Pillar Construction (p. 114). Prepare corn stalks. Cover pillars with tip 4 vertical lines, working from bottom to top. Pipe 2 or 3 rows of tip 352 pull-out leaves around top; finish with tip 4 lines for ties. For pumpkin, outline side sections and top leaves with tip 4; fill in with tip 16 stars. For stem, stack and attach 2 mini marshmallows with icing; cover with a tip 16 spiral.

For base board, tape three 14 in. cake circles together and wrap with foil. Ice 12 in. cake smooth; position on cake base. Divide cake into 8ths. Use round cutter to imprint 8 circles on sides, centering cutter at division marks and lining up at bottom edge. Mark tail shape with toothpick, continuing circle outer edges straight down. Pipe tip 352 pull-out leaves for feathers, 2 rows in each color; (begin at outer edge and work toward center). Sandwich 2 turkey cookies together using icing; position cut edge at center of tail. Cover cookies with tip 14 stars. Pipe tip 2 dot eyes with tip 1 dot pupils. Add tip 4 pull-out dot feet and beak; with tip 2 outline waddle. For wings, pipe tip 14 shells; overpipe for dimension. Pipe tip 5 ball border between feathers.

At party: Assemble cakes. Position corn stalk pillars on plate; sprinkle both 8 in. plates with coconut. Insert lollipops; attach pumpkin candies with icing. Serves 52.

*Combine White with a small amount of Red Candy Melts® for pink scarecrow cheeks. Combine White with small amounts of Light Cocoa and Yellow Candy Melts® for scarecrow faces.

†Brand confectionery coating.

▶ Pretzel Pop Present

Candy: Santa Pretzel Mold, Red, White, Green, Light Cocoa Candy Melts®†, p. 202

Also: Decorator Brush Set, p. 168 or Parchment Triangles, p. 143; Santa Party Bags, p. 201; pretzel rods

Use painting or piping method (p. 125) and melted candy to mold Santa pretzel candies in pretzel mold. (For light skin tone candy, add a small amount of red to white.) Refrigerate until firm; unmold. Place in party bag. Each serves 1.

†Brand confectionery coating.

◀ Chimney Champ

Pans: Step-By-Step Snowman, p. 200; Petite Loaf, p. 154

Tips: 1A, 1M, 5, 16, 18, p. 144-145

Colors: Red-Red, Kelly Green, Black, Copper (for skin tone shown), p. 134

Fondant: White Ready-To-Use Rolled Fondant (48 oz.), p. 130; Rolling Pin, Roll & Cut Mat, p. 133

Recipes: Buttercream Icing, p. 116; favorite crisped rice cereal treats (2½ recipes needed)

Also: Comfort-Grip™ Mitten Cutter, p. 204; 101 Cookie Cutters Set , p. 164; Cake Boards, Fanci-Foil Wrap, p. 232; 15 x 24 in. foamcore board (½ in. thick), knife, ruler, waxed paper, marshmallows, cornstarch

In advance: Make 20 bricks in Petite Loaf pan. Prepare cereal treat mixture and press into lightly greased cavities. Release immediately onto greased waxed paper-covered boards. Cut 2 bricks in half. Cover all with plastic wrap until needed. **Also:** Tint 24 oz. fondant red; roll out small portion ⅛ in. thick. Cut letters using cutters from 101 Cutter Set.

Bake and cool cake in snowman pan. Position on wrapped foamcore board. Lightly ice hat area. Use tip 5 to outline and fill in eyes and mouth (smooth with finger dipped in cornstarch). Cover face with tip 16 stars; overpipe nose for dimension. Use tip 18 to pipe reverse shell beard and moustache and elongated shell eyebrows. Roll out remaining red fondant ⅛ in. thick. Cut a 6 x 15 in. hat and attach; shape a tapered, pleated top and fold toward side. Pipe tip 1M zigzag brim and rosette pompom. Position bricks on board with icing "mortar." Pipe tip 1A pull-out snow on chimney top (smooth with finger). Tint 16 oz. fondant green. Roll out fondant 1 in. thick. Use mitten cutter to cut 2 shapes (reverse one shape for opposite mitten).

Position mittens and letters. Cake serves 12; each whole brick serves 1.

▶ Reindeer Mousse

Pan: Standard Muffin, p. 154

Candy: Light Cocoa, Red, Peanut Butter Candy Melts®†, Garden Candy Color Set, p. 166; Christmas Character Lollipop Mold, p. 202

Recipe: Chocolate Mousse, p. 116

Also: White Standard Baking Cups, p. 189; Decorator Brush Set, p. 168 or Parchment Triangles, p. 143; bite-size chocolate nougat candies, large chocolate chips

In advance: Prepare candy shells in baking cups (p. 125). Attach nougat candy feet to bottom with melted candy. Let set. **Also:** Mold reindeer heads using painting or piping method (p. 125) and Christmas Character Lollipop Mold without lollipop sticks. Fill cup with Chocolate Mousse; use spatula to smooth and round top.

Attach reindeer head to edge of candy shell with melted candy; refrigerate until firm. Attach large chocolate chip in back for tail. Each serves 1.

▲ Reindeer Race

Cookie: Cookie Sheet, Cooling Grid, p. 154; 18 Pc. Holiday Cutter Set, p. 204

Tip: 3, p. 144

Colors:* Christmas Red, Red-Red, Kelly Green, Brown, Black, p. 134

Recipes: Royal Icing, Roll-Out Cookies, p. 116

Also: 2009 Pattern Book (Sleigh Front/Bottom, Back), p. 128; White Nonpareils Sprinkles, Red Colored Sugar, p. 136; Shiver Me Snowman Fun Pix®, p. 201; Cake Board, Fanci-Foil Wrap, p. 232; Meringue Powder, p. 135; Parchment Triangles, p. 143; assorted candies, waxed paper

Make and decorate sleigh and reindeer cookies (p. 120). For each treat, cu a 2 x 6¾ in. board; wrap with foil. Spatula ice board fluffy. Position sleigh and reindeer; let set. Fill sleigh with candy. Position pick. Each serves 1.

*Combine Christmas Red with Red-Red for red shown. Combine Brown with a little Red-Red for brown shown.

▼ Claim Your Tree!

Pans: 13 x 9 x 2 in. Sheet, p. 153; Cooling Grid, p. 154
Candy: Red, Green, White Candy Melts®†, Primary Candy Color Set, p. 166; Christmas Trees Pretzel Mold, p. 202
Recipe: Favorite crisped rice cereal treats
Also: Shiver Me Snowman Fun Pix®, Party Bags, p. 201; Jumbo Stars Sprinkles, p. 136; Circle Metal Cookie Cutter, p. 165; Parchment Triangles, p. 143; pretzel rods, waxed paper, ruler

In advance: Use pretzel mold and melted candy in cut parchment bags to make decorated candy trees. Attach star to top with melted candy.

Prepare cereal treat mixture and press into pan, 1 in. deep. Unmold onto greased waxed paper. Cut circles using metal cutter. Place circles on cooling grid and cover with melted candy (p. 124). Cut a hole in center and insert tree and Fun Pix®, trimming pretzel as needed. Pipe snow using melted candy in cut parchment bag. Place in party bag. Each serves 1.

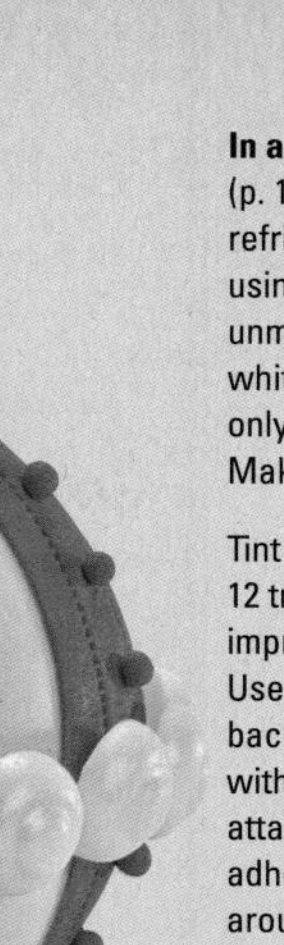

▲ Truffles on the Tree!

Pans: Sports Ball Pan Set, p. 161; 6 Cup Standard Muffin, Cookie Sheet (or warming tray), p. 154
Fondant: White Ready-To-Use Rolled Fondant, Brush Set, p. 130; Cutter/Embosser, p. 131; Rolling Pin, Roll & Cut Mat p. 133;
Colors:* Red-Red, Christmas Red, p. 134
Recipes: Truffles, p. 126; Thinned Fondant Adhesive, p. 117
Also: 2009 Pattern Book (Ornament Panel), p. 128; White (5 pks. makes 1 ornament), Lt. Cocoa (1 pk.) Candy Melts®†, Truffles Candy Mold, p. 166; White, Ruby Red Pearl Dust™, p. 130; White Standard Baking Cups, p. 189; Cake Dividing Set, p. 137; waxed paper, cornstarch, toothpicks, knife, chopped nuts

In advance: Use Sports Ball Pan to make candy shells (p. 125). Use ring from set to stabilize ball halves in refrigerator. **Also:** Make candy shell for ornament topper using Standard Baking Cup (p. 125). Refrigerate until firm; unmold, then brush on White Pearl Dust. **And:** Mold 20 white candies in Truffles Candy Mold (p. 125), filling cavities only ¾ full. Chill, unmold then brush on white Pearl Dust. Make cocoa truffles to fill ornament following recipe.

Tint 6 oz. fondant red; roll out 1⁄16 in. thick. Use pattern to cut 12 triangles. Roll with ridged wheel of Cutter/Embosser to imprint lines, starting ½ in. from edge and meeting at tip. Use Cake Divider to divide each shell half into 6ths. Brush backs of triangles with damp brush and attach to candy shell within divisions. Roll 48 red fondant balls, ¼ in. diameter; attach to fondant triangles, about ¾ in. apart, using fondant adhesive. Cut ¼ in. wide red fondant strips and attach around white section edges of bottom candy shell with melted candy to be even with red edges. Attach white candies around outside edge of shell using melted candy; position so half of candy extends above edge of candy shell. Fill bottom shell with cocoa truffles. Position top shell. Attach ornament topper with melted candy. Roll a 4 in. long fondant rope, ¼ in. diameter. Bend for ornament hook and let set about 1 hour. Attach to topper with melted candy; brush on white Pearl Dust. Brush red fondant triangles with red Pearl Dust. Each truffle serves 1.

*Combine Red-Red with Christmas Red for red shown.

▶ Happy to Help Santa

Pans: Teddy Bear Pan, p. 159; Cookie Sheet, Cooling Grid, p. 154
Tips: 3, 5, 12, 16, 21, 366, p. 144-145
Colors:* Kelly Green, Christmas Red, Black, Lemon Yellow, Golden Yellow, Brown, Copper (for skin tone shown), p. 134
Recipe: Buttercream Icing, Roll-Out Cookies, p. 116
Also: 2009 Pattern Book (Elf Hat, Elf Shoe Patterns), p. 128; Cake Boards, Fanci-Foil Wrap, p. 232; 18 Pc. Holiday Cutter Set, p. 204; spatula, toothpick, cornstarch, knife

In advance: Make cookies. Prepare and roll out dough. Use patterns to cut 3 hats and 4 shoes (reverse 2 shoes). Using mitten cutter from set, cut 6 mittens, reverse 3 for opposite hand. Using knife, cut 1⅜ in. round pompom. Bake and cool all cookies.

Position bear cake on foil-wrapped board, cut to fit design with hat, mittens and shoes. Trim off ears, square off arms, legs, and trim muzzle and eyes. Lightly ice cake smooth in buttercream. Using toothpick, mark suspenders, belt, pant leg, stockings and facial features. Using tip 16 stars, fill in shirt, pants and stockings. Pipe in tip 3 eyes, mouth and tongue; (pat smooth with finger dipped in cornstarch). Using tip 12, outline belt and fill in. Pipe tip 5 buckle; pat smooth. Build up ear area with tip 3. Cover face and ears and build up nose with tip 16 stars; overpipe cheeks.

Sandwich hat, shoe, and mitten cookies with icing. Position next to cake. Cover cookies with tip 16 stars. Pipe tip 366 pull-out leaf fringe. Add tip 21 pull-out star hair curl. Cover round pompom cookie with tip 21 swirls and position on hat. Cake serves 12; each cookie serves 1.

*Combine Lemon Yellow with Golden Yellow for yellow shade shown. Combine Brown with Christmas Red for brown shade shown.

Spirit-Lifting Gifts!

Pan: Cookie Sheet, Cooling Grid, p. 154

Tips: 2, 3, 6, p. 144

Colors: Kelly Green, Orange, Christmas Red, Violet, Golden Yellow, p. 134

Recipes: Color Flow Icing, Roll-Out Cookies, p. 116

Also: 18 Pc. Holiday Cutter Set, p. 204; Color Flow Mix, p. 135; Parchment Triangles, p. 143; White Candy Melts®†, p. 166

Prepare and roll out cookie dough. Cut cookies using package cutter from set. For every 2 treats, cut 1 extra package; cut in half vertically for easel back supports. Bake and cool cookies. Prepare Color Flow Icing and tint assorted colors. Use tip 3 and full-strength color flow to outline each package; flow in with Thinned Color Flow (p. 126). Let dry. Using full-strength color flow, use tip 3 to outline and pipe in bows and knots; use tip 2 to pipe dots and spirals; use tip 3 and tip 6 to pipe thin and wide ribbons. Let set. Attach easel back supports with melted candy. Each serves 1.

Energetic Elves

Pan: Cookie Sheet, p. 154

Tips: 1A, 3, 5, 7, 10, 12, p. 144

Colors:* Lemon Yellow, Golden Yellow, Violet, Rose, Orange, Royal Blue, Brown, p. 134

Fondant: White Ready-To-Use Rolled Fondant (24 oz.), Natural Colors Fondant Multi Pack, Brush Set, p. 130; Quick-Ease Roller, p. 131; Roll & Cut Mat, Gum-Tex™, p. 133

Recipes: Buttercream, Royal Icings, p. 116

Also: 2009 Pattern Book (Hat, Hand, Mouth), p. 128; Silly-Feet! Silicone Baking Cups, p. 148; Meringue Powder, p. 135; 101 Cookie Cutters Set, p. 164; 4 in. Lollipop Sticks, p. 169; Cake Boards, p. 232; spatula, knife, ruler, cornstarch, waxed paper

In advance: Make hats and heads. Add ½ teaspoon Gum-Tex to 8 oz. white fondant. Divide into 4ths; tint blue, yellow, orange, violet. Roll out colors ⅛ in. thick. Use pattern to cut out hats (reserve remaining fondant for collars). Add ¼ teaspoon Gum-Tex to 4 oz. of Natural Pink fondant from Multi Pack. Roll out ⅛ in. thick. Use pattern to cut 2 hands for each elf (reverse pattern for opposite hand). Use smallest round cutter from 101 Cookie Cutters Set to cut heads. Place heads on waxed paper-covered board. Attach hat using damp brush. Use royal icing to pipe tip 5 zig-zag pom-pom and fur trim. Pipe tip 3 pull-out hair. Roll out small amounts of white, pink and black fondant. Cut whites of eyes with tip 10, pupils with tip 7, cheeks with tip 12 and mouth using pattern. Attach features using damp brush. For nose, roll a ¼ in. ball of fondant and shape into a teardrop; attach with damp brush. For ears, roll ⅜ in. balls of fondant and shape into teardrops; attach with damp brush, positioning point at top. Let all dry.

Bake and cool cupcakes in silicone cups supported by cookie sheet. Using tip 1A and stiff consistency buttercream, pipe a mound of icing on top and smooth with spatula. For arms, cut lollipop sticks to 3 in.; insert 1½ in. into body. Cover arms with buttercream by inserting bag with tip 12 over stick and pulling out bag while using even pressure. Attach hands with icing dots. Push 4 in. lollipop stick into center of cupcake. Attach head and hat with icing. For collar, roll out reserved fondant colors. Cut a 1 x 3 in. strip; cut out V-shaped notches. Attach around neck and smooth seam with finger. Each serves 1.

*Combine Lemon Yellow with Golden Yellow for yellow shown. Combine Violet with Rose for violet shown.

Santa & Mrs. Claus

Pan: Stand-Up Cuddly Bear Set, p. 160

Tips: 1, 3, 6, 15, 16, 127D, p. 144-145

Colors:* Christmas Red, Red-Red, Kelly Green, Brown, Black, Copper (for skin tone shown), p. 134

Fondant: White Ready-To-Use Rolled Fondant (24 oz.), p. 130; Rolling Pin, Roll & Cut Mat, p. 133

Recipes: Buttercream Icing, p. 116

Also: Cake Boards, Fanci-Foil Wrap, p. 232; 6 Pc. Holiday Mini Cutter Set, p. 204; Parchment Triangles, p. 143; 4 in. Lollipop Sticks, p. 169; ruler, knife, scissors, cornstarch

In advance: Make tray with fondant cookies. For tray, cut cake board to 3¾ x 2¼ in.; wrap with foil. Tape 2 lollipop sticks to bottom of tray with 2¼ in. extending at back to insert into cake. Tint 1 oz. fondant brown; roll out ⅛ in. thick. Cut 2 gingerbread boys using cutter from set; position on tray. Use tip 1 to add zigzag trims, outline mouth and dot eyes, nose and buttons.

Bake and cool 2 bear cakes using firm-textured batter such as pound cake. For Santa, trim off ears, muzzle, paw going up to mouth and 1½ in. off horizontal paw. For Mrs. Claus, trim off ears, muzzle and both arms. On both cakes, spatula ice soles of shoes smooth. Using tip 3, pipe outline eyes; outline and fill in mouth and bead tongue (smooth with finger dipped in cornstarch). Use tip 6 to build up nose and ears for dimension. For Santa, roll a fondant log and add to arm to match shape of horizontal arm. Cover face, ears, shirt, overalls and shoes with tip 16 stars. Pipe tip 15 swirl beard and hair and pull-out shell mustache. Tint 8 oz. fondant red for hat. Shape into tapered cone and indent bottom for head shape. Position on head and fold over point. Pipe tip 6 zigzag brim and rosette pompom. Cut parchment triangle into a 9 x 2¾ in. scroll; curl ends. Attach against Santa; pipe tip 16 star hands. For Mrs. Claus, cover face, ears, dress and shoes with tip 16 stars. Pipe tip 16 swirl hair. Pipe tip 127D dress ruffle. Use tip 6 to outline and fill in apron (smooth with finger); pipe dot earrings. Roll 2 fondant logs, 3 x 1½ in., for arms; cut slit for thumb and insert tray with cookies. Cover dress and hands with tip 16 stars. Each cake serves 12.

*Combine Christmas Red with Red-Red for red shown. Combine Brown with Red-Red for brown shown.

Flavorful Fir Tree

Cookie: Pre-Baked Gingerbread Tree Kit, p. 203

Color: Lemon Yellow, p. 134

Also: Crystal-Look Bowl, p. 231; Cake Board, Fanci-Foil Wrap, p. 232; jelly spearmint leaves (15 oz.), knife

Using largest cookie as a pattern, cut a cake board to fit and wrap with foil (p. 110). Prepare white and green icings from kit. Assemble tree on wrapped board using dots of white icing. Cut spearmint leaves in half horizontally for thinner leaves. Trim ends to fit between points of tree, cutting leaves slightly shorter as you work your way up from the bottom row. Attach with green icing. Use round decorating tip to pipe pull-out snow. Attach round candies from kit with icing dots. Tint remaining white icing yellow; ice star. Attach to top of tree with icing. Position on base half of Crystal-Look Bowl.

†Brand confectionery coating.

▶ King of the Hill

Pans: Snowman Cookie Treat Pan, p. 203; Standard Muffin, p. 154

Tip: 1M, p. 145

Candy: White, Green, Light Cocoa Candy Melts®†, Primary Candy Color Set, p. 166

Recipe: Buttercream Icing, p. 116

Also: 13 Count Standard Cupcakes 'N More® Dessert Stand, p. 147; Winter Splendor Baking Cups, Petite Winter Splendor Icing Decorations, p. 201; Jumbo Snowflakes Sprinkle Decorations p. 202; Parchment Triangles, p. 143, small paring knife

In advance: Mold candy. For base, fill 1 muffin pan cavity ⅜ in. deep with melted white candy; tap, refrigerate until firm, then unmold. Use treat pan to mold snowman. Tint melted candy. Using piping method (p. 125), mold candy snowman. Refrigerate until firm then unmold. Trim bottom of snowman straight. Pipe facial features and buttons using melted candy. Let set. Attach snowman to candy base with melted candy; let set.

Bake and cool cupcakes. Ice with tip 1M swirl; add sprinkles, position icing decorations. Position cupcakes and snowman on stand. Each serves 1.

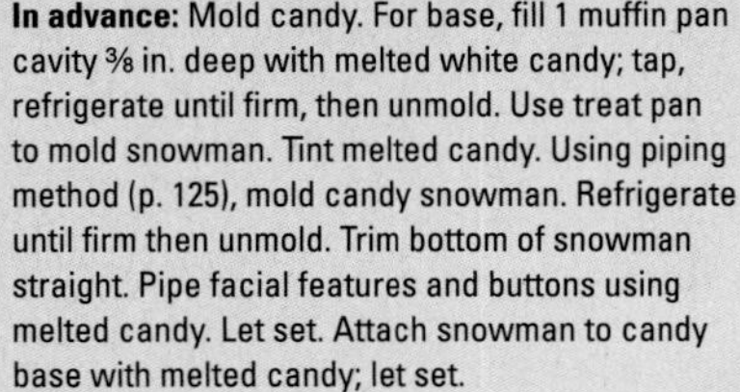

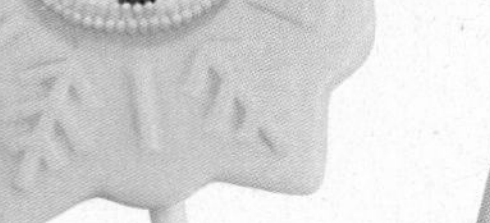

▲ Snowflake Suckers

Pan: Mini Snowflake Silicone Mold, p. 200

Candy: White Candy Melts®†, p. 166; 4 in. Lollipop Sticks, p. 169

Also: Shiver Me Snowman Icing Decorations, p. 201

Pour melted candy into mold cavities, filling ¼ in. thick. Refrigerate until firm; unmold. Attach icing decoration to center and lollipop stick to back with melted candy. Let set. Each serves 1.

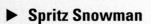

▶ Spritz Snowman

Pan: Cookie Sheet, Cooling Grid, p. 154

Colors: Orange, Kelly Green, Red-Red, p. 134

Fondant: White Ready-To-Use Rolled Fondant, p. 130; Cutter/Embosser, p. 131; Rolling Pin, Roll & Cut Mat, p. 133

Recipe: Spritz Cookies, p. 116

Also: 2009 Pattern Book (Snowman), p. 128; Cookie Pro™ Ultra II Deluxe Cookie Press, p. 162; White Candy Melts®† (1 pk.), p. 166; White Nonpareils Sprinkles, p. 136; Cake Boards, Fanci-Foil Wrap, p. 232; Parchment Triangles, p. 143; chocolate nougat candies, scissors, ruler, 18 x 12 in. foamcore board (½ in. thick)

In advance: Prepare board. Copy snowman pattern at 200%. Use pattern to cut foamcore board; wrap with foil (p. 110). **Also:** Make about 150 spritz cookies. Bake and cool. Using melted candy in cut parchment bag, pipe lines across top of cookie; immediately sprinkle on nonpareils. Let set.

Arrange cookies on board. Tint fondant as follows: ¾ in. ball orange, 7 oz. red and 6 oz. green. Roll a 1 in. high orange cone for nose. Roll out red fondant ½ in. thick. Using pattern as a guide, cut a curved cone shape for hat base. Roll out green fondant ⅛ in. thick. Cut a 2 x 9 in. strip and two 2 x 5½ in. strips for scarf. Knead nougat candies to soften. Roll ⅝ in. diameter balls for eyes. Roll ¾ in. diameter balls for buttons; flatten slightly. Roll a 3½ in. long ⅜ in. diameter log for mouth. Roll a 1¾ in. diameter white ball for hat pompom; shape with fingers for textured look. Roll a 6 x 1½ in. white log for hat brim; curve and flatten slightly.

Attach eyes, nose, mouth and buttons with dots of melted candy. Position hat base, brim and pompom on board. Position 9 in. scarf length; wrap over neck area. Use scissors to cut fringe on one end of each 5½ in. length. Position for scarf ends. Each cookie serves 1.

▶ A Winter Wonder

Pans: Dimensions® Snowflake, p. 200; Cookie Sheet, Cooling Grid, p. 154
Tips: 1A, 8, p. 144
Candy: Dark Cocoa Candy Melts®†, p. 166
Recipes: Royal Icing, p. 116; Ganache Glaze, p. 126
Also: 2009 Pattern Book (Snowflake Arms), p. 128; White Sparkling Sugar, p. 136; Cake Boards, Fanci-Foil Wrap, p. 232; Meringue Powder, p. 135; waxed paper

Several days in advance: Use royal icing to make 6 snowflake arms and center ball (p. 120).

Bake and cool cake. Position on cut-to-fit cake board; place on cooling grid set over drip pan. Cover with Ganache Glaze (p. 126); reserve any leftover glaze. Let set then position on plate or foil-covered board. Whip remaining glaze that has thickened to use as icing; pipe tip 8 ball bottom border. Position snowflake arms directly on cake top. Position ball in center. Serves 12.

†Brand confectionery coating.

▲ Fresh-Baked Flakes

Pans: Cookie Sheet, Cooling Grid, p. 154
Tip: 2, p. 144
Recipe: Shortbread Cookies, p. 116
Also: White Candy Melts®†, p. 166; Christmas Push 'N Print™ Cutter Set, Snowflakes 4 Pc. Nesting Cutter Set, p. 204; White Nonpareils Sprinkles, p. 136; Parchment Triangles, p. 143; tape

Prepare and roll-out cookie dough. For each treat, cut 1 cookie using largest snowflake cutter and 1 cookie using round snowflake cutter from Push 'N Print Set. Bake and cool cookies. Tape tip 2 to outside of parchment bag; fill with melted candy. Pipe melted candy around outside edge of round cookie; roll in nonpareils. Use melted candy to fill in snowflake impression on round cookie and to pipe vein lines on snowflake cookie; let set. Attach cookies using melted candy. Each serves 1.

▶ Colorful Cooler

Pan: Mini Snowflake Silicone Mold, p. 200
Colors: Rose, Kelly Green, p. 134
Recipe: Cream Cheese Mousse, p. 116
Also: vegetable oil pan spray

Prepare mousse recipe and divide in 3rds. Lightly spray mold cavities with pan spray; wipe out excess. Fill molds ⅓ deep with one portion of white mousse. Tint 2nd portion of mousse rose; fill molds ⅓ deep. Tint last portion of mousse green; fill molds to top and refrigerate overnight. Unmold. Serves 18.

◀ Snowflake Candy Box

Pan: Mini Snowflake Silicone Mold, p. 200
Also: White Candy Melts®†, p. 166; Petite Winter Splendor Icing Decorations, p. 201; Pastel Pearls Favor Candy, p. 237, spoon

In mold cavities, make 2 candy shells (p. 125) for each box. Fill cavities only halfway; refrigerate about 8-10 minutes until a ¼ in. shell has formed. Refrigerate until firm; unmold. Attach icing decoration to top with melted candy; let set. Fill bottom with mini pastels; position top. Each serves 1.

▲ Shiny and Bright!

Pans: Cookie Sheet, Cooling Grid, p. 154
Tip: 3, p. 144
Color: Red-Red, p. 134
Recipes: Buttercream Icing, Roll-Out Cookies, p. 116
Also: Blue, Green, Red Sparkle Gel, p. 135; Orange Tube Decorating Gel, p. 134; Jumbo Rainbow Nonpareils, p. 136; 18 Pc. Holiday Cutter Set, p. 204; shredded coconut

Prepare and roll out cookie dough. Cut into assorted shapes; bake and cool cookies. For stocking, wreath and tree outline and fill in cookies and most details with Sparkle Gel. For stocking, spatula ice top edge with buttercream and trim with coconut. For wreath, use tip 3 and buttercream to outline and fill in bow sides and dot center. For tree, position nonpareils. For candy cane, outline and fill in white stripes using tip 3 and buttercream; outline and fill in alternate stripes with red gel. For snowman, ice smooth with buttercream; pipe on dot, line and fill-in details with gels. Each serves 1.

▲ Snowmen That Stick Around

Cookie: Round Cookie Treat, 8 in. Cookie Treat Sticks, p. 163; Cookie Sheet, Cooling Grid, p. 154; Comfort Grip™ Santa Hat Cutter, p. 204
Recipes: Royal Icing, Roll-Out Cookies, p. 116
Also: White Candy Melts®†, p. 166; Red Colored Sugar, p. 136; Parchment Triangles, p. 143; Meringue Powder, p. 135; mini candy-coated chocolates, mini chocolate chips, candy corn

Prepare cookie dough. For heads, position cookie sticks and press dough into treat pan cavities. Roll out remaining cookie dough; cut hats using hat cutter. Sprinkle top with red sugar. Bake and cool cookies. Spatula ice hat brim and pompom. Ice round cookie smooth. Attach hat to head with melted candy. Position candy-coated chocolate eyes, mini chocolate chip smile and candy corn nose. Each serves 1.

▼ Making the Place Festive!

Pans: Non-Stick Mini Holiday, p. 200; Cookie Sheet, Cooling Grid, p. 154
Tips: 2, 3, p. 144
Colors: Christmas Red, Kelly Green, Brown, p. 134
Recipes: Royal Icing, Roll-Out Cookies, p. 116
Also: 2009 Pattern Book (Easel Back), p. 128; Rainbow Nonpareils Sprinkles, p. 136; ruler, knife, cornstarch

Make cookies. Prepare and roll out dough. Cut 2 x 5 in. bases; cut easel backs using pattern (2 for each card). For cookie accents, press dough into mini pan cavities. Bake and cool all cookies.

On cookie accents, use tip 3 to outline and fill in snowman body (smooth with finger dipped in cornstarch). Overpipe tip 3 arms (smooth with finger). Using tip 2, outline and pipe in hat brim, add dot eyes, mouth and buttons. For tree, cover with tip 2 pull-out branches; sprinkle on nonpareils. Using tip 2, pipe outline border and print name. Attach easel cookies to back with icing. Attach cookie accents. Each serves 1.

▶ Snow Globe Greetings

Pans: Jumbo Muffin, p. 146; Cookie Sheet, Cooling Grid, p. 154
Tips: 2, 3, p. 144
Colors: Christmas Red, Kelly Green, Orange, Lemon Yellow, Black, p. 134
Recipes: Royal Icing, Shortbread Cookies, p. 116
Also: Christmas Push 'N Print™ Cutter Set, p. 204; Meringue Powder, p. 135; Red, Green Candy Melts®†, p. 166; Jumbo Baking Cups, p. 148

In advance: Mold candy bases. Line muffin pan cavities with baking cups. Fill to ¾ in. deep with melted candy; refrigerate until firm. Unmold and peel off paper. **Also:** Make cookies. Prepare and roll out cookie dough. Use Push 'N Print set to cut and imprint assorted designs. Bake and cool.

For tree snow globe, decorate with tip 2 pull-out dot branches bead star and outline letters. Pipe tip 2 dots for ornaments and snowflakes. For snowman snow globe, outline and fill in body with tip 3; add tip 3 outline scarf, hat and snow. Use tip 2 to add dot and outline facial features, hat band and bead snowflakes. Cut 2 straight edges of a Candy Melts wafer to form a 90° angle easel. Attach globe cookie to candy base and candy easel using melted candy; let set. Each serves 1.

†Brand confectionery coating.

▲ Caroling Cookie Couple

Cookie: Christmas Tree, Snowman Cookie Treat Pans, 6 in. Cookie Treat Sticks, p. 203; Cookie Sheet, Cooling Grid, p. 154
Tips: 2, 3, 5, 6, 349, p. 144-145
Colors:* Christmas Red, Red-Red, Kelly Green, Brown, Copper (for skin tone shown), Black, p. 134
Recipes: Royal Icing, Roll-Out Cookies, p. 116
Also: Round Cut-Outs™, p. 132; Parchment Triangles, p. 143; Meringue Powder, p. 135; Cake Boards, p. 232; waxed paper, cornstarch

In advance: Make cookies. Prepare dough and press into pans inserting sticks, using tree for lady's body, snowman for man's body. Roll out remaining dough and cut heads using medium round Cut-Out. Bake and cool all cookies.

Ice heads and lady's body smooth. Position cookies on waxed paper covered board. For lady, pipe tip 6 arms; add tip 3 dot eyes, swirl hair, hat and fur hem. Using tip 3, outline and fill in muff. Pipe tip 349 leaves. Pipe tip 2 dot nose, berries and coat trim, outline mouth. Let dry. For man, pipe tip 6 arms. With tip 5, outline and fill in hat, shirt, pants and shoes (smooth with finger dipped in cornstarch). Using tip 3, pipe outline hat band and hair, dot eyes and buttons, outline and fill in mittens. Pipe tip 5 outline scarf. Pipe tip 2 dot nose and mouth, outline mustache and pull-out scarf fringe; let dry. Attach lady's head to body with icing. Each serves 1.

*Combine Christmas Red with Red-Red for shade shown.

▼ Cookie Gift Box

Pan: Cookie Sheet, Cooling Grid, p. 154
Tip: 3, p. 144
Colors*: Christmas Red, Red-Red, p. 134
Recipes: Royal Icing, Roll-Out Cookies, p. 116
Also: 2009 Pattern Book (Box Bottom), p. 128; 18 Pc. Holiday Cutter Set, p. 204; Meringue Powder, p. 135; Parchment Triangles, p. 143; Clear Party Bags, p. 189; knife, waxed paper, red mini candy-coated chocolates, assorted candies, silver curling ribbon, gift tag

Prepare and roll out cookie dough. For each treat, cut 4 gifts using cutter from set and 1 bottom using pattern. Thin a portion of dough to piping consistency and tint red. Using tip 3 and parchment bag, outline and pipe in bow and ribbon on gift cookies. Bake and cool cookies. Assemble box using royal icing; trim corners with tip 3 beads. Let dry then use royal icing to attach a mini chocolate to center of each bow. Fill treat bag with candy, tie ribbon and gift tag. Each serves 1.

*Combine Christmas Red with Red-Red for red shown.

▲ A Tempting Tree

Pans: Standard Muffin, Cookie Sheet, Cooling Grid, p. 154
Tip: 2, p. 144
Colors:* Kelly Green, Christmas Red, Red-Red, Royal Blue, Lemon Yellow, Violet, Rose, p. 134
Candy: White, Green Candy Melts®†, p. 166; 6 in. Lollipop Sticks, p. 169
Recipe: Buttercream, Royal Icings, Roll-Out Cookies (2 recipes), p. 116
Also: 4-Tier Stacked Dessert Tower, p. 147; Nesting Stars Metal Cutter Set, p. 165; 6 Pc. Holiday Mini Cutter Set, p. 204; Parchment Triangles, p. 143; Yellow, Light Green Colored Sugars, White Sparkling Sugar, p. 136; White Standard Baking Cups, p. 148; Round Cut-Outs™, p. 132; Meringue Powder, p. 135; hollow center round hard candy (45)

In advance: Make cookies. Prepare 2 recipes of dough; tint 1 recipe green. Roll out plain dough and cut treetop star using largest star cutter from set; sprinkle with colored sugar. Cut 38-40 ornaments using medium round Cut-Out. Roll out green dough and cut about 80 holly leaves using cutter from holiday set. Bake and cool all cookies. **Also:** Ice and decorate ornament cookies. To ice, outline edge using tip 2 and full-strength royal icing. Flow in centers using thinned royal icing. Let dry. Decorate with full-strength royal icing. Use tip 2 to pipe beads, zigzags and swirls; outline and fill in assorted geometric designs. Let dry. Attach hollow center candies to ornaments with melted white candy. Refrigerate until firm. **And:** Decorate leaves. Using melted candy in a cut parchment bag with tip 2 taped to outside, pipe veins. Immediately sprinkle with colored sugar. Refrigerate until firm. Cut cookie stick to 4 in.; attach to back of star cookie using melted candy.

Bake and cool 38-40 cupcakes. Spatula ice tops; sprinkle with white Sparkling Sugar. Position ornament cookies on cupcakes (reserve 1 cupcake); place cupcakes on stand. Position reserved cupcake on center column of stand; insert star. Using melted candy in cut parchment bag, attach leaves to outer rim of stand; let set. Hint: To help candy set more quickly, chill cookies in freezer for 5-10 minutes. Each serves 1.

*Combine Christmas Red with Red-Red for red shown. Combine Violet with Rose for violet shown.

▲ Holiday High-Rise

Pans: 16 x 2 in. Round, p. 153; Cookie Sheet, Cooling Grid, p. 154:
Tips: 2, 3, 4, 5, p. 144
Colors:* Christmas Red, Red-Red, Royal Blue, Kelly Green, Lemon Yellow, p. 134
Cookie: Pre-Baked Gingerbread House Kit (includes 8 x 7 x 6½ in. high house pieces, icing mix, assorted candies, decorating bag and round tip, cardboard base), p. 203; Gingerbread Boys 4 Pc. Nesting Cutter Set, p. 204
Recipes: Buttercream, Royal Icings, Grandma's Gingerbread, p. 116
Also: 2009 Pattern Book (Roof Scallops, Door, Windows), p. 128; 12 in. Crystal-Clear Cake Plate, 9 in. Crystal-Clear Twist Legs, p. 228; Cake Boards, Fanci-Foil Wrap, p. 232; Meringue Powder, p. 135; Jumbo Confetti Sprinkles, p. 136; 5 in. long candy canes (30), spice drops, spearmint leaves, mini multi-colored candies, candy-coated chocolates, granulated sugar, 18 in. diameter foamcore board (½ in. thick), waxed paper, knife, ruler, toothpicks, cornstarch

In advance: Bake gingerbread cookies. Prepare and roll out dough. Cut 8 each using 2 smallest cutters from set. Bake and cool cookies. Decorate with royal icing. Set cookies on waxed paper-covered boards. Outline and fill in dresses, vests and pants with tip 4 (smooth with finger dipped in cornstarch). Use tip 2 to pipe dot and outline facial features, dot buttons and zigzag trims. Pipe tip 3 swirl and zigzag hair, hair bows and bow ties. Let dry.

For gingerbread house: Prepare icing and assemble pre-baked pieces following directions in Gingerbread House Kit; assemble on a 12 in. plate. Decorate using icing and tip included in kit (or tip 5) unless otherwise specified. Using patterns, lightly mark door and windows (sides, front and back); outline in white. Tint a portion of icing red; outline and fill in door and curtains (smooth with finger). Pipe scallop trim around door and position mini multi-colored candies; attach spice drop half for window and mini multi-colored candy for doorknob. Cut Jumbo Confetti in half; attach around windows for shutters. Pipe C-scrolls above front and back windows; attach mini multi-colored candy trim. Using patterns, lightly mark scallops on roof; outline and fill-in areas between scallops (smooth with finger).

Edge scallops with tip 2 zigzags. Attach Jumbo Confetti to roof and jumbo spice drops from kit to roof peak. Cut 4 candy canes to 3 in. long and attach to corners of house; pipe outlines on each side. Attach whole candy canes to front edge of roof. Pipe pull-out dot icicles on window sills and roof edges. Using royal icing, spatula ice 12 in. plate; position house on plate. Cut spearmint leaves into slivers; toss with granulated sugar to coat cut edges then position around house. Position Jumbo Confetti flat for walkway and upright to edge plate.

Bake and cool 2-layer cake. Ice sides smooth. Ice top and outer edge of board fluffy. Position decorated gingerbread boys and girls against cake sides. Decorate board with spice drops and candy-coated chocolates. Position spice drops around top edge of cake. Prepare for Push-In Pillar Construction; insert pillars. Attach wrapped candy canes around pillars with royal icing. Position top plate at party. Cake serves 77; each cookie serves 1.

*Combine Christmas Red with Red-Red for red shown.

▶ Treasures Under the Tree

Cookie: Christmas Cookie Tree Cutter Kit, p. 203; Cookie Sheet, Cooling Grid, p. 154

Tips: 5, 21, p. 144-145

Colors:* Royal Blue, Kelly Green, Rose, Lemon Yellow, Golden Yellow, Brown, Red-Red, p. 134

Fondant: White Ready-To-Use Rolled Fondant (44 oz.), Brush Set, p. 130; Easy-Glide Fondant Smoother, p. 131; Gum-Tex™, Rolling Pin, Roll & Cut Mat, p. 133

Recipes: Buttercream, Royal Icings, Roll-Out Cookies (4 recipes), p. 116

Also: Pastel Silicone Baking Cups (2 sets), p. 210; Tall-Tier Cake Stand Set (8, 14 in. plates, 6½ in. column, top nut, bottom bolt used), Glue-On Plate Legs, p. 229; 6 in. (3) and 14 in. Cake Circles, Fanci-Foil Wrap, p. 232; Piping Gel, Meringue Powder, p. 135; Jumbo Stars, Jumbo Confetti Sprinkles, White Sparkling Sugar, p. 136; Jumbo Snowflakes Sprinkles, p. 202; mini candy-coated chocolates, spice drops, waxed paper, ruler, scissors, knife, tape, glue for plastic, cornstarch

In advance: Make fondant loops. Tint 5 oz. fondant to match each baking cup color; add ½ teaspoon Gum-Tex to each. Roll out ⅛ in. thick; cut seven ½ x 3 in. strips for each cupcake. Bend into loops; brush ends with water and secure. Let dry overnight on sides on waxed paper covered board dusted with cornstarch. Brush with piping gel and sprinkle with sparkling sugar. **Also:** Make cookies. Prepare and roll out dough. Cut using cutters from tree set. Using largest cutter as guide, use a knife to cut 3 cookies ¼ in. larger than cutter. Using 3 largest cutters, cut 3 cookies in each size. Using remaining 7 cutters, cut 2 cookies in each size and 1 star topper. Bake and cool cookies. **And:** Prepare stand (p. 122). Using royal icing, cover column of stand with tip 21 stripes for tree trunk. Prepare fondant-covered 14 in. cake circle (p. 124).

Assemble and decorate cookie tree with icing. Beginning with largest cookies and working up, build tree following package directions. Decorate with tip 21 pull-out stars and tip 5 pull-out dot snow. Position candies and sprinkles in icing. Spatula ice star cookie and attach to top with icing.

Bake and cool cupcakes in silicone cups supported by cookie sheet. Ice smooth. Trim ends of fondant loops to a point. Insert 6 loops in cupcake to form bow; add upright center loop with a dot of icing. **At party:** Position cupcakes and tree on stand. Each cupcake and cookie serves 1.

*Combine Lemon Yellow with Golden Yellow for yellow shown. Combine Brown with a little Red-Red for brown shown.

◀ A Place to Chill

Pans: 14 x 2 in. Round, p. 153; Soccer Ball, p. 161

Tips: 3, 5, p. 144

Colors: Royal Blue, Black, p. 134

Fondant: White Ready-To-Use Rolled Fondant (48 oz.), Primary Colors Fondant Multi Pack, Brush Set, p. 130; Fondant/Gum Paste Tool Set, p. 131; Rolling Pin, Roll & Cut Mat, p. 133

Recipe: Buttercream Icing, p. 116

Also: 2009 Pattern Book (Face, Chest, Wing, Doorway Arch), p. 128; 2 in. and 2½ in. Globe Pillar and Base Sets (2 sets of each), p. 228; 10 in. Decorator Preferred® Smooth Edge Plate, p. 230; Cake Circles, 16 in. Round Silver Cake Base, p. 232; knife, ruler

In advance: Make presents. Using 1½ in. balls of fondant from Multi Pack, shape into assorted squares and rectangles. Roll out small amounts of fondant 1⁄16 in. thick. Cut thin strips and attach around presents with damp brush for ribbon. Form small teardrop shapes and attach to tops for bows. **Also:** Make penguins (p. 122).

For 14 in. round, ice 2-layer cake smooth, sides in blue, top in white. Pipe tip 5 icicles. Roll ⅜ in. to ¾ in. diameter fondant balls; attach for bottom border with dots of icing. Pipe tip 3 message.

For igloo, bake and cool Soccer Ball cake. Prepare and cover with rolled fondant (p. 117). Position on plate, offset to back left edge of plate to allow room for doorway. Use small veining tool from set to score horizontal and then vertical lines. Roll out a small amount of fondant ½ in. thick; use pattern to cut doorway arch. Brush back with damp brush and attach to igloo. Roll out a small amount of fondant ⅛ in. thick; cut a 5 x 1 in. strip. Attach around doorway; score lines with veining tool. Spatula ice snow on plate around igloo.

Cut 4 pillars to 8 in. long; insert in 14 in. cake (see Globe Pillar Set Construction, p. 115). Cut 1 pillar to 7 in. long; insert in center of igloo cake. Position globe penguins on pillars. Position penguin feet. Position presents. Serves 75.

◀ Love from Above

Pan: Standard Muffin, p. 154

Tip: 2, p. 144

Colors:* Red-Red, Creamy Peach, Ivory, p. 134

Fondant: White Ready-To-Use Rolled Fondant (24 oz.), Brush Set, p. 130; Quick Ease Roller, p. 131; Gum-Tex™, Roll & Cut Mat, p. 133

Candy: Valentine Candy Making Kit Mega Pack (candy molds and Red, White, Pink and Light Cocoa Candy Melts®†), p. 208; Garden Candy Color Set (pink*), p. 166

Recipe: Buttercream Icing, p. 116

Also: 2009 Pattern Book (Wings), p. 128; 13 Count Standard Cupcakes 'N More® Dessert Stand, p. 147; Baby Face Cake Topper, p. 235; Nesting Hearts Cutter Set, p. 208; Hearts Remembered Standard Baking Cups, Hearts Mix Sprinkles, p. 207; Parchment Triangles, p. 143; Cake Boards, p. 232; craft knife, cornstarch

In advance: Make candies using Candy Making Kit. **Also:** Prepare fondant pieces. Tint 1 oz. fondant red and roll out ⅛ in. thick; cut heart using 2nd smallest cutter from set. Add ¼ teaspoon Gum-Tex to 2 oz. white fondant; roll out ⅛ in. thick. Use pattern to cut 2 wings (reverse pattern for 1). Let dry 24 hours on cornstarch-dusted board. **And:** Complete topper. Tint small amount of fondant Peach with Ivory for hands. Roll balls and flatten for hands; cut fingers using knife. Using melted candy in cut parchment bag, attach heart, wings and hands to topper; pipe on hair. Pipe tip 2 message on heart with icing.

Spatula ice cupcakes; sprinkle on Hearts Mix. Position candy. **At party:** Position cupcakes and topper on stand. Each serves 1.

*Add Pink candy color to Pink Candy Melts® for pink candy shown. Combine Peach with Ivory for fondant shade on hands.

▶ Love in His Eyes

Pans: 12-Cavity Petite Heart Silicone Mold, p. 206; Cookie Sheet, Cooling Grid, p. 154

Tip: 2, p. 144

Colors:* Rose, Christmas Red, Red-Red, Black, p. 134

Also: White Ready-To-Use Decorator Icing, p. 135; Jumbo Hearts Sprinkles, p. 207; Parchment Triangles, p. 143

Bake and cool cakes. Tint icing and follow can directions to heat to pouring consistency. Cover cakes with poured icing (p. 124); let set. Position heart sprinkles for lenses. Using tip 2, pipe outline mouth and eyeglass details; pipe dot nose and cheeks. Each serves 1.

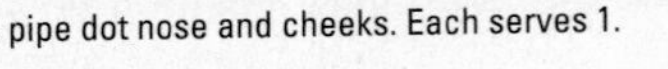

*Combine Christmas Red with Red-Red for red shown.

◀ Valentine Love-Bugs

Pans: Cookie Sheet, Cooling Grid, p. 154

Tips: 2, 12, p. 144

Colors:* Christmas Red, Red-Red, Rose, Black, p. 134

Recipe: Buttercream Icing, p. 116

Also: Heart Silicone Baking Cups, Jumbo Hearts Sprinkles, p. 207; red shoestring licorice, knife, ruler

Bake and cool cupcakes in silicone cups supported by cookie sheet. Ice smooth. Pipe tip 12 ball head; flatten slightly with finger. Using tip 2, pipe dot eyes, nose and spots; outline mouth and back division. Cut licorice to ¾ in. long; insert for antennae. Attach heart sprinkle to end with icing. Each serves 1.

*Combine Christmas Red with Red-Red for red shown.

◀ Bear Hugs and Hearts

Pans: Jumbo Muffin, Cookie Sheet, Cooling Grid, p. 154

Candy: Light Cocoa, White and Red Candy Melts®†, Garden Candy Color Set, p. 166; Heart Pretzel Mold, p. 208; Baby Candy Mold, p. 167

Recipe: Favorite crisped rice cereal treats

Also: Jumbo Hearts Sprinkles, p. 207; Decorator Brush Set, p. 168 or Parchment Triangles, p. 143; pretzel rods, non-stick cooking spray, curling ribbon, cardstock

Tint portions of melted white candy black and pink; reserve some white. Using painting or piping method (p. 125) and following mold instructions, mold pretzel candies and bears. Refrigerate until firm; unmold. For base, prepare cereal treat recipe and press into muffin pan ¾ deep; immediately remove from pan and insert pretzel rods to make hole. Remove pretzels. Cover cereal treats with melted pink candy (p. 125). Refrigerate until firm.

Attach confetti sprinkles to sides of base with dots of melted candy. Insert pretzel. Attach bear with dots of melted candy. Attach ribbon and tag. Each serves 1.

†Brand confectionery coating.

▶ Cupid's Cookie Cards

Pans: Cookie Sheet, Cooling Grid, p. 154

Tips: 2, 3, 4, 12, p. 144

Colors:* Rose, Christmas Red, Red-Red, Lemon Yellow, Copper (for skin tone shown), Black, Brown, p. 134

Recipes: Royal Icing, Shortbread Cookies, p. 116

Also: Valentine Push 'N Print™ Cutter Set, p. 208; Jumbo Hearts Sprinkles, Pink Colored Sugar, p. 207; Meringue Powder, p. 135; Parchment Triangles, p. 143; Cake Board, p. 232; waxed paper, cornstarch

In advance: Prepare and roll out cookie dough. Cut using heart cutters. Bake and cool cookies. Decorate cookies with royal icing following imprinted designs. Outline cookies with tip 4 and sprinkle with pink sugar. On double hearts design, pipe in center hearts with tip 4 and attach white heart sprinkles. On "Love" design, pipe tip 3 message. Place cookies on waxed paper-covered board dusted with cornstarch. For Cupid, pipe tip 12 ball head; flatten with finger. Using tip 2, pipe dot nose and eyes; pipe outline mouth. Pipe tip 3 outline arms and tip 2 pull-out dot fingers and hair. Pipe tip 4 pull-out wings. Let dry several hours. Each serves 1.

*Combine Christmas Red with Red-Red for red shown.

◀ Catch-a-Prince Kit

Cookie: Non-Stick Cookie Sheet, p. 150; Stackable! Teddy Bear Cookie Cutter Set, p. 165; Nesting Hearts Plastic Cutter Set, p. 164

Candy: White, Dark Cocoa Candy Melts®†, Primary and Garden Candy Color Sets, p. 166; Girl Power Candy Mold Set, p. 167; Tented Candy Gift Boxes, p. 169

Also: 2009 Pattern Book (Frog and Prince Crowns), p. 128; Groom Figurine, p. 224; Hearts Confetti Sprinkle Decorations, p. 207; Gold Fanci-Foil Wrap, p. 232; Parchment Triangles, p. 143; White Drawstring Sachet Bags, p. 223; candy hearts, mini candy-coated chocolates, waxed paper, cellophane tape, cardstock, marker, hole punch, scissors, glue

Use candy colors to tint portions of melted white candy green/yellow combination, yellow, red and pink. Mold candies on non-stick cookie sheet. For frog face, fill bear head cutter ⅛ in. deep with green/yellow candy. For frog crown, outline and pipe in pattern. Mold heart, filling 2nd smallest nesting cutter ⅛ in. deep. Refrigerate candies until firm. Overpipe crown; refrigerate until firm. Mold crown and ring in candy mold using piping method (p. 125); refrigerate until firm. Outline crown and attach mini chocolates to crown points; let set. On face, pipe outline mouth and dot eyes and pupils; attach crown to back. Outline and print message on heart; let set.

Write message on box with marker. Cut a 1½ x ¾ in. gift tag from cardstock; punch hole and write message. Attach heart confetti with glue. Fill sachet bag with confetti sprinkles and thread gift tag on ribbon; tie bag. Cut prince crown using pattern and gold foil. Attach around groomsman's head with glue. Attach frog and candy hearts to box with melted candy; let set. Place sachet and candies in box. Each serves 1.

▶ A Frog's Fancy

Pans: Heart Cookie Treat, p. 163; Cooling Grid, p. 154

Tips: 1, 2, 3, 9, p. 144

Colors: Rose, Leaf Green, Lemon Yellow, Black, p. 134

Recipes: Royal Icing, Roll-Out Cookies, p. 116

Also: 2009 Pattern Book (Frog), p. 128; Valentine Nonpareils, Hearts Confetti Sprinkles, Hearts Remembered Icing Decorations, p. 207; Meringue Powder, p. 135; 8 in. Cookie Treat Sticks, p. 163

Prepare dough. Press into pan with cookie sticks. Bake and cool cookies. Place on cooling grid. Cover with thinned royal icing (p. 124). Let dry.

Follow pattern to pipe royal icing frog directly on treat. Use tip 9 to outline and fill in body; position heart icing decoration. Use tip 3 to pipe dot eyes and elongated bead arms and legs. Use tip 2 to pipe pull-out dot crown, toes and fingers, dot eyes and pupils. Outline mouth with tip 1. Attach heart confetti with icing. Pipe tip 3 icing outline around outer edge; attach nonpareils. Each serves 1.

▶ Leaping Into Love!

Pans: Standard Muffin, Cookie Sheet, Cooling Grid, p. 154

Tips: 4, 6, 12, p. 144

Colors:* Leaf Green, Christmas Red, Red-Red, Rose, Black, p. 134

Fondant: White Ready-To-Use Rolled Fondant (2 oz.), Brush Set, p. 130; Round Cut-Outs™, p. 132; Quick Ease Roller, p. 131

Cookie: Hearts Plastic Nesting Cookie Cutter Set, p. 208; 8 in. Cookie Treat Sticks, p. 163

Candy: Red (1 pk.), White (2 pks.) Candy Melts®†, Primary and Garden Candy Color Sets, p. 166; Alphabet Candy Mold, Garden Goodies Lollipop Mold, p. 167; Kissy Lips Candy Mold, p. 208; 11¾ in. Lollipop Sticks, p. 169

Recipes: Buttercream, Royal Icings, Roll-Out Cookies, p. 116

Also: 2009 Pattern Book (Frog Leg, Crown), p. 128; Hearts Remembered Standard Baking Cups, Hearts Confetti Sprinkles, p. 207; Meringue Powder, p. 135; Cake Boards, 6 in. Cake Circle, Fanci-Foil Wrap, p. 232; Ceramic Pedestal Cake Stand, p. 226; Parchment Triangles, p. 143; 8 in. craft foam circle (2 in. thick), pink curling ribbon, 30 in. white ribbon (2 in. wide), mini candy-coated chocolates, knife, scissors, tape, cornstarch

In advance: Prepare candies, tinting portions of melted white candy using color sets. Mold lips; refrigerate until firm, unmold. Attach lollipop sticks to backs using melted candy. Mold frogs using piping method (p. 125); for lighter green lily pad, mix green with yellow candy color. Refrigerate until firm; unmold. Pipe dot eyes and outline mouth using melted, tinted candy in cut parchment bag. Mold letters using layering method (p. 125). Refrigerate until firm; unmold. For large crown, cover pattern with waxed paper. Using melted candy in cut parchment bag, outline and fill in area. Refrigerate until firm. Turn crown over and overpipe on back side. Refrigerate until firm. Attach mini chocolate candies at points of crown using melted candy. **Also:** Prepare cookie frog and heart (p. 121). **And:** Prepare base. Wrap craft foam circle with Fanci-Foil (p. 110). Attach white ribbon around outer edge, secure with tape. Attach message to front with melted candy.

Bake and cool cupcakes. Ice with buttercream; sprinkle on confetti. Make small candy crowns (p. 121). Insert frog cookie in base. Trim lips lollipop sticks to graduated lengths; insert into base behind frog. Curl curling ribbon and position on base. Position on pedestal cake stand. Surround pedestal with cupcakes. Each lollipop and cupcake serves 1; frog cookie serves 5.

*Combine Christmas Red with Red-Red for red shown.

◀ Cottontail Collection

Pans: Step-By-Step Bunny, p. 209; Cookie Sheet, Cooling Grid, p. 154
Tips: 3, 18, p. 144-145
Colors:* Rose, Royal Blue, Leaf Green, Violet, Lemon Yellow, Golden Yellow, Red-Red, Brown, p. 134
Recipes: Buttercream, Color Flow Icings, Roll-Out Cookies, p. 116
Also: 2009 Pattern Book (Arms, Feet, Base Board), p. 128; Hoppy Easter Cutter Set, p. 212; Blue Colored Sugar, Bright Sugars 4-Mix Assortment, p. 136; Color Flow Mix, p. 135; Fanci-Foil Wrap, p. 232; knife, confectioners' sugar, 24 x 36 x ½ in. foamcore board, cornstarch

In advance: Make cookies. Prepare and roll out dough. Cut 25 eggs using cutter from set. Use patterns to cut 3 each for left arm and foot; reverse patterns and cut 3 each for right arm and foot. Bake and cool cookies. **Also:** Decorate egg cookies. Place cookies on cooling grid over drip pan; cover with thinned color flow (p. 124); let dry 24 hours. Decorate using full-strength color flow and tip 3; sprinkle on colored sugar while icing is still wet. Let dry. **And:** Stack 3 like arm and foot cookies together using thin layer of color flow as glue. Let dry. **Also:** Prepare base board. Enlarge Base Board Pattern 200%. Position bunny pan and pattern on foamcore board. Cut base board and wrap with foil.

Bake and cool cake. Ice smooth inside ears. Using tip 3, pipe outline eyes; outline and pipe in mouth (pat smooth with finger dipped in cornstarch). Using tip 3, outline and pipe in nose and tongue (pat smooth). Cover remainder of cake and stacked cookies with tip 18 stars. Position cake and arms on base board. Position egg cookies and feet. Cake serves 12; each cookie serves 1.

*Combine Violet with Rose for violet shown. Combine Lemon Yellow with Golden Yellow for yellow shown. Combine Brown with Red-Red for brown shown.

▼ Chicks on a Half Shell

Pan: Mini Egg, p. 209
Candy: Fuzzy Bunny Lollipop Mold, p. 211; Yellow, White, Orange, Light Cocoa Candy Melts®†, Garden Candy Color Set, p. 166
Also: Decorator Brush Set, p. 168 or Parchment Triangles, p. 143; Pastel Mix Jelly Beans, p. 237; craft knife, spoon

In advance: Mold chick candies in lollipop mold without sticks. Using painting or piping method (p. 125), pipe in eyes and beak; let set before filling cavity with yellow. Refrigerate until firm; unmold. **Also:** Tint portion of white candy pink using candy colors. Make candy shells (p. 125) ¼ in. thick in pan. If excess candy pools in bottom of shell, scoop out with a spoon while soft. Place pan in freezer until candy is completely set then unmold. Use a craft knife to cut jagged top edge.

Attach chick candy inside shell using melted candy. Add jelly beans. Each serves 1.

▲ Bunny Totes a Basket

Pans: Cookie Sheet, Cooling Grid, p. 154
Candy: Fuzzy Bunny Lollipop Mold, White and Light Cocoa Candy Melts®†, Easter Candy Making Kit Mega Pack, p. 211; Primary and Garden Candy Color Sets, 166
Recipe: Roll-Out Cookies, p. 116
Also: Gingerbread Boy Metal Cookie Cutter, p. 165; Fuzzy Bunny Party Bags, p. 210; Parchment Triangles, p. 143; waxed paper

Mold candy using piping method (p. 125). Mold bunny heads in Fuzzy Bunny mold and Easter baskets using Mega Kit; refrigerate until firm and unmold. Prepare and roll out cookie dough. Cut cookies using boy cutter; bake and cool. Cover with melted candy (p. 124); let set. Pipe pants and suspenders on cookies with melted candy; let set. Attach candy head and basket with melted candy. Pipe candy bow tie and add dots to pants. Let set. Place in treat bag and close with tie. Each serves 1.

†Brand confectionery coating.

▼ Sparkle Shells

Pans: Decorated Egg Silicone Mold, p. 209; Cookie Sheet, Cooling Grid, p. 154

Recipe: Buttercream Icing, p, 116

Also: Pink, Yellow, Green Sparkle Gels, p. 135; spatula

Bake cakes in Silicone Egg Mold supported by cookie sheet; let cool. Ice smooth. Using sparkle gels, add zigzag and wavy lines on eggs. Each serves 1.

▶ Eggs-pressionist Painting

Pans: Mini Loaf, Cookie Sheet, Cooling Grid, p. 154

Candy: White and Light Cocoa Candy Melts®†, Primary and Garden Candy Color Sets, p. 166; Hoppy Easter Lollipop Mold, p. 211

Recipe: Shortbread Cookies, p. 116

Also: Easter Push 'N Print™ Cutter Set, p. 211; Parchment Triangles, p. 143; mini marshmallows

In advance: Tint portions of melted candy green, orange, yellow and pink. Use melted green candy to make candy plaque bases (p. 126) in Mini Loaf Pan. **Also:** Use piping method (p. 125) to mold sitting bunnies in lollipop mold. Pipe in eyes and nose before molding body; refrigerate until firm. Unmold; pipe on mouth and paint brush. **And:** Make cookies. Prepare and roll out dough. Cut using Push 'N Print Cutters. Bake and cool cookies.

Decorate cookies using melted candy in cut parchment bag; let set. Attach cookie, bunny and marshmallows to candy base using melted candy. Pipe candy on marshmallows for paint. Each serves 1.

▼ Lounging Lamb

Pans: Stand-Up Lamb, p. 209; Cookie Sheet, Cooling Grid, p. 154

Tips: 3, 16, 233, p. 144-145

Colors: Rose, Leaf Green, Brown, p. 134

Candy: White Candy Melts®† (2 pks.), Primary and Garden Candy Color Sets, p. 166; Fuzzy Bunny Lollipop Mold, p. 211; 4 in. Lollipop Sticks, p. 169

Recipe: Buttercream Icing, p. 116

Also: Pastel Silicone Baking Cups, p. 210; Decorator Brush Set, p. 168 or Parchment Triangles, p. 143; Fanci-Foil Wrap, p. 232; 11¼ x 5½ x 3 in. high craft foam block, 3 in. wide ribbon (1 yd. length), tape, knife, scissors, ruler, cornstarch

In advance: Make candies. Melt and tint candy pink, green, violet and yellow. Mold candies with lollipop sticks using painting or piping method (p. 125). Refrigerate until firm; unmold. **Also:** Make cupcakes. Bake and cool cupcakes in silicone cups supported by cookie sheet. Cover with tip 233 pull-out grass. Insert candies, trimming sticks as needed. **And:** Prepare base. Cover craft block with Fanci-Foil (p. 110). Wrap ribbon around sides and secure with tape.

Bake and cool lamb cake using firm-textured batter such as pound cake. Position on prepared base; ice face and inside ears smooth. Using tip 3, pipe outline eyes and mouth; outline and fill in nose (pat smooth with finger dipped in cornstarch). Cover cake with tip 16 rosettes. Cake serves 12; each cupcake serves 1.

◀ A Sprinkle of Springtime

Pan: Standard Muffin, p. 154
Tips: 2, 3, 352, p. 144-145
Colors:* Kelly Green, Violet, Rose, Royal Blue, p. 134
Fondant: White Ready-To-Use Rolled Fondant (6 oz.), p. 130; Round Cut-Outs™, p. 132; Rolling Pin, Roll & Cut Mat, Gum-Tex™, p. 133
Candy: Dancing Daisies Lollipop Mold, p. 167; Hoppy Easter Lollipop Mold, p. 211; White Candy Melts®† (3 pks.), Primary and Garden Candy Color Sets, p. 166
Recipes: Buttercream, Royal Icings, p. 116
Also: 2009 Pattern Book (Watering Can), p. 128; 38 Count Standard Cupcakes N' More® Dessert Stand, p. 147; Spring Party Standard Baking Cups, p. 210; Meringue Powder, p. 135; Decorator Brush Set, p. 168 or Parchment Triangles, p. 143; 22-gauge florist wire (five 8 in. lengths), white florist tape, waxed paper, scissors, ruler, tape

In advance: Using candy colors, tint portions of melted candy yellow, pink, violet and green. Mold candies without lollipop sticks using painting or piping method (p. 125). **Also:** Make fondant watering can topper (p. 122).

Bake and cool cupcakes. Ice smooth. Position candies. Pipe tip 352 leaves. Position cupcakes and topper on stand at party. Each serves 1.

*Combine Violet with Rose for violet shown.

†Brand confectionery coating.

▶ Hutch on a Hill

Pans: Standard Muffin, Cookie Sheet, Cooling Grid, p. 154
Tips: 3, 4, 233, p. 144-145
Colors: Rose, Leaf Green, Lemon Yellow, p. 134
Recipes: Buttercream Icing, Roll-Out Cookies, p. 116
Also: Fuzzy Bunny Standard Baking Cups, Fun Pix®, Spring Confetti Sprinkles, p. 210; Comfort Grip™ Egg Cutter, p. 211; 101 Cookie Cutter Set, p. 164; 23 Count Standard Cupcakes 'N More® Dessert Stand, p. 147; White Candy Melts®†, p. 166; Tapered Spatula, p. 138; sugar wafer cookies, knife, ruler, toothpicks

In advance: Make cookies. Prepare and roll out dough. Cut hutch using Egg Cutter and base using medium round cutter from 101 Cutter Set. Bake and cool cookies. **Also:** Prepare hutch. Lightly mark where door and windows will go; ice smooth. Outline door and windows with tip 4. Using tip 3, fill in door window and pipe pull-out dot grass under windows. Attach confetti sprinkle for door knob. Attach hutch to base with melted candy; spatula ice walkway and pipe tip 233 pull-out grass. Position confetti in grass. Cut 2 wafer cookies to 3 in. long; using melted candy, attach for roof. Cut a wafer cookie on an angle for 1½ in. tall chimney; attach using melted candy. Pipe tip 3 zigzag top trim.

Bake and cool cupcakes. Cover with tip 233 pull-out grass. Position Fun Pix®; sprinkle on confetti. Position cupcakes and hutch on stand at party. Each serves 1.

▲ Creamy Blossoms

Pan: 6-Cavity Silicone Mini Flowers Mold, p. 155
Tip: 21, p. 145
Colors: Lemon Yellow, Rose, p. 134
Candy: White Candy Melts®†, Garden Candy Color Set, p. 166; Decorator Brush Set, p. 168
Recipe: Cream Cheese Mousse, p. 116
Also: Vanilla Whipped Icing Mix, p. 135; Parchment Triangles, p. 143; non-stick cooking spray, lemon leaves

In advance: Make candy leaves (p. 125).

Prepare mousse recipe; divide in 3rds. Tint ⅓ yellow, ⅓ rose, leave remaining ⅓ white. Spray mold cavities with cooking spray and fill ⅓ full with yellow. Spoon in next ⅓ white then fill remainder with rose. Alternate colors as desired. Unmold mousse; pipe tip 21 whipped icing rosette. Position candy leaf before serving. Each serves 1.

▲ Grade-A Easter Treat

Pans: Jumbo Muffin, Cookie Sheet, Cooling Grid, p. 154
Tip: 6, p. 144
Colors:* Leaf Green, Brown, Red-Red, p. 134
Fondant: White Ready-To-Use Rolled Fondant (1 oz. for each handle), p. 130; Gum-Tex™, Roll & Cut Mat, p. 133
Recipes: Buttercream Icing, Roll-Out Cookies, p. 116
Also: 2009 Pattern Book (Handle), p. 128; Colored Sugars in Blue, Yellow, Pink, Lavender and Light Green, p. 136; Easter 12-Pc. Mini Cutter Collection, p. 212; Cake Board, p. 232; shredded coconut, knife, cornstarch, waxed paper

In advance: Make fondant handle. Add ½ teaspoon Gum-Tex to 6 oz. fondant; tint brown. Roll 1 oz. into a 9½ in. long rope, ⅜ in. thick. Score lightly with a knife, making diagonal lines about ¼ in. apart. Use pattern as guide for handle shape. Let dry 1-2 days on waxed paper-covered board dusted with cornstarch. **Also:** Make cookies. Prepare and roll out dough. Cut 11 eggs for each basket using mini cutter from set; sprinkle on colored sugars. Bake and cool cookies.

Bake and cool cupcakes. Ice tops fluffy. Cover sides with tip 6 basketweave (p. 119). Sprinkle tops with tinted coconut (p. 120). Position cookies (use more icing if necessary). Insert handles. Each serves 1.

*Combine Brown with Red-Red for brown shown.

▼ Plant a Sweet Surprise!

Pan: Dimensions® Multi-Cavity Mini Cupcakes, p. 151
Tips: 1B, 4, 352, p. 144-145
Colors: Rose, Violet, Lemon Yellow, Kelly Green, p. 134
Candy: White Candy Melts®†, Garden Candy Color Set, p. 166
Recipe: Royal Icing, p. 116
Also: Meringue Powder, p. 135; Parchment Triangles, p. 143; Cake Boards, p. 232; Pillow Mints, p. 237; waxed paper

In advance: Make flowers. Tint royal icing pink, yellow and violet; reserve a portion for green leaves. Pipe tip 1B drop flowers (p. 119) on waxed paper-covered board, 4 in each color for each treat; add tip 4 dot centers. Let dry. **Also:** Make candy shell (p. 125) cups and lid using pan bottom and top. Shells should be about ¼ in. thick. Refrigerate until firm; unmold.

Attach flowers to candy lid using royal icing or melted candy in cut parchment bag. Pipe tip 352 royal icing leaves. Let set. Fill bottom with mints; position lid. Each serves 1.

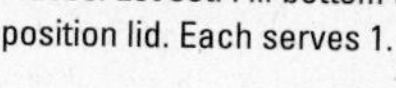

▲ Bird's Nest Fest

Candy: Easter Candy Making Kit Mega Pack, p. 211; Light Cocoa (2 pks.), White Candy Melts®†(2 pks.), Primary and Garden Candy Color Sets, p. 166; 1 in. Candy Cups, p. 169
Fondant: White Ready-To-Use Rolled Fondant (6 oz.), p. 130; Rose Leaf Fondant Cut & Press Set, p. 131; Flower Former Set, p. 137; Rolling Pin, Roll & Cut Mat, Gum-Tex™, p. 133
Color: Leaf Green, p. 134
Also: 13 Count Standard Cupcakes 'N More® Dessert Stand, p. 147; Parchment Triangles, p. 143; Cake Boards, p. 232; waxed paper, cornstarch, small jelly beans, shredded coconut (3¼ cups)

Two days in advance: Make leaves. Tint 6 oz. fondant; mix in 1 teaspoon Gum-Tex. Roll out ⅛ in. thick. Cut about 90 leaves using large leaf section of Cut & Press. Let dry overnight on medium Flower Formers dusted with cornstarch. **Also:** Make candies. Tint portions of white candy violet, blue and orange. Use mold, candy and instructions from kit to mold 13 hatching chicks. **And:** Prepare stand. Before assembling, lay each section of holder rings on a waxed paper-covered board. Open and flatten candy cups and slide 1 under each ring. Using melted candy in cut parchment bag, attach leaves to bottom of rings, letting candy cups catch excess candy. Let set completely before turning sections over and assembling stand. Leave candy cups on stand to hold nests. Add additional leaves on top side if desired.

For each nest, mix ¼ cup coconut with just enough melted candy to coat. Shape into a 2 in. diameter nest with center indentation to hold candies. Refrigerate until firm. Position chick candies and jelly beans in nests; position nests on candy cups on rings. Each serves 1.

▼ Broad Stripes, Bright Stars

Pans: #1, p. 159; Cookie Sheet, Cooling Grid, p. 154
Tips: 3, 4, 18, 21, p. 144-145
Colors: Christmas Red, Royal Blue, Golden Yellow, p. 134
Recipes: Buttercream Icing, Roll-Out Cookies, p. 116
Also: Nesting Stars Cutter Set, p. 164; Yellow Sparkle Gel, p. 135; Cake Boards, Fanci-Foil Wrap, p. 232; 8 in. Cookie Treat Sticks, p. 163; large marshmallows, ruler, toothpicks

Prepare and roll out cookie dough. Cut stars using cutters from set: 2 in smallest size, 3 in 2nd smallest, 3 in 3rd smallest (bake 1 on cookie stick), 1 in 3rd largest and 1 in 2nd largest. Bake and cool cookies. Outline with tip 3; fill in with Sparkle Gel.

Bake and cool cake. Position on wrapped, cut-to-fit cake board; ice smooth. Use tip 4 to pipe 2 vertical lines to define the firecracker's sides. Use ruler to mark 1 in. wide stripes, running across cake at a 45° angle. Cover stripes with tip 18 stars in alternating colors. Pipe tip 21 star bottom border. Insert cookie stick star into cake top. Attach remaining cookies with icing. For raised cookies, rest higher layers on marshmallows cut to the height needed. Pipe tip 3 message. Cake serves 12; each cookie serves 1.

▲ Festive Flag Wavers

Pans: Star, p. 161; Cookie Sheet, Cooling Grid, p. 154
Tips: 3, 5, 12, 16, 21, p. 144-145
Colors: Lemon Yellow, Orange, Kelly Green, Royal Blue, Brown, Black, Red-Red, Copper, p. 134
Recipes: Buttercream, Royal Icings, Roll-Out Cookies, p. 116
Also: Stars and Stripes Party Picks, Patriotic Mix Sprinkles, p. 214; 101 Cookie Cutters Set, p. 164; Cake Boards, Fanci-Foil Wrap, p. 232; Meringue Powder, p. 135; waxed paper, cornstarch

Two days in advance: Make cookies. Prepare and roll out dough. Cut 5 bodies using largest star cutter and 5 heads using smallest round cutter from 101 Cutter Set. Bake and cool cookies. **Also:** Decorate cookies with royal icing. Spatula ice all in light copper. Place on waxed paper to decorate. For heads, use tip 3 to pipe dot eyes, dot nose and outline mouth. Pipe hair using swirls, lines and pull-out dots; add tip 3 dot barrettes and pull-out bow. For bodies, use tip 16 to pipe green star shirt; outline and fill in other shirts and pants (smooth with finger dipped in cornstarch). Add tip 3 dot, line and zigzag trims. Pipe tip 12 bead shoes. Pipe tip 5 dot hands and position flag picks; pipe tip 3 pull-out fingers. Let dry overnight. **And:** Attach heads to bodies with royal icing. Let dry overnight.

Bake and cool 1-layer star cake. Ice smooth. Pipe tip 21 star bottom border. Use icing dots to attach cookies, letting heads extend slightly beyond cake points. Print tip 3 message; add sprinkles. Cake serves 12; each cookie serves 1.

◀ United Stars

Pans: Mini Star Pan, p. 156; Cookie Sheet, Cooling Grid, p. 154

Candy: White Candy Melts ®† (1 pk. will cover 4 to 5 treats), Garden and Primary Candy Color Sets, p. 166

Also: Patriotic Nonpareils, Stars and Stripes Party Picks, p. 214; Disposable Decorating Bags, Parchment Triangles, p. 143

Bake and cool cakes. Cover with melted candy (p. 125); let set. Use a spatula to add a thin layer of melted candy to sides; immediately sprinkle with nonpareils. Tint portions of melted candy blue and black using candy colors. Pipe dot and outline facial features using cut parchment bags. Insert cake pick. Each serves 1.

†Brand confectionery coating.

▶ Patriot Pops

Pan: 9 x 13 x 2 in. Sheet, p. 154

Color: Christmas Red, p. 134

Candy: Yellow Candy Melts®†, p. 166; 11¾ in. Lollipop Sticks, p. 169; Stars Candy Mold, p. 214

Recipe: Favorite crisped rice cereal treats (1 batch will make 8-10 treats)

Also: Round Cut-Outs™, p. 132; Patriotic Stars Icing Decorations, Party Bags, p. 214; Parchment Triangles, p. 143; non-stick pan spray, waxed paper, knife

In advance: Mold top star candies; refrigerate until firm, unmold.

Prepare cereal treats. Before mixing in cereal, divide marshmallow/butter mixture into 2 portions. Tint 1 red. Add ½ of cereal to each portion and mix per recipe. Keeping colors separated, press mixtures into waxed-paper lined pan; unmold by lifting waxed paper. Cut circles using medium round Cut-Out sprayed with pan spray; cut 3 red and 2 natural for each treat. Thread circles onto lollipop sticks, leaving 1½ in. extended at top; secure with dots of melted candy. Attach candy star to top of stick and icing decorations to treats using melted candy. Let set. Place treat in bag and tie. Each serves 1.

▶ Cookie Salute

Pan: Cookie Sheet, Cooling Grid, p. 154

Tips: 6, 8, p. 144

Color: Golden Yellow, p. 134

Recipes: Buttercream Icing, Roll-Out Cookies, p. 116

Also: Flag Comfort Grip™ Cutter, p. 213; Red, Blue Sparkle Gels, p. 135; White Nonpareils Sprinkles, p. 136

Prepare and roll out cookie dough. Cut with flag cutter. Bake and cool cookies. Pipe on icing using tip 8; smooth with spatula. Use blue gel to fill in upper corner; sprinkle with white nonpareils. Pipe red gel wavy stripes. Pipe tip 6 line for pole and dot on top. Each serves 1.

▶ Long May She Weave!

Pan: Stars & Stripes, p. 213

Tips: 12, 18, p. 144-145

Fondant: White Ready-to-Use Rolled Fondant (24 oz.) and Primary, Natural Color Fondant Multi Packs, Brush Set, p. 130; Star Cut-Outs™, p. 132; Fondant/Gum Paste Tool Set, Fondant Shaping Foam, Cutter/Embosser, p. 131; Rolling Pin, Roll & Cut Mat, p. 133

Recipes: Buttercream Icing, p. 116; Thinned Fondant Adhesive, p. 117

Also: 101 Cookie Cutters Set, p. 164; Cake Boards, Fanci-Foil Wrap, p. 232; Gum-Tex™, p. 133; 6 in. Cookie Treat Sticks, p. 163; ruler, craft knife, waxed paper, cornstarch

In advance: Use fondant to make figure, table, needles and spool of thread (p. 122). **Also:** Using pan as a pattern, prepare shaped board, allowing extra space where figure and table will stand. Wrap board with foil.

Bake and cool cake. Cut 1 in. off corner where figure will stand. Ice cake smooth. For flag, roll out all fondant ⅛ in. thick. Roll out 12 oz. white and place over flag pan. Cut out flag shape; place over cake top and smooth. Roll out blue; cut a 4½ x 3 in. rectangle. Attach with damp brush. Roll out red; cut 2 strips in each size: ⅞ x 7 in. and ⅞ x 12 in. Attach with damp brush. Roll out white fondant. Use smallest Cut-Out to cut 18 stars. Attach 13 stars in circle on blue background. Pipe tip 18 star bottom border. Position figure at corner. Place needle with thread in right hand and edge of flag in left hand. Position table on board; arrange stars, spool of thread and 2nd needle on tabletop. Serves 12.

Life's Landmarks

Will your guests take a sneak peek at the dessert table? If you've chosen your cake here, you can be sure they will! Our designs capture the thrill of the event—from a torrent of pastel umbrellas for the baby shower to a candy graduation cap cake framed with colorful imprinted fondant detail. They won't forget the Christening cake, topped by a 3-D carriage decked in swirls. Or the bold Bar Mitzvah design, which transforms a hexagon fondant cake into a scrolled Star of David. Make the moment a great memory!

Baby's Topping the Bill

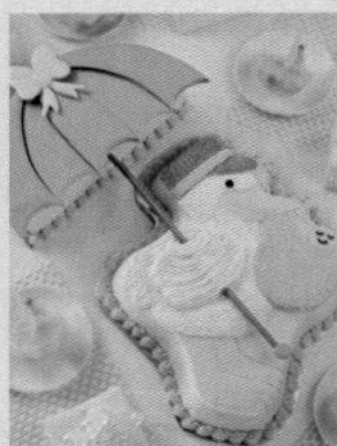

Pans: Stork Express, p. 235; 10 x 2 in. Round, p. 153
Tips: 3, 10, 16, 21, p. 144-145
Colors:* Violet, Royal Blue, Lemon Yellow, Rose, Kelly Green, Copper (for skin tone shown), Black, p. 134
Recipes: Buttercream, Color Flow Icings, p. 116
Also: 2009 Pattern Book (Umbrella Right, Left and Center Panels, Handle Tip and Base, Bow Knot, Bow), p. 128; Cake Boards, Fanci-Foil Wrap, p. 232; Color Flow Mix, p. 135; Wooden Dowel Rods, p. 230; Parchment Triangles, p. 143; waxed paper, ⅝ in. wide ribbon (20 in.), knife, waxed paper, cornstarch

In advance: Use patterns and tip 3 to make Color Flow umbrella and bow pieces (p. 126). Let dry 48 hours.
Also: Wrap dowel rod by rolling with ribbon held at a 45° angle. Secure ends with full-strength color flow.

Bake and cool 1-layer cakes (1½ in. high). Cut round cake in half and stack to make a 3 in. high half round; ice smooth. Pipe tip 21 shell bottom border. Trim wing section off stork cake. Ice sides and background areas smooth. Outline details with tip 3. Outline and pipe in stork's eye and inside of pink blanket; (pat smooth with finger dipped in cornstarch). Use tip 10 to pipe baby's head; add tip 3 outline features. Cover stork head, beak, body, feet, hat and blanket with tip 16 stars. Position dowel rod; overpipe tip 16 pull-out stars over rod for wing. Attach handle tip with full-strength color flow. Position umbrella base on half round cake; attach overlay panels, bow and knot with full-strength color flow.†† Position cakes by sliding dowel rod into umbrella cake. Serves 26.

*Combine Violet with Rose for violet shown.

††Buttercream icing will break down color flow. Position color flow pieces on a piece of plastic wrap cut to fit, on sugar cubes or on mini marshmallows.

Fast Favors

Candy: Mini Pastels Favor Candy, p. 237
Also: Umbrella Favor Kits, p. 236; Newborn Baby Figurines, p. 237; hot glue gun

Fill umbrellas with candy and close. Attach baby accents with dots of glue. Each serves 1.

Stroll in the Showers

Pans: Mini Ball, p. 161; Non-Stick Cookie Sheet, p. 150
Candy: White (2 pks.), Light Cocoa Candy Melts®†, Primary, Garden Candy Color Sets, p. 166; 4 in. Lollipop Sticks, p. 169
Also: 101 Cookie Cutters Set, p. 164; Parchment Triangles, p. 143; Rubber Ducky Candles, p. 185; ruler

Tint portions of melted white candy blue, pink, green and orange (for skin tone shown). For babies and circle bases, place small boy and largest circle cookie cutters from set on cookie sheet. Fill ¼ in. deep with melted candy. Refrigerate until firm, unmold and repeat. Make candy umbrellas (p. 125) using Mini Ball Pan and dividing into 10ths.

Using melted candy in cut parchment bag, add facial features to baby; outline and fill in diaper. Attach baby to base and umbrella to hand using melted candy. Position candles. Each serves 1.

▼ Joy Rains Supreme!

Pans: Standard Muffin, p. 154; Sports Ball Set, p. 161
Candy: White Candy Melts®† (2 pks.), Primary and Garden Candy Color Sets, p. 166; Baby Treats Candy Mold, p. 235
Recipe: Buttercream Icing, p. 116
Also: Cupcakes 'N More® Dessert Stand, p. 147; Baby Feet Standard Baking Cups, p. 233; Cake Dividing Set, p. 137; 8 in. Cookie Treat Sticks, p. 163; Decorator Brush Set, p. 168 or Parchment Triangles, p. 143; Spatula, p. 138; ⅛ in. wide ribbon (6 in. long)

In advance: Tint melted white candy using candy colors. Use painting or piping method (p. 125) to mold Baby Treats candies.
Also: Make candy umbrella (p. 125) using Sports Ball Pan and dividing into 16 sections. Tie on ribbon.

Spatula ice cupcakes. At shower, position candies on cupcakes and cupcakes on stand. Position umbrella in top cupcake. Each serves 1.

†Brand confectionery coating.

► Shakin' Up the Shower

Pan: Cookie Sheet, p. 163
Tips: 1, 3, 12, p. 144
Colors:* Brown, Red-Red, Royal Blue, Black, Rose, p. 134
Recipe: Buttercream Icing, p. 116
Also: Bear Silicone Baking Cups, p. 148; Shower Rattles, p. 237; cornstarch

Bake and cool cupcakes in silicone cups supported by cookie sheet. Cover cupcake using tip 12 and then ice smooth. Outline and fill in bib with tip 3; smooth with finger dipped in cornstarch. Edge bib with tip 3 balls; print tip 1 message. Attach rattle with icing. Each serves 1.

*Combine Brown with Red-Red and a little Black for brown shown.

▼ A Peek of Sunshine

Pan: Cookie Sheet, Cooling Grid, p. 163
Tips: 1, 2A, 3, 12, p. 144
Colors:* Kelly Green, Lemon Yellow, Brown, Red-Red, Black, Copper (for skin tone shown), p. 134
Recipes: Roll-Out Cookies, Color Flow Icing, p. 116
Also: 101 Cookie Cutters Set, p. 164; Color Flow Mix, p. 135; 4 in. Lollipop Sticks, p. 163; Parchment Triangles, p. 143; Cake Board, p. 232; ⅛ in. wide ribbon (6 in. for each treat), knife, waxed paper

In advance: Make umbrella buttons. Use thinned color flow in cut parchment bag to pipe ⅜ and ⅝ in. diameter puddle dots (p. 120) on waxed paper. Let dry 48 hours.

Prepare cookie dough and roll out. Cut a circle using largest circle cutter from set; cut in half. Cut scallops using open end of tip 2A. Bake and cool cookies. Outline umbrella and ribs with tip 3 and full-strength color flow; flow in with thinned color flow (p. 126). Let dry. Using full-strength color flow, attach lollipop stick to back; when set, turn over and attach ⅝ in. button at top and ⅜ in. button at bottom. Set on waxed paper-covered board. Use full-strength color flow and tip 12 to outline and pipe in head. Pipe tip 1 dot eyes, nose and outline mouth; pipe tip 3 dot hand and fingers over stick. Let dry. Tie ribbon onto stick. Each serves 1.

*Combine Brown with Red-Red for darker skin tone.

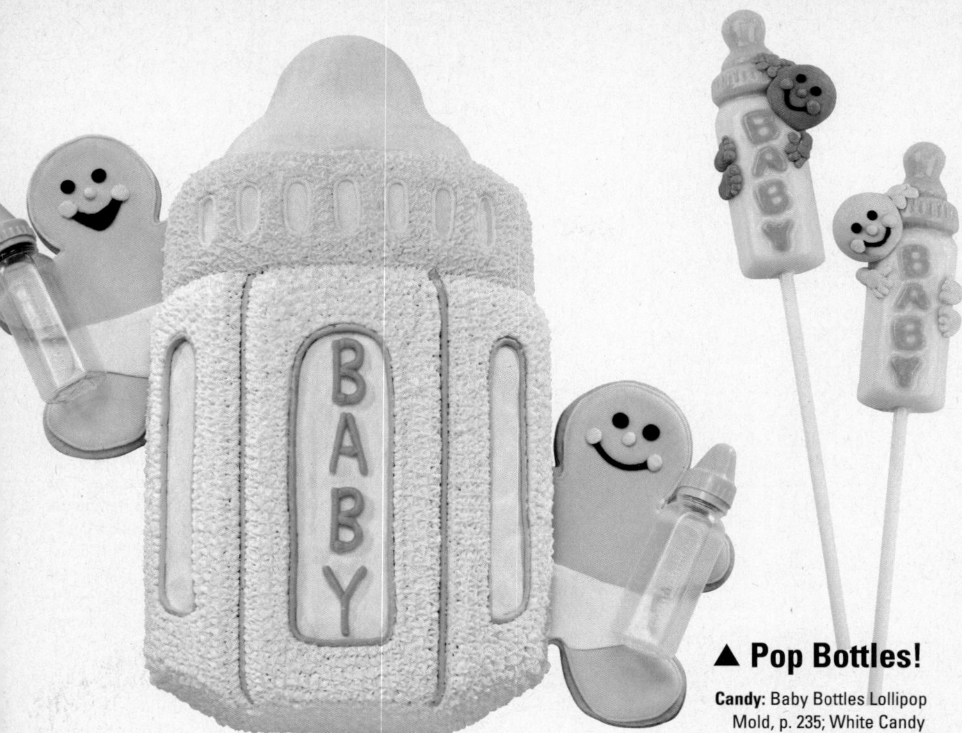

▲ Tall Order

Pans: Baby Bottle, p. 159; Cookie Sheet, Cooling Grid, p. 163

Tips: 3, 5, 16, p. 144-145

Colors:* Lemon Yellow, Rose, Royal Blue, Kelly Green, Black, Copper (for skin tone shown), p. 134

Recipes: Buttercream, Color Flow Icings, Roll-Out Cookies, p. 116

Also: 101 Cookie Cutters, p. 164; Baby Bottles, p. 236; Color Flow Mix, p. 135; Cake Boards, Fanci-Foil Wrap, p. 232; 10 x 5 x 1 in. craft block, waxed paper, cornstarch, knife

In advance: Make baby cookies. Prepare cookie dough and roll out. Cut using largest boy cutter from set; bake and cool. Decorate with color flow (p. 126).

Bake and cool 1-layer cake. On cake, ice smooth nipple, indented neck and bottle areas. Outline neck details with tip 3 and bottle with tip 5; fill in with tip 16 stars. Print tip 5 message. Position cake on craft foam block covered in foil. Position cookies; attach bottles with dots of icing. Cake serves 12, each cookie serves 1.

*Combine Kelly Green with Royal Blue for green shown.

▲ Pop Bottles!

Candy: Baby Bottles Lollipop Mold, p. 235; White Candy Melts®†, Primary and Garden Candy Color Sets, p. 166; 6 in. Lollipop Sticks, p. 163

Tips: 1, 2, 12, p. 144

Colors:* Copper (for skin tone shown), Brown, Red-Red, Black, p. 134

Recipe: Royal Icing, p. 116

Also: Parchment Triangles, p. 143 or Decorator Brush Set, p. 168; Meringue Powder, p. 135; waxed paper

Melt candy and tint portions pink and blue. Mold baby bottle lollipops using piping or painting method (p. 125). Refrigerate until firm; unmold onto waxed paper. Use royal icing to pipe tip 12 ball head, tip 2 ball, dot and pull-out hands and feet, tip 1 dot eyes, nose, cheeks and outline mouth. Let dry 24 hours before party.

*Combine Brown with Red-Red for brown shown.

◀ Baby Bear

Cookie: Cookie Sheet, Cooling Grid, p. 163; Teddy Bear Plastic Nesting Cutter Set, p. 164; Stackable! Teddy Bear Cookie Cutter Set, p. 165

Tips: 3, 5, p. 144

Colors:* Brown, Red-Red, Black, p. 134

Recipes: Roll-Out Cookies, Color Flow Icing, p. 116

Also: Color Flow Mix, p. 135; ⅝ in. wide ribbon (8 in. for each treat)

In advance: Prepare cookie dough and roll out. Cut cookies using 3-piece stackable set for head and largest nesting cutter for body; bake and cool. Outline all cookies with tip 3 and full-strength color flow; flow in with thinned color flow (p. 126). Let dry 24 hours.

Stack cookies and secure with icing. Outline and pipe in tip 5 eyes; add outline mouth. Tie ribbon into a bow and attach with a dot of full-strength color flow icing. Each serves 1.

*Combine Brown with Red-Red and Black for brown shown.

▼ Baby's Bird Bath

Pans: Baby Buggy, p. 235; Cookie Sheet, Cooling Grid, p. 163

Tips: 2, 3, 5, 12, 14, 16, p. 144-145

Colors: Royal Blue, Rose, Lemon Yellow, Kelly Green, Black, Copper (for skin tone shown), p. 134

Recipes: Buttercream, Color Flow Icings, Roll-Out Cookies, p. 116

Also: 2009 Pattern Book (Bird/Watering Can), p. 128; 101 Cookie Cutters, p. 164; Color Flow Mix, p. 135; Heart Drops Sprinkle Decorations, p. 136; Cake Boards, Fanci-Foil Wrap, p. 232; Disposable Decorating Bags, p. 143; white 18-gauge florist wire, white florist tape, knife, ruler, waxed paper, cornstarch, toothpicks

In advance: Make cookies. Prepare dough and roll out. Cut bird and watering can using pattern and knife. Cut baby head using medium round cutter from set. Bake and cool. Decorate blue bird and watering can (p. 126) with color flow; add wire water stream.

Ice cake sides and background areas smooth in blue, wheels in white. Mark umbrella with toothpick, about 3 in. from cake edge. Outline umbrella and buggy with tip 3; fill in with tip 16 stars. Overpipe umbrella for dimension. For buggy, pipe tip 12 spiral outline handle; trim with tip 3 zigzag scallops, ⅝ in. deep and 1½ in. wide. For wheels, pipe tip 5 outline spokes; add tip 12 outer rim and dot center (flatten and smooth with finger dipped in cornstarch). For baby, ice head smooth. Pipe tip 3 dot eyes, nose and cheeks; outline mouth and ears. Use tip 3 to outline and fill in shoulder area; position cookie head. Pipe tip 12 outline arm and umbrella handle. Use tip 5 to pipe dot hand over handle; pipe tip 3 dot fingers. Position bird cookie. Position additional heart drops on umbrella. Cake serves 12, cookie serves 1.

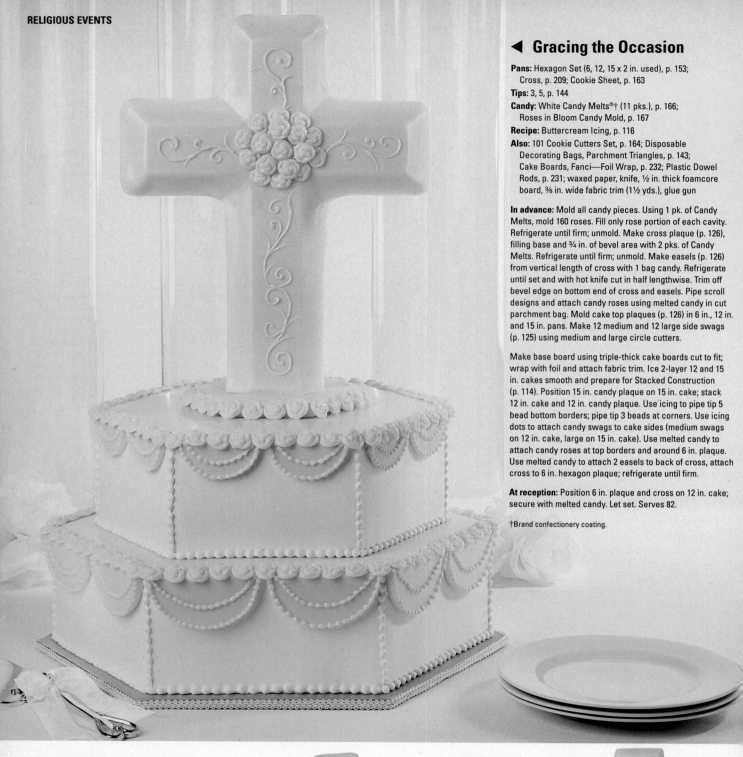

◀ Gracing the Occasion

Pans: Hexagon Set (6, 12, 15 x 2 in. used), p. 153; Cross, p. 209; Cookie Sheet, p. 163

Tips: 3, 5, p. 144

Candy: White Candy Melts®† (11 pks.), p. 166; Roses in Bloom Candy Mold, p. 167

Recipe: Buttercream Icing, p. 116

Also: 101 Cookie Cutters Set, p. 164; Disposable Decorating Bags, Parchment Triangles, p. 143; Cake Boards, Fanci—Foil Wrap, p. 232; Plastic Dowel Rods, p. 231; waxed paper, knife, ½ in. thick foamcore board, ⅜ in. wide fabric trim (1½ yds.), glue gun

In advance: Mold all candy pieces. Using 1 pk. of Candy Melts, mold 160 roses. Fill only rose portion of each cavity. Refrigerate until firm; unmold. Make cross plaque (p. 126), filling base and ¾ in. of bevel area with 2 pks. of Candy Melts. Refrigerate until firm; unmold. Make easels (p. 126) from vertical length of cross with 1 bag candy. Refrigerate until set and with hot knife cut in half lengthwise. Trim off bevel edge on bottom end of cross and easels. Pipe scroll designs and attach candy roses using melted candy in cut parchment bag. Mold cake top plaques (p. 126) in 6 in., 12 in. and 15 in. pans. Make 12 medium and 12 large side swags (p. 125) using medium and large circle cutters.

Make base board using triple-thick cake boards cut to fit; wrap with foil and attach fabric trim. Ice 2-layer 12 and 15 in. cakes smooth and prepare for Stacked Construction (p. 114). Position 15 in. candy plaque on 15 in. cake; stack 12 in. cake and 12 in. candy plaque. Use icing to pipe tip 5 bead bottom borders; pipe tip 3 beads at corners. Use icing dots to attach candy swags to cake sides (medium swags on 12 in. cake, large on 15 in. cake). Use melted candy to attach candy roses at top borders and around 6 in. plaque. Use melted candy to attach 2 easels to back of cross, attach cross to 6 in. hexagon plaque; refrigerate until firm.

At reception: Position 6 in. plaque and cross on 12 in. cake; secure with melted candy. Let set. Serves 82.

†Brand confectionery coating.

▶ Statements of Faith

Candy: Light Cocoa, White Candy Melts®†, p. 166; Cross/Bible Large Lollipop Mold, p. 167

Also: Silicone Standard Baking Cups, p. 155; Parchment Triangles, p. 143, ruler

Mold crosses without lollipop sticks using melted candy. Refrigerate until firm; unmold. Trim end where stick would go if necessary. Pipe flowers and scrolls using melted candy in cut parchment bag. For bases, fill silicone cups ¼ in. deep with melted candy. Refrigerate until firm; unmold. Attach cross to base with melted candy. To support cross, cut Candy Melts wafer in fourths; attach 1 piece behind cross with melted candy. Each serves 1.

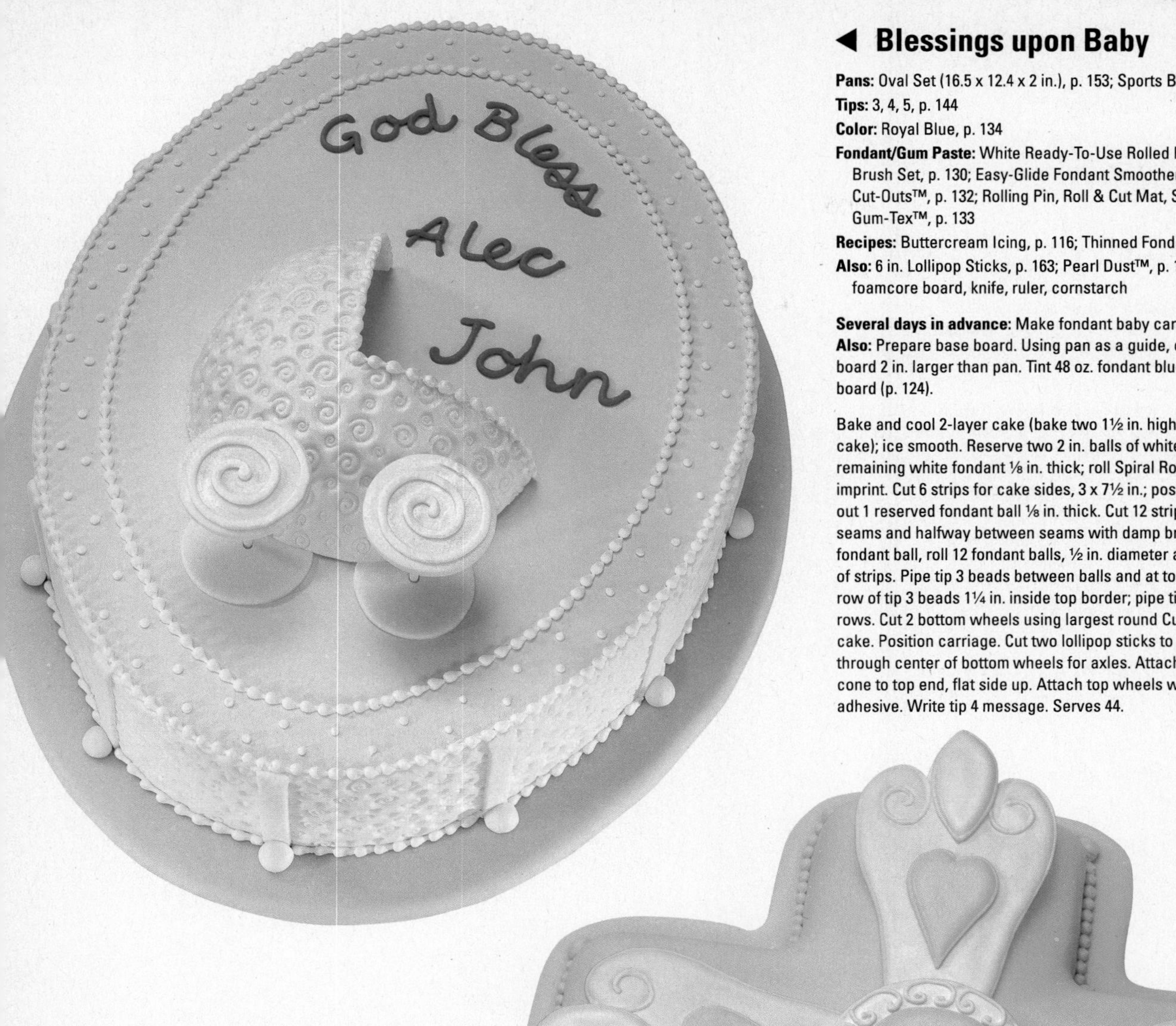

◀ Blessings upon Baby

Pans: Oval Set (16.5 x 12.4 x 2 in.), p. 153; Sports Ball Set, p. 161

Tips: 3, 4, 5, p. 144

Color: Royal Blue, p. 134

Fondant/Gum Paste: White Ready-To-Use Rolled Fondant (96 oz.), Brush Set, p. 130; Easy-Glide Fondant Smoother, p. 131; Round Cut-Outs™, p. 132; Rolling Pin, Roll & Cut Mat, Spiral Pattern Roller, Gum-Tex™, p. 133

Recipes: Buttercream Icing, p. 116; Thinned Fondant Adhesive, p. 117

Also: 6 in. Lollipop Sticks, p. 163; Pearl Dust™, p. 130; ½ in. thick foamcore board, knife, ruler, cornstarch

Several days in advance: Make fondant baby carriage (p. 123). **Also:** Prepare base board. Using pan as a guide, cut foamcore board 2 in. larger than pan. Tint 48 oz. fondant blue and cover board (p. 124).

Bake and cool 2-layer cake (bake two 1½ in. high layers for a 3 in. high cake); ice smooth. Reserve two 2 in. balls of white fondant. Roll out remaining white fondant ⅛ in. thick; roll Spiral Roller over top to imprint. Cut 6 strips for cake sides, 3 x 7½ in.; position on cake. Roll out 1 reserved fondant ball ⅛ in. thick. Cut 12 strips, ½ x 3 in.; attach at seams and halfway between seams with damp brush. With remaining fondant ball, roll 12 fondant balls, ½ in. diameter and attach at bottom of strips. Pipe tip 3 beads between balls and at top border. Pipe another row of tip 3 beads 1¼ in. inside top border; pipe tip 3 dots between rows. Cut 2 bottom wheels using largest round Cut-Out; position on cake. Position carriage. Cut two lollipop sticks to 5 in. and insert through center of bottom wheels for axles. Attach a ½ in. fondant cone to top end, flat side up. Attach top wheels with thinned fondant adhesive. Write tip 4 message. Serves 44.

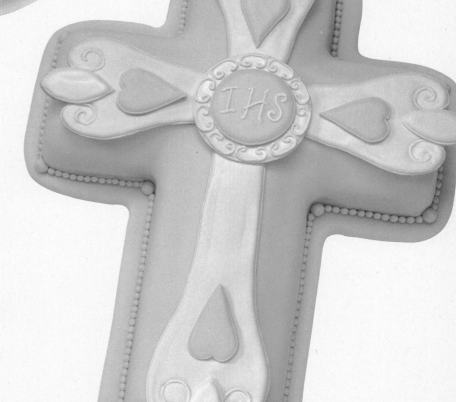

▶ Faith for the Future

Pans: Cross, p. 209; Cookie Sheet, p. 163

Tips: 2, 3, 5, p. 144

Color: Rose, p. 134

Fondant: White Ready-To-Use Rolled Fondant (72 oz.), p. 130; Rolling Pin, Roll & Cut Mat, p. 133; Cutter/Embosser, Easy-Glide Fondant Smoother, p. 131

Recipes: Buttercream, Color Flow Icings, p. 116

Also: 2009 Pattern Book (Long and Short Cross Arms, Long and Short Hearts and Teardrops, Small and Large Center Circles), p. 128; 13 x 19 in. Cake Boards, Fanci-Foil Wrap, p. 232; Color Flow Mix, Piping Gel, p. 135; Parchment Triangles, p. 143; waxed paper, cellophane tape, knife

2 days in advance: Make color flow cross (p. 126). Make extras of all pieces to allow for breakage. Attach with full-strength color flow icing. When dry, pipe scrolls and lettering with tip 2 and full-strength color flow icing.

1 day in advance: Prepare base board. Cut two cake boards ½ in. larger than cross pan; wrap with foil. Tint fondant pink; cover board (p. 124). Reserve remaining pink fondant for cake.

Prepare cake for rolled fondant (p. 117). Cover with reserved pink fondant; smooth with Fondant Smoother. Position cake on base board. Pipe a tip 5 ball at each corner, tip 3 balls between. Position color flow cross. Serves 12.

▶ Roses for La Quinceañera

Pans: 6, 10, 14 x 3 in. Round, 18 x 3 in. Half-Round, p. 152
Tips: 2, 4, 5, 12, 101, 104, 362, p. 144-145
Color: Rose, p. 134
Fondant: White Ready-To-Use Rolled Fondant (24 oz.), p. 130; Round and Oval Cut-Outs™, p. 132; Gum-Tex™, 9 in. Rolling Pin, Roll & Cut Mat, p. 133;
Recipes: Buttercream, Royal Icings, p. 116
Also: 2009 Pattern Book (Number "15"), p. 128; Cake Boards, Fanci-Foil Wrap, p. 232; Cake Dividing Set, Flower Nail No. 7, p. 137; Meringue Powder, p. 135; 8 in. Lollipop Sticks, p. 163; Wooden Dowel Rods, p. 231; 20 in. round plywood board ½ in. thick, sharp knife, ½ in. wide ribbon for cake board (63 in. long), double-stick tape, cornstarch

Several days in advance: Make cake top "15." Combine 6 oz. fondant with ½ teaspoon Gum Tex and tint rose. Roll out ¼ in. thick. Use numeral patterns and knife to cut numbers. Let dry on surface dusted with cornstarch. Attach 8 in. lollipop sticks to back of each number with royal icing; let dry. Pipe tip 4 dots, let dry. **Also:** Using rose royal icing, make 100 tip 101 roses with tip 5 bases and 10 tip 104 roses with tip 12 bases. Make extras to allow for breakage; let dry. **And:** Prepare 100 fondant circles using medium Round Cut-Out (p. 123).

Prepare 2-layer 6, 10, 14 in. cakes (bake two 2½ in. layers for each to make 5 in. high cakes) and 18 in. cake (bake 4 half rounds 2½ in. high for an 18 x 5 in. cake). Prepare for Stacked Construction (p. 114). Ice cake tops white and sides rose with buttercream.

For 6 in. cake, divide in 12ths with Cake Dividing Set. Roll out fondant ⅛ in. thick and use largest Oval Cut-Out to cut 6 ovals; trim ⅜ in. off top end. Assemble and decorate sides using royal icing. Attach ovals at every other division, lining up cut edge with top of cake. Attach fondant circle to each oval, with lower point 4¼ in. from bottom of cake. At remaining divisions, place fondant circles, 4 in. from bottom of cake. Attach a tip 101 rose to center of each fondant circle. Pipe tip 2 triple drop strings on each oval 2½, 3 and 3½ in. from bottom of cake. Add tip 2 dots at drop string points.

Divide 10 in. cake in 20th: First divide in 10ths, then divide each section in half. Divide 14 in. cake into 30ths: First divide in 10ths, then divide each section in thirds. Divide 18 in. cake in 32nds: first divide in 16ths, then divide each section in half. Decorate each cake as for 6 in. cake, attaching ovals at alternating division points, then attaching circles and roses same position; add drop strings and dots as above.

Pipe tip 362 shell bottom borders on all tiers. Insert numerals into cake and mound tip 104 roses around numerals. Attach ribbon around cake base using double-stick tape. Serves 21

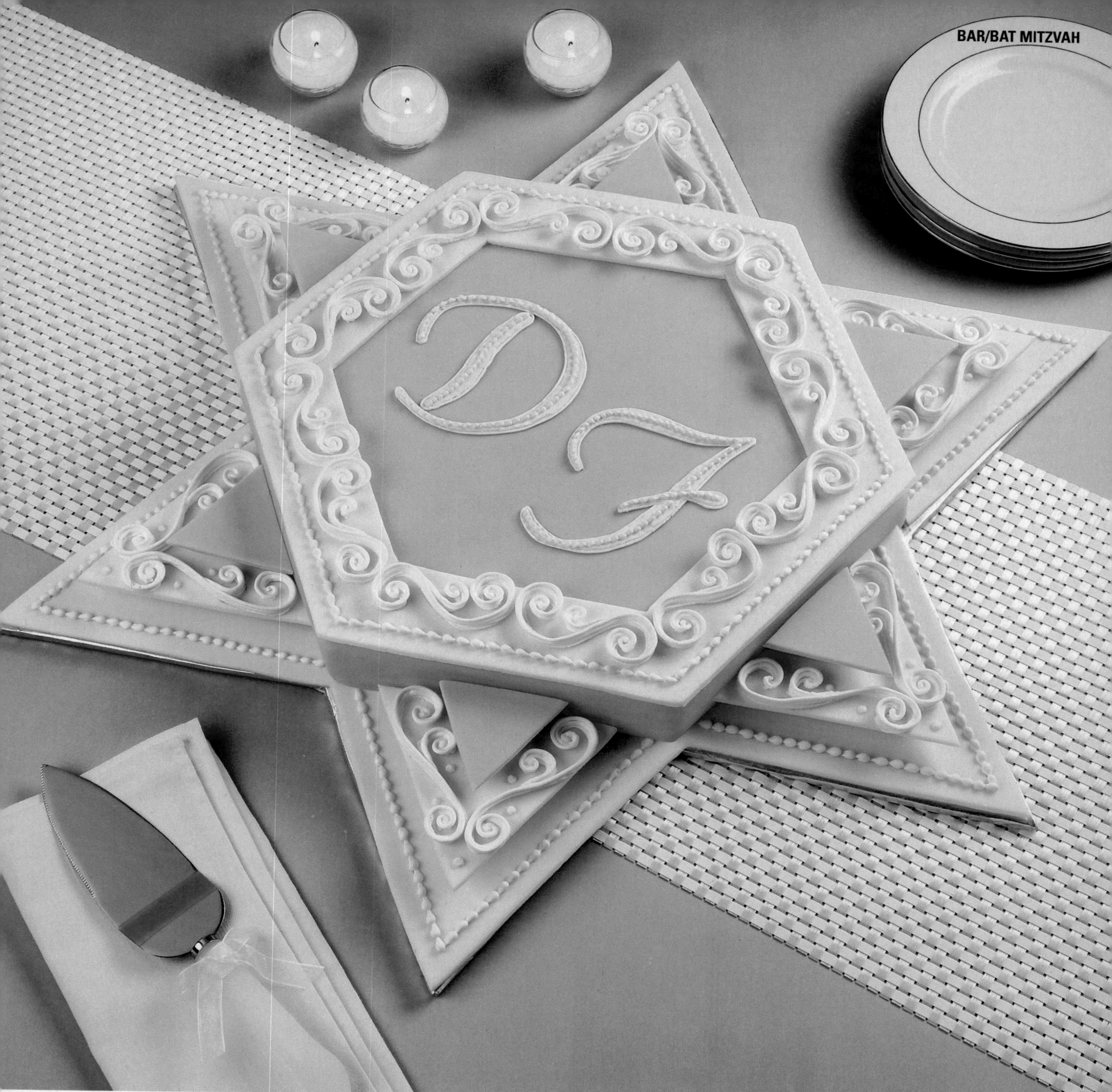

▲ As Your Journey Begins

Pan: Hexagon Set (15 x 2 in. used), p. 153

Tips: 2, 3, 5, 14, p. 144-145

Color: Royal Blue, p. 134

Fondant: White Ready-To-Use Rolled Fondant (120 oz.), p. 130; Cutter/Embosser, Easy-Glide Fondant Smoother, p. 131; Rolling Pin, Roll & Cut Mat, Gum-Tex™, p. 133

Recipes: Buttercream, Royal Icings, p. 116

Also: 2009 Pattern Book (Initials, Triangles, Open Hexagon Section), p. 128; Cake Boards, Fanci-Foil Wrap, p. 232; Meringue Powder, p. 135; 30 x 30 in. foamcore or plywood board (¼ in. thick), waxed paper, cornstarch, sugar cubes, toothpicks

Several weeks in advance: Knead 6 teaspoons Gum-Tex into 72 oz. fondant. Tint 3 oz. fondant blue. Roll out blue and white fondant ⅜ in. thick. Using patterns, cut 6 large white triangles, 6 medium white triangles, 6 small blue triangles. For open hexagon which frames initials, trace 15 in. hexagon pan on paper; cut. Mark 2 inches in from edge; cut and remove center. Let all dry on cornstarch-dusted cake boards.

Several days in advance: Use royal icing to add details and make initials. Pipe tip 3 beads ½ in. from edge on large triangles and on 15 in. hexagon. Use patterns to mark scrolls on medium triangles and on hexagon. Outline scrolls with tip 14; overpipe with tip 5, then overpipe again with tip 3. Add tip 3 dot accents to medium triangles; let dry. Tape letters to board and tape waxed paper over letters. Using tip 2, outline letters; let dry slightly. Fill in and pat smooth with finger dipped in cornstarch; let dry. Top with tip 2 beads; let dry. **Also:** Prepare foamcore board. Cut a star shape with points 5 in. larger than hexagon pan; wrap with Fanci-Foil.

Bake and cool 1-layer hexagon cake. Tint remaining fondant blue; cover cake (p. 117) and smooth with Fondant Smoother. Position cake in center of wrapped board. Position large triangles on each side of hexagon; secure with dots of icing. Attach 3 sugar cubes to large triangles with dots of icing; attach medium triangles to sugar cubes with icing. Repeat with sugar cubes and blue triangles. Attach fondant open hexagon to cake top with dots of icing. Position initials. Serves 24.

▶ Senior Scroll

Pan: 10.5 x 15 x 1 in. Jelly Roll/Cookie Pan, p. 154

Color: Black, p. 134

Fondant: White Ready-To-Use Rolled Fondant (96 oz.), Primary Colors Fondant Multi Pack, Gold Pearl Dust™, Brush Set, p. 130; Fondant/Gum Paste Tool Set, p. 131; Easy-Glide Fondant Smoother, p. 131; Alphabet/Number Cut-Outs™, p. 132; Rolling Pin, Roll & Cut Mat, p. 133

Ornament: Glowing Graduate, p. 216

Recipe: Buttercream Icing, p. 116

Also: 101 Cookie Cutters, p. 164; Cake Boards, Fanci-Foil Wrap, p. 232; confectioners' sugar, knife, ruler

Bake, fill and roll 2 jelly roll cakes. Prepare for rolled fondant (p. 117); cover each cake with 24 oz. fondant and smooth with Fondant Smoother. Roll out additional fondant ¼ in. thick. Using a small plastic lid or cookie cutter that matches diameter of cakes, cut a fondant circle for each end; attach with damp brush. Use veining tool to score ends with spiral pattern.

Prepare 12 x 18 in. base board using 3 cake boards. Position 1 cake at top edge of board. Roll out 36 oz. fondant ⅛ in. thick. Cut a rectangle the width of cake and 18 in. long. Position fondant up and over cake at top, extending down to bottom edge of board; attach to cake with damp brush. Position 2nd cake on bottom edge.

For message, roll out black fondant ⅛ in. thick. Cut letters with Cut-Outs; attach with damp brush. For ribbon, roll out blue fondant ⅛ in. thick. Cut base using starburst cookie cutter from set, cut center using small crinkle circle cutter. Cut two ¾ x 3½ in. strips for tails; cut a "V" shape at bottom. Position and attach starburst and tails on scroll with damp brush. Attach ribbon to cake. For scroll trim, roll two ¼ in. yellow ropes, 8 in. long. For petal designs, roll 3 ropes 2 in. long and loop. Attach trim with damp brush. Brush edges of scroll cakes with Pearl Dust. Position topper. Serves 18.

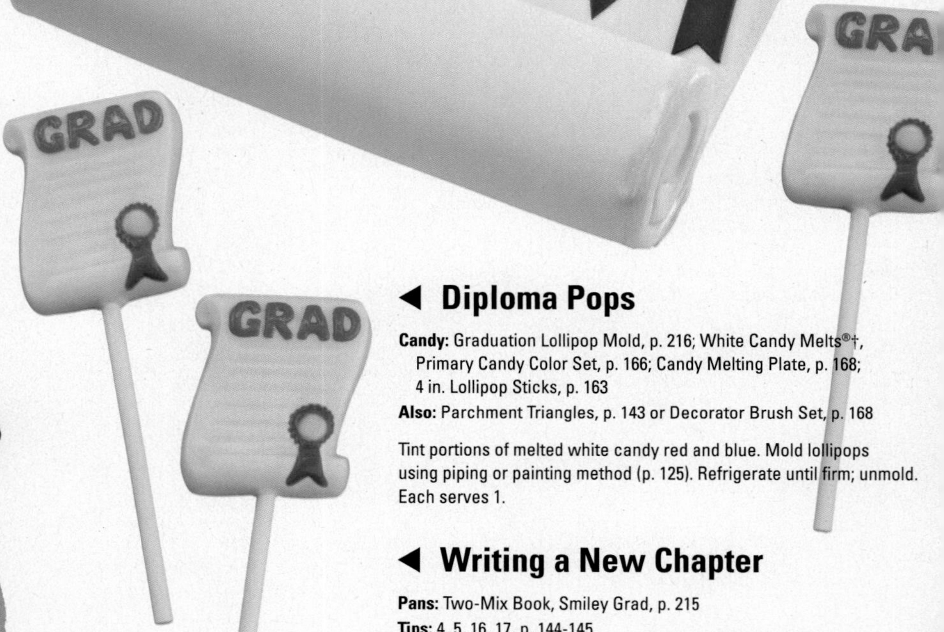

◀ Diploma Pops

Candy: Graduation Lollipop Mold, p. 216; White Candy Melts®†, Primary Candy Color Set, p. 166; Candy Melting Plate, p. 168; 4 in. Lollipop Sticks, p. 163

Also: Parchment Triangles, p. 143 or Decorator Brush Set, p. 168

Tint portions of melted white candy red and blue. Mold lollipops using piping or painting method (p. 125). Refrigerate until firm; unmold. Each serves 1.

◀ Writing a New Chapter

Pans: Two-Mix Book, Smiley Grad, p. 215

Tips: 4, 5, 16, 17, p. 144-145

Colors:* Royal Blue, Golden Yellow, Brown, Black, Red-Red, Rose, Copper, p. 134

Fondant: White Ready-To-Use Rolled Fondant (72 oz.), Brush Set, p. 130; Easy-Glide Fondant Smoother, p. 131; Rolling Pin, Roll & Cut Mat, p. 133

Recipe: Buttercream Icing, p. 116

Also: Decorating Comb, p. 137; Cake Boards, Fanci-Foil Wrap, p. 232; Piping Gel, p. 135; 12¼ x 16¼ in. foamcore board (½ in. thick), knife, ruler

In advance: Prepare base boards. For book, cut foamcore 1 in. larger than Book Pan on all sides. Tint 48 oz. fondant brown; cover board (p. 124). For grad cake, cut cake boards using Smiley Grad pan as a guide; wrap with foil.

Ice book cake smooth. Comb sides using small tooth edge of comb. Position on prepared board. Roll out white fondant ⅛ in. thick. Cut to cover cake top; position and trim as needed. Pipe tip 5 bead bottom border. For grad cake, outline features with tip 4. Pipe in pupils and whites of eyes with tip 5, mouth and tongue with tip 4. Cover face with tip 17 stars; overpipe nose and cheeks. Cover mortarboard top with tip 17 stars, base with tip 16 stars. Pipe button with tip 4. Pipe tip 4 lines for hair, tassel cord and pull-out fringe. Pipe tip 4 ball knot. For each hand, shape a 2 in. ball of fondant into a slightly flattened oval about 3 x 2 in.; use knife to cut and shape fingers. Position on book cake and cover with tip 17 stars. Add tip 4 message. Position cakes. Serves 36.

*Combine Brown with Black and Red-Red for brown fondant shown.

†Brand confectionery coating.

▶ Thinking Cap

Pans: 14 x 2 in. Square, p. 153; Topping Off Success, p. 215
Tips: 2, 8, p. 144
Colors:* Red-Red, Ivory, Black, Golden Yellow, p. 134
Fondant: White Ready-To-Use Rolled Fondant (96 oz.), Ruby Red, Yellow and Leaf Green Pearl Dust™, Brush Set, p. 130; Easy-Glide Fondant Smoother, Cutter/Embosser, p. 131; Graceful Vines Imprint Mat, Rolling Pin, Roll & Cut Mat, p. 133
Recipe: Buttercream Icing, p. 116
Also: Red Candy Melts®† (3 pks.), p. 166; Alphabet Candy Mold, p. 167; Piping Gel, p. 135; Cake Board, Fanci-Foil Wrap, p. 232; Plastic Dowel Rods, p. 231; 16 x 16 in. foamcore board (½ in. thick), fine-tip artist brush, lemon extract, scissors, ruler

In advance: Make base board. Tint 48 oz. fondant red. Cover foamcore board with fondant (p. 124). **Also:** Mold cap candy plaque (p. 126) using 2½ pks. of candy. Position on foil-covered cake board, cut to fit. Mold candy message, filling letter cavities ⅓ full.

Bake and cool 2-layer cake (trim 2 in. layers to 1½ in. for a 3 in. high cake). Ice smooth; position on prepared board. For cake side strips, tint 36 oz. fondant ivory; roll out ⅛ in. thick. Place on Imprint Mat and roll over once to imprint design. Remove from mat and cut into 3½ x 14½ in. strips. Attach strips to cake sides; trim as needed to fit. Mix Pearl Dust with lemon extract; paint over imprinted details on side panels with fine-tip brush. Using buttercream icing, pipe tip 8 bead top and bottom borders. Add tip 2 beads at corners; pipe dot flower centers. Position cap and letters. Tint remaining fondant yellow. Roll 2 ropes, ⅛ x 8 in. long; twist together for cord. Roll a ⅜ in. ball and flatten slightly for button. For tassel, roll out remaining yellow fondant ⅛ in. thick. Cut a 3 x 2 in. long rectangle. Use scissors to cut slits, ⅛ in. wide and 1¾ in. deep. Roll and pinch end to form tassel. Attach string, button and tassel with melted candy. Serves 63.

*Combine Red-Red with a little Black for red fondant.

◀ Filled with Pride

Pans: Non-Stick 17.25 x11.5 x 1 in. Jelly Roll/Cookie, Mini Muffin, Cooling Grid, p. 150
Colors: Red-Red, Royal Blue or others to match school colors, p. 134
Fondant: White Ready-To-Use Rolled Fondant, p. 130; Rolling Pin, Roll & Cut Mat, p. 133
Candy: White, Light Cocoa Candy Melts®†, Primary or Garden Candy Color Sets, p. 166
Recipe: Favorite crisped rice cereal treats
Also: 101 Cookie Cutters, p. 164; Parchment Triangles, p. 143; Graduation Icing Decorations, p. 216; Cake Boards, p. 232; sugar ice cream cones, cornstarch, waxed paper, knife, ruler, assorted small candies

In advance: Make candy base. With candy colors, tint portions of melted white candy red, blue or your school colors. Place medium round cutter from set on jelly roll pan and fill ⅜ in. high with candy. Refrigerate until firm; unmold.

For bodies, cut point off ice cream cones to make it 3¾ in. high. For heads, prepare cereal treats recipe and form 2¼ in. balls; make indentation for narrow end of cone. Using candy colors, tint portions of melted candy desired gown shade and orange for skin tone. Cover cones and heads with melted candy (p. 124); let set and repeat. Fill cone with assorted candies and attach base with melted candy; let set. Tint additional candy yellow and black. Pipe hair and facial features using melted candy in cut parchment bag; let set. Attach head to cone with melted candy. Using icing colors, tint 4 oz. fondant for each cap and gown. For base of cap, press a 1½ in. fondant ball into cornstarch-dusted mini muffin cavity; remove and trim to even edges. Indent center to fit head. For top of cap, roll out fondant ⅛ in. thick; cut a 2 in. square. Let cap pieces dry on cornstarch-dusted board. For arms, shape 3 in. logs, tapering at one end. Attach tapered end to cone with melted candy; let set. Position icing decoration between arms; attach with candy. Pipe hands using melted candy. Attach top to base of cap with melted candy; let set. For tassel roll a ½ x ¼ in. wide cone of yellow fondant; place on waxed paper and pipe lines of melted candy for fringe. Let set. Attach tassel and pipe button and cord on top of cap with melted candy; let set. Each serves 1.

▲ An Appetite for Learning

Cookie: Graduation Cap Colored Metal Cutter, p. 215
Also: Your favorite sandwich salad (ham, turkey or tuna), wheat bread, cheddar cheese, knife

Use cookie cutter and sliced bread to cut 1 whole cap and 1 diamond-shaped top for each sandwich. Spread salad on top part of whole cap and add top. Add cheese tassel. Stack ¼ in. wide strips next to sandwich until even with top. Cut cheese strips for string and tassel; use decorating tip to cut circles. Attach. Each serves 1.

Love Becomes Legend

Even after the last slice is cut, your cake will remain a perfect memory. Which design will define your day? It may be the quilling flower cake, with openwork pastel blossoms that march down 4 tall tiers. Or the masterful chocolate stairstep design, with a lush fondant carpet of embossed flowers. Or here, a high-rise classic with layers of scrolls dusted with bronze detail. A thrilling discovery awaits you.

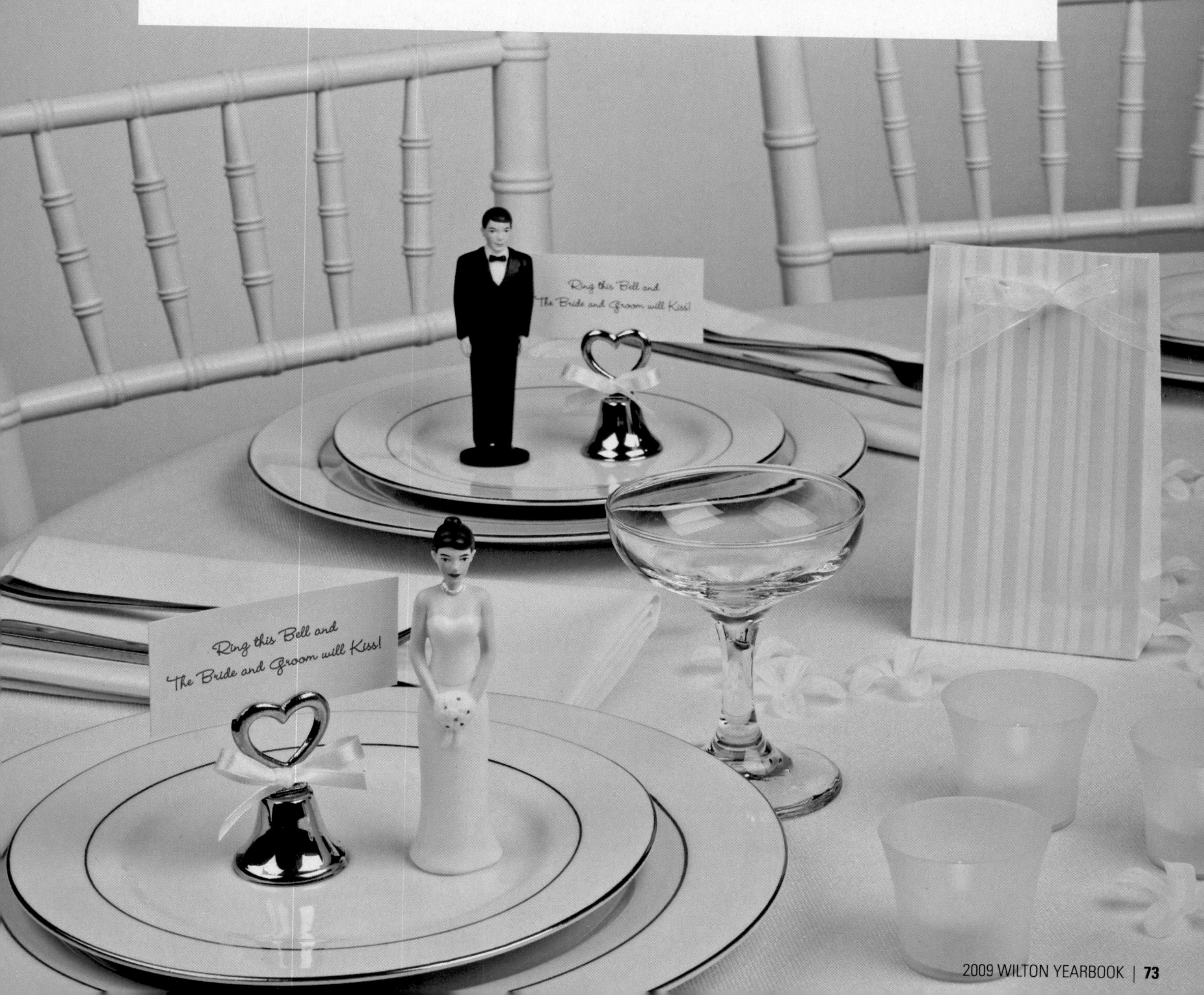

Their Peak Moment

Truly uplifting…each tier is topped by a ring of royal icing scrolls brushed with shimmering bronze Pearl Dust™.

Pans: Decorator Preferred® 6, 10 x 3 in. Rounds, 10 x 2 in. Square, p. 152; Petal Pan Set (15 in. used), p. 153

Tips: 2, 5, 16, 18, 224, 225, p. 144-145

Topper: First Kiss, p. 224

Recipes: Buttercream, Royal Icings, p. 116

Also: Bronze and White Pearl Dust™ (3 bronze, 5 white), Brush Set, p. 130; Decorator Favorites Pattern Press Set, p. 139; 5 in. Curved Pillars (2 pks.); 8, 12 in. Decorator Preferred® Smooth Edge Plates (2 each), p. 230; Meringue Powder, p. 135; Cake Dividing Set, p. 137; Dowel Rods, p. 231; Cake Boards, Fanci-Foil Wrap, p. 232; 22 in. square plywood board (½ in. thick), toothpicks, ruler, paper, waxed paper, ½ in. wide ribbon (80 in. long)

One week in advance: Use royal icing to make swirled drop flowers (p. 119) with tip 2 dot centers. Make 700 large with tip 224 and 200 small with tip 225. Let dry. **Also:** Use royal icing and pattern presses to make 84 small and 120 large scrolls (p. 120). Make extras to allow for breakage. Let dry. **And:** Mix 1 part bronze to 3 parts white Pearl Dust™ to create a softer shade. Dust all scrolls and flowers.

Wrap base board with foil. Bake and cool 5 in. high cakes. (Bake two 2½ in. layers for 6 in. and 10 in. round cakes. Bake one 2 in. and two 1½ in. layers for petal cake. Base cake is four 10 in. squares set side by side; bake one 2 in. and two 1½ in. layers for each square.) Position layered 10 in. squares on prepared base; ice smooth as one 20 in. square cake. Ice remaining cakes smooth and prepare for Combination Pillar and Stacked Construction (p. 114).

Pipe tip 5 bead bottom border on all cakes. For 20 in. base cake, divide each side into 8ths. Attach a row of large scrolls around bottom border at division points with icing; attach another row 1 in. down from top edge. Attach 3-flower clusters to cake sides midway between rows of scrolls with icing. For petal cake, attach large scrolls at petal centers, 1 at bottom and another 1 in. from top edge. Attach 1 small scroll on each side of large bottom scrolls. Attach 5-flower clusters at indentations above bottom scrolls and 4-flower clusters at indentations at top. Attach 3-flower clusters to cake sides midway between large scrolls.

Divide 10 in. round cake into 12ths. Divide 6 in. round cake into 8ths. On both cakes, attach top and bottom rows of large scrolls and 3-flower clusters between rows as for 20 in. base cake. On 10 in. cake, attach 5-flower clusters at bottom and 1 flower at top between scrolls. On 6 in. cake, attach 1 flower between each bottom scroll.

At reception: Position plates and pillars. Attach small upright scrolls to cake tops, about ½ in. inside cake edge. You will need 32 for base cake, 32 for petal cake, 12 for 10 in. round and 8 for 6 in. round. Assemble cakes. Position ornament.*** Serves 302.**

**The top tier is often saved for the first anniversary. The number of servings given does not include the top tier.

From page 73: Each plate is formally dressed with our Bride and Groom Figurines (p. 224) and Silver Bell Favor Kit (p. 222). The kit features favor bells, printable place cards and ribbons—it's an elegant way to mark places, continuing the tradition of ringing for a kiss from the bridal couple. Add a Simple Yet Elegant Favor Bag (p. 223) for each guest.

▲ A Home in Harmony

Pans: 6, 10, 14 x 2 in. Round, p. 153

Tip: 18, p. 145

Fondant: White Ready-To-Use Rolled Fondant (96 oz.), p. 130; Easy-Glide Fondant Smoother, p. 131

Topper: Spring Song, p. 225

Recipes: Buttercream, Royal Icings, p. 116

Also: 2009 Pattern Book (Small, Medium, Large Scrolls), p. 128; Tall Tier Cake Stand Basic Set (8, 12, 16 in. Separator Plates, Four 6 ½ in. Columns), Glue-On Plate Legs (6), Cake Corer Tube, p. 229; 10, 14, 18 in. Cake Circles, Cake Boards, p. 232; Meringue Powder, Piping Gel, p. 135; masking tape, waxed paper, vegetable pan spray

Several days in advance: Make scrolls using patterns (p. 121). Prepare fondant-covered cake circles (p. 124). Ice 2-layer cakes in buttercream and prepare for Tall Tier Construction (p. 115).

At reception: Assemble cakes on fondant-covered boards and Tall Tier Stand. Pipe tip 18 shell bottom borders. With buttercream, attach medium and small scrolls about 1 in. apart, in alternating fashion, on all cake sides. Attach large scrolls to columns with royal icing. Position topper.*** Serves 116.**

***Always place a separator plate, or cake board cut to fit, on the cake where you position any figurine or topper. This protects both the cake and your keepsake. For extra stability, secure topper to the plate with double-stick tape.

▶ Love Shines Through

Pans: Hexagon Pan Set (9, 12 and 15 x 2 in. used), p. 153
Tip: 3, p. 144
Fondant: White Ready-To-Use Rolled Fondant (312 oz.), Brush Set, p. 130; Easy-Glide Fondant Smoother, Cutter/ Embosser, p. 131; Rolling Pin, Roll & Cut Mat, p. 133
Topper: Rhinestone Heart Ornament, p. 225
Recipes: Buttercream, Royal Icings, p. 116
Also: 2009 Pattern Book (Triangles, Diamonds), p. 128; 8, 10 in. Plates from Crystal-Clear Cake Divider Set, 9 in. Twist Legs (2 pks.), p. 229; Silver Pearl Dust™ (4 bottles), p. 130; 12, 16 in. Cake Circles, 13 x 19 in. Cake Boards, p. 232; Piping Gel, Meringue Powder, Clear Vanilla Extract, p. 135; foamcore board (¼ in. thick), vegetable pan spray, waxed paper, scissors, ruler, toothpicks, double-stick tape, large fluffy brush

In advance: Prepare hexagon bases. Cut cake circles and foamcore 1 in. larger than corresponding pan size. Cover base boards with rolled fondant (p. 124) and set aside. **Also:** Make icing dots. Cover cake boards with waxed paper; lightly spray with vegetable pan spray. Use thinned royal icing to pipe 500 tip 3 dots, ¼ in. wide. Let dry 48 hours. While still attached to boards, brush dots with Pearl Dust mixed with extract. Let dry.

Bake and cool cakes; set each on a cut-to-fit hexagon cake board. Prepare and cover cakes with rolled fondant (p. 117); smooth with Fondant Smoother. Prepare cakes for Push-In Pillar Construction (p. 114). Cut triangle patterns in waxed paper and attach to cake sides with dots of icing; fondant triangles will later be positioned in these areas. Use large fluffy brush to cover background areas on cake sides with Pearl Dust. Remove waxed paper triangles. Position cakes on their covered boards.

Roll out fondant ⅛ in. thick. Use patterns and straight-edge wheel of Cutter/Embosser to cut 12 triangles in each size. Brush backs with damp brush and attach to cake sides, aligning widest edge of triangles with top and bottom edges of cake. Roll out fondant ⅜ in. thick. Use wide end of tip 3 to cut 18 buttons. Brush tops with Pearl Dust; brush backs with damp brush and attach over triangle points. Attach royal icing dots around triangles using 5 dots on each edge on 9 in. cake, 6 dots on 12 in. and 7 dots on 15 in. Roll out fondant ⅛ in. thick. Use pattern to cut 6 center diamonds in each size. Brush backs with damp brush and attach, centering over corners.

At reception: Using double-stick tape, attach 2 smallest covered hexagon boards to corresponding 8 and 10 in. plates. Assemble cakes. Position topper.*** Serves 110.**

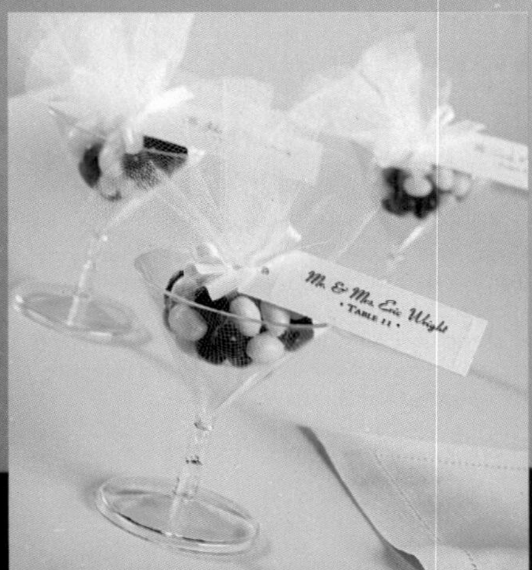

Pour on the charm with sophisticated favors using our Martini Glass Favor Kit (p. 222). Make a pretty tulle puff filled with Tuxedo Jelly Beans (p. 223) and finish with the elegant ribbon and tag included in the kit.

▲ Taking the Big Step

Pans: 8, 12, 16 x 2 in. Square, p. 153

Tips: 1, 5, p. 144

Colors:* Brown, Ivory, Black, Red-Red, p. 134

Fondant: White Ready-To-Use Rolled Fondant (192 oz.), p. 130; Floral Fantasy Fondant Imprint Mat, Rolling Pin, Roll & Cut Mat, Gum-Tex™, p. 133; Easy-Glide Fondant Smoother, Brush Set, Cutter/Embosser, p. 131

Recipes: Chocolate Buttercream, Royal Icings, p. 116

Also: White Candy Melts®† (1 pk.), p. 130; Meringue Powder, Piping Gel, p. 135; Dowel Rods, p. 231; Cake Boards, Fanci-Foil Wrap, p. 232; 20 x 20 x ½ in. foamcore or plywood board, tape, scissors, ruler

In advance: Tint 72 oz. fondant brown; cover base board (p. 124). Tint 96 oz. fondant ivory. Reserve 72 oz. for cake panels. Add 2 teaspoons Gum-Tex to 24 oz. ivory fondant; roll out into a 20 x 10 in. rectangle. Imprint design using Fondant Imprint Mat. Make 18-loop top bow (p. 124) using 1 x 9½ in. imprinted strips.

Ice 2-layer cakes smooth with Chocolate Buttercream. Prepare for Stacked Construction (p. 114) and position on fondant-covered base board. Roll out remaining ivory fondant 3⁄16 in. thick. Place on Imprint Mat and roll over once to imprint design. Cut two 4½ x 20 in. strips and two 4½ x 23 in. strips. Position 23 in. strips on opposite sides, matching ends on top of cake, then position two remaining strips. Roll out 24 oz. white fondant into a 5 x 20 in. rectangle, 3⁄16 in. thick. Cut eight ½ x 20 in. strips and position on cake sides about ½ in. away from edges of ivory fondant strips. Using tip 1 and thinned royal icing tinted brown, outline and fill in imprints on side strips and bow. Position bow on cake top. Use buttercream to pipe tip 5 bead bottom borders. Serves 200.**

*Combine Brown with Red-Red and Black for brown shown.

**The top tier is often saved for the first anniversary. The number of servings given does not include the top tier.

†Brand confectionery coating.

◀ Eternal Embrace

Pans: Oval Pan Set, p. 153

Tip: 5, p. 144

Colors:* Teal, Sky Blue, p. 134

Fondant/Gum Paste: White Ready-To-Use Rolled Fondant (300 oz.), Brush Set, p. 130; Daisy Cut-Outs™, p. 132; Ready-To-Use Gum Paste, Graceful Vines Fondant Imprint Mat, Rolling Pin, Roll & Cut Mat, p. 133; Fondant Shaping Foam, Easy-Glide Fondant Smoother, Fondant/Gum Paste Tool Set p. 131

Topper: Elegance, p. 224

Recipe: Buttercream Icing, p. 116

Also: White Pearl Beading, p. 232; 101 Cookie Cutters Set, p. 164; Cake Boards, p. 232; Dowel Rods, p. 231; two 21 x 17 in. foamcore or plywood boards (½ in. thick); cornstarch, knife, soft tissue

In advance: Make daisies (p. 124). **Also:** Prepare foamcore boards. Using largest pan as a pattern, cut one board 2 in. larger than pan and one 4 in. larger.

Tint 120 oz. fondant blue. Prepare 2-layer cakes in each size for Stacked Construction (p. 114) and rolled fondant (p. 117). Cover 7.75 x 5.5 in. and 13.5 x 9.8 in. cakes and small oval board with blue fondant; cover large oval board with white fondant. Smooth with Fondant Smoother. Roll out white fondant ⅛ in. thick. Following Imprint Mat package directions, imprint vine pattern and cover 10.75 x 7.8 and 16.5 x 12.4 in. cakes with fondant. Stack cakes. Pipe tip 5 ball bottom borders on all cakes. For swags, roll out white fondant ⅛ in. thick; imprint vine pattern. Cut a circle using largest round cutter from 101 Cutters Set; move cutter up ¾ in. and cut again. Trim ¼ in. off each tip to complete each 3¾ in. wide swag. Make 16 swags. Attach swags to blue cake sides using damp brush as follows: starting with a top point, move each garland end down ¾ in. on top tier and ½ in. down on larger tier in staggered formation from top to bottom and back to top. With dots of icing, attach a 1-layer daisy at each swag point; attach 2-layer flowers randomly on white tiers. Attach pearls at base of blue board with dots of icing.

At reception: Position topper.*** Serves 141.**

*Combine Teal with Sky Blue for blue shown.

***Always place a separator plate, or cake board cut to fit, on the cake where you position any figurine or topper. This protects both the cake and your keepsake. For extra stability, secure your figurine to the plate with double-stick tape.

▶ Petal Panorama

Pans: 6, 10, 14 x 3 in. Round, p. 153

Tips: 1A, 2, 3, 5, p. 144

Color: Rose, p. 134

Fondant/Gum Paste: White Ready-To-Use Rolled Fondant (192 oz.), Brush Set, p. 130; Easy-Glide Fondant Smoother, p. 131; Round Cut-Outs™, p. 132; Ready-To-Use Gum Paste, Rolling Pin, Roll & Cut Mat, Floral Fantasy Fondant Imprint Mat, p. 133

Recipes: Buttercream, Royal Icings, p. 116; Thinned Fondant Adhesive, p. 117

Also: 2009 Pattern Book (Large and Small Arches), p. 128; Floating Tiers Cake Stand, p. 227; White Pearl Beading, p. 232; Clear Vanilla Extract, Meringue Powder, p. 135; White Pearl Dust™, p. 130, Candy Melting Plate, p. 168; waxed paper, cornstarch, knife, ruler

In advance: Make Imprinted Arches and Buttons (p. 123).

Prepare 2-layer cakes for rolled fondant by icing lightly in buttercream. Tint 86 oz. of fondant rose. Cover cakes with rose fondant; smooth with Fondant Smoother. For cake sides, roll out white fondant ⅛ in. thick. Imprint floral design following instructions on Imprint Mat package. Cut cake side strips. For 6 in. tier, cut a 20 x 3 in. strip; for 10 in. tier, cut two 15 x 3 in. strips; for 14 in. tier, cut two 22 x 3 in. Attach strips to cake sides with damp brush and lightly press seams together. In melting plate cavity, mix Pearl Dust with a little vanilla; paint in imprinted designs.

Roll out remaining white and rose fondant ⅛ in. thick. Cut circles for center of each tier. Using knife and white fondant, cut a 2¼ in. circle for 6 in. tier, a 4 in. circle for 10 in. tier and a 5¾ in. circle for 14 in. tier. Attach to cake with damp brush. Using Cut-Outs and rose fondant, cut a small circle for 6 in. tier, medium for 10 in. tier and large for 14 in. tier. Attach to white circle with damp brush. Attach large imprinted arches from center circles to cake sides with thinned fondant adhesive, spacing all approximately 2 in. apart at cake sides. Attach buttons. Attach a small pearl-topped arch between each large arch. Roll ½ in. white fondant balls for bottom borders; attach with damp brush. Attach a ½ in. ball at end of each small arch on cake side. In buttercream, edge white circle with tip 5 balls and rose circles with tip 3 balls.

At reception: Position cakes on stand. Serves 116.**

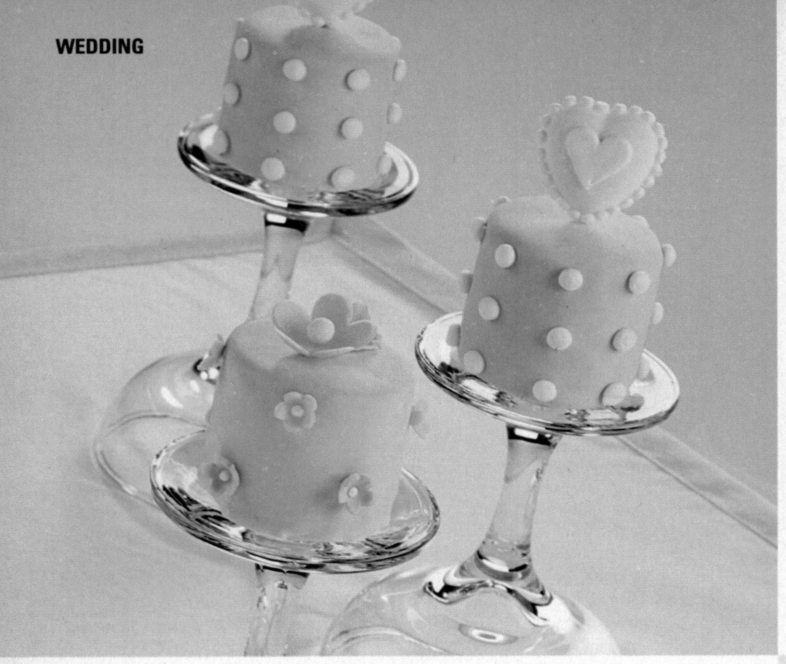

◀ Perfect Petits Fours

Pans: 9 x 13 x 2 in. Sheet (makes 16-18 petits fours), p. 153; Cooling Grid, p. 154
Tips: 2, 3, p. 144
Colors:* Rose, Kelly Green, Violet, Lemon Yellow, Golden Yellow, p. 134
Fondant: White Ready-To-Use Rolled Fondant, p. 130; Rolling Pin, Roll & Cut Mat, p. 133; Fondant/Gum Paste Tool Set, Flower Former Set, Floral Collection Flower Making Set, p. 131
Recipes: Buttercream, Poured Cookie Icings, p. 116
Also: 101 Cookie Cutters Set, p. 164; Hearts Candy Mold, p. 208; Candy Melting Plate, p. 168; waxed paper, toothpicks, cornstarch, knife

In advance: Make fondant hearts. Press fondant into Hearts Candy Mold dusted with cornstarch. Unmold; insert toothpick into bottom, leaving 1½ in. exposed. Let dry 48 hours. **Also:** Make fondant flowers and leaves (p. 124).

Make petits fours and cover with tinted cookie icing (p. 124). For rose cakes, use buttercream to pipe rows of tip 3 dots, about 1 in. apart, on cake sides. Outline and fill in center heart with tip 3; smooth with fingertip dipped in cornstarch. Pipe tip 2 dots around heart edge. Insert heart on top. For green cakes, attach flowers and leaves with tip 2 dots of buttercream. Each serves 1.

*Combine Lemon Yellow with Golden Yellow for yellow shown.

▶ A Signature Rose

Pans: 11 x 15 x 2 in. Sheet (makes 40-45 petits fours), p. 153; Cooling Grid, p. 154
Tips: 2, 12, 104, p. 144-145
Colors:* Lemon Yellow, Royal Blue, Rose, Violet, Brown, p. 134
Fondant: White Ready-To-Use Rolled Fondant, p. 130; Rolling Pin, Roll & Cut Mat, p. 133; Cutter/Embosser, Brush Set, p. 131
Recipe: Buttercream Icing, p. 116
Also: Light Cocoa Candy Melts®† (1 pk. covers 8-10 treats), p. 166; 101 Cookie Cutters Set, p. 164; Flower Nail No. 7, Flower Lifter, p. 137; Disposable Decorating Bags, p. 143; Cake Boards, p. 232; knife, ruler, toothpicks, waxed paper

Make petits fours and cover with melted candy (p. 124).

Tint portions of buttercream blue, yellow, rose, violet, green; reserve some white. Divide fondant and tint to match. Roll out fondant 1/16 in. thick. Cut a 1 x 6½ in. strip for each cake. Brush back with damp brush and attach around covered cake, trimming length if needed. Use buttercream to pipe tip 104 roses with tip 12 bases (p. 119); position on cakes using Flower Lifter. Tint reserved white buttercream brown; pipe tip 2 initial on front of cakes. Each serves 1.

†Brand confectionery coating.

*Combine Violet with Rose for violet shown.

◀ Sweetly Stated

Pans: Non-Stick Mini Heart Pan, p. 206; Cooling Grid, p. 154
Candy: Light Cocoa, White Candy Melts®† (1 pk. covers 8-10 hearts), Garden Candy Color Set, p. 166
Also: Parchment Triangles, p. 143; Cake Boards, p. 232; waxed paper

Bake and cool mini hearts. Cover with melted candy (p. 124). Let set on waxed paper-covered board. Pipe messages with melted candy in cut parchment bag. Each serves 1.

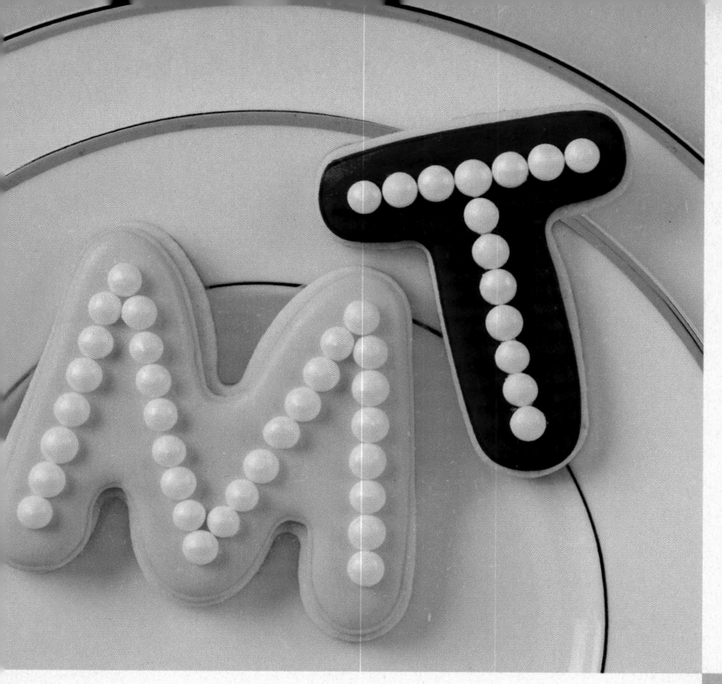

◄ Initial Impressions

Pans: Cookie Sheet, Cooling Grid, p. 154
Tips: 2, 4, p. 144
Colors:* Rose, Brown, Red-Red, p. 134
Recipes: Royal Icing, Roll-Out Cookies, p. 116
Also: A-B-C and 1-2-3 50-Pc. Cutter Set, p. 164; Meringue Powder, p. 135; Parchment Triangles, p. 143; White Pearl Dust™, p. 130; Decorator Brush Set, p. 168; waxed paper

In advance: Make ¼ in. puddle dots (p. 120) using thinned royal icing and tip 4. When dry, brush with white Pearl Dust. (Number of puddle dots needed will vary with each letter.)

Prepare and roll out dough. Cut letter cookies; bake and cool. Outline letters with tip 2 and full-strength royal icing. Flow in centers using thinned royal icing in a cut parchment bag. Let dry 48 hours. Attach puddle dots with dots of icing. Each serves 1.

*Combine Brown with Red-Red for brown shown.

► A Champagne Toast

Pan: Cookie Sheet, Cooling Grid, p. 154
Tip: 2, p. 144
Color: Lemon Yellow, p. 134
Recipes: Royal Icing, Roll-Out Cookies, p. 116
Also: Heart Plastic Nesting Cutter Set, p. 208; 6 in. Cookie Treat Sticks, p. 163; Gold Pearl Dust™, p. 130; Meringue Powder, p. 135; ribbon (12 in. per treat), knife, card stock or paper, hole punch, fine tip marker

Prepare and roll out dough. For each glass top, cut 1 heart using 2nd largest cutter from set. Use knife to cut off top curves (about ¾ in.); bottom of shape will be used for glass top. For base of glass, cut 1 heart using largest cutter from set. Cut across 1 top curve at a 45° angle to create a 1¼ in. deep semi-circle (each heart shape makes 2 bases). Bake and cool cookies.

Outline cookies using tip 2 and full-strength royal icing; let set. Prepare thinned royal icing (p. 116) in white and yellow. Flow in base and about ⅜ in. of glass top with white; flow in remainder of glass top with yellow. Let dry 48 hours. Brush yellow portion of glass top with Pearl Dust. Cut cookie sticks to 4 in. long. Attach to back of cookies using full-strength royal icing. Let dry. Cut 2 x 1½ in. tag; punch hole and add message. Tie onto cookie stick with ribbon. Each serves 1.

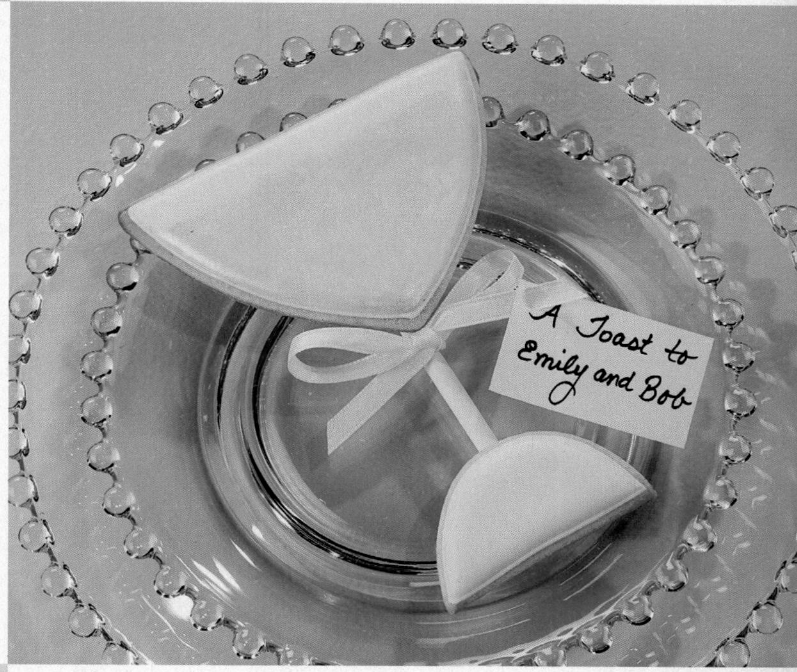

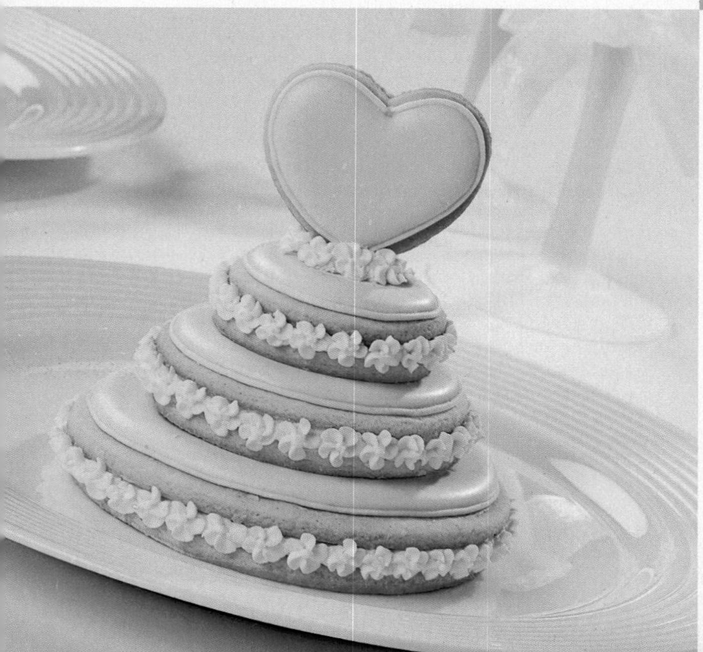

◄ Tiers of Joy

Cookies: Cookie Sheet, Cooling Grid, p. 154; 101 Cookie Cutters Set, p. 164
Tips: 2, 24, p. 144-145
Color: Rose, p. 134
Recipes: Buttercream, Royal Icings, Roll-Out Cookies, p. 116
Also: Meringue Powder, p. 135; Parchment Triangles, p. 143

In advance: Use royal icing to make about 100 tip 24 swirl drop flowers (p. 119) with tip 2 dot centers. Make extras to allow for breakage; let dry. **Also:** Make cookies. Prepare and roll out dough. Cut 1 heart with smallest heart cutter and 2 rounds each with small, medium and large round cutters from set. Bake and cool cookies. **And:** Use tip 2 and full-strength royal icing to outline heart and 1 of each size round; fill in using thinned royal icing. Let dry 48 hours.

Layer pairs of round cookies with buttercream icing; attach drop flowers around edge with icing. Using royal icing, stack and secure cookie pairs; attach upright heart to top and surround base with drop flowers. Each serves 1.

▶ Tiers & Boutonnieres

Pans: 6, 8, 10 x 2 in. Round, p. 153

Tip: 5, p. 144

Color: Kelly Green, p. 134

Topper: Single Figurines, p. 224

Fondant/Gum Paste: White Ready-To-Use Rolled Fondant (24 oz.), p. 130; Button Flower Fondant Cut & Press Set, Flower Forming Cups, p. 131; Ready-To-Use Gum Paste, Rolling Pin, Roll & Cut Mat, p. 133

Recipe: Buttercream Icing, p. 116; Thinned Fondant Adhesive, p. 117

Also: Fancy Scrolls Cake and Dessert Stand, p. 226; Round Comfort Grip™ Cutter, p. 165; Cake Boards, p. 232; Wooden Dowel Rods, p. 231; confectioners' sugar, cornstarch

In advance: Make fondant press flowers. Combine 16 oz. each of fondant and gum paste; roll out ⅛ in. thick. Following Cut & Press package directions, make 35 each large flowers, small flowers and center buttons. Set large flowers and button centers flat on cornstarch-dusted board. Set small flowers on small forming cups. Let dry.

Attach small flowers and buttons to large flowers with thinned fondant adhesive; let dry. Bake and cool two 1-layer 6 in. cakes and one each 1-layer 8 and 10 cakes. Using round cutter, cut a circle from one 6 in. cake for top tier. Ice cakes smooth and prepare for Stacked Construction (p. 114). Stack 6 in. tier on 8 in. tier; position small round for top tier; stacked tiers will be positioned on 10 in. tier at reception. On top tier and 6 in. tier, pipe tip 5 bead bottom borders and attach flowers to cake sides, 5 for top, 8 for 6 in. tier.

At reception: On stand, stack top 3 tiers on 10 in. tier. Pipe tip 5 bead bottom borders on 8 and 10 in. tiers. Attach 10 flowers to 8 in. tier, 12 flowers to 10 in. tier. Position topper.*** Serves 31.**

**The top tier is often saved for the first anniversary. The number of servings given does not include the top and 6 in. tier.

***Always place a separator plate or cake board cut to fit, on the cake where you position any figurine or topper. This protects both the cake and your keepsake. For extra stability, secure topper to the plate with double-stick tape.

◀ Bridal Path

Pans: 3-Pc. Paisley Set, p. 153; Cooling Grid, p. 154

Tip: 3, p. 144

Colors:* Leaf Green, Lemon Yellow, Royal Blue, Rose, Orange, Violet, p. 134

Fondant: White Ready-To-Use Rolled Fondant (265 oz.), Brush Set, p. 130; Button Flower, Rose Leaf Fondant Cut & Press Sets, Easy-Glide Fondant Smoother, Cutter/Embosser, Flower Former Set, Flower Forming Cups (2 pks.), p. 131; Rolling Pin, Roll & Cut Mat, Gum-Tex™, p. 133;

Topper: Just Married Cake Pick, p. 226

Recipes: Buttercream Icing, p. 116; Thinned Fondant Adhesive, p. 117

Also: Flower Spikes, p. 231; Piping Gel, p. 135; Cake Boards, p. 232; Spatula, p. 138; Wooden Dowel Rods, p. 231; 14 x 19 x ½ in. foamcore or plywood board, ruler, cornstarch, waxed paper, 18-gauge florist wire (56 6 in. pieces, one 12 in., one 14 in., one 20 in. piece), wire cutters, moss green florist tape, craft knife

A week in advance: Make fondant press flowers, leaves and wire vines (p. 124).
2 days in advance: Tint 48 oz. fondant green. Cover base board with fondant. Using ruler and ridged wheel of Cutter/Embosser, score diagonal lines 1 in. apart on board.

Prepare 2-layer cakes for Stacked Construction (p. 114) and rolled fondant (p. 117); cover cakes with fondant and smooth with Fondant Smoother. Pipe tip 3 dots randomly on cake sides. For rope bottom borders, roll 8 oz. of fondant into ¼ in. diameter logs; for smallest cake, roll two 23 in. long logs, for medium cake, two 33 in., for large cake, two 46 in. Twist 2 logs together; attach to bottom borders with fondant adhesive. Make main vines using wires wrapped in florist tape, 20 in. for bottom cake, 14 in. for center cake, 12 in. for top cake. Attach flowers, leaves and tendrils with florist tape. Insert flower spikes in each cake to hold vines; insert a small piece of fondant in spikes as needed to secure vines. Insert pick in cake top. Serves 94.**

*Combine Leaf Green with Lemon Yellow for green shown. Combine Violet with Rose for violet shown.

▶ Breezy Blossoms

Pans: 6, 8, 10 x 3 in. Round, 12 x 2 in. Round, p. 153

Tips: 1A, 2A, 6, p. 144-145

Colors:* Rose, Sky Blue, Violet, Leaf Green, Lemon Yellow, p. 134

Fondant/Gum Paste: White Ready-To-Use Rolled Fondant (24 oz.), Brush Set, p. 130; Rose Leaf Fondant Cut & Press Set, Cutter/Embosser, p. 131; Ready-To-Use Gum Paste (1 lb.), Rolling Pin, Roll & Cut Mat, p. 133

Recipe: Buttercream Icing, p. 116

Also: White Candy Melts®†, p. 166; Wooden Dowel Rods, p. 231; Cake Boards, 14 in. Round Silver Cake Base, p. 232; Yellow Colored Sugars, p. 136; 11¾ in. Lollipop Sticks, p. 169; Clear Vanilla Extract, p. 135; Parchment Triangles, p. 143, ½ in. wide ribbon (48 in. long), cornstarch

Two days in advance: Make Quilling Flowers (p. 123).

Bake and cool 1-layer 12 x 2 in. cake and 2-layer 6, 8, 10 in. cakes (bake 2 layers 2½ in. high for 5 in. high cakes). Prepare for Stacked Construction (p. 114). Ice cakes smooth and stack in cascading fashion: 10 in. at back right of 12 in. cake, 8 in. at back center of 10 in. cake, 6 in. at the back left of 8 in. cake. Randomly pipe tip 6 dots on cake sides; pipe tip 6 bead bottom borders on all tiers. Insert flowers cascading from top to bottom tier; trim sticks as needed. Serves 90.**

*Combine Violet with Rose for violet shown. Combine Leaf Green with Lemon Yellow for green shown.

†Brand confectionery coating.

Love has blossomed...and our Flower Favor Kit (p. 222) creates a lovely remembrance of the day. With frosted containers, ribbon and tags (all included in kit), it's a sweet gift you can fill with Pastel Pearls Favor Candies (p. 223).

◀ The Picture of Romance

Pans: 8, 10, 12, 14 x 2 in. Square, p. 153
Tip: 2D, p. 144
Colors:* Brown, Black, Red-Red, p. 134
Fondant: White Ready-To-Use Rolled Fondant (60 oz.), Brush Set, p. 130; Rolling Pin, Roll & Cut Mat, p. 133
Topper: Photo Frame Topper, p. 225
Recipe: Buttercream Icing, p. 116
Also: 5 in. Curved Pillars (3 sets), p. 230; 8, 10, 12 in. Decorator Preferred® Square Plates (2 each), p. 230; Fanci-Foil Wrap, p. 232; Wooden Dowel Rods, p. 231; 16 x 16 x ½ in. foamcore board, ½ in. brown ribbon (64 in. long), knife, ruler, double-stick tape

Bake and cool 2-layer cakes. Ice smooth and prepare for Separator Plate and Pillar Construction (p. 114). Tint 48 oz. fondant brown and roll out ⅛ in. thick. Cut ¾ in. strips and attach to all edges of cake sides with dots of icing; trim as needed to fit. Roll out white fondant ⅛ in. thick. Use wide end of tip 2D to cut brown and white circles. Brush backs with water, attach brown circles at corners to cover seams and white circles on cake sides. Attach ribbon to base board with tape.

At reception: Assemble cakes. Insert favorite photo and position topper.*** Serves 220.**

*Combine Brown with a little Black and Red-Red for brown shown.

**The top tier is often saved for the first anniversary. The number of servings given does not include the top tier.

***Always place a separator plate, or cake board cut to fit, on the cake where you position any figurine or topper. This protects both the cake and your keepsake. For extra stability, secure topper to the plate with double-stick tape.

Bows and bouquets are a can't-miss combination! We love the delicate stripes and blossoms of the Flirty Fleur Favor Box (p. 223). Top it with a silk flower bow for a favor with the elegant look of a wedding gift.

◄ Pearl Dust™ Perfection

Pans: 6, 10, 14 x 2 in. Round, p. 153; 18 x 3 in. Half-Round, p. 152

Tips: 2, 3, 5, 6, 7, 10, 14, 16, 101, 101s, 102, 103, 224, p. 144-145

Fondant: White Ready-To-Use Rolled Fondant (280 oz.), Brush Set, p. 130; Rolling Pin, Roll & Cut Mat, p. 133; Easy-Glide Fondant Smoother, Cutter/Embosser, p. 131

Recipes: Buttercream, Royal Icings, p. 116

Also: Tailored Tiers Cake Display Set, p. 228; Flower Nail No. 7, p. 137; White Pearl Dust™ (5 pks.), p. 130; Meringue Powder, Piping Gel, p. 135; Silver Fanci-Foil Wrap, p. 232; Dowel Rods, p. 231; Clear Vanilla Extract, p. 135; 20 in. round ½ in. plywood board, waxed paper, 24-gauge white wire (24 5 in. long pieces), white florist tape, double-stick tape, craft block, ⅜ in. white ribbon (10½ ft. long), ½ in. white ribbon (64 in. long), wire cutters

Several days in advance: Using royal icing, make 125 each of the following roses: tip 101 with tip 5 bases, tip 101s with tip 3 bases, tip 102 with tip 7 bases, tip 103 with tip 10 bases. Use royal icing to make 150 each of the following drop flowers: tip 224 with tip 3 dot centers, tip 14 and 16, each with tip 2 dot centers. Using royal icing, make 45 tip 6 calyxes on 5 in. lengths of wire. Pipe tip 6 cone-shaped bases on waxed paper. Insert hooked wire and brush with damp brush to blend. Insert in craft block to dry overnight. Mix Pearl Dust with vanilla and brush on all flowers; let dry. Attach the following roses to calyxes using tip 3 and royal icing: 20 tip 103, 15 tip 102 and 10 tip 101. Let dry.

Bake 2-layer 6, 10, 14 and 18 in. cakes (for 18 in. cake, bake 4 half-rounds 2 in. high to create an 18 x 4 in. cake). Prepare cakes for rolled fondant (p. 117) and Tailored Tiers and Stacked Construction (p. 114-115). Cover cakes with fondant; smooth with Fondant Smoother. Remove fabric from separators; brush sides lightly with piping gel and cover sides with fondant. In buttercream, pipe tip 6 bead bottom border on all tiers. Randomly attach roses and drop flowers to cake sides with royal icing. Tape wired flowers together to form a bouquet. Arrange 9 groups of 5 various-size roses. Tape each group together, then arrange in a bouquet and tape all groups together. Attach ribbon to each separator and base board with double-stick tape.

At reception: Assemble cakes; position bouquet. Serves 262.**

Destination Weddings

You've picked the perfect spot to tie the knot! Shouldn't your wedding cake take on some of the local color? The designs here are departures from the classic wedding cake, but each travels well to the reception and captures your special place forever. Whether you're hitting the jackpot in Vegas or basking in a tropical paradise, these cakes are first-class all the way.

◀ Love's Perfect Setting

Pans: 6 x 3, 8 x 2, 12 x 2 in. Round, p. 153

Tips: 2, 5, 12, p. 144

Colors:* Leaf Green, Violet, Rose, Lemon Yellow, Golden Yellow, Creamy Peach, Ivory, Brown, Black, Royal Blue, p. 134

Fondant/Gum Paste: White Ready-To-Use Rolled Fondant (48 oz.), Brush Set, p. 130; Ready-To-Use Gum Paste (16 oz.), Rolling Pin, Roll & Cut Mat, Fondant/Gum Paste Tool Set, p. 133; Flower Former Set, p. 131, Floral Collection Flower Making Set, p. 132

Topper: Sweet Couple, p. 224

Recipes: Buttercream, Royal Icings, p. 116

Also: Seashells Candy Mold, p. 167; White Pearl Dust™, p. 130; Piping Gel, Meringue Powder, p. 135; Wooden Dowel Rods, p. 231; 16 in. Cake Circles (3), Gold Fanci-Foil Wrap, p. 232; embroidery scissors, knife, granulated brown sugar, tissue, fabric trim, double-stick tape

In advance: Make fondant flowers. Knead together 4 oz. balls of fondant and gum paste. Divide into 4 pieces and tint yellow, rose, violet and green; reserve green for small flower leaves. Roll out 1/16 in. thick. Using cutters from Flower Making Set, make the following flowers: 12 large with pansy cutter, 8 medium with apple blossom cutter and 6 small with forget-me-not cutter. Pipe tip 2 dot centers in royal icing. Let dry in cornstarch-dusted flower formers. Using reserved green, make 20 small flower leaves using small rose leaf cutter. **Also:** Make 40 fondant seashells. Marbleize fondant (p. 124) using 6 oz. white and 4 oz. peach. Press firmly into candy mold dusted with cornstarch. Unmold and let dry. Brush with white Pearl Dust. **And:** Use fondant/gum paste mixture to make 5 palm trees (p. 123).

For base: Cut 3 cake boards to 15 in. diameter; stack, tape and wrap with foil. Bake and cool 1-layer cakes using firm-textured batter such as pound cake. Ice smooth and prepare for Stacked Construction (p. 114). Center 12 in. cake on cake board; position 8 and 6 in. cakes so edges of all 3 cakes align at the back. Spatula ice waterfall area light blue; cover with blue tinted piping gel. Sprinkle cake tops with brown sugar "sand." Pipe tip 5 bead bottom borders on all tiers. Attach flowers, leaves and seashells with tip 2 dots of buttercream. Attach trim to base board with double-stick tape.

At reception: Insert palm trees; position additional flowers and leaves at base of trunks. Position topper. Serves 40.**

*Combine Violet with Rose for violet shown. Combine Ivory with Golden Yellow for tan shown. Combine Brown with Black, Ivory and Golden Yellow for brown shown.

**The top tier is often saved for the first anniversary. The number of servings given does not include the top tier.

▲ A Romantic Getaway?

Pan: 18 x 3 in. Half Round, p. 153

Tips: 1, 2, 3, 5, p. 144

Colors:* Rose, Violet, Christmas Red, Black, Leaf Green, Royal Blue, Lemon Yellow, Orange, p. 134

Fondant/Gum Paste: White Ready-To-Use Rolled Fondant (24 oz.), Brush Set, p. 130; Hearts Cut-Outs™, p. 132; Ready-To-Use Gum Paste, Rolling Pin, Roll & Cut Mat, p. 133; Cutter/Embosser, Fondant/Gum Paste Tool Set, p. 131

Topper: Oh No You Don't, p. 225

Recipes: Buttercream, Royal Icings, p. 116

Also: 2009 Pattern Book (Slot Machine, Sign, Chapel Doorway and Sign, Carpet), p. 128; Meringue Powder, p. 135; Silver, White Pearl Dust™, p. 130; 8 in. Cookie Treat Sticks, p. 163; yellow spice drops, uncooked spaghetti, cornstarch, craft block

Several days in advance: Make fondant Slot Machines, Sign and Chapel Doorway with sign (p 123).

Ice 1-layer (3 in. high) cake smooth in buttercream. For carpet, tint 4 oz. fondant red, roll out 1/8 in. thick. Using pattern and straight-edge wheel of Cutter/Embosser, cut carpet and position on cake. Pipe tip 5 dots around front message area of cake. Print tip 5 message. Pipe tip 5 ball top and bottom borders on remainder of cake. Position slot machines. Insert chapel doorway and sign. Position topper. Serves 55.

*Combine Violet and Rose for violet shown.

Please join us
for a Bridal Shower honoring

Sue Vogt

Saturday, September 28th
3:00

Rosalind's Tea Room, Atlanta

Hosted by: Catherine, Sarah and Marcia

RSVP by September 1st, 446-672-2534

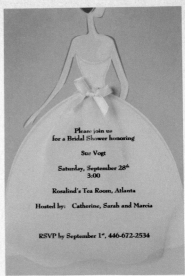

When the cookies and cake match the invitations, you know the shower hostess has everything under control! See our Print Your Own Stationery selection on page 217 for some great theme ideas, like the fun Bride Invitation design here. It's easy to bring stationery design elements such as bows, hearts and flowers into your desserts.

◀ Her High Profile Day

Pans: Oval Pan Set (16.5 x 12.4 in. used), p. 153

Tips: 2, 6, 10, 103, 352, p. 144-145

Colors: Royal Blue, Moss Green, Copper, Brown, p. 134

Fondant: White Ready-To-Use Rolled Fondant (118 oz.), Brush Set, p. 130; Rolling Pin, Roll & Cut Mat, p. 133; Easy-Glide Fondant Smoother, p. 131

Recipes: Buttercream, Royal Icings, p. 116

Also: 2009 Pattern Book (Bride's Torso, Dress), p. 128; Flower Nail No. 7, p. 137; Cake Board, Fanci-Foil Wrap, p. 232; Meringue Powder, Piping Gel, p. 135; 13 x 19 x ¼ in. foamcore board, 8 in. white ribbon (⅜ in. wide), ½ yd. tulle, non-toxic copper chalk, straight pins, waxed paper, knife, dental floss or thin cord

In advance: Using royal icing, make about 36 tip 103 roses (p. 119) with tip 10 bases. Make extras to allow for breakage; let dry. **Also:** For base, cut foamcore board 1½ in. larger than pan size. Use about 36 oz. fondant to cover base (p. 124). Let dry overnight. **And:** Make fondant bride (p. 123).

Bake and cool 1-layer cake. Prepare cake for rolled fondant (p. 117). Tint approx. 56 oz. fondant blue; cover cake (p. 124). Smooth with Fondant Smoother. Position cake on prepared base. Attach torso to cake top with dots of icing. Roll out 12 oz. fondant ⅛ in. thick. Use pattern to cut out dress; attach over torso, then smooth and shape edges. Pin dress pattern to 2 layers of tulle; cut 1½ in. wider than dress on each side to allow for gentle folds. Gather layers of tulle at top and tie with dental floss. Attach at waist with icing. Pipe tip 2 royal icing dots on top layer of tulle; make small ribbon bow and attach with icing. Pipe tip 6 bead bottom border; position roses. Pipe tip 352 leaves. Serves 22.

▶ Perfect Attendants

Cookies: Cookie Sheet, Cooling Grid, p. 154; Heart Plastic Nesting Cutter Set, p. 164;

Tips: 1, 3, 8, 12, p. 144-145

Colors:* Violet, Rose, Lemon Yellow, Kelly Green, Brown, Red-Red, Orange, Copper, p. 134

Fondant/Gum Paste: Ready-To-Use Gum Paste, Rolling Pin, Roll & Cut Mat, p. 133

Recipes: Roll-Out Cookies, Color Flow Icing, p. 116

Also: 2009 Pattern Book (Bridesmaid, Dress, Large and Small Bows), p. 128; Color Flow Mix, p. 135; confectioners' sugar, knife, cornstarch

In advance: Prepare gum paste pieces. Tint gum paste and roll out 1/16 in. thick. Use patterns to cut body, bodice overlay, dress and large and small bow pieces. Use small ends of tips 8 and 12 to cut knots for large and small bows. Cut a ½ x 3½ in. strip base for each figure and ¼ x 1½ in. tails for large bows. Let dry on cornstarch-dusted surface.

Make cookie skirts. Prepare dough and roll out; cut using largest heart cutter from set. Cut off top curves to shape straight hem of skirt; bake and cool. Using full-strength color flow icing, outline skirt with tip 3; let set, then flow in with thinned color flow. Let dry. Assemble using dots of full-strength color flow. Attach body and skirt to base strip. Attach bodice overlay, then dress bow pieces. Pipe tip 1 curly hair with full-strength color flow; attach hair bow pieces. Let dry 24 hours. Each serves 1.

*Combine Violet with Rose for violet shown. Combine Brown with Red-Red for brown shown. Combine Orange with Red-Red for orange shown.

◀ Love's in the Stars!

Pans: 6, 10 x 2 in. Round, p. 153

Tip: 5, p. 144

Fondant/Gum Paste: Gold Pearl Dust™, Brush Set, p. 130; Star Cut-Outs™, p. 132; Ready-To-Use Gum Paste, Rolling Pin, Roll & Cut Mat, p. 133

Topper: Sweet Couple, p. 224

Recipes: Buttercream Icing, p. 116; Gum Paste Adhesive, p. 117

Also: 2009 Pattern Book (Moon), p. 128; 11¾ in. Lollipop Sticks, p. 169; Ceramic Pedestal Cake Stand, p. 226; Meringue Powder, p. 135; Dowel Rods, p. 231; Cake Boards, p. 232; toothpick, knife, cornstarch

Two days in advance: Cut gum paste pieces. Roll out gum paste 1⁄16 in. thick. Cut 7 stars using large Cut-Out, 12 stars using medium Cut-Out and 10 stars using small Cut-Out. Trace moon pattern using toothpick; cut using knife. Roll out additional gum paste 1⁄16 in. thick. Cut a 1 x ¾ in. rectangle bench seat. Let all pieces dry overnight on cornstarch-dusted surface. **One day in advance:** Cut lollipop stick to 8½ in.; wrap a small amount of gum paste around top 3½ in. and attach to back of moon using gum paste adhesive. Cut 2 sticks to 5½ in.; wrap gum paste around tops; attach to bottom of bench seat with adhesive. Let dry overnight.

Ice 2-layer cakes smooth and prepare for Stacked Construction (p. 114). Position on Cake Stand. Pipe tip 5 bead bottom borders. Lightly brush stars with Pearl Dust. Attach stars to cake and plate with dots of icing. Insert moon in cake top; insert bench behind it. Position topper.** Serves 40.

▶ Linked by Love

Pans: 9 x 2 in. Round, p. 153, Cookie Sheet, Cooling Grid, p. 154

Tips: 3, 18, p. 144-145

Colors:* Rose, Violet, Lemon Yellow, Kelly Green, p. 134

Topper: Two Rings Topper, p. 225

Recipes: Buttercream, Color Flow Icings, Roll-Out Cookies, p. 116

Also: Fancy Scrolls Cake and Dessert Stand, p. 226; White Candy Melts®†, p. 166; Heart Plastic Nesting Cutter Set, p. 164; 11¾ in. Lollipop Sticks, p. 169; Neon Colors FoodWriter™ Edible Color Markers, p. 130; Color Flow Mix, p. 135; Cake Boards, p. 232

In advance: Prepare dough and roll out. Cut cookies using Nesting Cutters (2 each of smallest and 3rd largest, 1 each all other sizes). Bake and cool. Outline and fill in using tip 3 and Color Flow Icing (p. 126). Let dry 48 hours.

Spatula ice 2-layer cake. Pipe tip 18 shell bottom border. Attach lollipop sticks to back of cookies using melted candy. For cookies on cake sides, cut sticks to 2½ in. and attach to back of cookie at a 90° angle. Write message with FoodWriter marker.

At reception: Position cake on stand. Position topper** and insert cookies, trimming sticks as needed. Cake serves 24; each cookie serves 1.

*Combine Violet with Rose for violet shown.

**Always place a separator plate, or cake board cut to fit, on the cake where you position any figurine or topper. This protects both the cake and your keepsake. For extra stability, secure topper to the plate with double-stick craft tape.

†Brand confectionery coating.

◀ Flourishing Together

Pans: 6, 12 x 2 in., 8 x 3 in. Round, p. 153

Tips: 3, 5, p. 144

Color: Moss Green, p. 134

Fondant/Gum Paste: Ready-To-Use Gum Paste (3 pkgs.), p. 133; Fondant/Gum Paste Tool Set, p.131; Floral Collection Flower Making Set, p. 132; White (2), Yellow and Orchid Pink Pearl Dust™, p. 130

Topper: 25th Anniversary Cake Pick, p. 226

Recipes: Buttercream, Royal Icings, p. 116; Gum Paste Adhesive, p. 117

Also: Candlelight Cake Stand Set (includes flameless votives), p. 226; 14 in. Decorator Preferred® Smooth Edge Plate, p. 230; Flower Stamen Assortment, Flower Former Set, Dowel Rods, p. 131; Cake Dividing Set, p. 137; Meringue Powder, p. 135; Cake Circles, p. 232; Heart Plastic Nesting Cutter Set, p. 164; cornstarch, plastic drinking straws, paper drink cones, toothpicks

Several days in advance: Make gum paste flowers (p. 120) and leaves (p. 124). You will need: 34 small roses (dust edges of half with yellow Pearl Dust, half with orchid Pearl Dust); 16 plain and 16 ruffled calla lilies (dust all with white Pearl Dust); and 55 large rose leaves. Make extras to allow for breakage. Let dry for several days.

Bake and cool 2-layer 6 in., 2-layer 8 in. (bake 2 layers, 2½ in. each, for a 5 in. high cake) and 1-layer 12 in. cake. Ice smooth and prepare for Stacked Construction (p. 114). Use Cake Dividing Set to divide 6 in. cake into 8ths, 10 in. cake into 10ths and 12 in. cake into 16ths (mark 8ths then divide each section in half). Using tip 3, pipe triple drop strings on 6 in. and 8 in. cakes (1, 1¼, 1½ in. deep); pipe double drop strings on 12 in. cake (1, 1¼ in. deep). Pipe tip 5 bead border around base of 12 and 6 in. cakes; pipe tip 3 bead border on top of 8 in. cake. Position flowers and leaves, securing with icing. Cut drinking straws to 5 in. long; slide onto bottom of cake pick for extra length.

At reception: Position cake on stand. Insert pick in cake top. Serves 52.

▶ Packed with Memories

Pan: Oval Pan Set (16.5 x 12.4 in. used), p. 153

Tips: 2, 3, 16, 18, 55, 129, 131, 352, p. 144-145

Colors:* Golden Yellow, Rose, Moss Green, Brown, Red-Red, Black, p. 134

Fondant/Gum Paste: Fine Tip Neon Colors FoodWriter™ Edible Color Markers, Gold Pearl Dust™, Brush Set, p. 130; Ready-To-Use Gum Paste, Rolling Pin, Roll & Cut Mat, p. 133; Fondant/Gum Paste Tool Set, p. 131

Topper: Wedding Gown and Tuxedo Topper, p. 225

Recipes: Buttercream, Royal Icings, p. 116

Also: Champagne Bottle Candles, p. 190; Parchment Paper, p. 140; Cake Boards, Fanci-Foil Wrap, p. 232; 4 in. Lollipop Sticks, p. 169; Meringue Powder, p. 135; black fine tip permanent marker, foamcore board (¼ in. thick), lemon extract, cornstarch, double-stick tape, knife, ruler, scissors

In advance: Use royal icing to make 50 tip 129 and 50 tip 131 drop flowers with tip 2 dot centers. Let dry. Make gum paste chest, album, purse, shoes and champagne glasses (p. 123).

Bake and cool 1-layer cake; ice smooth. Pipe tip 3 double drop strings 2 in. apart, ¾ in. and 1 in. deep. Pipe tip 16 shell top border and tip 18 shell bottom border. Attach flowers with icing dots; pipe tip 352 leaves. Position chest base on cake top; insert topper. Pipe tip 55 message. Position album, purse, shoes, champagne glasses (trim sticks to fit) and bottle candle. Cut 1¼ x 9 in. strip of parchment paper; print message with marker. Attach to topper with double-stick tape. Attach lid to chest with royal icing. Serves 44.

*Combine Brown with Red-Red for brown shown.

▶ Golden Scrolls

Pans: 6, 8, 10 x 2 in. Round, p. 153

Tip: 2, p. 144

Fondant/Gum Paste: White Ready-To-Use Rolled Fondant (96 oz.), Brush Set, p. 130; Ready-To-Use Gum Paste (1 pk.), Rolling Pin, Roll & Cut Mat, p. 133; Easy-Glide Fondant Smoother, Cutter/Embosser, p. 131

Topper: Gold 50th Anniversary Cake Pick, p. 226

Recipes: Buttercream, Royal Icings, p. 116

Also: Graceful Tiers Cake Stand, p. 226; Gold Pearl Dust™ (2 pks.), p. 130; Meringue Powder, p. 135; Cake Circles, p. 232; 4 in. Lollipop Sticks, p. 169; 2 white plastic drinking straws, ruler, lemon extract, cornstarch

In advance: Make spirals for cake top. Roll out portion of gum paste ⅛ in. thick. Cut five strips ¼ in. wide in various lengths from 9 to 11 in. For each, wrap ¾ in. of one end around a lollipop stick and smooth. Set on cornstarch-dusted board and shape into spiral. Make extras to allow for breakage. Let dry.

Prepare 2-layer cakes for rolled fondant (p. 117). Cover with fondant and smooth with Fondant Smoother. Knead remaining gum paste into 16 oz. fondant; roll out ⅛ in. thick. Cut ⅝ in. wide strips 19, 25½ and 32 in. long for bottom borders; brush backs with water and attach. Cut ¼ in. wide strips in various lengths from 6 to 12 in. Set strips on side on cornstarch-dusted surface and shape into spirals; let set 15 to 30 minutes. Use royal icing to pipe tip 2 outline on back edge; attach to cake sides in random order. Mix Pearl Dust with small amount of lemon extract; brush onto bottom borders and edges of all spirals.

At reception: Position cakes on stand. Insert top spirals. Cut drinking straws to 5 in. long; attach to 50th pick for extra height. Insert pick. Serves 60.

A bubbly personality is just what you want in a favor—our Champagne Bottle Favor Kit (p. 222) is overflowing with fun! Fill the bottles with Peppermint Pearls (p. 223), add personalized labels and a perky ribbon included in kit. Then place in a champagne glass with Sparkling Ice (p. 220).

Desserts in 3-D!

Party cakes don't have to lay flat—these designs demand to stand up and be noticed! In this special section, you'll see that cakes can become almost any object you can imagine. You'll discover amazing architecture, from a giant cupcake barn and circus tent to an incredible doll house filled with fondant furniture. Next, enter new dimensions with stacked cakes like our towering rocket ship or the fun-loving robot. Or, decorate the colorful cupcake menagerie shown here, surrounding a big birthday cupcake with Teddy popping from the top. It's the shape of cakes to come!

HAPPY
BIRTHDAY

FROM OUR COVER

King of Cupcakes!

Pan: Dimensions® Large Cupcake, p. 151

Tip: 4, p. 144

Colors:* Violet, Rose, Royal Blue, Orange, Brown, Red-Red, Black, p. 134

Recipe: Buttercream Icing, p.116

Fondant/Gum Paste: White Ready-To-Use Rolled Fondant (24 oz), Brush Set, p. 130; Fondant Ribbon Cutter/Embosser Set, Flower Former Set, p. 131; 9 in. Rolling Pin, Roll & Cut Mat, Gum-Tex™, p. 133

Also: Jumbo Confetti Sprinkles, p. 136; Cake Boards, Fanci-Foil Wrap, p. 232; Small Angled Spatula, p. 138; ruler, cornstarch

In advance: Make fondant paper tears. Combine 4 oz. white fondant with ¼ teaspoon Gum Tex. Roll out fondant ⅛ in. thick and cut 8 triangles 1½ in. wide in various lengths from 2 to 2½ in. Let dry 48 hours in medium and large flower formers dusted with cornstarch. **Also:** Make fondant bear. Tint 4 oz. fondant brown ⅛ oz. light brown and ½ oz. orange. Use brown fondant to make a 1¾ in. ball for torso and a 1½ in. ball for head. Shape and attach together with damp brush. Roll and attach 1 x ½ in. logs for arms, ½ in. flattened balls for ears. For muzzle, roll out light brown fondant ⅛ in. thick; cut ½ x ¾ in. oval and attach. Using buttercream icing and tip 1, pipe dot eyes, pipe-in nose and string mouth. Using orange fondant, shape a ½ in. wide x ¾ in. high cone for hat; attach. Pipe tip 1 pull-out fringe.

Bake and cool cake. Trim ½ in. off top of cupcake. Ice bottom section smooth; position top section and use spatula to ice with swirl effect. Tint 8 oz. fondant blue; roll out ⅛ in. thick. Cut 16 strips, 3½ in. long using Cutter/Embosser with 2 zigzag wheels and ¼ in. spacer; attach to bottom section sides with dots of icing. Attach confetti sprinkles. Pipe tip 4 message. Position bear and fondant paper tears. Serves 12.

*Combine Violet with Rose for violet shown.

Cupcake Critters

Pans: Cookie Sheet, Cooling Grid, p. 163

Tips: 1, 2A, 3, p. 144

Colors: Golden Yellow, Lemon Yellow, Brown, Red-Red, Rose, Royal Blue, Violet, Orange, Kelly Green, p. 134

Fondant: White Ready-To-Use Rolled Fondant (24 oz. for 10-12 animals), p. 130; Fondant/Gum Paste Tool Set, p. 131; Round and Heart Cut-Outs™, p. 132

Recipes: Buttercream, Royal Icings, p. 116

Also: Silly-Critters! Silicone Baking Cups, p. 148; 4 in. Lollipop Sticks, p. 169; Meringue Powder, p. 135; knife, ruler, waxed paper, cornstarch

In advance: Make fondant hats. Tint portions of fondant green, rose and violet. Shape a fondant cone ¾ in. high, ½ in. diameter at base. Stand on waxed paper-covered board. Use royal icing and tip 1 to pipe pull-out fringe at base and tip. Let dry. **Also:** Make fondant animal heads and tails (p. 124). Tint about 1½ oz. fondant for each. Attach fondant pieces using a damp brush. Pipe details using royal icing. Let heads dry on cornstarch-dusted surface at least 24 hours.

Bake and cool cupcakes in silicone cups supported by cookie sheet. Tint icing to match heads. Cover tops and build up icing with tip 2A; smooth with spatula. Position heads; insert tails. Pipe tip 3 pull-out dot fringe for lion's mane and tip of lion, cow and elephant tails. Outline and fill in spots on cow. Each serves 1.

*Combine Golden Yellow with Lemon Yellow for yellow shown. Combine Brown with Red-Red for brown shown.

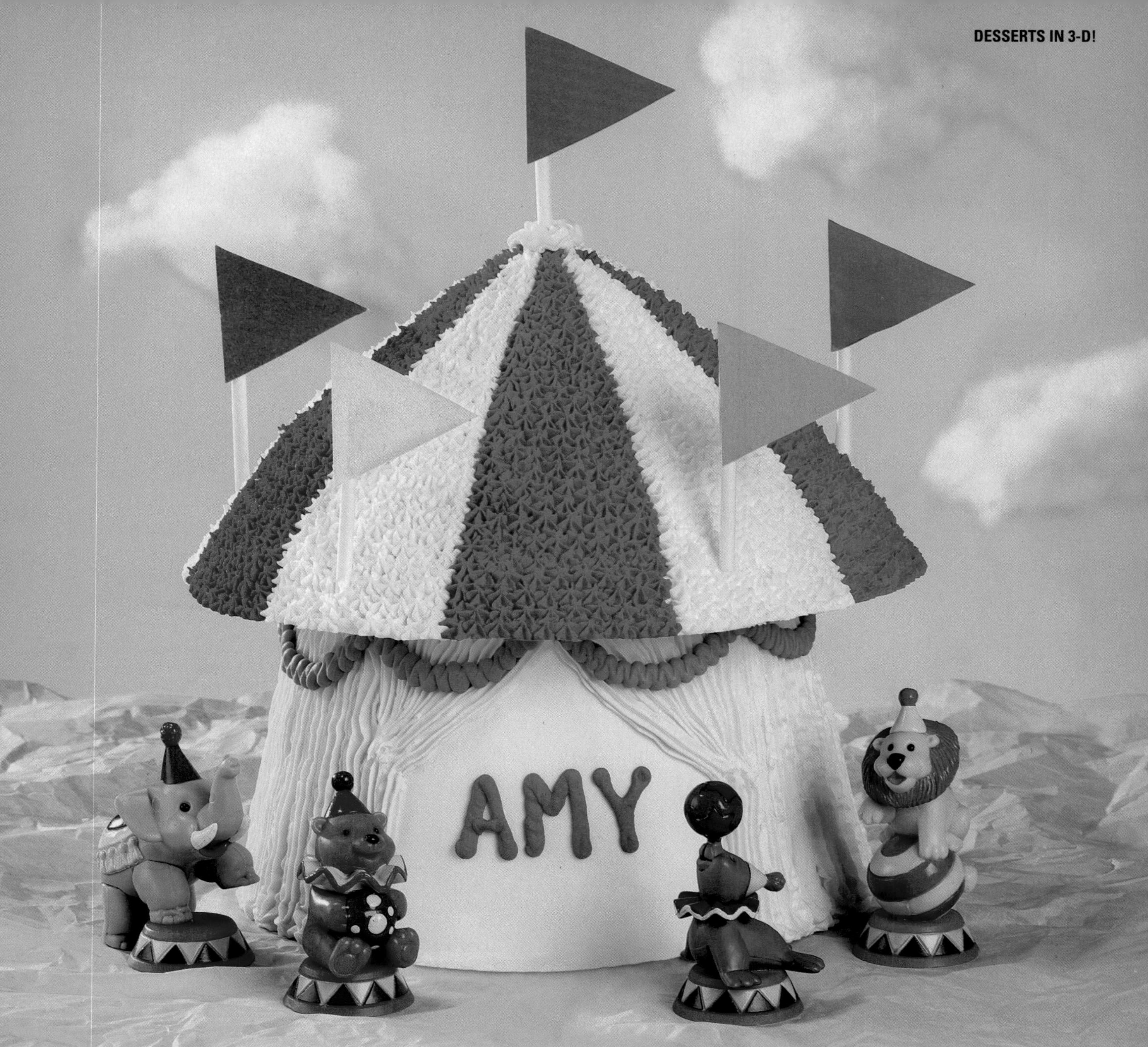

◀ Barn Raising

Pans: Dimensions® Large Cupcake, p. 151; Cookie Sheet, Cooling Grid, p. 163

Tips: 2B, 3, 5, 8, 12, p. 144

Colors:* Red-Red, Black, Golden Yellow, Brown, Rose, p. 134

Fondant: White Ready-To-Use Rolled Fondant (24 oz. for 10-12 animals), pg. 130; Fondant/Gum Paste Tool Set, p. 131; Rolling Pin, Roll & Cut Mat, p. 133

Recipes: Buttercream, Royal Icings, p. 116

Also: Silly-Critters! Silicone Baking Cups, p. 148; Meringue Powder, p. 135; Cake Boards, Fanci-Foil Wrap, p. 232; 4 in. Lollipop Sticks, p. 169; toothpick, cornstarch, knife

In advance: Make fondant animal heads (p. 124). Tint about 1½ oz. fondant for each. Attach fondant pieces using a damp brush. Pipe details using royal icing. Let heads dry on cornstarch-dusted surface at least 24 hours.

Bake and cool large cupcake in pan and Silly-Critters cupcakes in silicone cups supported by cookie sheet. For barn, turn bottom cupcake section narrow side up on prepared board. Mark 2 x 3 in. door and 1½ in. square windows with toothpick. Pipe in openings and bottom of door with tip 5 (smooth with finger dipped in cornstarch). Cover barn bottom with tip 12 lines. Outline door and windows with tip 8. Pipe tip 3 pull-out hay. Position barn top on same size board; stack top on bottom. Pipe rows of tip 2B lines starting at bottom edge for roof. For animals, tint icing to match heads. Cover tops and build up with tip 2A; smooth with spatula. Position heads; insert tails. Pipe tip 3 pull-out dot fringe for tip of cow tail; outline and fill in spots on cow. Cake serves 12; each cupcake serves 1.

*Combine Brown with Red-Red for brown shown.

▲ Big Top Buddies

Pan: Dimensions® Large Cupcake, p. 151

Tips: 4, 16, p. 144-145

Colors: Red-Red, Lemon Yellow, Royal Blue, p. 134

Recipe: Buttercream Icing, p. 116

Also: Circus Animals Cake Toppers Set, p. 192; Cake Dividing Set, p. 137; 6 in. Lollipop Sticks, p. 169; Cake Circles, Fanci-Foil Wrap, p. 232; construction paper, ruler, scissors, tape, toothpicks

Bake and cool cake. Position bottom on foil-wrapped cake circle with wider side down. Ice smooth in white. Lightly mark 4 in. wide opening. Use tip 16 lines to pipe curtain. Divide top of cake into 10ths and pipe tip 4 zigzag swags, ¾ in. deep. Print tip 4 name. Position top section on same size board. Ice top cake smooth; divide into 10ths and mark lines to top. Position on base cake. Fill in sections, alternating colors, with tip 16 stars. Pipe tip 1 rosette on top. Cut 6 paper triangles for flags; tape onto lollipop sticks cut to 3 in. long. Insert flags in cake. Arrange toppers around cake. Serves 12.

◀ Party Whole Hog!

Pan: Sports Ball Set, p. 161

Tip: 16, p. 145

Colors:* Rose, Violet, Lemon Yellow, Brown, Kelly Green, p. 13

Fondant: White Ready-To-Use Rolled Fondant (12 oz.), Brush Set, p. 130; Rolling Pin, Roll & Cut Mat, p. 133

Recipes: Buttercream Icing, p. 116; Thinned Fondant Adhesive p. 117

Also: 2009 Pattern Book (Ear), p. 128; Green Candy Melts®†, p. 166; "Hidden" Pillars, p. 230; Wooden Dowel Rods, p. 231; 4 in. Lollipop Sticks, p. 169; Jumbo Confetti Sprinkles, Flowerful Medley Sprinkles, p. 136; Cake Circles, Cake Boards, Fanci-Foil Wrap, p. 232; Piping Gel, p. 135; sugar cone, large marshmallow, knife, ruler, scissors, shredded coconut, cornstarch, waxed paper

In advance: Prepare board with legs (p. 121). **Also:** Make party hat: tint 3 oz. fondant violet, 2 oz. yellow. Roll out ⅛ in. thick. Cut 1 in. off bottom of sugar cone; lightly brush with piping gel. Wrap fondant around cone; trim to fit and smooth seam with hand. Use Thinned Fondant Adhesive to attach Jumbo Confetti. For fringed brim, cut 1 in. wide strips. Use scissors to cut ⅛ in. wide slits, ¾ in. deep. Cut strips into 2½ in. lengths. Roll into tufts and fluff ends with fingers. Brush with a damp brush and attach around bottom for brim. For pompom, cut a ¾ in. wide strip, 1½ in. long. Use scissors to cut ⅛ in. wide slits, ½ in. deep. Roll into tuft and fluff ends. Brush with a damp brush and attach to tip. Let dry on waxed paper-covered board. **And:** Make curlique tail and 2 ears. Tint 2 oz. fondant pink. Roll out ⅛ in. thick. For tail, cut a ¼ x 6 in. strip. Loosely wrap around wooden dowel rod. Let stand 5-10 minutes then slide off rod. Let dry on cornstarch-dusted board. Use pattern to cut 2 ears; curve slightly and let dry. Attach tail to a 4 in. Lollipop Stick using Thinned Fondant Adhesive. Let dry.

Bake and cool cake using firm-textured batter such as pound cake. Attach halves with icing. Position on prepared board. Cover body with tip 16 stars. Attach ears to cake with icing. For nose, cut ⅓ off bottom of marshmallow; attach top to cake with icing. Cover nose and outer edges and back of ears with tip 16 stars. Tint small amount of fondant brown; roll into 2 balls ½ in. diameter. Flatten and attach for eyes. Insert tail; position hat. Sprinkle serving platter with green tinted coconut (p. 120). Add confetti from Flowerful Medley assortment.Serves 12.

*Combine Violet with Rose for violet shade shown.

†Brand confectionery coating.

◀ He Gets Around!

Pan: Mini Ball, p. 161
Tip: 16, p. 145
Colors:* Lemon Yellow, Rose, Sky Blue, Leaf Green, Violet, Orange, p. 134
Recipe: Buttercream Icing, p. 116
Also: Black twist licorice, large spice drops, candy-coated chocolates, jelly bean, knife, ruler

Bake and cool 2 halves for each ball; attach with icing. Cover with tip 16 stars. Attach candy facial features and 2¼ in. long twist for mouth. For antennae, cut spice drops in half and position on end of 2½ in. licorice twist; insert in top of head. Each ball serves 1.

*Combine Violet with Rose for violet shade shown.

It's Great to Bee 3-D!

'an: Stand-Up Cuddly Bear Set, p. 160
'ips: 3, 5, 12, 16, p. 144-145
:olors:* Black, Lemon Yellow, Golden Yellow, Violet, Leaf Green, Rose, Royal Blue, p. 134
ondant: White Ready-To-Use Rolled Fondant (36 oz.), p. 130; Cutter/Embosser, p. 131; Gum-Tex™, Rolling Pin, Roll & Cut Mat, p. 133
lecipe: Buttercream Icing, p. 116
Ilso: 2009 Pattern Book (Wings), p. 128; Jumbo Stars Sprinkles, p. 136; White Candy Melts®†, p. 166; Decorator Brush Set, p. 168; 6 in. Lollipop Sticks, p. 169; Wooden Dowel Rods, p. 231; Piping Gel, p. 135; Celebration Candles, p. 191; Cake Boards, Fanci-Foil Wrap, p. 232; sugar cone, ruler, knife, lemon extract, scissors, cornstarch, toothpicks

n advance: Make wings (p. 123). **Also:** Make hat. Cut 1 in. off ottom of sugar cone. Tint 4 oz. fondant green, roll out ⅛ in. thick. ightly brush cone with piping gel and cover with fondant. For ringe, tint 4 oz. fondant violet, roll out ⅛ in. thick and cut 1 x 1 ⅜ 1. wide strips; cut ⅛ in. wide slits, ¾ in. deep. Roll into small tufts, uff with fingers. Attach to bottom of hat with damp brush; repeat o cover entire edge. For pompom, cut fondant strips ¾ in. wide x in. long; cut ⅛ in. slits, shape and attach to hat with damp brush. ttach star sprinkles to hat with dots of icing. Let dry on waxed aper-covered cake circles. **And:** Make fondant arms, hands, egs, feet, antennae and birthday cake. Tint 10 oz. fondant black. hape 2¼ x 2 x ½ in. thick feet and 1½ x 2 x ½ in. thick hands. Roll in. ball for each antenna. Cut 4 wooden dowel rods to 5 in. for rms and legs. Roll out remaining black fondant ⅛ in. thick. Brush owel rods with piping gel and cover each with fondant; smooth t seams. For antennae stems, bend lollipop sticks slightly. Dilute lack icing color with water and brush on sticks; let dry. Make ondant birthday cake (p. 123).

'repare cake using firm-textured batter such as pound cake. Fill repared pan, bake without core at 325°F for 90 minutes. Cool ompletely. Position cake on prepared board. Trim off ears, feet, rms and muzzle. Lightly ice cake. Use toothpick to trace face utline and mark 1 in. wide stripes on body. Pipe tip 3 outline nouth and dot eyes, tip 5 dot nose (smooth nose and eyes with nger dipped in cornstarch). Cover head and body with tip 16 tars. Overpipe cheeks with tip 16 stars. Insert prepared dowel ods ½ in. deep in hands and feet; secure with icing. Insert other nd 2½ in. deep in cake. Insert prepared lollipop sticks into ntenna balls, then into cake. Insert wings, large side up, into back f cake. Insert plain lollipop stick into head to support hat; position at; position birthday cake. Serves 12.

Combine Lemon Yellow with Golden Yellow for yellow shown.
Combine Violet with Rose for violet shade shown.

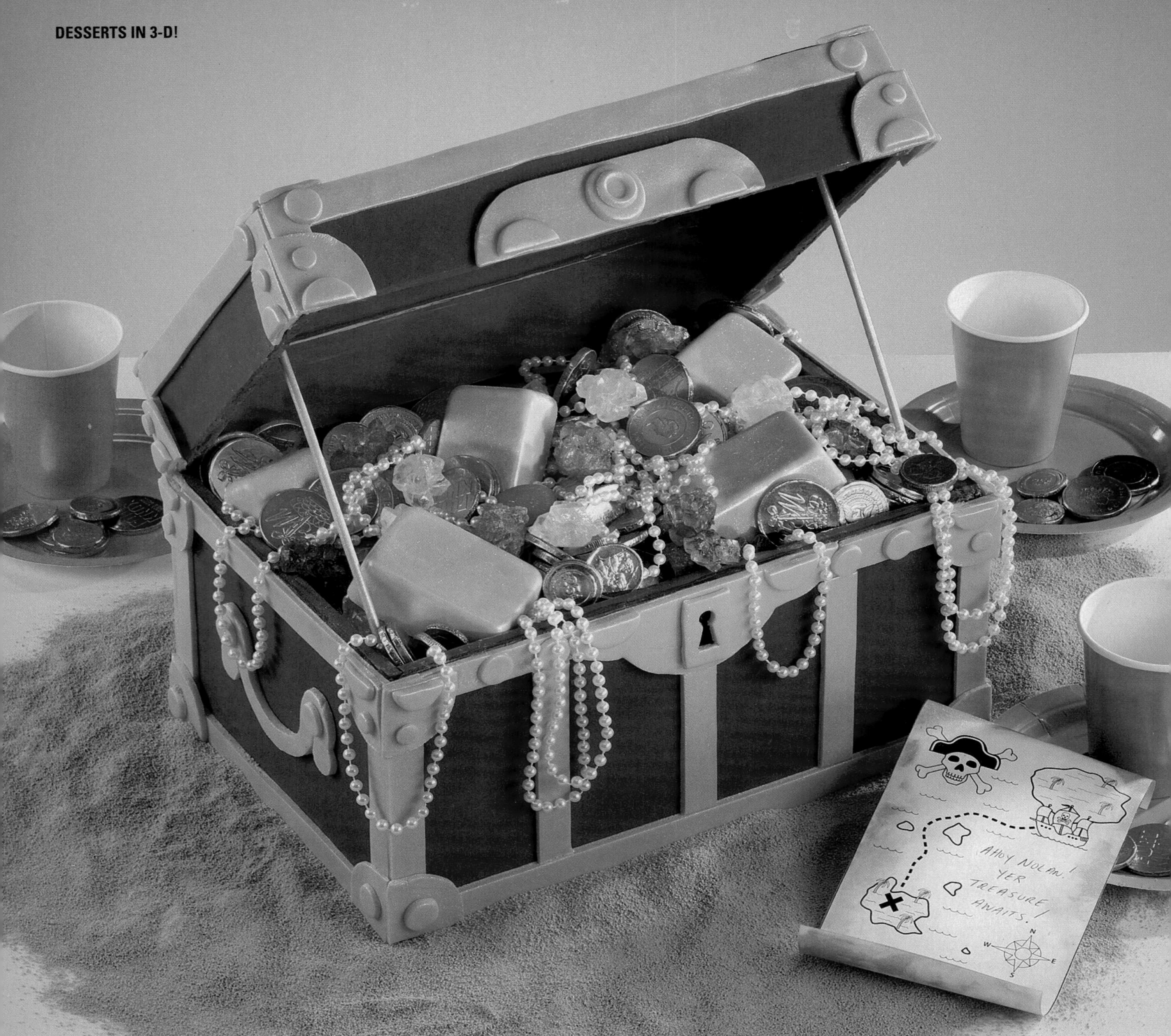

▲ How Pirates Party

Pans: 9 x 13 x 2 in. Sheet (2), p. 152; Non-Stick Large Cookie/Jelly Roll (2), p. 150; Petite Loaf, Cooling Grid, p. 154

Tips: 1A, 2A, 12, p. 144

Colors:* Golden Yellow, Black, Brown, Red-Red, p. 134

Recipes: Chocolate Buttercream, Royal Icings, p. 116

Fondant: White Ready-To-Use Rolled Fondant (48 oz.), Gold (3) and Bronze Pearl Dust™, p. 130; Rolling Pin, Roll & Cut Mat, p. 133

Candy: Light Cocoa (3 pks.), White (6 pks.), Yellow (4 pks.) Candy Melts®†, p. 166; Decorator Brush Set, p. 168; 11¾ in. Lollipop Sticks, p. 169

Also: 2009 Pattern Book (Top and Bottom Lock Plates, Handle, Corner Plates, Treasure Map), p. 128; Cake Boards, Fanci-Foil Wrap, White Pearl Beading, p. 232; Wooden Dowel Rods, p. 231; Meringue Powder, p. 135; knife, foil-wrapped chocolate coins, rock candy, granulated brown sugar, fine point marker, ruler, waxed paper

In advance: Prepare candy chest pieces. Melt and combine the Light Cocoa and White candy and make 2 candy plaques (p. 126) each in 9 x 13 in. and Non-Stick Jelly Roll pans, each ¼ in. deep. Refrigerate until firm; unmold and turn over 9 x 13 in. plaques. Bring to room temperature and cut the Jelly Roll plaques into 2 in. wide strips, 2–9 in. and 2–13 in. long. Attach the strips to the backside of 9 x 13 in. plaques at inside edges, using melted candy to create 1 box for lid and 1 box to top cake and hold candy. For lid, ice the outside top and sides of one candy box using royal icing. Let dry. **Also:** Using melted yellow candy, mold gold bars 1 in. deep in Petite Loaf Pan. Refrigerate until firm; unmold and brush with Gold Pearl Dust. Cut 2 lollipop sticks to 9½ in. Brush with Golden Yellow icing color, then with Gold Pearl Dust. Let dry on waxed paper-covered board. Make a copy of Treasure Map pattern and trim to size. Write message on map with marker. Brush map edges with Bronze Pearl Dust. Roll up ends around a dowel rod to curl.

Bake and cool two 9 x 13 in. sheet cakes; prepare for Stacked Construction (p. 114). Ice smooth in chocolate buttercream. Stack one candy box on cake top, open side up, and ice cake and candy sides smooth. For chest trim, tint 36 oz. fondant Golden Yellow. Roll out ⅛ in. thick. Cut ¾ in. wide strips in lengths to fit height and width of box and lid sides. Use patterns to cut Top and Bottom Lock Plates, 2 Handles, and 16 Corner Plates. Use wide opening of tips 1A and 12 and both openings of tip 2A to cut circle trims. Cut a 1 x ½ in. rectangle for keyhole plate. Using a knife, cut out a triangle shape and use tip 12 to cut top hole. Tint a small piece of fondant black and attach to back of keyhole plate with damp brush. Attach circles and half circles with damp brush. Brush all trim with Gold Pearl Dust.

Attach fondant pieces to chest with icing. Fill treasure chest with gold bars, chocolate coins, rock candy and pearl beading. Position lid on cake top. Attach lollipop sticks to lid with melted candy for support. Pipe melted candy along lid and chest seam to secure. Ice edge of cake board and immediately sprinkle with granulated brown sugar. Position treasure map. Cake serves 45.

*Combine Black, Brown and Red-Red for brown icing shown.

†Brand confectionery coating.

▼ Dynamic Dino!

Pans: 3-D Rubber Ducky, p. 159; Oval Set (2nd largest used), p. 153; Cooling Grid, p. 154

Tips: 3, 5, 16, p. 144-145

Colors:* Violet, Rose, Kelly Green, Leaf Green, Lemon Yellow, p. 134

Fondant: White Ready-To-Use Rolled Fondant (10 oz.), Gum-Tex™, p. 130; Rolling Pin, Roll & Cut Mat, p. 133

Recipe: Buttercream Icing, p. 116

Also: "Hidden" Pillars, p. 231; Rainbow Colors Lattice Candles, p. 191; Cake Boards, Fanci-Foil Wrap, p. 232; Dinosaur Party Set, p. 192; paring knife, waxed paper, pencil, hot glue gun, ruler, cornstarch

In advance: Make dinosaur spikes. Tint 4 oz. fondant violet; add ½ teaspoon Gum-Tex. Roll out ⅛ in. thick. Use paring knife to cut three 1¼ in. wide and four 1 in. wide triangles. Let dry on surface dusted with cornstarch. **Also:** Make legs. Cover 4 in. of hidden pillars with white fondant, leaving 2 in. at bottom to insert in cake; smooth seams. Cover fondant area on legs with tip 16 stars. Trace bottom of Rubber Ducky Pan on cake board and cut board to fit. Wrap board with foil and attach tops of legs to bottom of board with hot glue.

Bake 1-layer oval and Rubber Ducky cake (using firm-textured batter such as pound cake). Cut 2 cake boards to fit under dinosaur cake using Ducky pan as pattern; wrap with foil and position under cake. Trim 1 in. off top of tail and slightly round back of head. Fill space between cake bottom and board with icing. Build up icing on face with spatula to resemble a dinosaur. Pipe tip 5 dot eyes, nostrils and outline mouth. Cover cake with tip 16 stars. Insert 1 small and 3 large spikes in head and remaining small spikes in back. Ice oval cake smooth and prepare for Push-In Pillar Construction (p. 114). Insert hidden pillar legs into oval cake; position dinosaur cake on leg base, securing with icing. Insert candles. Pipe tip 16 pull-out grass on cake top, around candles and for bottom border. Print tip 3 message. Position toppers. Serves 27.

*Combine Violet with Rose for violet shown. Combine Kelly Green with Lemon Yellow for light green shown on dinosaur.

◀ He's Bolting for the Party!

Pans: 6, 8 x 2 in. Round, p. 153; Sports Ball Set, p. 161
Tips: 1A, 2A, 3, p. 144
Colors:* Royal Blue, Red-Red, Christmas Red, Violet, Rose, Leaf Green, Lemon Yellow, Orange, Black, p. 134
Fondant: White Ready-To-Use Rolled Fondant (34 oz.), Brush Set, p. 130; Easy-Glide Fondant Smoother, p. 131; Round Cut-Outs™, p. 132; Rolling Pin, Roll & Cut Mat, p. 133
Recipe: Buttercream Icing, p. 116
Also: Silly-Feet! Cake Stand, p. 192; Plastic and Wooden Dowel Rods, p. 231; 6 in. Cookie Treat Sticks, p. 163; Cake Circles, p. 232; Piping Gel, p. 135; knife, ruler, cornstarch

Bake and cool three 1-layer 6 in. and two 1-layer 8 in. rounds plus ½ Sports Ball. Set each round on a matching cake circle; stack Sport Ball half with 1 of the 6 in. rounds. Ice all smooth. Prepare all cakes for Stacked Construction (p. 114). Tint fondant as follows: 18 oz. lime; 6 oz. violet; 3 oz. blue; 3 oz. red; 3 oz. orange; 1 oz. green. Roll out fondant ¼ in. thick unless otherwise specified. Roll out lime ⅛ in. thick; cover plate portion of stand. Stack tiers on stand. Use wide end of tip 1A to cut 6 circles in each color for sides of 8 in. rounds. Attach with damp brush. Use narrow end of tip 1A to cut 24 circles for sides of 6 in. rounds; attach. Push a 12 in. plastic dowel rod through top 6 in. round for arms; cover exposed ends with ⅛ in. thick fondant. Roll out portions of violet fondant ¼ and ½ in. thick. Cut 5 x ½ in. wide strips for connectors; attach around arms with damp brush, using ¼ in. thick fondant for inner and outer connectors, ½ in. thick for center connectors. Use fondant to secure cookie sticks inside arms, leaving ½ in. exposed. Shape 1¾ in. balls of fondant into U-shaped hands; push onto cookie sticks. Using ⅛ in. thick fondant, cut a 20 x ¼ in. wide strip and attach around bottom of head; cut whites of eyes using medium round Cut-Out and attach. Using wide end of decorating tips, cut tip 3 pupils, tip 1A nose and tip 2A cheeks; attach. Cut a 4 x ¼ in. wide strip and attach for mouth. Cut cookie sticks to 4 in. long and insert into top and sides of head, leaving 1¾ in. exposed. Attach ¼ in. diameter logs around base of sticks. Attach 1½ in. fondant ball to top stick and 1¼ in. fondant balls to side sticks. Serves 44.

*Combine Violet with Rose for violet shown. Combine Leaf Green with Lemon Yellow for lime shade shown. Combine Red-Red with Christmas Red for red shown.

▶ Time for Launch!

Pans: Classic Wonder Mold, p. 156; 8 x 3,10 x 2 in. Round, p. 152; Jumbo Muffin, p. 146; Cookie Sheet, Cooling Grid, p. 163

Tips: 2, 3, 5, 6, 8, 10, 18, p. 144-145

Colors:* Royal Blue, Violet, Rose, Leaf Green, Lemon Yellow, Copper (for skin tone shown), Brown, Black, p. 134

Recipes: Buttercream Icing, Roll-Out Cookies, p. 116

Also: 2009 Pattern Book (Door, Window), p. 128; 101 Cookie Cutters Set, p. 164; 12 in. Decorator Preferred® Smooth Edge Plates (2), 3 in. Crystal-Look Pillars, p. 230; Decorating Comb, Cake Dividing Set, p. 137; Cake Circles, p. 232; Dowel Rods, p. 231; Cake Corer Tube, p. 229; 15 in. Angled and 9 in. Tapered Spatulas, p. 138; Cake Leveler, p. 140; candy-coated chocolates (mini, regular), spice drops (large, regular), curling ribbon (25 yards each red, yellow, orange); waxed paper, cornstarch, ruler, toothpicks, knife

For astronaut: Prepare cookie dough and roll out. Cut cookie using largest gingerbread boy cutter from set. Bake and cool cookie. Outline details with tip 3. Fill in with tip 5 (pat smooth with finger dipped in cornstarch). Add tip 3 dot and outline facial features; add tip 2 pull-out hair.

For spaceship: Bake and cool 10 x 2 in. round, four 8 x 3 in. rounds, 1 Wonder Mold and 4 jumbo cupcakes (use firm-textured batter such as pound cake). Trim 8 in. rounds to 2½ in. high; stack for 2 cakes 5 in. high. Trim bottom of Wonder Mold for 6 in. high top cone. Place all 4 cakes on matching cake circles. Prepare cakes for Stacked Construction (p. 114). Stack 8 in. rounds for 10 in. high capsule; ice smooth. Ice top cone smooth, adding icing to shape top. Place 10 in. round cake on 12 in. separator plate; ice cake and plate smooth. Divide top cone into 10 sections; mark lines to top. Cover lines with tip 18 outlines. Use patterns to mark door and windows on capsule; outline with tip 5. Fill in centers with zigzag motion; smooth with tapered spatula. Outline door and door windows with tip 6 and side windows with tip 8. Stack top cone, capsule and base. Using tip 10, add ball borders to base and capsule; pipe zigzag border on top cone.

Attach candies with icing. Use mini chocolates over door and around windows. Use regular chocolates for door knob and between divisions of top cone. Attach large spice drop on cone tip. Cut ¼ in. off bottom of large spice drops. Attach bottoms to zigzag of top cone; attach tops around base. Cut ⅓ off bottom of regular spice drops; attach tops under door. For exhaust cones, return jumbo cupcakes to pan and use corer tube to cut away centers; insert pillars. Set each cupcake on a same-size waxed paper circle; cut slit where plate feet will go. Ice and comb sides using large tooth edge of decorating comb. Set exhaust cones in position on bottom plate, feet side up. Position space capsule on pillars at party. Pipe tip 5 zigzag around edge of base plate; attach mini chocolates. Position curled ribbon and cookie. Cake serves 66, cupcakes and cookie each serve 1.

*Combine Violet with Rose for violet shown. Combine Leaf Green with Lemon Yellow for green shown.

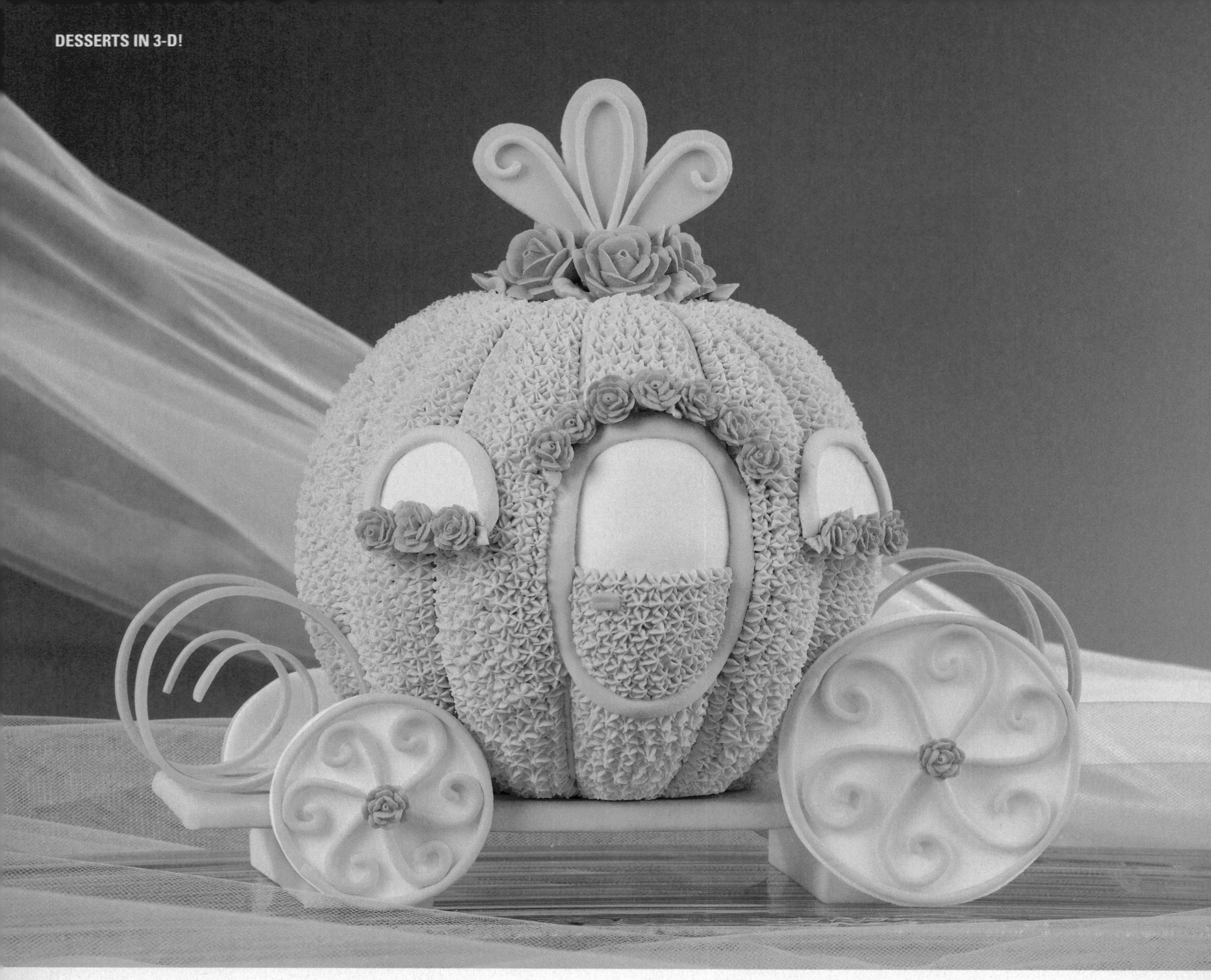

▲ Princess Coach

Pan: Dimensions® Large Pumpkin, p. 151

Tips: 4, 5, 8, 10, 16, 101s, 103, 349, 352, p. 144-145

Colors: Rose, Kelly Green, p. 134

Fondant: White Ready-To-Use Rolled Fondant (24 oz.), Brush Set, p. 130; Easy-Glide Fondant Smoother, Cutter/Embosser, p. 131; Rolling Pin, Roll & Cut Mat, Gum-Tex™, p. 133

Recipes: Buttercream, Royal Icings, p. 116

Also: 2009 Pattern Book (Wheels, Spirals, Door, Windows, Fleur-de Lis), p. 128; 101 Cookie Cutters Set, p. 164; Flower Nail No. 7, p. 137; Cake Boards, Fanci-Foil Wrap, p. 232; 4 in. Lollipop Sticks, p. 169; Meringue Powder, Piping Gel, p. 135; Parchment Triangles, p. 143; glue gun, 2 craft foam blocks (1 x 1 x 3½ in.), ruler, knife, tape, waxed paper, cornstarch, toothpicks

Several days in advance: Make roses (p. 119) using royal icing. Make 30 tip 101s roses with tip 5 bases, 6 tip 103 roses with tip 10 bases (make extras to allow for breakage); let dry. **Also:** Prepare base. Tint 12 oz. fondant rose; reserve 3 oz. for trims. Cut 2 boards 10 x 3¾ in. wide; tape together and wrap with foil. Roll out fondant ⅛ in. thick. Brush boards with piping gel and wrap with fondant; smooth and trim as needed. Wrap craft blocks with foil; cover with fondant. Position and attach blocks on bottom of board, 1½ in. from left and 1 in. from right, using glue gun. **And:** Use patterns to make wheels, spirals and fleur-de-lis. Add ¼ teaspoon Gum-Tex to reserved 3 oz. rose fondant and ½ teaspoon to 6 oz. white fondant. For wheels, roll out white fondant 3⁄16 in. thick. Using cutters from 101 Cookie Cutters Set, cut 2 large and 2 medium circles. Let dry 2 days. Outline rim and pipe spirals using patterns, royal icing and tip 5; attach tip 101s rose to center of each wheel. Let dry. For spirals on front and back of coach, trace patterns (2 large, 2 small) and tape to cake board; cover with waxed paper. Roll out rose fondant 3⁄16 in. thick. Cut ¼ x 14 in. strips. Set on sides and follow patterns to form spirals; trim as needed. Let dry 2 days. For fleur-de-lis, roll out rose fondant ⅛ in. thick and cut using pattern. Let dry 2 days. Using royal icing, attach 4 in. lollipop stick to back, leaving 2 in. exposed at bottom. Pipe loop and spirals using pattern and tip 5. Let dry.

Bake and cool cake using firm-textured batter such as pound cake. Trim off top stem and leaves. Center cake on prepared base. Use patterns to mark doors and windows on both sides. Outline and fill in with tip 4; smooth with finger dipped in cornstarch. Outline doors with tip 10, windows with tip 8, side pumpkin indentations with tip 4. Cover cake and door bottoms with tip 16 stars. Use icing to attach small roses under windows and over doors; add tip 349 leaves. Pipe tip 4 door handles. Insert fleur-de-lis on top and surround with large roses; pipe tip 352 leaves. Using royal icing, attach wheels and spirals to board. Let dry. Serves 12.

▼ Dream Dollhouse

Pans: Stand-Up House, p. 157; 9 x 5 in. Loaf, p. 154; Medium Non-Stick Cookie Pan, p. 150

Tips: 1, 3, 7, 13, 16, 103, 233, 348, p. 144-145

Colors:* Violet, Rose, Kelly Green, Lemon Yellow, Golden Yellow, Brown, Red-Red, Royal Blue, p. 134

Fondant: White Ready-To-Use Rolled Fondant (48 oz.), Primary and Neon Colors FoodWriter™ Edible Color Markers, Brush Set, p. 130; Cutter/Embosser, p. 131; Rolling Pin, Roll & Cut Mat, p. 133

Recipes: Buttercream, Royal Icings, p. 116

Also: 2009 Pattern Book (Ceiling, Side Wall, Back Wall, Upper Floor), p. 128; White Candy Melts®† (5 pks.), p. 166; Meringue Powder, p. 135; Cake Boards, Fanci-Foil Wrap, p. 232; Cake Leveler, p. 140; Parchment Triangles, p. 143; 12 x 20 x ½ in. foamcore board, knife, ruler, cornstarch, mini marshmallows, oval mini breath mints (2 pks.), ½ in. wide ribbon (64 in.), waxed paper

Several days in advance: Make royal icing flowers. Make 35 each in violet, pink and yellow using tip 13; add tip 1 dot centers. Make extras to allow for breakage and let dry. **Also:** Make candy shell and panels for back half of house. Brush melted candy over inside of house pan to make a 3-D candy shell ⅜ in. thick (p. 125); chill and repeat as needed. Refrigerate until completely set; unmold carefully. Use cookie sheet to mold a sheet of candy ¼ in. thick. Unmold and bring to room temperature. Use patterns and warm knife to cut upper floor of main house plus 2 each side wall, back wall and ceiling sections for kitchen and dining room (reverse pattern for 2nd piece) and a 1 x 6 in. rectangle. **And:** Make your furniture (p. 102-103).

Now let's build your dream house: Bake and cool house cake and loaf cake using firm-textured batter such as pound cake. Trim house to 2½ in. deep. Raise cake up slightly by attaching 1 x 6 in. candy strip underneath front side of house with melted candy. Attach candy house shell at backside of cake house using melted candy. Cut loaf cake to make 2 rectangles, 4½ x 2½ x 3 in. high. Attach one half on each side of cake house, lining up at front. Use melted candy to attach prepared candy panels to candy shell at back of house. Attach upper floor inside house candy shell. Attach back and side walls to house. Attach ceiling panels; let set.

For outside of house: Use toothpicks to mark details. Large windows at left, right and on both sides of house are 2 x 1½ in. high; shutters are ¾ x 1½ in. high. Ice smooth roof, decks, door and all window areas. Using tip 3, pipe drapes; outline and fill in shutters then overpipe for dimension (smooth top layer with finger dipped in cornstarch); pipe bead hearts on shutters. Use tip 7 to outline door and window, pipe dot doorknob. Cover house front and sides with tip 7 bricks; pat smooth. Pipe tip 3 zigzag over roof peak. Pipe tip 103 scallops on roof and eaves. Pipe tip 7 outline around decks; position upright mini mints every ¼ in. Pipe tip 7 outline over top of mints to complete railing. Use fondant to shape front steps; ice smooth. Pipe cobblestone walk with tip 7 balls (flatten with finger). Spatula ice grass areas. For bushes, line house and walkway with mini marshmallows; cover with tip 233 pull-out leaves. Pipe tip 16 pull-out star trees (work from bottom up). Attach flowers to bushes and under windows; trim with tip 349 leaves. Add ribbon around base board.

Position furniture inside and start the housewarming party! Serves 20.

*Combine Violet with Rose for violet shown. Combine Lemon Yellow with Golden Yellow for yellow shown. Combine Brown with Red-Red for brown shown.

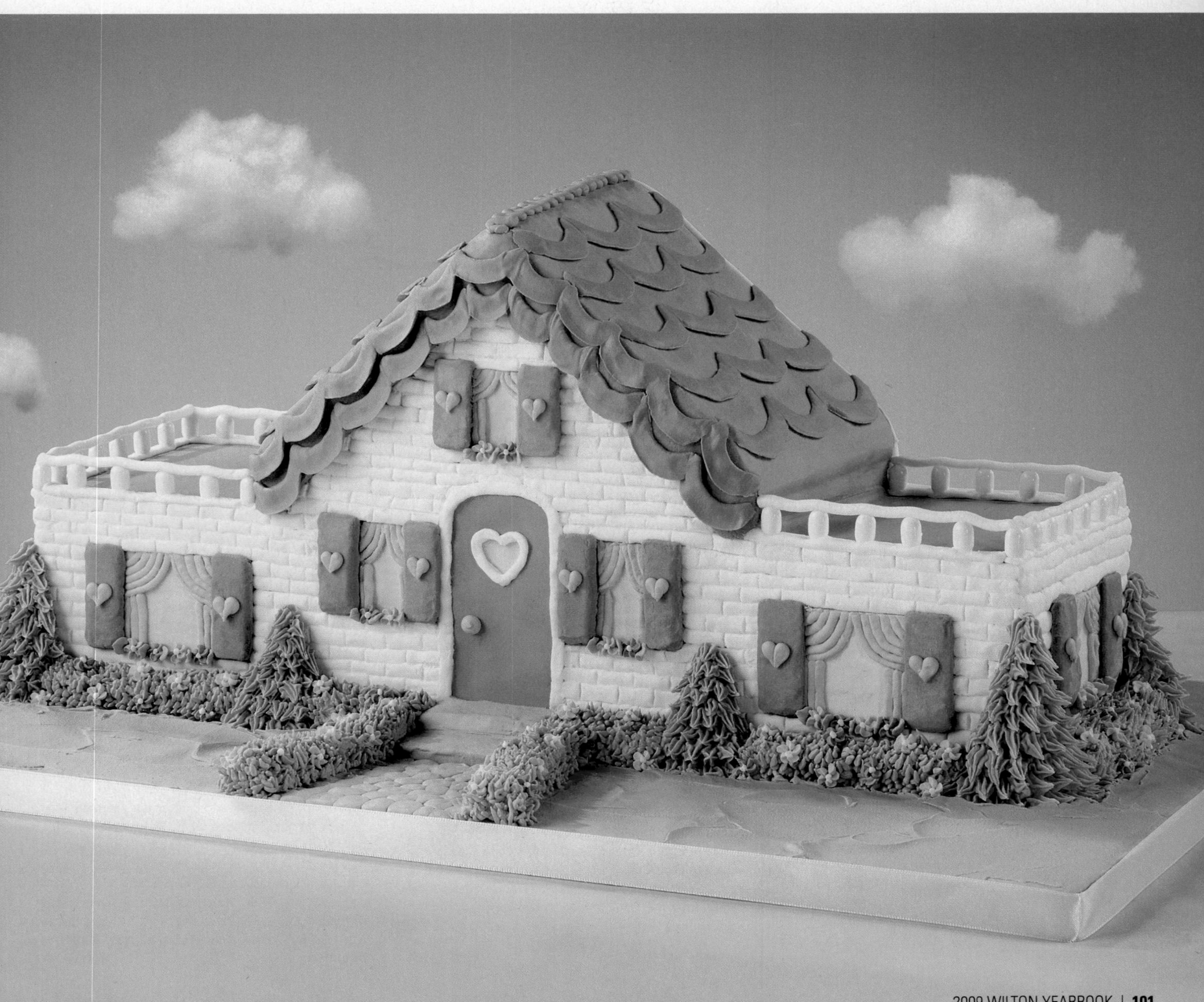

Surprise–it's an Open House!

Wait until the kids see your interior decorating! It's easy to furnish every room with colorful fondant pieces they'll be marveling at throughout the celebration. All the decorating details are below, so get ready to become the perfect homemaker!

For inside of house: Rooms are lined with fondant rolled ⅛ in. thick. Brush back with damp brush and attach. Ceilings are white, walls are assorted colors (pink, yellow, beige and blue), floors are brown (score lines with knife every ¼ in. for hardwood look). Add royal icing details. Use tip 3 to outline and pipe in windows: 1 x 1 in. high in bedroom; 1 x 1¼ in. high in living room; 1⅜ x 1¼ in. high in kitchen and dining room; 1 x 1¼ in. high for kitchen and dining room side walls. Smooth with finger dipped in cornstarch. Pipe tip 3 drapes. Use tip 3 to outline and pipe in door; smooth with finger. Use tip 3 to outline door frame and pipe dot door knob and bead heart window (flatten with finger). Attach strips of fondant to outside edges to hide seams.

Furnish your house in a rainbow of fondant colors! Tint fondant as follows: 4 oz. each pink, yellow, ivory, light brown; 6 oz. each dark brown, blue. Make 4 legs for each table and chair: ⅜ in. high for living room table; ⅝ in. high for dining room table; ⅜ in. high for each dining chair. Roll a ¼ in. high base for bedroom lamp. Let dry.

Time to tour the house! Let's start in the bedroom: Shape a 1½ x 2 x ¾ in. high block for bed. Roll out pink fondant ⅛ in. thick; cut a 2½ in. square for bedspread and attach. Cut a 1¾ x ¼ x 1⅛ in. high block for headboard; attach. Shape and attach 2 pillows, ⅝ x ⅜ x ¼ in. Shape a ⅞ x ½ x1 in. high block for dresser and a ⅝ x ½ x ½ in. high block for nightstand. Use knife to score lines for drawers. Roll a ¼ in. high vase. Roll a ¾ in. diameter ball for lamp shade; taper top and flatten.

Now move to the kitchen: Shape a 1 x ⅝ x 1¾ in. high refrigerator, ⅞ x ¾ x ¾ in. high stove base (attach a thin ⅞ in. square to back), 2 x ⅝ x ¾ in. high back cabinets, 1⅛ x ¼ x ¾ in. high floor cabinets and 1 x ⅛ x 1 in. high wall cabinets (for back and side). Use knife to score lines for doors and drawers. Roll small amount of blue 1⁄16 in. thick. Cut an L-shaped countertop.

Check out the living room: Shape 1¾ x1¾ in. block that tapers from ½ to ¼ in. thick; bend into L-shaped sofa and score lines for cushions. Shape a ⅞ x 1⅝ in. block that tapers from ½ to ¼ in. thick; bend into L-shaped chair and score lines for cushions. Shape a ½ x ⅝ x ¼ in. high block for ottoman; score lines for cushion. Cut a 1 x ¾ x ⅛ in. thick table top; attach legs. Roll small amount of fondant 1⁄16 in. thick. Cut 1¼ x ⅞ in. high picture frames with smaller white overlays; draw pictures using FoodWriters.

Enter the dining room: Roll out brown fondant ⅛ in. thick. Cut a 1 x ¾ in. rectangle for table top; attach legs with royal icing. Cut a ⅞ x 1⅝ in. rectangle for each chair (make extras if company is expected!). Bend to shape; attach legs. Cut ½ x ⅞ in. high picture frames with smaller white overlays; if desired, paint pictures using FoodWriters. Roll a ¾ in. ball; flatten slightly and indent center for vase.

Add royal icing details: Use tip 1 to pipe dot knobs on bedroom furniture, kitchen cabinets and stove; pipe outline stove handle and burners; pipe lines on lamp shade. Use tip 3 to pipe refrigerator handles. Attach lamp base to nightstand and shade to base. Attach bedroom vase to dresser and drop flower to top. Add drop flowers to dining room vase; pipe tip 349 leaves.

◀ Springtime Baskets

Pan: Dimensions® Multi-Cavity Mini Flower Basket, p. 151

Tips: 2, 7, 102, 352, p. 144-145

Colors: Rose, Kelly Green, Lemon Yellow, p. 134

Fondant: White Ready-To-Use Rolled Fondant (4 oz. for each treat), Gum-Tex™, p. 130

Recipes: Buttercream, Royal Icings, p. 116

Also: Flower Former Set, Flower Nail No. 7, p. 137; Meringue Powder, p. 135; Cake Board, p. 232; knife, waxed paper, ruler, cornstarch

In advance: Use tip 102 and royal icing to make 45-50 wild roses (p. 120) for each basket. Add tip 2 dot centers. Make extras to allow for breakage and let dry on medium flower formers. **Also:** Make fondant rope handle. Add ½ teaspoon Gum-Tex to 4 oz. white fondant. Roll fondant into two ¼ x 12 in. long pieces. Lay pieces together side by side and press together to join at one end. Holding the joined end stationary, twist other end to form rope. Form a curved shape 3 x 3¼ in. wide and let dry on board dusted with cornstarch.

Bake and cool cakes. Trim off ribbon and bow from cakes. Cover bottom half of cake with tip 7 basketweave. Attach top of cake with icing. Lightly ice top half of cake. Attach handle to cake with icing. Attach flowers to cake with icing and add tip 352 leaves. Each serves 1.

▶ A Shower for Flowers

Pan: Jumbo Muffin, p. 146

Tips: 3, 5, 352, p. 144-145

Colors: Rose, Leaf Green, Lemon Yellow, p. 134

Fondant: White Ready-To-Use Rolled Fondant (5 oz. for each treat), Brush Set, p. 130; Easy-Glide Fondant Smoother, Quick Ease Roller, p. 131; Rolling Pin, Roll & Cut Mat, Gum-Tex™, p. 133

Recipes: Buttercream Icing, p. 116; Thinned Fondant Adhesive, p. 117

Also: 4 in. Lollipop Sticks, p. 169; sugar cone, cornstarch, waxed paper, ruler, knife

In advance: Make handles and spout. For each treat, add ½ teaspoon Gum-Tex to 2 oz. fondant. For handles, roll ¼ in. diameter logs. Cut a 6 in. section for top handle, a 4 in. section for side handle. Using bottom of pan as a guide, bend into C-shapes. For spout, trim ½ in. off tip of sugar cone, then cut cone to 2 in. long, angling at wide opening. Fill cone with fondant and insert lollipop stick. Roll out portion of fondant ⅛ in. thick. Cut a 2 x 4 in. section and wrap around cone, smoothing with hands. Shape a 1 in. diameter circle, ¼ in. thick; brush with damp brush and attach to top of spout. Let all pieces dry on waxed paper-covered board dusted with cornstarch.

Bake and cool cupcakes. Lightly ice with buttercream. Roll out fondant ⅛ in. thick. Cover cakes with fondant and smooth with Fondant Smoother; trim bottom as needed. Use tip 5 to pipe bead flower with dot center (flatten slightly); add tip 352 leaves. Pipe tip 3 dots on top border. Attach handles with Fondant Adhesive. Insert spout. Each serves 1.

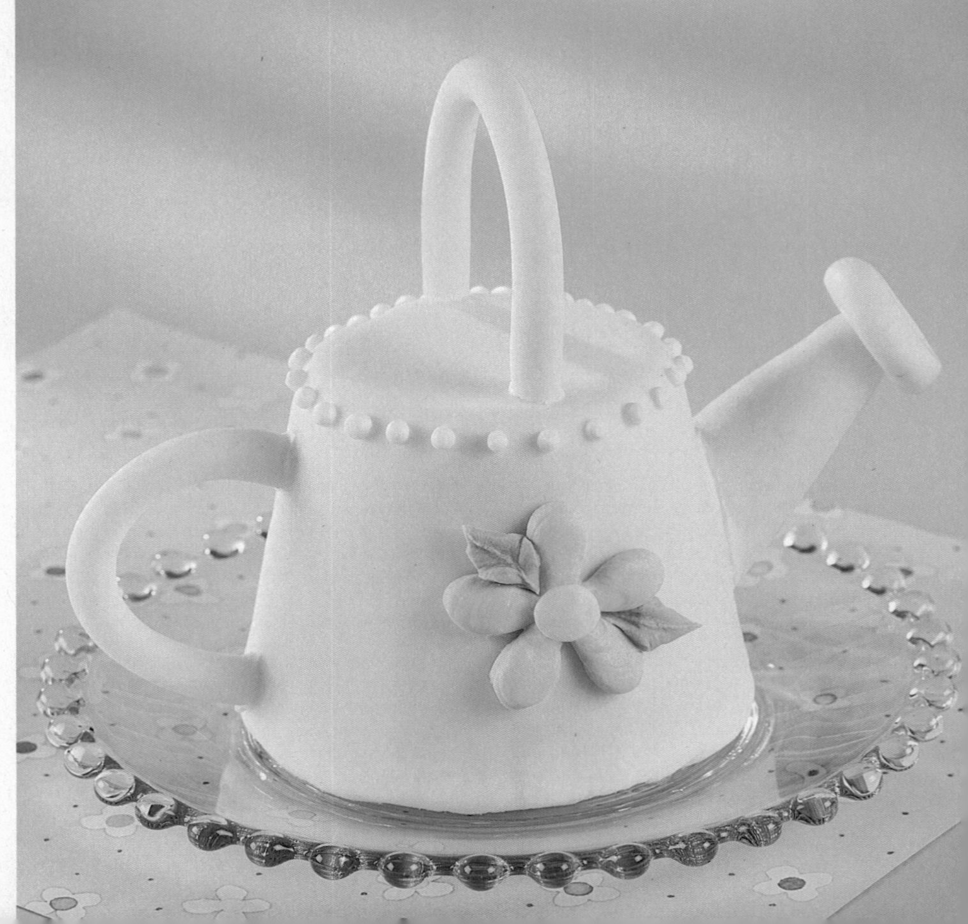

▶ Tea Cozy

Pans: 8 x 3 in. Round, p. 152; Soccer Ball, p. 161

Tips: 1A, 2, 2D, p. 144

Colors:* Rose, Violet, p. 134

Fondant/Gum Paste: White Ready-To-Use Rolled Fondant (80 oz.), p. 130; Easy-Glide Fondant Smoother, Fondant/Gum Paste Tool Set, Fondant Shaping Foam, Brush Set, Cutter/Embosser, p. 131; Round Cut-Outs™, p. 132; Rolling Pin, Roll & Cut Mat, Ready-To-Use Gum Paste, p. 133

Recipe: Buttercream Icing, p. 116

Also: 2009 Pattern Book (Umbrella Panel, Chair Back & Legs), p. 128; White Candy Melts®†, p. 166; "Hidden" Pillars, p. 231; Tall Tier Cake Stand (8, 14 in. plates, two 6½ in. columns, top nut and bottom bolt), Glue-On Plate Legs (6), Cake Corer Tube, p. 229; Circle Metal Cutter, p. 165; Piping Gel, p. 135; Cake Circles, p. 232; 4 in. Lollipop Sticks, p. 169; glue for plastic, cornstarch, knife, craft knife, ruler

Several days in advance: Make chairs (p. 124). **Also:** Make tea set. Tint 1 oz. fondant rose. Roll a portion very thin. Cut saucers with wide end of tip 1A, cups with wide end of tip 2D (shape with ball tool on thick foam). Let dry on cornstarch-dusted surface for 2 days. **And:** Prepare base plate. Glue 6 legs onto bottom of 14 in. plate; let dry. Tint 24 oz. fondant violet; roll out ⅛ in. thick. Mark and cut out center of 14 in. circle for tall tier column opening. Brush circle with piping gel; cover with fondant. Position on stand.

Bake and cool soccer ball and 8 x 3 in. round cake. Trim soccer ball to 3¼ in. Prepare cakes for rolled fondant (p. 117). Prepare 8 in. cake for Center Column Construction (p. 115) on two 8 in. boards wrapped with foil. Cover with a 14 in. circle of fondant, letting fondant hang over sides. Cut hidden pillars into six 2 in. lengths. Attach with melted candy around center column on fondant covered board. Position cake over column to rest on hidden pillars. Add 6½ in. column. Place soccer ball cake on 8½ in. foil-wrapped board with center hole cut out for top nut. Tint 12 oz. fondant rose. Roll out rose and 12 oz. white fondant ⅛ in. thick. Use pattern to cut 4 white and 4 rose panels; position on soccer ball cake. Pipe tip 2 dot lace on rose panels. Roll a small ball of fondant and attach to umbrella top with damp brush. Roll ¼ in. diameter rope of fondant and attach around column where it meets the table.

At reception: Position 8 in. plate and top nut to secure stand; position umbrella cake. Position cups and saucers on table. Position chairs around table. Serves 26.

*Combine Violet with Rose for violet shown.

†Brand confectionery coating.

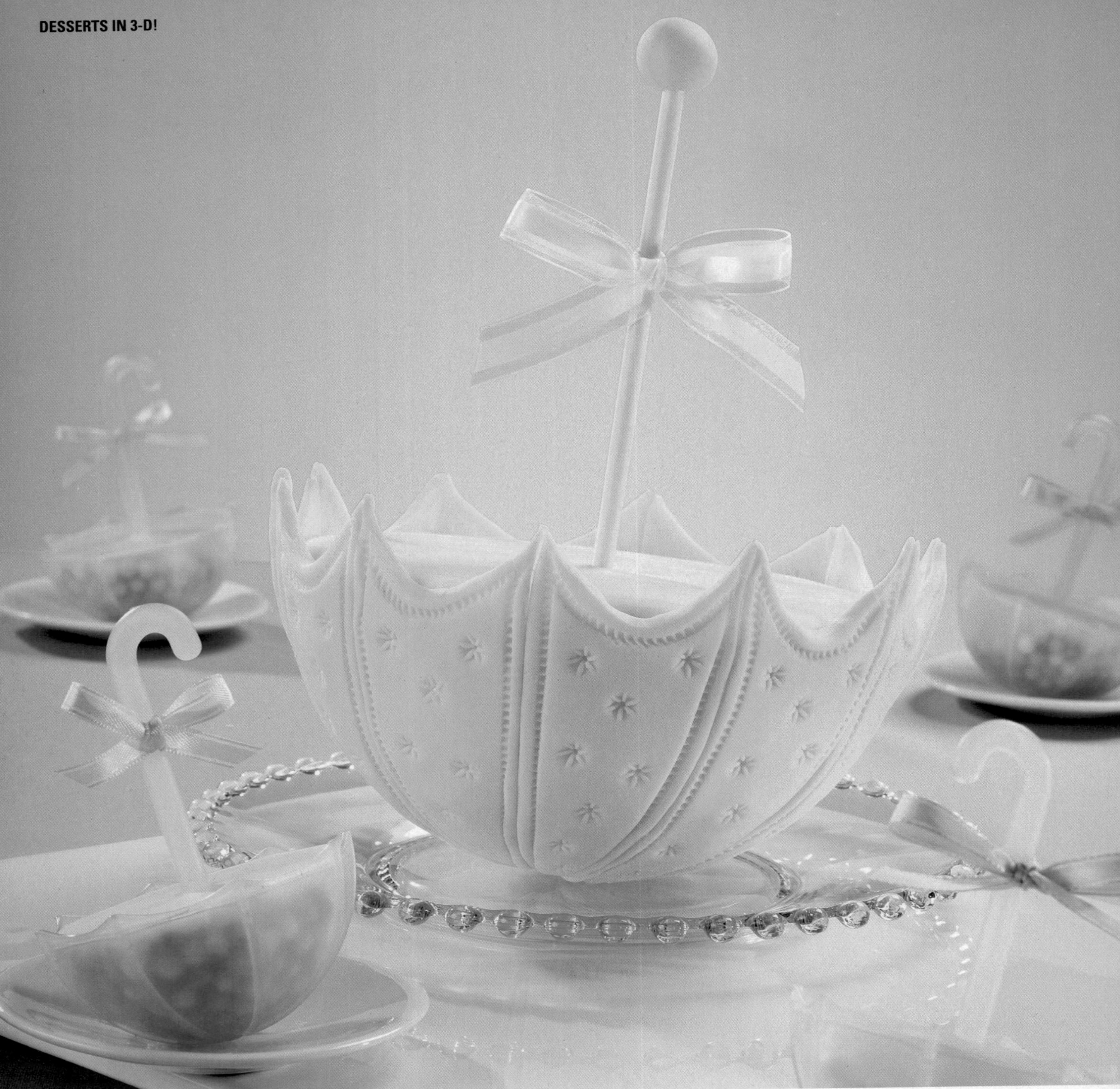

▲ Do Showers in Style!

Pan: Sports Ball Set, p. 161

Tip: 131, p. 144

Color: Lemon Yellow, p. 134

Fondant: White Ready-To-Use Rolled Fondant (12 oz.), Brush Set, p. 130; Cutter/Embosser, p. 131; Gum-Tex™, Rolling Pin, Roll & Cut Mat, p. 133

Recipes: Buttercream Icing, p. 116

Also: 2009 Pattern Book (Umbrella Panel), p. 128; White Candy Melts®† (1 pk.), p. 166; Cake Dividing Set, p. 137; 8 in. Cookie Treat Sticks, p. 163; Umbrella Baby Favor Kit, p. 236; Pastel Pearls, p. 237; ½ in. wide ribbon (18 in.), knife, ruler, toothpicks, waxed paper, 4 to 5 in. diameter container

Bake and cool cake using ½ of Sports Ball pan. Cover flat side with melted candy. Before candy hardens, make a small hole in center where handle will go. Refrigerate until firm.

Lightly ice remainder of cake with buttercream. Use Dividing Wheel to divide ball into 10ths. Set on waxed paper-covered container, candy side down. Tint fondant yellow; add ½ teaspoon Gum-Tex to 12 oz. of fondant. Roll out ⅛ in. thick. Use pattern to cut 10 panels for each cake. Use ridged wheel with Cutter/Embosser to imprint design ⅛ in. from edges. Imprint floral designs with tip 131. Attach panels to cake, beginning at top, with points extending beyond edge of cake; smooth lightly. Fill umbrella favor containers with Pastel Pearls; assemble and position around cake. Roll a ¾ in. ball of fondant; insert Cookie Stick for handle. Insert in cake; tie on ribbon. Each serves 6.

†Brand confectionery coating.

▶ A Sweet Stroller

Pans: Oval Pan Set (2nd smallest and largest used), p. 153; 3-D Egg, p. 208

Tips: 2, 14, 17, 127, 127D, 352, p. 144-145

Colors: Golden Yellow, Leaf Green, p. 134

Fondant: White Ready-To-Use Rolled Fondant (8 oz.), p. 130; Rolling Pin, Roll & Cut Mat, Gum-Tex™, p. 133; Floral Collection Flower Making Set, p. 137

Recipes: Buttercream, Royal Icings, p. 116

Also: Crystal-Clear Cake Divider Set (7½ in. Twist Legs, 8 in. Plate), p. 228; Round Comfort Grip™ Cutter, p. 165; Candy Melting Plate, p. 168; Meringue Powder, p. 135; Dowel Rods, p. 231; Cake Boards, Fanci-Foil Wrap, p. 232; ¼ in. thick foamcore board, cornstarch, ruler, knife, ½ in. wide white ribbon (2 ft. long)

In advance: Make flowers. Add ½ teaspoon Gum-Tex to 8 oz. fondant; roll out 1⁄16 in. thick. Cut 35 flowers using pansy cutter from Flower Making Set. Place on thick foam and cup centers using dogbone tool. Let dry in Candy Melting Plate dusted with cornstarch. Add tip 2 dot centers with royal icing. Let dry. **Also:** Make wheels. Roll out remaining fondant ⅛ in. thick. Cut 8 rounds for wheels using Comfort Grip cutter. Let dry 24 hours on cornstarch-dusted board. Decorate with royal icing. Divide wheel into 8ths; pipe spokes with tip 14 outlines. Add tip 14 shell border. Attach flower to center. Let dry. **And:** Prepare foamcore board. Also cut 3 cake boards to fit 10¾ x 7⅞ in. oval cake with ¾ in. clearance on all sides. Tape together and wrap with foil.

Bake and cool 1-layer large oval, 2-layer smaller oval; bake and cool ½ egg cake using firm-textured batter such as pound cake. Position 2-layer oval on prepared board; ice smooth. Add dowel rods for support where egg cake will sit. Trim 2½ in. off narrow end of egg cake; position on oval for hood. Ice hood smooth, adding icing as needed for rounded shape. Pipe 2 rows of tip 127 ruffles around hood; pipe 3 rows of tip 127D ruffles around sides (work from bottom up). Add tip 14 shell borders on hood and around oval. Ice large oval smooth. Pipe tip 17 shell top and bottom borders. Use icing to attach flowers. Pipe tip 352 leaves. Make 2 bows using ribbon and attach to hood and stroller with icing. At party, use 8 in. plate to mark legs; push in pillars. Use icing to attach 2 wheels to each pillar. Position plate on pillars; attach stroller cake to plate with icing. Serves 48.

▲ Snuggly Warm

Pan: Stand-Up Cuddly Bear Set, p. 158

Tips: 4, 6, 16, p. 144-145

Colors: Copper (for skin tone shown), Royal Blue, Rose, Kelly Green, Lemon Yellow, Black, p. 134

Fondant: White Ready-To-Use Rolled Fondant (24 oz.), Brush Set, p. 130; Rolling Pin, Roll & Cut Mat, p. 133

Recipe: Buttercream Icing, p. 116

Also: Mini Geometric Crinkle Cookie Cutters (square used), p. 165; Cake Board, Fanci-Foil Wrap, p. 232

Bake and cool cake using firm-textured batter such as pound cake. Position on prepared board. Trim off ears. Build up ear shapes with tip 16 stars. Pipe tip 4 string mouth and dot eyes (smooth with finger dipped in cornstarch). Cover head, body, diaper, right arm and bottoms of feet with tip 16 stars; pipe tip 6 dot toes. Overpipe tip 16 star nose and cheeks. Tint 2 oz. fondant each: rose, blue, yellow and green. Roll out ⅛ in. thick and use square crinkle cutter to cut 7 squares of each color. Cover squares with plastic wrap or place in plastic bag until ready to use. Roll out white fondant ⅛ in. thick and cut into 10 in. x 15 in. rectangle for blanket. Position alternating color fondant squares on blanket and attach with damp brush. Drape blanket over left leg and arm area and across in front of right leg. Trim as needed to fit. Overpipe left arm and hand with tip 16 stars. Serves 12.

▶ Getting His Bearings

Pans: 6, 10 x 2 in. Square, p. 153
Tips: 1A, 2A, 12, p. 144
Colors*: Brown, Red-Red, Lemon Yellow, Golden Yellow, Royal Blue, Rose, Kelly Green, Black, p. 134
Fondant: White Ready-To-Use Rolled Fondant (36 oz.), Fine Tip Neon Colors FoodWriter™ Edible Color Markers, Brush Set, p. 130; Cutter/Embosser, p. 131; Rolling Pin, Roll & Cut Mat, p. 133
Topper: Baby Face Topper, p. 235
Recipe: Buttercream Icing, p. 116
Also: 101 Cookie Cutters Set, p. 164; 2 in. and 2½ in. Globe Pillar and Base Sets, p. 228; 6 in. Decorator Preferred® Square Plate, p. 230; Cake Boards, Fanci-Foil Wrap, p. 232; Piping Gel, p. 135; ruler, knife, toothpicks

In advance: Tint 16 oz. fondant as follows: 12 oz. brown, 2 oz. light brown, 1 oz. black; reserve 1 oz. white. Make bears (p. 124).

Bake and cool 3-layer cakes using firm-textured batter such as pound cake (use three 2 in. high layers; trim 1 layer to 1 in. high to create 5 in. high cakes). Use knife to trim sides of 6 in. cake to create a 5 x 5 in. square. Ice cakes smooth and prepare for Globe Pillar Set Construction (p. 115).

Tint 20 oz. fondant as follows: 8 oz. yellow, 4 oz. green, 4 oz. rose, 4 oz. blue. Roll out ⅛ in. thick. Cut 10 each ¾ x 5 in. and ¾ x 3½ in. yellow strips. Attach to top and side edges of 5 in. cake with dots of icing. Divide 10 in. cake top and sides into 5 in. squares. Mark pillar placement on top of 10 in. cake using 6 in. square plate. Cut 6 each ¾ x 5 in. and ¾ x 3½ in. strips in each color; attach to cake top and side edges as for 5 in. cake. Use cutters from set to cut 2 each B, A, B, Y, small heart and small star in assorted colors; cut 1 medium circle to place under baby topper. Attach all with icing. Insert pillars into 10 in. cake over marked areas and position bears. Use remaining fondant colors to cut 2 triangles (½ x 1 in.) and a tip 12 circle for each bow tie. Attach to bears with damp brush.

At party: Position 5 in. cake and plate. Position baby topper. Serves 42.

*Combine Brown with Red-Red for dark brown shown. Combine Lemon Yellow with Golden Yellow for yellow shown.

▼ Block Party

Candy: Peanut Butter, Light Cocoa Candy Melts®†, p. 166; Baby 2-Pack Candy Mold Set, p. 167
Also: Baby Blocks Containers, p. 236; Mini Pacifiers Candy, p. 237; Parchment Triangles, p. 143

Mold bear candies using melted candy. Refrigerate until set then unmold. Pipe on features with melted candy in cut parchment bag. For open blocks, fill with candy and position bear. For closed blocks, fill with candy and replace lid; attach bear to lid with melted candy. Each serves 1.

†Brand confectionery coating.

Step-By-Step

Decorating Guide

Decorating help starts here! Whatever cake you want to make from this Yearbook, you'll find out how to make it happen on the following pages. Whether you're creating a cake for the first time or need a quick brush-up on a technique, it's easy when you use this handy guide as you decorate.

Want to learn more?

Find Wilton Cake Decorating Classes in your area or register for The Wilton School in Darien, Illinois on line at **www.wilton.com**. Our website is also a great place to explore decorating techniques, find recipes and chat with other decorators. Visit us regularly!

Cake Preparation

Think of your cake as the canvas on which you will create beautiful icing decorations. To achieve the masterpiece you want, it is essential that your canvas be smooth and free of crumbs. These steps for preparing and icing your cake will result in the perfect decorating surface essential for your work of art.

BAKING THE CAKE

Follow recipe directions for specific baking instructions and recommended batter amounts for the pan size you choose. Prepare the pan by generously greasing the inside using a pastry brush or paper towel and solid vegetable shortening. For best results, do not use butter, margarine or liquid vegetable oil. Spread the shortening so that all indentations are covered. Sprinkle about 2 Tablespoons of flour inside the pan and shake so that the flour covers all greased surfaces. Turn pan upside down and tap lightly to remove excess flour. If any uncovered spots remain, touch up with shortening and flour. Or use Bake Easy™ Non-Stick Spray or Cake Release (p. 140) to coat the pan—no grease or flour needed. Pour batter into pan and place in pre-heated oven.

After cake has baked the specified time, remove it from the oven and let it cool in the pan on a cake rack for 10 minutes. Run a thin knife between the cake and side of the pan. Unmold from pan by placing cooling rack against cake and turning both cooling rack and pan over. Lift pan off carefully. Cool at least one hour and brush off loose crumbs prior to icing.

CUTTING AND WRAPPING A CAKE BOARD

For round, square and sheet cakes, you don't need to cut a cake board. Simply buy a ready-made board that is 2 in. larger than your cake. (For example, if the cake is 8 in. diameter, buy a 10 in. round board.) For shaped cakes, cut a board to fit. Turn pan upside down and trace outline onto your cake board. Cut board with a craft knife, leaving 1 in. extra around outline.

To wrap, trace your cut board onto Fanci-Foil, making the outline 3-4 in. larger than the board. Cut Fanci-Foil along the outline. Place your board, white side down, on top of your cut foil. Cut deep slits at several points along foil edge, creating tabs of foil to wrap neatly around the board. Secure foil tabs to the board with tape.

LEVELING THE CAKE

After the cake has cooled at least one hour, you'll need to level the top of the cake. This can be done using a serrated knife or the Cake Leveler (p. 140).

Using a Serrated Knife

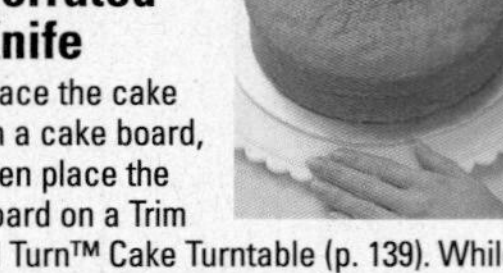

Place the cake on a cake board, then place the board on a Trim 'N Turn™ Cake Turntable (p. 139). While slowly rotating the turntable, move the knife back and forth across the top of cake in a sawing motion to remove the crown. Try to keep knife level as you cut.

Using the Wilton Cake Leveler

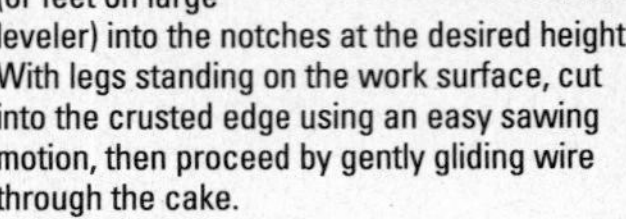

Position the ends of the cutting wire (or feet on large leveler) into the notches at the desired height. With legs standing on the work surface, cut into the crusted edge using an easy sawing motion, then proceed by gently gliding wire through the cake.

TORTING THE CAKE

Torting adds extra height, drama and taste to the cake when the layers are filled with icing, pudding or fruit filling. A serrated knife or the Cake Leveler may be used to cut a cake into multiple layers.

Using a Serrated Knife

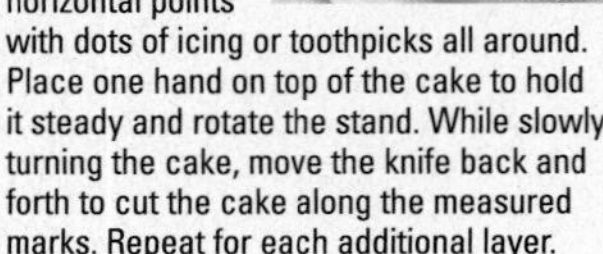

Divide cake sides and mark equal horizontal points with dots of icing or toothpicks all around. Place one hand on top of the cake to hold it steady and rotate the stand. While slowly turning the cake, move the knife back and forth to cut the cake along the measured marks. Repeat for each additional layer.

Using the Cake Leveler

Torting is easily accomplished with the Cake Leveler. Simply follow the same directions as for leveling.

Separating the Layers

Carefully slide the top torted layer onto a cake board to keep it rigid and safe from breakage. Repeat for each additional layer.

FILLING THE LAYERS

Fill a decorating bag with medium consistency icing and use a large round tip, like tip 12. Or simply use the coupler without mounting a tip.

Starting with the bottom layer, leveled side up, create a dam of icing just inside the edge of the cake (about 3/4 in. high and 1/4 in. from the outside edge). Fill with icing, preserves or pudding. Place next layer on top, level; repeat. Finish with top layer leveled side down.

ICING THE CAKE

For better results, use a revolving turntable like professional decorators do…see our Trim 'N Turn™ Cake Turntables on p. 139.

Using a Spatula

The trick to keeping crumbs out of your icing is gliding your spatula on the icing—*never allow it to touch the surface of the cake.* Place a large amount of thin consistency icing on the center of the cake.

Spread icing across the top, pushing toward edges. Smooth the top using the edge of the spatula.

Sweep the edge of the spatula from the rim of the cake to its center then lift it off and remove excess icing.

Cover the sides with icing. Smooth sides by holding the spatula upright with the edge against the icing and slowly spinning the turntable without lifting the spatula from the icing surface. Return excess icing to the bowl and repeat until sides are smooth.

Rotate the cake slightly and repeat the procedure, starting from a new point on the rim until you have covered the entire top surface. Smooth the center of the cake by leveling the icing with the edge of your spatula. For easier smoothing, it may help to dip the spatula into hot water, wipe dry and glide it across the entire surface. Set the cake aside and allow the icing to crust over for at least 15 minutes before decorating. At that point you may also lay Non-Stick Parchment Paper (p. 140) on the iced cake top and gently smooth with the palm of your hand.

Using a Decorating Tip

Trim a 16 in. Featherweight bag to fit tip 789. Fill bag half full with icing. Hold bag at 45° angle and lightly press tip against cake. Squeeze a ribbon of icing in a continuous spiral motion to cover cake top, with last ribbon forcing icing over edge of cake top.

To ice the sides, squeeze icing as you turn the cake slowly. Repeat the process until the entire cake side is covered.

Smooth sides and top with spatula, same as above.

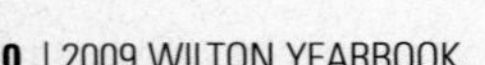

Icing Basics

In this section, we've listed general descriptions of icings, their uses, qualities and consistencies. Use this information to determine the right icing for your cake. Refer to our recipes for homemade icings (p. 116) along with color instructions below, to create the look and taste you want.

ICING USAGE GUIDE

Icing Type	Flavor/Description	Consistency	Best Used For...	Coloring	Storage/Freshness	Special Information
Buttercream (Wilton Mix or homemade)	Sweet, buttery flavor. Tastes/looks great for most decorating.	Thin-to-stiff depending on amount of corn syrup or sugar added (sugar stiffens).	Icing cakes smooth. Borders, writing, flowers, decorations.	Yields all colors. Most deepen upon setting. Let set 2-3 hours for deep color. Some may fade in bright light.	Can be refrigerated in airtight container for 2 weeks. Iced cake stores at room temperature for 2-3 days.	Flowers remain soft enough to be cut with a knife.
Snow-White Buttercream (homemade)	Sweet, almond flavor. Ideal for wedding cakes.	Thin-to-stiff depending on amount of corn syrup or sugar added (sugar stiffens).	Icing cakes smooth. Borders, writing, flowers, decorations.	Yields truer colors due to pure white base color. Creates deep colors. Most colors deepen upon setting.	Can be refrigerated in airtight container for 2 weeks. Iced cake stores at room temperature for 2-3 days.	Air-dried flowers have translucent look. Flowers remain soft enough to be cut with knife.
Wilton Ready-To-Use Decorator White (4½ lb. tub)	Sweet, vanilla flavor. Convenient, ready-to-spread icing. Pure white color ideal for tinting.	Thin-to-medium. No need to thin for spreading.	Spreading on cakes right from the can. Piping stars, shells, messages and more.	Yields truer colors due to pure white base color. Creates deep colors. Most colors deepen upon setting.	Leftover icing can be refrigerated for 2 weeks. Iced cake stores at room temperature for 2-3 days.	Available for purchase through Wilton Yearbook, at www.wilton.com or any authorized Wilton retailer.
Wilton Ready-To-Use Decorator White (1 lb. can)	Sweet, vanilla flavor. Convenient, ready-to-spread icing. Pure white color ideal for tinting.	Stiff. Make roses right from the can.	Shells, stars, flowers—use from container. Icing cakes, writing, leaves—thin with milk, water or corn syrup.	Yields truer colors due to pure white base color. Creates deep colors. Most colors deepen upon setting.	Leftover icing can be refrigerated for 2 weeks. Iced cake stores at room temperature for 2-3 days.	Available for purchase through Wilton Yearbook, at www.wilton.com or any authorized Wilton retailer.
Wilton Ready-To-Use Decorator Chocolate (1 lb. can)	Sweet chocolate flavor. Convenient ready-to-spread icing.	Stiff. Make roses right from the can.	Shells, stars, flowers—use from container. Icing cakes, writing, leaves—thin with milk, water or corn syrup.	Recommended when black or brown icing is needed. Add a little black icing color to chocolate for a better tasting black icing.	Leftover icing can be refrigerated for 2 weeks. Iced cake stores at room temperature for 2-3 days.	Available for purchase through Wilton Yearbook, at www.wilton.com or any authorized Wilton retailer.
Royal (made with Wilton Meringue Powder)	Very sweet flavor. Dries candy-hard for lasting decorations.	Thin-to-stiff, depending on the amount of water added.	Flower making, figure piping, making flowers on wires. Decorating cookies and gingerbread houses.	Yields deep colors. Some colors may fade in bright light. Requires more icing color than buttercream to achieve the same intensity.	Icing can be stored in airtight, grease-free container at room temperature for 2 weeks. Air-dried decorations last for months.	Bowls and utensils must be grease-free. Cover icing with damp cloth to prevent crusting.
Rolled Fondant (homemade or Wilton Ready-To-Use Rolled Fondant)	Covers cakes with a perfectly smooth, satiny surface. Easy and fast to use. Knead in flavor of your choice.	Dough-like. Fondant Is rolled out before being applied to cake. Stays semi-soft on cake.	Any firm-textured cake, pound cake or fruit cake. Cutting, molding and modeling decorations.	White yields pastels to deep colors. Wilton pre-colored fondant is also available in Multi Packs for fondant decorations in a variety of colors.	Excess can be stored 2 months in an airtight container. Do not refrigerate or freeze. Iced cake stores at room temperature for 3-4 days.	Prior to applying fondant, cake should be lightly covered with a glaze or buttercream icing to seal in freshness and moisture.
Whipped Icing Mix (Wilton Mix)	Light, delicate vanilla flavor. Holds shape like no other mix. **For chocolate icing**, add ½ cup of sifted cocoa powder.	Velvety, perfect for stars, roses, borders, garlands and writing.	Icing cakes. Most decorations. Toppings on pies, puddings, tarts and more.	Yields any color.	Can be refrigerated in airtight container. Iced cake stores at room temperature for 2-3 days.	Exclusive Wilton formula. Available for purchase through Wilton Yearbook, at www.wilton.com or any authorized Wilton retailer.
Fluffy Boiled Icing (homemade)	Marshmallow-like flavor. 100% fat-free.	Very fluffy. Sets quickly.	Icing cakes smooth and fluffy. Borders, figure piping, writing, stringwork.	Yields pastels to deep colors.	Use immediately. Iced cake can be stored at room temperature.	Serve within 24 hours.
Stabilized Whipped Cream (homemade)	Creamy, delicate sweetness.	Light, thin-to-medium.	All cakes but especially those decorated with fruits. Borders, large tip work, writing.	Yields pastels only.	Use immediately. Iced cake must be refrigerated.	Texture remains soft on decorated cake.

COLORING ICING

Mixing Colors

Begin with white icing and use concentrated Icing Colors (p. 134) which will not affect your icing consistency. (Using ordinary liquid food colors can thin your icing and affect your ability to pipe certain decorations.) If you are tinting icing dark brown or black, begin with chocolate icing—your icing will not have the aftertaste that large amounts of icing color can produce. If you are tinting a large area red, use No-Taste Red.

Dip a fresh toothpick into the color, then swirl it into the icing. Add color a little at a time until you achieve the shade you desire. Always use a new toothpick each time you add color; you want to avoid getting icing in your jar of color. Blend the icing well with a spatula.

Consider the type of icing you are using when mixing color. Icing colors intensify or darken in buttercream icing about 1-2 hours after mixing. Royal icing requires more color than buttercream icing to achieve the same color intensity.

Always mix enough of each icing color to complete your entire cake. For example, if you are going to decorate a cake with pink flowers and borders, color enough icing for both. It is difficult to duplicate an exact shade of any color, and you will want to keep your colors consistent on your cake.

Bag Striping Effects

You can easily pipe two-tone decorations just by adding a different color inside the bag before you put in your tinted icing. This is how you pipe flowers with natural light and dark tones or make a rainbow-colored clown suit to brighten up the party.

Brush Striping

Produces more intense multiple colors because it is done with straight icing color brushed into the bag. Apply one or more stripes of icing color with a decorating brush, then fill the bag with white or pastel-colored icing. As the icing is squeezed past the color, your decorations will come out striped.

Spatula Striping

Produces two-tone and realistic pastel tones for flowers and figure piping. It is done with pastel-colored icing, striped inside the decorating bag with a spatula. After striping, fill the bag with white icing or another shade of the same color as the striping. Squeeze out decorations with soft contrasts.

Brush Striping

Spatula Striping

MIXING SKIN SHADES

It's easy to create a wide variety of skin shades using various Wilton Icing Colors. Simply add desired color to white icing with a toothpick. If you wish to reach a shade lighter or darker than what is indicated, add slightly less or more of the icing color. Color listings for projects in this book reflect skin shade shown; feel free to choose your own shade.

1. To reach desired skin tone color, start with enough icing to cover the entire area, as matching shades later may be difficult.
2. Dip the end of a toothpick into the color or colors indicated, and swirl into icing and blend well.
3. Add color a little at a time until you achieve the shade you desire. Always use a new toothpick each time you add color to keep icing out of your jar of color.

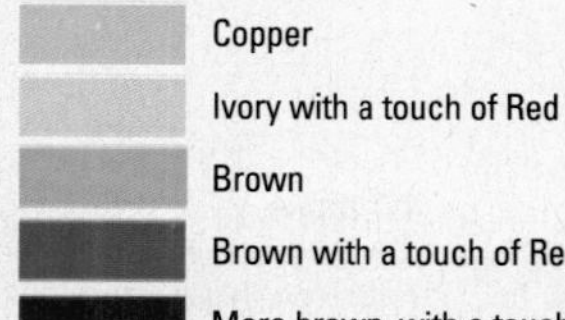

Skin Shade	Icing Colors
	Copper
	Ivory with a touch of Red
	Brown
	Brown with a touch of Red
	More brown, with a touch of Red

Three Essentials of Cake Decorating

Every decoration you make is the result of three things working together: the consistency of your icing, the position of the bag (that is, the way you are holding it) and the amount and type of pressure you apply to the bag. You'll know when you have everything right because you'll get perfect results time after time. This will take practice. The more you concentrate on perfecting these three essentials, the sooner you will achieve perfect results.

ICING CONSISTENCY

If the consistency of your icing is not right, your decorations will not be right either. Just a few drops of liquid can make a great deal of difference in your decorating results. Many factors can affect icing consistency, such as humidity, temperature, ingredients and equipment. You may try using different icing consistencies when decorating to determine what works best for you. As a general guideline, if you are having trouble creating the decorations you want and you feel your icing is too thin, add a little more confectioners' sugar; if you feel your icing is too thick, add a little more liquid. In royal icing recipes, if adding more than ½ cup confectioners' sugar to thicken icing, also add 1-2 additional teaspoons of Meringue Powder (p. 135).

Stiff icing is used for figure piping and stringwork and for decorations like roses, carnations and sweet peas with upright petals. If icing is not stiff enough, flower petals will droop. If icing cracks when piped out, icing is probably too stiff. Add light corn syrup to icing used for stringwork to give strings greater elasticity so they will not break.

Medium icing is used for decorations such as stars, shell borders and flowers with flat petals. If the icing is too stiff or too thin, you will not get the uniformity that characterizes these decorations.

Thin icing is used for decorations such as printing and writing, vines and leaves. Leaves will be pointier, vines will not break and writing will flow easily if you add 1-2 teaspoons light corn syrup to each cup of icing. Thin icing is used to ice cakes smooth. Begin with your prepared icing recipe, then add small amounts of the same liquid used in the recipe (usually milk or water) until the proper spreading consistency is reached.

CORRECT BAG POSITION

The way your decorations curl, point and lie depends not only on icing consistency but also on the way you hold the bag and the way you move it. Bag positions are described in terms of both angle and direction.

Angle

Angle refers to the position of the bag relative to the work surface. There are two basic angle positions, 90° (straight up) and 45° (halfway between vertical and horizontal).

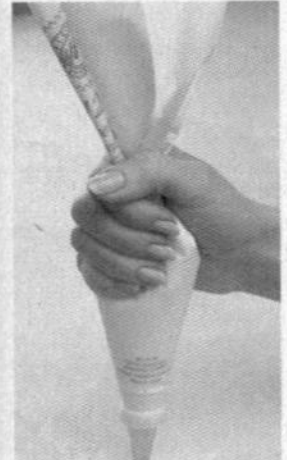

90° angle
or straight up, perpendicular to the surface.

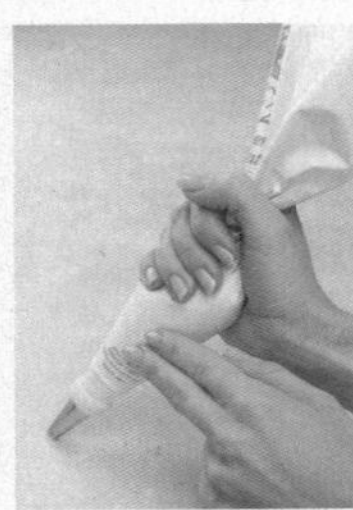

45° angle
or halfway between vertical and horizontal.

Direction

The angle in relation to the work surface is only half the story on bag position. The other half is the direction in which the back of the bag is pointed.

Correct bag direction is easiest to learn when you think of the back of the bag as the hour hand of a clock. When you hold the bag at a 45° angle to the surface, you can sweep out a circle with the back end of the bag by rolling your wrist and holding the end of the tip in the same spot. Pretend the circle you formed in the air is a clock face. The hours on the clock face correspond to the direction you point the back end of the bag.

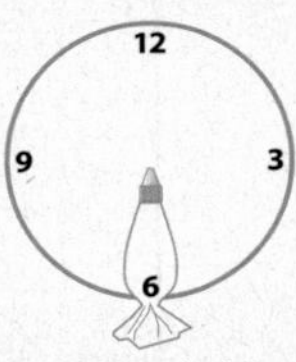

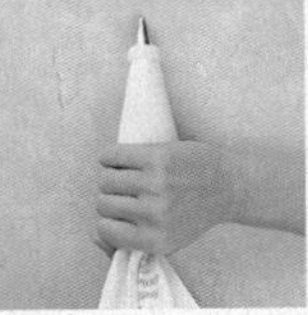

Back of bag at 6:00

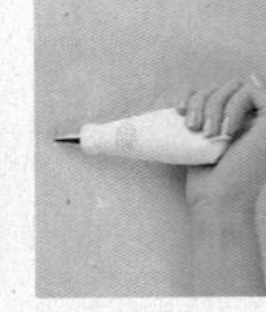

Back of bag at 3:00

The technique instructions in this Decorating Guide will list the correct direction for holding the bag. When the bag direction differs for left-handed decorators, that direction will be listed in parentheses. For example, when a bag is to be held at 3:00 for a right-handed decorator, it should be held at 9:00 for a left-handed decorator.

One more thing…since most decorating tip openings are the same shape all the way around, there's no right side and wrong side up when you're squeezing icing out of them. However, some tips, such as petal, ruffle, basketweave and leaf have irregularly shaped openings. For those you must watch your tip position as well as your bag position. If the tip opening must be in a special position, the instructions will tell you.

PRESSURE CONTROL

In addition to having the proper icing consistency and the correct bag position, you'll need to master three types of pressure control: heavy, medium and light. The size and uniformity of your icing designs are affected by the amount of pressure you apply to the bag and the steadiness of that pressure. (In other words, how you squeeze and relax your grip on the decorating bag.) Your goal is to learn to apply pressure so consistently that you can move the bag in a free and easy glide while just the right amount of icing flows through the tip. Practice will help you achieve this control.

Heavy Pressure | **Medium Pressure** | **Light Pressure**

Storing Cakes

Take some final precautions and store your cake the best way possible. After all, your time, effort and creativity have made it very special! Beware of the following factors, which can affect the look of your decorated cake.

Sunlight and fluorescent lighting will alter icing colors. Keep your cake stored in a covered box and out of direct sunlight and fluorescent lighting.

Humidity can soften royal icing, fondant and gum paste decorations. If you live in a climate with high humidity, prepare your royal icing using only pure cane confectioners' sugar (not beet sugar or dextrose), add less liquid and add 1 more teaspoon Meringue Powder (p. 135) to the recipe.

Heat can melt icing and cause decorations to droop. Keep your decorated cake as cool as possible and stabilize buttercream icing by adding 2 teaspoons Meringue Powder per recipe. Protect your cake by placing it in a clean, covered cake box. Avoid using foil or plastic wrap to cover a decorated cake—these materials can stick to icing and crush delicate decorations. The icing that covers your cake determines how it should be stored—in the refrigerator, at cool room temperature, or frozen, if storing for longer than 3 days. If you want to store your iced cake in a different way than noted, make a small test cake.

Icing type determines care. See chart on p. 111 for storage information.

NOTE: Cakes with thoroughly-dried royal icing decorations should be stored according to the type of icing that covers the cake. However, if royal icing decorations are to be put on a cake that will be frozen, it is recommended that these decorations be placed on the cake after thawing so that they don't bleed from condensation or become soft.

Transporting Tiered Cakes

Moving a tiered cake from one location to another does not have to be difficult. It can be quite easy! Following some simple guidelines ensures that your cake will arrive safely—whether you are traveling hundreds of miles or just a few.

Before Moving Cakes

Be certain the cake is constructed on a sturdy base made of three or more thicknesses of corrugated cardboard. Base tiers of very heavy cakes should be placed on a foam core or plywood base, ½ in. thick. Cakes on pillars must be transported unassembled. Toppers, candles and ornaments should be removed from cakes when they are being moved. For stacked cakes, move the entire assembled cake. Or, for a larger quantity of tiers, transport unassembled and assemble at the reception. Be sure to have with you the equipment and icings you will need to finish any decorating needed after assembly at the reception.

For a cake which combines stacked and 2-plate construction, take tiers apart, keeping stacked tiers as units. Boxing the cake makes transportation easier. Not only does it protect the tiers from damage, but it keeps the tiers clean—free from dirt, dust and bugs. Place the boxes on carpet foam or a non-skid mat on a level surface in the vehicle to prevent shifting. Keep the boxes flat; never place on a car seat. Boxed cakes can also be transported in the trunk of the car, except in hot weather, because air conditioning will not reach the trunk area. It's also important to find out about the reception location before the event. Knowing what to expect when you arrive can make your delivery and setup so much easier. Call the reception hall a few days before the event to get an idea of the conditions you will encounter there. Ask whether the room is located upstairs or downstairs. Find out what is the best location for bringing the cake into the building. That way you can park in the right place the first time and minimize the distance your cake has to travel from your car. Also ask how far in advance the cake can be set up so that you can plan your day and reduce the stress.

In Pan

Take tiers apart if constructed in Center Column or Push-In Leg method. Leave columns or legs in place. Position the plates on crumpled foil or in shallow pans if they do not sit level. Remove pillars from tier plates; plates stay in position.

In Box

Place the cakes in clean, covered, sturdy boxes that are sized to the base board of each cake. This prevents shifting within the box and possibly crushing the sides of the cake. If the box is too big, roll pieces of masking tape sticky side out and attach to the inside bottom of the box. Position the cake base on top of the tape, securing the base in the box. For taller decorations, prop up box top and sides, secure with masking tape.

On Non-Skid Foam

If tiers cannot be boxed, they can be transported on large pieces of non-skid foam. Place the foam on the floor of the vehicle, then carefully place the tiers centered on each piece of foam. Remove any ornament or fragile decorations before transporting.

At Your Destination

Before you bring in the cake from your car, walk the path you will have to travel to the set-up site. Be alert for any bumps along the way and note any tight spaces you will have to maneuver around. Make sure the cake table is level—it's a good idea to bring a level to check this on setup day. Request a cart on wheels to move the cake into the reception area. This is easier and safer than carrying by hand. Remove the cakes from the boxes on the reception table by cutting the sides of the boxes and sliding the cakes out. Bring along a repair kit, including extra icing, prepared decorating bags and tips, flowers and spatulas, just in case it is necessary to make any repairs. Once the cake is assembled, take a picture to establish that the cake was in perfect condition when you left it.

Cake Baking and Serving Guides

The charts below are based on baking recommendations from the Wilton Test Kitchen; your results may vary depending on oven performance or altitude in your area. For large cakes, always check for doneness after they have baked for 1 hour.

Serving amounts are based on party-sized portions of 1.5 x 2 in. or smaller wedding-sized portions of approximately 1 x 2 in. Cakes from 3 to 6 in. high, baked in the same size pan, would yield the same number of servings because they follow the same pattern of cutting. Cakes shorter than 3 in. would yield half the number of servings indicated for that pan. Number of servings are intended as a guide only.

Icing amounts are very general and will vary with consistency, thickness applied and tips used. Icing amounts allow for top and bottom borders.

4 IN. HIGH CAKES (using 2 in. high pans)

The figures for 2 in. pans are based on a 2-layer, 4 in. high cake. Fill pans ½ to ⅔ full.

PAN SHAPE	SIZE	NUMBER SERVINGS PARTY	NUMBER SERVINGS WEDDING	CUPS BATTER 1 LAYER, 2 IN.	BAKING TEMP. (F.)	BAKING TIME MINUTES	APPROX. CUPS ICING TO ICE AND DECORATE
Round	6 in.	12	12	2	350°	25-30	3
	8 in.	20	24	3½	350°	30-35	4
	9 in.	24	32	5½	350°	30-35	4½
	10 in.	28	38	6	350°	35-40	5
	12 in.	40	56	7½	350°	35-40	6
	14 in.	63	78	10	325°	50-55	7½
	16 in.	77	100	15	325°	55-60	9
Square	6 in.	12	18	2	350°	25-30	3½
	8 in.	20	32	4	350°	35-40	4½
	10 in.	30	50	6	350°	35-40	6
	12 in.	48	72	10	350°	40-45	7½
	14 in.	63	98	13½	325°	45-50	9½
	16 in.	80	128	15½	325°	50-55	11
Heart	6 in.	8	14	1½	350°	25-30	3½
	8 in.	18	22	3½	350°	30-35	4½
	9 in.	20	28	4	350°	30-35	6
	10 in.	24	38	5	350°	30-35	8½
	12 in.	34	56	8	325°	45-50	9
	14 in.	48	72	10	325°	45-50	10
	15 in.	50	74	11	325°	40-45	11
	16 in.	64	94	12½	325°	40-45	12
Petal	6 in.	6	8	1½	350°	25-30	4
	9 in.	14	18	3½	350°	35-40	6
	12 in.	38	40	7	350°	35-40	9
	15 in.	48	64	12	325°	50-55	11
Hexagon	6 in.	10	12	1¾	350°	30-35	3
	9 in.	20	26	3½	350°	35-40	5
	12 in.	34	40	6	350°	40-45	6
	15 in.	48	70	11	325°	40-45	9
Oval	7.75 x 5.5 in.	9	13	2½	350°	25-30	3
	10.75 x 7.8 in.	20	26	5	350°	25-30	4
	13.5 x 9.8 in.	30	45	8	350°	35-40	5½
	16.5 x 12.4 in.	44	70	11	325°	40-45	7½
Sheet	7 x 11 in.	28	32	5½	350°	30-35	5
	9 x 13 in.	45	50	7	350°	35-40	6
	11 x 15 in.	60	74	11	325°	35-40	8
	12 x 18 in.	72	98	14	325°	45-50	10
Paisley	Small	9	13	3	350°	35-40	5
	Medium	28	38	7	350°	45-50	6
	Large	40	56	10½	325°	55-60	8

3 IN. HIGH CAKES (using 3 in. high pans)

The figures for 3 in. pans are based on a 1-layer cake which is torted and filled to reach 3 in. high; fill pans ½ full.

PAN SHAPE	SIZE	NUMBER SERVINGS PARTY	NUMBER SERVINGS WEDDING	CUPS BATTER 1 LAYER, 2 IN.	BAKING TEMP.	BAKING TIME MINUTES	APPROX. CUPS ICING TO ICE AND DECORATE
Round	6 in.	12	12	3	350°	35-40	3
	8 in.	20	24	5	350°	55-60	4
	10 in.	28	38	8	325°	65-75	5
	12 in.	40	56	10½	325°	60-65	6
	14 in.	63	78	15	325°	75-85	8
	16 in.	77	100	18	325°	75-85	9
	18 in. Half, 2 in. layer	110*	146*	9**	325°	60-65	10½
	18 in. Half, 3 in. layer	110*	146*	12**	325°	60-65	10½
Sheet	9 x 13 in.	45	65	11½	325°	70-75	5
	11 x 15 in.	60	90	16	325°	80-85	6½
	12 x 18 in.	72	108	20	325°	85-90	8
Square	8 in.	20	32	6½	350°	60-65	4½
	10 in.	30	50	9	325°	65-75	6
	12 in.	48	72	14	325°	65-75	7½
	14 in.	63	98	19	325°	65-75	9½
Contour	7 in.	6	11	3½	350°	45-50	2
	9 in.	11	17	5½	350°	45-50	2½
	11 in.	16	24	8	325°	80-85	3
	13 in.	22	39	13	325°	75-80	4
	15 in.	32	48	16	325°	75-80	5

For pans 10 in. and larger, we recommend using a heating core (p. 147) to insure even baking. Use 2 cores for 18-in. pans.

*Two half rounds. **For each half round pan.

For additional pan information, check out ***www.wilton.com***

General Cake Cutting Guides

The diagrams below will give you a general plan for cutting the most popular cake shapes. They will help you serve more attractive, uniform pieces while reaching your targeted number of servings. Diagrams show only one size in each shape; you will use the same general technique to cut each size cake in that shape.

WEDDING CAKES—1 x 2 in. slices

The diagrams show how to cut popular shaped wedding tiers into slices approximately 1 x 2 in. and 2 layers high (about 4 in.) For cakes shorter than 3 in. you will need to cut wider slices to serve a proper portion; even if a larger serving size is desired, the order of cutting is still the same. Before cutting the cake, remove the top tier, which is usually saved for the first anniversary and is not included in our serving amounts for wedding cakes in this book. Begin by cutting the 2nd tier, followed by the 3rd, 4th and so on.

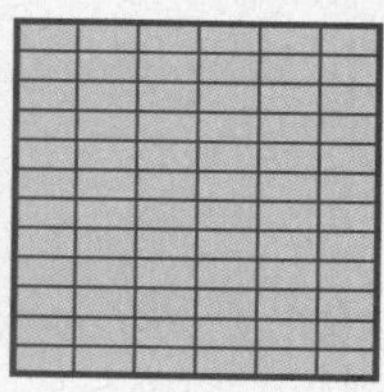

12 in.

Square Tiers:

Move in 2 in. from the outer edge and cut vertically, top to bottom. Slice and serve 1 in. pieces of cake. Now move in another 2 in. and repeat process until the entire tier is cut.

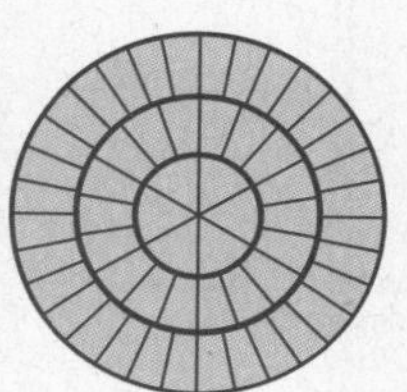

12 in.

Round Tiers:

Move in 2 in. from the tier's outer edge and cut a circle. Slice and serve 1 in. pieces from around the circle. Now move in another 2 in. and cut another circle. Repeat process until the tier is completely cut. The center core of each tier and the small top tier can be cut into 4ths, 6ths, or more, depending on size.

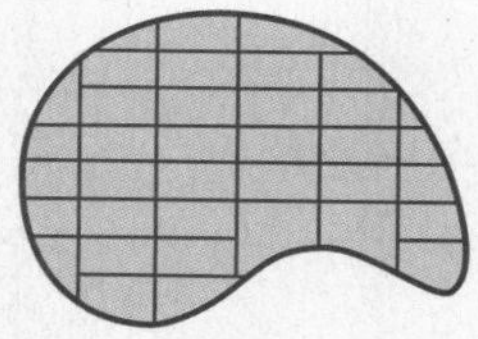

Large

Paisley Tiers:

Move in 2 in. from the outer edge and cut across. Slice and serve 1 in. pieces of cake, similar to oval tiers as diagram shows. Now move in another 2 in., repeat process until the entire tier is cut.

12 in.

Heart Tiers:

Divide the tiers vertically into 2 in. wide rows. Within rows, slice and serve 1 in. pieces of cake.

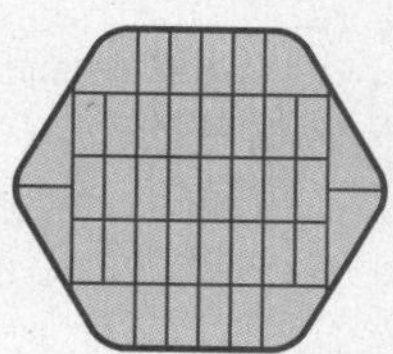

12 in.

Hexagon Tiers:

Move in 2 in. from the outer edge and cut across. Slice and serve 1 in. pieces of cake. Now move in another 2 in., repeat process until the entire tier is cut.

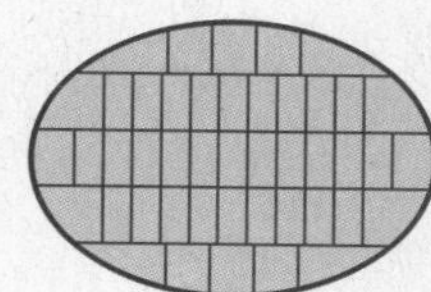

13.5 x 9.8 in.

Oval Tiers:

Move in 2 in. from the outer edge and cut across. Slice and serve 1 in. pieces of cake. Now move in another 2 in., repeat process until the entire tier is cut.

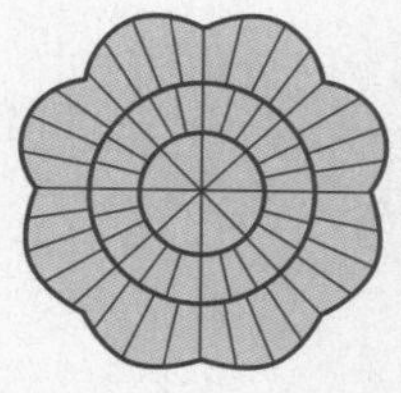

15 in.

Petal Tiers:

Cut similar to round tiers as diagram shows.

PARTY CAKES—1.5 x 2 in. slices

Follow the diagrams above to cut party cakes (from 3 to 6 in. high), but adjust for the larger party-size slices. For cakes shorter than 3 in. you will need to cut wider slices to serve a proper portion; even if a larger serving size is desired the order of cutting is still the same.

Rounds:

To cut round cakes, move in 2 in. from the cake's outer edge; cut a circle and then slice approximately 1.5 in. pieces within the circle. Now move in another 2 in. and cut another circle; slice approximately 1.5 in. pieces. Continue until the cake is completely cut. Note: 6 in. diameter cakes should be cut in wedges, without a center circle. Cut petal and hexagon cakes similar to round cakes.

Squares:

To cut square cakes, move in 2 in. from the outer edge and cut top to bottom, then slice approximately 1.5 in. pieces. Now move in another 2 in. and continue until the entire cake is cut.

Sheets: Cut sheet cakes similar to square cakes.

Tiered Cake Construction

There are many methods of constructing tiered cakes. Here are some used in this book. Visit **www.wedding.wilton.com** *for more construction methods.*

TO PREPARE CAKE FOR ASSEMBLY

Place base tier on a sturdy base plate of 3 or more thicknesses of corrugated cardboard. For heavy cakes, use foam core or plywood. Base can be covered with Fanci-Foil Wrap and trimmed with Tuk-'N-Ruffle or use Ruffle Boards® (p. 232). Each tier of your cake must be on a cake circle or board cut to fit. Place a few strokes of icing on boards to secure cake. Fill and ice layers before assembly.

Adding Dowel Rods to Tiered Cakes

Use the upper tier for size reference when determining dowel rod placement. All the dowel rods must be placed within the area you will mark (see steps below) to provide adequate support.

1. Center a cake board the same size as the tier above it on base tier and press it gently into icing to imprint an outline. Remove. Use this outline to guide the insertion of the dowel rods.

2. Insert one dowel rod into cake straight down to the cake board. Make a knife scratch on the rod to mark the exact height. Pull dowel rod out.

3. Cut the suggested number of rods (see note below) the exact same length, using the mark on the first one as a guide.

4. Insert rods into tier, spacing evenly 1½ inches in from the imprinted outline. Push straight down until each touches the cake board. Repeat this procedure for every stacked or pillared tier on the cake.

NOTE: The larger and more numerous the tiers, the more dowels needed. If the tier above is 10 in. or less, use six ¼ in. wooden dowels. Use 8 dowel rods for 16 in. and 18 in. cakes; on these larger tiers, use ½ in. plastic dowel rods in the base tier. When using white plastic dowel rods that are wider and provide more support, the number needed may be less.

Stacked Construction

Stacking is the most architectural method of tiered cake construction. Tiers are placed directly on top of one another and pillars are not used. Cakes are supported and stabilized by dowel rods and cake boards.

1. Dowel rod all tiers except top tier.

2. Position the middle tier on the base tier, centering exactly.*

3. Repeat with the top tier.

4. To stabilize tiers further, sharpen one end of a long dowel rod and push it through all tiers and cake boards to the base of the bottom tier. To decorate, start at the top and work down.

*Finely shredded coconut or confectioners' sugar, placed in area where cake circles or plastic plates will rest, helps prevent icing on the cake from sticking.

Separator Plate (2-Plate) and Pillar Construction

This most dramatic method features 2, 3 or more single cakes towered together. Use separator plates and pillars (p. 229-230). Check pillars and plates for correct fit before constructing your cake.

1. Set cake tiers on separator plates 2 in. larger in diameter than cakes.

2. Dowel rod cakes and position separator plates on tiers with feet up. (Note: Connect only same size separator plates with pillars.)

3. Position pillars over feet on separator plates.

4. Carefully set cake plate on pillars. Continue adding tiers this way.**

**Assemble cakes when you arrive at the reception or party.

Push-In Pillar Construction

Simple assembly—no dowel rods needed! Use any type of Wilton push-in pillars and plates (p. 231). Check pillars and plates for correct fit before constructing your cake.

1. Mark tier for push-in pillar placement. Use the separator plate for the next tier above, gently pressing it onto the tier, feet down, making sure it is centered. Lift plate away. The feet will leave marks on the icing to guide the position of pillars when you assemble the tier. Repeat this process for each tier, working from largest to smallest tier. The top tier is left unmarked.

2. Place each tier on its separator plate, securing with icing.

3. Position push-in pillars at marks, and insert into tiers. Push straight down until pillars touch the cake plate.

4. To assemble, start with the tier above the base tier. Place the feet of the separator plate on the pillar openings. Continue adding tiers in the same way until the cake is completely assembled.**

Center Column Construction (Tall Tier Stand) (p. 229)

1. Use boards the same size as tiers, or if tiers are shaped, cut boards to fit. Make a waxed paper pattern for each tier except the top tier in order to find the exact center for the columns. Fold the pattern in quarters. Snip the point to make a center hole. Test the hole for size by slipping it over a column, adjust size if necessary. Trace hole pattern on prepared cake board and cut out. Also cut a hole in the top tier board to allow for the column cap nut. Save patterns for marking cake tops later.

2. The base tier of the cake will rest on a 14, 16 or 18 in. plate. (18 in. plate is footed. Do not use a bottom plate smaller than 14 in.) To add legs to bottom plate, turn it upside down; using extra-strength glue designed for plastic, attach the six legs, positioning the legs over each of the ribs on the plate.

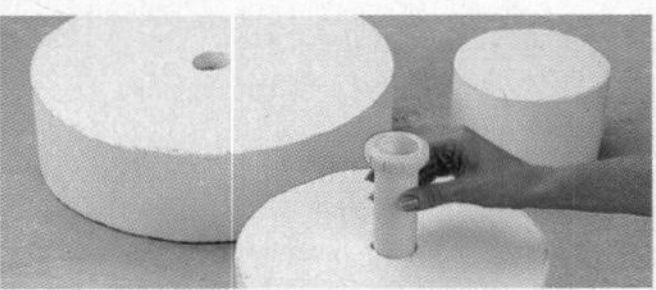

3. Prepare and ice tiers and position on prepared cake boards. Make the center holes for the columns in all tiers except the top tier. Mark the top of the cakes with corresponding waxed paper pattern. Cut the hole by pressing the Cake Corer Tube (p. 229) through the tier right down to the bottom. Hold the corer upright, remove cake corer and push the upper part down to eject the cake center.

4. Screw in a column to the prepared base plate and bottom column bolt from underneath the plate. Slip the next size tier on its plate over the column.

5. Add a second column and position the next size tier on its plate, slipping it over the column. Finally, add on the top plate only, securing the top column nut. Place the top tier on the plate and decorate bottom border.**

Globe Pillar Set Construction

These elegant pearl-look globes (p. 228) are available in separate sets of four 2 in., 2½ in. or 3 in. globes. The 3 in. globes are to be used to support the base cake only. They have a reinforced center channel which eliminates the need for pillars. The 2 and 2½ in. sets should be used with 9 in. "Hidden" Pillars (included in set); do not use these sets to support the base cake. Your cake design may use a base board instead of the 3 in. globes to support the base cake as shown below.

1. Position separator plate holding base cake on 3 in. Globe Base Set or a thick base board. Using the separator plate which will hold the cake above, mark base cake for pillar placement (see Push-In Pillar construction, p. 114). Lift plate away.

2. Insert pillars through cake centered over marked area to rest on its separator plate or base board. Place the correct size globe (2½ in. for cake shown here) over the pillars. Mark pillars where they extend above globes. The cut pillars should be equal to the height of the base cake plus the height of each globe.

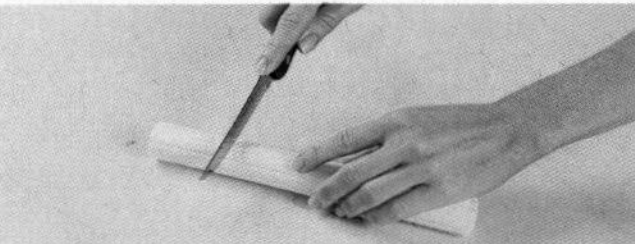

3. Trim pillars at markings with craft knife or serrated edge knife.

4. Insert pillars in base cake. Position globes over pillars.

5. Position the tier above on globes.

6. Add additional sets for more tiers.

Tailored Tiers Construction

Our Tailored Tiers Cake Display Set (p. 228) features fabric-wrapped separators which add great texture to your tiered design. The top 2 tiers are decorated on same-size boards, then transported to the reception on larger boards, so that cakes can be easily transferred to the separator plates during assembly. Bottom borders are then added to these tiers. The recommended display for Tailored Tiers separators includes a 14 in. base cake, a 10 in. center cake and a 6 in. top cake.

1. Ice cakes; place 14 in. base cake on 16 in. base board wrapped in foil or 16 in. Silver Cake Base (p. 232). Place 10 in. center and 6 in. top cakes on same size boards. Mark 14 in. and 10 in. cakes for placement of dowel rods. Center the 8 in. plate from the Tailored Tiers set on top of the 14 in. cake and press it gently into icing to imprint an outline. Remove. Use this outline to guide the insertion of dowel rods.

2. Dowel rod 14 in. cake (see page 114). Place the 6 in. plate from set on top of the 10 in. cake and repeat process for marking and inserting dowel rods. Complete decorating on cakes, except bottom borders of 10 in. center and 6 in. top cakes, which will be done at reception. Attach 10 in. and 6 in. cakes to larger boards before transferring to reception.

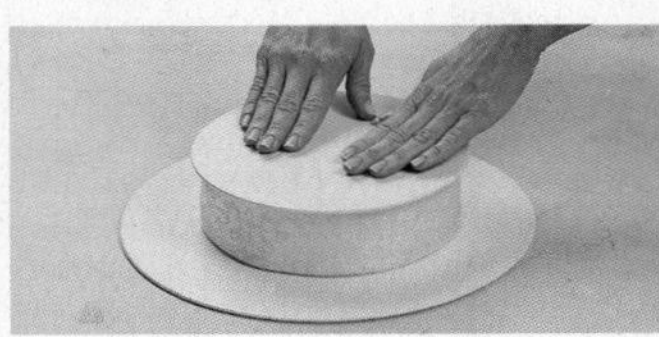

3. Place the 12 in. plate (spikes up) on table. Center the large (7¼ in.) separator over the plate and press down over the spikes. Position one 8 in. plate (spikes down) on top of the large separator. Place the second 8 in. plate (spikes up) on table. Center the small (4¼ in.) separator over the plate and press down over the spikes. Position the 6 in. plate (spikes down) on top of the small separator.

4. At reception: Position the large separator, with 8 in. plate on bottom and 12 in. plate on top, on the base cake. Remove 10 in. and 6 in. cakes from their larger boards. Position 10 in. cake on large separator.

5. Add bottom border to 10 in. cake. Position the small separator, with 6 in. plate on bottom and 8 in. plate on top, on the 10 in. cake. Position 6 in. cake on small separator. Add bottom border.

To Use Acetate Wrap for Tailored Tiers

1. Insert photos, patterned paper or fabric in pockets of acetate wrap. Trim inserted items as needed to fit.
2. Wrap acetate around separator and fasten Velcro® ends.

Alternate 2-Plate Set-Ups

The Fluted Bowl and Spiral Separator Sets shown below are assembled similar to 2-Plate and Pillar Construction (p. 114)—the separators provide support instead of pillars; each set includes 2 separator plates. Cakes must still use dowel rods to support cakes and secure the separators.

Fluted Bowl Separator Set (p. 228)

Spiral Separator Set (p. 228)

Dowel rod base cake as for 2-Plate & Pillar Construction. Position smaller plate from set on base cake (spikes up). Position Fluted Bowl or Spiral Separator over spikes. Position next tier on larger plate from set. Position plate (spikes down) on separator.

Recipes

The cakes, cookies and other desserts in this Yearbook were made using our favorite kitchen-tested recipes. Follow these instructions for decorated desserts that look and taste their best!

ICING RECIPES

*Buttercream Icing (Medium consistency)

½ cup solid vegetable shortening
½ cup butter or margarine, softened
1 teaspoon Clear Vanilla Extract (p. 135)
4 cups sifted confectioners' sugar (about 1 lb.)
2 tablespoons milk

In large bowl, cream shortening and butter with electric mixer. Add vanilla. Gradually add sugar, one cup at a time, beating well on medium speed. Scrape sides and bottom of bowl often. When all sugar has been mixed in, icing will appear dry. Add milk and beat at medium speed until light and fluffy. Keep bowl covered with a damp cloth until ready to use. For best results, keep icing bowl in refrigerator when not in use. Refrigerated in an airtight container, this icing can be stored 2 weeks. Rewhip before using.

Makes about 3 cups.

For thin (spreading) consistency icing, add 2 tablespoons light corn syrup, water or milk.

For Pure White Icing (stiff consistency), omit butter; substitute an additional ½ cup vegetable shortening for butter and ½ teaspoon No-Color Butter Flavor (p. 135). Add up to 4 tablespoons light corn syrup, water or milk to thin for icing cakes.

Chocolate Buttercream Icing

Add ¾ cup cocoa powder (or three 1 oz. squares unsweetened chocolate, melted) and an additional 1-2 tablespoons milk to buttercream icing. Mix until well blended. For a unique change of pace, substitute ⅛ to ¼ teaspoon Wilton Candy Flavors (p. 166) for vanilla extract.

Chocolate Mocha Icing: Substitute brewed strong coffee for milk in Chocolate Buttercream recipe.

Darker Chocolate Icing: Add an additional ¼ cup cocoa powder (or 1 additional 1 oz. square unsweetened chocolate, melted) and 1 additional tablespoon milk to Chocolate Buttercream Icing.

*Snow-White Buttercream Icing (Stiff consistency)

⅔ cup plus 3 tablespoons water, divided
¼ cup Meringue Powder (p. 135)
12 cups sifted confectioners' sugar (about 3 lbs.), divided
1¼ cups solid vegetable shortening
3 tablespoons light corn syrup
¾ teaspoon salt
¾ teaspoon No-Color Almond Extract
¾ teaspoon Clear Vanilla Extract
½ teaspoon No-Color Butter Flavor

In large bowl, combine ⅔ cup water and meringue powder; whip with electric mixer at high speed until peaks form. Add 4 cups sugar, one cup at a time, beating at low speed after each addition. Add remaining 8 cups sugar and 3 tablespoons water, shortening and corn syrup in 3 additions, blending well after each. Add salt and flavorings; beat at low speed until smooth.

Makes about 7 cups icing.

For thin (spreading) consistency icing, add up to 4 more tablespoons each water and corn syrup.

NOTE: Recipe may be doubled or halved.

Royal Icing

3 tablespoons Meringue Powder (p. 135)
4 cups sifted confectioners' sugar (about 1 lb.)
6 tablespoons water [1]

Beat all ingredients at low speed for 7-10 minutes (10-12 minutes at high speed for portable mixer) until icing forms peaks. Makes 3 cups.

[1] When using large countertop mixer or for stiffer icing, use 1 tablespoon less water.

Thinned Royal Icing: To thin for pouring, add 1 teaspoon water per cup of royal icing. Use grease-free spoon or spatula to stir slowly. Add ½ teaspoon water at a time until you reach proper consistency.

Stabilized Whipped Cream Icing

½ pint (1 cup) heavy whipping cream
2 tablespoons confectioners' sugar
2 tablespoons Piping Gel (p. 135)
½ teaspoon Clear Vanilla Extract (p. 135)

Combine whipping cream and sugar in mixing bowl. Whip to soft peak stage. Add Piping Gel and vanilla, then continue to whip until stiff peaks form. Do not overbeat. Makes 1½ to 2 cups.

As an alternative, you can use frozen non-dairy whipped topping or packaged topping mix. Thaw frozen whipped topping in refrigerator before coloring or using for decorating. Use packaged topping mix immediately after preparing. Do not allow either to stay at room temperature, as it becomes too soft for decorating. Store decorated cake in refrigerator until ready to serve.

Heated Wilton Ready-To-Use Decorator Icing (p. 135)

Open icing container, remove foil. Microwave at 30% (Defrost) Power for 20-30 seconds, stirring at least once, until ready to pour. If a microwave is unavailable, icing container can be heated on a warming tray or in a pan of hot water on a stove.

Color Flow Icing Recipe (full-strength for outlining)

¼ cup + 1 teaspoon water
4 cups sifted confectioners' sugar (about 1 lb.)
2 tablespoons Color Flow Mix (p. 135)

With electric mixer, using grease-free utensils, blend all ingredients on low speed for 5 minutes. If using hand mixer, use high speed. Color flow icing "crusts" quickly, so keep bowl covered with a damp cloth while using. Stir in desired icing color. Makes approx. 2 cups color flow icing.

Thinned Color Flow: In order to fill in an outlined area, the recipe above must be thinned with ½ teaspoon of water per ¼ cup of icing (just a few drops at a time as you near proper consistency). Use grease-free spoon or spatula to stir slowly. Color flow is ready for filling in outlines when a small amount dropped into the mixture takes a count of ten to disappear.

NOTE: Color flow designs take a long time to dry, so plan to do your color flow piece up to 1 week in advance.

Poured Cookie Icing

This icing dries to a shiny, hard finish. Great to use as icing or to outline and fill in with tip 2 or 3.

1 cup sifted confectioners' sugar
2 teaspoons milk
2 teaspoons light corn syrup

Place sugar and milk in bowl. Stir until thoroughly mixed. Add corn syrup; mix well. For filling in areas, use thinned icing (add small amounts of light corn syrup until desired consistency is reached).

COOKIE RECIPES

Roll-Out Cookies

1 cup (2 sticks) unsalted butter, softened
1½ cups granulated sugar
1 egg
1½ teaspoons Clear Vanilla Extract (p. 135)
½ teaspoon No-Color Almond Extract (p. 135)
2¾ cups all-purpose flour
2 teaspoons baking powder
1 teaspoon salt

Preheat oven to 400°F. In large bowl, cream butter with sugar with electric mixer until light and fluffy. Add egg and extracts; mix well. Combine flour, baking powder and salt; add to butter mixture 1 cup at a time, mixing after each addition. Do not chill dough. Divide dough into 2 balls. On a floured surface, roll each ball into a circle approximately 12 in. wide and ⅛ in. thick. Dip cookie cutter in flour before each use. Bake cookies on ungreased cookie sheet 6-7 minutes or until cookies are lightly browned.

Makes about 3 dozen cookies. Recipe may be doubled.

Chocolate Roll-Out Cookies

¾ cup (1½ sticks) butter or margarine, softened
1 cup granulated sugar
2 eggs
1 teaspoon vanilla extract
3 squares (3 oz.) unsweetened chocolate, melted and cooled
3 cups all-purpose flour
1 teaspoon baking powder

Preheat oven to 375°F. In large bowl, cream butter with sugar using mixer until light and fluffy. Add eggs and vanilla; mix well. Blend in chocolate. Combine flour and baking powder; add to butter mixture, 1 cup at a time, mixing after each addition. Cover and chill until firm, about 1 hour.

Roll out dough approximately ⅛ in. thick. Dip cookie cutter in flour before each use. Bake cookies on ungreased cookie sheet 8-10 minutes or until cookies are lightly browned. Remove to rack and cool thoroughly. Makes 2-2 ½ dozen cookies.

Spritz Cookies

1½ cups (3 sticks) butter, softened
1 cup granulated sugar
1 egg
2 tablespoons milk
1 teaspoon Clear Vanilla Extract (p. 135)
½ teaspoon No-Color Almond Extract (p. 135)
3½ cups all-purpose flour
1 teaspoon baking powder

Preheat oven to 375°F. In large bowl, beat butter and sugar with electric mixer until light and fluffy. Add egg, milk, vanilla and almond extract; mix well. Combine flour and baking powder; gradually add to butter mixture, mixing to make a smooth dough. Do not chill. Place dough into cookie press and press cookies onto ungreased cookie sheet.

Bake 10-12 minutes or until lightly browned around edges. Remove cookies from cookie sheet; cool on cooling grid. Makes 7-8 dozen cookies.

Grandma's Gingerbread

5 to 5½ cups all-purpose flour
1 teaspoon baking soda
1 teaspoon salt
2 teaspoons ground ginger
2 teaspoons ground cinnamon
1 teaspoon ground nutmeg
1 teaspoon ground cloves
1 cup solid vegetable shortening
1 cup granulated sugar
1¼ cups unsulphured molasses[2]
2 eggs, beaten

Preheat oven to 375°F. Thoroughly mix flour, baking soda, salt and spices. Melt shortening in large saucepan. Cool slightly. Add sugar, molasses and eggs to saucepan; mix well. Add 4 cups dry ingredients and mix well.

Turn mixture onto lightly floured surface. Knead in remaining dry ingredients by hand. Add a little more flour, if necessary, to make firm dough.

On floured surface, roll out ⅛ to ¼ in. thick for cut-out cookies. Bake on ungreased cookie sheet, small and medium-sized cookies for 6-10 minutes, large cookies for 10-15 minutes. Makes 40 medium-sized cookies.

NOTE: If you're not going to use your gingerbread dough right away, wrap in plastic and refrigerate. Refrigerated dough will keep for a week.

[2] Substitute 1¼ cups light corn syrup for molasses to make Blonde Gingerbread.

SPECIALTY RECIPES

Cream Cheese Mousse

2½ cups whipping cream
4 envelopes (.25 oz. ea.) unflavored gelatin
1 cup cold water
2 packages (8 oz. ea.) cream cheese, softened
1¾ cups granulated sugar
1 tablespoon Pure Vanilla Extract
2 tablespoons lemon juice
1½ tablespoons lemon zest

Spray pan with vegetable pan spray; if desired, line with plastic wrap and spray wrap.

In large bowl, whip cream with electric mixer until soft peaks form; chill until ready to use. In medium saucepan, combine gelatin with water; let stand 5 minutes. Cook on low heat 5 minutes, stirring constantly, or until gelatin is completely dissolved. In large bowl, beat cream cheese and sugar with electric mixer until light and fluffy; add vanilla, lemon juice and zest, mixing well. Beat in dissolved gelatin; immediately fold in whipped cream. Pour into prepared pan. Refrigerate until firm, at least 6 hours or overnight.

Makes 18-20 servings.

Creamy Cheesecake

Crust:

1½ cups graham cracker crumbs
2 tablespoons granulated sugar
4 tablespoons butter, melted

Filling:

3 packages (8 oz. ea.) cream cheese, softened
1 cup granulated sugar
4 eggs
2 teaspoons Pure Vanilla Extract
1 cup sour cream
½ cup heavy cream

Preheat oven to 325°F. Spray 9 in. springform pan with vegetable pan spray. In medium bowl, combine the graham cracker crumbs, sugar and butter until well blended. Press into bottom of prepared pan; set aside.

Beat cream cheese and sugar with electric mixer on medium speed until smooth and creamy, about 5 minutes, scraping down bowl several times. Add eggs, one at a time, beating well after each. Add vanilla; blend well. On low speed, add sour cream until just combined, and then slowly pour in heavy cream. Pour filling over crust.

Place cheesecake in center of oven. Fill a large, deep pan with hot water and place on rack underneath cheesecake. Bake for 1½ hours or until firm. Turn off oven and let cheesecake stand for 30 minutes. Remove from oven and cool completely. Refrigerate until ready to serve.

Makes 10 to 12 servings.

Chocolate Mousse

1½ cups heavy cream
2 envelopes (.25 oz.) unflavored gelatin
6 tablespoons cold water
6 ounces cream cheese, softened
1 cup granulated sugar
½ teaspoon Clear Vanilla Extract
2½ cups milk
2 boxes (3.4 oz. ea.) instant chocolate fudge pudding

Whip cream until soft peaks form; set aside. Soften gelatin in cold water, heat in microwave on high 20-30 seconds; stir until dissolved. Set aside to cool. Beat cream cheese and sugar until light and fluffy. Add vanilla and milk; mix well. Add gelatin mixture; stir. Add pudding mix. Fold in whipped cream; immediately spoon into prepared cups. Refrigerate until firm, at least 3 hours.

Shortbread Cookies

Use with Push 'N Print Cutter Sets (p. 162).

1½ cups (3 sticks) butter, softened
1 cup granulated sugar
½ teaspoon salt
6 egg yolks
2 teaspoons Pure Vanilla Extract
4 cups all-purpose flour

In large bowl, cream butter, sugar and salt with electric mixer until light and fluffy. Add egg yolks one at a time, mixing well after each addition. Add vanilla. Add flour: mix just until combined. (Note: Dough can be tinted with Wilton Icing Color. Add small amounts until desired color is reached.) Divide dough in half. Press dough to flatten; wrap with plastic wrap. Refrigerate at least 2 hours or overnight.

Preheat oven to 375°F. Work with one dough disk at a time. Let chilled dough stand at room temperature for 10 minutes. Lightly flour work surface and roll dough ⅛ to ¼ in. thick. Depress imprint disk into flour, then cut and imprint cookies. Gather scraps and roll dough again to make more cookies. For best results, depress disk into flour after each use.

Carefully transfer cookies to an ungreased cookie sheet, leaving 1 in. between cookies. Bake 14-16 minutes or until edges are lightly browned. Remove cookies from cookie sheet and cool completely on cooling grid.

Makes about 2 dozen cookies.

*Changes in Wilton's traditional recipes have been made due to Trans Fat Free Shortening replacing Hydrogenated Shortening

ROLLED FONDANT AND GUM PASTE RECIPES

Fondant is rolled out and used as a covering for any firm-textured cake, pound cake or fruit cake, which is traditionally first covered with a layer of marzipan to seal in flavor and moistness of the cake. A light layer of buttercream icing or apricot glaze may also be used. Cakes covered with rolled fondant can be decorated with royal or buttercream icing. Wilton also offers convenient Ready-To-Use Rolled Fondant (p. 130) for easy-to-handle fondant with no mixing.

Rolled Fondant

1 tablespoon plus 2 teaspoons unflavored gelatin
¼ cup cold water
½ cup Wilton Glucose (p. 133)
2 tablespoons solid vegetable shortening
1 tablespoon Wilton Glycerin (p. 133)
Icing color and flavoring, as desired
8 cups sifted confectioners' sugar (about 2 lbs.)

Combine gelatin and cold water; let stand until thick. Place gelatin mixture in top of double boiler and heat until dissolved. Add glucose, mix well. Stir in shortening and just before completely melted, remove from heat. Add glycerin, flavoring and color. Cool until lukewarm. Next, place 4 cups confectioners' sugar in a bowl and make a well. Pour the lukewarm gelatin mixture into the well and stir with a wooden spoon, mixing in sugar and adding more, a little at a time, until stickiness disappears. Knead in remaining sugar. Knead until the fondant is smooth, pliable and does not stick to your hands. If fondant is too soft, add more sugar; if too stiff, add water (a drop at a time). Use fondant immediately or store in airtight container in a cool, dry place. Do not refrigerate or freeze. When ready to use, knead again until soft. This recipe makes approx. 36 oz., enough to cover a 10 x 4 in. round cake.

Extra-Firm Rolled Fondant

Use this recipe for a fondant with the extra body and pliability ideal for making drapes, swags and elaborate decorations.

1 to 2 teaspoons Gum-Tex™ (p. 133)
24 oz. Ready-To-Use Rolled Fondant (p. 130)

Knead Gum-Tex™ into fondant until smooth. Store in an airtight container or tightly wrapped in plastic.

Gum Paste

Clay-like gum paste can be rolled thinner than fondant for finer detail. Gum paste dries hard and is meant for decoration only; remove from cake before serving. For perfectly mixed gum paste whenever you need it, try Wilton Ready-To-Use Gum Paste (p. 133)

1 tablespoon Gum-Tex™ (p. 133)
3 cups sifted confectioners' sugar (about ¾ lb.)
1 heaping tablespoon Glucose (p. 133)
4 tablespoons warm water
1 cup sifted confectioners' sugar (about ¼ lb.; save until ready to use)

In a large bowl, mix Gum-Tex™ into 3 cups confectioners' sugar. Make a well in the center and set aside. Mix water and glucose in a glass measuring cup and blend; heat in microwave on high for about 30 seconds until mixture is clear. Pour into well of 3 cups confectioners' sugar and mix until well blended (mixture will be very soft). Place mixture in a plastic bag and seal tightly; let mixture rest at room temperature for 8 hours or overnight. Knead remaining confectioners' sugar into gum paste when you are ready to use it. As you work it in, gum paste will whiten and soften.

Apricot Glaze

Ideal for preparing a cake for fondant or for crumb-coating cakes before icing.

1 cup apricot preserves

Heat preserves to boiling, strain. Brush on cake while glaze is still hot. Let dry. Glaze will dry to a hard finish in 15 minutes or less. Makes enough to cover a 10 x 4 in. cake.

Thinned Fondant Adhesive

Use this mixture when attaching dried fondant to other fondant decorations or for attaching freshly-cut fondant pieces to lollipop sticks or florist wire.

1 oz. Wilton Ready-To-Use Rolled Fondant (p. 130) (1½ in. ball)
¼ teaspoon water

Knead water into fondant until it becomes softened and sticky. To attach a fondant decoration, place mixture in decorating bag fitted with a small round tip, or brush on back of decoration. Recipe may be doubled.

Gum Paste Adhesive

1 tablespoon Wilton Meringue Powder (p. 135)
1 tablespoon water

This easy-to-make "glue" will hold your gum paste flowers and other decorations together. Mix Meringue Powder and water together; add more water if mixture is too thick. Brush on decorations.

Chocolate Fondant

1 pk. (14 oz.) Dark Cocoa Candy Melts®* (p. 166)
½ cup light corn syrup
24 oz. White Ready-To-Use Rolled Fondant (p. 130)
Brown or Black Icing Color (p. 134, optional)

Melt Candy Melts® following package directions. Add corn syrup; stir to blend. Turn out mixture onto waxed paper; let stand at room temperature to dry and harden several hours. Wrap well and store at room temperature until ready to continue with recipe.

Knead small portions of candy mixture until soft and pliable. Knead softened mixture into fondant until smooth and evenly colored. If darker color is desired, knead in icing color.

Quick-Pour Fondant Icing

6 cups sifted confectioners' sugar (about 1½ lbs.)
½ cup water
2 tablespoons light corn syrup
1 teaspoon No-Color Almond Extract (p. 135)
Wilton Icing Colors (p. 134)

Cakes should be covered with apricot glaze (see recipe above) or a thin coating of buttercream icing. Let set 15 minutes before covering with fondant.

Place sugar in saucepan. Combine water and corn syrup. Add to sugar and stir until well mixed. Place over low heat. Don't allow temperature of fondant to exceed 100°F. Remove from heat, stir in flavor and icing color. To cover, place cake or cookies on cooling grid over a drip pan. Pour fondant into center and work towards edges. Touch up bare spots with spatula. Let set. Excess fondant can be reheated. Makes 2½ cups.

*Brand confectionery coating.

HOW TO COLOR AND FLAVOR FONDANT

You can easily tint our White Ready-To-Use Rolled Fondant (p. 130) or the Rolled Fondant recipe (above) using Wilton Icing Colors (p. 134). Using a toothpick, add icing color, a little at a time, and knead into fondant until color is evenly blended. Wilton Ready-To-Use Rolled Fondant has a mellow flavor which can be enhanced using Wilton No-Color Butter Flavor, Clear Vanilla Extract or No-Color Almond Extract (p. 135). Knead flavor into fondant until well blended.

Using Rolled Fondant

The dough-like consistency of fondant makes it the perfect medium for creating ruffles and braids, stately molded accents, distinctive borders, fun trims and beautiful flowers. Decorators agree that fondant is an icing that is truly easy to work with. It's even easier with Wilton Ready-To-Use Rolled Fondant (p. 130)—no mixing, no mess!

COVERING THE CAKE

Just follow our instructions for the right ways to knead, roll out and lift the fondant, and you'll find that covering a cake is easy. For instructions on covering Square, Petal and other cake shapes, see the *Celebrate® With Fondant* book, p. 128.

1. Prepare cake by lightly covering with buttercream icing.
2. Before rolling out fondant, knead it until it is a workable consistency. If fondant is sticky, knead in a little confectioners' sugar. Lightly dust your smooth work surface or the Roll & Cut Mat and your rolling pin with confectioners' sugar to prevent sticking. Roll out fondant sized to your cake (see "Fondant Amounts," at right). To keep fondant from sticking, lift and move as you roll. Add more confectioners' sugar if needed.

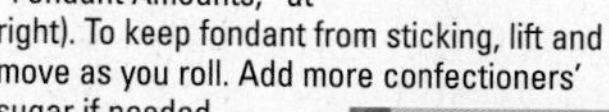

3. Gently lift fondant over rolling pin and position on cake.
4. Shape fondant to sides of cake with Easy-Glide Smoother. We recommend using the Smoother because the pressure of your hands may leave impressions on the fondant. Use the straight edge of the Smoother to mark fondant at the base of cake. Trim off excess fondant using a spatula or sharp knife.
5. Smooth and shape fondant on cake using Easy-Glide Smoother. Beginning in the middle of the cake top, move the Smoother outward and down the sides to smooth and shape fondant to the cake and remove air bubbles. If an air bubble appears, insert a pin on an angle, release air and smooth the area again.

FONDANT AMOUNTS

Use this chart to determine how much Ready-To-Use Rolled Fondant to buy. Wilton Fondant is available in 24 oz. (1 lb., 8 oz.) or 80 oz. (5 lb.) packages. Amounts listed do not include decorations.

Cake Shape	Cake Size	Fondant
Rounds 4 in. high	6 in.	18 oz.
	8 in.	24 oz.
	10 in.	36 oz.
	12 in.	48 oz.
	14 in.	72 oz.
	16 in.	108 oz.
	18 in.	140 oz.
Rounds 3 in. high	6 in.	14 oz.
	8 in.	18 oz.
	10 in.	24 oz.
	12 in.	36 oz.
	14 in.	48 oz.
	16 in.	72 oz.
	18 in.	108 oz.
Sheets 2 in. high	7 x 11 in.	30 oz.
	9 x 13 in.	40 oz.
	11 x 15 in.	60 oz.
	12 x 18 in.	80 oz.
Ovals 4 in. high	7.75 x 5.5 in.	24 oz.
	10.75 x 7.8 in.	36 oz.
	13.5 x 9.8 in.	48 oz.
	16.5 x 12.4 in.	72 oz.
Hearts 4 in. high	6 in.	18 oz.
	8 in.	26 oz.
	9 in.	32 oz.
	10 in.	36 oz.
	12 in.	48 oz.
	14 in.	72 oz.
	16 in.	96 oz.
Petals 4 in. high	6 in.	18 oz.
	9 in.	30 oz.
	12 in.	48 oz.
	15 in.	72 oz.
Squares 4 in. high	6 in.	24 oz.
	8 in.	36 oz.
	10 in.	48 oz.
	12 in.	72 oz.
	14 in.	96 oz.
	16 in.	120 oz.
Hexagons 4 in. high	6 in.	18 oz.
	9 in.	36 oz.
	12 in.	48 oz.
	15 in.	84 oz.
Paisley 4 in. high	9 x 6 in.	20 oz.
	12.75 x 9 in.	48 oz.
	17 x 12 in.	72 oz.

COVERING LARGE CAKES

In most cases, the smaller your cake, the easier it will be to cover with rolled fondant. However, there is an easy way to position and smooth fondant on cakes that are 12 in. diameter or larger. Follow the steps below to lift fondant onto the cake without tearing.

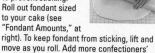

1. Cover cake lightly with buttercream icing. Roll out fondant sized to fit your cake.
2. Slide a large cake circle that has been dusted with confectioners' sugar under the rolled fondant. Lift the circle and the fondant and position over cake. Gently shake the circle to slide the fondant off and into position on the cake. Smooth and trim as described at left.

USING FONDANT IMPRINT MATS (p. 133)

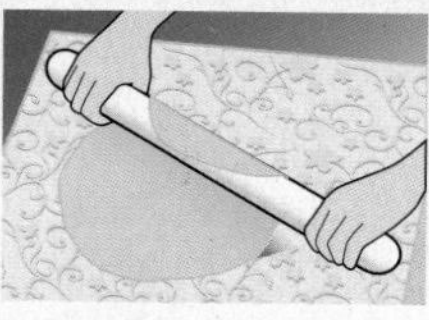

1. Roll out fondant ⅛ in. thick using rolling pin.
2. Lift fondant onto Fondant Imprint Mat using rolling pin. Or, place Fondant Imprint Mat on top of rolled fondant.

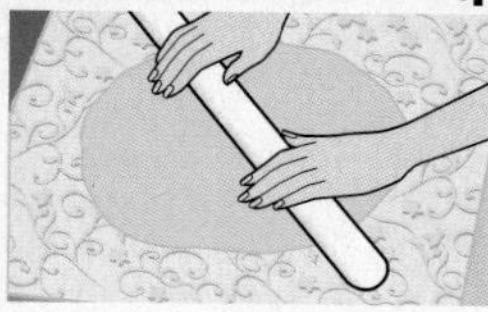

3. If fondant is on top of Fondant Imprint Mat, smooth by pressing firmly with Wilton Easy-Glide Fondant Smoother (p. 131) or roll with rolling pin. If fondant is below Fondant Imprint Mat, roll with rolling pin.

4. Lift Fondant Imprint Mat with fondant attached and center imprinted fondant on cake. Peel back mat. Smooth fondant around cake by gently pressing with heel of hand.

Tip Techniques

Your icing turned out great—now you're ready to learn how to pipe beautiful shapes on your cake. Stars, shells, dots, lines and other techniques are the foundation of your decorating knowledge. We'll tell you step-by-step how to pipe each one, including the angle, pressure and movement to use for a uniform look. With practice, you can build on these basics to create many other impressive designs.

ROUND TIPS

Dot

Pipe dots for flower centers, faces, figure piping and border effects. When making large dots, lift the tip as you squeeze to allow icing to fill out completely.

Practice With: Tip 3
Icing Consistency: Medium
Bag Position: 90°
Hold Tip: Slightly above surface

1. Hold the bag straight up with the tip slightly above the surface. Squeeze the bag and keep point of the tip in icing until the dot is the size you want.
2. Stop squeezing the bag completely before you lift the tip from the dot.
3. Lift tip up and pull away from piped dot.

Ball

An important technique to master, the ball shape makes bold borders and is the first step to learn for figure piping. Vary the basic look by adding stars, dots or spirals on the ball shapes.

Practice With: Tip 9
Icing Consistency: Medium
Bag Position: 90°
Hold Tip: Slightly above surface

1. Squeeze the bag, applying steady even pressure. As the icing begins to build up, raise the tip with it, but keep the tip end buried in the icing.
2. Stop squeezing as you bring the end of the tip to the surface.
3. Lift the tip up and pull away from your piped ball. Use the edge of the tip to shave off any point so that your ball is nicely rounded.

Bead

If you can pipe a shell, you can pipe a bead—the movements are similar. To pipe a bead heart, simply pipe one bead, then a second, joining the tails. Smooth together using a decorator's brush.

Practice With: Tip 5
Icing Consistency: Medium
Bag Position†: 45° at 3:00 (9:00)
Hold Tip: Slightly above surface

1. Squeeze as you lift tip slightly so that icing fans out.
2. Relax pressure as you draw the tip down and bring the bead to a point.
3. To make a bead border, start the end of your next bead so that the fanned end covers the tail of the preceding bead to form an even chain.

†The technique instructions in this Decorating Guide will list the correct direction for holding the bag. When the bag direction differs for left-handed decorators, that direction will be listed in parentheses. For example, when a bag is to be held at 3:00 for a right-handed decorator, it should be held at 9:00 for a left-handed decorator.

Printing

Practice With: Tip 3 with message press
Icing Consistency: Thin
Bag Position†: 45° at 3:00 (9:00)
Hold Tip: Lightly touching surface

You may pipe letters freehand, pipe over a pattern traced with a toothpick, or pipe after imprinting letters with a pattern press. If you are using a pattern press, let icing crust slightly, then imprint the message. With a steady, even pressure, squeeze out a straight line, lifting the tip off the surface to let icing string drop. To prevent tails from forming, be careful to stop squeezing before you touch tip to surface and pull away. Be sure the end of the tip is clean before you go on to another line.

Writing

Practice With: Tip 5
Icing Consistency: Thin
Bag Position†: 45° at 3:00 (6:00)
Hold Tip: Lightly touching surface

You may pipe letters freehand, pipe over a pattern traced with a toothpick, or pipe after imprinting letters with a pattern press. If you are using a pattern press, let icing crust slightly, then imprint the message. Steadily squeeze, gliding along the surface in a smooth, continuous motion. Use your arm, not your fingers, to form each line, letter or word. Keep your wrist straight, moving your entire forearm as a single unit. After you begin to master the curves and swings of the letters, lift the tip up slightly as you write. You'll find you have more control if you let the icing draw out slightly over the surface as you write.

Note: Left-handed decorators may have to adjust the bag position to fit their writing style.

Outline

Characters or designs are often outlined first, then piped in with stars or zigzags. Outlines are used for facial features, too. Color Flow plaques are also outlined before icing is flowed into the shape.

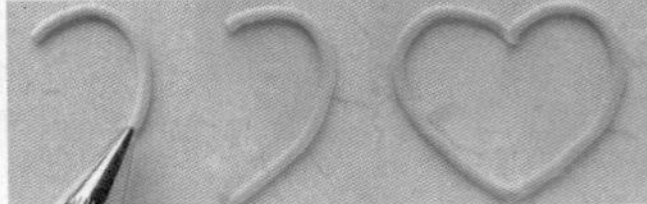

Practice With: Tip 3
Icing Consistency: Thin
Bag Position†: 45° at 3:00 (9:00)
Hold Tip: Slightly above surface

1. Touch tip to surface. Raise the tip slightly and continue to squeeze.
2. The icing will flow out of the tip while you direct it along the surface.
3. To end, stop squeezing, touch tip to surface and pull away.

To Pipe-In
After outlining, using the same tip, squeeze out rows of lines to fill area. Pat icing down with fingertip dipped in cornstarch or smooth with dampened art brush.

Drop Strings

These flowing strings are a beautiful way to adorn the sides of a cake. The trick to making drop strings is to pull the bag toward you as the string drapes down. If you "draw" the string with the tip, you won't achieve a pretty curve and your strings will tend to break. Pipe at eye level to your cake so that strings line up evenly. The Cake Dividing Set (p. 137) is a great help in accurately dividing and marking your cake for even drop strings.

Single Drop Strings

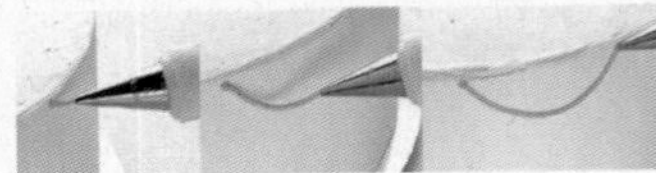

Practice With: Tip 3
Icing Consistency: Stiff
Bag Position†: Shoulder level at 4:30 (7:30)
Hold Tip: Lightly touching surface to attach

1. With a toothpick, mark horizontal divisions on cake in the width you desire. Touch tip to first mark and squeeze, pausing momentarily so that icing sticks to surface.
2. While squeezing, pull the bag toward you. Continue squeezing to allow the icing to drape naturally into an arc. Icing will drop by itself—do not move the tip down with the string. The end of the tip should be the same distance from the surface as the width from point to point on your cake.
3. Stop pressure before you touch tip to second mark to end string. Repeat, keeping drop strings uniform in length and width.

Multiple Drop Strings

Try a different color for each row of multiple drop strings—put holiday colors together to really dress up your cake.

To add multiple rows of strings, mark the cake for the deepest row and pipe that row. Return to the first drop string point, squeeze the bag, and drop a string with a slightly shorter arc than in the first row. Join the end of this string to the end of the corresponding string in the first row. Repeat the process for a third row of drop strings above the second.

STAR TIPS

Star

Practice With: Tip 16
Icing Consistency: Medium
Bag Position: 90°
Hold Tip: Between ⅛ and ¼ in. above surface

1. Hold the decorating bag straight up, with the tip between ⅛ and ¼ in. above the surface, while using your other hand to hold the tip steady. Squeeze the bag to form a star. Increasing or decreasing the pressure changes the size of the star.
2. Stop squeezing the bag completely before you lift the tip from the star.
3. Lift the tip up and pull away from piped star.

Pull-out stars add even more dimension to your cake. To make them, hold bag at a 45° angle to surface. As you squeeze out icing, pull tip up and away from cake. When your mound is high enough, stop pressure and pull tip away. Work from bottom to top of area to be covered with pull-out stars.

Star Fill In

Because these close-together stars require so much piping from the same bag, it's a good idea to keep replenishing the icing. Replenish icing when it gets soft or stars will be poorly defined.

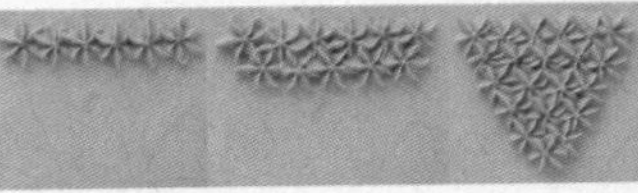

Practice With: Tip 16
Icing Consistency: Medium
Bag Position: 90°
Hold Tip: ¼ in. above surface

1. Pipe a row of stars evenly and close together, adjusting the tip position slightly each time so that the points of the stars interlock and cover the area without gaps.
2. Pipe a row of stars beneath the first, again adjusting tip position to close any gaps.
3. Continue to fill in entire area.

Zigzag

A quick and popular way to fill in outlined areas, perfect for ribbed sweater and cuff effects. You can use tight zigzags to cover the entire side of your cake—they look great!

Practice With: Tip 16
Icing Consistency: Medium
Bag Position†: 45° at 3:00 (9:00)
Hold Tip: Lightly touching surface

1. Steadily squeeze and move your hand in a tight up and down motion.
2. Continue piping up and down with steady pressure. To end, stop pressure and pull tip away. For more elongated zigzags, move your hand to the desired height while maintaining a steady pressure. For a more relaxed look, just increase the width as you move the bag along.
3. Repeat as you move in a straight line with consistent up/down motion.

Shell

Most popular icing technique of all, the shell is the basis for many borders. Lift tip slightly when piping shells to avoid a bumpy look.

Practice With: Tip 21
Icing Consistency: Medium
Bag Position: 45° at 6:00
Hold Tip: Slightly above surface

1. Hold the bag in the 6:00 position so that you can pull the bag toward you. The tip should be slightly above the surface.
2. Squeeze hard, letting the icing fan out generously as it lifts the tip—do not lift the bag. Gradually relax your pressure as you lower the tip until it touches the surface.
3. Stop pressure and pull the tip away, without lifting it off the surface, to draw the shell to a point.
4. To make a shell border, start the end of your next shell so that the fanned end covers the tail of the preceding shell to form an even chain.

Rope

Finish your piped baskets with pretty edging and handles. Excellent for western or nautical themed cakes. You can make a great-looking rope with star or round tips (or basketweave tips, ridged or smooth side up).

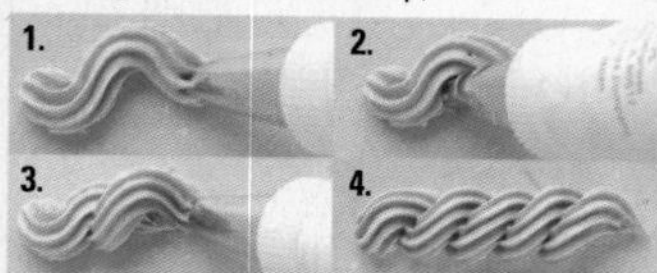

Practice With: Tip 21
Icing Consistency: Medium
Bag Position†: 45° at 4:30 (7:30)
Hold Tip: Lightly touching surface

1. Using a steady, even pressure, move the tip in a gentle sideways "S" curve. Stop pressure and pull tip away.
2. Insert tip under the bottom curve of the "S" shape.
3. Squeeze the bag with steady pressure as you pull down, then lift the tip. Move up and over the tail of the "S" as you continue to squeeze and form a hook.
4. Keep spacing as even as possible and "S" curves uniform in thickness, length and overall size. Be sure to tuck the tip into the bottom curve of the previous "S" before you begin squeezing to insure the clean, continuous look of a rope.

Rosette

Practice With: Tip 16
Icing Consistency: Medium
Bag Position: 90°
Hold Tip: Lightly touching surface

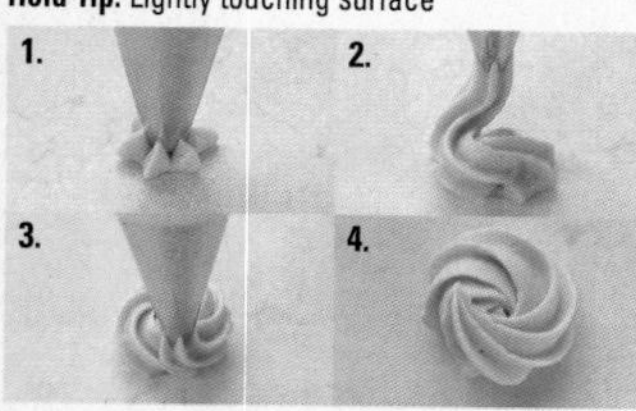

1. Keeping the tip slightly above the surface, squeeze out icing to form a star and, without releasing pressure, move the tip in a tight, complete rotation, starting at 9:00 (3:00), moving to 12:00. . .
2. then to 3:00 (9:00) and 6:00. . .
3. and ending back at 9:00 (3:00).
4. Stop pressure and lift tip away.

MULTIPLE TIPS

Swirl Drop Flower

The swirled look adds a nice motion effect to the cake. You must squeeze and turn at the same time.

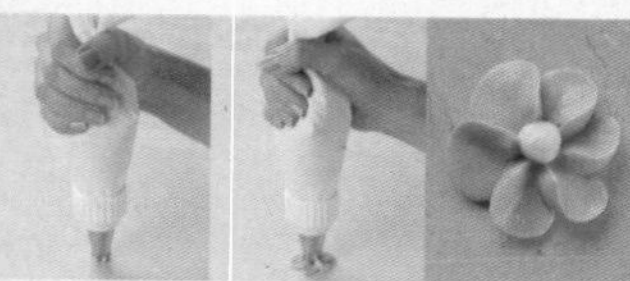

Practice With: Tips 2D, 3; use Large Coupler
Icing Consistency: Use royal icing: medium for flower, thin for center
Bag Position: 90°
Hold Tip: Slightly above surface

1. Turn your wrist in toward you before piping. Hold bag straight up, just touching the surface. You will turn wrist a full twist. Starting with the flat of your knuckles at 9:00 (3:00). As you squeeze out the icing, slowly turn your hand, with knuckles ending at 12:00.
2. Stop squeezing and lift the tip away.
3. Make a tip 3 dot flower center, holding your bag straight up and keeping the tip buried as you squeeze. Stop squeezing, then pull your tip up and away.

BASKETWEAVE TIPS

Try using different tips to vary the woven effects.

Practice With: Tip 47
Icing Consistency: Medium
Bag Position†: 45° at 6:00 for vertical stripes; at 3:00 (9:00) for horizontal bars
Hold Tip: Lightly touching surface, serrated side up

1. Squeeze out a vertical stripe of icing from top to bottom (shown ridged side up).
2. Squeeze out short horizontal stripes of icing across the vertical stripe starting at the top. Spacing between stripes should be the same as the width of the tip opening. Squeeze next vertical stripe over ends of horizontal stripes. Start next set of horizontal stripes by burying the tip under the first vertical stripe.
3. Repeat vertical lines then horizontal lines until you achieve basketweave effect. Each new set should fit between the previous set.

PETAL TIPS

Ruffle

Everyone loves a ruffle's graceful motion—ruffles always add interest to your cake. Use them as a top border, to frame a plaque or to trim doll dresses and baby bonnets.

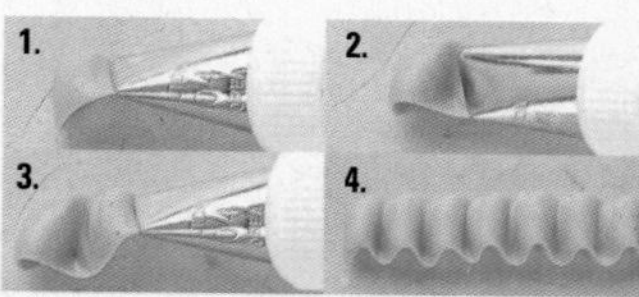

Practice With: Tip 104
Icing Consistency: Medium
Bag Position†: 45° at 3:00 (9:00)
Hold Tip: Wide end lightly touching surface with narrow end facing down and away from surface

1. Keep the wide end of your tip touching the cake with the narrow end down. Move wrist up to pull up icing.
2. Move wrist down to complete one curl of the ruffle.
3. Repeat up and down motion.
4. Raise and lower the narrow end as you move around the cake. Repeat this motion for the entire ruffle.

Wild Rose

A pretty year-round flower piped about the size of a flower nail. If you prefer a more cupped shape, increase the angle of the tip.

Practice With: Tips 103, 1
Icing Consistency: Medium royal icing
Bag Position: For petals 45° at 3:00 (9:00); for center 90°
Hold Tip: For petals, wide end lightly touching center of nail, narrow end pointing out and raised ⅛ in. above nail surface; for centers, slightly above flower
Flower Nail: #7

1. Use tip 103 at a 45° angle. Touch nail with wide end of tip, keeping narrow end just slightly above nail surface. Begin at center of flower nail and squeeze out first petal, turning nail ⅕ turn as you move tip out toward edge of nail. Relax pressure as you return to center of nail, curving tip slightly upward to create a cupped shape. Stop squeezing as wide end touches center of nail and lift up.
2. Repeat step 4 more times.
3. Pipe tiny pull-out dot stamens with tip 1.

Flower-Making Techniques

Explore beautiful flowers like the sweet pea or carnation, which add lovely color to your cake design. Create the magnificent rose—the most popular icing flower of all. With practice, your flowers will have the just-picked look of real garden flowers.

FLOWER NAIL FLOWERS

Using a Flower Nail

The nail is a revolving platform you hold in your hand to conveniently build roses and other flowers. It allows you to work close up, to turn for easy piping and to remove your completed flowers without damage, to dry.

The key to making the flower on the nail is to coordinate the turning of the nail with the formation of each petal.

Attach a square of waxed paper on the flat surface of the flower nail using a dot of icing. Pipe your flower directly on the waxed paper. Hold the flower nail between the thumb and forefinger of your left (right) hand (use other fingers to support nail) and roll it slowly counterclockwise (clockwise for lefties) as you press out icing with the decorating bag held in the right (left) hand. Your right (left) hand moves in and out, or up and down, as it holds the decorating bag and tip at just the right angle (in most cases 45°) and keeps the icing flowing at an even speed. After piping, slide the waxed paper with flower off the nail to dry.

The Wilton Rose

NOTE: If you are going to be placing your roses on your cake immediately, waxed paper squares are not needed. To remove finished roses, use the Flower Lifter (p. 137). Slide flower from lifter onto cake, using a spatula.

Practice With: Tips 104, 12
Icing Consistency: Royal or stiff buttercream
Bag Position†: Base 90° (straight up); petals 45° at 4:30 (7:30)
Hold Tip: For base, slightly above nail; for petals, wide end touching base
Flower Nail: #7

1. Make the rose base, using tip 12 and flower nail #7. Hold the bag straight up, the end of tip 12 slightly above the center of your waxed paper-covered flower nail, which is held in your other hand. Using heavy pressure, build up a base, remembering to keep your tip buried as you squeeze. Start to lift the tip higher, gradually raise the tip, and decrease the pressure.
2. Stop pressure, pull up and lift away. The rose base should be 1½ times as high as the rose tip opening.

3. Make the center bud, using tip 104. Hold nail containing base in your left (right) hand and bag with rose tip 104 in right (left) hand. Bag should be at a 45° angle to the flat surface of the nail and in the 4:30 (7:30) position. The wide end of the tip should touch the cone of the icing base at or slightly below the midpoint, and the narrow end of the tip should point up and angled in over top of base.
4. Now you must do 3 things at the same time: squeeze the bag, move the tip and rotate the nail. As you squeeze the bag, move the tip up from the base, forming a ribbon of icing. Slowly turn the nail counterclockwise (clockwise for lefties) to bring the ribbon of icing around to overlap at the top of the mound, then back down to starting point. Move your tip straight up and down only; do not loop it around the base.
5. Now you have a finished center bud.

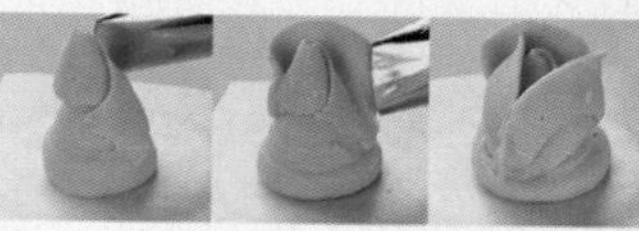

6. Make the top row of 3 petals. Touch the wide end of tip to the midpoint of bud base, narrow end straight up.
7. Turn nail, keeping wide end of tip on base so that petal will attach. Move tip up and back down to the midpoint of mound, forming the first petal.
8. Start again, slightly behind end of first petal, and squeeze out second petal. Repeat for the third petal, ending by overlapping the starting point of the first petal. Rotate the nail ⅓ turn for each petal.

9. Make the middle row of 5 petals. Touch the wide end of tip slightly below center of a petal in the top row. Angle the narrow end of tip out slightly more than you did for the top row of petals. Squeeze bag and turn nail moving tip up, then down, to form first petal.
10. Repeat for a total of 5 petals, rotating the nail ⅕ turn for each petal.
11. The last petal end should overlap the first's starting point.

12. Make the bottom row of 7 petals. Touch the wide end of tip below the center of a middle row petal, again angling the narrow end of tip out a little more. Squeeze bag and turn nail to end of fingers, moving tip up, then down to form first petal.
13. Repeat for a total of 7 petals, rotating the nail ⅐ turn for each petal.

14. The last petal end should overlap the first's starting point.
15. Slip waxed paper and completed rose from nail. This is the completed Wilton Rose.

†The technique instructions in this Decorating Guide will list the correct direction for holding the bag. When the bag direction differs for left-handed decorators, that direction will be listed in parentheses. For example, when a bag is to be held at 3:00 for a right-handed decorator, it should be held at 9:00 for a left-handed decorator.

Flower-Making Techniques (cont.)

Gum Paste Roses
(see Flourishing Together, p. 88)

1. Make rose bases. Roll a ⅝ in. ball of gum paste into a teardrop shape, 1¼ in. high. Dip toothpick in Gum Paste Adhesive (p. 117) and insert into bottom. Insert toothpick in craft block and let dry 48 hours.

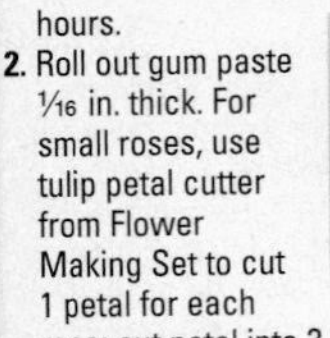

2. Roll out gum paste 1/16 in. thick. For small roses, use tulip petal cutter from Flower Making Set to cut 1 petal for each rose; cut petal into 3 separate petals.

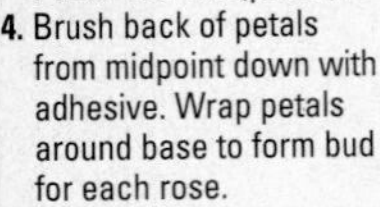

3. Place petals horizontally on thin foam dusted with cornstarch. Soften top petal edge with large ball tool from Fondant/Gum Paste Tool Set (p. 131).
4. Brush back of petals from midpoint down with adhesive. Wrap petals around base to form bud for each rose.
5. Cut another set of 3 petals to add to each base. Slightly widen and elongate each petal using modeling stick. Turn petals so the rounded end is the top of petal and the point is the bottom. Soften top petal edge with ball tool on thin foam. Turn petals over. Add adhesive to bottom half of petals; position and press onto rose base. This completes the small rose.

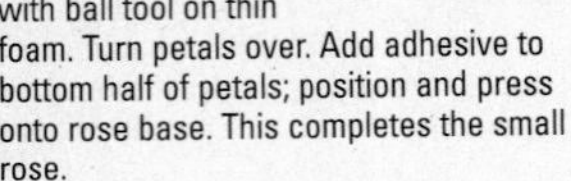

6. For medium and large roses, cut and attach a second row of 5 petals. For large roses, cut and attach a third row of 7 petals.

Calla Lilies
(see Flourishing Together, p. 88)

1. Roll out gum paste ⅛ in. thick. Use tulip leaf cutter from Floral Collection Flower Making Set (p. 132) to cut 1 leaf for each. Cut ¾ in. off tapered bottom. Use rolling pin to widen to approximately 3 in. across. Place on thin foam lightly dusted with cornstarch; soften side edges with large ball tool from Fondant/Gum Paste Tool Set (p. 131).

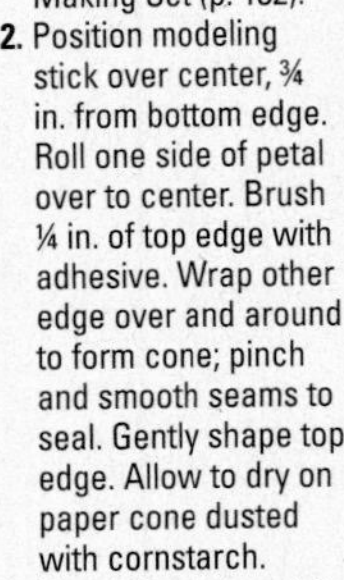

2. Position modeling stick over center of petal, ¾ in. from bottom edge. Roll one side of petal over to center. Brush ¼ in. of top edge with adhesive. Wrap opposite edge over to form cone; pinch and smooth seams to seal. Gently shape top edge. Let dry on paper cone dusted with cornstarch.

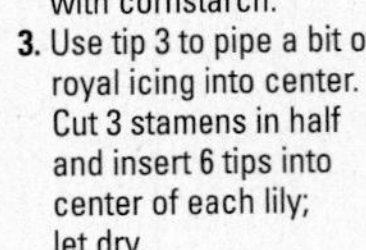

3. For centers, roll a ¼ in. thick rope; cut a 1½ in. length for each lily. Smooth and taper tip; let dry. Dust with yellow Pearl Dust (p. 130). Attach to calla lily with dot of royal icing; let dry.

Ruffled Calla Lilies
(see Flourishing Together, p. 88)

1. Roll out gum paste 1/16 in. thick. Using 3rd largest heart from Nesting Heart Set, cut one heart for each lily. Trim off rounded bottom to make a straight edge. Place on thin foam lightly dusted with cornstarch and ruffle sides using pointed modeling stick from Floral Collection Flower Making Set (p. 132).

2. Position modeling stick over center, ¾ in. from bottom edge. Roll one side of petal over to center. Brush ¼ in. of top edge with adhesive. Wrap other edge over and around to form cone; pinch and smooth seams to seal. Gently shape top edge. Allow to dry on paper cone dusted with cornstarch.

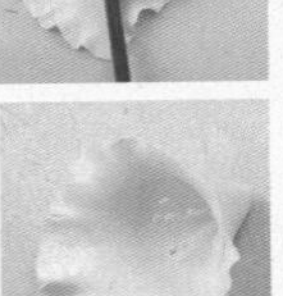

3. Use tip 3 to pipe a bit of royal icing into center. Cut 3 stamens in half and insert 6 tips into center of each lily; let dry.

FLORAL GREENERY

Leaves
Practice With: Tips 352, 67, 366
Icing Consistency: Buttercream thinned with corn syrup
Bag Position: 45° at 6:00
Hold Tip: Lightly touching surface; wide opening parallel to surface

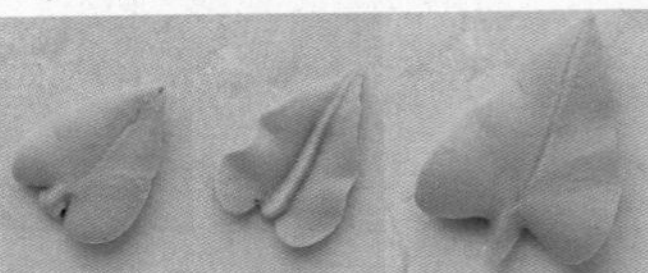

Basic Leaf Tip 352 | **Veined Leaf Tip 67** | **Large Leaf Tip 366** Use large coupler

1. Squeeze hard to build up the base and, at the same time, lift the tip slightly.
2. Relax pressure as you pull the tip toward you, drawing the leaf to a point.
3. Stop squeezing and lift away.

Vines
Practice With: Tip 3
Icing Consistency: Thin
Bag Position: 45° at 3:00 (9:00)
Hold Tip: Lightly touching surface

1. Touch your tip lightly to the surface as you start to squeeze, then lift slightly above the surface as you draw out the stem.
2. Move tip gently up and down to form "hills and valleys." To end the line, stop squeezing and pull the tip along the surface.
3. Add secondary curved stems, starting at main stem, stopping pressure as you pull to a point.

Other Decorating Techniques

Combing
Practice With: Icing Sculptor™, Decorating Comb or Triangle (p. 137), Trim 'N Turn™ Cake Turntable (p. 139)
Icing Consistency: Medium-to-thin buttercream

Cover the cake with a slightly thicker coating of icing so the comb's ridges will not touch the cake. Hold comb at 45° angle. Comb immediately after icing cake, while icing is soft. Using a turntable helps to keep the movement smooth. Use the Icing Sculptor™, Decorating Comb or Decorating Triangle to add different contoured effects to your iced cake. Choose the type of effect you want—wide or narrow—then run that edge around your cake to form ridges. Ridges will be deep or shallow depending on the Icing Sculptor™ blade or the side of Decorating Comb or Triangle you use.

Icing Sculptor™
Select the sculpting blades you want and slide into holder. Press sculptor into iced cake as you rotate cake on turntable. Mix and match between the 64 blades to achieve the perfect look for your cake.

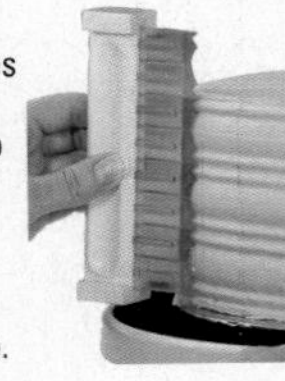

Pattern Press
The trick to uniform designs and steady writing and printing is using a pattern press (p. 139). Simply imprint the press on any icing, including fondant. Use the vine pattern press

on cake sides for a beautiful botanical effect.
Practice With: Tips 3, 16
Icing Consistency: Medium
Bag Position: 45° at 3:00
Hold Tip: Slightly above surface

1. Lightly press pattern onto your iced cake to imprint the design.
2. Outline the imprinted design with icing, using the tip of your choice. Change the tip to change the look of each pattern.

Tinting Shredded Coconut
Place desired amount of coconut in plastic bag, add a few drops of color and knead until color is evenly blended. Dry on waxed paper.

Coating Spaghetti

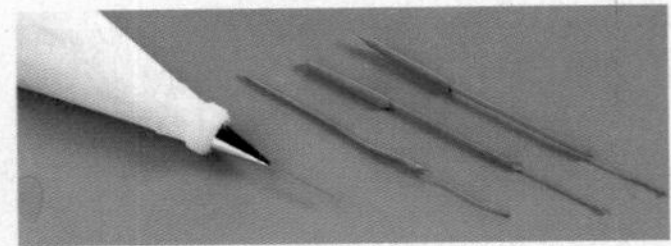

Break pieces of uncooked spaghetti into desired lengths. Use decorating bag with specified tip, and royal or buttercream icing as specified in cake directions. Insert a piece of spaghetti into open end of tip, then as you squeeze bag, pull spaghetti out of tip, coating spaghetti with icing. Push uncoated end into craft block to dry.

Sponging on Texture
(see A Piece of Perfection, p. 7)

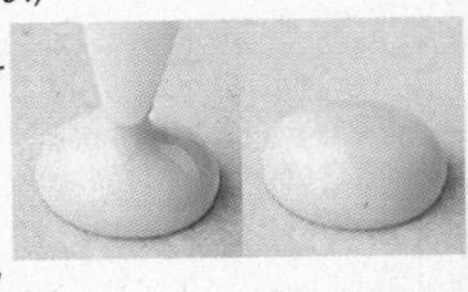

Textured highlights are easy to create. Thin buttercream icing. Dampen paper towel and lightly dip into icing. Using a quick pulling motion, blot icing onto iced cake surface to produce spackled effect. Different spackled effects can be achieved using crushed waxed paper, plastic wrap or a new sponge.

Puddle Dots
(see Initial Impressions, p. 79; A Peek of Sunshine, p. 64)

Thin royal icing (or color flow), adding ½ teaspoon water per ¼ cup of icing. Icing is ready for flowing when a small amount dripped back into mixture takes a count of 10 to disappear. On waxed paper, pipe a ball, ¼ to 1¼ in. diameter, depending on project instructions, using thinned icing in a cut parchment bag. Let dry 48 hours. Decorate following project instructions.

Sleigh and Reindeer Cookies
(see Reindeer Race, p. 44)

In advance: Make cookies. Prepare dough.

Tint a portion brown for reindeers (use Brown with a little Red-Red). Roll out dough. For each treat, cut: 2 sleighs using sleigh cutter from set (reverse 1 before baking); 1 each front, back and bottom panels using patterns; 1 reindeer using cutter from set (reverse before baking). Sprinkle sleigh sides, front and back panels with red sugar. Bake and cool cookies. Also: Decorate cookies using royal icing and tip 3. Place cookies on waxed paper-covered board. Pipe top borders on sleigh sides; immediately dip in nonpareils. Pipe bottom runners on sleigh and harness on reindeer. Add dot eyes, nose and harness trim; outline and fill in hooves and antlers. Let dry overnight then assemble using royal icing. Let dry.

Snowflake
(see A Winter Wonder, p. 49)

Copy Snowflake Arms pattern and tape onto cake boards; cover with waxed paper. Using royal icing and tip 8, outline 1 snowflake arm at a time; immediately sprinkle on Sparkling Sugar. Excess sugar can be collected and reused. Repeat until you have completed 6 arms (make extras to allow for breakage). Use tip 1A to pipe a 1½ in. diameter ball; immediately sprinkle on Sparkling Sugar. Let all pieces dry 1 to 2 days. Carefully remove arms from waxed paper by sliding a small spatula underneath.

Ice Cream Sandwiches

(see Ice Scream Sandwiches, p. 38)

For candy corn cookie design: Use tip 2 and buttercream to outline and fill in candy corn and letters. **For pumpkin cookie design** (shown in treat bag): Outline and fill in pumpkin with tip 3 (smooth with finger dipped in cornstarch). Use tip 2 to fill in eyes, nose and mouth; add tip 3 dot pupils and outline stem. **For ghost cookie design:** Outline and fill in ghost with tip 3 (smooth with finger). Use tip 2 to pipe outline and dot facial features and to fill in letters. **To assemble sandwiches:** Use metal section of Push 'N Print cutter to shape ice cream. Remove plastic disk and spring handle. Line deeper half of holder with plastic wrap, then pack with slightly softened ice cream. Place an undecorated cookie on top of cutter. Lift plastic wrap to remove cookie and ice cream; remove plastic wrap and turn over treat. Top ice cream with decorated cookie; immediately roll in sprinkles to cover edges. Place in freezer 5 to 10 minutes to set, then wrap individually in plastic wrap. Freeze until serving time.

Cookie Frog and Heart

(see Leaping into Love, p. 55)

Prepare and roll out dough. Cut heart using largest cutter from set. Cut 2 eyes using largest round Cut-Out. Use pattern to cut 2 legs (reverse pattern for 2nd leg). Using 6 in. cake circle as pattern, cut body. Bake and cool cookies. Decorate and assemble frog on waxed paper-covered board using royal icing. Spatula ice frog pieces green, heart red; let dry. Position eyes and legs; attach body on top. Attach heart to body. Pipe arms using tip 12 and fingers using tip 6. Using tip 4, outline mouth; outline and pipe in whites of eyes, pupils and tongue (smooth all with finger dipped in cornstarch). Let dry. Attach 2 cookie treat sticks to back of frog with melted candy, leaving 2 in. extended to insert into craft foam circle.

Small Crowns

(see Leaping into Love, p. 55)

Tint a small amount of fondant yellow; roll out ⅛ in. thick. Use knife to cut ¾ in. high crowns for candy frogs. Brush bottom with damp brush and press onto frog's head. Position candy frogs on cupcakes.

Royal Icing Clowns

(see It's Fun Being #1!, p. 9)

Place prepared #1 candy plaque face up on waxed paper-covered board. Position candy clown heads by attaching sticks to back of plaque with melted candy, leaving space for piped bodies; let set. Use tip 12 to pipe bodies over sticks; pipe arms and legs. Use tip 6 to pipe hands and cone-shaped hats. Pipe tip 3 swirl hair and dot noses; pipe tip 2 outline mouth, dot eyes and cheeks and pull-out dot trims on hats. Pipe tip 8 shoes, tip 13 rosette buttons, tip 101 ruffles. Let dry 2 days before reinforcing clowns and attaching dowel rods to back.

Board with Legs

(see Party Whole Hog, p. 94)

Wrap a 4 in. cake circle with foil to support cake. Cut hidden pillars into 1½ in. high lengths for the 4 legs. Attach legs to back side of circle with melted candy, 1¼ in. inside edge. Refrigerate until firm. Wrap an 8 in. diameter cake circle with Fanci-Foil Wrap. Mark a 4 in. diameter circle in the center. Ice the marked circle with melted candy and position legs. Refrigerate until firm. Position Sports Ball cake on prepared 4 in. cake board and decorate following project instructions.

Monkey's Head and Gift Bows

(see In the Birthday Swing, p. 6)

On waxed paper covered board, using royal icing, pipe tip 2A ball head (flatten and smooth with finger dipped in cornstarch) and tip 3 outline bow. Pipe tip 5 ears. Add tip 5 muzzle and tip 3 inner ears. Pipe tip 2 dot nose and outline mouth and eyes. Attach icing decoration hat to top of head and let dry overnight.

Scrolls

(see Their Peak Moment, p. 72 and A Home in Harmony, p. 74)

For *Their Peak Moment,* use large and small "C" scroll pattern presses from Decorator Favorites Set (p. 139) to transfer patterns to paper. Tape paper to cake board; tape and smooth waxed paper over. **For large scrolls,** pipe over patterns with tip 18 "C" shells, tails meeting at the center. Pipe tip 16 "C" shells underneath, curving 3 to the left and 3 to the right. Attach 1 large and 2 small drop flowers to cover tails. **For small scrolls,** pipe over pattern with tip 18 "C" shells, tails meeting at the center. Attach 1 large drop flower to cover tails. Let all dry then dust with Pearl Dust™ mixture per instructions.

For *A Home in Harmony,* place large, medium and small scroll patterns on cake boards; cover with waxed paper. Lightly spray with vegetable oil pan spray; wipe off excess spray. Using tip 18 and royal icing, pipe 20 large and 60 each medium and small scrolls. Make extras to allow for breakage and let dry overnight. Turn scrolls over and overpipe backs; let dry overnight.

BRUSHING DECORATIONS WITH PEARL DUST™

It's easy to add a shimmering touch to fondant and candy decorations with Wilton Pearl Dust (p. 130). This **food-safe** powder creates rich, lustrous highlights on flowers, bows, letters and more. To apply, just brush onto your decoration with a soft artist brush. Or, to paint decorations, pour a small amount of clear vanilla, lemon juice or vodka into a Color Tray (p. 130) cavity; stir in a small amount of Pearl Dust and brush onto your decoration.

Fondant/Gum Paste Techniques

Fondant Monkeys

(see Monkeys Get Funky, p. 4)

For 2 monkeys, add ½ teaspoon Gum-Tex™ to 6 oz. fondant. Tint as follows: 2½ in. ball brown, ½ in. balls each light brown, yellow and pink. Using brown fondant, press ¾ in. ball into cavity of Candy Melting Plate for each head; unmold. Shape a 1½ in. round body, ⅜ in. thick. Attach to head with damp brush. Roll out a small amount of fondant ⅛ in. thick. Cut ears using wide end of tip 1, inner ears using narrow end of tip 2A. Trim and attach to head. Cut muzzle using wide end of tip 1; roll into oval ¾ in. wide and attach. Roll ¼ in. diameter fondant ropes. Cut off a 2½ in. length for tail, 1¾ in. for arms and 2 in. for bent leg. Shape and attach to body. Bend and flatten foot; cut slits for toes. Roll out brown fondant ⅛ in. thick for straight leg. Cut a 1¼ x ½ in. rectangle. Wrap around lollipop stick middle, starting ¾ in. from top end. Brush ¾ in. end with damp brush and insert stick into monkey body. Shape and flatten small ball of fondant into foot; thread into position on stick and cut slits for toes. Attach package with melted candy. Bend arms into position over package and attach; cut slits for fingers. For hats, roll ¾ in. high cones of tinted fondant; attach. Using royal icing, pipe tip 2 pull-out dot fringe on hat brim and tip; pipe tip 1 dot and outline facial features. Let dry 3 or more days.

Race Track Board

(see Lightning Laps the Field, p. 24)

Wrap foamcore board with foil (p. 110). Tint fondant per instructions. Roll out ⅛ in. thick; attach with piping gel. Cover board in light gray up to top of track border; smooth. Use patterns to cut away gray from track border and grass areas. Use patterns to cut grass, track border, stands and sky; attach with damp brush. Cut assorted narrow green triangles for blades of grass and attach. Cut ⅛ in. wide strips for track details; trim to fit and attach. Using smallest Cut-Out, cut black and white squares and attach for finish line. Attach Jumbo Confetti for people in stands with dots of icing. Pipe tip 2 puffy outline message. Position cake on board at party.

Care Bears™ Box, Trims, Hat and Ribbons

(see Care Package, p. 31)

Tint fondant and add Gum-Tex according to instructions. Use patterns to cut box pieces and hat. Use smallest heart and star Cut-Outs to cut decorations for box. **For gift tag,** cut a 2 x 2½ in. rectangle. **For streamers,** cut 4 strips, ⅛ x 6 in.; wrap around cookie stick to curl; let set 5-10 minutes. Slide off and let all dry 48 hours. **For ribbons,** cut 1 in. wide fondant strips. Cut 2 strips 4¾ in. long; brush backs with damp brush and attach to box. Trim ends on an angle, just a bit smaller than box. **For bottom curls,** cut 2 strips 3 in. long. Cut a V into 1 end; bend into C-shape. **For top curls,** cut 2 strips 4 in. long. Cut a V into 1 end; bend into wavy shape. Let curls dry on their sides on cornstarch-dusted board for 2 days. Attach lollipop sticks to back of hat, box sides and ribbons using Thinned Fondant Adhesive (p. 116). Attach small heart and star decorations to box. Attach confetti sprinkles from Flowerful Medley Assortment to ribbons. Use FoodWriter to print message on gift tag.

Fondant Bows

(see Cheer Bear™ Leads the Team, p. 31)

Add 1 teaspoon Gum-Tex™ to 12 oz. White Ready-To-Use Fondant. Divide into 4ths and tint to match the Pastel Silicone Baking Cups. Roll out ¹⁄₁₆ in. thick. Cut a ½ x 3¼ in. strip for each loop; make 6 loops for each cupcake. Bend into loop, dampen ends and attach; let dry on sides on cornstarch-dusted board for at least 24 hours. To assemble bows, trim ends to a point and position on iced cupcake.

Fondant/Gum Paste Techniques

Girl and Guy Golfers

(see Glee on the Green, p. 20)

Add 1 teaspoon Gum-Tex™ to 12 oz. fondant. Tint 4 oz. gray for putter and putter head, 1 oz. black for handle, 2 oz. skin tone for hands, 1 oz. light gray or dark blue for shoe overlays. Roll out ⅛ in. thick (unless otherwise specified) when needed.

For putter: Cut wooden dowel rod to 10 in. long. Cut a 1½ x 10 x 1⁄16 in. thick strip of gray fondant; brush back with damp brush, wrap around dowel rod to attach and smooth seam. Cut a 1½ x 2½ x 1⁄16 in. thick strip of black fondant; brush back with damp brush, wrap around dowel rod to attach for handle and smooth seam. Score lines for texture using edge of spatula. Use pattern to cut ¼ in. thick putter head. Score lines for grooves; attach with Thinned Fondant Adhesive. Let dry. Brush club head and shaft to handle with Pearl Dust. Attach hand (see below). Let dry on cornstarch-dusted surface.

For hands: Use pattern to cut left hand; reverse pattern and cut right hand. Let 1 hand dry flat on cornstarch-dusted surface. Wrap other hand around prepared putter (thumb on top); attach with damp brush. Let dry. Use Thinned Fondant Adhesive (p. 116) to attach 2 cookie sticks trimmed to 4 in. to the back of each hand, leaving 2 in. extended. Let dry.

For visor brim: Cut using pattern. Set plastic container (5½ to 6 in. diameter) upside down on board; curve fondant around outside; let dry.

For shoes: Use pattern to cut shoe and overlay; reverse pattern and cut 2nd shoe and overlay. Attach overlays to shoes using damp brush. Brush her overlays with Pearl Dust™. Cut eyelet holes using narrow end of tip 5. Let dry. Use Thinned Fondant Adhesive to attach 2 cookie sticks, trimmed to 4 in., to the back of each shoe, leaving 2 in. extended to insert into cake. Let dry.

Palm Trees

(see Volcanic, Jurassic Treats, p. 13; Pirate Treat Fleet, p.16; Treasure Cruise, p. 18)

Cut spearmint leaf into 4 thin slices; dip cut sides in granulated sugar to prevent sticking. Arrange 3 slices in Flower Forming Cup; freeze for 5-10 minutes. Pipe dot of melted candy onto center; position pretzel stick in candy and hold until set. Chill until completely set then unmold carefully.

Strawberry Top

(see Berry-Go-Round, p. 30)

Lighten green fondant from Multi Pack by blending in a small amount of white fondant; roll out ⅛ in. thick. Cut 11 daisies for leaves using smallest cutter from set. Cut a slit to center and use ball tool from tool set to elongate petals. Shape a ⅜ in. long stem and attach. Brush backs with damp brush and attach tops to strawberries.

Strawberry Shortcake Guitar

(see Strawberry Strums Along, p. 30)

Roll out fondant ⅛ in. thick as needed. Use pattern at 90% to cut white guitar base; cut off small strawberry. Use pattern at 100% to cut red and green guitar pieces. Cut dark red rectangle for bridge; cut a matching rectangle in large strawberry and inlay bridge in opening (smooth edges to join seams). Let pieces dry overnight on waxed paper-covered boards dusted with cornstarch. Position and attach guitar pieces using Thinned Fondant Adhesive (p. 116). Use ruler and black FoodWriter™ marker to draw guitar strings. Pipe tip 2 beads on large strawberry and end of guitar strings.

Tree Trunk, Leaves & Flowers

(see Treetop Tink, p. 32)

For tree trunk: Tint 48 oz. fondant brown. Roll out ¼ in. thick; cut a 5 x 8 in. rectangle. Brush plastic column with Piping Gel; cover the complete column with fondant and smooth seam. Cut a 3½ x 6 in. rectangle, ⅛ in. thin at the top tapering to ¾ in. thick at the bottom. Brush back with damp brush and wrap around bottom of tree trunk for tapered shape; smooth seam. Roll 10 logs, 9 in. long, tapering from ½ in. at top to 1 in. diameter at the bottom. Brush with damp brush and attach around tree, bending bottoms onto cake top for roots. Use veining tool from Fondant/Gum Paste Tool Set to imprint vertical lines for bark. For tree limbs, cut 7 lollipop sticks to lengths from 4 to 5 in. Cover with fondant rolled ¼ in. thick; smooth seams. Position to fit between tree trunk sides and bottom of top plate; attach with melted candy.

For flowers, add ¾ teaspoon Gum-Tex™ to 8 oz. fondant; tint violet. Roll out ⅛ in. thick. Cut using Flower Cut-Outs™: cut 35 medium and 25 small flowers. Place on thick Shaping Foam and cup using ball tool from Fondant/Gum Paste Tool Set. Set in Flower Forming Cup dusted with cornstarch for 10-15 minutes to shape. Tint 2 oz. fondant yellow. Roll tiny balls and attach for flower centers using a damp brush. Let dry, then brush on Pearl Dust™.

For leaves, add 1 teaspoon Gum-Tex™ to 14 oz. fondant; tint green. Roll out ⅛ in. thick. Using Leaf Cut-Outs™; cut 130 medium leaves and 60 small leaves. Place on thin Shaping Foam and score lines using small veining tool from Fondant/Gum Paste Tool Set. Let dry in various positions on cornstarch-dusted Flower Formers. Grate green and yellow non-toxic chalk over tea strainer to create a powder; brush on leaves, then brush again with white Pearl Dust™.

Fondant Pumpkins

(see Spin a Scary Tale, p. 38)

Roll out orange fondant ⅛ in. thick. Use 2 smallest cutters from set to cut 8 pumpkins in each size; use 3rd smallest cutter to cut 4. Cut off stems. Trim sides of largest pumpkins to make thinner version. Attach pumpkins around cake sides using damp brush. Pipe tip 3 stems; smooth with finger. Use tip 1 to pipe rib lines and to outline features; fill in features and pat smooth.

Globe Spiders

(see Spin a Scary Tale, p. 38)

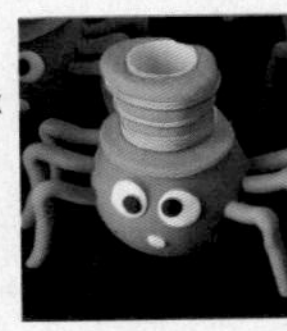

Add ½ teaspoon Gum-Tex to 6 oz. violet fondant for 24 legs. Roll ¼ x 3 in. logs; bend at 1 in. Let dry on cornstarch-dusted surface. Cut hidden pillars to 7½ in. Use 12 in. plate to mark plate leg positions, then insert pillars into base cake. Cover globes with fondant for spider bodies, leaving openings for pillars clear; slide globes onto pillars. Roll out orange fondant ⅛ in. thick. For hat brim, cut a circle using largest Cut-Out; use pillar end to cut away center. Slide brim over pillar and onto spider. For top of hat, use a 1¼ in. ball of fondant; roll out, leaving top edge thicker. Brush pillar area with piping gel, then wrap around pillar and shape. Cut 4 x 1¼ in. long green strips and attach to hats with damp brush. Roll and flatten small balls of fondant for eyes, pupils and nose; attach with damp brush. Attach spider legs with Thinned Fondant Adhesive (p. 116). At party, position 12 in. plate on spider pillars; position pumpkin cake on top.

Penguins

(see A Place to Chill, p. 52)

Tint 12 oz. fondant black; roll out ⅛ in. thick. Cut a 2½ x 8 in. strip to wrap a 2½ in. globe for each body; cut a 2 x 7 in. strip to wrap a 2 in. globe for each head. Brush globes with piping gel and attach fondant; smooth with hands. Leave opening for pillars clear of fondant; for top penguin's head, cover globe top hole with tape before covering over with fondant. Roll out white fondant ⅛ in. thick. Use patterns to cut face and chest. Brush backs with damp brush and attach. Roll small white fondant balls for eyes; flatten slightly and attach. Roll tiny balls for pupils; attach. Using yellow fondant from Multi Pack, roll ½ in. diameter balls; shape into cones for beaks. Roll ¾ in. long flattened teardrops for feet. Score toes with knife. Roll out black fondant ¼ in. thick. Use pattern to cut wings; round edges then brush with damp brush and attach to sides. To make hat, shape a 1 in. diameter ball of red fondant into a slightly curved cone; attach for hat. Roll out white fondant 1⁄16 in. thick; cut a ⅛ x 10 in. long strip and wrap around hat for stripe. Shape a 5 x ¼ in. long log and attach for hat brim; attach a small ball for pompom.

Tree Stand

(see Treasures Under the Tree, p. 53)

Use craft knife to cut 1½ in. diameter center holes in 14 in. and three 6 in. cake circles. Cover 14 in. circle with fondant (p. 117); use knife to clear center hole). Tape three 6 in. circles together and wrap with foil; use knife to clear center hole. Glue legs onto 14 in. Tall-Tier plate; let dry. Assemble stand with 6½ in. column and bottom bolt (add 14 in. plate, then 14 in. fondant covered circle, 8 in. plate and top nut). Position wrapped 6 in. circles over top nut to level surface.

Fondant Watering Can

(see A Sprinkle of Springtime, p. 58)

Add ½ teaspoon Gum-Tex™ to 6 oz. fondant. Roll out fondant ⅛ in. thick. Use pattern to cut out watering can. Use largest round Cut-Out™ to cut circle for base. For easel back, roll out additional fondant ½ in. thick. Shape a 90° triangular wedge of fondant, ¾ in. wide x 1½ in. high. Let all pieces dry for 24 hours on cornstarch-dusted board. Using full-strength royal icing, outline watering can with tip 3. Using thinned royal icing and tip 3, pipe bead flower petals; add dot centers. Let dry.

Water Spray: Use thinned royal icing to pipe about 30 water beads, ¼ in. long, on waxed paper-covered board. Let dry. Cut florist wire into two 6 in. and three 8 in. lengths. Group and tape ends together. Tape end to waxed paper–covered board and arrange spray. Using full-strength royal icing, attach water beads to wires, about ½ to ¾ in. apart; let set. Attach spray to back of spout; let dry. Attach watering can and wedge to base; let set.

Betsy Ross, Table, Needles, Thread

(see Long May She Weave, p. 61)

For Figure: Mix ½ teaspoon Gum-Tex™ into 1 pk. pink fondant from Natural Multi Packs; roll out ⅛ in. thick. Cut body using largest girl cutter from 101 Cookie Cutters Set; set on cornstarch-dusted surface. Trim ⅜ in. off end of each arm; smooth cut edge with finger. Knead together a 1½ in. ball each of blue and white until evenly blended. Roll out ⅛ in. thick. Cut dress using girl cutter. Cut slits under arms and shape sleeves; build up shoulders with a bit of fondant. Attach to body with damp brush. Roll out white fondant ⅛ in. thick. Cut with girl cutter then cut to shape apron. Attach over dress. Pinch sleeve ends to thin at wrists. Shape hands from small balls of pink fondant; attach under sleeves. For hat base, roll out white fondant ¼ in. thick. Use girl cutter to cut just top of head; move cutter down ¾ in. and cut again for crescent shape. Attach on head and shape. Roll out white fondant 1⁄16 in. thick; cut a ½ x 3 in. strip. Place on shaping foam and use ball tool to soften edge and shape ruffle. Attach to hat. For shoes, shape 2 brown teardrops 1½ in. long and attach over feet. For hair, roll a ¼ in. diameter brown rope. Gather into zigzags and attach. Roll ¼ in. white balls for eyes; attach and flatten slightly. Roll ⅛ in. balls for pupils and nose; attach. Roll thin log and attach for mouth. Cut 2 triangular supports for figure, each 1 x 3 in. high. Let all pieces dry 48 hours. Attach supports to back of figure using Thinned Fondant Adhesive. Let dry.

For Table: Cut cookie sticks into four 2 in. lengths. Mix ¼ teaspoon Gum-Tex™ into 2 oz. brown fondant. Roll out ⅛ in. thick. Cut 1¾ x 2½ in. rectangular tabletop; set on cornstarch-dusted surface. Roll out remaining brown mixture 1⁄16 in. thick. Cut strips and wrap around cookie stick legs; secure using damp brush. Smooth seams and trim as needed. Roll a

(continued on p. 123)

(continued from p. 122)

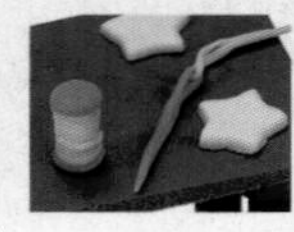

¼ in. diameter rope. Cut and curve into rings that fit around legs. Attach rings and legs to tabletop using damp brush. Let dry 48 hours.

For Spool of Thread: Roll white fondant into ½ x ¼ in. log; flatten ends. Roll out brown fondant 1⁄16 in. thick. Use tip 12 to cut 2 circles; attach to ends of white log. Use craft knife to score thread lines in white section. Roll a 1 in. long, very thin strand of white fondant; attach to spool for loose thread.

For Needles: Roll a 1⁄16 x 1½ in. brown rope. Flatten one end and cut slit for eye. Taper opposite end to a point. Roll a very thin strand of white fondant and attach for thread. Make 2.

Baby Carriage

(see Blessings upon Baby, p. 67)

Mix 1 teaspoon Gum-Tex™ into 12 oz. White Ready-To-Use Rolled Fondant. Roll out ⅛ in. thick; imprint using Spiral Roller. Dust outside of Sports Ball Pan half with cornstarch; cover pan with fondant. Trim bottom edge with knife; trim away opening about 5¾ and 4¾ in. away from edges. Let dry 2-3 days then remove pan. Roll out a small amount of fondant ⅛ in. thick; use largest round Cut-Out™ to cut 2 top wheels. Use buttercream to pipe tip 3 bead border around carriage; pipe tip 5 spirals on wheels. Let dry. Use dry brush to dust carriage and wheels with Pearl Dust.

Fondant Circles

(see Roses for La Quinceañera, p. 68)

Roll out fondant ⅛ in. thick. Cut 100 circles using medium Round Cut-Out; let dry on cornstarch dusted surface. In royal icing, pipe 12 tip 2 dots, approximately ¼ in. apart on edge of circles. Make extras to allow for breakage; let dry.

Imprinted Arches, Buttons

(See Petal Panorama, p. 77)

Knead together 16 oz. each of fondant and gum paste. Roll out ⅛ in. thick. Imprint floral design following instructions on Imprint Mat package. Cut out strips for large arches: **For 6 in. tier**, cut six 3¾ x 1 in. strips; for 10 in. tier, cut ten 4½ x 1 in. strips; for 14 in. tier, cut fourteen 5¾ x 1 in. strips. Let strips dry on sides overnight on corresponding large arch patterns covered with waxed paper and dusted with cornstarch. Cut out strips for small arches: For 6 in. tier, cut six 2½ x ¼ in. strips; for 10 in. tier, cut ten 3½ x ¼ in. strips; for 14 in. tier, cut fourteen 4¾ x ¼ in. strips. Let dry on sides overnight on small arch patterns as above. Reserve remaining mixture to make buttons. When dry, attach pearls to small arches with royal icing: Use 9 pearl lengths for 6 in. tier arches, 12 for 10 in. and 16 for 14 in. Let dry overnight.

For Buttons: Roll out reserved fondant/gum paste mixture ⅛ in. thick. Using wide end of tip 1A, cut 30 circles. Tint reserved mixture rose; roll out ⅛ in. thick. Using narrow end of tip 1A, cut 30 circles. Attach rose circles to white using damp brush. Edge rose circles with tip 2 balls in royal icing; let dry on cornstarch-dusted surface.

Quilling Flowers

(see Breezy Blossoms, p. 81)

Two days in advance:

Make petals, flower centers and leaves (make extras of all to allow for breakage). Mix 1½ oz. of fondant with 1½ oz. of gum paste for each color (yellow, rose, violet, blue, green). Roll out fondant/gum paste ⅛ in thick. **For large flowers,** cut 2¾ x ¼ in. strips for inner petals and 3½ x ¼ in. strips for outer petals; cut 12 of each size in violet, 6 blue, 6 rose and 6 yellow. **For medium flowers,** cut 2 x ¼ in. strips for inner petals and 3 x ¼ in. strips for outer petals; cut 12 of each size in blue, 6 of each size in violet, rose and yellow. **For small single-petal flowers,** cut 2¼ x ¼ in. strips, 12 each in rose and blue, 6 each in violet and yellow. **For double-petal flowers,** brush ends with damp brush and pinch ends of smaller strips together to form loop. Position larger strip around loop; brush ends with damp brush and pinch ends together; repeat to form loops for small flowers. Let petals dry on sides on cornstarch-dusted board. **For flower centers,** roll out yellow fondant/gum paste ⅛ in. thick. **For small flowers,** cut 12 circles with narrow end of tip 1A. **For medium flowers,** cut 6 circles with wide opening of tip 6. **For large flowers,** cut 10 circles with wide end of tip 2A. Brush half the number of circles in each size with water and immediately sprinkle with yellow sugar; let dry. **For leaves,** roll out green fondant/gum paste ⅛ in. thick. Follow press set directions to make 6 medium and 9 large leaves; let dry. **Also:** Prepare stems. Tint small amount of clear vanilla extract with leaf green and yellow icing colors. Brush onto 15 lollipop sticks; let dry.

One day in advance: Assemble flowers. Put 6 petals together of same color and size to form flower. Attach petal ends together with melted candy; let dry. Attach plain flower center circles with melted candy where petals meet in back; attach sugared flower centers in front. With melted candy, attach lollipop sticks to flowers, medium leaves to small flower stems and large leaves to medium and large flower stems. Let dry.

Palm Trees

(see Love's Perfect Setting, p. 84)

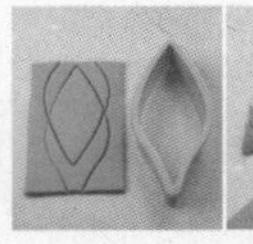

For 5 fondant/gum paste trees, combine equal parts of gum paste and fondant, tint 6 oz. of mixture green and 5 oz. brown. Roll out ⅛ in. thick.

For Leaves: Cut leaves using tulip leaf cutter from set. Turn cutter and cut again to make diamond-shaped leaves in various lengths from 2 to 3¼ in. You will need 6 to 9 leaves for each tree. On thin foam, use veining tool to mark center vein. Use scissors to cut small angled slits. Let dry on medium and large Flower Formers dusted with cornstarch. **For tree trunks:** Cut dowel rods to lengths from 6 to 8½ in. Cover with fondant mixture, leaving 2 to 3 in. exposed to insert into cake. Score with knife to make trunk rings. Let dry. **To assemble:** For leaf base, roll out a small amount of green fondant mixture ¼ in. thick. Use small carnation cutter from Flower Making Set to cut 1 circle for each tree. Insert 3 or 4 leaves. Use tip 12 to pipe a mound of royal icing in the center. Insert additional leaves in icing; tuck tissue under leaves to hold raised position and let dry at least 24 hours. Later, turn grouped leaves over and pipe a tip 12 mound of brown royal icing in the center. Insert tree trunk and prop to hold in position; let dry at least 24 hours.

Fondant Slot Machines, Sign, Chapel Doorway with Sign

(see A Romantic Getaway?, p. 85)

For each of slot machines: Knead together 2 oz. each of fondant and gum paste; tint gray with a small amount of black icing color. Roll out 1⁄16 in. thick. Using patterns and straight-edge wheel of Cutter/Embosser, cut 2 sets of slot machine panels (front, slanted results window panel, top, 2 sides, back); let dry on cornstarch-dusted board. Use tip 1 and royal icing to assemble both slot machines; let dry a few hours. Brush machines with Silver Pearl Dust™. Outline and pipe in details with tip 1 and royal icing (smooth larger areas such as results window, fruit, numbers and payout slot with finger dipped in cornstarch). Score lines between results window with spatula. **For handles,** coat spaghetti (p. 120) using black royal icing and tip 3; let dry in craft block. Attach handle to side and yellow spice drop light to top of machine with tip 3 dots of royal icing. Pipe tip 3 red trim on light and black ball knob on end of handle.

For sign: Knead together ¾ in. balls of fondant and gum paste; roll out 1⁄16 in. thick. Cut sign using pattern and straight-edge wheel of Cutter/Embosser. Decorate with royal icing. Pipe tip 5 dot arrow; let dry. Brush with White Pearl Dust. Print tip 2 message. Trim cookie stick to 5 in. and attach to back of sign with tip 3 dots; let dry.

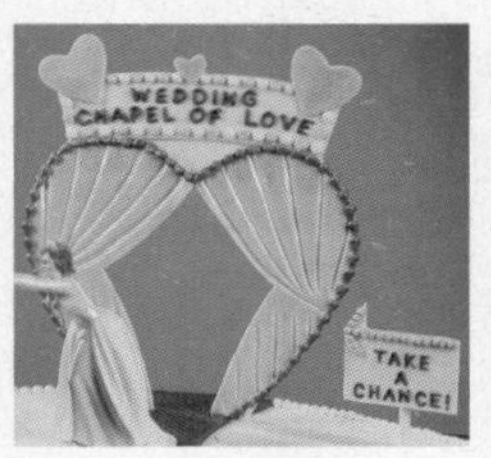

For chapel doorway: Combine 4 oz. each of fondant and gum paste; roll out 1⁄16 in. thick. Using pattern and straight-edge wheel of Cutter/Embosser, cut chapel doorway with sign area. Cut a separate sign area and attach with damp brush. Tint remaining fondant/gum paste mixture rose; roll out ⅛ in. thick. Separately cut 2 sides of heart; score curtain pleats with veining tool from set and attach to doorway with damp brush. Reserve remaining mixture. Decorate doorway with royal icing. Pipe tip 3 bead border around heart and dots around sign. Brush dots on sign with White Pearl Dust™; print tip 2 message. Let all dry for 2 days. **For hearts on doorway sign,** roll out reserved rose mixture ⅛ in. thick. Using Cut-Outs, cut 2 medium and 1 small heart; let dry on cornstarch-dusted board. Attach hearts to front and cookie sticks to back of chapel with royal icing and let dry overnight.

Fondant Bride

(see Her High Profile Day, p. 86)

Tint 6 oz. fondant skin tone; roll out ⅛ in. thick. Use pattern to cut bride's torso; transfer to waxed paper-covered board dusted with cornstarch and let dry overnight. Rub torso edge with side of chalk; blend with soft tissue to create shadow effect. Using royal icing and tip 2, pipe zigzag hair and outline hair ribbon.

Gum Paste Chest and Accessories

(see Packed with Memories, p. 88)

Chest: Tint 12 oz. gum paste brown; roll out ⅛ in. thick. Cut 2 of each size panel: 6½ x 2 in., 3 x 2 in. and 6¾ x 3¼ in. (lid and bottom); reserve remaining gum paste. Set panels on cornstarch-dusted cake board; let dry at least 48 hours. Attach 4 upright panels to bottom using tip 3 lines of royal icing; reinforce inside seams with extra icing. Let dry. Roll out reserved brown gum paste ⅛ in. thick. Cut 6 strips ⅜ in. wide for bars on front, back and lid. Cut 4 small triangles for lid corners; cut 8 larger triangles to wrap around corners of base. Attach details by brushing backs with a damp brush. For lock, cut a circle using open end of a decorating tip; roll slightly into an oval shape. Cut in half and attach to edges of front and lid. Score inner circle of lock with knife tip. Use dry brush to dust all panels of chest with dry Gold Pearl Dust™. Mix Pearl Dust with a little lemon extract; brush on chest corners and lock. Let dry.

Album: Roll out white gum paste ⅜ in. thick. Cut a 1¾ x 1¼ in. wide rectangle for inside pages. Tint a small amount of gum paste rose; roll out ⅛ in. thick. Cut a 1⅞ x 3 in. wide rectangle for cover; wrap and attach over inside pages using damp brush. Use knife tip to score thin lines for white pages; use brush handle to score binding lines on pink cover. Let dry. Use FoodWriter™ markers to print message and draw hearts.

Purse: Roll out white gum paste ⅛ in. thick. Cut a 2¾ x 1⅛ in. wide rectangle. Fold up 1 in.; pinch sides. Trim top to shape flap; fold over and secure using damp brush. Paint clasp using Pearl Dust mixed with lemon extract. Let dry.

Shoes: For her shoes, roll 2 white gum paste logs 1½ x ⅜ in. and shape into tapered high heels. For his shoes, tint gum paste black. Roll 2 logs 1½ x ⅜ in. and shape into shoes. Hollow out inside of all shoes using small end of dog bone tool from Fondant/Gum Paste Tool Set. Let dry.

Champagne Glasses: Press a ⅜ in. ball of gum paste onto top of 4 in. lollipop stick. Use ball tool from Fondant/Gum Paste Tool Set to indent center; pinch to shape top of glass. Wrap ½ x ¼ in. log around stick, ½ in. lower. Pinch to shape glass base. Trim as needed to push into cake. Let dry.

Bee Wings and Birthday Cake

(see It's Great to Bee 3-D!, p. 94)

For Bee Wings: Mix 2 teaspoons Gum-Tex with 24 oz. fondant. Roll out 8 oz. fondant ⅛ in. thick. Use pattern to cut wings; reverse pattern for opposite wing. Let dry on cornstarch-dusted surface. When completely dry, attach lollipop sticks to back of wings with melted candy; let set.

For Birthday Cake: Tint ¼ oz. fondant each in rose and blue, ½ oz. each in green and violet. Roll 3 oz. of white fondant into a ball, flatten ends to shape cake 1 in. thick. Insert candle. Roll out green and rose fondant ⅛ in. thick. Use wide end of tip 12 to cut curve of scallops; move up tip ¼ in. and cut to complete scallop. Use narrow end of tip 12 to cut dots. With violet and blue fondant, roll ¼ in. ropes to wrap around bottom border and candle. Let dry.

Fondant/Gum Paste Techniques *cont.*

Fondant Animal Heads and Tails

(see Cupcake Critters, p. 90 and Barn Raising, p. 92)

Dog: Roll a 1⅜ in. ball of fondant for head and flatten slightly. Shape 1¾ x ¾ in. wide ears; attach. Pipe tip 3 dot nose (overpipe in black), eyes and tongue, outline mouth and eyebrows. Roll a 2½ x ⅜ in. fondant log for tail; curve and taper tip. Let dry. Insert 3 in. lollipop stick in back of head.

Pig: Roll a 1½ in. ball of fondant for head and flatten slightly. Use knife to cut mouth. Roll 2 teardrops ⅜ x ½ in. high for ears; pinch to shape and attach. Roll a ½ in. ball for nose; flatten and attach. Use round end of thin handle modeling stick to indent nostrils. Pipe tip 3 features. Roll a 3/16 x 4¼ in. fondant log for tail; wrap around lollipop stick to curl then remove stick. Let dry.

Horse: Roll a 1¾ in. ball of fondant into oblong shape. Use knife to cut mouth. Roll out fondant 1/16 in. thick. Cut two ⅝ in. high triangles for ears; attach. Use round end of thin modeling stick to shape inner ears and indent eyes and nostrils. Cut two 1¼ x ¾ in. rectangles for sides of mane; cut partial slits ⅛ in. wide with knife and attach. Cut two 2½ x 1½ in. rectangles for center mane areas and one 1 x ¾ in. rectangle for forehead. Cut slits as above and attach. Cut a 2½ x 1¾ in. rectangle for tail; cut partial slits, roll and pinch to secure end. Pipe tip 3 features. Let dry.

Cow: Roll a 1½ in. ball of fondant into oblong shape. Use knife to cut mouth and indent cheeks. Shape ⅜ in. long ears. Use round end of thin modeling stick to shape inner ears and indent eyes and nostrils. Cut a ¾ x ¾ in. square of fondant for hair; cut partial slits and attach. Pipe tip 3 features. Roll a 2 x ¼ in. log for tail; curve. Let dry.

Lion: Roll out fondant 1/16 in. thick. Using large round Cut-Out, cut back mane support base. For head, roll a 1½ in. ball of fondant; flatten slightly. Attach to mane base with damp brush. Shape ½ in. balls for ears; cut 1 side and attach. Roll a ½ in. long teardrop for nose; attach. Pipe tip 3 features. Roll a 3 x ¼ in. fondant log for tail; curve. Let dry.

Elephant: Roll out fondant 1/16 in. thick. Cut 2 ears using medium heart Cut-Out. Flatten top half of heart with finger for upper ear section. Reverse for opposite ear. For head, roll a 1¼ in. ball of fondant; flatten slightly. Attach to ears with damp brush. Roll and curve a 1 x ½ in. log for nose; indent tip with round end of thin modeling stick and attach. Pipe tip 3 features; outline and fill in inner ears. Roll a 1¾ x ¼ in. long for tail; curl. Let dry. Attach a 3 in. lollipop stick to back of all heads for inserting into cupcake.

Fondant Flowers and Leaves

(see Perfect Petits Fours, p. 78)

Tint portions of fondant violet, yellow and green; roll out 1/16 in. thick. For each cake, cut 8 small flowers using forget-me-not cutter and 1 large flower using pansy cutter from Flower Making Set. Pipe tip 2 dot centers in buttercream. Let dry in cavities of Candy Melting Plate. Cut 1 leaf for each cake using small rose leaf cutter from set. Place leaf on thin foam and soften edges with ball tool. Imprint center vein with small end of veiner tool. Let dry on flower formers dusted with cornstarch.

Petits Fours

(see Perfect Petits Fours and A Signature Rose, p. 78)

Bake and cool 1½ in. high sheet cake using firm-textured batter such as pound cake. Freeze for easier cutting. **For rounds**, cut cakes using smallest round cookie cutter from 101 Cutters Set as guide; **for squares** in *A Signature Rose*, use knife to cut 1½ in. squares. Place on cooling grid set over drip pan. Cover cakes with melted candy (*A Signature Rose*) or tinted cookie icing (*Perfect Petits Fours*). Let dry on waxed paper.

Fondant Press Flowers, Leaves and Wire Vines

(see Bridal Path, p. 80)

A week in advance:
Make flowers and leaves. Tint 12 oz. portions of fondant each in orange, yellow, rose, blue and violet; tint an 8 oz. portion green. Add 1 teaspoon Gum-Tex to each portion.* Roll out fondant ⅛ in. thick. . Following Cut & Press package directions, make 30 each large and small flowers, 30 button centers, 20 large leaves and 15 small leaves. Dry flowers in cornstarch-dusted forming cups. Dry button centers on wax paper-covered board dusted with cornstarch. Dry leaves on cornstarch-dusted medium flower formers, curved side up. For shallower curve, lay leaves at an angle. Let all dry overnight. Assemble flowers and make vines. Attach button centers to small flowers and some small flowers to large flowers with Thinned Fondant Adhesive (p. 117). For vines, using fondant adhesive, attach flowers and leaves separately to 6 in. lengths of wire wrapped in florist tape; let dry. For tendrils, use fifteen 6 in. lengths of wrapped wire; curl one end of each using wire cutters.

***Hint:** You may substitute Wilton Ready-To-Use Gum Paste and tint with colored fondant.

Curliques

(see His Star is Rising, p. 7)

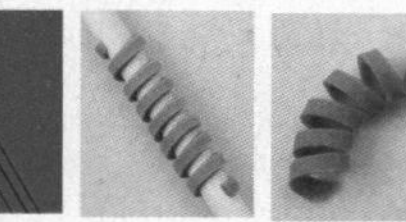

1. Roll out fondant 1/16 in. thick on Roll & Cut Mat lightly dusted with cornstarch. Cut into thin strips.
2. Loosely wrap strips around a dowel rod several times to form curls. Let set 5 to 10 minutes.
3. Slide curl off dowel rod and let dry. Attach to cake with Thinned Fondant Adhesive (p. 117).

Chairs

(see Tea Cozy, p. 105)

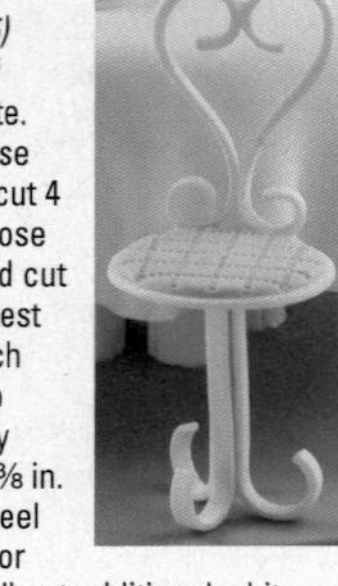

Combine 6 oz. each of fondant and Gum Paste. Roll out ⅛ in. thick. Use metal circle cutter to cut 4 chair seats. Roll out rose fondant ⅛ in. thick and cut 4 seat pads using largest round Cut-Out™. Attach pad to seat with damp brush and immediately emboss quilting lines ⅜ in. apart using ridged wheel on Cutter/Embosser. For seat back and legs, roll out additional white fondant/gum paste mixture ⅛ in thick. Cut strips ¼ in. wide. Shape strips using patterns and let dry on sides several days.

To assemble: Cut 4 lollipop sticks to 2½ in. lengths. Make an indentation at bottom center of each seat and attach a stick using melted candy at a 90° angle (straight up and down). Position 3 chair legs around each stick, making sure they are level, and secure with melted candy. Let candy set. Attach 2 chair back pieces together at top and bottom; let set. Attach bottom to chair. Let set.

Fondant Bears

(see Getting His Bearings, p. 109)

Tint fondant per instructions. Roll out brown ⅛ in. thick. Cut a 2½ x 8 in. strip to wrap a 2½ in. globe for each head; cut a 2 x 7 in. strip to wrap a 2 in. globe for each body. Brush globe with piping gel and attach fondant; smooth with hands. Leave opening for pillars clear of fondant; slide body then head onto pillars and cut off any excess fondant. Cut circles with open end of tip 1A; cut in half and attach for ears. Roll 2 logs 2 x ¾ in. for legs and 2 logs 1¾ x ⅝ in. for arms; shape and attach with damp brush. Roll out light brown ⅛ in. thick. Cut circles with narrow end of tip 2A; attach for snout. Cut circles with open end of tip 12; cut in half and attach for inner ears. Cut 1 x 1½ in. ovals; attach for tummy. Cut tip 1A circles for bottom paw pads and tip 2A circles for top paw pads; attach with damp brush. Roll small white balls for eyes; attach. Roll smaller black balls for pupils and nose; attach. Use black FoodWriter™ to draw curved mouth. (Bow ties will be made later using fondant tinted for cake.)

Daisies

(see Eternal Embrace, p. 77)

Roll out gum paste 1/16 in. thick. Cut 16 single-layer daisies using smallest Cut-Out. On thick shaping foam, curve flowers using ball tool from Fondant/Gum Paste Tool Set (p. 131). Let dry on cornstarch-dusted surface. Cut 10 large, 21 medium and 30 small 2-layer daisies using Cut-Outs. Let bottom layer dry flat overnight. Curve top layer flowers with petals at various positions; let dry overnight, supporting petals with soft tissue. Tint a portion of gum paste blue. Roll small ball flower centers and attach with icing. Attach top and bottom layers with icing. Let dry.

Rose Leaves

(see Flourishing Together, p. 88)

1. Tint gum paste a light moss green. Roll out 1/16 in. thick. Cut leaves using largest rose leaf cutter from Floral Collection Flower Making Set (p. 132). Vary sizes by rolling slightly wider or longer.
2. Imprint veins using veiner mold from set. Place on thin foam and vein edges using thin edge of veiner tool from set. Set in various positions on flower formers; let dry.

Top Bow

(see Taking the Big Step, p. 76)

1. Bow can be assembled directly on the cake or made ahead of time using a 2 to 2½ in. fondant circle as a base. Roll out a fondant rectangle, ¼ in. thick. Place on Imprint Mat and roll over one time to imprint design. Cut strips for bow loops using dimensions listed in project instructions. Your bow may use more loops than shown here, Fold strips over to form loops. Brush ends with damp brush. Align ends and pinch slightly to secure. Stand loops on side to dry.
2. Position 6 or 7 bow loops in a circle over fondant circle. Attach with Thinned Fondant Adhesive (p. 117) or melted candy.
3. Attach remaining loops to fill center of bow. Trim loop ends, if needed, to fit.

Covering Base Boards with Fondant

Cut cake boards 2 in. larger in diameter than your cake, unless otherwise directed, then roll out fondant about 1 in. larger than board size. Wrap board with foil.

1. Lightly coat board with piping gel to help the fondant stick to the foil.
2. Roll out fondant to desired size, ¼ in. thick. Position over board using a rolling pin, draping fondant over edge.
3. Trim excess fondant from edges under bottom of board. Smooth top and sides with Easy-Glide Smoother.

Preparing Fondant-Covered Cake Circles for Tall Tier Construction

(see A Home in Harmony, p. 74)

Using columns from Tall-Tier Stand as a guide, cut a center hole in each cake circle. Tape edges of cake circles with masking tape. Brush boards with piping gel. Roll out fondant and cover cake circle. Smooth fondant with Fondant Smoother, overlapping edges of circle. Smooth fondant around edges and center hole.

Marbleizing Fondant

Using Icing Color: Roll fondant into a ball, kneading until it's soft and pliable. Using a toothpick, add dots of icing color in several spots. Knead fondant slightly until color begins to blend in, creating marbleized streaks. Roll out fondant to desired shape.

Using Pre-Tinted Fondant and White Fondant: Roll a log each of tinted and white fondant. Twist one log around the other several times. Knead fondant slightly until color begins to blend in, creating marbleized streaks. Roll out fondant to desired shape.

Candy Making Techniques

USING CANDY MELTS®*

Fast-melting confectionery coating wafers are the key to easy candy making. Smooth texture and great taste make Candy Melts® your most convenient option for molding. Check out all the great colors on p. 166.

To Melt

Chocolate Pro® Electric Melting Pot (p. 166): The most convenient way to melt—no microwave or double boiler needed! Melts large amounts of Candy Melts® in minutes.

Double boiler method: Fill lower pan with water to below level of top pan. Bring water to simmer, then remove from heat. Put Candy Melts® in top pan and set in position on lower pan. Stir constantly, without beating, until smooth and completely melted.

Microwave method: In microwave-safe container, microwave 1 package Candy Melts® at 50% power or defrost setting for 1 minute. Stir thoroughly. Continue to microwave and stir at 30 second intervals until smooth and completely melted. Candy Melts® may also be melted in Candy Decorating Bags (p. 168). Melt as described above, squeezing bag between heating intervals to blend Candy Melts® together. When completely melted, snip off end of bag and squeeze melted Candy Melts® into molds. Throw away bag when empty.

NOTE: Confectionery coating will lose its pouring and dipping consistency if overheated, or if water or other liquid is added. If coating is overheated, add 2 teaspoons hydrogenated vegetable shortening per 14 oz. Candy Melts®.

To Mold (1 color candies)

Pour melted candy into clean, dry mold; tap lightly to remove air bubbles. Place mold on level surface in refrigerator until bottom of mold appears frosty or until candy is firm. Pop out candy. For lollipops, fill molds, tap to remove air bubbles, then position sticks in mold. Rotate sticks to thoroughly cover with candy so they remain securely in place. Refrigerate to set then unmold.

To Color

Add Candy Colors (p. 166) to melted Candy Melts® a little at a time. Mix thoroughly before adding more color. Colors tend to deepen as they're mixed. Pastel colored candies are most appetizing, so keep this in mind.

To Flavor

The creamy, rich taste of Candy Melts® can be enhanced by adding approx. ¼ teaspoon oil-based Candy Flavor (p. 166) to 14 oz. (one pack) of melted Candy Melts®. Never use alcohol based flavorings; they will cause candies to harden.

Multi-colored candy

"Painting" Method: Before filling mold cavity, use a decorator brush dipped in melted Candy Melts® to paint features or desired details; let set. Fill mold and refrigerate until firm as described above.

Piping Method: Use a parchment or Candy Decorating Bag filled halfway with melted candy. Cut small hole in tip of bag and gently squeeze to add candy detail to mold; let set. Fill mold and refrigerate until firm as described above.

Marbleizing Method

Separately melt 2 different colors of Candy Melts®. Stir colors together, using a lollipop stick to draw lines in mixture. Do not overmix. Quickly spoon or place into molds while mixture is still soft. Tap. Refrigerate until firm; unmold.

Layering Method

Pour melted Candy Melts® into dry molds to desired height. Refrigerate until partially set. Pour melted contrasting color to desired height. Refrigerate until partially set. Repeat until desired number of layers are formed; refrigerate until firm and unmold.

SPECIALTY TECHNIQUES

Candy Shells

Fill pan cavity to the top edge with melted candy. Tap on counter to remove air bubbles. Let chill for 8 to 10 minutes or until a ⅛ to ¼ in. shell has formed. Pour out excess candy then return shell to refrigerator to chill completely. Carefully unmold shells (if you have difficulty removing shells, place pan in freezer for 2-3 minutes, then unmold). Smooth top edges by sliding across warmed cookie sheet or warming plate. Excess candy can be reheated and reused.

Candy Shells in Baking Cups

Spoon or pipe 1 to 2 tablespoons of melted candy into the bottom of a standard baking cup. Brush candy up sides, to desired height, forming an even edge. Refrigerate 5 to 8 minutes. Repeat process if a thicker shell is needed. Refrigerate until firm. Carefully peel baking cup off candy shell.

Candy Umbrellas

(see Stroll in the Showers, p. 63, Joy Rains Supreme!, p. 64)

For Stroll in the Showers: Divide inside of Mini Ball Pan cavity into 10ths. Using melted candy in cut parchment bag, pipe scalloped edging within divisions, starting ½ in. down from top edge. Pipe in below scallops to create a candy shell. Let set, unmold and repeat. Decorate with melted candy in cut parchment bag. Pipe button and rib lines over umbrella top; let set. Cut lollipop sticks to 3 in. long; attach inside umbrella with melted candy. Let set.

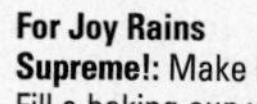

For Joy Rains Supreme!: Make base. Fill a baking cup with melted candy; place cookie stick in center and secure to hold in position. Set in freezer until firm. Make umbrella top. Divide inside of Sports Ball Pan into 16ths. Follow instructions above for piping scallops, starting about 2 in. down from pan edge. Follow instructions above for filling in and decorating candy shell. Attach to cookie stick using melted candy; let set.

*Brand confectionery coating

Candy Curls

(see Mane Attraction, p. 11)

Melt 1 package Candy Melts®; add 2 tablespoons shortening. Pour candy into 2 Mini Loaf Pan cavities, 1 in. deep. Refrigerate until set, then unmold and let come to room temperature. Run cheese plane or potato peeler across narrow edge of candy blocks to make curls in various sizes. For more open curls, use cheese plane; for tighter curls, use potato peeler. Position curls on cake as instructed.

Pretzel Spider Legs and Spider Hats

(see Spiders Step Lively, p. 38)

For Spider Legs: Cut pretzel sticks to 1¾ in. for top of leg, 2 in. for bottom of leg. Hold by end and dip in melted candy to coat; let set on waxed paper. Cut ⅓ off bottom of black spice drop. Push uncoated pretzel ends into spice drop top.

For Spider Hats: For hat top, pour melted candy into Cordial Cups mold. Let set, unmold. For brim, draw 1¾ in. diameter circles on paper; tape paper to cookie sheet and cover with waxed paper. Use melted candy in cut parchment bag to outline and pipe in circles. Let set. Attach top to brim with melted candy. Pipe lines using melted candy in cut parchment bag.

Candy Swags

(see Gracing the Occasion, p. 66)

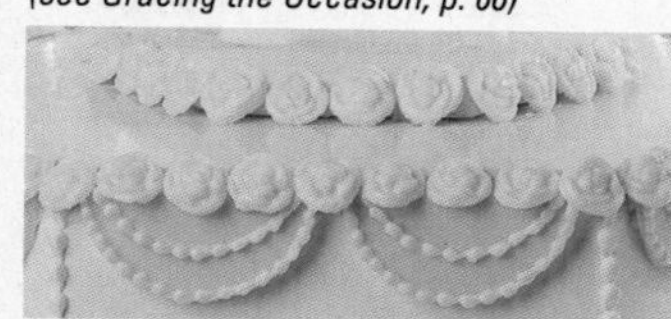

You will need 2 packs of candy to make 12 medium and 12 large swags. Use medium and large circle cutters from 101 Cookie Cutters set. Place cutter on cookie sheet and pour in melted candy to ¼ in. deep. Refrigerate until firm then unmold. Repeat so you have 6 of each size. Let candy circles return to room temperature then cut in half using a warm knife. Using melted candy in a cut parchment bag, pipe a row of beads at the curved edge. Pipe a second row of beads, 1 in. down from straight edge on large swags, ⅜ in. down on medium swags. Let set.

Cowl

(see He's Counting on You, p. 40)

Stack 3-4 jumbo baking cups in your hand so that pleats align. Mark 24 pleats for cowl area and place face down on waxed paper-covered board. Slightly flatten cups to expand marked area to 5 in. wide. Using Candy Decorating Bag, pipe melted cocoa candy over marked area and on bottom circle of cup. Do not spread beyond marked area. Refrigerate until firm. Repeat with 2 more layers of candy. Peel cups from candy.

Coffins

(see Sweet Dreams, p. 41)

Melt 10 oz. cocoa candy and pour into biscuit/brownie pan until ¼ in. thick. Refrigerate until firm. Unmold on waxed paper-covered board; let come to room temperature. Using pattern and knife, cut coffin bottom and lid. Also cut ¾ in. high pieces for sides, 2 each 1⅝ in., 1 ½ in. and 3⅛ in. wide. To attach sides to bottom, start with a 1⅝ in. top piece; run edge of piece along warming tray and position on coffin bottom. If a warming tray is not available, pipe a line of melted cocoa candy using a cut parchment bag and attach side piece. Repeat to attach two 1 ½ in. sides, two 3⅛ in. sides and remaining 1⅝ in. side. Let set. To smooth gap between bottom and sides, run area along warming tray or use a hot knife.

Candy Leaves

(see Creamy Blossoms, p. 59)

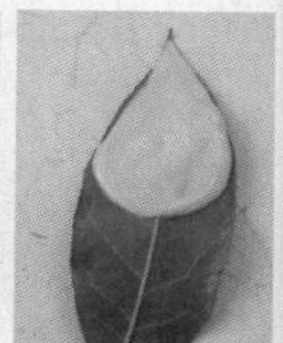

Clean lemon leaves with damp cloth. Tint melted white candy green. Brush onto back of lemon leaf; let dry in medium flower former. When dry, peel off leaf. Paint vein lines on candy using fine tip brush and green candy color or using FoodWriters™.

Covering Cakes and Cookies with Candy Melts®* or Poured Icings

A quick and easy way to give a professional-looking finish to all your baked goods! For Candy Melts®, melt following package directions. For icing recipes, follow recipe directions to reach pouring consistency. For canned icing, heat in microwave at Defrost setting (30% power) for 20-30 seconds; stir. Repeat until consistency of icing will pour. Place cooled cakes or cookies on cooling grid positioned over cookie sheet or pan. Pour or pipe candy or icing on center of item, spreading to edges with a spatula so that candy or icing drips down and covers sides. Let dry.

CANDY PLAQUES

You can use pans as candy molds to make solid decorative plaques. If your pan has detail, it may be painted or filled in desired colors as you would for any candy mold.

Pour melted candy into center of pan cavity. Tap pan gently on counter to eliminate bubbles. Candy should be ¼ to ¾ in. thick, depending on project instructions. Place pan in refrigerator for about 15-30 minutes until firm (check occasionally; if candy becomes too chilled, it may crack). Unmold onto hand or soft towel (tap gently if necessary).

Monkey Candy Plaque, Candy Faces and Balloons

(see Monkey Shines, p. 4)

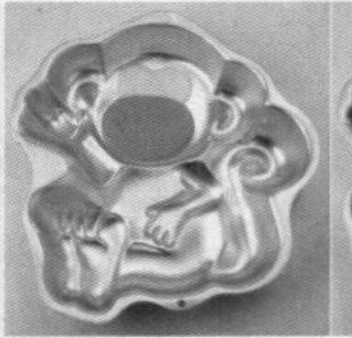

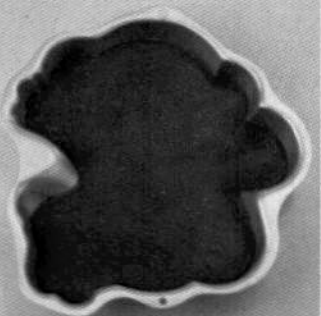

Tint candy as follows: 2 oz. black, 4 oz. light brown (white with some light cocoa Candy Melts®*) for monkey plaque; 5 oz. yellow for hat; 4 oz. each pink, violet and green for balloons; 1 oz. blue for small hats; enough orange to make letters of name. Using melted candy in cut parchment bags, fill in pupils, muzzle, inner ears and background areas of Monkey Pan; refrigerate until firm. Fill in eyes and let set. Melt 3 packs of light cocoa Candy Melts; pour into pan. Refrigerate until completely set, then unmold. Lay hat pattern on board and cover with waxed paper. Position candy plaque on paper then outline and pipe in hat with melted candy. Use letters and largest circle cutter from 101 Cookie Cutters Set to mold name and 3 balloons. Place cutters on non-stick cookie sheet; fill ¼ in. deep with melted candy. Refrigerate until firm; unmold. Using Candy Melting Plate cavities, mold 12 small monkey faces. Refrigerate until firm; unmold. Place on waxed paper-covered board. Pipe ears and hat using melted candy in cut parchment bags. Let set.

Disney Princess Candy Plaque

(Ariel's Splashy Celebration, p. 33)

Melt 2 oz. white Candy Melts®* and tint pink. Pipe in lips; refrigerate until set. Melt 14 oz. white Candy Melts and tint Ariel skin tone using orange candy color. Pipe in face and skin; refrigerate until set. Melt 2 packages of red Candy Melts. Pipe in hair; refrigerate until firm then unmold. Pipe on details using royal icing. Outline and fill in flower, flower center and bikini using tip 6; smooth with finger. Pipe whites of eyes with tip 2, iris with tip 3, pupil with tip 2. Pipe eyelid and lashes with tip 1, eyebrows with tip 3. Pipe dot highlights on eyes and flower with tip 1.

Spider-Man Candy Plaque

(see Take His Gift for a Spin, p. 34)

Melt 14 oz. white Candy Melts®*. Tint 5 oz. black and 6 oz. blue (combine blue with violet candy color). Using Spider-Man pan and melted candy in cut parchment bag, pipe in blue areas and black around eyes; chill until set. Pipe in whites of eyes; chill until set. Melt 20 oz. red candy; fill in remainder of pan, tap to eliminate bubbles. Refrigerate until firm. Unmold onto soft towel and set on waxed paper-covered cake board. Using melted black candy in cut parchment bag, pipe all web lines.

Candy Plaque Crown and Color Flow Slipper

(see Accessorize the Princess, p. 14)

You will need about 3 packages melted white Candy Melts®*. Tint 14 oz. pink using candy color. Mold 7 large pink roses and 1 white rose in Roses in Bloom mold; 5 pink roses using only rose portion of Roses mold; and 5 pink hearts using Hearts mold. Use painting method (p. 125) to mold 2-tone letters using Letters & Numbers set. Use about 28 oz. melted white candy to mold ½ in. thick candy plaque in Crown pan. Refrigerate all until firm; unmold. Use melted candy to attach 2 plastic dowel rods, 6 in. long, to back of crown, about 1 in. from outer edges with 2 in. exposed at bottom. Refrigerate until firm. Turn crown over and attach roses, hearts and letters using melted candy; let set several hours. Brush entire plaque with Pearl Dust™. **For color flow slipper,** copy shoe pattern and tape to board; cover with waxed paper. Outline using tip 2 and full-strength color flow icing (p. 116). Fill in with thinned color flow. Use tip 2 and thinned color flow to pipe about 28 puddle dots, ¼ in. diameter, on waxed paper. Let all dry 2 days. Use full-strength color flow to attach dots and prepared white candy rose to slipper. Brush white Pearl Dust™ over all except inside shoe (area above dots).

Hexagon Cake Top Plaques

(see Gracing the Occasion, p. 66)

You will need 5 packages of candy to make 3 plaques: 6 in., 12 in. and 15 in. Use 9 oz. of candy for 6 in. pan, 28 oz. for 12 in. pan and 33 oz. for 15 in. pan. Pour into pans, refrigerate until firm and unmold.

Candy Easels

(see Gracing the Occasion, p. 66)

Melt 1 pk. white Candy Melts and pour into vertical section of cross; refrigerate until firm and unmold. Cut diagonal line from top corner to opposite bottom corner with a hot knife. Trim tops and bottoms flat. Attach to back of cross with melted candy, wide end at bottom end of cross.

COLOR FLOW

Working With Color Flow

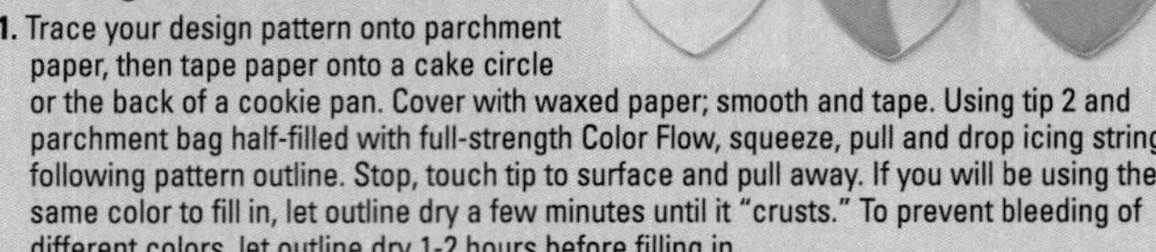

1. Trace your design pattern onto parchment paper, then tape paper onto a cake circle or the back of a cookie pan. Cover with waxed paper; smooth and tape. Using tip 2 and parchment bag half-filled with full-strength Color Flow, squeeze, pull and drop icing string following pattern outline. Stop, touch tip to surface and pull away. If you will be using the same color to fill in, let outline dry a few minutes until it "crusts." To prevent bleeding of different colors, let outline dry 1-2 hours before filling in.
2. Thin Color Flow mixture with water. Cut opening in parchment bag to the size of tip 2. Fill in design with thinned Color Flow.
3. Let decorations air dry thoroughly, at least 48 hours. To remove, cut away waxed paper from board, then turn over and peel waxed paper off the Color Flow piece.

Hint: For curved decorations, dry pieces on flower formers. To easily remove dried Color Flow, pull waxed paper backing over the edge of a table with one hand, while holding decoration with other hand. Waxed paper will pull off naturally. Or, with dried Color Flow resting on cookie sheet, place cardboard sheet over Color Flow, lift and turn over so that top of decoration rests on cardboard. Lift off waxed paper.

Since any moist icing will break down Color Flow, either position Color Flow decorations on cake shortly before serving or place on sugar cubes, attaching with full-strength Color Flow.

Color Flow Umbrella, Bow

(see Baby's Topping the Bill, p. 62)

Trace patterns from *2009 Pattern Book* (p. 128). **For Umbrella:** Trace umbrella base, 3 overlay panels (right, left, center) and puddle dot handle tip. **For bow:** Trace bow and puddle dot knot. Tape patterns to cake boards; cover with waxed paper and tape to hold smooth. Outline using tip 3 and full-strength Color Flow Icing, (p. 116) let set. Flow in using Thinned Color Flow Icing (p. 116) in a cut parchment bag. Let dry 48 hours.

Color Flow Blue Bird with Watering Can

(see Baby's Bird Bath, p. 65)

Prepare cookie dough and roll out. Use pattern to cut out bird with watering can. Bake and cool cookie. Outline details with tip 2 and full-strength Color Flow (p. 116). Flow in with Thinned Color Flow; let dry several hours. Continue using full-strength Color Flow. Pipe tip 14 pull-out feathers; pipe tip 2 dot eye, outline and fill in beak. Cut white wire into four 4 in. lengths; secure ends by wrapping with florist's tape. Set on waxed paper-covered board and fan wires. Attach Heart Drops to wires and to top of watering can with dots of icing. Let dry. Use full-strength Color Flow to attach end of wires under watering can.

Color Flow Cross

(see Faith for the Future, p. 67)

Tint portion of Color Flow (p. 116) pink and reserve remainder white. Using full-strength Color Flow and waxed paper-covered pattern, outline 1 Cross Long Arm, 3 Cross Short Arms, 1 Long Arm Teardrop, 3 Short Arm Teardrops, 1 each Outer and Inner Disk with tip 2. Flow in center of patterns with thinned color flow in cut parchment bag. Let dry 48 hours. Divide outer disk into 10ths, marking divisions with a small dot of Color Flow icing in cut parchment bag. Using tip 2 and full-strength Color Flow icing, pipe scroll at division points and print letters on inner disk. Attach pieces together to form cross with full-strength color flow icing; let set.

CANDY RECIPES

Basic Ganache and Truffles

14 oz. Candy Melts®* (p. 166)
½ cup heavy whipping cream

Chop candy (you can use a food processor). Heat whipping cream in saucepan just to boiling point. Do not boil. Remove from heat and add chopped candy, stir until smooth and glossy.

Whipped Ganache: Follow recipe above, using 1 cup whipping cream. Allow mixture to set and cool to room temperature (mixture will have the consistency of pudding; this may take 1-2 hours). Whip on high speed with an electric mixer until light and soft peaks form.

Truffles: Add 1 tablespoon liqueur for flavor, if desired. Stir until smooth and creamy. Refrigerate until firm. Roll into 1 in. diameter balls. Can be used as center for dipped candies, served plain or rolled in nuts, coconut or cocoa powder. Store truffles in refrigerator up to 3 weeks. Makes about 2 dozen (1 in.) balls.

Ganache Glaze: If mixture is too thick, add 1 to 2 tablespoons whipping cream. Position cake on wire rack over drip pan. Pour glaze onto center and work out toward edges.

NOTE: Cake may be iced first in buttercream. Let icing set, then pour on ganache glaze. If cake has a perfect surface, no other icing is needed.

Ready-In-Minutes Cocoa Fudge

(see Fall for Fudge, p. 42)

20 oz. (approximately 4 ½ cups) Dark Cocoa Candy Melts®* (p. 166)
1 can (14 oz.) sweetened condensed milk (not evaporated)

Melt Candy Melts® in microwave-safe container using microwave on low power. Add milk; stir until blended. Microwave an additional 2 to 3 minutes on medium power; stir until fudge develops a sheen. Pour mixture into buttered 7 x 11 in. non-stick Biscuit/Brownie pan and refrigerate until firm.

*Brand confectionery coating

2009 PRODUCT SHOPS

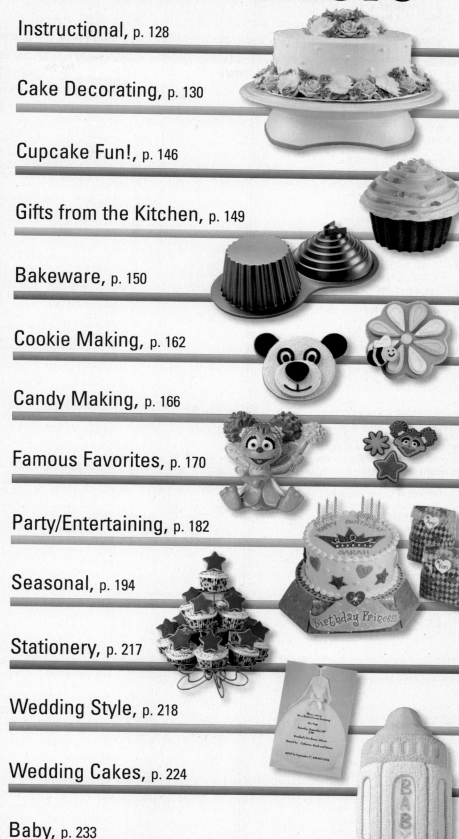

FIND IT FAST... ORDER WITH EASE!

Welcome to the most complete selection of cake decorating products anywhere! Here you'll find all the great Wilton tools, ingredients, accents and more you need to create every design in this Yearbook.

Go ahead and browse! Our shops are conveniently organized to help you find what you need fast. Whether you're decorating a batch of holiday cookies or creating a 3-tiered wedding cake, it's easy to find everything on your list.

When you're ready to buy, we make it a breeze! Charge your order 4 easy ways at your convenience:

PHONE TOLL-FREE
800-794-5866
8:00 am-4:30 pm, Monday-Friday CST
(RETAIL CUSTOMERS ONLY)

FAX TOLL-FREE
888-824-9520
24 HOURS A DAY/7 DAYS A WEEK

ORDER ON-LINE
www.wilton.com
24 HOURS A DAY/7 DAYS A WEEK

MAIL YOUR ORDER
Use the convenient retail order form in this book.

Se Habla Español!
Para mas informacion, marque 800-436-5778

Prices in this Yearbook were accurate at the time of printing and supersede all previous Wilton publications. Due to dynamic market conditions, the price of some items may have changed. Please check **www.wilton.com** for the most up-to-date prices before placing an order.

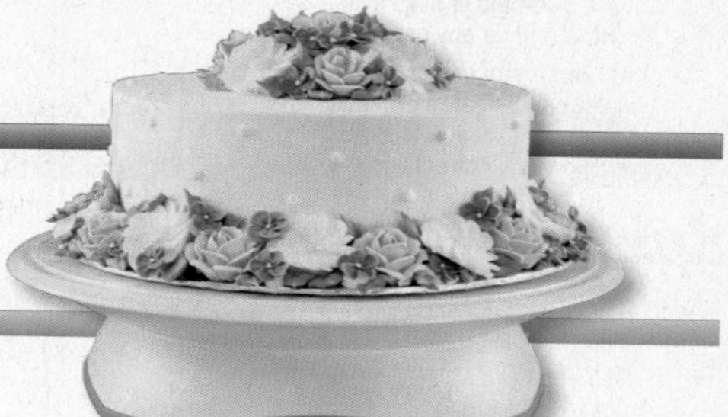

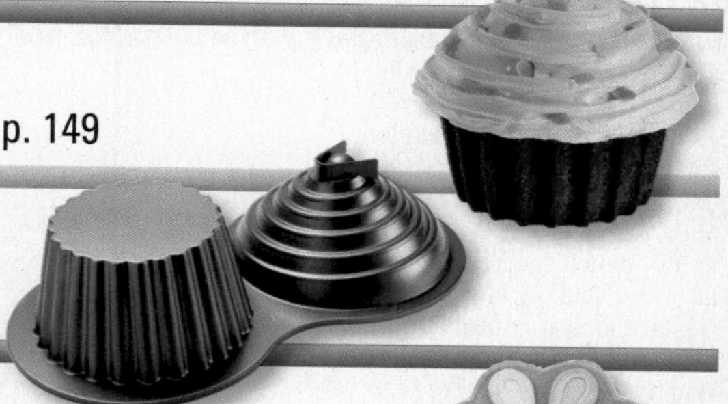

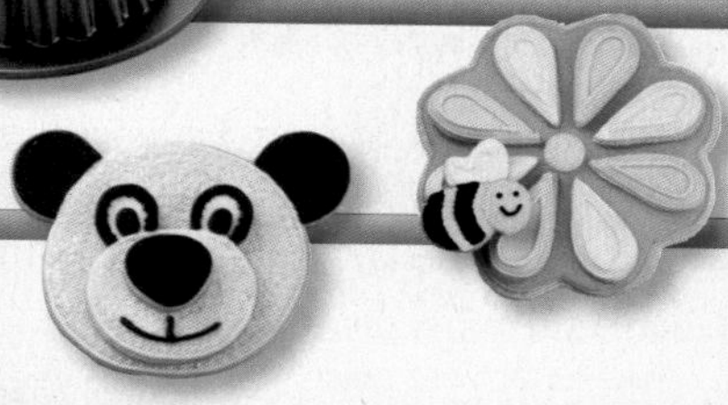

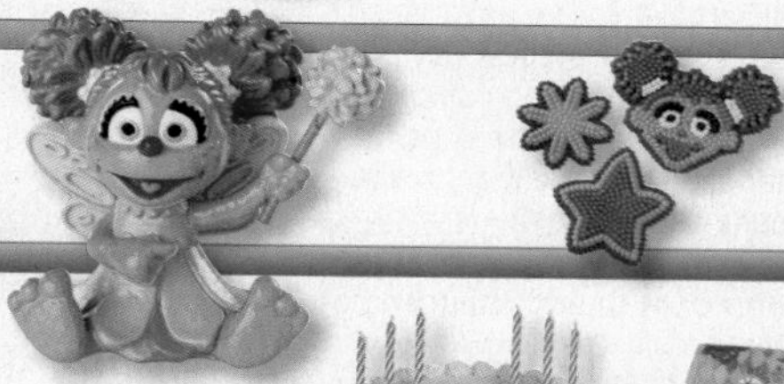

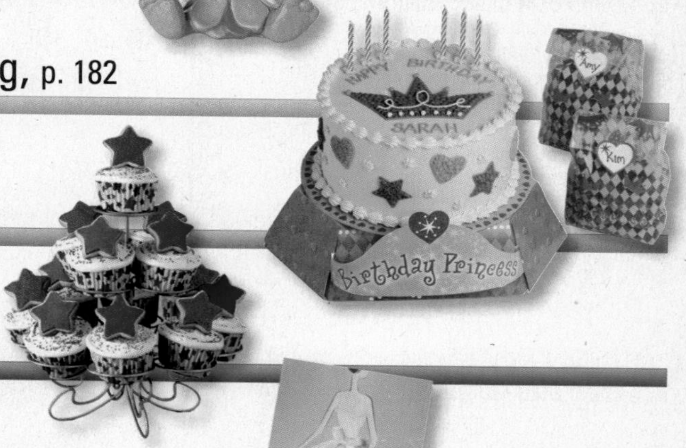

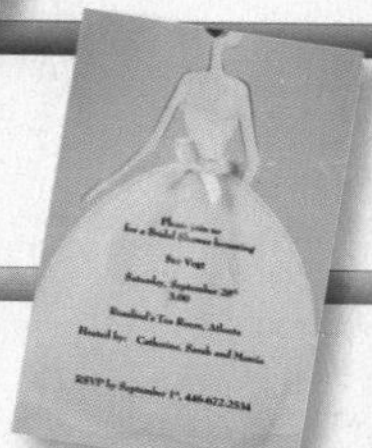

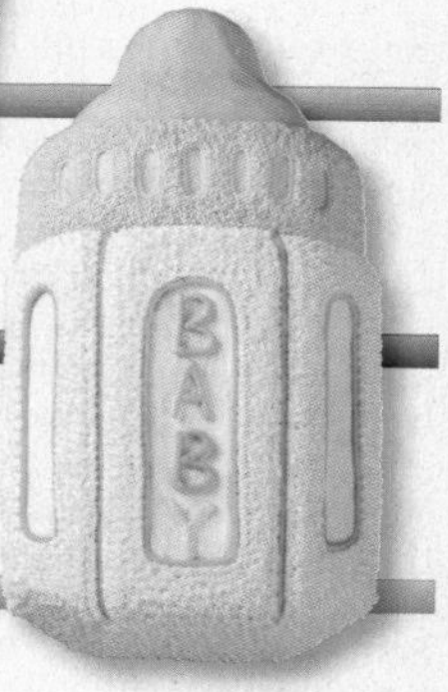

Instructional

Find inspiration with Wilton how-to books and videos. There's something perfect for your next celebration, from kids' birthday cakes to multi-tiered wedding designs.

Specialty Publications

NEW!

Gifts from the Kitchen

Wrap up your homemade food gifts with pizzazz! *Wilton Gifts from the Kitchen* shows you dozens of great ways to package and present a food gift that is as welcoming and tasteful as the good things inside. This book makes it easy, using supplies you may already have on hand, along with convenient Wilton accents. *Wilton Gifts from the Kitchen* is also a great recipe book, with over 50 easy-to-prepare foods—you'll find delicious tastes for every season, fancy dipped treats, special occasion desserts, fun food gifts for kids and more. With *Wilton Gifts from the Kitchen,* you'll find the perfect food to please the eye and warm the heart. Soft cover, 96 pages.
902-U-1225 $12.99

Cupcake Fun!

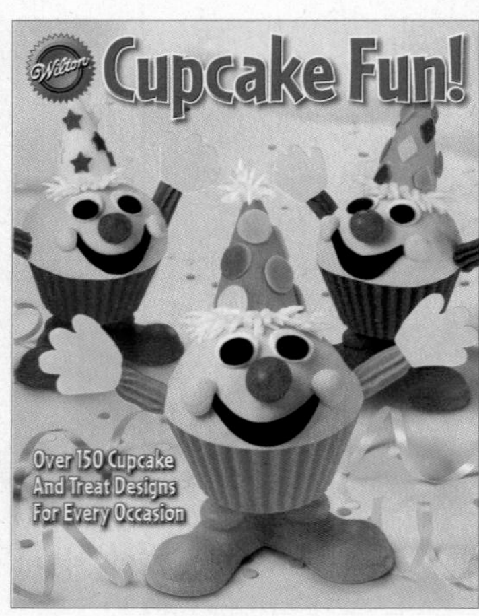

Wilton presents today's hottest party dessert like you've never seen it before. This all-new collection features over 150 exciting cupcake and treat ideas for all occasions, with complete baking and decorating instructions to make them easy. Discover captivating new shapes from coffee cups to flying saucers, plus a great recipe section with delicious surprises like Key Lime Cupcakes, Mocha Icing and more. Great baking and decorating products, too! *Cupcake Fun!* is the book you need to create the ultimate cupcake celebration. Look for many more great cupcake ideas and recipes at www.cupcakefun.com. Soft cover, 128 pages.
902-U-795 $12.99

Wilton Tiered Cakes

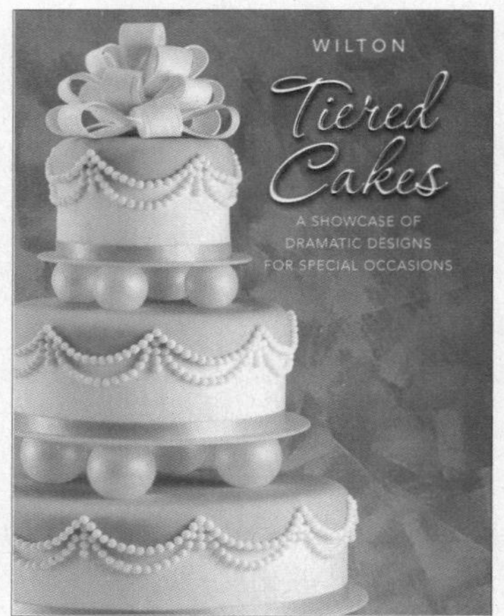

If you are planning a wedding, a shower or any big event, *Wilton Tiered Cakes* will show you the perfect way to top it off. Experience today's most contemporary looks in reception cakes! See how exciting it can be to mix colors on a wedding cake using textured fondant or floral accents. Discover creative new construction ideas like our cute teddy bear tower with fondant baby blocks used as separators. It's all here—38 amazing cake designs—along with complete instructions, techniques, construction and cutting guides, plus great Wilton products. Soft cover, 128 pages.
902-U-1108 $14.99

NEW!

2009 Yearbook of Cake Decorating

Your most exciting celebrations begin here! This new edition of the *Wilton Yearbook* is filled with one-of-a-kind designs for decorated cakes and desserts that will make the party unforgettable. You'll discover over 200 amazing cakes, cookies, candies and more that set the tone for your event. From birthday cakes for kids and adults to festive holiday desserts for each season, you'll find the perfect design. Our 3-D Cakes special section presents incredible dimensional designs like rocket ships, a stand-up bumble bee—even an enchanting doll house, with fantastic fondant furniture. As always, you'll find the best in traditional and contemporary wedding designs, today's hottest character cakes, fun cupcake creations and more. Featuring step-by-step instructions, technique resource guide, complete product section and a website link to more great designs.
Soft cover; 240 pages.
English 1701-U-2041 $11.99
Spanish 1701-U-2043 $11.99

2009 Pattern Book

Wilton Pattern Book
FOR THE 2009 WILTON YEARBOOK

Duplicate many of the beautiful cake designs featured in the *2009 Yearbook* and on the Wilton website. Includes over 100 decorating outlines to transfer to your cake. Easy-to-follow instructions. Soft cover; 50 pages of patterns.
408-U-2009 $8.99

Wilton Wedding Cakes—A Romantic Portfolio

Our exciting collection of tiered cakes makes the romantic wedding of every bride's dreams a reality. *A Romantic Portfolio* sets the bride's imagination free, with 38 exquisite cakes that express love in many ways. It's all here—beautiful seasonal designs, elegant shapes, classic and contemporary looks. There is a cake for every taste—along with coordinating ornament, favor suggestions and tiered cake accessories.

A Romantic Portfolio will inspire decorators as well as brides. Every design includes step-by-step decorating instructions, product checklists and serving amounts. Used with our comprehensive construction guide, patterns, techniques and recipes, *A Romantic Portfolio* has everything decorators need to recreate each cake to perfection. Soft cover, 144 pages.
902-U-907 $16.99

Celebrate!® With Fondant

It's the first book to feature fondant done the Wilton way—using our exciting cake designs, step-by-step instructions and convenient fondant products. *Celebrate!® with Fondant* makes fondant cakes easy and fun for everyone. See how to make more than 40 terrific cakes, along with alternate ways to decorate every design and suggestions for the perfect occasions to serve them.
Soft cover, 120 pages.
902-U-911 $14.99

The Wilton School—Decorating Cakes

- 30 exciting cakes with complete instructions and product listings
- 103 technique instructions, shown step-by-step, including borders, flowers, fondant and more
- Helpful recipes, tip chart, serving and cutting guides, glossary of terms
- In-depth sections on baking cakes, preparing icing, using tips, cutting and transporting cakes
- Product guide, which shows and explains the equipment and ingredients required for decorating

This exciting book presents what Wilton has learned in 79 years of teaching cake decorating. *Decorating Cakes* is designed to appeal to anyone who wants to make great-looking cakes for families and friends. Soft cover, 116 pages.
902-U-904 $14.99

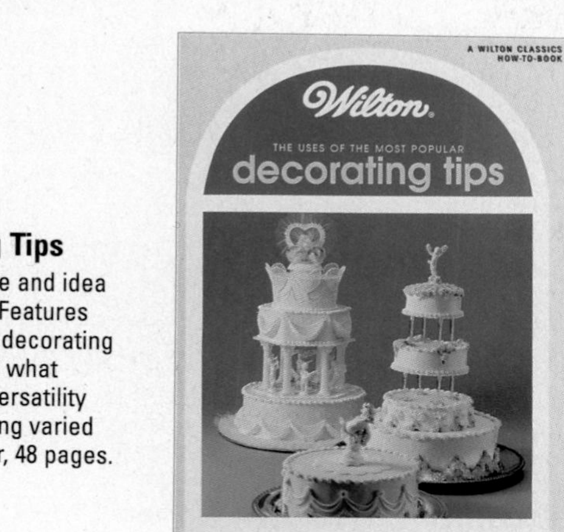

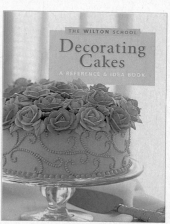

Uses of Decorating Tips

Valuable quick reference and idea book for any decorator. Features five of the most popular decorating tip families and explains what each does. Shows the versatility of many tips by presenting varied cake designs. Soft cover, 48 pages.
902-U-1375 $9.99

Instructional Videos

Winner of 2 Telly Awards

BAKE DECORATE CELEBRATE!™ Seasons 1-3 on DVD!

It's the ultimate introduction to cake and dessert decorating on video! Each boxed set includes a complete 13-episode season of the popular Telly Award-winning Public Television series, which makes it easy for anyone to create something great to serve.
In every episode, hosts Nancy Siler and Melanie Glasscock focus on a specific theme, such as Kids' Birthdays, Shaped Pans or Whimsical Cupcakes. They'll decorate specialty projects based on that theme and give you related decorating ideas to make the celebration complete. Special segments in each episode include Decorating Basics, featuring essential techniques, and Decorating Tips, with a variety of designs made using one specific tip. Each set includes 4 DVDs, approx. 6 hours total.

Season 1

Garden Party Desserts, Chocolate Treats, Fruits, Easy Flowers and more.
DVD 901-U-121 Set/4 $39.99

Season 2

Roses, Tarts, Pool & Beach, Patriotic and more. Closed captioned.
DVD 901-U-131 Set/4 $39.99

Season 3

Apples, Apples, Apples, Tropical & Tasty, Critters You Can Eat, Quick Change Cakes and more. Closed captioned.
DVD 901-U-132 Set/4 $39.99

Cake Decorating Basics

See and learn the essentials of creating amazing cakes and desserts, step by step! Everything from tools to icings, baking perfect cakes, decorating stars, shells, flowers and more, is covered in this 60-minute program.
DVD 901-U-120 $19.99

How to Make Wedding Cakes

Invaluable lessons on how to design and assemble tiered cakes for weddings, showers, anniversaries and other special occasions. Hints for transporting and serving are also included in this 60-minute video. DVD material matches VHS.
DVD 901-U-256 $19.99

How to Make Icing Flowers

Learn how to make roses, Easter lilies, violets, pansies, daisies, poinsettias and more! Five cake designs incorporate all the flowers included in this 60-minute video. DVD material matches VHS.
DVD 901-U-258 $19.99

Cake Decorating Beginner's Guide

- How to bake and ice perfect cakes
- How to mix any color icing with ease
- 15 fantastic cake ideas to decorate in 6 steps or less
- Step-by-step decorating instructions for stars, rosettes, drop flowers and more

Wilton, the #1 name in cake decorating, shows beginners everything they need to know, step-by-step. The *Beginner's Guide* makes decorating easy to learn and fun to do for everyone!
Soft cover, 40 pages.
902-U-1232 $3.99

Candy Making Beginner's Guide

- 20 incredible candy ideas—all made in a few easy steps
- Easy ways to melt perfectly every time
- Painting color details in candy
- How to make classic creme-filled and dipped candies
- Great candy gift and favor ideas

You'll be amazed at the fantastic candies you can make using this book. The possibilities are endless, using the great selection of Wilton Candy Melts®* and Candy Molds. The *Beginner's Guide* shows you how, step-by-step, so you will make great-looking candies your very first time. The *Beginner's Guide* has the information you need to start making candy like a pro.
Soft cover, 40 pages.
902-U-1231 $3.99

*Brand confectionery coating.

Cake Decorating

Create your greatest cakes with the essentials decorators count on. Time-saving tools. Precise tips. Quality icings. Plus, exciting new products for fondant and gum paste decorating!

Rolled Fondant

White Ready-To-Use Rolled Fondant

Fondant has never been more convenient and easy to use for decorating! With Wilton Ready-To-Use Rolled Fondant, there's no mess, no guesswork. The 24 oz. (1.5 lbs.) package covers an 8 in. 2-layer cake plus decorations; the 80 oz. (5 lbs.) package covers a 2-layer 6 in., 8 in. and 10 in. round tiered cake plus decorations. Pure white. Certified Kosher.

1. Roll out.
2. Layer over cake.

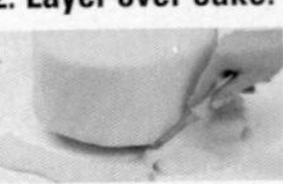

3. Trim and decorate.

24 oz. (1.5 lbs.) Pk.
710-U-2076 $6.79

80 oz. (5 lbs.) Pk.
710-U-2180 $22.99

Color Fondant Multi Packs

Convenient four-pouch assortments are perfect for multicolored flowers and borders. Each 17.6 oz. package contains four 4.4 oz. packs. Certified Kosher.
$10.49

Primary Colors Green, Red, Yellow, Blue **710-U-445**

Neon Colors Purple, Orange, Yellow, Pink **710-U-446**

Pastel Colors Blue, Yellow, Pink, Green **710-U-447**

Natural Colors Light Brown, Dark Brown, Pink, Black **710-U-448**

PEARL DUST™

Give your fondant, gum paste, royal icing and molded Candy Melts®* decorations a beautiful, glittering finish! Wilton Pearl Dust creates rich, lustrous highlights on flowers, bows, letters and more. Easy to use, just brush onto your decoration with a soft artist brush. Or, to paint decorations, pour a small amount of lemon extract into a a Color Tray cavity; stir in Pearl Dust and brush onto your decoration. Edible; FDA-approved. Certified Kosher (except Orchid Pink and Lilac Purple). .05 oz. bottle. **$3.99**

NEW! **Leaf Green 703-U-215**
NEW! **Lilac Purple 703-U-221**
NEW! **Sapphire Blue 703-U-222**
NEW! **Ruby Red 703-U-223**
Gold 703-U-216
Yellow 703-U-213
Bronze 703-U-214
Orchid Pink 703-U-217
Silver 703-U-218
White 703-U-219

Fondant Tools and Accessories

NEW!

Quick Ease Roller

Makes it easy to prepare small pieces of fondant and gum paste for cutting flowers and designs. Wooden roller fits comfortably in palm of hand. 4.2 in. wide.
1907-U-1202 $5.49

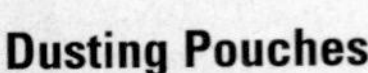

Dusting Pouches

Essential for rolling out gum paste or fondant! Fabric pouch dusts surfaces with a cornstarch/confectioners' sugar mixture to prevent your rolling pin from sticking. Gathering cord closes bag securely—just tap lightly on the pouch to sprinkle. 7 in. diameter.
417-U-106 Pk./4 $3.29

Brush Set

Fine-bristle brushes in three tip designs (round, square and bevel) help you achieve different painted effects. Use with Icing Writer (p. 135); or attach fondant decorations with water or adhesive.
1907-U-1207 Set/3 $3.29

Color Tray

Become a true fondant artist with this convenient tray! Pour in Icing Writer™ (p. 135) and use with the Brush Set to add vivid designs to your fondant cakes.
1907-U-1208 $3.29

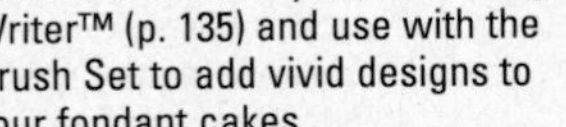

FoodWriter™ Edible Color Markers

Use like ink markers to add fun and dazzling color to countless foods. Kids love 'em! Decorate on fondant, color flow, Wilton Cookie Icing, royal icing, even directly on cookies. Brighten everyday foods like toaster pastries, cheese, fruit slices, bread and more. Each set includes five .07 oz. FoodWriter markers. Certified Kosher.

Primary Colors Sets

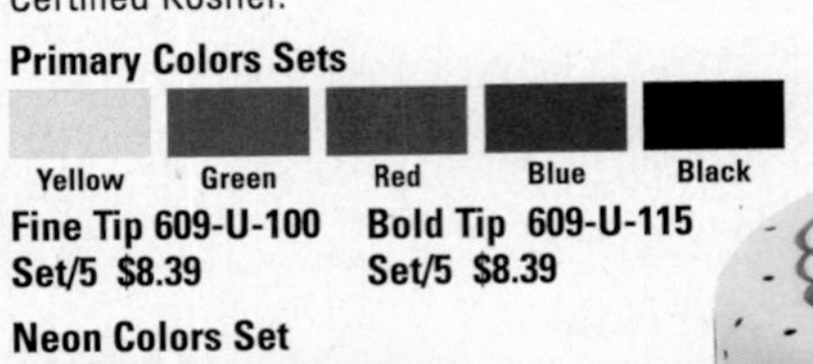

Yellow, Green, Red, Blue, Black

Fine Tip 609-U-100 Set/5 $8.39
Bold Tip 609-U-115 Set/5 $8.39

Neon Colors Set

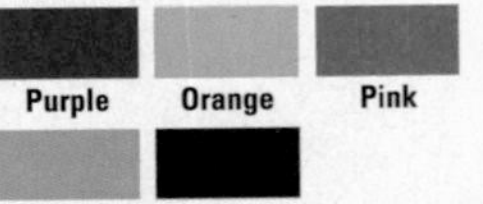

Purple, Orange, Pink, Light Green, Black

Fine Tip 609-U-116 Set/5 $8.39

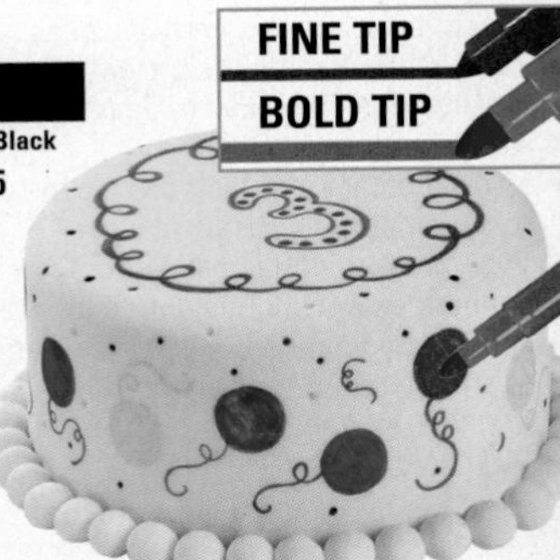

*Brand confectionery coating.

Fondant Tools and Accessories

NEW!

10-Pc. Fondant/Gum Paste Tool Set

Here are the tools every decorator needs to create breathtaking gum paste and fondant flowers, leaves and accents. Precise modeling tools feature comfortable grips for easy handling. Colored grips and numbered tip designs make tools easy to identify. Convenient case keeps the collection organized and handy. Includes large/small veining tool, shell tool/knife, large/small dogbone tool, serrated quilting/cutting wheel, umbrella tool with 5 and 6 divisions, scriber/cone tool, large/small ball tool, palette knife and modeling sticks #1 and #2.
1907-U-1107 Set/10 $29.99

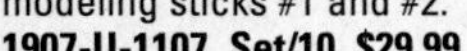

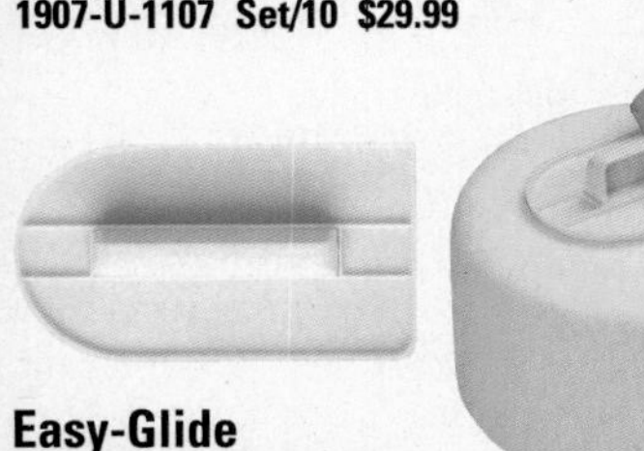

Easy-Glide Fondant Smoother

Essential tool for shaping and smoothing rolled fondant on your cake. Works great on top, edges and sides! Shapes fondant to sides of cake so that no puffed areas appear. Trim off excess with a sharp knife. 6.25 x 3.35 in. wide.
1907-U-1200 $5.49

Fondant Shaping Foam

Thick and thin squares are the ideal soft surface for shaping flowers, leaves and other fondant or gum paste cutouts. Use the thin square for thinning petal edges with a ball tool, carving vein lines on leaves and making ruffled fondant strips. Use the thick square for cupping flower centers. Thin: 4 x 4 x .2 in. Thick: 4 x 4 x 1 in.
1907-U-9704 Set/2 $3.29

Flower Stamen Assortment

Finish your royal icing or gum paste flowers with these 3 lovely stamen styles. Cut stamens to desired size and insert in flower center. Includes 60 each Pearl, Glitter and Fluffy. May be tinted (except Pearl) with Wilton Icing Colors added to vanilla. 2.5 in. long.
1005-U-410 Pk./180 $3.19

NEW!

FONDANT CUT & PRESS SETS

Give your cake the perfect finish! Create a beautifully-textured fondant and/or gum paste design in seconds with the Fondant Cut & Press. It's easy—just roll out fondant, gum paste or a 50/50 mixture, cut with the rectangular cutting edge, then place between the two sides and press sides together to imprint. Includes 2 piece cutter/press, instructions.

Button Flower
1907-U-1306 $6.99

Rose Leaf
1907-U-1300 $6.99

Flower Forming Cups

Curved round shape is ideal for drying gum paste, fondant and royal icing flowers and leaves. Openings in bottom center make it easy to pull wires through and adjust for the perfect drying position. Includes 2.5 and 3 in. diameter cups for drying everything from simple blossoms and briar roses to large daisies.
1907-U-118 Set/6 $5.49

Flower Former Set

Dry fondant or icing leaves and flowers in a convex or concave shape. Three each of 1.5, 2 and 2.5 in. wide holders, all 11 in. long.
417-U-9500 Set/9 $6.29

Cutter/Embosser

Three detachable wheels (straight, wavy and ridged) for cutting and for embossing patterns on fondant. Light, easy-rolling design cuts at the perfect angle. Comfortable handle also stores wheels.
1907-U-1206 $4.49

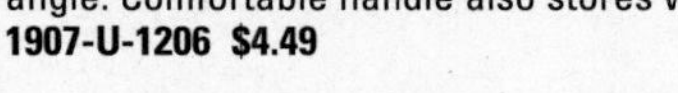

Fondant Ribbon Cutter/ Embosser Set

Add beautiful textured fondant ribbons, stripes and bows to your cake! Just choose the cutting and embossing wheel designs you want, slide the washer, core, wheels and spacers on the roller handle, and roll on fondant. Produces ribbon widths from ¼ in. to 3¾ in. when combining spacers. Complete set includes: 8 embossing wheels; 9 spacers; 9 cutting wheels; roller handle with detachable core; assembly hardware.
1907-U-1203 Set/26 $16.49

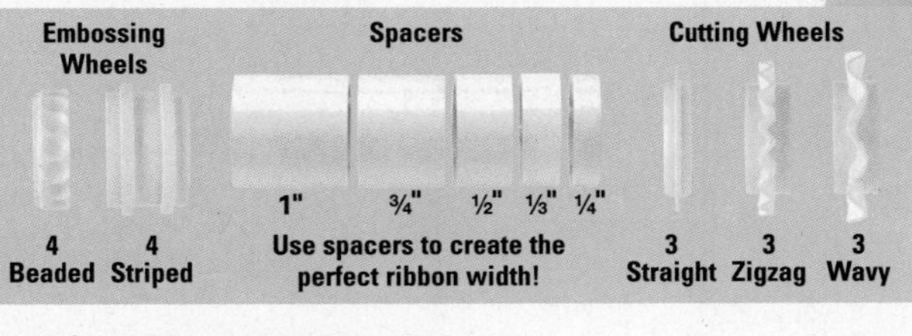

Fondant Decorative Punch Set

Add exciting 3-dimensional decorations in fondant. Punch out fondant accents with elegant openwork shapes. As you punch, the disk imprints a detailed design that adds a pretty touch of texture. The comfortable angled handle holds 8 design disks. Disks turn to lock into place.
1907-U-1204 Set/9 $9.99

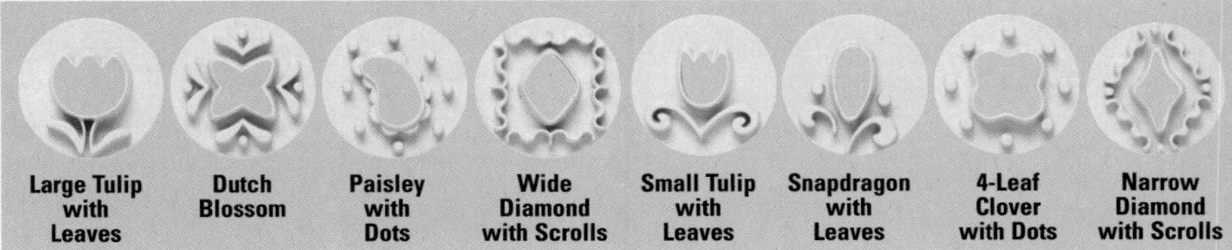

CAKE DECORATING

Fondant Tools and Accessories

Cut-Outs ™

- Fast, fun way to brighten any fondant cake!
- Great assortment of shapes for any occasion.

With Cut-Outs, it's easy to make fun 3-D shapes for your fondant cakes and cupcakes. Just roll out fondant, press down with Cut-Out and lift away. Remove shapes with a small spatula. Stainless steel (except for plastic Daisy) shapes range from .6 in. to 2.5 in.

Crinkle Shapes
Circle, Square, Triangle, Heart
417-U-444 Set/4 $3.19

Fancy Shapes
Flower, Leaf, Oval, Heart
417-U-445 Set/4 $3.19

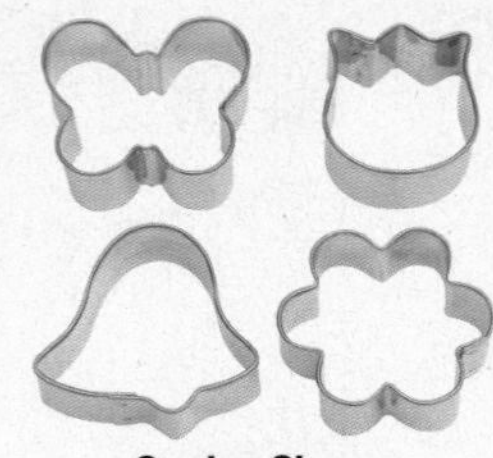

Garden Shapes
Butterfly, Tulip, Bell, Flower
417-U-443 Set/4 $3.19

Daisy
Durable plastic.
417-U-439 Set/3 $2.59

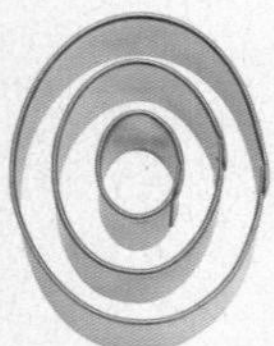

Oval
417-U-438
Set/3 $2.59

Round
417-U-432
Set/3 $2.59

Square
417-U-431
Set/3 $2.59

People
417-U-441
Set/6 $4.19

Heart
417-U-434
Set/3 $2.59

Star
417-U-433
Set/3 $2.59

Flower
417-U-435
Set/3 $2.59

Funny Flower
417-U-436
Set/3 $2.59

Leaf
417-U-437
Set/3 $2.59

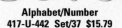

Alphabet/Number
417-U-442 Set/37 $15.79

FONDANT AND GUM PASTE DECORATING SETS

Floral Collection Flower Making Set

Make incredibly lifelike gum paste flowers. Full-color how-to book includes many arranging ideas and step-by-step instructions. Kit includes 24 plastic cutters, 1 leaf mold, 3 wood modeling tools, protector flap, 40-page instruction book and 2 foam squares for modeling.
1907-U-117 Set/32 $21.99
Book only 907-U-117 $9.99

Stepsaving Rose Bouquets Flower Cutter Set

Create gorgeous fondant and gum paste roses and forget-me-nots using book and cutters in this set. Cutters include large and small rose, rose leaf, calyx and forget-me-not.
1907-U-1003
Set/6 $8.99

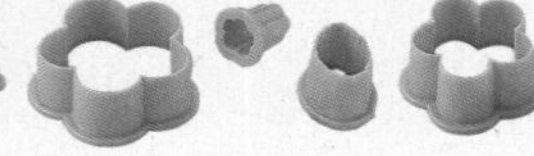

Floral Garland Cutter/ Ejector Set

Quickly and easily cuts and positions fondant or gum paste flowers on cakes. Includes ejector, 5 cutters and instructions.
1907-U-1001
Set/7 $10.99

Letters & Numbers Gum Paste & Fondant Mold Set

With this set, it's easy to put the finishing touches on your cakes with a beautiful 3-dimensional message or monogram. Just fill molds with a 50/50 gum paste and fondant blend, press and smooth with tool included and release. Great for 2-tone letters and numbers, a perfect way to personalize cake and cupcakes. Includes 11 mold sheets with 52 alphabet molds (upper and lower case A-Z), 3 punctuation marks and 10 numeral molds, stainless steel smoothing/releasing tool, molding instructions.
2104-U-3070 Set/13 $21.99

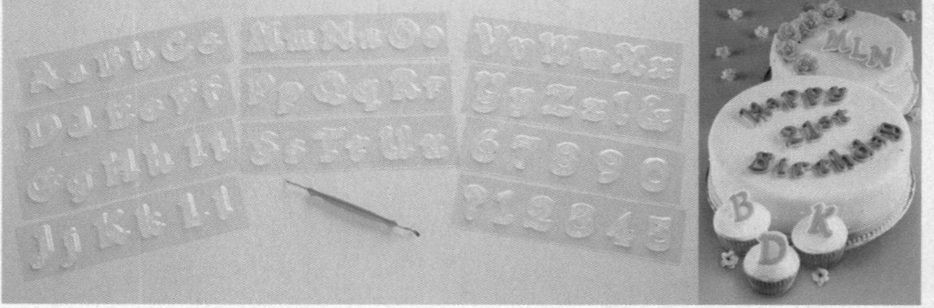

Mats and Rolling Pins

FONDANT IMPRINT MATS

NEW!

Imprint a beautiful recessed pattern to cover your cake! Just smooth your rolled fondant over the mat, place on your cake and peel back the mat. The recessed design imprinted in the fondant adds beautiful definition, so even white cakes stand out. Also great for textured fondant ribbons and edging. 20 x 20 in. **$19.99**

Floral Fantasy
409-U-415

Graceful Vines
409-U-414

20 in. Rolling Pin

Its extra-wide, smooth design is perfect for covering cakes with rolled fondant. The non-stick surface makes handling large pieces of fondant easy—just dust the surface with confectioners' sugar and roll out fondant to the size you need, then use the Rolling Pin to lift the fondant from your work surface to the cake. Great for rolling out pastry dough and pie crusts too. 20 x 1.5 in. diameter. (Mat sold below.)
1907-U-1210 $21.99

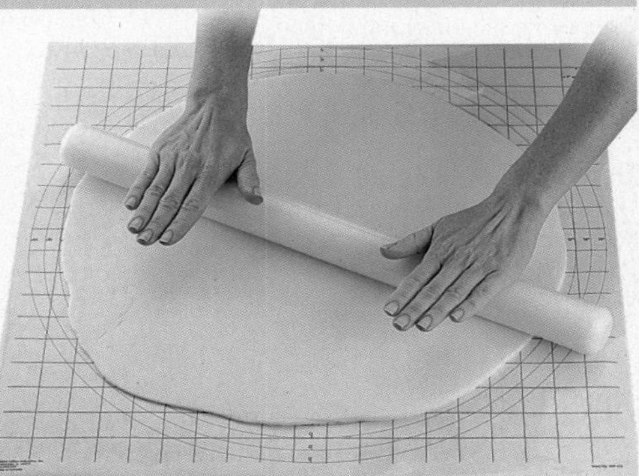

Roll & Cut Mat

For precise measuring, rolling and cutting of fondant or dough. Pre-marked circles for exact sizing. Square grid helps you cut precise strips. Non-stick surface for easy release. 20 in. square with circles from 3 in. to 19 in. diam.
409-U-412 $9.49

9 in. Rolling Pin

Roll out fondant evenly, in the perfect thickness for easy cutting and shaping, with this 3-piece non-stick roller. Roll to the perfect ⅛ or 1⁄16 in. height used for cutting many fondant decorations, using the slide-on guide rings. Easy to handle—just the right size for preparing small amounts of fondant to place on your cake. Perfect for use with Fondant Multi Packs and Cut-Outs™. 9 x 1 in. diameter. Includes ⅛ and 1⁄16 in. rings.
1907-U-1205 $6.99

Spiral Pattern Roller

This easy-to-use roller adds an exciting swirled texture to fondant cake decorations. Its lightweight design makes it easy to imprint evenly, creating a perfect look for your cake. Sized just right for preparing small amounts of fondant to create bow loops, swags, flat flowers and more. Perfect for use with Wilton Ready-To-Use Rolled Fondant, Fondant Multi Packs and Cut-Outs™. Just roll out fondant with a smooth rolling pin, then re-roll with the Spiral Pattern Roller to imprint incredible texture. Imprint width is 9¼ in.; 2 in. diameter.
1907-U-1224 $10.99

20 in. Rolling Pin Guide Rings

Slip these easy-to-use guide rings onto the ends of your 20 in. rolling pin to achieve the perfect thickness every time. Includes 1⁄16 in. (blue) for flower petals and leaves, 3⁄16 in. (gold) for letters, numbers and appliqué shapes, ⅛ in. (orange) for shapes cut with Wilton Cut-Outs™ or cookie cutters and for covering cakes with fondant.
1907-U-1010 Set/3 $4.49

Gum Paste and Ingredients

Ready-To-Use Gum Paste

Create beautiful hand-molded flowers right from the package.
Now you can have gum paste on hand whenever you need it! With Ready-To-Use Gum Paste, there's no mixing, no mess—just tint, roll out and cut to create incredible floral bouquets for your cakes. Follow the easy instructions included and use with Wilton Gum Paste Decorating Sets to make roses, daisies, apple blossoms, tulips and many more beautiful blooms. 1 lb. Certified Kosher.
707-U-130 $9.99

Gum Paste Mix

Just add water and knead. Workable, pliable dough-like mixture molds beautiful flowers and figures. 1 lb. Certified Kosher.
707-U-124 $5.99

Gum-Tex™

Makes fondant and gum paste pliable, elastic, easy to shape. Plastic resealable lid. 6 oz. Certified Kosher.
707-U-117 $7.99

Glucose

Essential ingredient for making fondant and gum paste from scratch. Use with Wilton Gum-Tex™. 12 oz. Certified Kosher.
707-U-107 $3.99

Glycerine

Stir into dried out fondant, gum paste or icing color to restore consistency. 2 oz. Certified Kosher.
708-U-14 $1.99

All-Purpose Decorating Gloves

Food-safe disposable gloves keep your hands clean, odor-free and protected in and out of the kitchen. Prevent color stains when tinting fondant, keep fingerprints off homemade candy, eliminate burning of skin when cutting spicy foods. Great when working with craft paint and glue too. Easy to slip-on, gloves fit either hand.
417-U-1642 Pk./20 $3.29

Icing Colors

Wilton colors are made to produce deeper, richer color by adding just a small amount. Our concentrated gel formula helps you achieve the exact shade you want without thinning your icing. You'll find a rainbow of colors, ready to blend together to create your own custom shades.

*Note: Large amounts of these colors may affect icing taste.

Use No-Taste Red for large areas of red on a cake. When using Black, start with chocolate icing to limit the amount of color needed.

‡Daffodil Yellow is an all-natural color. It does not contain Yellow #5. The color remains very pale.

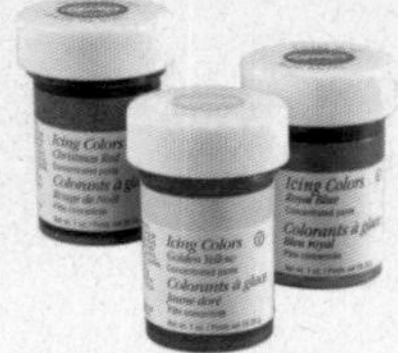

Single Bottles
1 oz. Certified Kosher.
$1.99

Ivory	Daffodil Yellow‡	Buttercup Yellow	Golden Yellow	Lemon Yellow	Copper	Creamy Peach	Rose Petal Pink	Terra Cotta	Orange
610-U-208	610-U-175	610-U-216	610-U-159	610-U-108	610-U-450	610-U-210	610-U-410	610-U-206	610-U-205

Red-Red*	Christmas Red*	Red (no-taste)	Rose	Burgundy	Pink	Violet	Delphinium Blue	Cornflower Blue	Royal Blue
610-U-906	610-U-302	610-U-998	610-U-401	610-U-698	610-U-256	610-U-604	610-U-228	610-U-710	610-U-655

Sky Blue	Teal	Kelly Green	Leaf Green	Moss Green	Juniper Green	Brown	Black*
610-U-700	610-U-207	610-U-752	610-U-809	610-U-851	610-U-234	610-U-507	610-U-981

Primary 4-Icing Colors Set
Lemon Yellow, Sky Blue, Christmas Red, Brown in .5 oz. jars. Certified Kosher.
601-U-5127 Set/4 $4.99

Pastel 4-Icing Colors Set
Creamy Peach, Rose Petal Pink, Willow Green, Cornflower Blue in .5 oz. jars. Certified Kosher.
601-U-25588 Set/4 $4.99

Garden Tone 4-Icing Colors Set
Buttercup Yellow, Delphinium Blue, Aster Mauve, Juniper Green in .5 oz. jars. Certified Kosher.
601-U-4240 Set/4 $4.99

8-Icing Colors Set
Lemon Yellow, Sky Blue, Christmas Red, Brown, Orange, Violet, Pink and Leaf Green in .5 oz. jars. Certified Kosher.
601-U-5577 Set/8 $9.99

White-White Icing Color
Stir in to whiten icing made with butter or margarine. Perfect for wedding cakes. 2 oz. Certified Kosher.
603-U-1236 $2.99

12-Icing Colors Set
Our most popular collection creates the spectrum of primary colors plus light and dark skin tones, teal and burgundy. Lemon Yellow, Teal, No-Taste Red, Brown, Copper, Violet, Pink, Burgundy, Golden Yellow, Royal Blue, Black, Kelly Green in .5 oz. jars. Certified Kosher.
601-U-5580 Set/12 $13.99

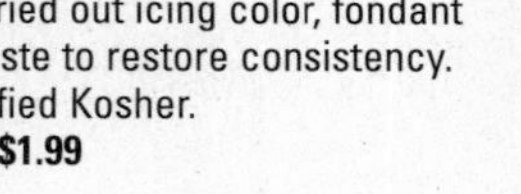

Glycerine
Stir into dried out icing color, fondant or gum paste to restore consistency. 2 oz. Certified Kosher.
708-U-14 $1.99

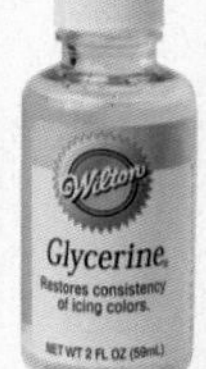

COLOR MIST™ FOOD COLOR SPRAY

This easy-to-use spray gives decorators the versatility and dazzling effects of an airbrush in a convenient can! Creates a rainbow of excitement on so many desserts. Use it to transform a plain iced cake with sensational color, add splashes of holiday color to iced cookies and cupcakes. Great for party desserts—highlighting whipped topping or ice cream with color. No mess, taste-free formula; add a little color or a lot. Colors match Wilton Icing Colors above. 1.5 oz. Certified Kosher. **$3.29**

Red	Blue	Yellow	Green
710-U-5500	710-U-5501	710-U-5502	710-U-5503
Violet	**Pink**	**Black**	**Orange**
710-U-5504	710-U-5505	710-U-5506	710-U-5507

Icings

All Wilton icings are formulated for easy decorating as well as great taste. Our convenient ready-to-use icings are the perfect medium consistency for decorating, so you don't need to worry about mixing or measuring.

TUBE ICINGS, GELS

Tube Decorating Icings

The same high quality as our Ready-To-Use Decorator Icing, in a convenient tube. Create flowers, borders and more. Ideal for small areas of color on character cakes. Use with the Tip and Nail Set or Coupler Ring Set (below) and any standard-size Wilton metal tip (not included). Colors match Wilton Icing Colors shown at left. 4.25 oz. Certified Kosher. **$1.99**

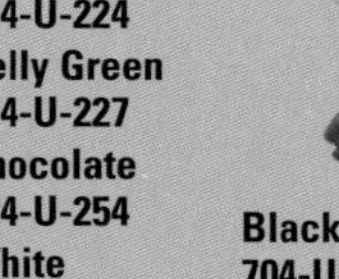

Red 704-U-218	**Royal Blue** 704-U-248	
Violet 704-U-242	**Leaf Green** 704-U-224	
Lemon Yellow 704-U-236	**Kelly Green** 704-U-227	
Orange 704-U-212	**Chocolate** 704-U-254	
Pink 704-U-230	**White** 704-U-200	**Black** 704-U-206

Coupler Ring Set

Attach Wilton standard size metal decorating tips onto Wilton tube icings to create any technique.
418-U-47306 Set/4 $2.19

Tip and Nail Set

Tips easily twist onto Wilton tube icings to create many decorating techniques. Includes Star, Round, Leaf and Petal Tips, Flower Nail.
418-U-47300 Set/5 $2.19

Tube Decorating Gels

Add shimmering accents, colorful highlights and sparkle to your decorating with these transparent gels. Create a beautiful stained-glass effect and add distinctive writing and printing. Great for cakes and cookies. Colors match Wilton Icing Colors shown at upper left. .75 oz. Certified Kosher. **$1.49**

Red 704-U-318	**Orange** 704-U-312	
Pink 704-U-330	**Royal Blue** 704-U-348	
Violet 704-U-342	**Leaf Green** 704-U-324	**White** 704-U-302
Lemon Yellow 704-U-336	**Brown** 704-U-354	**Black** 704-U-306

Tube Icing and Gel Color Chart

Lemon Yellow	Orange	Red	Pink
Violet	Royal Blue	Leaf Green	† Kelly Green
† Chocolate	Brown	White	Black

†Not available in gel.

SPARKLE GEL

Make your cake decorations more dynamic! Squeeze on sparkling color effects with our ready-to-use gel. Great for dots, messages, water effects and fondant accents. Try it on cookies, cupcakes, ice cream and more! Resealable 3.5 oz. tubes. Certified Kosher.
$2.99

Pink	Blue	
704-U-356	704-U-110	
Red	**Yellow**	**Green**
704-U-112	704-U-108	704-U-111

READY-TO-USE DECORATOR ICINGS

Wilton makes the only ready-to-use icing that is the perfect consistency for decorating. The pure white color is best for creating true vivid colors using Wilton Icing Colors. Rich and creamy, with a delicious homemade taste.

Large Tub

Ideal thin-to-medium consistency for use in Wilton Method Cake Decorating Classes in a convenient easy-carry tub. Great for icing cakes, making borders, messages and more. Contains 9 cups—enough to decorate ten 8 or 9 in. round cake layers. Certified Kosher.
White 704-U-680 $14.99

1 lb. Can

Ideal stiff consistency for making roses and flowers with upright petals. One 16 oz. can covers two 8 or 9 in. layers or one 9 x 13 in. cake.
White 710-U-118 $3.29
Chocolate 710-U-119 $3.29

White Cookie Icing

Quick-setting microwavable icing covers cookies with a shiny finish—perfect for decorating with colorful Wilton Icing Writer™ accents or FoodWriter™ markers! Easy to use—just heat and squeeze onto cookies using the convenient cap. Sets smooth in just 45 minutes. 10 oz. bottle covers approx. 12 cookies, 3 in. each; 20 oz. covers approx. 24. Certified Kosher.
10 oz. Bottle **704-U-481 $4.49**
20 oz. Bottle **704-U-492 $7.99**

Icing Writer™

Squeeze colorful accents onto fondant and Wilton Cookie Icing with this ready-to-use icing! It's easy to control, just squeeze the bottle and icing flows smoothly from the built-in round tip. Dries to a smooth, satin finish. 3 oz. bottle. Certified Kosher.
$2.49

Blue	Red	Yellow	
710-U-2227	710-U-2225	710-U-2226	
White	**Green**	**Pink**	**Violet**
710-U-2228	710-U-2229	710-U-2230	710-U-2231

Creamy White Buttercream Icing Mix

Our convenient mix has the delicious taste and creamy texture of homemade buttercream icing. Use just as you would your favorite buttercream recipe. Makes 1½ to 2 cups. Enough to ice a 2-layer 8 in. cake. Certified Kosher Dairy.
710-U-112 $2.99

Vanilla Whipped Icing Mix

Our light, whipped icing provides the ideal texture for decorating in an easy-to-make, delicious mix. Just add ice water and it whips up velvety-smooth for icing or decorating. Light and delicate flavor. Makes 5 cups. Certified Kosher Dairy.
710-U-1241 $4.99

Meringue Powder

Primary ingredient for royal icing. Stabilizes buttercream, adds body to boiled icing and meringue. Replaces egg whites in many recipes. Resealable top opens for easy measuring. 4 oz. can makes 5 recipes of royal icing; 8 oz. can makes 10 recipes. 16 oz. can makes 20 recipes. Certified Kosher.
4 oz. can 702-U-6007 $5.29
8 oz. can 702-U-6015 $8.49
16 oz. can 702-U-6004 $16.99

Color Flow Mix

Create dimensional flow-in designs for your cake. Just add water and confectioner's sugar. 4 oz. can makes ten 1½ cup batches. Certified Kosher.
701-U-47 $7.49

Piping Gel

Pipe messages and designs or glaze cakes before icing. Use clear or tint with icing color. 10 oz. Certified Kosher.
704-U-105 $3.99

Ready-To-Decorate Icing

Add an exciting finishing touch to treats, without mixing or mess. Just slip one of the four free tips over the nozzle and start the fun. Colors match Wilton Icing Colors (p. 134). 6.4 oz. Certified Kosher.
$4.29

Red	Green	White
710-U-4400	710-U-4401	710-U-4402
Black	**Pink**	**Blue**
710-U-4404	710-U-4406	710-U-4407
Violet	**Yellow**	**Orange**
710-U-4408	710-U-4409	710-U-4410

Four FREE decorating tips included:
Small Round Tip For dots and outlining
Leaf Tip For basic and ruffled leaves
Large Round Tip For writing and printing
Star Tip For stars, swirls and pretty borders

Flavorings

Decorators trust Wilton flavorings for great taste that won't change icing consistency. Wilton flavors are concentrated—only a drop or two adds delicious taste to icings, cakes, beverages and other recipes.

Pure Vanilla Extract

The world's finest vanilla is from Madagascar. Unmatched flavor and aroma to enhance cakes, puddings, pie fillings, custards, salad dressings and more. 4 oz. Certified Kosher.
604-U-2270 $7.99

No-Color Flavorings

Recommended and used in Wilton Method Classes, these delicious flavors won't change your icing color. Essential for making pure white icings for wedding cakes and maintaining vibrant colors in all your decorating. Certified Kosher.

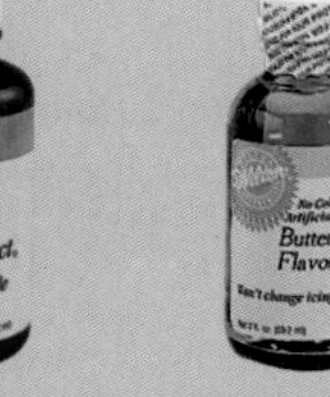

Clear Vanilla Extract
2 oz.
604-U-2237 $1.99
8 oz.
604-U-2269 $4.99

No-Color Butter Flavor
2 oz.
604-U-2040 $1.99
8 oz.
604-U-2067 $4.99

No-Color Almond Extract
2 oz.
604-U-2126 $1.99

Sprinkles

CUPCAKE CRUNCHES

Add delicious flavor and a colossal crunch to your cupcakes! Sprinkle over iced cupcakes. Certified Kosher.
$3.99

Toffee
3.5 oz. Naturally and artificially flavored.
710-U-023

Almond
3.5 oz. Artificially flavored.
710-U-024

Chocolate
3.5 oz.
710-U-025

JUMBO SPRINKLES

Give your cupcakes a big finish! Top them with our new Jumbo Sprinkles in exciting shapes and colors. These big and bold decorations are perfect for cupcakes, mini cakes, jumbo and king-size cupcakes, brownies and cookies. Innovative shapes for birthday, holiday or any celebration. Certified Kosher. **$4.09**

Jumbo Hearts
3.25 oz.
710-U-032

Heart Drops
5.25 oz.
710-U-035

Jumbo Stars
3.25 oz.
710-U-026

Jumbo Confetti
3.25 oz.
710-U-029

Jumbo Diamonds
3.5 oz.
710-U-027

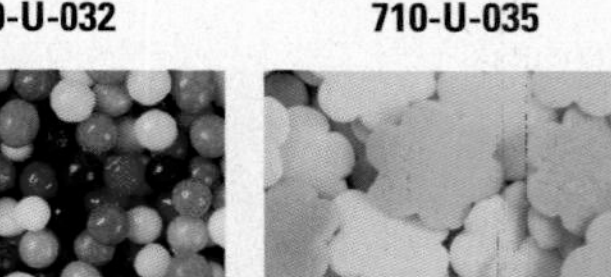

Jumbo Rainbow Nonpareils
4.8 oz. **710-U-033**

Jumbo Daisies
3.25 oz.
710-U-028

SPRINKLES

Pour on the fun! Great shapes and colors add a dash of excitement to cakes, cupcakes, ice cream and more. Certified Kosher. **$2.29**

Chocolate Hearts
2.5 oz. Naturally and artificially flavored.
710-U-622

Cinnamon Drops
3 oz.
710-U-769

White Nonpareils
3 oz.
710-U-773

Rainbow Nonpareils
3 oz.
710-U-772

Chocolate Flavored Jimmies
2.5 oz. **710-U-774**
6.25 oz.
710-U-168 $4.49

Rainbow Jimmies
2.5 oz. **710-U-776**
6.25 oz.
710-U-994 $4.49

SPARKLING SUGARS

Put extra dazzle in your decorating! These easy-pour sugars have a coarse texture and a brilliant sparkle that makes cupcakes, cookies and cakes really shine. 5.25 oz. bottle. Certified Kosher. **$3.99**

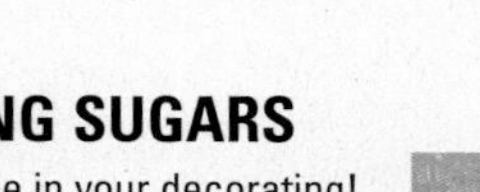

Yellow
710-U-036

Blue
710-U-039

Lavender
710-U-037

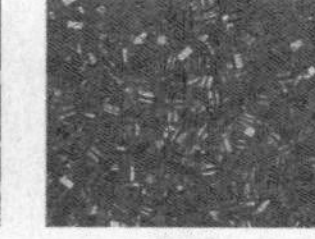

Pink
710-U-038

8 oz. bottle. Certified Kosher. **$4.49**

White
710-U-992

Lavender/White
710-U-993

Rainbow
710-U-991

Colored Sugars

Extra-fine sugar is excellent for filling in brightly colored designs on cakes, cupcakes and cookies. 3.25 oz. bottle. Certified Kosher.
$2.29

Blue 710-U-750	**Yellow** 710-U-754	**Orange** 710-U-759
Pink 710-U-756	**Red** 710-U-766	**Lavender** 710-U-758
Light Green 710-U-752	**Dark Green** 710-U-764	**Black** 710-U-762

Cake Sparkles™

Add shimmering color to cakes, cupcakes, cookies and ice cream! Brilliant edible glitter in a great variety of colors, great for stencilling, highlighting messages, snow scenes. .25 oz. Certified Kosher. **$3.19**

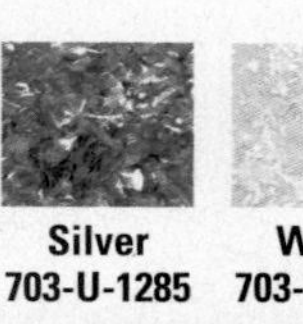

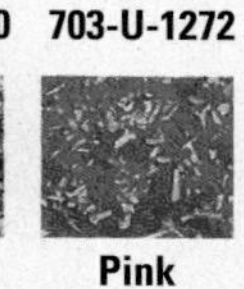

Silver 703-U-1285	**White** 703-U-1290	**Yellow** 703-U-1272	**Purple** 703-U-1266	**Blue** 703-U-1314
Red 703-U-1284	**Green** 703-U-1278	**Pink** 703-U-1260	**Orange** 703-U-1308	**Black** 703-U-1302

6-Mix Assortments

They're so convenient! Assorted fun shapes in an easy-pour flip-top bottle. Top cupcakes, ice cream and other goodies. Certified Kosher. **$4.99**

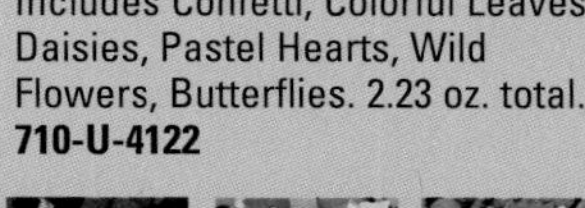

Flowerful Medley
Includes Confetti, Colorful Leaves, Daisies, Pastel Hearts, Wild Flowers, Butterflies. 2.23 oz. total.
710-U-4122

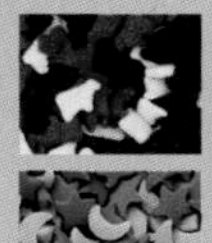

Animals and Stars
Includes Cows, Stars, Dinosaurs, Stars and Moons, Bears, Dolphins. 2.1 oz. total. **710-U-4123**

Nonpareils
Includes Pink, Orange, Green, Red, Yellow, Purple. 3 oz. total.
710-U-4125

Jimmies
Includes Pink, Orange, Green, Red, Yellow, Blue. 2.52 oz. total.
710-U-4127

4-Mix Assortments

They're so convenient! Assorted sugars in an easy-pour flip-top bottle. Top cupcakes, ice cream and other goodies. 4.4 oz. total. Certified Kosher. **$4.99**

Bright Sugars
Includes Yellow, Light Green, Lavender, Pink. **710-U-651**

Primary Sugars
Includes Red, Dark Green, Blue, Yellow. **710-U-650**

CAKE STENCILS VARIETY PACK

Our collection of 4 stencil designs gives you several ways to make birthday and everyday cakes more festive. It's so easy—just place on your iced cake, then sprinkle with Wilton Cake Sparkles™, add exciting Wilton Sugars in a rainbow of colors or use Color Mist™ Food Color Spray. Also works beautifully with Wilton Rolled Fondant—fill in designs with sugars or decorate with FoodWriter™ Markers. Includes Happy Birthday, Flower, Swirl and Heart designs.

417-U-148 Pk./4 $7.99

Decorating Tools

Icing Sculptor®

Now your cakes can have an elegant sculpted finish that will give them a beautiful professional look. It's easy with the Icing Sculptor. Just insert any combination of the 64 design blades—mix and match between the 14 sculpting edges to create your favorite customized effects. Then glide the comb over the iced cake sides to create attractive ridges that will beautifully frame your design. Create hundreds of pattern combinations—wide or narrow ridges, dramatic swirls and vertical designs too. Also includes sculptor handle and complete instructions. This versatile tool has a patent pending.

2104-U-12 Set/66 $13.69

Includes 8 of each 2-Sided Design Blade

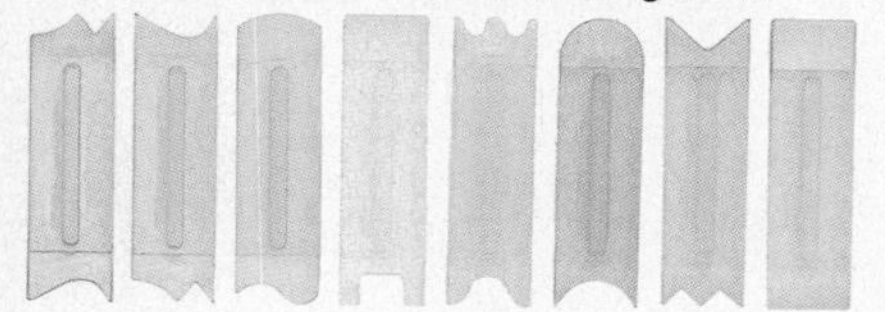

So Easy!
Select the sculpting blades you want and slide into handle. Press sculptor into iced cake as you rotate cake on turntable.

So Versatile!
Mix and match between the 14 edge designs on 64 blades to achieve the perfect look for your cake.

6-Piece Covered Mixing Bowl Set

Perfect for preparing decorating icings—clear lids snap on tight to keep icing the right texture. Includes one each 1, 2 and 3 quart nesting bowls with easy-grip handles and easy-pour spouts for better control. Rubberized base keeps bowls from sliding on countertops. Measurements clearly marked for precise mixing. Dishwasher safe.

417-U-469 Set/6 $13.69

Cake Dividing Set

Measures equal sections of your cake for precise placement of garlands, stringwork and other designs.
Cake Dividing Wheel marks up to 16 divisions on cakes up to 20 in. diameter. Garland Marker adjusts to 7 widths. Instructions included.

409-U-806 Set/2 $9.99

Practice Board with Patterns Set

Includes stand and 20 full-size patterns. 9 x 6 in.

406-U-9464 $7.99

Decorating Comb

Run edge across your iced cake to form perfect ridges. Plastic, 12 x 1½ in.

417-U-156 $1.69

Decorating Triangle

Each side adds a different contoured effect to iced cakes. Easy to hold. Plastic, 5 x 5 in.

417-U-162 $1.19

Garland Marker

Adjusts to 7 preset widths and varying depths to easily mark perfectly uniform garlands on cake sides. Instructions included.

409-U-812 $4.49

Flower-Making Accessories

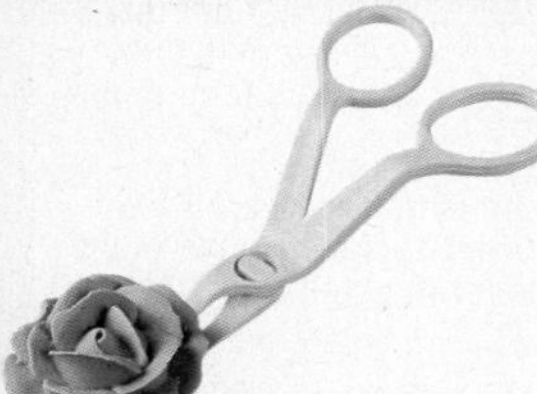

Flower Lifter

Easily transfers buttercream flowers from nail to cake without damage. Angled design keeps your hands from touching the cake. Detachable blades for easy cleaning. Plastic. 5¼ in. long.

417-U-1199 $3.29

Flower Nail No. 7

For basic flower making. Provides the control you need when piping icing flowers. Just rotate the nail between your thumb and fingers as you pipe a flower on the head. Stainless steel. 1½ in. wide.

402-U-3007 $1.19

Lily Nail Set

Essential for making cup flowers. Includes ½, 1¼, 1⅝ and 2½ in. diameter cups.

403-U-9444 Set/8 $2.19

Flower Stamen Assortment

Finish your royal icing or gum paste flowers with these 3 lovely stamen styles. Cut stamens to desired size and insert in flower center. Includes 60 each Pearl, Glitter and Fluffy. May be tinted (except Pearl) with Wilton Icing Colors added to vanilla. 2.5 in. long.

1005-U-410 Pk./180 $3.19

Flower Former Set

Dry icing leaves and flowers in a convex or concave shape. Three each of 1½, 2 and 2½ in. wide holders, all 11 in. long.

417-U-9500 Set/9 $6.29

Spatulas

Decorate with more control and less fatigue. The ergonomic handle features a finger pad, which tapers to the flexible stainless steel blade for better control.

Straight
NEW!

Great for spreading and smoothing fillings and all-around kitchen use.

9 in.
409-U-6045
$7.99
11 in.
409-U-6046
$9.99
15 in.
409-U-6047
$13.99

Angled
NEW!

Ideal angle for smoothing cake sides and spreading fillings.

9 in.
409-U-6040
$7.99
13 in.
409-U-6041
$9.99
15 in.
409-U-6042
$13.99

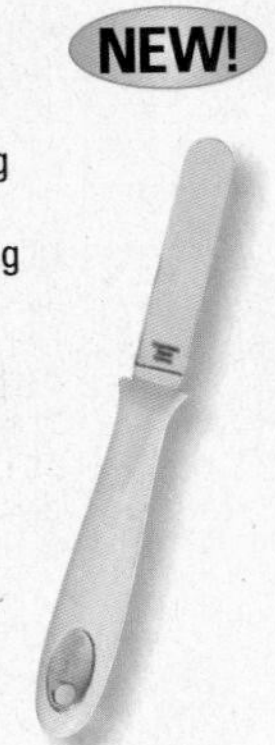

Tapered
NEW!

Easily ices hard-to-reach spots on your cake.

9 in.
409-U-6057
$7.99

Cake Knife/Spatula

This stainless steel knife is perfect for torting cakes—it cuts layers cleanly and has the width you need to transfer layers without breakage. Use the smooth edge for spreading icing or filling on cake layers. It's easy to control, with a lightweight nylon handle that is comfortable in any hand. 15 in. long
409-U-6048 $9.99

CONTOURED HANDLES

Decorate with greater comfort, more control and less fatigue, thanks to contoured handle with finger pad. Flexible stainless steel blade is perfect thickness for gliding over icing.

Straight Blade

15 in.; 10⅛ in. blade.
409-U-6030 $10.49
11 in.; 6 in. blade.
409-U-6018 $6.29
9 in.; 4½ in. blade.
409-U-6006
$4.19

Angled Blade

15 in.; 9⅞ in. blade.
409-U-6036 $10.49
13 in.; 7¾ in. blade.
409-U-6024 $6.79
9 in.; 4½ in. blade.
409-U-6012
$4.79

Tapered Blade

9 in.; 4 in. blade.
409-U-6003
$4.19

Basic Dessert Decorator

Give your cakes and pastries a beautiful finishing touch in seconds. The easy-to-control lever helps you fill and decorate all kinds of desserts. The 4 decorating nozzles included let you pipe stars, rosettes, shells and many other accents. Works great with Wilton Icing Mixes (p. 135).
415-U-825 $11.59

ROSEWOOD HANDLES

Quality rosewood handle spatulas have been favorites for years. They have strong, flexible stainless steel blades and sturdy riveted handles.

Straight Blade

11 in.; 6 in. blade.
409-U-7695 $5.29
8 in.; 4¼ in. blade.
409-U-6044
$3.19

Angled Blade

12 in.; 6¼ in. blade.
409-U-135 $6.29
8 in.; 4½ in. blade.
409-U-739
$3.19

Tapered Blade

8 in.; 4 in. blade.
409-U-518
$3.19

Dessert decorator Pro™

It's easy to add beautiful decorations to any dessert or appetizer in minutes! Designed for comfortable one-hand decorating and effortless tip positioning, this is the most convenient dessert tool you'll ever use. Create beautiful decorations—shells, stars, rosettes, leaves. The recipe book included is filled with fabulous ideas to tempt your family and friends. Decorate desserts with elegant whipped cream or icing designs. Dress up pastry shells with dramatic swirls of mousse. With Dessert Decorator Pro, you can do it all!
415-U-850 $31.49

Rotating Cylinder
Just turn to place the tip in the correct position for any decoration.

Ergonomic Design
Easy, comfortable grip for right or left hand. Outer sleeve fits your fingers like a glove.

Stainless Steel Cylinder
Preferred by pastry chefs because stainless won't transfer flavors and it maintains temperature of fillings.

Fits Virtually Any Tip/Coupler
Use with the tips included or with most other Wilton tips.

Pull-Out Plunger
Inner ring pushes filling smoothly through cylinder.

Convenient Thumb Lever
The ideal distance from cylinder for comfortable one-handed decorating.

Durable Construction
Cylinder and plunger are housed in an impact-resistant sleeve for years of great decorating performance.

Easy To Fill and Clean
Most parts detach with ease; wash in warm, soapy water.

Dessert Decorator Pro includes all this:

Two Tip Couplers
Two sizes to hold standard (small) and large tips.

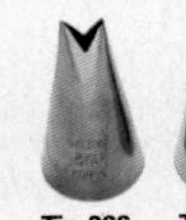
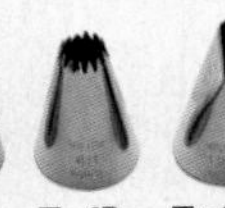
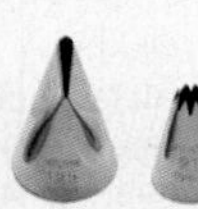

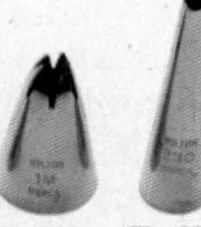

Tip 366 Leaf | Tip 4B Star | Tip 125 Petal | Tip 21 Star | Tip 1M Star | Tip 230 Bismarck

Six Durable Nickel-Plated Tips
Quality metal tips produce perfectly-shaped decorations every time.

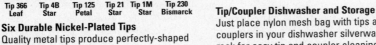

Tips in bag for size reference only. Tips included are shown at left.

Tip/Coupler Dishwasher and Storage Bag
Just place nylon mesh bag with tips and couplers in your dishwasher silverware rack for easy tip and coupler cleaning.

Recipes and Instructions
Includes delicious recipes and easy decorating instructions for elegant desserts and appetizers.

Cake Decorating Turntables

A quality cake turntable is a must for easy decorating. Turntables lift your cake off the work surface so you can create borders conveniently. And they rotate, allowing you to decorate all the way around the cake without straining.

Trim ´n Turn® ULTRA Cake Turntable

NEW!

Experience the ultimate in turntable control. The Trim ´n Turn® ULTRA combines an extra-high smooth-turning platform with non-slip detail for secure performance. The easy- locking platform keeps your cake steady as you create delicate flowers and writing. Platform turns in either direction for easy icing, borders, combing and leveling. Great for left-hand or right-hand users.

- Non-slip design with soft-grip ring molded into platform to keep cake in place
- 3 in. raised base with arched sides for easy grip
- Hidden ball bearing track for smooth turning
- Lock platform with ease using the pull-out tab
- 12 in. platform removes from base for easy cleaning
- Holds cakes up to 11 in. with platform visible—holds larger cakes if needed

307-U-301 $20.99

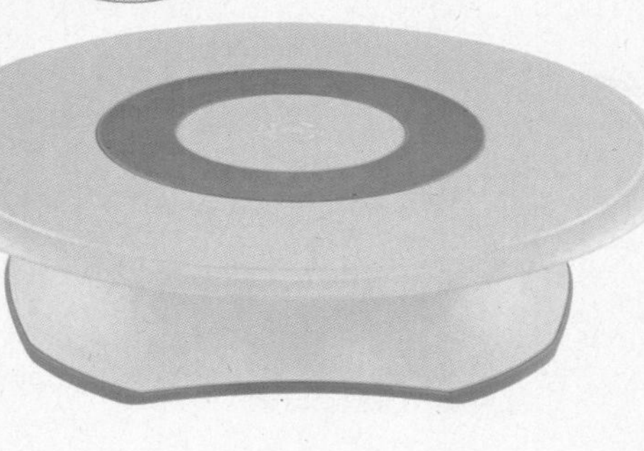

NEW!

Trim ´n Turn® PLUS Cake Turntable

Decorate with more convenience and control with the Trim ´n Turn PLUS. Its smooth-turning performance puts your cake in the ideal position for decorating beautiful borders and icing sides perfectly smooth.

- Non-slip base is raised for better control.
- Arched sides for easy lifting
- Removable 12 in. platform for easy cleaning
- Hidden ball-bearing track for smooth turning
- Holds cakes up to 11 in. with platform visible—holds larger cakes if needed

307-U-303 $13.69

CAKE DECORATING

Tilting Cake Turntable

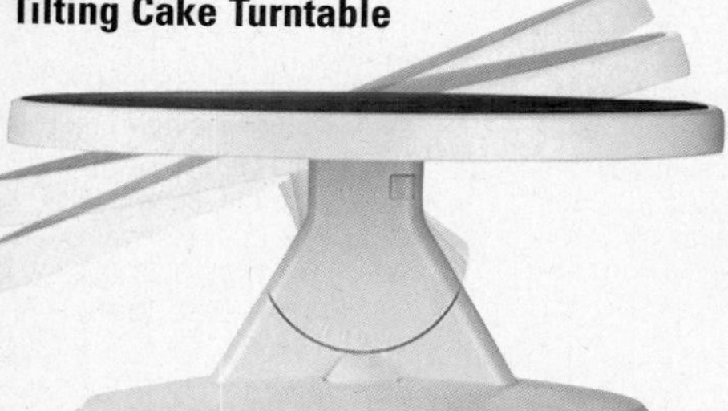

It tilts! Decorate any part of your cake conveniently!

The Tilting Cake Turntable moves to 3 preset angles (12°, 24°, and level) and locks in place, making every decorating technique easier! 6 in. high turntable smoothly rotates in any of the angled positions for effortless decorating of top borders, stringwork, lettering on top and sides of cake, more. Includes lock to prevent rotation. Non-slip bottom, 12 in. diameter.

307-U-894 $69.99

Professional Turntable

Extra strength and effortless turning for decorating tiered wedding cakes. Heavy-duty aluminum stand is 4½ in. high with 12 in. diameter plate. Holds cakes up to 16 in. diameter.

307-U-2501 $69.99

Trim ´N Turn™ Cake Stand

Turns smoothly on hidden ball bearings for easy decorating and serving. Flute-edged 12 in. plate is white molded plastic. Holds cakes up to 10 in. diameter.

2103-U-2518 $8.39

Press Sets

Block Message Press Set

Includes Best, Happy, Wishes, Anniversary, Birthday and Congratulations. Message holder. Word height ⅞ in.

2104-U-2077 Set/6 $4.09

Italic Make-Any-Message Press Set

Pretty and sophisticated letters for a custom message. Press words up to 10½ in. wide, letters ¾ in. high. Includes letter holder.

2104-U-2277 Set/58 $8.99

Decorator Favorites Pattern Press Set

Includes: fleur-de-lis; double heart; medallion; open heart; closed scroll; heart; large, medium and small C-scrolls; crest; double scroll; vine.

2104-U-3160 Set/12 $6.99

Designer Pattern Press Set

Imprints elegant designs for easy overpiping. Includes: symmetrical swirl; small and large fleurs de lis; corner flourish; flower; heart bow; scroll; curlicues.

2104-U-3112 Set/8 $6.99

Make-Any-Message Letter Press Set

Imprint the perfect sentiment! Press words up to 10½ in. wide, letters ¾ in. high. Includes letter holder.

2104-U-10 Set/56 $8.99

Script Message Press Set

Combine the words Best, Happy, Wishes, Birthday, Anniversary, and Congratulations. Word height ⅞ in.

2104-U-2061 Set/6 $4.09

Kitchen Tools

Make decorating and kitchen tasks easier! Lightweight, comfortable tools with contoured handles and quality blades of stainless steel and silicone heads suited for the task.

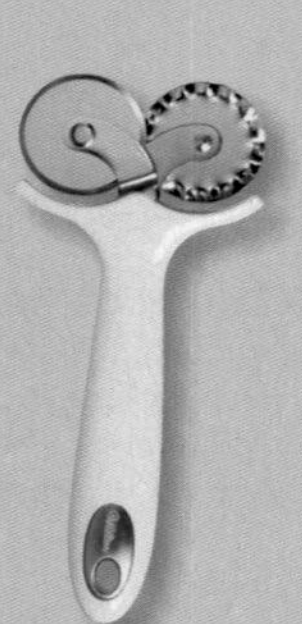

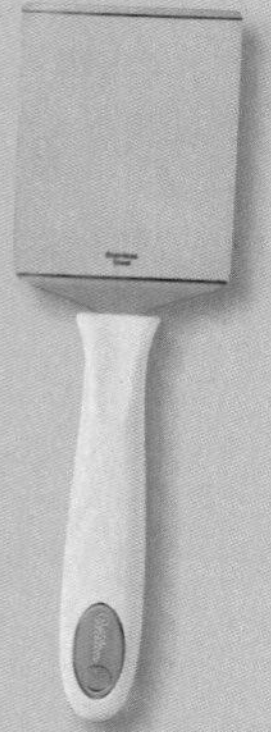

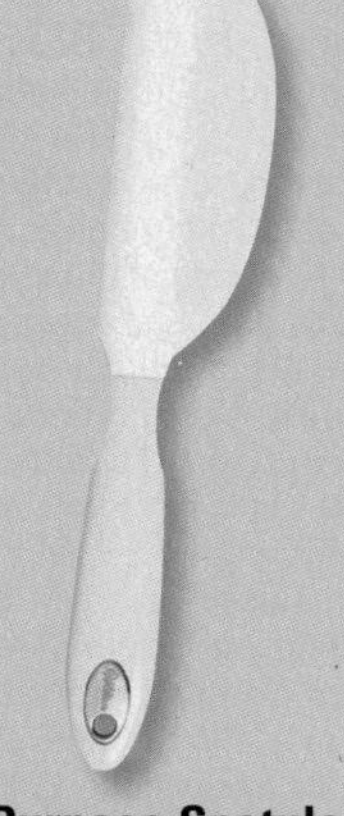

Pastry Wheel
Create crisp straight or graceful scalloped edges with this smooth-rolling pastry wheel. Comfortable handle with finger/thumb guard. 6.5 in. long.
2103-U-315 $8.99

Pastry Brush
Flexible silicone bristles are great for brushing on Cake Release, shortening or hot glazes. More durable than nylon bristles. Comfortable ergonomic handle. 8.5 in. long.
409-U-6056 $5.99

Cookie Spatula
Angled stainless steel blade moves cookies from pan to plate with ease. Slides easily under cookies—great for serving brownies and bar cookies too. Comfortable ergonomic handle with thumb rest. 9 in. long.
409-U-6054 $6.99

Cake and Pie Server
Slice and serve with greater control. The comfortable ergonomic handle with thumb rest and angled blade makes lifting every slice easier. Serrated stainless steel blade cuts even the first slice cleanly. 9 in. long.
409-U-6058 $6.99

All-Purpose Spatulas
Blend and mix with greater comfort, more control and less fatigue, thanks to the contoured Comfort Grip™ handle. Flexible silicone blade is ideal for blending and removing icing from bowls or containers—great for all-around kitchen use. Stain and odor resistant.
9 in. 409-U-6050 $7.99
12 in. 409-U-6052 $8.99

Baking Accessories

Bake Easy!™ Non-Stick Spray
For cakes that turn out beautifully every time, start by spraying pans with Bake Easy. This convenient non-stick spray helps your cakes release perfectly with fewer crumbs for easier icing and a flawless look for decorating. Just a light, even coating does the job. Use for all mixes and recipes, versatile for all types of baking and cooking. 6 oz.
702-U-6018 $3.29

NEW!

Pastry Mat
Non-stick mat with pre-marked measurements for easy rolling and precise cutting! Includes circles for pie, tart and pizza crusts from 6 to 16 in. diameter, pre-marked inches and centimeters for exact cutting of lattice strips. Delicious cookie and pie crust recipes are printed on the mat. Non-stick surface for easy release. 18 x 24 in.
409-U-413 $9.49

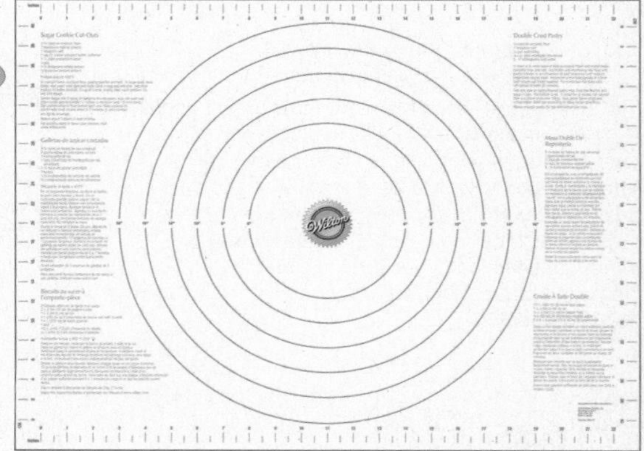

Cake Release
No need to grease and flour your baking pan—Cake Release coats in one step. Simply spread Cake Release lightly on pan bottom and sides with a pastry brush and add batter. Cakes release perfectly every time without crumbs, giving you the ideal surface for decorating. In convenient dispensing bottle. 8 oz. Certified Kosher.
702-U-6016 $3.49

Bake-Even Strips
Cakes bake perfectly level and moist, without cracking, when you wrap these strips around the pan before baking. Oven-safe, instructions and clips included.

Small Set
Two 1½ in. high strips, 30 in. long. Enough for two 8 or 9 in. round pans.
415-U-260 Set/2 $8.99

Large Set
Four 1½ in. high strips, 36, 43, 49 and 56 in. long. Enough for one each: 10, 12, 14, 16 in. round pans.
415-U-262 Set/4 $18.99

Cake Leveler
Make your cake top perfectly level for precise decorating—just place adjustable wire in notches to desired height up to 2 in. and glide through the cake. Makes torting easy, too! For cakes up to 10 in. wide.
415-U-815 $3.19

Non-Stick Parchment Paper
Use Wilton silicone-treated non-stick parchment to line baking pans and cookie sheets—a non-fat alternative that saves cleanup time. Roll out cookie dough between 2 sheets, dough won't stick and will easily transfer to your cookie sheet. You can even reuse it for the next batch. Oven-safe to 400°F, great for conventional ovens, microwaves and the freezer. Double roll is 41 square feet, 15 in. wide. Certified Kosher.
415-U-680 $5.29

Large Cake Leveler
Blade easily levels and torts cakes up to 18 in. wide. Adjusts up to 3 in. high—just twist feet to lock into notch at desired height then glide the stainless steel blade through your cake.
417-U-1198 $23.09

Better Baking Tools

Essential tools designed to do more! Wilton's new Better Baking Tools are designed with exclusive features that make baking easier:

- *The patented Twist 'N Measure has a rotating dial to create 6 cups in 1*
- *The unique patented clip slides along the wires of the Baker's Pastry Blender to remove butter and dough*
- *The Cyclone Whisk has an innovative center spiral that incorporates more air into batters*
- *The Rolling Pin has removable handles making it fully submersible and dishwasher safe*

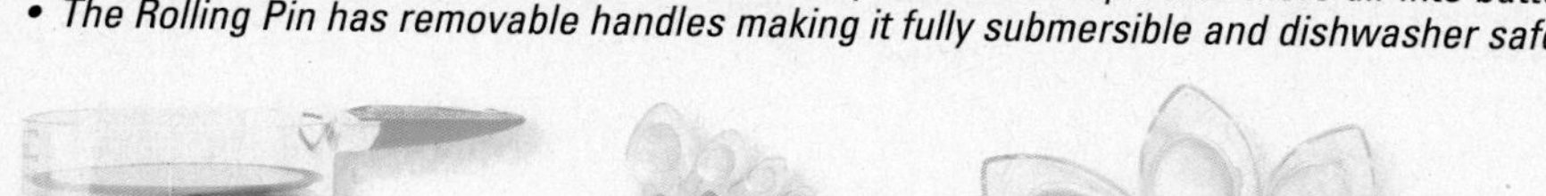

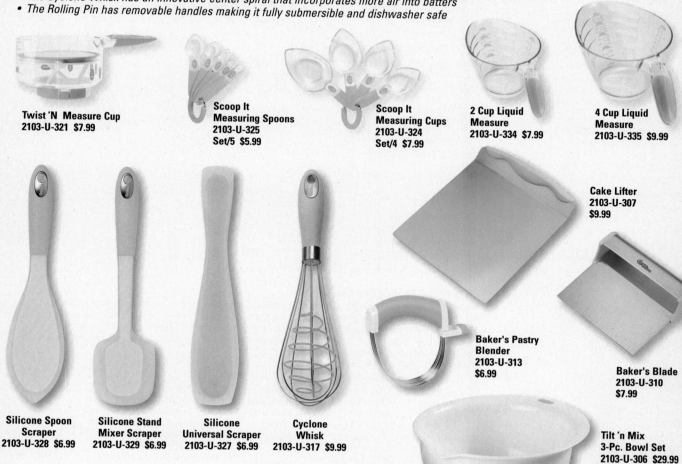

Twist 'N Measure Cup
2103-U-321 $7.99

Scoop It Measuring Spoons
2103-U-325
Set/5 $5.99

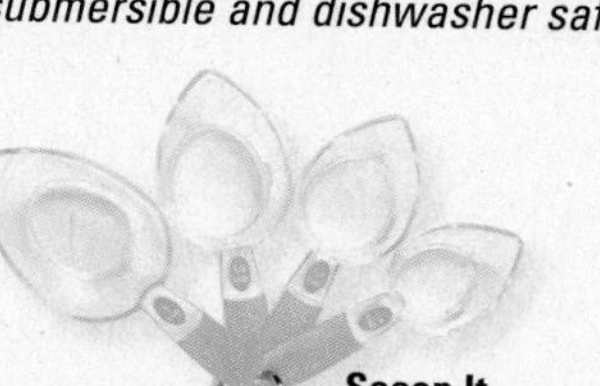

Scoop It Measuring Cups
2103-U-324
Set/4 $7.99

2 Cup Liquid Measure
2103-U-334 $7.99

4 Cup Liquid Measure
2103-U-335 $9.99

Cake Lifter
2103-U-307
$9.99

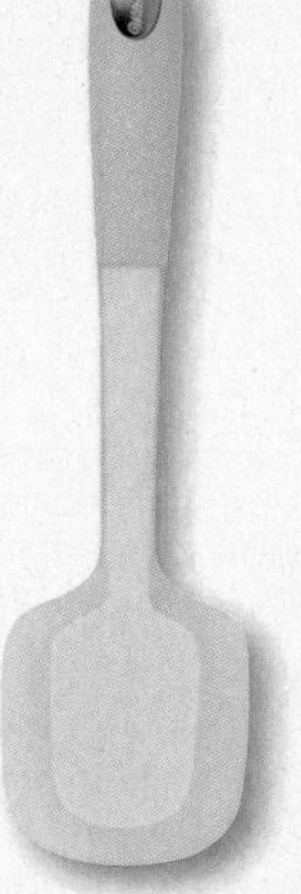

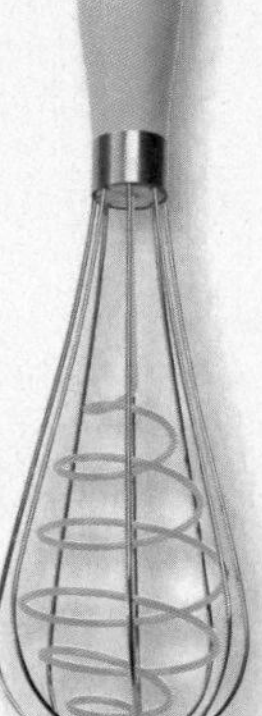

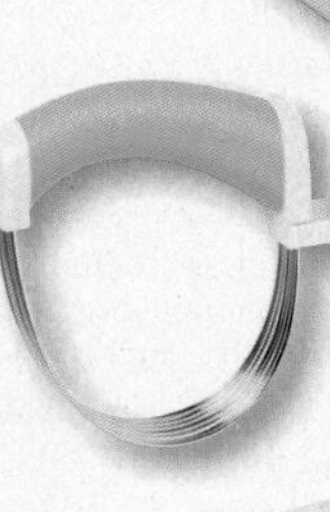

Baker's Pastry Blender
2103-U-313
$6.99

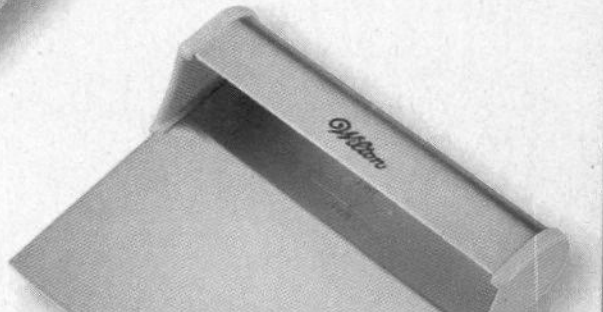

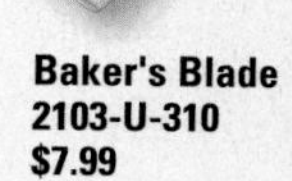

Baker's Blade
2103-U-310
$7.99

Silicone Spoon Scraper
2103-U-328 $6.99

Silicone Stand Mixer Scraper
2103-U-329 $6.99

Silicone Universal Scraper
2103-U-327 $6.99

Cyclone Whisk
2103-U-317 $9.99

Tilt 'n Mix 3-Pc. Bowl Set
2103-U-306 $29.99

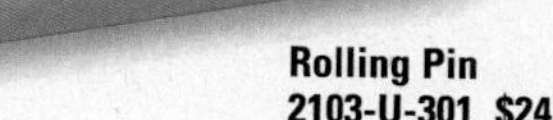

Rolling Pin
2103-U-301 $24.99

Cake Carriers

Cake Caddy™

The 6 in. high see-through plastic dome has 3 locking latches that hold the base securely in place wherever you go. Convenient handle gives you a firm grip. The elegant base is approximately 13 in. diameter and holds and stores up to 10 in. round cake or pie, cupcakes, cookies and more.
2105-U-9952 $14.99

THE ULTIMATE 3-IN-1 CADDY™

The versatile and safe way to carry cakes and deserts.

Take along cakes, cupcakes, muffins and more!
The Ultimate 3-In-1 Caddy features an exclusive reversible cupcake tray which holds 12 standard or 24 mini cupcakes. Or, remove the tray to carry up to a 9 x 13 in. decorated cake on the sturdy locking base. The see-through cover has higher sides to protect icing flowers and tall decorations. You can also use the caddy at home, to keep pies, cookies and brownies fresh for days after baking. 18 x 14⅛ x 5½ in. high.
2105-U-9958 $19.99

Tool Caddies

Ultimate Tool Caddy™

It's the storage solution designed specifically for cake decorators! Perfect for keeping your decorating space neat—or take it with you for touching up your cake at the event. The Ultimate Tool Caddy features 3 levels of organization to help you find your tools and accessories with ease.
409-U-623 $59.99

Top level:
Tip & Accessory Organizer Compartments
36 pegs hold virtually any size tip including wired drop flower tips, and let you stack to hold more! Tip organizer compartments allow for stacking of tips, which increases holding capacity. Two tip accessory compartments hold couplers, brushes and more.

Middle level:
Flip-top and Icing Color Drawers
Two slide-out drawers feature 3 compartments with snap-open tops. The perfect space for Fondant Cut-Outs™, stamens, flower nails, decorating bags, candles and more.
Icing color drawer holds up to 24 - ½ oz. jars or 10 each 1 oz. and ½ oz. jars.

Bottom level:
Oversized Drawer
Large pull-out drawer is ideal for oversized items. Create customized spaces with 3 dividers! Use the recessed lid to hold cake leveler.

Plus:
Spatula Slots on both sides for straight and angled spatulas.

NEW!

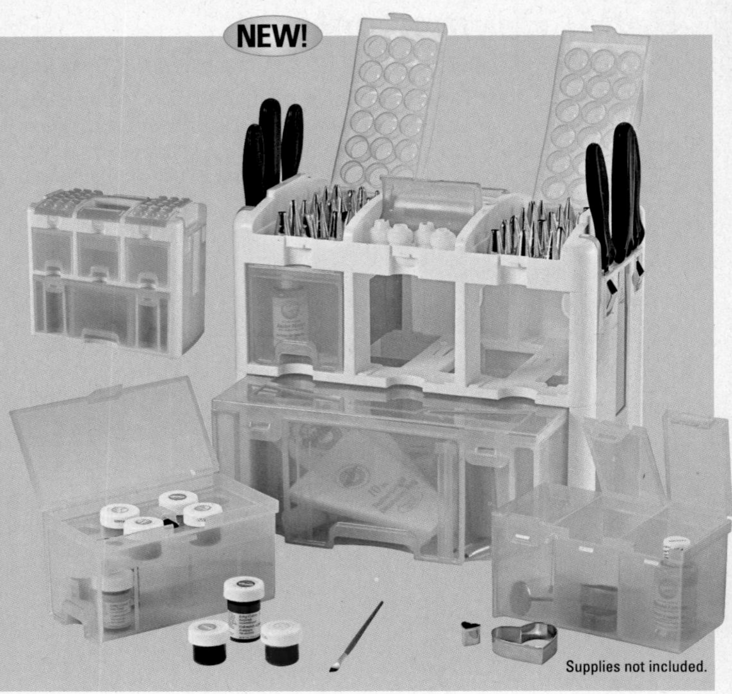

Supplies not included.

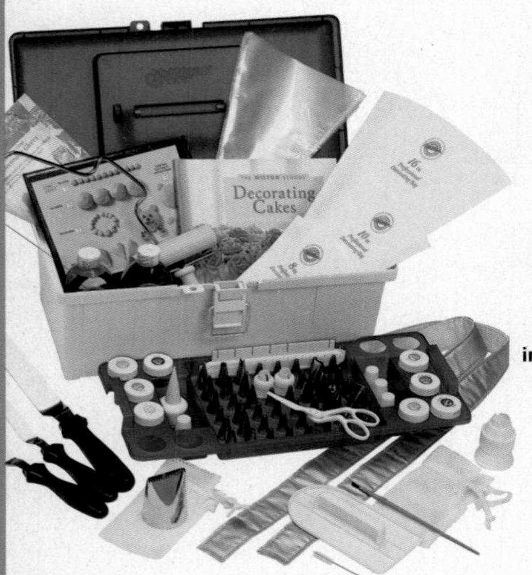

101 Piece Tool Caddy Collection

This convenient caddy contains our most complete collection of tools, colors and flavors for the cake decorator. It's a great way to organize, carry and store the essentials—tips, couplers, colors, spatulas and more. Lift-out tray holds tips, couplers, brushes and colors securely. Upright storage prevents spills and makes it easy to find what you need. Generous storage area keeps books, spatulas, bags and other large supplies neatly organized.
2109-U-861 Set/101 $144.99

Save over $43
Compared to individual prices

Includes These Tools:
- Eight .5 oz. Icing Colors: Golden Yellow, No-Taste Red, Brown, Violet, Pink, Royal Blue, Black, Kelly Green
- 3 Couplers (2 standard, 1 large)
- 2 Tip/Coupler Dishwasher and Storage Bags
- Tip Cleaning Brush
- 24 Disposable 12 in. Decorating Bags
- 3 Professional Reusable Decorating Bags (8, 10 and 16 in.)
- 4 Tip Covers
- Tip Saver
- 1½ in. Flower Nail No. 7
- 3 Spatulas (8 and 13 in. Angled, 8 in. Tapered)
- Flower Lifter
- Garland Marker
- *Decorating Cakes* Book
- 20 All-Purpose Disposable Decorating Gloves
- Practice Board with Patterns
- 2 Bake-Even Strips
- 8 oz. Clear Vanilla and No-Color Butter Flavors
- Cake Leveler
- Quick Ease Roller
- Easy-Glide Fondant Smoother
- Decorating Brush

Plus 18 Tips:
- Round: 1, 2, 2A, 3, 12
- Star: 16, 18, 21, 32
- Basketweave: 48
- Leaf: 67, 352
- Petal: 102, 103, 104, 125
- Drop Flower: 2D
- Cake Icer: 789

50 Piece Tool Caddy Decorating Set

We've put together the perfect set for both beginning and advanced decorators. The generous selection of tips, colors and tools gives you the flexibility to decorate virtually any kind of cake. There's also plenty of room to add new items and keep everything organized to save you time. Set includes all tools specified as needed in our Course I class.
2109-U-859 Set/50 $61.99

Save $27
Compared to individual prices

Includes These Tools:
- Tip Brush
- Decorating Brush
- 1½ in. Flower Nail No. 7
- 2 Standard Couplers
- 18 Disposable 12 in. Bags
- One 10 in. Professional Bag
- 8 in. Angled Spatula
- Four .5 oz. Icing Colors: Lemon Yellow, Christmas Red, Royal Blue, Leaf Green
- Practice Board with Stand
- *Cake Decorating Beginner's Guide*

Plus 19 Tips:
- Round: 2, 3, 5, 7, 12
- Leaf: 67, 352
- Drop Flower: 225
- Closed Star: 133
- Basketweave: 47
- Open Star: 16, 18, 21, 32
- Petal: 101, 103, 104
- Large Drop Flower: 2004 (2D)
- Multi-Opening: 233

Tool Caddy Only

Lift out tray keeps 48 tips and 12 color jars within reach (tips and colors not included). Stores colors upright to prevent spilling. Plastic.
409-U-860 $26.29

Decorating Sets

12 Piece Cupcake Decorating Set

Create all kinds of fun cupcake designs perfect for celebrations or everyday treats! Includes star tips 1M (rosettes, stars, drop flowers), star tip 22 (zigzags, pull-out stars), round tip 12 (outlines, dots, messages) and Bismarck tip 230 for exciting filled cupcakes, plus 8 disposable bags, instruction booklet.
2104-U-6667 Set/12 $8.39

53 Piece Cake Decorating Set

The works! Decorate many advanced wedding, floral and basketweave cakes as well as basic cakes. Set includes: metal decorating tips 2, 3, 5, 7, 12, 16, 18, 21, 32, 48, 67, 101, 103, 104, 129, 225, 349 and 352; 24 disposable 12 in. decorating bags, two tip couplers; 5 icing colors (.5 oz. each: Golden Yellow, Moss Green, Rose Petal, Cornflower Blue, Violet); one 1¼ in. flower nail No. 9; 8 in. angled spatula; storage tray; and 40-page *Cake Decorating Beginner's Guide*.
2104-U-2546 Set/53 $32.99

25 Piece Cake Decorating Set

A solid foundation set for decorating. Set includes: metal decorating tips 3, 16, 32, 104 and 352; 12 disposable 12 in. decorating bags; two tip couplers; 4 icing colors (.5 oz. each: Lemon Yellow, Pink, Sky Blue, Violet, Leaf Green); 1¼ in. flower nail No. 9; instruction booklet.
2104-U-2536 Set/25 $12.99

18 Piece Cake Decorating Set

Perfect for Wilton character cakes! Set includes: metal decorating tips 4, 12, 18 and 103; 6 disposable 12 in. decorating bags; 2 tip couplers; 5 liquid color packets (.067 fl. oz. each: Yellow, Red, Green, Orange, Blue); instruction booklet.
2104-U-2530 Set/18 $7.99

Decorating Bags

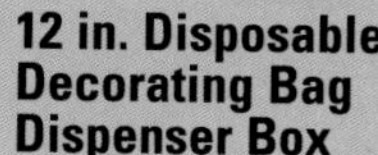

Featherweight® Decorating Bags

Use these easy-handling bags over and over. Lightweight, strong and flexible polyester will never get stiff. Coated to prevent grease from seeping through. May be boiled; dishwasher safe. Instructions included. Sold singly.

8 in. 404-U-5087 $3.19
10 in. 404-U-5109 $4.79
12 in. 404-U-5125 $5.79
14 in. 404-U-5140 $6.79
16 in. 404-U-5168 $8.39
18 in. 404-U-5184 $9.49

Disposable Decorating Bags

Just use, then toss. Strong, flexible plastic. Both 12 and 16 in. bags fit standard tips and couplers. Also perfect for melting Candy Melts®* in the microwave. Instructions included.

16 in.
2104-U-1357 Pk./12 $5.29

12 in.
2104-U-358 Pk./12 $4.19
2104-U-1358 Pk./24 $6.79

*Brand confectionery coating.

12 in. Disposable Decorating Bag Dispenser Box

50 Pack

Now in convenient Value Packs! Dispenser boxes make it easy to pull out one bag at a time, so you can keep your decorating space uncluttered. Instructions included.
2104-U-1273 Pk./50 $13.19
2104-U-1249 Pk./100 $20.99

15 in. Parchment Triangles

Make your own disposable decorating bags with our grease-resistant vegetable parchment triangles. The professional's choice for convenience and quick bag preparation. Instructions included.
2104-U-1508 Pk./100 $6.99

Icing Bag Ties

Convenient bands wrap around the twist of your decorating bag, then lock to prevent icing from oozing out of the top. As you squeeze out icing, slide the tie down to maintain the pressure.
417-U-173 Pk./12 $4.49

Deluxe Tip Set

Includes: 26 metal decorating tips (2, 4, 7, 13, 16, 17, 18, 30, 42, 46, 47, 61, 65, 66, 67, 74, 78, 97, 98, 101, 102, 103, 104, 106, 107 and 199); 1¼ in. flower nail No. 9; tip coupler; plastic tipsaver case.
2104-U-6666 Set/28 $28.59

Master Tip Set

Includes: 52 metal decorating tips: (1, 2, 3, 4, 6, 7, 12, 13, 16, 17, 18, 22, 24, 27, 30, 31, 32, 42, 45, 46, 47, 48, 54, 59, 61, 65, 66, 67, 68, 69, 70, 73, 74, 78, 96, 97, 98, 101, 102, 103, 104, 106, 108, 109, 123, 124, 129, 134, 136, 195, 199 and 2C); two standard tip couplers; two 1¼ in. flower nails No. 9; plastic tipsaver case.
2104-U-7778 Set/56 $49.49

Tip Accessories

Maintain the quality of your Wilton metal decorating tips with these tools.

Tip/Coupler Dishwasher and Storage Bag

Place nylon mesh bag in dishwasher silverware rack for easy tip and coupler cleaning. Tips not included. 5¾ x 6 in.
417-U-1640
Pk./2 $3.29

Decorating Couplers

Couplers make it easy to change decorating tips on the same icing bag.

Standard
Fits all decorating bags and standard tips.
411-U-1987 $0.69

Large
Use with large decorating tips and 14 to 18 in. Featherweight Bags.
411-U-1006 $1.69

Tip Saver

Restores bent tips to their proper shape; opens clogged tips. Place tip over pointed or cone-shaped end, put on cover and twist back and forth to reshape. Heavy-duty plastic.
414-U-909 $3.09

Tip Covers

Take filled bags along for touch ups—just slip over tip and go. Plastic.
414-U-915 Pk./4 $1.09

Tip Brush

Great for cleaning small tip openings. Plastic bristles. ¼ x 4 in. long.
418-U-1123 $1.59

Tipsaver Cases

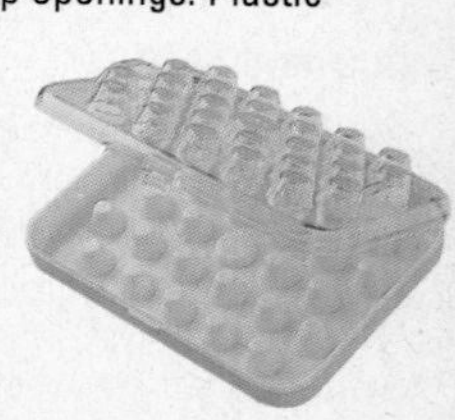

Small case holds 26 tips; large case holds 52 tips
Tips not included.
Small 405-U-8773 $6.99
Large 405-U-7777 $8.49

Decorating Tips

All tips work with standard bags and couplers, unless otherwise indicated. Nickel-plated brass. Dishwasher safe.

ROUND TIPS

Outline, lettering, dots, balls, beads, stringwork, lattice, lacework.

402-U-1 $0.99

402-U-901** $1.89

402-U-1009 $1.59

402-U-2 $0.99

402-U-3 $0.99

402-U-4 $0.99

402-U-5 $0.99

402-U-6 $0.99

402-U-7 $0.99

402-U-8 $0.99

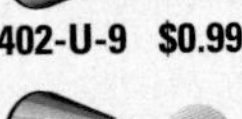
402-U-9 $0.99

402-U-10 $0.99

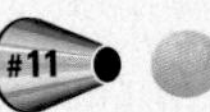
402-U-11 $0.99

402-U-12 $0.99

Smaller version of 1A.
402-U-2001* $1.69

Bold borders, figure piping.
402-U-1001* $1.89

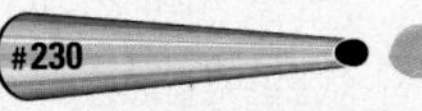

Fill eclairs and bismarcks.
402-U-230** $2.19

402-U-55 $0.99

402-U-57 $0.99

For flat lettering.
402-U-301 $0.99

DROP FLOWER TIPS

Small (106-225); medium (131-194); large (2C-1G, great for cookie dough).

402-U-106 $1.69

402-U-107 $1.69

402-U-108** $1.69

402-U-109** $1.89

402-U-129 $1.69

402-U-224 $1.69

402-U-225 $1.69

402-U-131 $1.69

402-U-190** $1.89

402-U-191 $1.69

402-U-193 $1.69

402-U-194** $1.89

402-U-140 $1.89

402-U-195** $1.69

402-U-2003* $1.69

402-U-2004* $1.69

402-U-2005* $1.69

402-U-2006* $1.69

402-U-1002* $1.89

402-U-1003* $1.89

402-U-1005* $1.89

402-U-1006* $1.89

402-U-1007* $1.89

PETAL TIPS

Realistic flower petals, dramatic ruffles, drapes, swags and bows.

402-U-594 $0.99

402-U-59 $0.99

402-U-60 $0.99

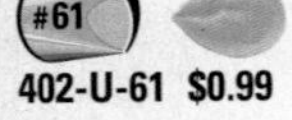
402-U-61 $0.99

402-U-62 $0.99

402-U-64 $0.99

402-U-97 $0.99

402-U-1019 $1.59

402-U-101 $0.99

402-U-102 $0.99

402-U-103 $0.99

402-U-104 $0.99

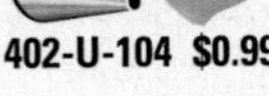

402-U-150 $1.69

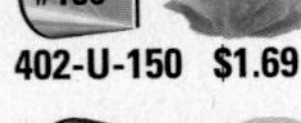
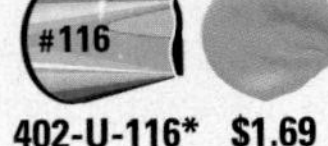
402-U-116* $1.69

402-U-121* $1.69

402-U-123* $1.69

402-U-124* $1.69

402-U-125* $1.69

402-U-126* $1.69

402-U-127* $1.69

Giant Rose**
402-U-1274
$1.89

BASKETWEAVE TIPS

Tips 44, 45 make only smooth stripes; rest of basketweave tips and Cake Icer make both smooth and ribbed stripes.

402-U-44 $0.99

402-U-45 $0.99

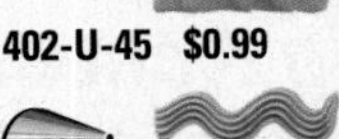
402-U-46 $0.99

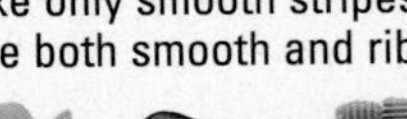
402-U-47 $0.99

402-U-48 $0.99

402-U-1004** $1.89

402-U-2002*
$1.69

Cake Icer**
409-U-789 $3.29

MULTI-OPENING TIPS

Rows and clusters of strings, beads, stars, (Use 233 for grass).

402-U-42 $0.99

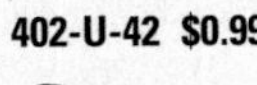
402-U-89 $0.99

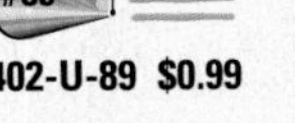
402-U-134** $1.89

402-U-233 $1.69

402-U-234* $1.89

402-U-235* $1.69

Triple Star*
402-U-2010 $2.89

*Fits large coupler.

**Tip does not work with coupler. Use with parchment or uncut bags only. Cake Icer Tip should be used with bags 14 in. or larger.

OPEN STAR TIPS

Star techniques, drop flowers; the finely cut teeth of 199 through 364 create decorations with many ridges; use 6B and 8B with pastry dough too.

402-U-13 $0.99

402-U-14 $0.99

402-U-15 $0.99

402-U-16 $0.99

402-U-17 $0.99

402-U-18 $0.99

402-U-19 $0.99

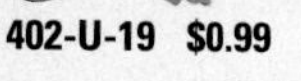

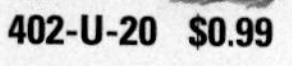
402-U-20 $0.99

402-U-21 $0.99

402-U-22 $0.99

402-U-32 $0.99

402-U-199 $1.69

402-U-362 $1.69

402-U-363 $1.69

402-U-364 $1.69

402-U-172** $1.69

402-U-2110* $1.69

402-U-4400** $1.69

402-U-6600** $1.69

402-U-8800** $1.89

LEFT-HANDED TIP SETS

Now left-handers can achieve the same beautiful flowers as right-handed decorators! Nickel-plated brass tips fit standard bags and couplers.

Drop Flower Set
Includes Left tips 106 and 107 for making small swirled flowers.
418-U-613† Set/2 $3.29

Petal Set
Includes Left tip 59° for violets, Left tip 97 for Victorian roses and Left tip 116** for large Wilton roses.
418-U-612† Set/3 $3.29

CAKE DECORATING

SPECIALTY TIPS

Shells, ropes, hearts, Christmas trees, ring candle holders!

402-U-98 $0.99

402-U-347 $1.69

402-U-136 $1.89

402-U-77 $0.99

402-U-78 $0.99

402-U-83 $0.99

402-U-96 $0.99

402-U-79 $0.99

402-U-105 $0.99

402-U-80 $0.99

402-U-81 $0.99

402-U-250* $1.89

402-U-252* $1.89

402-U-95 $0.99

LEAF TIPS

So realistic! Ideal for shell-motion borders too.

402-U-659 $1.59

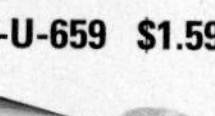
402-U-65 $0.99

402-U-66 $0.99

402-U-67 $0.99

402-U-68 $0.99

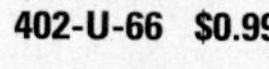

402-U-69 $0.99

402-U-73 $0.99

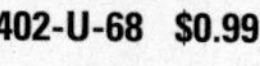
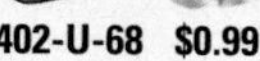
402-U-74 $0.99

402-U-75 $0.99

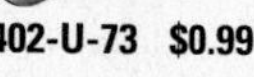
402-U-349 $1.59

402-U-352 $1.59

402-U-326 $1.59

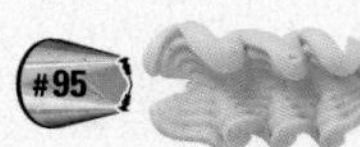
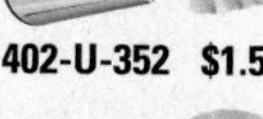
402-U-70 $0.99

402-U-112** $1.69

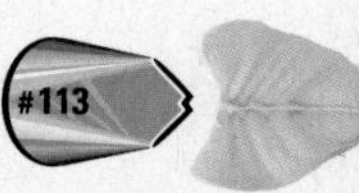
402-U-113* $1.69

402-U-115* $1.69

Makes leaves for larger flowers.
402-U-366* $1.89

CLOSED STAR TIPS

Create deeply grooved shells, stars and fleurs de lis.

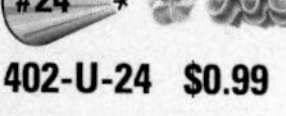
402-U-24 $0.99

402-U-26 $0.99

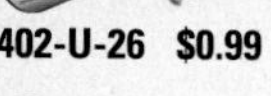
402-U-27 $0.99

402-U-28 $0.99

402-U-29 $0.99

402-U-30 $0.99

402-U-31 $0.99

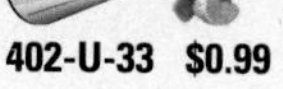

402-U-33 $0.99

402-U-35 $0.99

402-U-133 $0.99

402-U-54 $0.99

RUFFLE TIPS

Plain, fluted, shell-border, special effects.

402-U-86 $0.99

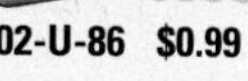
402-U-87† $0.99

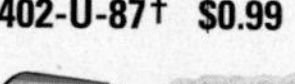
402-U-88† $0.99

402-U-100 $0.99

402-U-353 $1.59

402-U-340 $1.59

402-U-401 $1.59

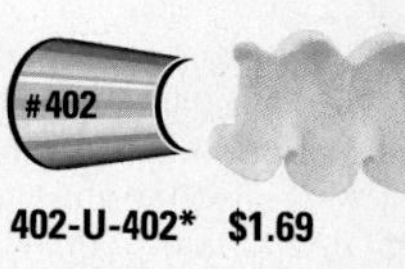
402-U-402* $1.69

402-U-406* $1.89

402-U-403** $1.89

†For left-handers.

*Fits large coupler.

Cupcake Fun!

What makes Wilton cupcakes more fun? It's our exciting products, which make baking, decorating and serving one-of-a-kind cupcakes a pleasure! See www.cupcakefun.com, for more great products and ideas!

NEW!

SILICONE BUILD-A-CAKE SETS

Enjoy the fun of a party cake with the convenience of cupcakes! Arrange the shaped silicone cups on a baking pan, fill and bake, then decorate and serve. Decorating Puzzle Cakes!™ is easy! Check the instructions inside for 3 fun designs you can create using simple icing techniques and colorful candies. Or, use your imagination and create more fun shapes of your own.

Transportation
415-U-9453 Set/24 $14.99

Animal
415-U-9452 Set/24 $14.99

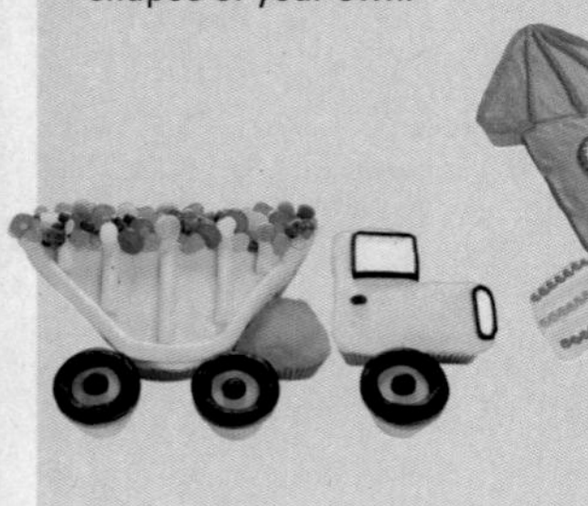

6-Cup King-Size Muffin Pan

Create extra-tall treats! Great for cupcakes, ice cream, molded gelatin, mini angel food cakes, and mousse. Heavy-gauge premium non-stick for quick release and easy clean-up.
2105-U-9921 $9.99

Jumbo Muffin Pan

Make super-size cupcakes and muffins. Six cups, each 4 x 2 in. Heavy-gauge premium non-stick for quick release and easy clean-up.
2105-U-955 $6.99

Cupcake Pedestals

Perfectly display cupcakes, muffins, party favors and more —or turn the pedestal over for the perfect ice cream cone holder! 5.2 in. high.
307-U-839 Pk./4 $7.99

The Ultimate 3-In-1 Caddy™

It's the most convenient way to take along cakes, cupcakes, muffins and more! The Ultimate 3-In-1 Caddy features an exclusive reversible cupcake tray which holds 12 standard or 24 mini cupcakes. Or, remove the tray to carry up to a 9 x 13 in. decorated cake on the sturdy locking base. The see-through cover has higher sides to protect icing flowers and tall decorations. You can also use the caddy at home, to keep pies, cookies and brownies fresh for days after baking. 18 x 14 x 6.75 in. high.
2105-U-9958 $19.99

Cupcake Fun!

Wilton presents today's hottest party dessert like you've never seen it before. This all-new collection features over 150 exciting cupcake and treat ideas for all occasions, with complete baking and decorating instructions to make them easy. Discover captivating new shapes from coffee cups to flying saucers, plus a great recipe section with delicious surprises like Key Lime Cupcakes, Mocha Icing and more. Great baking and decorating products, too. *Cupcake Fun!* is the book you need to create the ultimate cupcake celebration. Look for many more great cupcake ideas and recipes at **www.cupcakefun.com**. Soft cover, 128 pages. **902-U-795 $12.99**

12-Piece Cupcake Decorating Set

Wait until you see how much fun cupcakes can be using the decorating tips in this set! You'll create all kinds of fun designs perfect for celebrations or everyday treats! Includes star tip 1M (rosettes, stars, drop flowers), star tip 22 (zigzags, pull-out stars), round tip 12 (outlines, dots, messages) and Bismarck tip 230 for exciting filled cupcakes; 8 disposable bags, instruction booklet.
2104-U-6667 Set/12 $8.39

CUPCAKES 'N MORE® DESSERT STANDS

The look is fresh and fun, featuring bold silver-finished wire spirals to securely hold each cupcake. The twisting, towering design is perfect for any setting—showers, kids' birthdays, weddings, holidays and more.

13 Count Standard
9.25 in. high x 9 in. wide.
Holds 13 standard cupcakes.
307-U-831 $13.69

24 Count Mini
10.5 in. high x 9 in. wide.
Holds 24 mini cupcakes.
307-U-250 $15.79

19 Count Standard
18 in. high x 12 in. wide.
Holds 19 standard cupcakes.
307-U-666 $20.99

23 Count Standard
12 in. high x 13 wide.
Holds 23 standard cupcakes.
307-U-826 $31.49

38 Count Standard
15 in. high x 18 wide.
Holds 38 standard cupcakes.
307-U-651 $41.99

NEW!

Collapsible for easy storage

4-Tier Stacked Dessert Tower

Great way to display cupcakes, appetizers, brownies and other party treats! Four plastic stacking sections with angled tiers for the best view of decorated desserts. Sections easily disassemble and nest for storage; assembled tower is 16.25 in. high x 12 in. wide. Holds 36 standard cupcakes.
307-U-856 $19.99

JUMBO SPRINKLES

Give your cupcakes a big finish! Top them with Jumbo Sprinkles in exciting shapes and colors. These big and bold decorations are perfect for cupcakes, mini cakes, jumbo and king-size cupcakes, brownies and cookies. Innovative shapes for holiday, birthday or any celebration. Certified Kosher.
$4.09

Jumbo Stars
3.25 oz. **710-U-026**

Jumbo Confetti
3.25 oz. **710-U-029**

Jumbo Diamonds
3.5 oz. **710-U-027**

Jumbo Daisies
3.25 oz. **710-U-028**

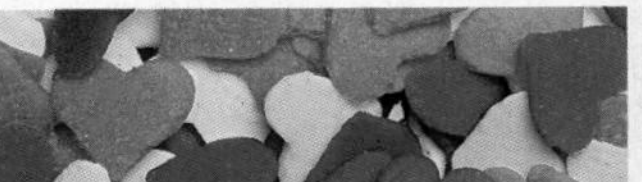

Jumbo Hearts
3.25 oz. **710-U-032**

Jumbo Rainbow Nonpareils
4.8 oz. **710-U-033**

Heart Drops
5.25 oz. **710-U-035**

CUPCAKE CRUNCHES

Add delicious flavor and a colossal crunch to your cupcakes! Sprinkle over iced cupcakes. Certified Kosher.
$3.99

Chocolate
3.5 oz. **710-U-025**

Almond
3.5 oz. Artificially flavored. **710-U-024**

NEW!

Toffee
3.5 oz. Naturally and artificially flavored. **710-U-023**

SILICONE BAKING CUPS

Discover the convenience and easy release of flexible silicone! Reusable oven-safe cups in fun colors and exciting shapes are perfect for baking and serving. All have convenient batter fill line.

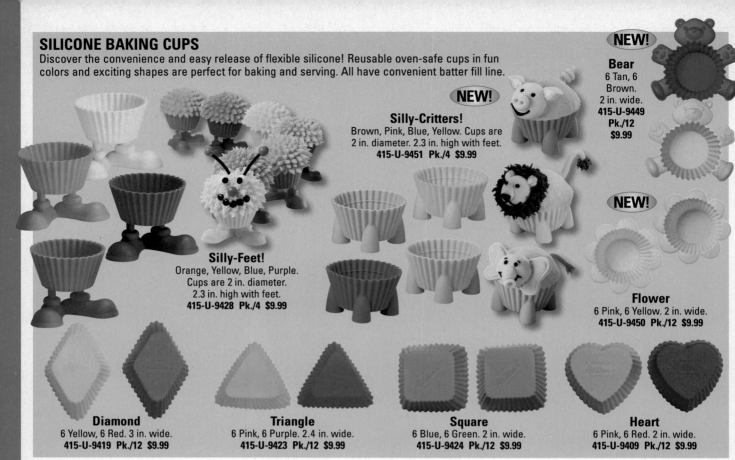

NEW!
Bear
6 Tan, 6 Brown. 2 in. wide.
415-U-9449 Pk./12 $9.99

NEW!  
Silly-Critters!
Brown, Pink, Blue, Yellow. Cups are 2 in. diameter. 2.3 in. high with feet.
415-U-9451 Pk./4 $9.99

Silly-Feet!
Orange, Yellow, Blue, Purple. Cups are 2 in. diameter. 2.3 in. high with feet.
415-U-9428 Pk./4 $9.99

NEW! 
Flower
6 Pink, 6 Yellow. 2 in. wide.
415-U-9450 Pk./12 $9.99

Diamond
6 Yellow, 6 Red. 3 in. wide.
415-U-9419 Pk./12 $9.99

Triangle
6 Pink, 6 Purple. 2.4 in. wide.
415-U-9423 Pk./12 $9.99

Square
6 Blue, 6 Green. 2 in. wide.
415-U-9424 Pk./12 $9.99

Heart
6 Pink, 6 Red. 2 in. wide.
415-U-9409 Pk./12 $9.99

Baking Cups

Microwave-safe paper. Standard size, 2 in. dia., Mini size, 1.25 in. dia., King and Jumbo size, 2.25 in. dia.

NEW!
Be My Cupcake $2.09
Standard
415-U-127 Pk./75
Mini
415-U-128 Pk./100

NEW!
Bubble Stripes $2.09
Standard
415-U-114 Pk./75
Mini
415-U-115 Pk./100

Cupcake Heaven $2.09
Standard
415-U-422 Pk./75
Mini
415-U-426 Pk./100

Snappy Stripes $2.09
Standard
415-U-5381 Pk./75
Mini
415-U-5380 Pk./100

White
King-Size $2.09
415-U-2118 Pk./24
Jumbo $2.09
415-U-427 Pk/75
Standard $1.59
415-U-2505 Pk./75
Mini $1.59
415-U-2507 Pk./100

Add-A-Message Fun Pix®
Clip on messages, pictures and more with these colorful plastic picks! Great for place markers, announcing awards at banquets and favorite sayings. Four fun colors to go with your favorite baking cups. 3 in. high.
2113-U-7611 Pk./12 $2.09

CUPCAKE BOXES

Brightly-patterned window boxes are the perfect way to hold and display your cupcakes! Each box includes an insert with recessed space to hold standard cupcakes safely in place. Easy folding assembly; great for gifts and favors! Choose single, 4-cupcake size or 6-cupcake size.

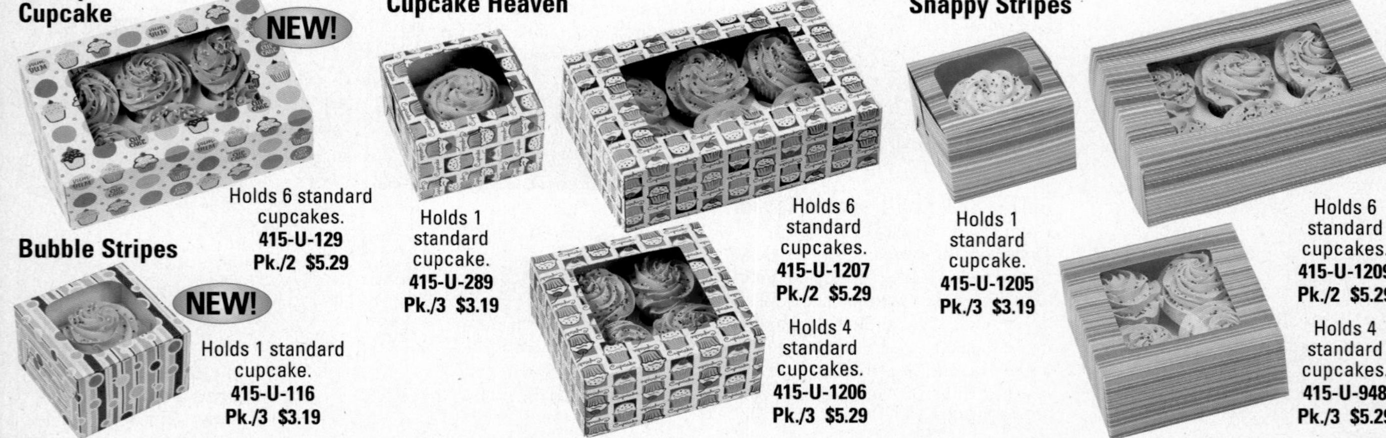

Be My Cupcake
NEW!
Holds 6 standard cupcakes.
415-U-129
Pk./2 $5.29

Bubble Stripes
NEW!
Holds 1 standard cupcake.
415-U-116
Pk./3 $3.19

Cupcake Heaven
Holds 1 standard cupcake.
415-U-289
Pk./3 $3.19

Holds 6 standard cupcakes.
415-U-1207
Pk./2 $5.29

Holds 4 standard cupcakes.
415-U-1206
Pk./3 $5.29

Snappy Stripes
Holds 1 standard cupcake.
415-U-1205
Pk./3 $3.19

Holds 6 standard cupcakes.
415-U-1209
Pk./2 $5.29

Holds 4 standard cupcakes.
415-U-948
Pk./3 $5.29

Gifts from the Kitchen

Your homemade treats are even more welcome when packaged in our boxes, bags and accessories. We make it easy to present your delicious foods with pride!

Gift-Giving Containers

Create a custom food gift with our crisp white containers! Add color and flair with your own gift wrap, ribbon, tissue and tags.

Treat Boxes
Create the perfect gift with window boxes. Great for candies or 3.5 in. cookies. Includes seals/sticker sheet. 4.5 x 4.5 x 1.5 in.
415-U-102 Pk./3 $3.19

Hexagon Treat Boxes
Self-closing top forms a pretty petal box top. Great for cookies, candy and favors. 4 x 6.25 in. high.
415-U-105 Pk./4 $5.29

Popcorn Treat Boxes
Classic shape stands up tall to hold popcorn, nuts and other snacks. 3.75 x 2.25 x 5.25 in. high.
1904-U-1141 Pk./4 $3.19

Paper Treat Bags
Versatile way to give, ready for your favorite embellishments. 4.5 x 2.8 x 8.5 in. high.
1912-U-1144 Pk./4 $3.19

Treat Basket
Roomy handled basket is ideal for your gifts. Great for muffins, mini loaves and more. 6.5 x 6.5 x 3 in.
415-U-104 Pk./2 $5.29

Clear Treat Bags

Find the perfect size to wrap up any treats.

10 x 16 in. Treat Bags
Wrap up bread loaves, smaller bowls and plates of treats. Includes 4 - 10 x 16 in. bags; 4 - 18 in. ribbons, 4 gift tags.
1912-U-1142 $3.19

16 x 20 in. Treat Bags
Ideal size for Treat Baskets (above) filled with muffins. Great for a cookie platter, pie, scones and more. Includes 3 - 16 x 20 in. bags; 3 - 18 in. ribbons, 3 gift tags.
1912-U-1143 $4.19

ACCESSORIES

Tissue Paper
Line bags or boxes with this heavyweight tissue to protect and present your food gift with flair. 12 x 24 in. Food safe.
1904-U-1294 Pk./10 $4.19

Bakers Twine
Strong,colorful twine has so many uses in the kitchen. From trussing turkey to wrapping breads and gifts of food, it's a necessity you'll want to keep on hand. 3 colors (75 ft. each).
1904-U-1026 $4.19

Bakeware

Wilton is the #1 bakeware brand in America. From fun novelty shapes for birthday cakes to dramatic cast aluminum styles for elegant desserts, count on Wilton for the best results.

Non-Stick Bakeware

Our premium non-stick bakeware combines superior non-stick performance, serving convenience and elegant design, to provide the highest level of baking satisfaction.

- *Oversized handles for safe lifting of the pan*
- *Pan dimensions permanently stamped into handles*
- *Heavy-duty steel construction prevents warping*
- *Durable, reinforced non-stick coating offers superior release and easy cleanup*
- *10-Year Warranty*

Cookie Pans and Sheets

Small Cookie
13.25 x 9.25 x .5 in.
2105-U-436 $13.99

Medium Cookie
15.25 x 10.25 x .75 in.
2105-U-412 $14.99

Large Cookie/Jelly Roll
17.25 x 11.5 x 1 in.
2105-U-413 $16.99

Jumbo Air Insulated Sheet
18 x 14 in.
2105-U-422 $23.99

2105-U-412

2105-U-422

Specialty Pans

Fluted Tube
9.75 x 3.4 in.
2105-U-416 $16.99

6 Cavity Mini Fluted Tube
4.2 x 2 in.
2105-U-445 $21.49

Angel Food
9.4 x 4.25 in.
2105-U-415 $19.99

14 in. Pizza Crisper
14 x .5 in.
2105-U-420 $16.99

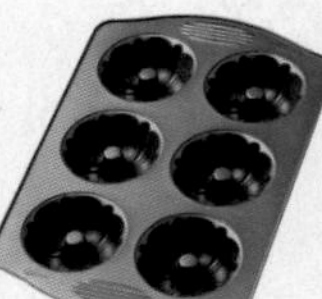

2105-U-445

2105-U-420

Cake and Pie Pans

9 x 1.5 in. Round Cake
2105-U-408 $9.99

9 x 9 x 2 in. Square Cake
2105-U-407 $10.99

11 x 7 x 1.5 in. Biscuit/Brownie
2105-U-443 $11.99

13 x 9 x 2 in. Oblong Cake
2105-U-411 $14.99

13 x 9 x 2 in. Oblong Cake w/Plastic Cover
2105-U-423 $19.99

9 x 1.5 in. Pie w/Fluted Edges
2105-U-438 $9.99

2105-U-408

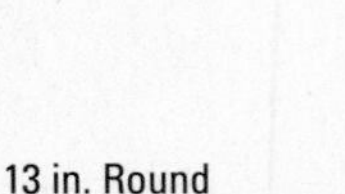

2105-U-411

Cooling Grids

10 x 16 in. Rectangle
2305-U-228 $9.99

14.5 x 20 in. Rectangle
2305-U-229 $14.49

13 in. Round
2305-U-230 $10.49

3-Tier Stackable
15.8 x 9.8 in.
2105-U-459 $11.99

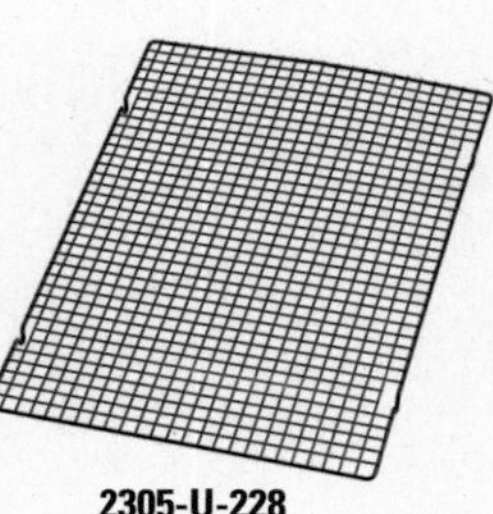

2305-U-228

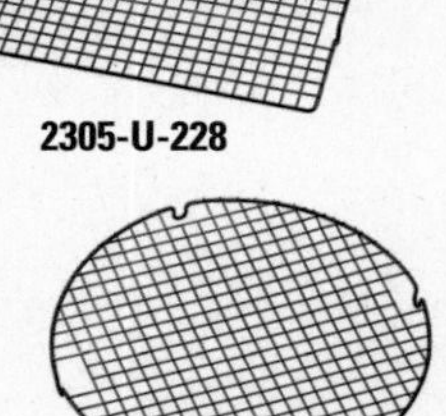

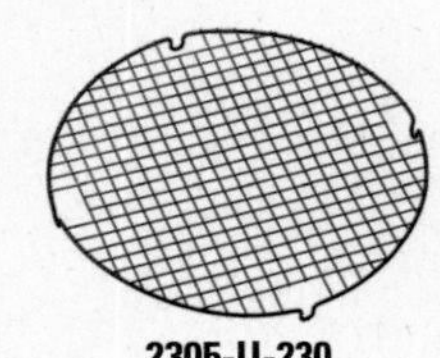

2305-U-230

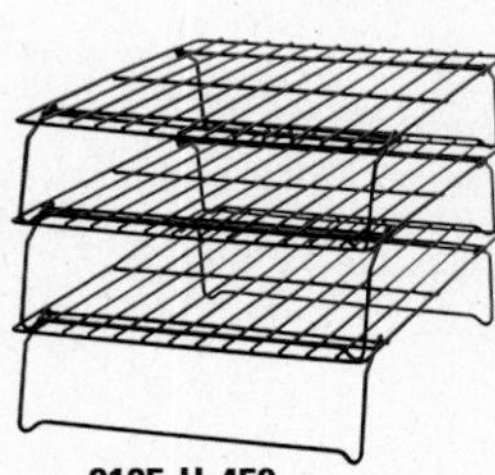

2105-U-459

Tart/Quiche Pans

9 x 1.2 in. Round
2105-U-442 $11.99

11 x 1.2 in. Round
2105-U-450 $13.99

10 x 1.2 in. Heart
2105-U-452 $11.99

Round 3-Pc. Set
8 x 1.2 in., 9 x 1.2 in., and 10 x 1.2 in.
2105-U-451 Set/3 $26.99

4 in. Tart 4-Pc. Set
4 x .75 in. with removable bottom.
2105-U-466 $11.99

4 in. Tart/Quiche 6-Pc. Set 4 x .75 in. with removable bottom.
2105-U-441 $17.99

2105-U-450

2105-U-452

Muffin and Loaf Pans

6 Cup Regular Muffin
2105-U-405 $11.99

12 Cup Mini Muffin
2105-U-403 $8.99

12 Cup Regular Muffin
2105-U-406 $16.99

Large Loaf
9.25 x 5.25 x 2.75 in.
2105-U-402 $9.99

4 Cavity Mini Loaf
5.75 x 3 x 2.2 in.
2105-U-444 $21.49

2105-U-405

2105-U-402

Springform Pans

4 x 1.75 in. Round
2105-U-453 $6.99

6 x 2.75 in. Round
2105-U-447 $11.99

9 x 2.75 in. Round
2105-U-414 $16.99

10 x 2.75 in. Round
2105-U-435 $17.99

4 x 1.75 in. Heart
2105-U-457 $9.99

9 x 2.75 in. Heart
2105-U-419 $21.49

2105-U-435

2105-U-419

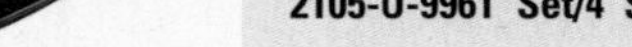

CHECKERBOARD CAKE SET

With this unique baking set, you'll create cakes with an exciting multicolored pattern—there's style in every slice! Baking is easy with the Batter Dividing Ring included. Just place the Dividing Ring in one of the three 9 x 1.5 in. pans in the set and follow instructions for adding dark and light colors of batter in the divisions. Use the easy-lift handles to lift out ring and repeat for 2 more layers, pouring the dark and light batters in opposite sections for the middle layer. Lift out ring, bake cakes, then stack cakes to form the checkerboard. Enjoy two tastes in one cake—try the Golden Yellow/Chocolate recipe on the package. Great for colorful holiday cakes too! Three pans feature oversized handles for safe lifting from the oven; each takes 5½ cups batter. Non-stick steel pans; plastic Dividing Ring.
2105-U-9961 Set/4 $15.99

Dimensions®
DECORATIVE BAKEWARE

Heavyweight cast aluminum conducts heat evenly and provides uniquely sculpted shapes. Bake in non-stick cast aluminum as you would in any aluminum pan. The premium non-stick surface means foods release perfectly and cleanup is a breeze. Lifetime Warranty.

Perennial
9.5 x 3.2 in.; 9 cup capacity.*
2105-U-5031 $30.99

Tulip
9.5 x 4 in.; 11 cup capacity.*
2105-U-5032 $30.99

2-LAYER CAKE SETS
Assemble shaped top and bottom cake halves with a thin layer of icing.

FEATURED ON OUR COVER!

NEW!

Multi-Cavity Mini Cupcakes
Finished cakes 3.8 x 4 in.; 6 cup total capacity.*
2105-U-5043 $30.99

Large Cupcake
Finished cake 8.25 x 7.5 in.; 10 cup total capacity.*
2105-U-5038 $30.99

NEW!

Multi-Cavity Mini Pumpkins
Finished cakes 3.4 x 3.4 in.; 5 cup total capacity.*
2105-U-1183 $30.99

NEW!

Large Pumpkin
Finished cake 6.75 x 6 in.; 10 cup total capacity.*
2105-U-1184 $30.99

NEW!

Multi-Cavity Mini Flower Baskets
Finished cakes 3.9 x 4.2 in.; 6 cup total capacity.*
2105-U-5029 $30.99

NEW!

Multi-Cavity Mini Ice Cream Cones
Finished cakes 3.9 x 4.7 in.; 6 cup total capacity.*
2105-U-5010 $30.99

Gift
11.2 in. x 9.5 in. x 1.5 in.; 11 cup capacity.*
2105-U-5027 $30.99

Snowflake
12 x 10.5 x 2.75 in.; 11 cup capacity.*
2105-U-5030 $30.99

4 Cavity Mini Snowflakes
Each 5 x 2.25 in.; 7 cup total capacity.*
2105-U-5028 $30.99

Crown of Hearts
11 x 2.5 in.; 11 cup capacity.*
2105-U-5011 $30.99

6 Cavity Mini Hearts
Each 4 in. x 2 in.; 7 cup total capacity.*
2105-U-5012 $30.99

Queen of Hearts
9 x 3.25 in.; 11 cup capacity.*
2105-U-5001 $30.99

Antoinette
9 x 4 in.; 11 cup capacity.*
2105-U-1189 $30.99

Cascade
9.5 x 4.75 in.; 11 cup capacity.*
2105-U-1199 $30.99

Belle
9 x 3.75 in.; 11 cup capacity.*
2105-U-1186 $30.99

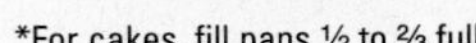

*For cakes, fill pans ½ to ⅔ full.

OUR MOST POPULAR BAKEWARE!

Decorator Preferred®

Professional Aluminum Bakeware

Built with the most features to help decorators bake their best! Compare these benefits to any brand:

STRAIGHT SIDES

Bake perfect 90° corners for the precise look wedding cakes require. Ordinary bakeware has rounded corners, giving cakes rounded edges.

GRIP LIP EDGES

Extra-wide rims make heavy filled pans easy to handle.

PURE ALUMINUM

The best material for baking cakes—creates a light, golden brown cake surface, beautiful for decorating.

SUPERIOR THICKNESS

Thicker than ordinary bakeware, built to distribute heat evenly for more consistent baking.

HANDCRAFTED CONSTRUCTION

Sheets and squares are handwelded for excellent detail and durability.

LIFETIME WARRANTY

Superior construction and performance designed and guaranteed to last a lifetime.

Rounds

What a selection of sizes—including the hard-to find 18 in. Half Round, which lets you bake and ice two halves to create one 18 in. round cake.

6 x 2 in.
2105-U-6122 $7.99

8 x 2 in.
2105-U-6136 $8.99

9 x 2 in.
2105-U-6137 $9.99

10 x 2 in.
2105-U-6138 $11.99

12 x 2 in.
2105-U-6139 $14.49

14 x 2 in.
2105-U-6140 $19.99

16 x 2 in.
2105-U-6141 $21.99

6 x 3 in.
2105-U-6106 $9.99

8 x 3 in.
2105-U-6105 $10.99

10 x 3 in.
2105-U-6104 $12.99

12 x 3 in.
2105-U-6103 $16.49

14 x 3 in.
2105-U-6102 $19.99

16 x 3 in.
2105-U-6101 $22.99

18 x 3 in.
Half Round
2105-U-6100 $26.99

3-Pc. Round Set

6, 10 and 14 in. diameter x 3 in. deep.
2105-U-6114
Set/3 $40.99

Hearts

Ultimate heart cake is beautiful for showers, weddings, more!

6 x 2 in.
2105-U-600 $7.49

8 x 2 in.
2105-U-601 $8.49

10 x 2 in.
2105-U-602 $10.99

12 x 2 in.
2105-U-607 $12.99

14 x 2 in.
2105-U-604 $15.49

16 x 2 in.
2105-U-605 $17.99

4-Pc. Heart Set

Now redesigned for a perfect fit when used with our Decorator Preferred® Heart Separator Plates shown on page 230. Includes 6, 10, 12 and 14 in. pans. Aluminum.
2105-U-606 Set/4 $41.99

Contour

Create cakes with an elegant, rounded top edge. This is the perfect shape for positioning rolled fondant. 9 x 3 in. deep.
2105-U-6121 $14.49

Heating Core

Distributes heat to bake large cakes evenly. Recommended for pans 10 in. diameter or larger. Releases easily from cake. 3.5 x 3.5 x 4 in. diameter.
417-U-6100 $8.49

Sheets

Extra-thick aluminum distributes heat efficiently on these large pans.

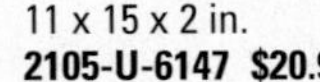

9 x 13 x 2 in.
2105-U-6146 $18.99

11 x 15 x 2 in.
2105-U-6147 $20.99

12 x 18 x 2 in.
2105-U-6148 $25.49

Squares

Perfect 90° corners give you the flawless look necessary for wedding tiers.

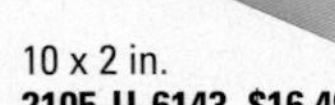

8 x 2 in.
2105-U-6142 $11.99

10 x 2 in.
2105-U-6143 $16.49

12 x 2 in.
2105-U-6144 $19.99

Springform Pans

When shopping for a springform pan, you want strong construction and an easy-release design that will let you remove a perfect cheesecake every time. Wilton springform pans are built tough, with strong springlocks that hold up year after year. The removable waffle-textured bottom design keeps crusts from sticking while distributing heat evenly. Springlock releases sides. Aluminum.

6 x 3 in.
2105-U-4437 $12.99

8 x 3 in.
2105-U-8464 $14.49

9 x 3 in.
2105-U-5354 $15.49

10 x 3 in.
2105-U-8465 $15.49

Performance Pans™

The classic aluminum pans—durable, even-heating and built to hold their shape through years of use. We named them Performance Pans because they perform beautifully. These are great all-purpose pans. You'll use them for casseroles, entrees, baked desserts and more. Wilton has sold millions of Performance Pans because decorators and bakers know they can depend on them.

SweetHeart

A gently curving shape gives the classic heart a more romantic flair. Whether you accent it with pretty icing flowers or pair it with bold fondant decorations, this cake will charm guests for birthdays, Mother's Day, Valentine's Day, showers and more. Takes 1 standard mix. 10.25 x 11 x 2 in.
2105-U-1197 $12.99

Squares

6 x 2 in.
507-U-2180 $7.99

8 x 2 in.
2105-U-8191 $9.99

10 x 2 in.
2105-U-8205 $11.99

12 x 2 in.
2105-U-8213 $16.49

14 x 2 in.
2105-U-8220 $20.99

16 x 2 in.
2105-U-8231 $22.99

Rounds

6 x 2 in.
2105-U-2185 $7.99

8 x 2 in.
2105-U-2193 $8.99

10 x 2 in.
2105-U-2207 $9.99

12 x 2 in.
2105-U-2215 $12.99

14 x 2 in.
2105-U-3947 $16.49

16 x 2 in.
2105-U-3963 $19.99

2-Pan Round Set

9 x 2 in. deep
2105-U-7908 $14.49

Sheets

9 x 13 x 2 in.
2105-U-1308 $12.99

11 x 15 x 2 in.
2105-U-158 $17.99

12 x 18 x 2 in.
2105-U-182 $19.99

Covered Baking Pan

Clear, durable cover makes it easy to transport desserts and keep them fresh at home. 11 x 15 x 2 in.
2105-U-3849 $22.99

PERFORMANCE PANS™ SETS

These are the classic shapes every baker needs. Wilton has them in convenient graduated-size sets, to help you create fabulous tiered cakes or individual cakes in exactly the size you want. Quality aluminum holds its shape for years. Each pan is 2 in. deep, except where noted.

3-Pc. Paisley Set

Create a beautiful tiered cake with graceful curves unlike any other. Ideal for cascading floral arrangements—perfect for weddings, showers and more. Includes 9 x 6 in., 12.75 x 9 in. and 17 x 12 in. pans.
2105-U-4039
Set/3 $47.99

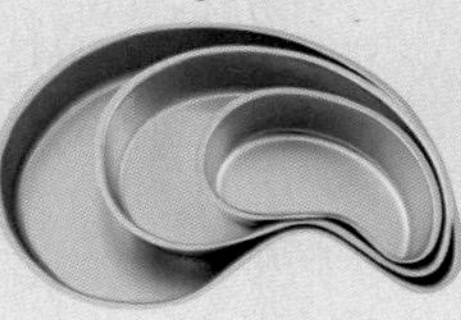

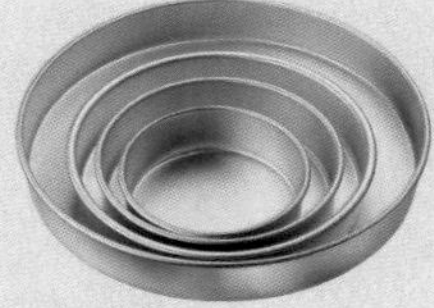

Round Set

Includes 6, 8, 10, 12 in. pans.
2105-U-2101 Set/4 $35.49

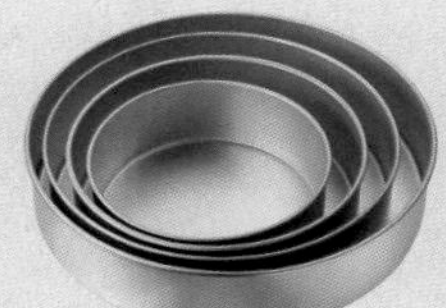

Round Set, 3 in. Deep

Includes 8, 10, 12, 14 in. pans.
2105-U-2932 Set/4 $47.99

Oval Set

Includes 7.75 x 5.5 in.; 10.75 x 7.8 in.; 13.5 x 9.8 in. and 16.5 x 12.38 in. pans.
2105-U-2130 Set/4 $41.99

Square Set

Includes 8, 12, 16 in. pans.
2105-U-2132 Set/3 $47.99

Hexagon Set

Includes 6, 9, 12, 15 in. pans.
2105-U-3572 Set/4 $41.99

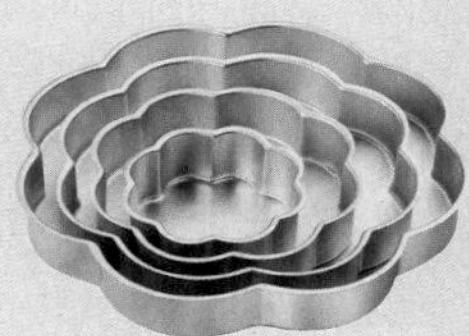

Petal Set

Includes 6, 9, 12, 15 in. pans.
2105-U-2134 Set/4 $41.99

Specialty Pans

Classic Angel Food

If you're looking for a healthy dessert, you can't do better than angel food! It's delicious with a simple fresh fruit topping. Removable inner core sleeve, cooling legs. Aluminum.

7 x 4.5 in. deep
Takes ½ standard mix.
2105-U-9311 $15.49

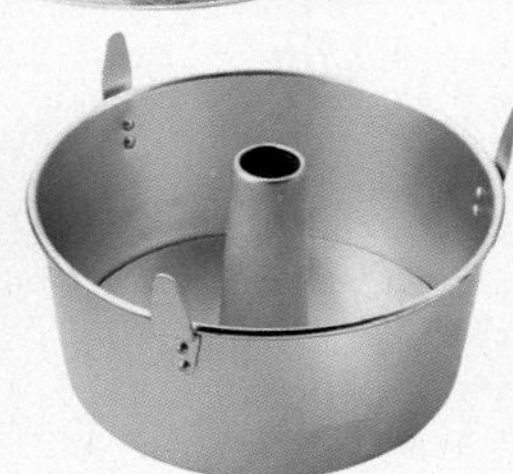

10 x 4 in. deep
Takes 1 standard mix.
2105-U-2525 $18.99

Fancy Ring Mold

Beautiful sculpted pan, ideal for pound cakes, mousse and more! Takes 1 standard mix. 10 in. diameter x 3 in. Aluminum.
2105-U-5008 $12.99

Ring Mold

Turn out spectacular cakes, gelatin molds and more. Takes approx. 1.5 standard cake mixes. 10.5 x 3 in. Aluminum.
2105-U-4013 $12.99

Cookie Sheets and Pans

A warped sheet can ruin a batch of cookies. With Wilton Cookie Sheets, you won't worry about warping. The extra-thick aluminum heats evenly for perfectly browned bottoms. Versatile sheets are great for baking appetizers, turnovers and more.

Aluminum Sheet
Extra-thick construction heats evenly for perfectly browned bottoms.
Jumbo 14 x 20 in.
2105-U-6213
$19.99

Insulated Aluminum Sheet
Two quality aluminum layers sandwich an insulating layer of air for perfect browning without burning.
14 x 16 in.
2105-U-2644
$20.99

Jelly Roll and Cookie Pans
Wilton pans are 1 in. deep for fuller-looking desserts.
10.5 x 15.5 x 1 in.
2105-U-1269 $14.49
12 x 18 x 1 in.
2105-U-4854 $16.49

Muffin Pans

With so many great Wilton muffin pans to choose from, you'll be making muffins and cupcakes more often. You'll love our mini pans for the perfect brunch muffins and the jumbo size pan for bakery-style muffins and cupcakes.

Standard Muffin
Most popular size for morning muffins, after-school cupcakes and desserts. Twelve cups, each 3 in. diameter x 1 in. Aluminum.
2105-U-9310 $18.99

White Standard Baking Cups **(shown on p. 189)**
Microwave-safe paper. 2 in. diameter.
415-U-2505 Pk./75 $1.59

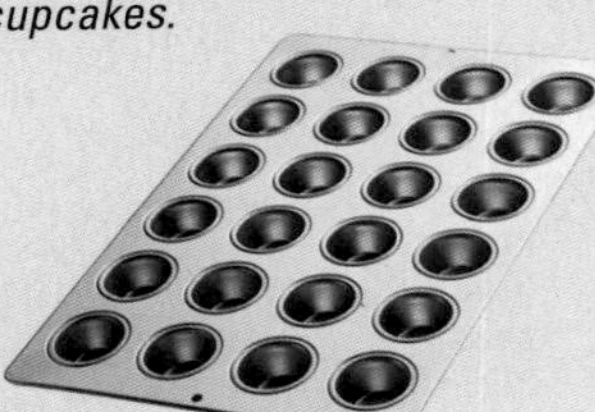

Mini Muffin
Great for mini cheesecakes, brunches, large gatherings. Cups are 2 in. x .75 in. Aluminum.
12 Cup 2105-U-2125 $12.99
24 Cup 2105-U-9313 $19.99

White Mini Baking Cups **(shown on p. 189)**
Microwave-safe paper. 1.25 in. diameter.
415-U-2507 Pk./100 $1.59

Jumbo Muffin
Make super-size cupcakes and muffins. Six cups, each 4 x 2 in. Aluminum.
2105-U-1820 $18.99

White Jumbo Baking Cups **(shown on p. 189)**
Microwave-safe paper. 2.25 in. diameter.
415-U-2503 Pk./50 $1.59

Loaf Pans

It's all in the crust. Wilton Loaf Pans bake bread with hearty, crisp crusts and soft, springy centers. Our superior anodized aluminum promotes better browning, resulting in the perfect texture for all your breads.

Petite Loaf
Great for single-size dessert cakes, frozen bread dough. Nine cavities, each 2.5 x 3.38 x 1.5 in. Aluminum.
2105-U-8466 $11.99

Mini Loaf
Everyone loves personal-sized nut breads or cakes. Six cavities are 4.5 x 2.5 x 1.5 in. Aluminum.
2105-U-9791 $11.99

9 x 5 in. Loaf
Favorite size for homemade breads and cakes. 2.75 in. Aluminum.
2105-U-3688 $8.49

Long Loaf
Legs provide support for cooling angel food cakes, breads or classic cakes. 16 x 4 x 4.5 in. deep. Aluminum.
2105-U-1588 $15.49

Chrome-Plated Cooling Grids

Sturdy design will never rust. Great selection of popular sizes.

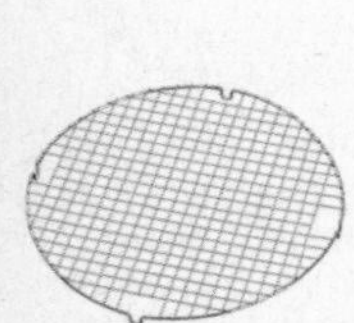

13 in. Round
2305-U-130 $8.99

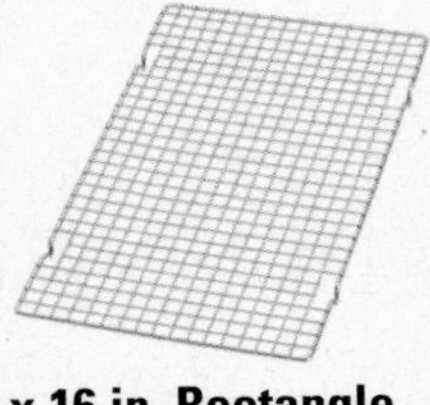

10 x 16 in. Rectangle
2305-U-128 $6.99

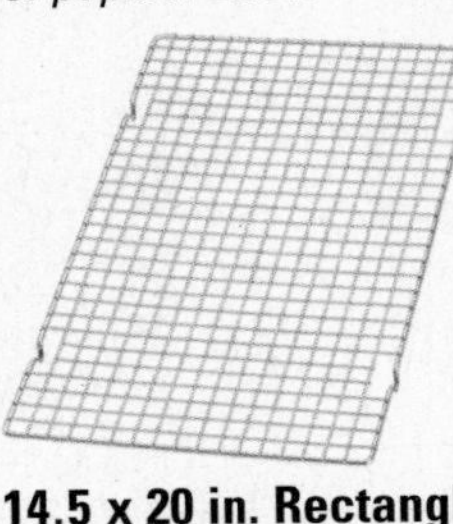

14.5 x 20 in. Rectangle
2305-U-129 $9.99

3-Tier Stackable
Use singly or stack to save space while cooling three cake layers or batches of cookies at the same time. Individual grids are 13.5 x 9.75 x 3 in. high; stacked grids are 9.75 in. high.
2305-U-151 $14.49

Wilton
EASY-Flex
SILICONE BAKEWARE
Flexible pans and tools for great baking performance

Silicone Bakeware

Discover the convenience and easy release of flexible silicone bakeware!

- Exceptional baking performance for your favorite recipes
- Freezer, refrigerator, oven, microwave and dishwasher safe*
- Resists stains and odors
- Oven safe to 500°F
- Easy and convenient storage
- Limited lifetime warranty

Fluted Tube
2105-U-4806 $12.99

9 in. Round
2105-U-4800 $9.99

8 in. Square
2105-U-4801 $9.99

9 x 5 in. Loaf
2105-U-4804 $9.99

6 Cup Muffin
2105-U-4802 $9.99

12 Cup Mini Muffin
2105-U-4829 $9.99

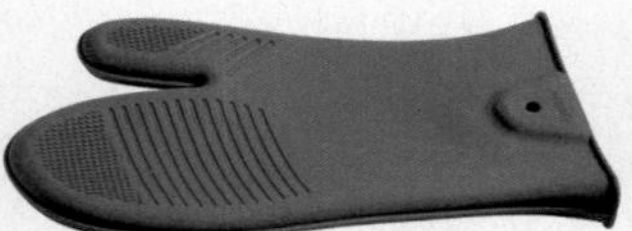

Silicone Oven Mitt
Silicone provides better protection from oven heat! Flexible design with interior and exterior textured grip for better control.
570-U-1127 $9.99

Baking Mat
Line cookie sheets—protects against burned bottoms and cleans up with ease! Or, use as a pastry mat to roll out dough without sticking.
10 x 15 in. **2105-U-4808 $9.99**
11 x 17 in. **2105-U-4809 $12.99**

Trivet
An excellent hot pad for tables or buffets; also great as a jar opener.
570-U-1111 $4.99

Standard Baking Cups
2 in. diameter. Convenient fill line.
415-U-9400 Pk./12 $9.99

Silicone Molds

Make treats in favorite party shapes using these colorful, easy-release molds! Great for baking mini cakes and brownies, molding ice cream, gelatin and more.

Silicone Mini Stars
One cake mix makes 20 to 24 mini stars. Six-cavity pan is 10.5 x 7 in.; individual cavities are 2.5 x 2.5 x 1.25 in. deep.
2105-U-4819 $9.99

Silicone Mini Rounds
One cake mix makes 20 to 24 mini rounds. Six-cavity pan is 10.5 x 7 in.; individual cavities are 2.5 in. diameter x 1.5 in. deep.
2105-U-4832 $9.99

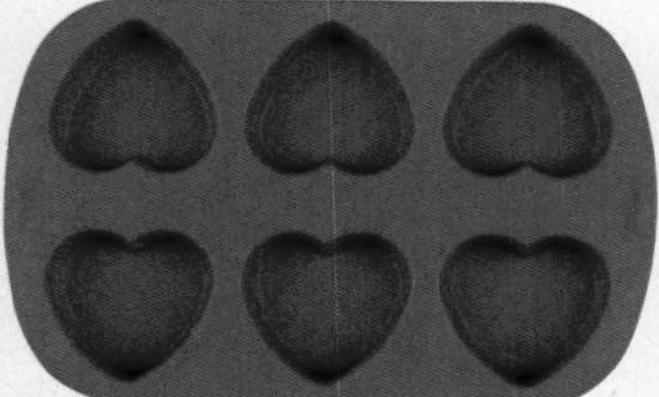

Silicone Mini Hearts
One cake mix makes 20 to 24 mini hearts. Six-cavity pan is 10.5 x 7 in.; individual cavities are 2.5 x 2.5 x 1.25 in. deep.
2105-U-4824 $9.99

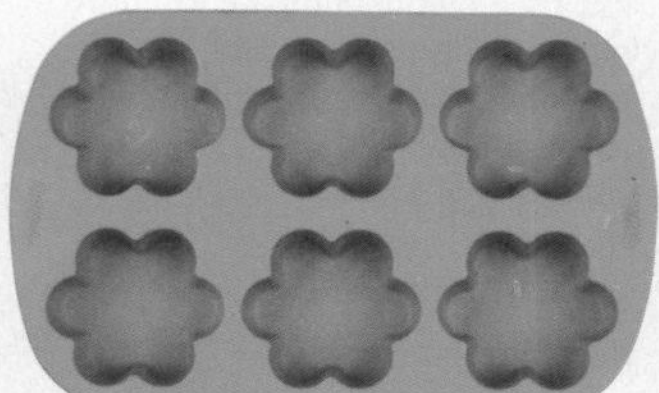

Silicone Mini Flowers
One cake mix makes 20 to 24 mini flowers. Six-cavity pan is 10.5 x 7 in.; individual cavities are 2.5 x 2.5 x 1.25 in. deep.
2105-U-4825 $9.99

*Always place silicone bakeware on a cookie sheet for easy removal from oven.

Non-Stick Oven Liner

Never Scrub Your Oven Again!

- EASY TO CLEAN
  Spills or burned-on foods wipe away with a soft, damp cloth.
- CUT TO FIT
  Use as is or trim with scissors to custom fit ovens.
- OVEN-SAFE UP TO 500°F
  Withstands high baking temperatures while maintaining non-stick performance.

23 x 16.25 in. Oven Liner
2102-U-1021 $14.99

Keeps oven clean!

Filled Cake Pan Sets

Serve delicious filling in every slice! Create filled cakes and entrees with incredible flavor combinations using these convenient non-stick pans. The patented recessed design creates a contour you can fill with ice cream, fruit, mousse and more—just bake, fill, flip and frost! The premium non-stick coating provides easy release so cakes unmold perfectly from the pan. Also great for pasta and potato entrees, molded salads and appetizers.

Fanci-Fill™
Set includes two 8.75 x 2 in. non-stick pans, bonus recipe booklet with 12 delicious ideas and complete instructions. Non-stick steel.
2105-U-150 Set/2 $17.99

Mini Tasty-Fill™
Set includes four 4 x 1.25 in. non-stick pans, bonus recipe booklet with 12 delicious ideas and complete instructions. Non-stick steel.
2105-U-155 Set/4 $11.99

NEW!

Heart Tasty-Fill™
It's easy to create delicious cakes with a heart-shaped filled center! Set includes two 8.5 x 2.75 in. non-stick pans, bonus recipe book with delicious recipe ideas and complete instructions. Non-stick steel.
2105-U-157 Set/2 $17.99

Mini Shaped Pans

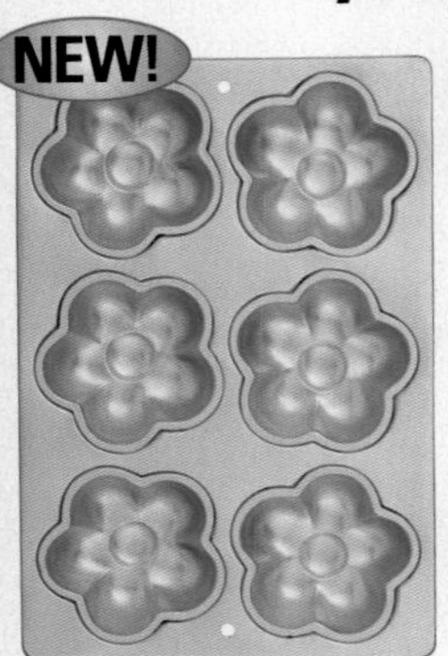

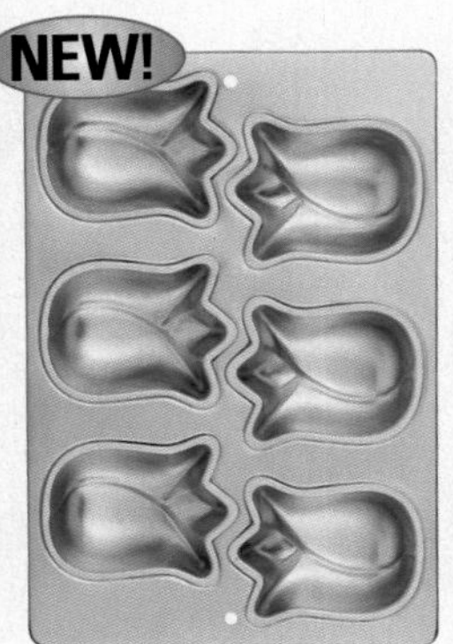

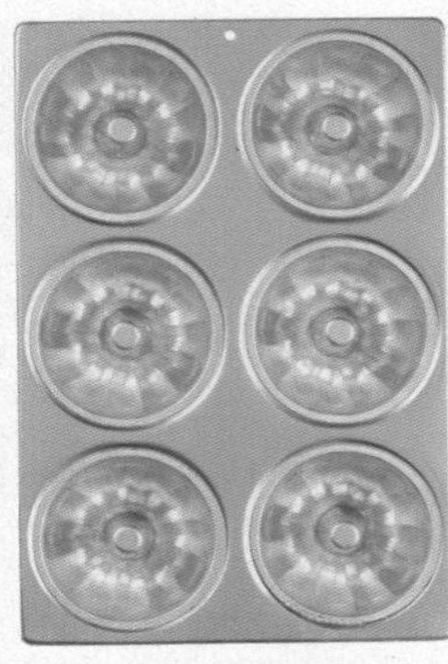

Mini Daisy (NEW!)
One cake mix makes 12-14 mini daisy cakes. Six cavity pan is 12.25 x 8.2 x 1.5 in.; individual cavities are 3 x 3.25 x 1.5 in. deep.
2105-U-1239 $14.49

Mini Tulip (NEW!)
One cake mix makes 12-14 mini tulip cakes. Six cavity pan is 12.25 x 8.2 x 1.75 in.; individual cavities are 3.5 x 2.5 x 1.75 in. deep.
2105-U-1233 $14.49

Mini Tiered Cakes
One cake mix makes 10-15 mini tiered cakes. Six cavity pan is 14 x 10.75 in.; individual cavities are 4 x 4.75 x 1.25 in. deep. Aluminum.
2105-U-3209 $14.49

Mini Fluted Mold
One cake mix makes 12-14 mini fluted molds. Six cavity pan is 14.75 x 9.75 in.; individual cavities are 4 x 1.25 in. deep. Aluminum.
2105-U-2097 $20.99

Mini Star
One cake mix makes 12-14 mini stars. Six cavity pan is 14.5 x 11 in.; individual cavities are 4.75 x 1.25 in. deep. Aluminum.
2105-U-1235 $14.49

Wonder Mold Pans

Mini Wonder Mold
Use with Mini Doll Picks for a quartet of party treats. Great with the Wilton Classic Wonder Mold (at right) for a color-coordinated bridal party centerpiece. One cake mix makes 4 to 6 cakes. Pan is 10 x 10 x 3 in. deep. Individual cakes are 3.5 x 3 in. Aluminum.
2105-U-3020 $12.99

Mini Doll Picks
4¼ in. high with pick.
1511-U-1019
Pk./4 $6.29

Classic Wonder Mold
Creates an elegant 3-D shape for decorating fabulous dress designs. Use with our Teen Doll Pick to make the doll of your dreams. Pan is 8 in. diameter and 5 in. deep; takes 5–6 cups of firm-textured batter. Heat-conducting rod assures even baking. Kit contains pan, rod, stand, 7 in. brunette doll pick and instructions. Aluminum/plastic.
2105-U-565 $19.99

Teen Doll Picks
Her hair and face are prettier than ever to give your Wonder Mold cakes a realism and sophistication unlike anything you've seen. 7¼ in. high with pick.
$3.19
Brunette 2815-U-101
Blond 2815-U-102

Ethnic Doll Pick
Beautiful face for realistic doll cakes. 7¾ in. high with pick.
2815-U-103
$3.19

Novelty Shaped Pans

Princess Carriage

Create a birthday celebration fit for a princess! Give it the royal treatment with dazzling windows and wheels decorated in her favorite colors. Or, decorate a classic carriage cake for the bridal shower, with flowers and accents to match your colors. One-mix pan is 13.75 x 12 x 2 in. deep. Aluminum.

2105-U-1027 $12.99

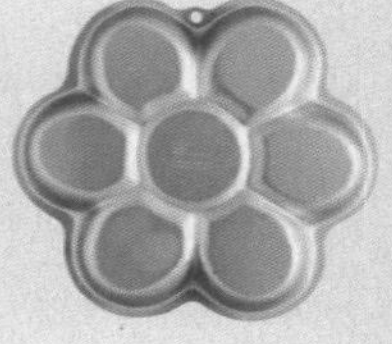

Dancing Daisy

One perfect flower makes bunches of great desserts! It's a big, bouncy blossom that's the perfect shape for cakes, molded gelatin and ice cream, brunch breads and more. Pick this daisy for Mother's Day, wedding showers and birthdays for any garden-lover. One-mix pan is 12 x 12 x 2 in. deep. Aluminum.

2105-U-1016 $12.99

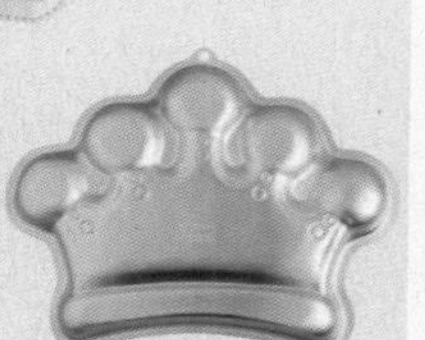

Crown

Treat your little princess (or prince) like royalty at their next celebration! This majestic crown cake is a fun way to honor both kids and adults alike—perfect for birthdays, school parties, Mother's and Father's Day, more! One-mix pan is 14.25 x 10.5 x 2 in. deep. Aluminum.

2105-U-1015 $12.99

Sunflower

There's no better way to spread sunshine at the celebration! Ideal for cakes, mousse, gelatin and salad molds. Center can be filled with fruit and whipped topping. One-mix pan is 10 in. round x 2 in. deep. Aluminum.

2105-U-1019 $12.99

Enchanted Castle

Royal treat for little girls' birthdays or any event. Wonderful for molded sugar or ice cream. One-mix pan is 11.5 x 11.75 x 2 in. deep. Aluminum.

2105-U-2031 $12.99

Topsy Turvy

Our topsy turvy "tiered" cake is just the right look for wacky birthdays, wild parties or special occasions. One-mix pan is 10.25 x 12 x 2 in. deep. Aluminum.

2105-U-4946 $12.99

Purse

Fun is in the bag with a cake that carries excitement galore for birthday parties, showers and school celebrations. Accessorize the event with custom colors and designs. One-mix pan is 10.5 x 8 x 2 in. deep. Aluminum.

2105-U-1192 $12.99

Stand-Up House

A delightful "welcome home". Haunted houses, Easter hutches, Christmas cottages, school houses and dog houses are a few ideas for this pan. Cakes can stand up or lay flat. One-mix pan is 9 x 3 x 8.75 in. high. Aluminum.

2105-U-2070 $15.49

Novelty Shaped Pans

Pirate Ship
Your ship has come in with this favorite kids' shape and its cargo of great decorating ideas on the label! Birthdays, movie parties and school celebrations provide a bounty of decorating opportunities. One-mix pan is 13.2 x 11.25 x 2 in. deep. Aluminum.
2105-U-1021 $12.99

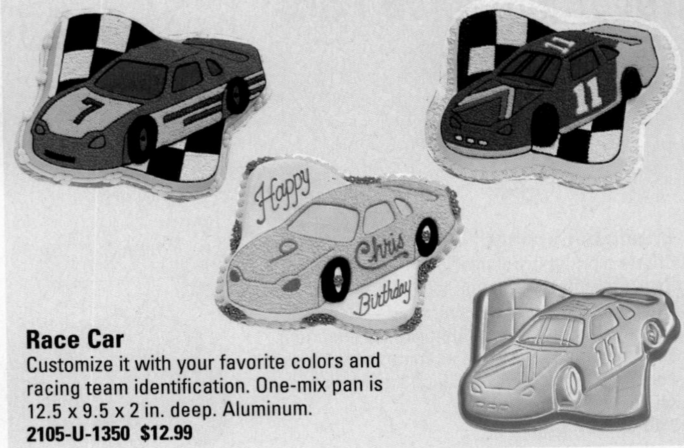

Race Car
Customize it with your favorite colors and racing team identification. One-mix pan is 12.5 x 9.5 x 2 in. deep. Aluminum.
2105-U-1350 $12.99

Train
Load with delicious cargo! One-mix pan is 14 x 7.25 x 2 in. deep. Aluminum.
2105-U-2076 $12.99

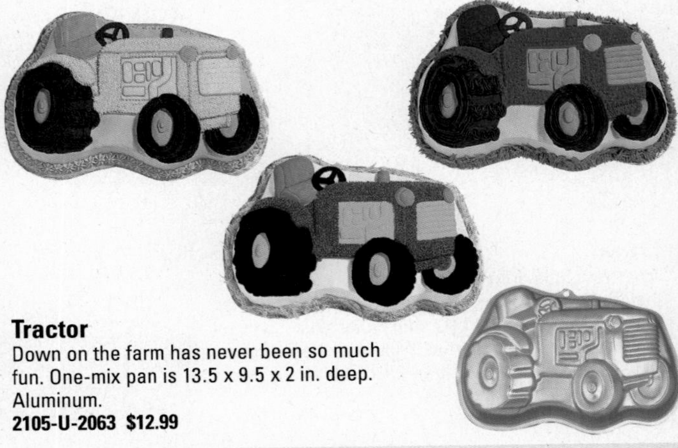

Tractor
Down on the farm has never been so much fun. One-mix pan is 13.5 x 9.5 x 2 in. deep. Aluminum.
2105-U-2063 $12.99

Choo-Choo Train Set
Two-piece pan snaps together to create a cake 10 x 4 x 6 in. high. Takes 6 cups batter. Aluminum.
2105-U-2861 Set/2 $14.49

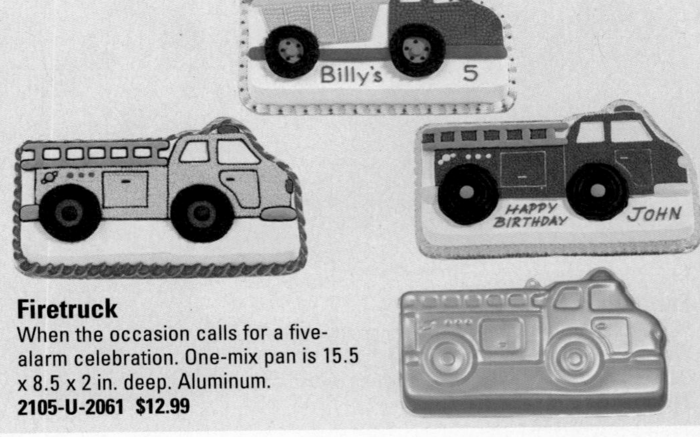

Firetruck
When the occasion calls for a five-alarm celebration. One-mix pan is 15.5 x 8.5 x 2 in. deep. Aluminum.
2105-U-2061 $12.99

3-D Cruiser
Bake exciting 3-D cakes, ready to customize for all occasions. One-mix pan is 11 x 6.75 x 4 in. deep. Aluminum.
2105-U-2043 $12.99

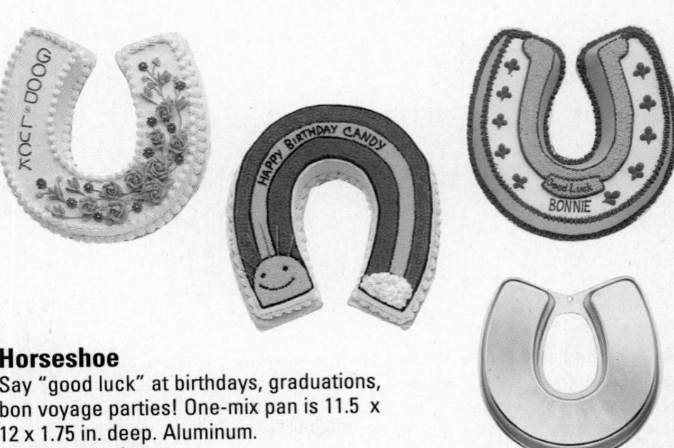

Horseshoe
Say "good luck" at birthdays, graduations, bon voyage parties! One-mix pan is 11.5 x 12 x 1.75 in. deep. Aluminum.
2105-U-3254 $12.99

Novelty Shaped Pans

Baby Bottle

Here's the formula for a great shower or baby naming celebration—serve a delightful dessert made in this adorable Baby Bottle Pan! Its outstanding detail creates exciting cakes along with molded mousse, gelatin and ice cream. One-mix pan is 13.75 x 7.25 x 2.5 in. deep. Aluminum.

2105-U-1026 $12.99

Teddy Bear

Everybody just loves teddy bears. This cutie will be busy all year 'round with birthdays, school parties and baby showers. No time for hibernating with all these fun events on the agenda. One-mix pan is 13.5 12.25 x 2 in deep. Aluminum.

2105-U-1193 $12.99

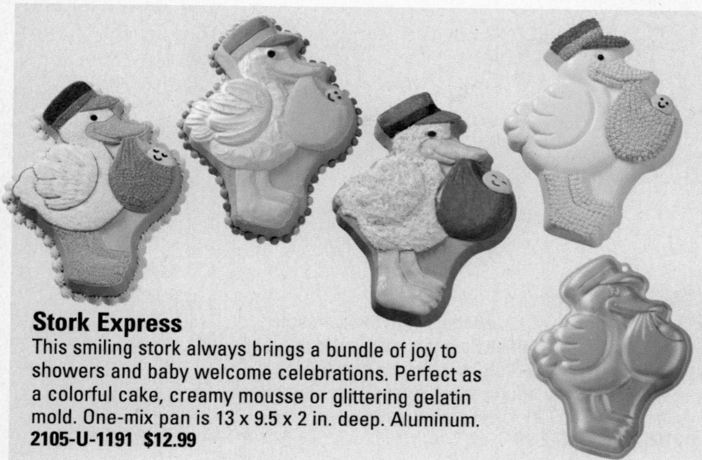

Stork Express

This smiling stork always brings a bundle of joy to showers and baby welcome celebrations. Perfect as a colorful cake, creamy mousse or glittering gelatin mold. One-mix pan is 13 x 9.5 x 2 in. deep. Aluminum.

2105-U-1191 $12.99

Baby Buggy

These wheels will bring squeals of delight from shower and christening guests. It's a precious carriage design fit for royalty and ready to dress up for colorful cakes or elegant salads and gelatins. One-mix pan is 11.25 x 11.25 x 2 in. deep. Aluminum.

2105-U-3319 $12.99

#1

Add the #1 cake to all the important first celebrations. Great for kids' birthdays, first anniversary, contest winners, first place teams—or just to let someone know they're #1 with you! One-mix pan is 12.75 x 8.5 x 2 in. deep. Aluminum.

2105-U-1194 $12.99

3-D Rubber Ducky

This bathtime favorite will make the biggest splash for birthdays, baby showers and school celebrations. Five adorable designs included. Two-piece pan takes 5½ cups batter, 9 x 5 x 7 in. high. Aluminum.

2105-U-2094 $16.49

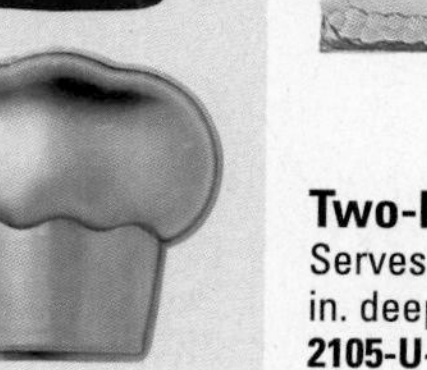

Cupcake

Here's a "cupcake" cake that's big enough for the whole crowd to eat. Bake and decorate it to look like your favorite party cupcake—only bigger! Create endless color and flavor combinations, including the luscious Chocolate Supreme design on the label. One-mix pan is 9.75 x 9.5 x 2 in. deep. Aluminum.

2105-U-3318 $12.99

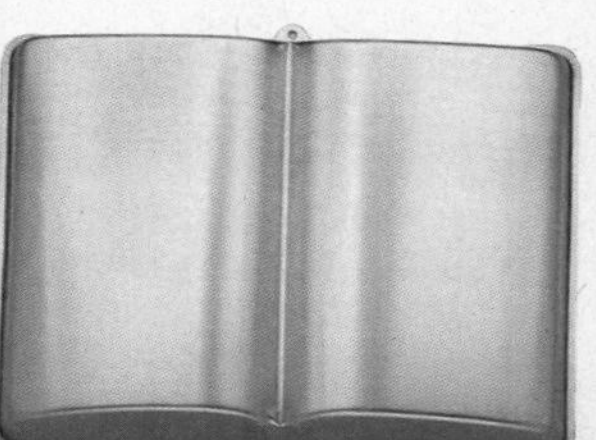

Two-Mix Book

Serves up to 30. 15 x 11.5 x 2.75 in. deep. Aluminum.

2105-U-2521 $17.99

BAKEWARE

Novelty Shaped Pans

Monkey
He'll be the top banana at so many fun occasions! Kids will just love him at birthday parties, school celebrations and jungle-themed events. One-mix pan is 12.75 x 11.25 x 2 in. deep. Aluminum.
2105-U-1023 $12.99

Dinosaur
Our prehistoric party pal has a fun-loving look that's just right for kids birthdays, school functions and animal-themed celebrations. One-mix pan is 12.75 x 11 x 2 in. deep. Aluminum.
2105-U-1022 $12.99

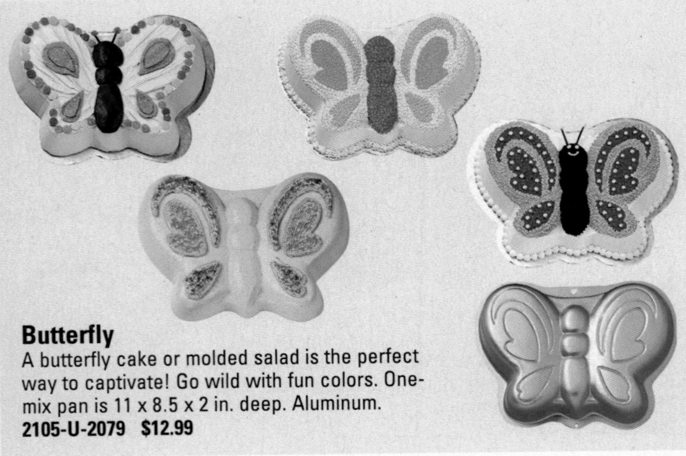

Butterfly
A butterfly cake or molded salad is the perfect way to captivate! Go wild with fun colors. One-mix pan is 11 x 8.5 x 2 in. deep. Aluminum.
2105-U-2079 $12.99

Animal Crackers
Make a zoo full of fun animals with this versatile pan! Pick your favorite from the menagerie of critters on the box—pig, cat, giraffe or panda bear—or create a furry face of your own. One-mix pan is 10.75 x 9.25 x 2 in. deep. Aluminum.
2105-U-4945 $12.99

Lady Bug
These critters are so cute, you'll want them dropping in at all your celebrations. It's a pan that adapts to any environment—try it as a birthday bee, a Valentine love bug or even a friendly fly for that special gardener in your life. One-mix pan is 12 x 10 x 2 in. deep. Aluminum.
2105-U-3316 $12.99

Mini Stand-Up Bear Set
Includes baking stand, four clips and instructions. Two-piece pan takes 1 cup of batter; standard pound cake mix makes about 4 cakes. Assembled cakes are 4 x 3.25 x 4.75 in. high. Aluminum.
2105-U-489 Set/8 $14.49

Tropical Fish
Everyone at the party will be hooked by this fish! Catch it at kids' celebrations and school events—it's a great cake for that special fisherman's birthday. It's a keeper! One-mix pan is 12.5 x 11.5 x 2 in. deep. Aluminum.
2105-U-1014 $12.99

Stand-Up Cuddly Bear Set
Five decorating ideas on the box! Two-piece pan takes 6.75 cups of firm textured batter. Includes 6 clips, heat-conducting core and instructions. Pan is 9 x 6.75 x 8.5 in. high. Aluminum.
2105-U-603 Set/10 $26.99

Novelty Shaped Pans

Golf Bag
A stroke of genius for your favorite golfer's birthday, group golf outings, awards dinners and more. Whether decorated for men or women, it always shows perfect form. One-mix pan is 13.25 x 8.25 x 2 in. deep. Aluminum.
2105-U-1024 $12.99

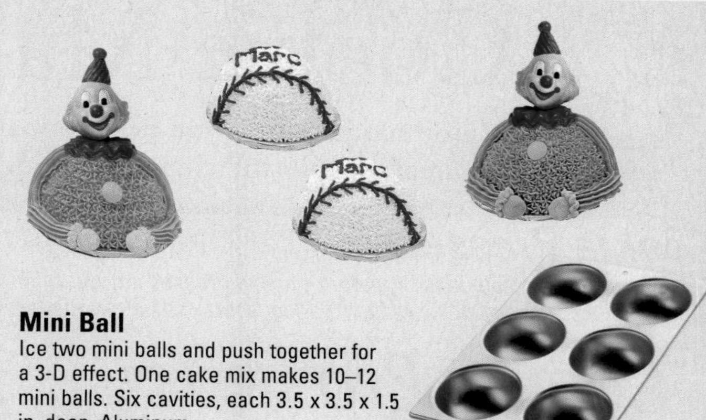

Mini Ball
Ice two mini balls and push together for a 3-D effect. One cake mix makes 10–12 mini balls. Six cavities, each 3.5 x 3.5 x 1.5 in. deep. Aluminum.
2105-U-1760 $12.99

First and Ten Football
Touching down at Super Bowl parties, homecomings, award dinners and much more. One-mix pan is 12 x 7.75 x 3 in. deep. Aluminum.
2105-U-6504 $12.99

Guitar
Whatever your musical choice, a guitar cake sets the tone for fun at your next party! Celebrate school band concerts, kid and adult birthdays! One-mix pan is 16.5 x 8.5 x 2 in. deep. Aluminum.
2105-U-570 $12.99

Soccer Ball
A great way to reward a season or a game well done! One-mix pan is 8.75 x 8.75 x 3.5 in. deep. Aluminum.
2105-U-2044 $12.99

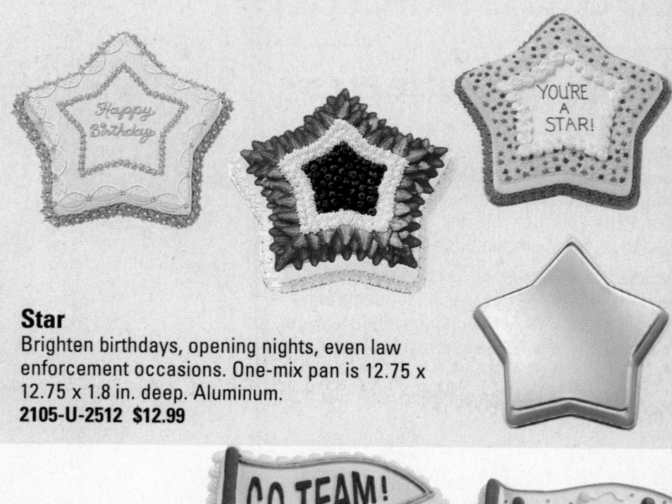

Star
Brighten birthdays, opening nights, even law enforcement occasions. One-mix pan is 12.75 x 12.75 x 1.8 in. deep. Aluminum.
2105-U-2512 $12.99

Sports Ball Set
Use this four-piece set to create a perfect sports cake centerpiece. Includes two 6 in. diameter half-ball pans and two metal baking stands. Each pan half takes 2.5 cups batter. Aluminum.
2105-U-6506 Set/4 $12.99

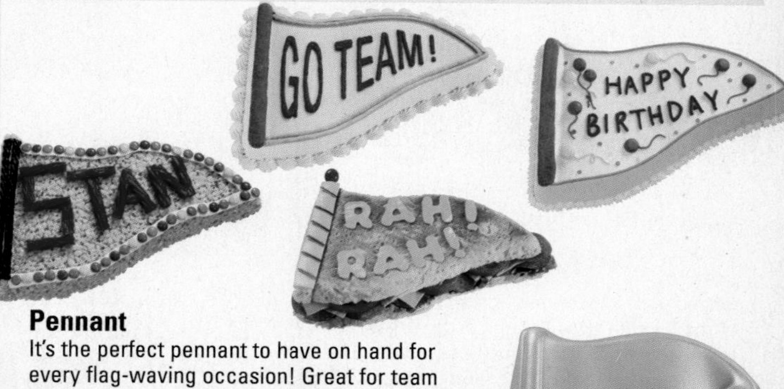

Pennant
It's the perfect pennant to have on hand for every flag-waving occasion! Great for team sports, birthday greetings, tailgate parties and homecomings. One-mix pan is 12.5 x 8.5 x 2 in. deep. Aluminum.
2105-U-1190 $12.99

BAKEWARE

Cookie Making

Wilton has just what you need to make cookies fun! Easy-to-use presses, colossal cutter sets, fun stencils, colorful icings and unique toppings sure to create unforgettable cookies!

Cookie Presses

Wilton has the best selection of feature-packed presses anywhere! From our Comfort Grip™ Press, designed for easy handling and filling, to our powerful cordless Cookie Master® Plus, spritz cookie-making has never been easier!

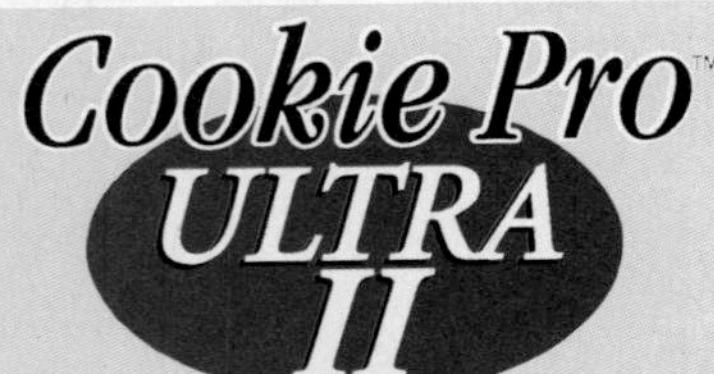

Making traditional spritz cookies has never been so easy! Cookie Pro Ultra II is designed to be the easiest to fill, most comfortable press you've ever used. And, with 12 terrific shapes, plus 4 fun mini cookie designs, your holiday cookie baskets will be more festive than ever! Includes complete instructions and delicious recipes.
2104-U-4018 Set/17 $24.99

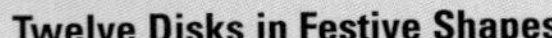

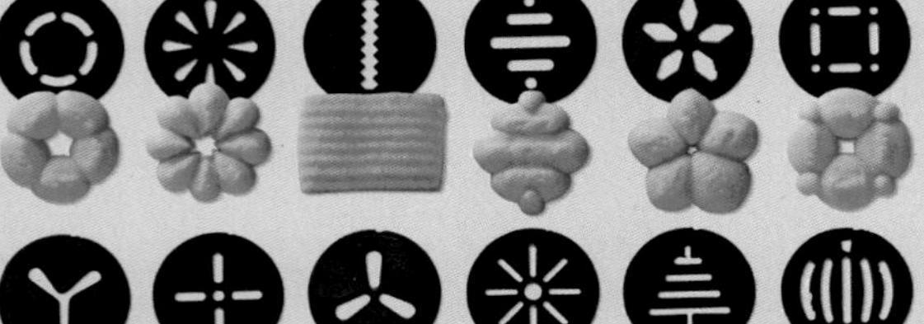

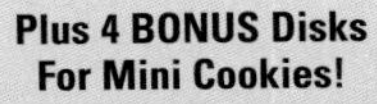

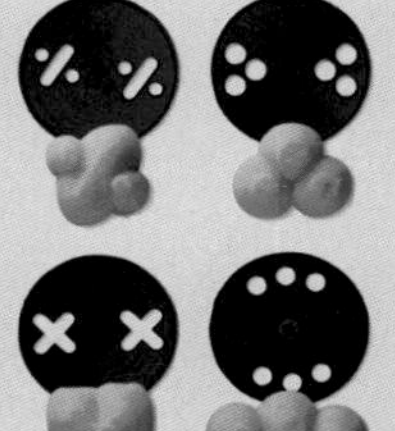

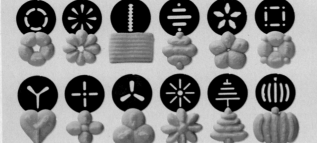

COOKIE MASTER® Plus

Cordless Cookie Press

Our cordless cookie press is so powerful and easy to operate, you'll use it all year to create cookies, appetizers, desserts and more. Exclusive patented reverse action means there's no need to take press apart for refilling. Ergonomic design is shaped to fit in your hand for excellent comfort.

Includes 12 aluminum disks in classic and seasonal shapes, 4 accent tips for decorating and filling and 2 bonus recipe booklets—sweet and savory. Uses 4 AA batteries, not included.
2104-U-4008 Set/19 $39.99

4 Accent Tips

12 Disk Designs

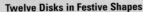

COMFORT GRIP™ Cookie Press

Experience a classic press that is truly comfortable. Its ergonomic handle feels great in your hand and the easy-squeeze action releases perfectly shaped dough. Clear barrel takes the guesswork out of refilling. Fluted bottom raises press off the cookie sheet for better-defined shapes. Includes 12 cookie disks in a variety of shapes and our classic spritz recipe.
2104-U-4011 Set/13 $12.99

12 Disk Designs

Push 'N Print Cutter Set

Serve cookies that make a great impression—use Push 'N Print Cutters to emboss a fun message before baking! It's so easy! Load one of the 3 cutter disk designs in the press, cut the cookie, then press the plunger with disk in place to imprint the design. Bake, cool and serve a treat that's perfect for celebrations and cookie gift baskets. Great for embossed fondant decorations, too! Disks are 3 in. diameter. Recipe included.
2308-U-4004 Set/4 $7.99

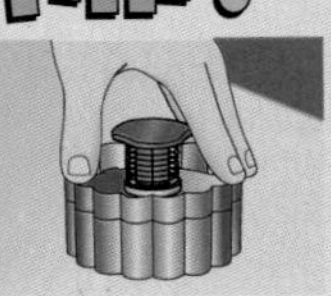

Cookie Bakeware and Accessories

Cookie Treat Pans

Cookie treats on a stick are so easy! Just press cookie dough into pan, insert a cookie stick, then bake, cool and decorate. Create your own cookie blossoms for that special someone; also great for rice cereal treats and candy. Recipe included. Each pan makes 6 individual treats, 3.5 in. x .25 in. deep. Aluminum.
Each $9.99

Star
2105-U-8102

Round
2105-U-8105

Heart
2105-U-8104

Blossom
2105-U-8109

Cookie Treat Sticks

For fun cookie pops.
6 in. **1912-U-9319**
Pk./20 $1.99
8 in. **1912-U-9318**
Pk./20 $2.99

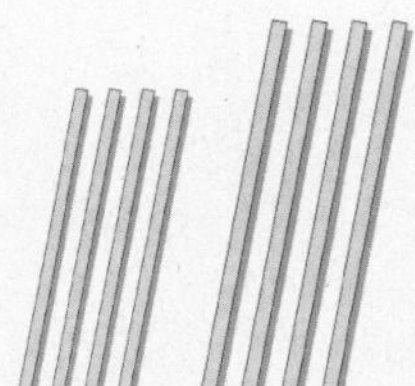

Clear Party Bags

4 x 9.5 in. Each pack contains 25 bags and 25 ties.
1912-U-1240
Pk./25 $2.09

Round
2105-U-6201

Heart
2105-U-6203

Giant Cookie Pans

Our Giant Cookie Pans help you create a jumbo pan cookie in a shape that will be a big hit for any occasion. Specially designed for one package of refrigerated dough, they are also great for brownies and pizza! Each shape is approximately .75 in. deep and can be used with recipes that call for a standard 13 x 9 in. pan. Aluminum. **Each $7.49**

Cookie Sheets

Wilton Cookie Sheets are extra thick aluminum to heat evenly for perfect, evenly-browned bottoms.

Aluminum
Extra-thick construction.
Jumbo 14 x 20 in.
2105-U-6213 $19.99

Insulated Aluminum
Two quality aluminum layers sandwich an insulating layer of air for perfect browning without burning.
16 x 14 in.
2105-U-2644 $20.99

Cooling Grids

Chrome-Plated
Sturdy design will never rust.
13 in. Round
2305-U-130 $8.99
10 x 16 in.
2305-U-128 $6.99
14.5 x 20 in.
2305-U-129 $9.99

Non-Stick
Cookies and cakes won't stick with our slick non-stick coating.
13 in. Round
2305-U-230 $10.49
10 x 16 in.
2305-U-228 $9.99
14.5 x 20 in.
2305-U-229 $14.49

3-Pc. Stackable Chrome-Plated
Use singly or stack to save space while cooling three batches of cookies at the same time. Individual grids are 13.5 x 9.75 x 3 in. high; stacked grids are 9.75 in. high.
2305-U-151 $14.49

See p. 150-161 for the full line of Wilton Bakeware.

NEW!

Jumbo Cookie Spatula

Generously-sized spatula is great for handling multiple or oversized cookies, brownies, pastries and large treat bars. The easy-grip handle helps balance large cookies and desserts. Stainless steel; dishwasher safe.
570-U-2018 $6.99

FOODWRITER™ EDIBLE COLOR MARKERS

Use like ink markers to add fun and dazzling color to countless foods. Kids love 'em! Decorate on cookie icing, fondant, color flow and royal icing designs. Brighten everyday foods like toaster pastries, cheese, fruit slices, bread, more. Each set includes five .07 oz. FoodWriter pens. Certified Kosher.

Primary Colors Sets

Yellow, Green, Red, Blue, Black
Bold Tip 609-U-115 Set/5 $8.39
Fine Tip 609-U-100 Set/5 $8.39

Neon Colors Set

Purple, Orange, Pink, Light Green, Black
Fine Tip 609-U-116 Set/5 $8.39

WHITE COOKIE ICING

Use this quick-setting microwavable icing to cover your cookies with a shiny finish—perfect for decorating with colorful Wilton Icing Writer™ (p. 135) accents! Easy to use—just heat and squeeze onto cookies using the convenient cap. Sets smooth in just 45 minutes. 10 oz. bottle covers approximately 12 (3 in.) cookies; 20 oz. bottle covers approximately 24 (3 in.) cookies. Certified Kosher.
10 oz. Bottle **704-U-481 $4.49**
20 oz. Bottle **704-U-492 $7.99**

Colored Sugars

Brighten up plain cookies fast with our colorful decorating sugars. Just sprinkle these extra-fine sugars on cookies before baking. Certified Kosher. 4.4 oz. bottles.

Brights 4-Mix
Contains Pink, Yellow, Light Green, Lavender.
710-U-651 $4.99

Primary 4-Mix
Contains Red, Dark Green, Blue, Yellow.
710-U-650 $4.99

Cookie Cutters

Versatile designs sure to spark your creativity!

PLASTIC CUTTER SETS

101 Cookie Cutters

With this set, you're covered! Make cookies featuring popular holiday and theme shapes like sports, flowers, animals and more. Or use the complete alphabet and numeral collections included to create the perfect cookie message. Great for cutting all kinds of food into fun shapes—perfect for crafting, too. Average cutter size approx. 3.5 x 3.5 in. Recipe included.

2304-U-1050 Set/101 $14.99

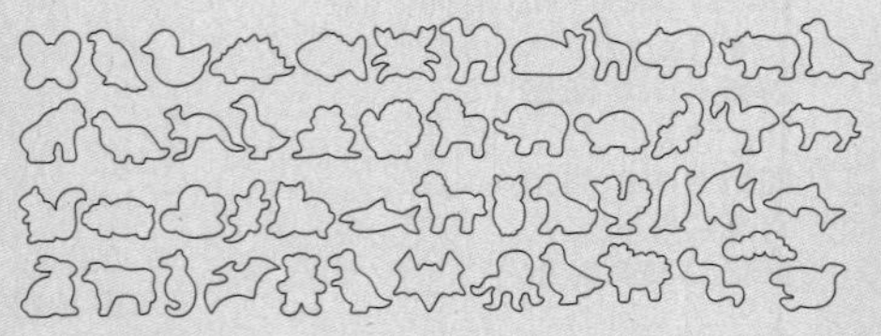

Animal Pals 50-Piece Cutter Set

Everyone will go wild for cookies, foods and crafts made with this menagerie of favorite animal shapes. Shapes include fish, dog, cat, birds, butterflies, reptiles and more. Average cutter size approx. 3.5 x 3.5 in. Recipe included.

2304-U-1055 Set/50 $8.99

A-B-C and 1-2-3 50-Piece Cutter Set

Complete alphabet and numeral collection, great for cookies, brownies, gelatin treats, learning games, crafts and more. Average cutter size approx. 3.5 x 3.5 in. Recipe included.

2304-U-1054 Set/50 $8.99

Plastic Cutters

With our large variety of brightly-colored cutter shapes, the making is as much fun as the eating! Child-safe design means kids can help. Each approx. 3 x 4 in. **Each $0.69**

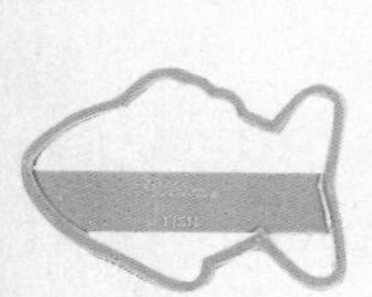

Fish
2303-U-128

Dinosaur
2303-U-112

Teddy Bear
2303-U-133

Butterfly
2303-U-116

Puppy
2303-U-137

Dog Bone
2303-U-123

Star
2303-U-135

Hand
2303-U-147

Foot
2303-U-113

Girl
2303-U-120

Boy
2303-U-124

Airplane
2303-U-101

Flower
2303-U-117

Locomotive Engine
2303-U-139

Heart
2303-U-100

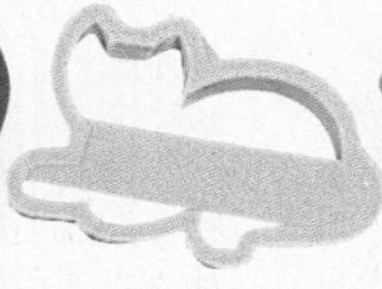

Cat
2303-U-118

Duck
2303-U-148

Four-Leaf Clover
2303-U-134

Cross
2303-U-141

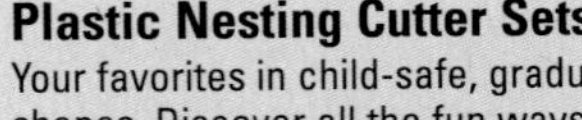

Plastic Nesting Cutter Sets

Your favorites in child-safe, graduated shapes. Discover all the fun ways to use our cutters—for bread shapes, stencils, sun catchers and so much more.

Teddy Bear
1.75 to 6.4 in.
2304-U-1520
Set/4 $2.99

Blossom
1.2 to 4.5 in.
2304-U-116
Set/6 $2.99

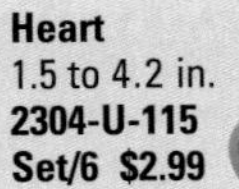

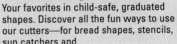

Heart
1.5 to 4.2 in.
2304-U-115
Set/6 $2.99

Star
1.6 to 4.6 in.
2304-U-111
Set/6 $2.99

Cookie Cutters

STACKABLE! COOKIE CUTTER SETS

Use these fun shaped cutters to create a sensational, stackable 3-D cookie design! Just cut and bake the cookies using your favorite roll-out recipe, decorate with icing and stack them to make a terrific treat. Let the kids help—they'll love to create their own cookie bears or flowers. Stackable cookies are perfect for parties, favors and gift baskets. Other cutters just don't stack up!
Set/3 $3.99

Teddy Bear
2308-U-1287

Flower
2308-U-1288

COMFORT GRIP™ CUTTERS

Easy-grip stainless steel cutters with extra-deep sides are perfect for cutting so many favorite foods into spectacular shapes. Ideal for brownies, biscuits, sandwiches, sheet cakes, cheese, crispy rice treats, fudge and much more. The cushion grip gives you comfortable control even when cutting into thick desserts. Each approximately 4 x 4 x 1.75 in. Recipe included.
Each $3.19

Star
2310-U-605

Flower
2310-U-613

Teddy Bear
2310-U-609

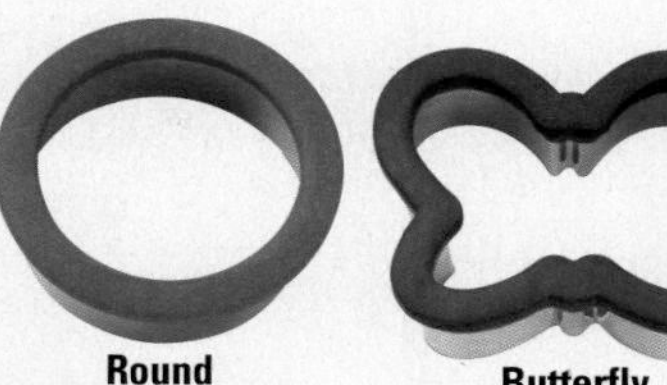

Round
2310-U-608

Butterfly
2310-U-614

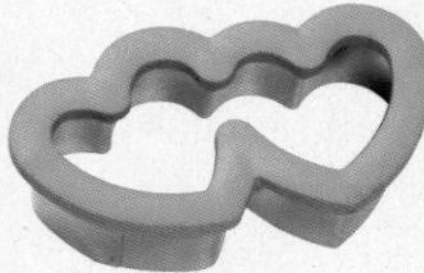

Heart
2310-U-616

Double Heart
2310-U-647

Daisy
2310-U-619

METAL CUTTER SETS

Multi-piece sets add variety. Built to last, they cut cleanly and release easily. Recipe included.

Mini Romantic

Butterfly, heart, bell, crinkled heart, tulip, and blossom. Each approx. 1.5 in.
2308-U-1225
Set/6 $3.19

Mini Noah's Ark

Horse, ark, elephant, bear, giraffe and lion. Each approx. 1.5 in.
2308-U-1206
Set/6 $3.19

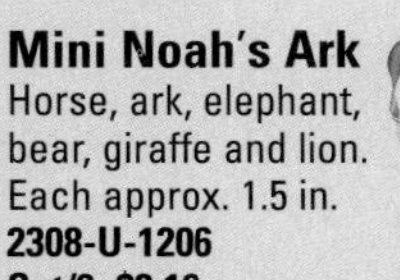

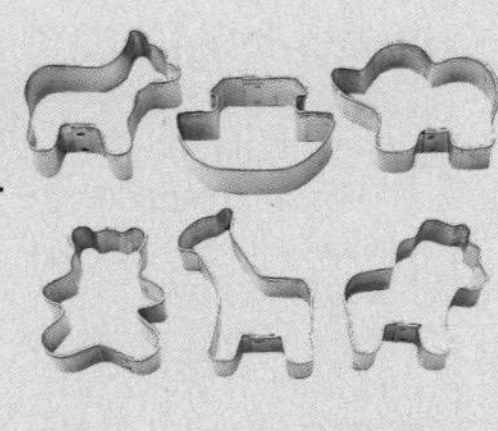

Mini Geometric Crinkle

Square, circle, heart, diamond, oval and triangle. Each approx. 1.5 in.
2308-U-1205
Set/6 $3.19

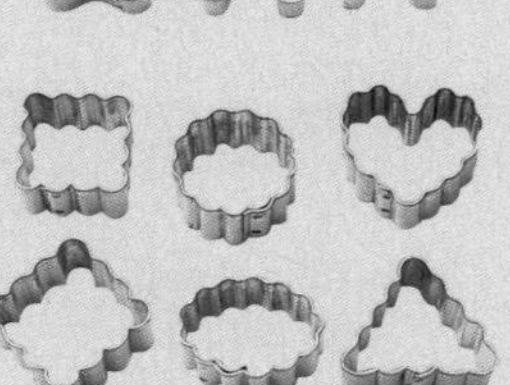

Classic

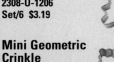

Geometric, crinkle diamond, heart, half moon, star and flower. Each approx. 3 in.
2308-U-1235
Set/6 $5.29

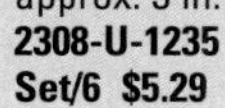

Animals

Horse, dove, lion, duck, pig and cat. Each approx. 3 in.
2308-U-1236
Set/6 $5.29

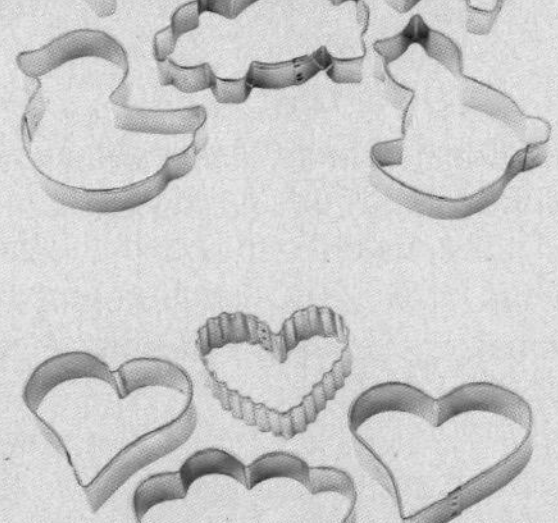

Hearts

Seven different heart cutter designs from stylized to traditional. Sizes range from 1.5 to 3 in.
2308-U-1237
Set/7 $5.29

Bug Buddies

Caterpillar, dragonfly, spider, butterfly, bee and ladybug. Each approx. 3 in.
2308-U-1245
Set/6 $5.29

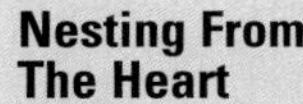

Nesting From The Heart

Two crinkled, two smooth. Largest is approx. 5 in.
2308-U-1203
Set/4 $4.79

Nesting Stars

For holidays and more! Largest is approx. 5 in.
2308-U-1215
Set/4 $4.79

Nesting Blossoms

Flowers in four sizes. Largest is approx. 5 in.
2308-U-1204
Set/4 $4.79

METAL CUTTERS

Metal cutters from Wilton are built to last through years of cookie making; they cut cleanly and release with ease. Each shape is approximately 3 in.
Each $0.69

Star
2308-U-1008

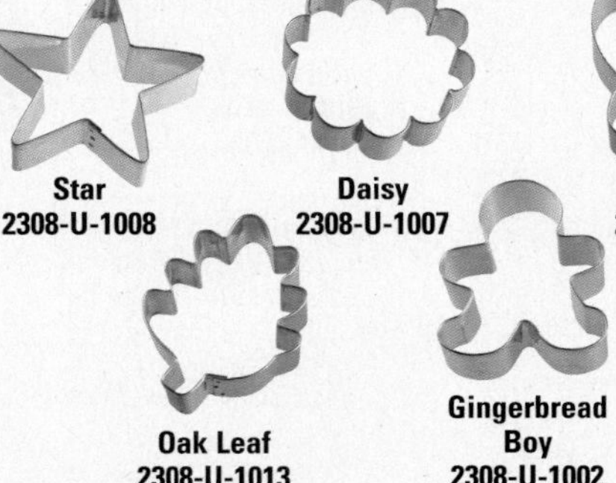

Daisy
2308-U-1007

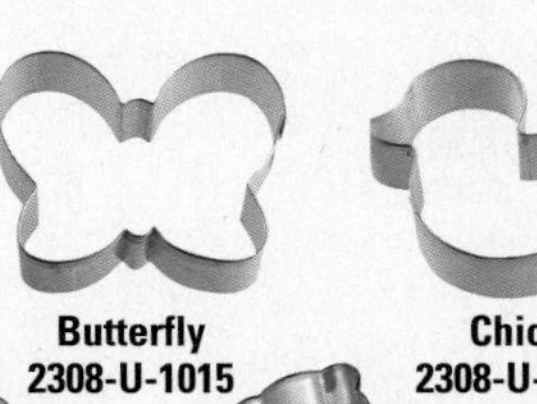

Butterfly
2308-U-1015

Chick
2308-U-1000

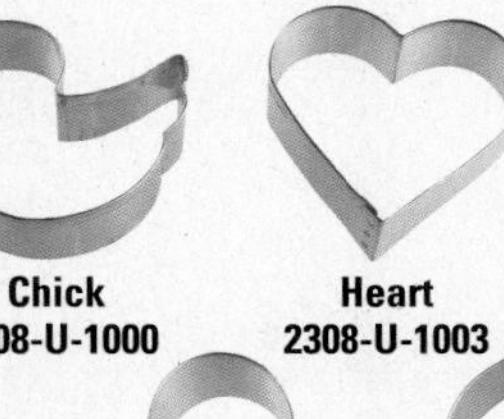

Heart
2308-U-1003

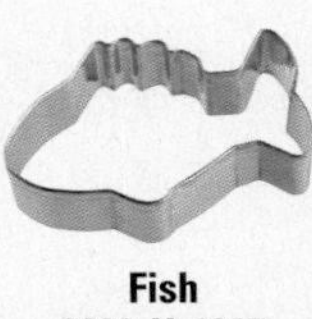

Fish
2308-U-1017

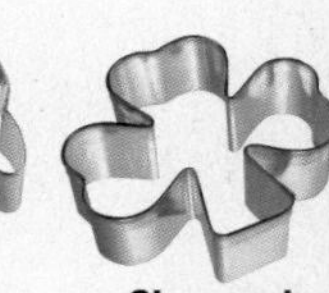

Shamrock
2308-U-1011

Oak Leaf
2308-U-1013

Gingerbread Boy
2308-U-1002

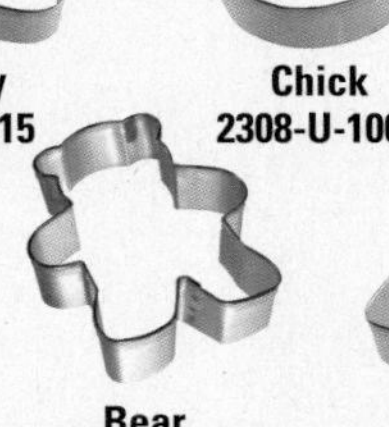

Bear
2308-U-1009

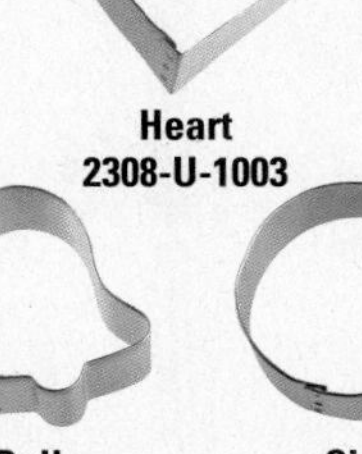

Bell
2308-U-1006

Circle
2308-U-1010

Cross
2308-U-1018

Candy Making

Let Wilton show you how much fun candy making can be! Use our Candy Melts®* and molds for beautiful candy in 3 easy steps—just melt, mold and serve.

*Candy Melts®**

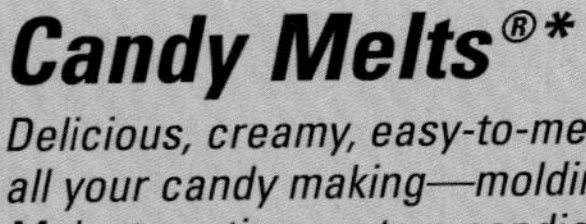

Delicious, creamy, easy-to-melt wafers are ideal for all your candy making—molding, dipping or coating. Make tempting custom candies using the Candy Flavoring Set below.

14 oz. bag. Certified Kosher Dairy. **$2.79**

Peanut Butter 1911-U-481 · **Dark Cocoa 1911-U-358** · **Light Cocoa 1911-U-544** · **Dark Cocoa Mint 1911-U-1920** · **Lavender 1911-U-403** · **Pink 1911-U-447**

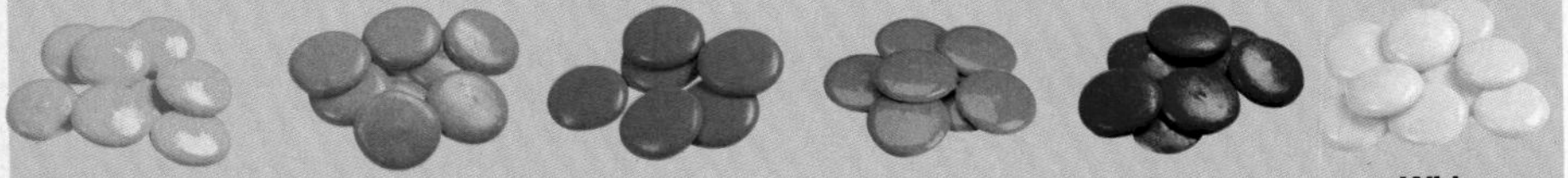

Yellow 1911-U-463 · **Orange 1911-U-1631** · **Blue 1911-U-448** · **Red 1911-U-499** · **Green 1911-U-405** · **White 1911-U-498**

Candy Decorating Pen Set

Give your homemade candies a delicious touch of color with these easy-melting candy pens. Just melt in hot water and squeeze into detailed areas of candy mold. The snip-off tip makes it easy to control the flow and add great-looking details just where you want them. Add excitement to all kinds of treats—drizzle on fruit, ice cream, cookies, pretzels and more. Includes 1.6 oz. tubes of Red, Yellow, Blue and White.

1914-U-1285 Set/4 $9.49

Cookie Candy Molds

NEW!

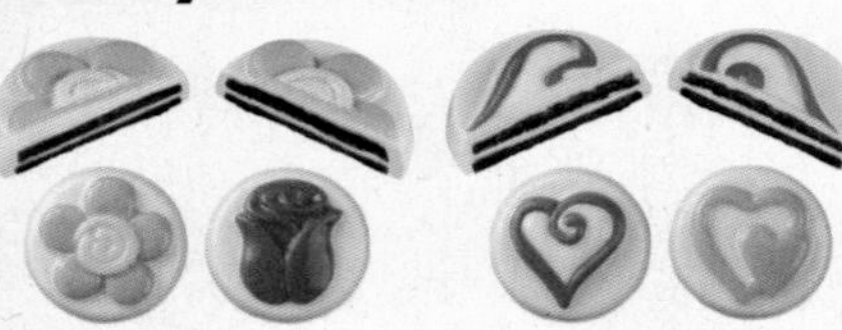

Flowers 2115-U-1351 · **Hearts 2115-U-1352** · **Animals 2115-U-1354** · **Sports 2115-U-1353**

Turn store-bought cookies into candy-coated treats! With Cookie Candy Molds and easy-melting Wilton Candy Melts®, it's a breeze to add a great tasting and colorful candy design to your favorite cookies. Just brush colored candy details in the mold, let set, then add more melted candy and position your cookie in the mold. Great for sandwich cream cookies or any round cookie 2 in. diameter or less. Hearts and Flowers molds have 2 designs, 8 cavities, Sports and Animals molds have 4 designs, 8 cavities. **$1.99**

Pretzel Molds

Easy to mold: add your favorite melted Candy Melts®*, position pretzel rod and refrigerate to set. **$1.99**

NEW!

Race Car 2 designs, 6 cavities. **2115-U-1034**

NEW!

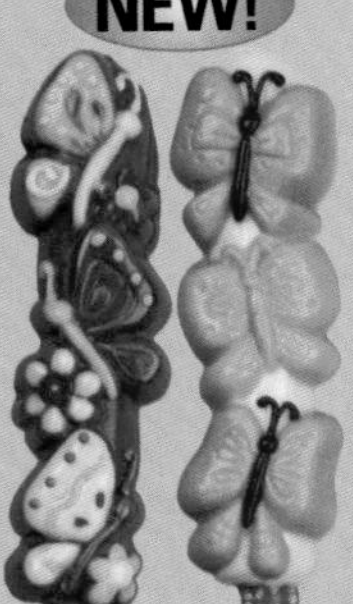

Butterfly 2 designs, 6 cavities. **2115-U-1032**

Smiley Face 1 design, 6 cavities. **2115-U-4437**

Flowers 1 design, 6 cavities. **2115-U-4436**

Celebration Cakes 1 design, 6 cavities. **2115-U-4429**

Presents 1 design, 6 cavities. **2115-U-4442**

Candy Color and Flavoring Sets

Primary Candy Color Set

Concentrated oil-based colors blend easily with Candy Melts®. Includes Yellow, Orange, Red and Blue in .25 oz. jars. Certified Kosher.

1913-U-1299
Set/4 $3.99

Garden Candy Color Set

Create pretty pastel colors! Concentrated oil-based colors blend easily with Candy Melts®. Includes Pink, Green, Violet and Black in .25 oz. jars. Certified Kosher.

1913-U-1298
Set/4 $3.99

Candy Flavoring Set

Includes Peppermint, Cherry, Cinnamon and Creme de Menthe in .25 oz. bottles. Certified Kosher.

1913-U-1029 Set/4 $5.49

*Brand confectionery coating.

Candy Molds

More fun shapes and greater detail make Wilton Candy Molds the perfect way to create candy. Look at the variety! You can do it all, from exciting kids' party treats to elegant wedding and shower favors. Molding and coloring couldn't be easier when you use Candy Melts®. Look for terrific design ideas and molding instructions on every mold package.* *For specific Holiday designs, see our Seasonal Section, p. 194-216.*

LARGE LOLLIPOP MOLDS

Fairy Tale
3 designs, 3 cavities.
2115-U-1033 $1.99

Sports
4 designs, 4 cavities.
2115-U-4432 $1.99

Party/Birthday
4 designs, 4 cavities.
2115-U-4434 $1.99

Double Heart
2 designs, 4 cavities.
2115-U-4440 $1.99

Pinwheel
2 designs, 3 cavities.
2115-U-4443 $1.99

Cross/Bible
4 designs, 6 cavities
(2 lollipop, 4 candy).
2115-U-4435 $1.99

Springtime Treats Lollipop
8 designs, 9 cavities.
2115-U-1716 $1.99

Transportation
5 designs, 5 cavities.
2115-U-1413 $1.99

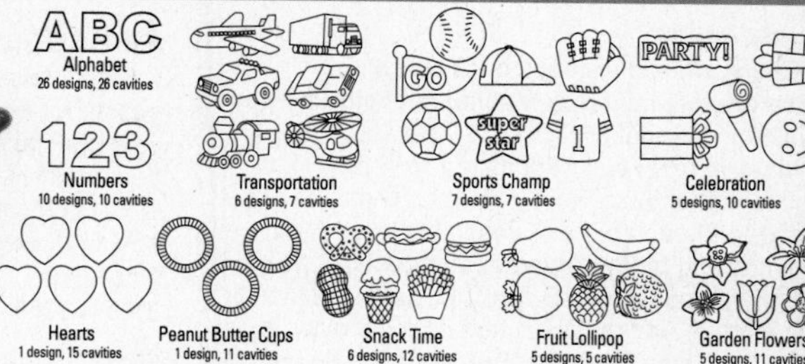

10-PACK CANDY MOLD SET

Be ready for any celebration with this great variety of theme molds! Includes 72 total shapes and 114 total cavities for fun candy messages, sports treats, flowers and more.
2115-U-1724 Pk./10 $9.99

Sea Creatures Lollipop
5 designs, 5 cavities.
2115-U-1414 $1.99

Seashells
5 designs, 11 cavities.
2115-U-1561 $1.99

Alphabet
26 designs, 26 cavities.
2115-U-1563 $1.99

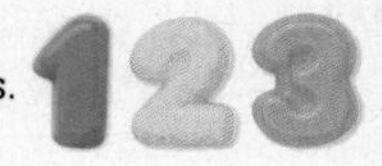

Numerals
10 designs, 10 cavities.
2115-U-1564 $1.99

Summer Fun
5 designs, 11 cavities.
2115-U-1741 $1.99

Baby Treats
5 designs, 5 cavities.
2115-U-4447 $1.99

Stars
1 design, 12 cavities,
2115-U-1554 $1.99

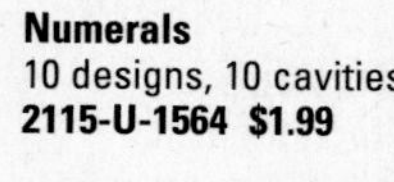

Roses in Bloom
1 design, 10 cavities.
2115-U-1738 $1.99

Rubber Ducky
1 design,
6 cavities.
2115-U-1565 $1.99

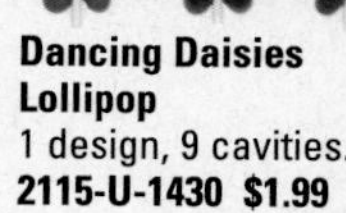

Dancing Daisies Lollipop
1 design, 9 cavities.
2115-U-1430 $1.99

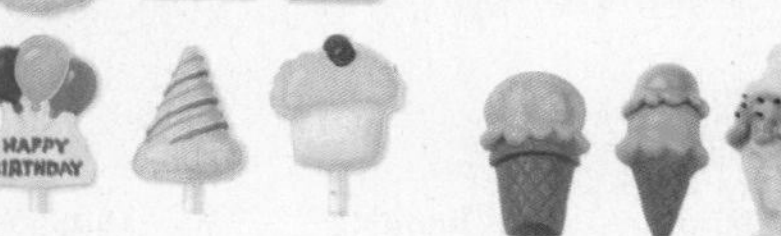

Party Time Lollipop
6 designs, 8 cavities.
2115-U-1516 $1.99

Ice Cream
3 designs, 9 cavities.
2115-U-4367 $1.99

Wedding Favor
3 designs, 6 cavities.
2115-U-4446 $1.99

Wedding Shower Lollipop
5 designs, 10 cavities.
(4 lollipop, 6 candy).
2115-U-1711 $1.99

Roses and Buds Lollipop
3 designs, 9 cavities.
(4 lollipop, 5 candy).
2115-U-1708 $1.99

Smiley Face Lollipop
1 design,
9 cavities.
2115-U-1715 $1.99

2-PACK CANDY MOLD SETS

Girl Power
10 designs, 10 cavities.
2115-U-1604 Pk./2 $2.99

Baby
10 designs, 10 cavities.
2115-U-1605 Pk./2 $2.99

Pets
10 designs, 11 cavities.
2115-U-1606 Pk./2 $2.99

Garden Goodies Lollipop
10 designs, 10 cavities.
2115-U-1607 Pk./2 $2.99

Summer Fun Lollipop
10 designs, 10 cavities.
2115-U-1608 Pk./2 $2.99

CANDY MAKING

Candy Melting Accessories

CHOCOLATE PRO® ELECTRIC MELTING POT

The fast and easy way to melt chocolate and Candy Melts®*!

- Melting base stays cool to the touch
- Removeable non-stick Melting Pot holds 2½ cups
- Easy-pour spout
- Non-skid feet keep Chocolate Pro® steady

It's the fast and fun way to mold candies like a pro. With the Chocolate Pro®, you'll be able to mold lollipops and fancy dipped-center candies. Serve elegant dipped desserts like fruit, cake, cookies and fondue. Add the great taste of chocolate to potato chips and pretzels. Create flavored chocolate sauces for ice cream or silky ganache glaze to pour over cakes. 120 volts. CUL Listed.
2104-U-9004 $32.99

STAY-WARM CERAMIC CANDY MELTING CUPS & BOWLS

Ceramic keeps candy melted longer for easier candy-making because microwave-safe ceramic retains heat. Great for heating and pouring dessert toppings too.

Candy Melting Cups

Cups are great for melting colors separately. Use them like an art palette for painting colors. Holds heat up to ½ hour. Includes 6 cups (2 x 1.5 in. deep) and 6 decorating brushes.
1904-U-1067 Set/12 $10.49

Candy Melting Bowls

Ideal for filling all types of Wilton molds. Take them to the table for easy dipping. Holds heat up to 1 hour. Two, 4 x 3.5 in. deep.
1904-U-1076 Set/2 $10.49

Candy Decorating Bags

NEW!

The convenient way to melt small amounts of Candy Melts and pipe color detail in your molds! Flexible 12 in. plastic bags—just use, then toss.
2104-U-4825 Pk./12 $4.19

Classic Candy Molds

Wilton has a great selection of traditional shapes to create elegant gift assortments and party trays.

Peanut Butter Cups

1 design, 10 cavities.
2115-U-1522 $1.99

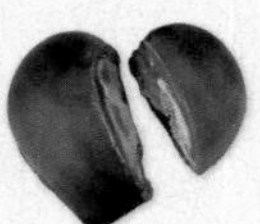

Deep Heart Truffles

1 design, 7 cavities.
2117-U-100 $1.99

Truffles

1 design, 12 cavities.
2115-U-1521 $1.99

NEW!

Dessert Shells

2-piece mold
1 design, 3 cavities.
2115-U-1035 $2.99

Roses

3 designs, 12 cavities.
2115-U-1713 $1.99

Gift Truffles

1 design, 13 cavities.
2115-U-1728 $1.99

Mint Discs

1 design, 16 cavities.
2115-U-1739 $1.99

Cordial Cups

Mold a candy "glass" for dessert liqueurs, or fill with whipped cream and float in cocoa or coffee. 1 design, 6 cavities.
2115-U-1535 $1.99

Add-A-Message Candy Bar

Create a sweet memory for your guests . . . a candy bar featuring your special message. Present them beautifully in Candy Bar Boxes (p. 169). Each candy bar measures 3.75 x 1.75 x .25 in. deep. Mold has 1 design, 4 cavities.
2115-U-1356 $1.99

Candy Bar

1 design, three 4-block cavities.
2115-U-4431 $1.99

Candy Making Tools

Silicone Dipping Bowls

NEW!

Colorful bowls are great for dipping treats into melted candy or toppings. The oval shape is ideal for dipping cookies, fruit, cake and more in chopped nuts, sprinkles, shredded coconut or cocoa powder. Silicone bowls are dishwasher safe.
1904-U-3231 Set/2 $3.99

Candy Thermometer

Precise measurement essential for preparing hard candy, nougat, more.
1904-U-1200 $14.99

Candy Dipping Set

Easy-handling spoon and fork, each 7.75 in. long.
1904-U-3230 Set/2 $3.19

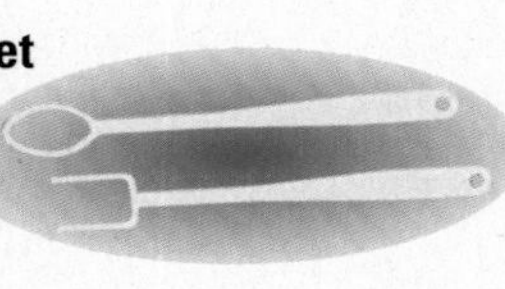

Metal Dipping Set

Professional-quality stainless steel with wooden handles. 8.75 in. long.
1904-U-925 Set/2 $10.49

Easy-Pour Funnel

Push-button controls flow of candy. 5 x 4 in. diameter, nylon.
1904-U-552 $4.19

Squeeze Bottles

Melt candy with ease, then fill your mold without mess! Our convenient bottles are available in 3 sizes so you can melt just the amount of Candy Melts®* you need, right in the bottle. Great way to store and reheat leftover candy.

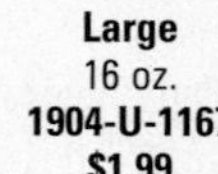

Mini	Regular	Large
6 oz.	12 oz.	16 oz.
1904-U-1166	**1904-U-1189**	**1904-U-1167**
Pk./2 $1.99	**$1.69**	**$1.99**

Candy Melting Plate

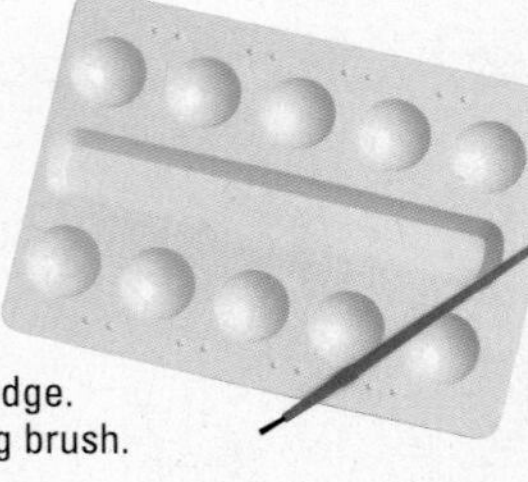

Microwave-melt up to 11 Candy Melts®* colors at one time with less mess! Plastic with non-slip grip edge. Includes decorating brush.
1904-U-8016 $3.19

Decorator Brush Set

Plastic, durable bristles, easy-to-hold handle.
2104-U-9355 Set/3 $1.69

*Brand confectionery coating.

Candy Wraps and Boxes

Your homemade candy deserves a beautiful presentation. Wilton has everything you need to wrap and package your candy gifts like a pro.

Love Chocolate Candy Gift Boxes and Bags

NEW!

Bright, fun pattern makes your gift even sweeter!

½ lb. Candy Boxes
1904-U-4242
Pk./3 $2.09

Lollipop Bags
Contains 25 bags, 25 twist ties.
1912-U-1092
Pk./25 $2.09

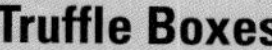

Truffle Boxes

An elegant look, with a lock-close top that forms a perfect "bow." Holds 2-3 pieces of candy.
Pk./4 $2.09
White 1904-U-1154
Silver 1904-U-1155
Gold 1904-U-1156

Candy Bar Boxes

Designed to hold candies made in our Candy Bar Molds (p. 168), the window displays your special message.
Pk./10 $4.19
White 1904-U-1157
Silver 1904-U-1159

Gold Elastic Ties

Pre-tied with a bow. Use with Candy Gift Boxes.
1904-U-1186 Pk./5 $1.59

Candy Gift Boxes

For attractive gift giving.
1 lb. White Candy Boxes
1904-U-1344 Pk./2 $2.09
½ lb. Candy Boxes Pk./3 $2.09
White 1904-U-1150 **Silver 1904-U-1153**
Red 1904-U-1152

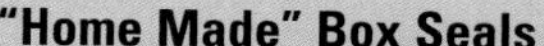

Tented Candy Gift Boxes

Stand-up design with front window will give your homemade candy gift the ideal showcase. 3.25 x 1.6 x 5.75 in. high. White.
1904-U-1087
Pk./3 $2.09

Candy Box Liners

Padded paper liners cushion candy and prevent breakage. Fits ½ lb. Candy Gift Boxes.
1904-U-1191 Pk./4 $1.59

"Home Made" Box Seals

Let everyone know the care you put into your candy gift with these embossed seals. Add this "homemade" touch whenever you give baked goods too!
1904-U-8936
Pk./24 $1.09

Glassine Candy Cups

Crisply-pleated, just like professionals use. White glassine-coated paper. **$1.59**
1.25 in. Diameter.
1912-U-1245 Pk./75
1 in. Diameter.
1912-U-1243 Pk./100

Foil Wrappers

Bright, shiny coverings for candy and lollipops! 4 x 4 in. squares.
Pk./50 $1.99
Gold 1904-U-1197
Silver 1904-U-1196
Red 1904-U-1198

Foil Candy Cups

NEW!

Crisply-pleated, just like professionals use. Wax-laminated paper on foil.
Pk./75 $1.59
Blue 415-U-313
Red 415-U-314
Pink 415-U-315
Gold 415-U-306
Silver 415-U-307

LOLLIPOP AND TREAT STAND

Show off your fun lollipops and other treats! This lively looping metal stand neatly serves up to 18 treats for the ideal celebration centerpiece. Great for marshmallows, jelly candies and caramels too—just insert 4 in. sticks. Use the top slot to add a fun message! Assembled size 6 x 14 in. high.
1904-U-1068 $10.99

CANDY MAKING

Accessories

Create the perfect pop with sticks in every size, cool colors too! Clear wrappers and tags make giving easy.

Lollipop Tags

Write a name or a message, then slide the tag onto your lollipop stick. Perfect for party lollipops, cookie pops and more.
Pk./12 $2.09
Pennant 1904-U-1088
Star 1904-U-1089
Flower 1904-U-1071

Drawstring Lollipop Bags

Fill with your favorite candies, then pull the drawstring to close—a fun way to give your goodies. Clear bags are also great for cookies, nuts and other treats. 4.5 x 5.5 in.
1912-U-9469 Pk./15 $2.09

Rainbow Lollipop Sticks

Add pizzazz to your pops! Food-safe plastic sticks; 5 each red, yellow, blue and green. Not for oven or microwave use. 4 in.
1912-U-9316 Pk./20 $1.99

Lollipop Sticks

Sturdy paper sticks in 4 sizes. Not for oven use.
4 in.
1912-U-1006 Pk./50 $1.99
6 in.
1912-U-1007 Pk./35 $1.99
8 in.
1912-U-9320 Pk./25 $1.99
11¾ in.
1912-U-1212 Pk./20 $3.99

Lollipop Wrapping Kit

Cover your candy lollipops and special treats for gift-giving! Contains 18 sticks, (4 in.) 18 bags, 18 twist ties.
1904-U-1193 $2.09

Clear Treat Bags Only
3 x 4 in. **1912-U-2347**
Pk./50 $2.89

Pretzel Bags

See-through bags are ideal for showing off your candy-coated pretzels—great for favors and gifts. 20 plastic bags, 20 twist ties. 2.25 x 9.75 in.
1912-U-5911 Pk./20 $2.09

Famous Favorites

Wilton helps you make kids feel like stars! We have a great cast of today's favorite faces and themes on fun party products for cakes, cookies and more.

123 SESAME STREET

NEW!

Cake Pan
Kids everywhere have fallen for *Abby Cadabby*! This 3-year-old fairy-in-training has moved to Sesame Street and is winning new friends every day. She's here on a cake pan that captures all her magic and fun. One-mix pan is 9.5 x 11.75 x 2 in. deep. Aluminum.
2105-U-4444 $14.49

Party Toppers
Abby Caddaby casts magic and excitement on your treats with a wave of her fairy wand! Handpainted, food-safe plastic is great on cupcakes, brownies, cakes and more. 1¾ in. high.
2113-U-1901 Set/6 $4.19

Candle
Handpainted, clean-burning with fun details. 2¾ in. high.
2811-U-4444
$4.39

Icing Decorations
Mint-flavored edible sugar shapes to decorate cupcakes, cookies, ice cream and cake. Certified Kosher.
710-U-4444
Pk./9 $2.49

Baking Cups
Standard size, microwave-safe paper. 2 in. diameter.
415-U-4444
Pk./50 $1.79

Icing Color Set
Includes four .5 oz. jars: Pink, Purple, Blue and Yellow. Certified Kosher.
601-U-4444
Set/4 $4.99

Treat Bags
Fill with candy, cookies and other goodies; great for gifts and surprises, too! Includes sixteen 4 x 9.5 in. bags with closures.
1912-U-4444 Pk./16 $2.09

Sesame Workshop, the nonprofit educational organization behind Sesame Street, puts the proceeds it receives from sales of its products right back into Sesame Street and its other projects for children at home and around the world.
Learn more at www.sesameworkshop.org

Disney • PIXAR
WALL•E

Cake Pan
Meet the newest star from Disney/Pixar! It's *WALL•E*, an industrial robot from the future who brings the excitement and fun of his hit movie to your celebration. This fun shaped pan is programmed to make a kid's birthday unforgettable! One-mix pan is 10 x 11 x 2 in. deep. Aluminum.
2105-U-9999 $14.49

Party Toppers
WALL•E is no wallflower! He greets your guests with a friendly wave that invites everyone to join in the fun. Handpainted, food-safe plastic is great on cupcakes, brownies, cakes and more. 2 in. high.
2113-U-9999 Set/6 $4.19

Icing Decorations
Mint-flavored edible sugar shapes to decorate cupcakes, cookies, ice cream and cake. Certified Kosher.
710-U-9999 Pk./9 $2.49

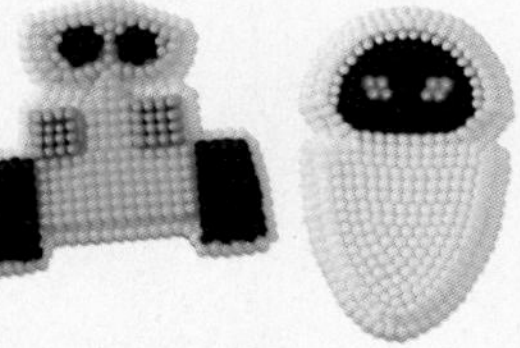

Baking Cups
Standard size, microwave-safe paper. 2 in. diameter.
415-U-9999
Pk./50 $1.79

Candle
Handpainted, clean-burning with fun details. 2¾ in. high.
2811-U-9999
$4.39

Icing Color Set
Includes four .5 oz. jars: Red, Black and two Yellow. Certified Kosher.
601-U-9999
Set/4 $4.99

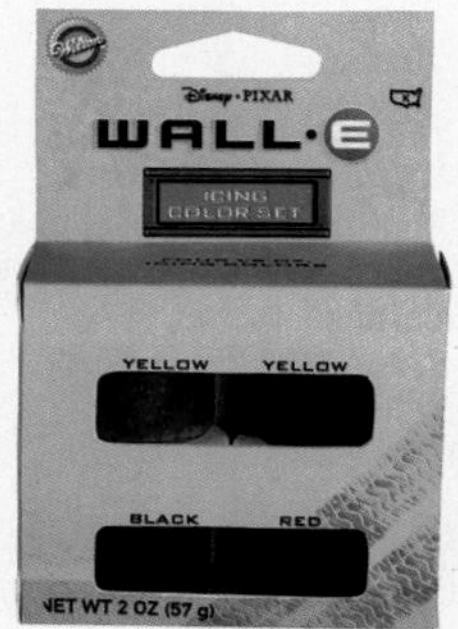

Treat Bags
Fill with candy, cookies and other goodies; great for gifts and surprises too! Includes sixteen 4 x 9.5 in. bags with twist ties.
1912-U-9999 Pk./16 $2.09

Care-Bears™ NEW!

Cheer Bear™

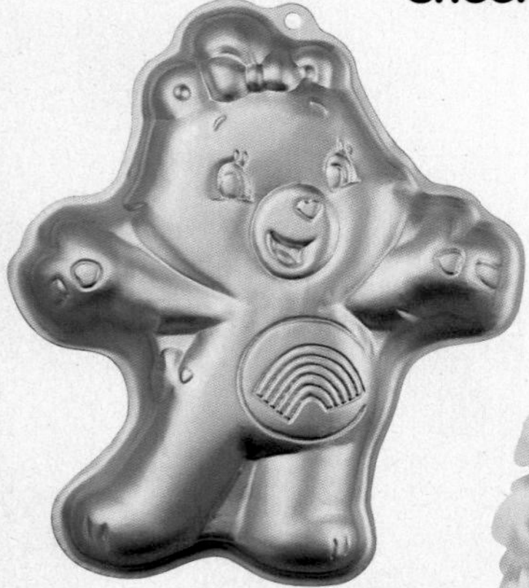

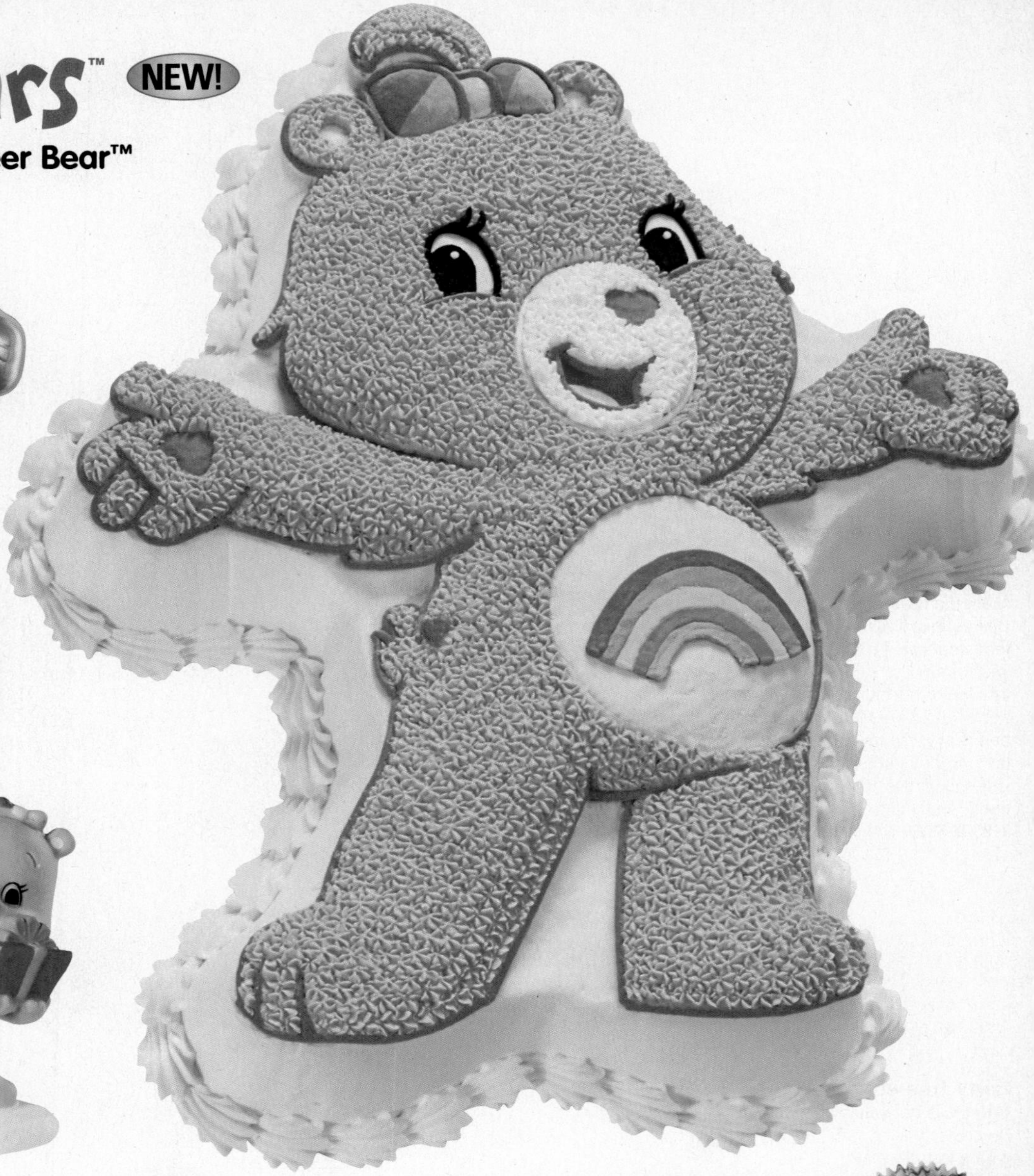

Cake Pan
Everyone will give a cheer when they see a *Cheer Bear*™ cake! With her sunny attitude and lively rainbow colors, she's the perfect birthday party guest! One-mix pan is 10.6 x 13 x 2 in. Aluminum.
2105-U-5555 $14.49

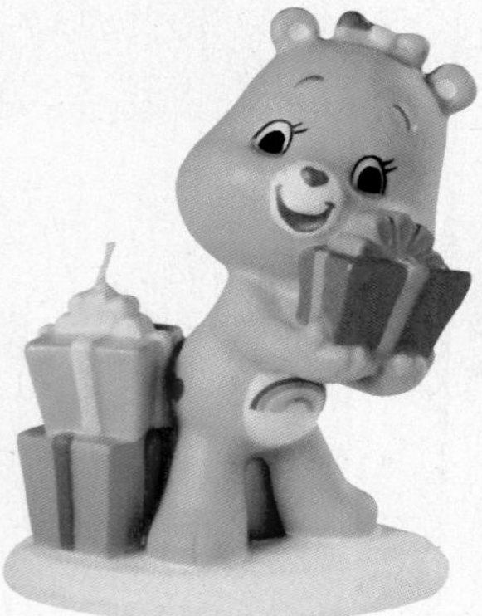

Candle
Handpainted, clean-burning with fun details.
2¾ in. high.
2811-U-5555
$4.39

Baking Cups
Standard size, microwave-safe paper.
2 in. diameter.
415-U-2424
Pk./50 $1.79

Icing Color Set
Includes four .5 oz. jars: Pink, Blue, Yellow and Black. Certified Kosher.
601-U-5555
Set/4 $4.99

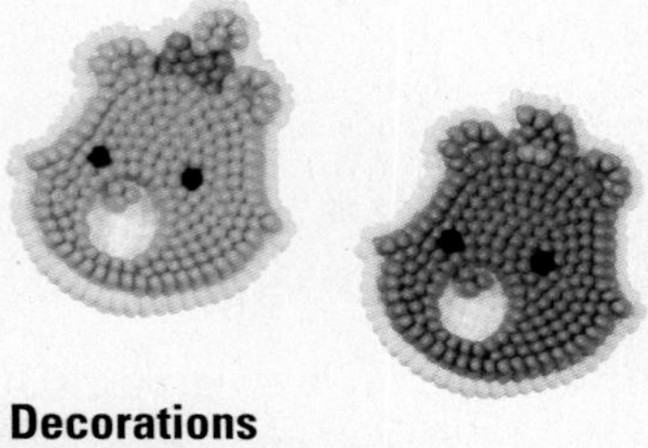

Icing Decorations
Mint-flavored edible sugar shapes to decorate cupcakes, cookies, ice cream and cake. Certified Kosher.
710-U-2424 Pk./9 $2.49

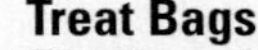

Treat Bags
Fill with candy, cookies and other goodies—great for gifts and surprises too! Includes sixteen 4 x 9.5 in. bags with twist ties.
1912-U-2424 Pk./16 $2.09

NEW!

Cake Pan
It's a whole new, "berry" exciting shape for this kids' favorite! *Strawberry Shortcake* strikes a fun-loving pose that's perfect for birthday cakes, ice cream molds and more. One-mix pan is 11.25 x 11.5 x 2 in. Aluminum.
2105-U-7050 $14.49

Candle
Handpainted, clean-burning with fun details. 2½ in. high.
2811-U-7050
$4.39

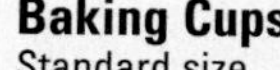

Baking Cups
Standard size, microwave-safe paper. 2 in. diameter.
415-U-7040
Pk./50 $1.79

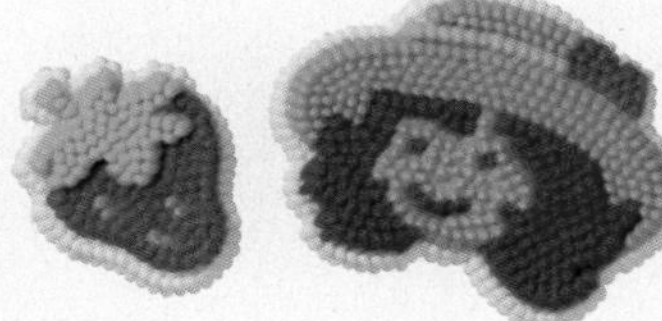

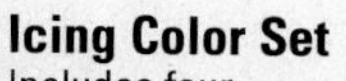

Icing Color Set
Includes four .5 oz. jars: Orange, Pink, Green and *Strawberry Shortcake* Skin Tone. Certified Kosher.
601-U-7050
Set/4 $4.99

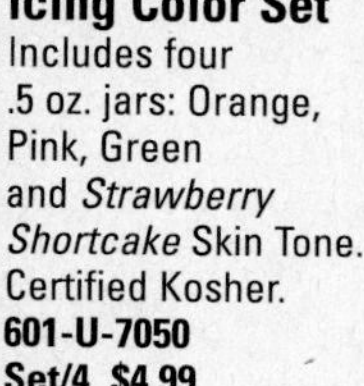

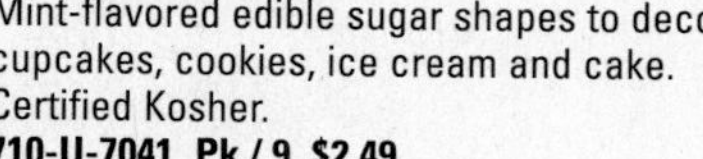

Icing Decorations
Mint-flavored edible sugar shapes to decorate cupcakes, cookies, ice cream and cake. Certified Kosher.
710-U-7041 Pk./9 $2.49

Treat Bags
Fill with candy, cookies and other goodies; great for gifts and surprises too! Includes sixteen 4 x 9.5 in. bags with twist ties.
1912-U-7040 Pk./16 $2.09

Cake Pan

Kids will follow *Diego* everywhere—they've watched him race to the rescue on TV, and now he's ready to save the party with the perfect birthday cake! The fun detailed design really captures his adventurous attitude. One-mix pan is 16 x 10 x 2 in. Aluminum.
2105-U-4250 $14.49

Party Toppers

Diego scopes out all the party fun on these colorful toppers. They're easy ways to complete your treats! Handpainted, food-safe plastic is great on cupcakes, brownies, cakes and more. 2 in. high.
2113-U-4250 Set/6 $4.19

Candle

Handpainted, clean-burning with colorful details.
3¼ in. high.
2811-U-4250
$4.39

Fun Pix®

Fun for cupcakes, brownies, ice cream and more. Paper, 3¼ in. high.
2113-U-4251
Pk./24 $1.49

Icing Decorations

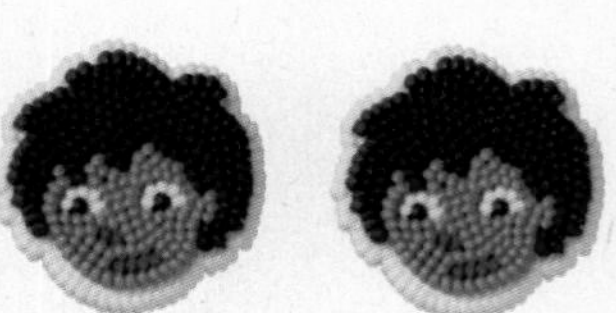

Mint-flavored edible sugar shapes to decorate cupcakes, cookies, ice cream and cake. Certified Kosher.
710-U-4250 Pk./9 $2.49

Icing Color Set

Includes four .5 oz. jars: *Diego* Skin Tone, Brown, Blue and Black. Certified Kosher.
601-U-4250
Set/4 $4.99

Baking Cups

Standard size, microwave-safe paper. 2 in. diameter.
415-U-4250
Pk./50 $1.79

Treat Bags

Fill with candy, cookies and other goodies; great for gifts and surprises too! Includes sixteen 4 x 9.5 in. bags with twist ties.
1912-U-4250
Pk./16 $2.09

NICKELODEON

DORA the EXPLORER™

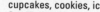

Cake Pan

Wherever *Dora* goes, it's always "una fiesta"! Discover a world of party excitement with this great pan. One-mix pan is 13.75 x 10 x 2 in. deep. Aluminum.
2105-U-6300 $14.49

Party Toppers

Dora is ready to top your delightful party treats! Handpainted, food-safe plastic is great on cupcakes, brownies, cakes and other treats. 2¼ in. high.
2113-U-6300 Set/6 $4.19

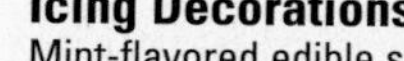

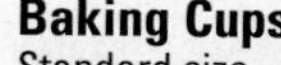

Icing Decorations

Mint-flavored edible sugar shapes to decorate cupcakes, cookies, ice cream and cake. Certified Kosher.
710-U-6300 Pk./8 $2.49

Baking Cups

Standard size, microwave-safe paper. 2 in. diameter.
415-U-6300
Pk./50 $1.79

Candle

Handpainted, clean-burning with colorful details.
3¼ in. high.
2811-U-6300
$4.39

Icing Color Set

Includes four .5 oz. jars: Red, Pink, Brown and *Dora* Skin Tone. Certified Kosher.
601-U-6300
Set/4 $4.99

Treat Bags

Fill with candy, cookies and other goodies; great for gifts and surprises too! Includes sixteen 4 x 9.5 in. bags with twist ties.
1912-U-6300
Pk./16 $2.09

Cake Pan
Tink makes birthday wishes come true! She brings fun to the celebration on a cake that captures the twinkle in her eye and the magic in her smile. One-mix pan is 10.5 x 12 x 2 in. Aluminum.
2105-U-5110 $14.49

Icing Decorations
Mint-flavored edible sugar shapes to decorate cupcakes, cookies, ice cream and cake. Certified Kosher.
710-U-5110
Pk./9 $2.49

Fun Pix®
Fun for cupcakes, brownies, ice cream and more. Paper, 3½ in. high.
2113-U-5111
Pk./24 $1.49

Candle
Handpainted, clean-burning with colorful details.
3 in. high.
2811-U-5110
$4.39

Party Toppers
Top your treats with *Tink* and create enchantment! Handpainted, food-safe plastic is great on cupcakes, brownies, cakes and other treats. 2¼ in. high.
2113-U-5110 Set/6 $4.19

NEW!

Cakescapes™ Cake Stand Kit
Her cake will look great on this easy-to-assemble cake stand with colorful decorative panels and cake board. Serve favors and snacks to match in bright treat bags with ties. Includes 11.5 x 3.25 in. high cake stand, 10 in. diameter cake board, 8 treat bags (4 x 9.5 in.) with ties, instruction sheet.
1509-U-1003 $9.99

NEW!

Treat Bags
Stand-up bags with a fun *Fairies* design. Perfect for food treats, cookies, candy, brownies and more! 4.5 x 1.75 x 4.75 in. high.
1904-U-1208
Pk./4 $2.59

Baking Cups
Standard size, microwave-safe paper. 2 in. diameter.
415-U-5110
Pk./50 $1.79

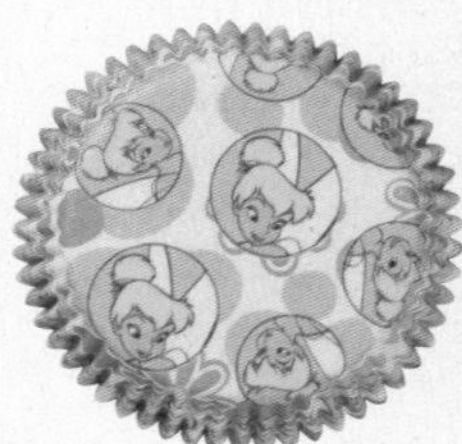

Icing Color Set
Includes four .5 oz. jars: Blue, Yellow, Red, *Tink* Skin Tone. Certified Kosher.
601-U-5110
Set/4 $4.99

NEW!

Cupscapes™ Cupcake Stand Kit
It's an instant *Disney Fairies* party, with a bright 3-tier cupcake stand, fun decorative topper, colorful baking cups and Fun Pix®. Includes 12 x 15 in. high stand, and 24 each 2 in. diameter cups and 3.5 in. high picks. Holds up to 24 cupcakes.
1510-U-1003 $9.99

Treat Bags
Fill with candy, cookies and other goodies; great for gifts and surprises too! Includes sixteen 4 x 9.5 in. bags with twist ties.
1912-U-5110
Pk./16 $2.09

Please visit Disney Fairies at DisneyFairies.com

Cake Pan
Enter *Ariel's* world of enchantment under the sea! Her sweet look will captivate kids and bring all the thrills of *The Little Mermaid* story to your celebration. One-mix pan is 10.5 x 11.75 x 2 in. Aluminum.
2105-U-4355 $14.49

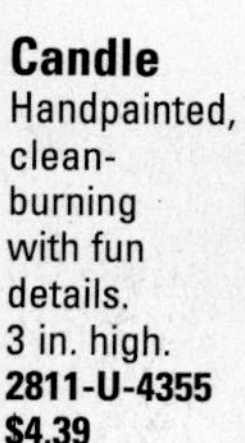

Candle
Handpainted, clean-burning with fun details. 3 in. high.
2811-U-4355 $4.39

Party Toppers
When *Ariel* surfaces on party desserts, there's a new wave of birthday excitement! Handpainted, food-safe plastic is great on cupcakes, brownies, cakes and other treats. 1¾ in. high.
2113-U-4355 Set/6 $4.19

Icing Decorations
Mint-flavored edible sugar shapes to decorate cupcakes, cookies, ice cream and cake. Certified Kosher.
710-U-4355
Pk./9 $2.49

Baking Cups
Standard size, microwave-safe paper. 2 in. diameter.
415-U-4355
Pk./50 $1.79

Icing Color Set
Includes four .5 oz. jars: *Ariel* Skin Tone, Teal and 2 Red. Certified Kosher.
601-U-4355
Set/4 $4.99

Treat Bags
Fill with candy, cookies and other goodies; great for gifts and surprises too! Includes sixteen 4 x 9.5 in. bags with twist ties.
1912-U-4355 Pk./16 $2.09

Please visit DisneyPrincess.com and LittleMermaidDVD.com

Fun Pix®
Fun for cupcakes, brownies, ice cream and more. Paper, 3 in. high.
2113-U-6402 Pk./24 $1.49

Cake Pan
Any party is a joy ride when you serve a cake starring *Lightning McQueen*! All the fun details you love on the big screen are here. One-mix pan is 13.75 x 6.25 x 2.75 in. Aluminum.
2105-U-6400 $14.49

Icing Decorations
Mint-flavored edible sugar shapes to decorate cupcakes, cookies, ice cream and cake. Certified Kosher.
710-U-6400 Pk./9 $2.49

Party Toppers
Rev up the fun with treats topped with your favorites from *Disney/Pixar Cars*! Handpainted, food-safe plastic is great on cupcakes, brownies, cakes and other treats. 1¼ in. high.
2113-U-6400 Set/6 $4.19

Baking Cups
Standard size, microwave-safe paper. 2 in. diameter.
415-U-6400 Pk./50 $1.79

Candle
Handpainted, clean-burning with fun details. 3½ in. high.
2811-U-6400 $4.39

Icing Color Set
Includes four .5 oz. jars: Red, Blue, Yellow, Black. Certified Kosher.
601-U-6400 Set/4 $4.99

Treat Bags
Fill with candy, cookies and other goodies; great for gifts and surprises too! Includes sixteen 4 x 9.5 in. bags with twist ties.
1912-U-6400 Pk./16 $2.09

Cake Pan
Everyone's favorite seafaring star will make a big splash at the party. One-mix pan is 13.5 x 11.75 x 2 in. deep. Aluminum.
2105-U-5130 $14.49

Party Toppers
He's surfing your party goodies on these cool handpainted toppers. Food-safe plastic to use on cupcakes, brownies, cakes and other treats. 2 in. high.
2113-U-5130
Set/6 $4.19

Candle
SpongeBob is swimming in loot—giving you a cake to treasure! Handpainted, clean-burning with colorful details. 3½ in. high.
2811-U-5130
$4.39

NEW!

Cakescapes™ Cake Stand Kit
Their cake will look great on the easy-to-assemble cake stand with colorful decorative panels and cake board. Serve favors and snacks to match in bright treat bags with ties. Includes 11.5 x 3.25 in. high cake stand, 10 in. diameter cake board, 8 treat bags (4 x 9.5 in.) with ties, instruction sheet.
1509-U-1005 $9.99

Treat Bags
Stand-up bags with a fun *SpongeBob* design. Perfect for food treats, cookies, candy, brownies and more! 4.5 x 1.75 x 4.75 in. high.
1904-U-1210 Pk./4 $2.59

Baking Cups
Standard size, microwave-safe paper. 2 in. diameter.
415-U-5130
Pk./50 $1.79

Icing Color Set
Includes four .5 oz. jars: Yellow, Red, Blue and Brown. Certified Kosher.
601-U-5130
Set/4 $4.99

Icing Decorations
Mint-flavored edible sugar shapes to decorate cupcakes, cookies, ice cream and cake. Certified Kosher.
710-U-5130 Pk./9 $2.49

Cupscapes™ Cupcake Stand Kit
It's an instant *SpongeBob SquarePants* party, with a bright 3-tier cupcake stand, fun decorative topper, colorful baking cups and Fun Pix®! Includes 12 x 15 in. high stand, and 24 each 2 in. diameter cups and 3.5 in. high picks. Holds up to 24 cupcakes.
1510-U-1005 $9.99

NEW!

Treat Bags
Fill with candy, cookies and other goodies; great for gifts and surprises too! Includes sixteen 4 x 9.5 in. bags with twist ties.
1912-U-5130
Pk./16 $2.09

THE AMAZING SPIDER-MAN

Cake Pan
The Wizard of Webs is back in action, on a pan that will grab every guest! Kids will love the great costume detail. One-mix pan is 9 x 12 x 2 in. Aluminum.
2105-U-5052
$14.49

Party Toppers
He's ready to sling his next web on these exciting handpainted toppers. Food-safe plastic to use on cupcakes, brownies, cakes and other treats. 2¼ in. high.
2113-U-5052 Set/6 $4.19

Candle
Handpainted, clean-burning with exciting details.
3½ in. high.
2811-U-5052
$4.39

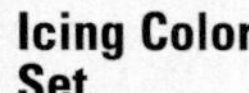

Icing Color Set
Includes four .5 oz. jars: Light Blue, Dark Blue, Red and Black. Certified Kosher.
601-U-5052
Set/4 $4.99

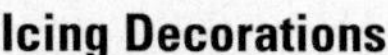

Icing Decorations
Mint-flavored edible sugar shapes to decorate cupcakes, cookies, ice cream and cake. Certified Kosher.
710-U-5052 Pk./9 $2.49

Baking Cups
Standard size, microwave-safe paper. 2 in. diameter.
415-U-5052 Pk./50 $1.79

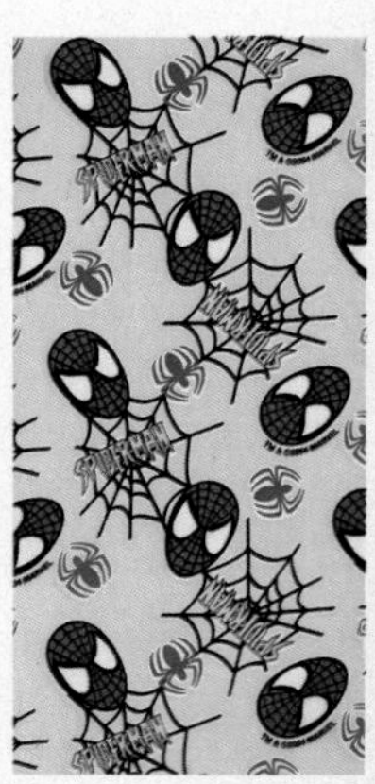

Treat Bags
Fill with candy, cookies and other goodies; great for gifts and surprises too! Includes sixteen 4 x 9.5 in. bags with twist ties.
1912-U-5052 Pk./16 $2.09

MARVEL

SCOOBY-DOO!™

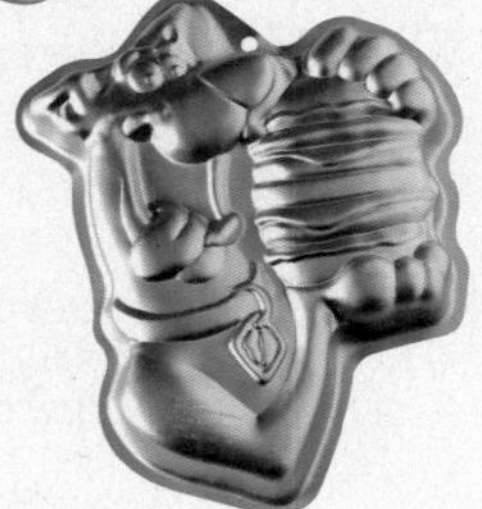

Candle
Handpainted, clean-burning with colorful details. 3¾ in. high.
2811-U-3227 $4.39

NEW!

Baking Cups
Standard size, microwave-safe paper. 2 in. diameter.
415-U-3227
Pk./50 $1.79

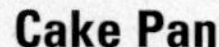

Cake Pan
As usual, *Scooby* gets right next to the food! This fun pan shows him about to put his canines into a big burger. One-mix pan is 10.5 x 12 x 2 in. Aluminum.
2105-U-3227 $14.49

NEW!

Icing Color Set
Includes four .5 oz. jars: Brown, Yellow, Black, Teal. Certified Kosher.
601-U-3206 Set/4 $4.99

Party Toppers
Scooby-Doo! is begging for attention on these fun handpainted toppers. Food-safe plastic to decorate cupcakes, brownies, cakes and other treats. 2½ in. high.
2113-U-3206 Set/6 $4.19

NEW!

Treat Bags
Fill with candy, cookies and other goodies; great for gifts and surprises too! Includes sixteen 4 x 9.5 in. bags with twist ties.
1912-U-3227
Pk./16 $2.09

Icing Decorations
Mint-flavored edible sugar shapes to decorate cupcakes, cookies, ice cream and cake. Certified Kosher.
710-U-3206 Pk./9 $2.49

FAMOUS FAVORITES

123 SESAME STREET®

Elmo with Crayons Candle
Elmo brings smiles to the party. Handpainted, clean-burning with colorful details. 3½ in. high.
2811-U-3463 $4.39

Icing Decorations
Mint-flavored edible sugar shapes to decorate cupcakes, cookies, ice cream and cakes. Certified Kosher.
710-U-3460
Pk./9 $2.49

NEW!

Baking Cups
Standard size, microwave-safe paper. 2 in. diameter.
415-U-3461
Pk./50 $1.79

Elmo Face Cake Pan
He's sweet, lovable and popular with kids of all ages. One-mix pan is 13.5 x 10.5 x 2 in. Aluminum.
2105-U-3461 $14.49

Parade Cake Top Set
A fun birthday parade right on your cake. *Cookie Monster, Zoe, Elmo, Big Bird* in food-safe plastic. 1½ to 4 in. high.
2113-U-3460 Set/4 $5.29

NEW!

Treat Bags
Fill with candy, cookies and other goodies; great for gifts and surprises too! Includes sixteen 4 x 9.5 in. bags with closures.
1912-U-3461
Pk./16 $2.09

Sesame Workshop, the nonprofit educational organization behind Sesame Street, puts the proceeds it receives from sales of its products right back into Sesame Street and its other projects for children at home and around the world.
Learn more at www.sesameworkshop.org

Party

You've written the guest list—now start your decorating list here! From baking cups to candles, cake toppers to treat bags, Wilton has the great-looking designs you want.

Theme Party Products

Give your party personality! See how easy it is to pull your look together with the great selection of Wilton theme products. You'll discover favorite subjects including jungle animals, colorful flowers, over-the-hill tombstones and sports for every season. Find candles, party bags, baking cups, candy molds, cake pans and more—all with the Wilton touch of fun design and detail.

PRINCESS

The royal treatment for any birthday girl begins here, with colorful treats and cakes that rule!

NEW!

Princess Carriage Pan
Create a birthday celebration fit for a princess! Give it dazzling windows and wheels decorated in her favorite colors. Or, decorate a classic carriage cake for the bridal shower, with flowers and accents to match your colors. One-mix pan is 12.25 x 9.5 x 2 in. deep. Aluminum.
2105-U-1027 $12.99

Romantic Castle Cake Set
Everything you need to transform your tiered cake into a fantasy castle is included: three sizes of detailed turret towers with removable peak pieces, lattice windows, a paneled door and roof pieces. Complete assembly and decorating ideas included. For design ideas visit **www.wilton.com**!
301-U-910 Set/32 $20.99

NEW!

Fairy Tale Lollipop Mold
3 designs, 3 cavities.
2115-U-1033 $1.99

NEW!

Princess Cake Stand Kit
Her cake will look great on the easy-to-assemble cake stand with colorful decorative panels and cake board. Serve favors and snacks to match in bright treat bags with ties. Includes 11.5 x 3.25 in. high cake stand, 10 in. diameter cake board, 8 - 4 x 9.5 in. treat bags with ties, instruction sheet.
1509-U-1008 $9.99

NEW!

Princess Cupcake Stand Kit
It's an instant princess party, with a bright 3-tier cupcake stand, fun decorative topper, colorful baking cups and Fun Pix®! Includes 12 x 15 in. high stand, 24 - 2 in. diameter cups and 24 - 3 in. high picks. Holds up to 24 cupcakes.
1510-U-1008 $9.99

NEW!

Princess Favor Bags
Dazzling bags are big enough to hold a treasure of treats for her highness. 4.5 x 1.75 x 4.75 in., Velcro close.
1904-U-1213 Pk./4 $2.09

NEW!

Cupcake Combo Pack
Quick and colorful way to serve cupcakes that set the tone for your celebration. Contains 24 each 2 in. diameter baking cups and 3 in. high paper party picks.
415-U-1313 Pk./24 $2.09

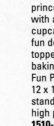

OVER THE HILL

The secret of aging is keeping your sense of humor! These Wilton products help anyone face those big birthdays with a smile!

Candle Picks
1¾ in. high.
2811-U-786 Set/13 $2.19

Icon Candles
Candles that feature a fun hand-carved tombstone. Instant fun, great size for cupcakes too!
2½ in. high.
2811-U-8417
Pk./10 $2.19

Candle
2¼ in. high.
2811-U-553 $2.19

NEW!

Cupcake Combo Pack
Quick and colorful way to serve cupcakes that set the tone for your celebration. Contains 24 each 2 in. diameter baking cups and 3 in. high paper party picks.
415-U-1315 Pk./24 $2.19

JUNGLE PALS

Kids will just love these adorable creatures for birthdays, school parties and special events.

NEW!

Animals Cookie Candy Molds
With Cookie Candy Molds and easy-melting Wilton Candy Melts®, it's a breeze to add a great tasting and colorful candy design to your favorite cookies. Great for sandwich cream cookies or any round cookie 2 in. diameter or less. 4 designs, 8 cavities.
2115-U-1354 $1.99

Monkey Pan
He'll be the top banana at so many fun occasions! Kids will just love him at birthday parties, school celebrations and jungle-themed events. One-mix pan is 12.75 x 11.25 x 2 in. deep. Aluminum.
2105-U-1023 $12.99

NEW!

Baking Cups
Standard size 2 in. diameter.
415-U-1012
Pk./50 $1.59

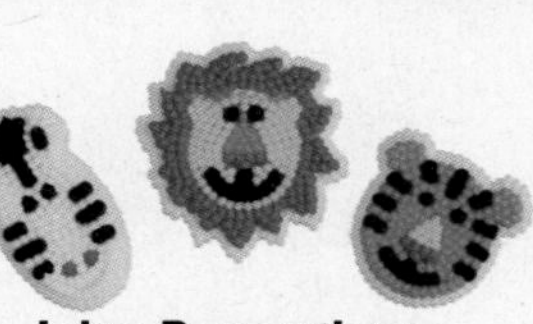

Icing Decorations
Certified Kosher.
710-U-1012 Pk./12 $2.29

Party Bags
20 plastic bags, 20 ties included.
4 x 9.5 in.
1912-U-1012
Pk./20 $2.09

Fun Pix®
Approx. 3¼ in. high.
2113-U-1012 Set/24 $2.09

Jungle Animals Topper Set
1.75 to 3 in. high.
2113-U-2095 Set/4 $4.19

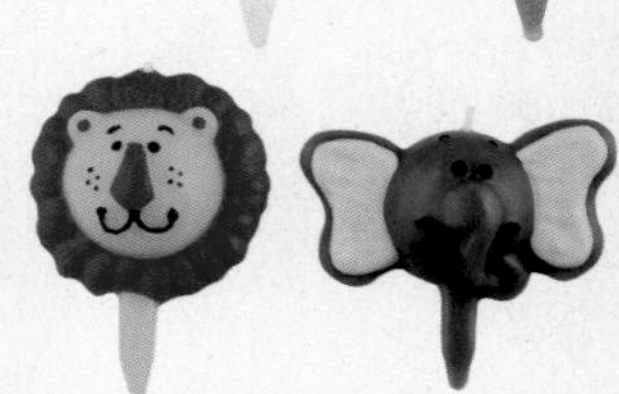

Candle Picks
Approx. 2 in. high.
2811-U-1012
Set/4 $3.89

ICE CREAM

A refreshing look for any celebration, from birthdays to backyard barbecues.

Candy Mold
3 designs, 9 cavities.
2115-U-4367 $1.99

Candles
Approx. 2¼ in. high.
2811-U-9349 Set/4 $3.89

Baking Cups
Standard size 2 in. diameter.
415-U-121
Pk./50 $1.59

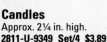

Party Bags
20 plastic bags, 20 ties included.
4 x 9.5 in.
1912-U-3106
Pk./20 $2.09

PARTY

Theme Party Products

PARTY TIME

What a great way to cap off any celebration, from birthdays to that New Year's Eve bash!

Party/Birthday Large Lollipop Mold
4 designs, 4 cavities.
2115-U-4434 $1.99

Topsy Turvy Pan
Our topsy turvy "tiered" cake is just the right look for wacky birthdays, wild parties or special occasions. One-mix pan is 10.25 x 12 x 2 in. deep. Aluminum.
2105-U-4946 $12.99

Icing Decorations
Certified Kosher.
710-U-7205 Pk./12 $2.29

Party Bags
20 plastic bags, 20 ties included. 4 x 9.5 in.
1912-U-4365 Pk./20 $2.09

Baking Cups
Standard size 2 in. diameter.
415-U-5365 Pk./50 $1.59

Candles
Approx. 1½ in. high.
2811-U-860 Set/4 $3.89

DANCING DAISY FLOWER

Pick this daisy for Mother's Day, wedding showers and birthdays for any garden-lover.

Lollipop Mold
1 design, 9 cavities.
2115-U-1430 $1.99

Pan
One perfect flower makes bunches of great cakes and desserts! One-mix pan is 12 x 12 x 2 in. deep. Aluminum.
2105-U-1016 $12.99

Icing Decorations
Certified Kosher.
710-U-353 Pk./12 $2.29

Party Bags
20 plastic bags, 20 ties included.
4 x 9.5 in.
1912-U-7813
Pk./20 $2.09

Baking Cups
Standard size 2 in. diameter.
415-U-7812
Pk./50 $1.59

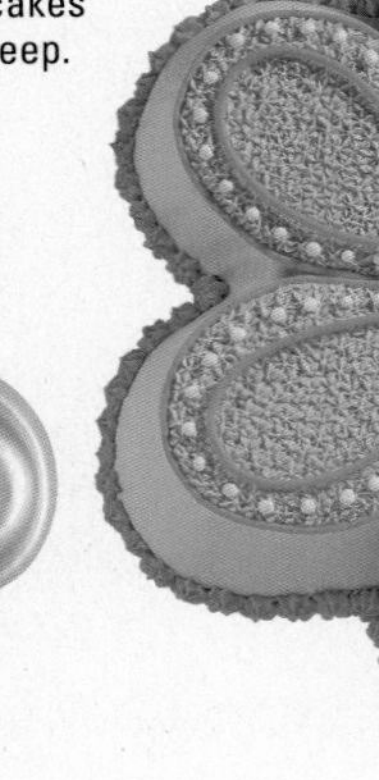

Candle Picks
Approx. 2 in. high.
2811-U-217
Set/6 $3.89

SMILEY FACE

Have a nice party! This friendly face has a way of making everyone happy at birthdays, housewarmings and welcome home parties.

Pretzel Mold
Easy to mold;
1 design,
6 cavities.
2115-U-4437
$1.99

Lollipop Mold
1 design, 10 cavities.
2115-U-1715 $1.99

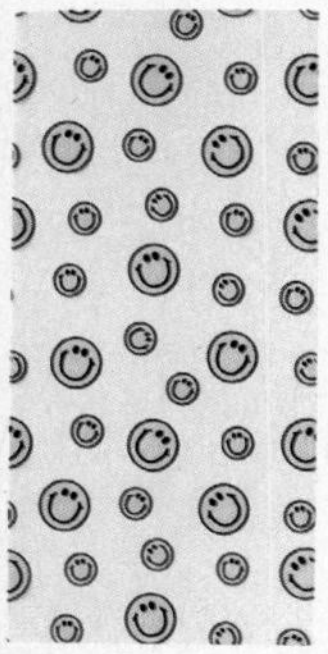

Party Bags
20 plastic bags, 20 ties included. 4 x 9.5 in.
1912-U-2361
Pk./20 $2.09

Baking Cups
Standard size 2 in. diameter.
415-U-261 Pk./50 $1.59

Candles
1½ in. high.
2811-U-9351 Set/6 $3.89

Candle Picks
2½ in. high.
2811-U-6327
Set/4 $3.89

Chunky Candles
Thicker candles to energize any cake! They feature bold textured spirals and a fun hand-carved shape on top.
3¼ in. high.
Pk./4 $3.89

Smiley Stars
2811-U-6325

Smiley Flames
2811-U-6326

RUBBER DUCKY

This bath-time favorite will make the biggest splash for birthdays, baby showers and school celebrations.

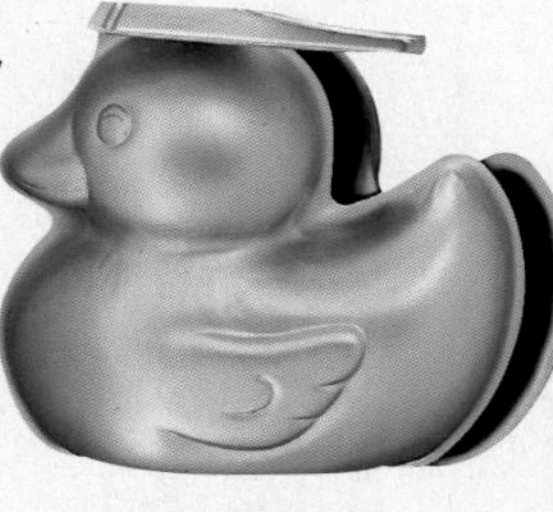

NEW!

Announcement Magnets
Printable magnets are easy to create online at **www.wiltonprint.com**. Includes 7.25 x 5.25 in. magnets and mailing envelopes, 3 test sheets.
3302-U-5523 Set/12 $9.99

3-D Cake Pan
Five adorable designs included. Two-piece pan takes 5½ cups batter. Aluminum.
2105-U-2094 $16.49

Candy Mold
1 design, 6 cavities.
2115-U-1565 $1.99

Candles
Handpainted details, clean-burning design.
1½ in. high.
2811-U-9337
Set/6 $3.89

Party Bags
20 plastic bags, 20 ties included.
4 x 9.5 in.
1912-U-1275
Pk./20 $2.09

Icing Decorations
Certified Kosher.
710-U-293 Pk./12 $2.29

NEW!

Baking Cups
Microwave-safe paper. Standard size, 2 in. diameter, mini size, 1.25 in. diameter.

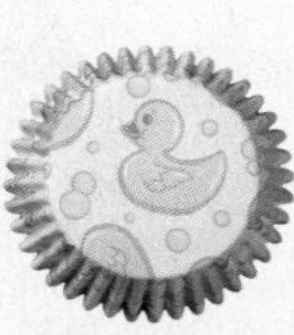

Ducky Standard
415-U-1016
Pk./75 $2.09
Mini 415-U-1017
Pk./100 $2.09

Rubber Ducky Standard
415-U-378
Pk./50 $1.59

NEW!

Guest Book
60 printed pages record guests' names, gifts received and good wishes. Perfect keepsake of the baby shower. 7.6 in x 5.75 in. x 0.3 in.
1003-U-1074 $5.99

PARTY

Theme Party Products

SPORTS

Here's the perfect game plan for your next party, whatever sport you favor: Action-packed, colorful ways to serve cakes, cupcakes or treats.

Sports Ball Pan Set
Includes two 6 in. diameter half-ball pans and two metal baking stands. Each pan half takes 2½ cups batter. Aluminum.
2105-U-6506 Set/4 $12.99

Mini Ball Pan
Ice two mini balls and push together for a 3-D effect. One cake mix makes 10–12 mini balls. Six cavities, each 3.5 x 3.5 x 1.5 in. deep. Aluminum.
2105-U-1760 $12.99

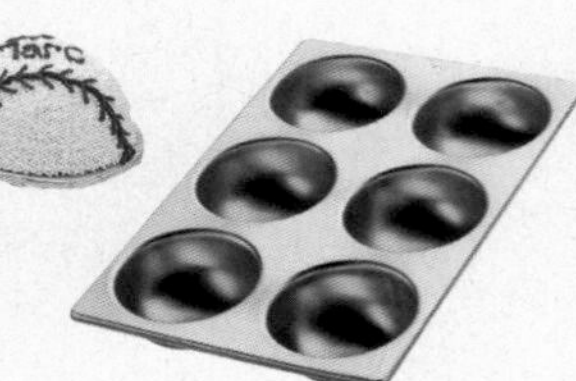

NEW!

Sports Cookie Candy Molds
With Cookie Candy Molds and easy-melting Wilton Candy Melts®, it's a breeze to add a great tasting and colorful candy design to your favorite cookies. Great for sandwich cream cookies or any round cookie 2 in. diameter or less. 4 designs, 8 cavities.
2115-U-1353 $1.99

NEW!

Sports Cake Stand Kit
The cake will look great on the easy-to-assemble cake stand with colorful decorative panels and cake board. Serve favors and snacks to match in bright treat bags with ties. Includes 11.5 x 3.25 in. high cake stand, 10 in. diameter cake board, 8 - 4 x 9.5 in. treat bags with ties, instruction sheet.
1509-U-1009 $9.99

NEW!

Cupcake Combo Pack
Quick and colorful way to serve cupcakes that set the tone for your celebration.
Contains 24 each 2 in. diameter baking cups and 3 in. high paper party picks.
415-U-1314 Pk./24 $2.19

NEW!

Sports Cupcake Stand Kit
It's an instant sports celebration, with a bright 3-tier cupcake stand, fun decorative topper, colorful baking cups and Fun Pix®! Includes 12 x 15 in. high stand, 24 - 2 in. diameter cups and 24 - 3 in. high picks. Holds up to 24 cupcakes.
1510-U-1009 $9.99

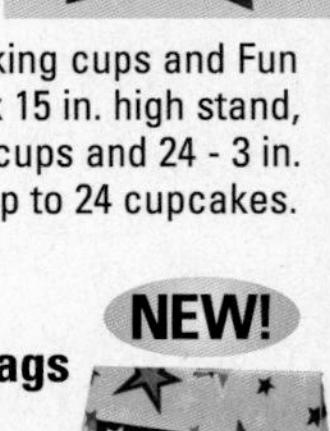

NEW!

Sports Favor Bags
Bring cheers with a bold bag at everyone's place! 4.5 x 1.75 x 4.75 in., Velcro close.
1904-U-1214 Pk./4 $2.09

BASEBALL/SOFTBALL

From Little League to World Series celebrations, cover the bases with 3-D cakes, bobbling player toppers and hit candles.

Take Me Out To The Ballgame Candles
Approx. 2 in. high.
2811-U-9341 Set/4 $3.89

Sports Lollipop Mold
Makes favorite sports balls from every season. 4 designs, 4 cavities.
2115-U-4432 $1.99

Baking Cups
Standard size 2 in. diameter.
415-U-298 Pk./50 $1.59

Icing Decorations
Certified Kosher.
710-U-475 Pk./9 $2.29

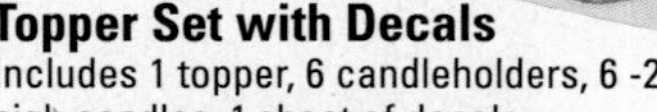

Topper Set with Decals
Includes 1 topper, 6 candleholders, 6 -2 in. high candles, 1 sheet of decals.
2811-U-8425 Set/14 $5.49

Baseball Topper Set*
Batter, catcher, three fielders and pitcher, 2.1 to 2.75 in. high.
2113-U-2155 Set/6 $3.19

Soccer Ball Pan
One-mix pan is 8.75 x 8.75 x 3.5 in. deep. Aluminum.
2105-U-2044 $12.99

*CAUTION: Contains small parts. Not recommended for use by children 3 years and under.

FOOTBALL

Touching down at Super Bowl parties, homecomings, award dinners and much more.

Sports Lollipop Mold
Makes favorite sports balls from every season.
4 design, 4 cavities.
2115-U-4432 $1.99

Baking Cups
Standard
2 in. diameter.
415-U-5152
Pk./75 $2.09
Mini
1.25 in. diameter.
415-U-5154
Pk./100 $2.09

Party Bags
20 plastic bags, 20 ties included. 4 x 9.5 in.
1912-U-1053
Pk./20 $2.09

First and Ten Football Pan
One-mix pan is 12 x 7.75 x 3 in. deep. Aluminum.
2105-U-6504
$12.99

Icing Decorations
Certified Kosher.
710-U-478
Pk./9 $2.29

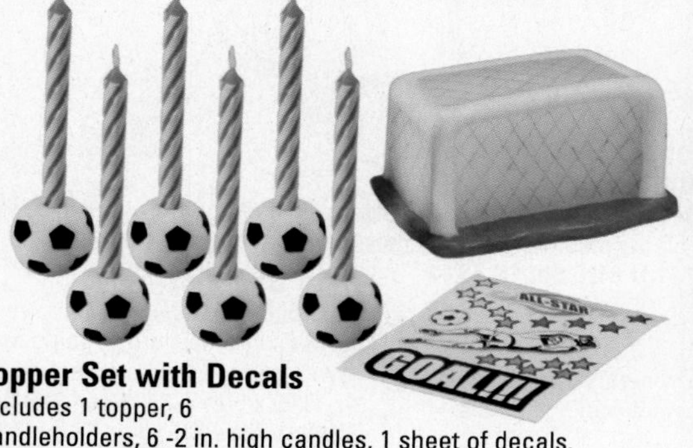

Topper Set with Decals
Includes 1 topper, 6 candleholders, 6 - 2 in. high. candles, 1 sheet of decals.
2811-U-8424
Set/14 $5.49

Football Topper Set*
Eight players and two goal posts, 1.5 to 4.5 in. high.
2113-U-2236
Set/10 $3.19

SOCCER

A great way to reward a season or a game well played!

Sports Lollipop Mold
Makes favorite sports balls from every season.
4 design, 4 cavities.
2115-U-4432 $1.99

Topper Set with Decals
Includes 1 topper, 6 candleholders, 6 -2 in. high candles, 1 sheet of decals.
2811-U-8421 Set/14 $5.49

Soccer Topper Set*
Seven players and two nets, 1.75 to 2 in. high.
2113-U-9002
Set/9 $3.19

Soccer Ball Pan
One-mix pan is 8.75 x 8.75 x 3.5 in. deep. Aluminum.
2105-U-2044 $12.99

Baking Cups
Standard size 2 in. diameter.
415-U-296 Pk./50 $1.59

Icing Decorations
Certified Kosher.
710-U-477
Pk./9 $2.29

HOCKEY

Topper Set With Decals
Includes 1 topper, 6 candleholders, 6 - 2 in. high candles, 1 sheet of decals.
2811-U-8422 Set/14 $5.49

*CAUTION: Contains small parts. Not recommended for use by children 3 years and under.

Theme Party Products

BASKETBALL

Slam dunk winners! Create thrilling cakes and candies.

Sports Lollipop Mold
Makes favorite sports balls from every season.
4 design, 4 cavities.
2115-U-4432 $1.99

Topper Set with Decals
Includes 1 topper, 6 candleholders, 6 - 2 in. high candles. 1 sheet of decals.
2811-U-8423 Set/14 $5.49

Basketball Topper Set*
Includes 1 forward, 2 centers, 3 guards and 1 hoop, 2.25 to 4 in. high.
2113-U-2237 Set/7 $3.19

Soccer Ball Pan
One-mix pan is 8.75 x 8.75 x 3.5 in. deep. Aluminum.
2105-U-2044 $12.99

GOLF

Great ways to top cakes with perfect form.

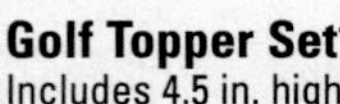

Topper Set with Decals
Includes 1 topper, 6 candleholders, 6 - 2 in. high candles. 1 sheet of decals.
2811-U-8420 Set/14 $5.49

NEW!

Golf Bag Pan
A stroke of genius for your favorite golfer's birthday, group golf outings, awards dinners and more. One-mix pan is 13.25 x 8.25 x 2 in. deep. Aluminum.
2105-U-1024 $12.99

Golf Topper Set*
Includes 4.5 in. high golfer plus three each: 2.5 in. wide greens, 4 in. high flags, 5 in. clubs and golf balls.
1306-U-7274 Set/13 $3.19

FISHING

Land the perfect cake for your angler, with bright candles and toppers.

Tropical Fish Pan
Everyone will be hooked by this fish—it's a keeper! One-mix pan is 11.5 x 12.5 x 2 in. deep. Aluminum.
2105-U-1014 $12.99

Frustrated Fisherman Topper*
4.5 in. high.
2113-U-2384 $3.69

Tropical Fish Candles
Approx. 1½ in. high.
2811-U-9333 Set/4 $3.89

*CAUTION: Contains small parts. Not recommended for use by children 3 years and under.

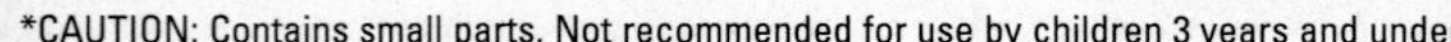

Baking Cups

The easiest way to dress up a cupcake! Ideal for holding candy and nuts, too.

Made of microwave-safe paper unless otherwise noted. Jumbo cups are 2.25 in. diameter, standard cups are 2 in. diameter, mini cups are 1.25 in. diameter, candy cups are 1 in. diameter.

NEW!

Lilac Polka Dots $2.09
Mini
120-U-168 Pk./100

NEW!

Pink Polka Dots $2.09
Standard
120-U-169 Pk./75

Dazzling Dots $1.59
Standard
415-U-582 Pk./50
Mini
415-U-1141 Pk./75

Snappy Stripes $1.59
Standard
415-U-581 Pk./50
Mini
415-U-1140 Pk./75

White $1.59
Jumbo 415-U-2503 Pk/50
Standard 415-U-2505 Pk./75
Mini 415-U-2507 Pk./100

Assorted Pastel $1.59
25 pink, 25 yellow, 25 blue.
Standard 415-U-394
Pk./75

Gold Foil $1.59
Wax-laminated paper on foil.
Standard 415-U-206 Pk./24
Candy 415-U-306 Pk./75

Silver Foil $1.59
Wax-laminated paper on foil.
Standard 415-U-207 Pk./24
Candy 415-U-307 Pk./75

Petite Loaf Cups*
Microwave-safe paper.
White
415-U-450 Pk./50 $1.59

Nut and Party Cups
Mini 1.25 oz.
415-U-500 Pk./36 $1.79
Standard 3.25 oz.
415-U-400 Pk./24 $1.79

*Petite Loaf Cups are 3¼ x 2 in. and fit Petite Loaf Pan p. 154.

Add-A-Message Fun Pix®

Serve party cupcakes in an exciting new way —clip on messages, pictures and more with these colorful plastic picks! Great for place markers, announcing awards at banquets and favorite sayings. Four fun colors to go with your favorite baking cups. 3 in. high.
2113-U-7611 Pk./12 $2.09

Party Bags

Wrap up cookies, candies, favors and more with color and fun!

Contains 20, 4 x 9.5 in. bags and 20 twist ties, unless otherwise noted.
Pk./20 $2.09

Clear (not shown)
1912-U-1240
Pk./25 $2.09

Dazzling Dots
1912-U-1090

Snappy Stripes
1912-U-1089

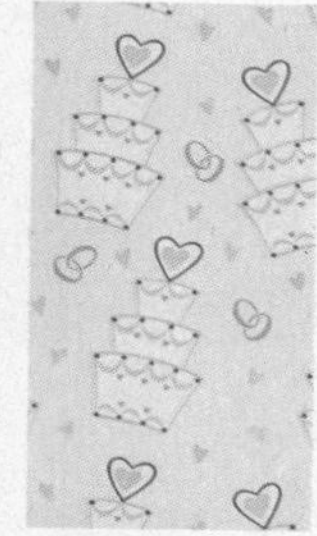

Wedding Cake
1912-U-1086

Wedding
1912-U-2364

Colorful Stars
1912-U-2362

Baby
1912-U-2365

Blue
1912-U-2356

Yellow
1912-U-2359

Pink
1912-U-2363

Red
1912-U-2357

Icing Decorations

Wilton Icing Decorations are perfect for topping cupcakes, cookies and ice cream. Mint-flavored edible shapes are Certified Kosher.

HAPPY BIRTHDAY

Alphabet/Numerals
710-U-494 Pk./70 $2.29

HAPPY BIRTHDAY

Script Alphabet
710-U-546 Pk./62 $2.29

Happy Birthday with Balloons
710-U-547 Pk./21 $2.29

NUMERALS

Festive way to mark age or year. Edged in green unless specified. 3 in. high.
$0.89

#1	**Pink #1**	**Blue #1**
2811-U-9101	**2811-U-240**	**2811-U-241**

#2	**2811-U-9102**	**#6**	**2811-U-9106**	**#9**	**2811-U-9109**
#3	**2811-U-9103**	**#7**	**2811-U-9107**	**#0**	**2811-U-9100**
#4	**2811-U-9104**	**#8**	**2811-U-9108**	**?**	**2811-U-9110**
#5	**2811-U-9105**				

PARTY

Candles

CANDLE SETS

Wilton gives you more choices! Top your cake with candles in the perfect colors—and check out our exciting designs.

Farm
Approx. 1⅝ in. high.
2811-U-9347
Set/4 $3.89

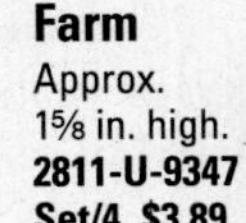

Firefighting
Approx. 1½ in. high.
2811-U-9339
Set/4 $3.89

Baby Things
Approx. 2 in. high.
2811-U-855 Set/4 $3.89

Fiesta
Approx. 1¾ in. high.
2811-U-9345 Set/4 $3.89

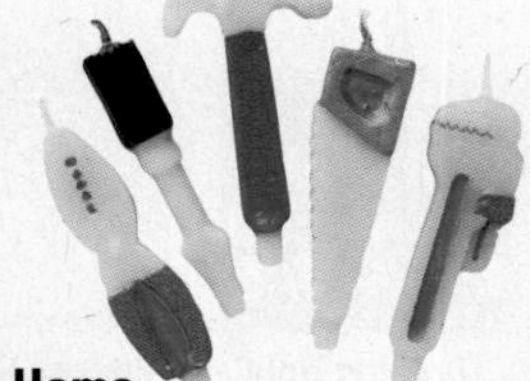

Home Improvement Tools
Approx. 2¼ in. high.
2811-U-9136 Set/5 $3.89

Construction Vehicles
Approx. 1¾ in. long.
2811-U-858 Set/4 $3.89

Race Cars
Approx. 1¾ in. high.
2811-U-9135 Set/4 $3.89

Beach Sandals
⅜ in. high,
⅞ in. long.
2811-U-9352
Set/6 $3.89

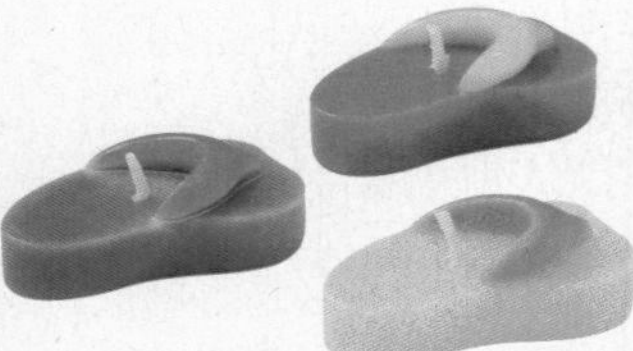

Margaritas
1¼ in. high.
2811-U-9343
Set/6 $3.89

Champagne Bottles
2 in. high.
2811-U-163 Set/6 $3.89

Beer Cans
1¾ in. high.
2811-U-9326
Set/6 $3.89

NOVELTY

Glow-in-the-Dark
They light up the room even before you light them! These luminous candles will lend an extra touch of fun to any celebration. Assorted colors: white, yellow, green, blue.
2½ in. high.
2811-U-165
Pk./10 $2.19

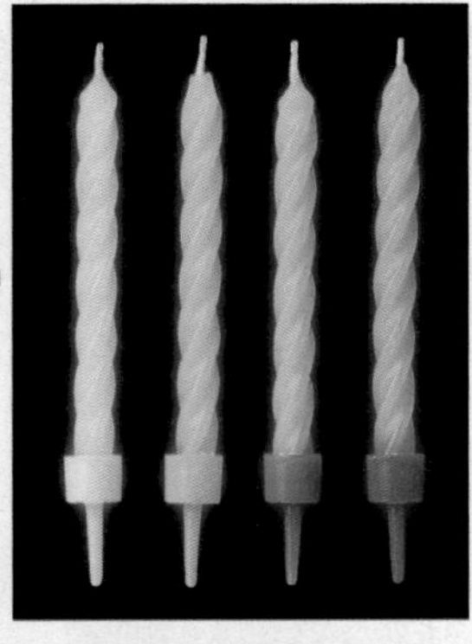

Glow Candle Set
Turn out the lights and get ready to serve your cake in a thrilling glow of color. Set of 4 light stick candle holders with candles gives cakes an aura of excitement that lasts up to 6 hours. No batteries needed—the glow starts when you bend the light sticks. Includes 4 each light sticks, connectors and candles.
6½ in. high.
2811-U-6215
Set/4 $5.59

PICK SETS

Put your celebration message in lights! These bright candle picks are a unique and easy way to pick up the party theme on your cake top. Fun colors are just right for the occasion.

Happy Birthday
1¾ in. high.
2811-U-785
Set/15 $2.19

Congratulations
1¾ in. high.
2811-U-787 Set/15 $2.19

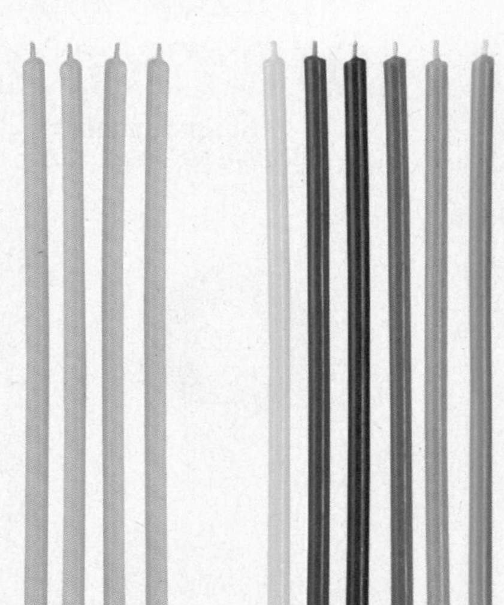

Longs
Sized right for larger cakes or for making a bold statement on any cake. 5⅞ in. high. **Pk./12 $2.19**

White **2811-U-773**
Multicolor **2811-U-777**

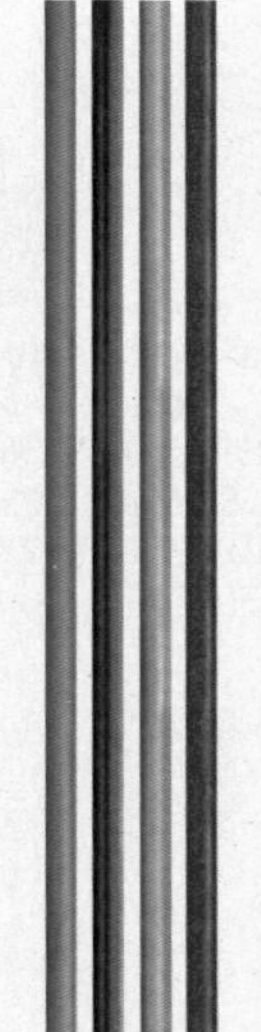

Slenders
6½ in. high.
2811-U-1188
Pk./24 $0.89

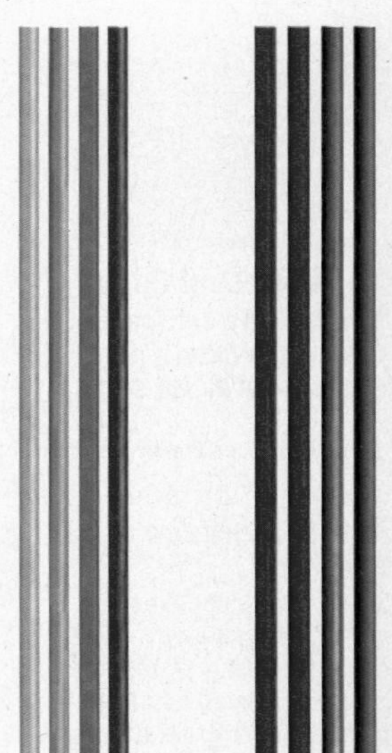

"Trick" Sparklers
Blow 'em out—they relight!
6½ in. high. **Pk./18 $1.09**

Assorted **2811-U-1230**
Red and Blue **2811-U-704**

RAINBOW COLORS

Curly
Twisting, turning fun. 3 in. high.
2811-U-9127
Pk./12 $1.69

Candle Holders
Protect cakes and keep candles secure. Great colors, 1 in. high.
2811-U-552
Pk./24 $1.09

CLASSIC

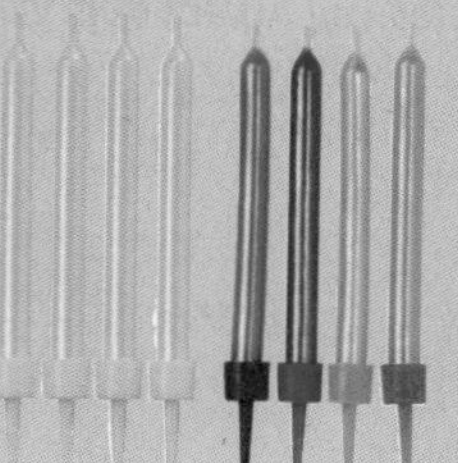

Pearlized
Watch them shimmer from the moment you light them! 2½ in. high.
Pk./10 $2.19
White
2811-U-3658
Multicolor
2811-U-3665

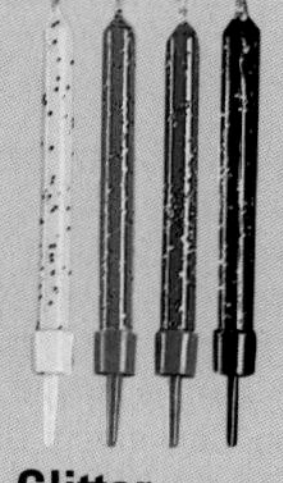

Glitter
2½ in. high.
Pk./10 $1.09
White
2811-U-248
Pink 2811-U-244
Blue 2811-U-246
Black
2811-U-247

Celebration
2½ in. high.
Pk./24 $0.79
White 2811-U-207
Pink 2811-U-213
Red 2811-U-209
Blue 2811-U-210
Black 2811-U-224

Assorted Celebration
Classic spirals in attractive two-tones.
2½ in. high.
2811-U-215
Pk./24 $0.79

"Trick"
Blow 'em out —they relight!
2½ in. high.
Assorted: White, Yellow, Pink, Blue.
2811-U-220
Pk./10 $1.09

Silver and Gold
2¼ in. high.
Pk./10
$1.69
Silver
2811-U-9123
Gold
2811-U-9122

Shimmer
2½ in. high.
2811-U-3663
Pk./10 $2.19

Lattice
2½ in. high.
2811-U-3656
Pk./10 $2.19

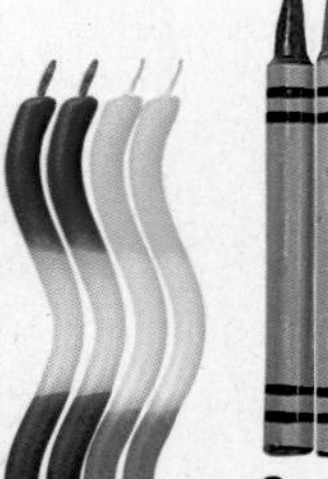

Tricolor
2½ in. high.
2811-U-779
Pk./10 $2.19

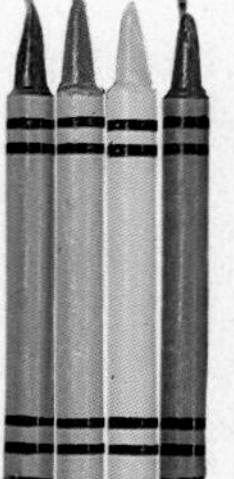

Crayons
3¼ in. high. **$1.69**
2811-U-226 Pk./8
2½ in. high. **$1.69**
2811-U-227 Pk./10

Triangle "Trick" Sparklers
2½ in. high.
2811-U-278
Pk./9 $1.09

Wavy "Trick" Sparklers
2½ in. high.
2811-U-272
Pk./10 $2.19

Rounds
2½ in. high.
2811-U-284
Pk./24
$0.79

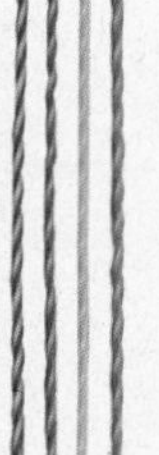

Party Thins
8 in. high.
2811-U-239
Pk./20
$1.09

HOT COLORS

Shimmer
2½ in. high.
2811-U-3662
Pk./10 $2.19

Lattice
2½ in. high.
2811-U-3655
Pk./10 $2.19

Twist
2½ in. high.
2811-U-3659
Pk./8 $2.79

Rounds
2½ in. high.
2811-U-225
Pk./24 $0.79

Tricolor
2½ in. high.
2811-U-781
Pk./10
$2.19

Crayons
3¼ in. high.
2811-U-282
Pk./8 $1.69

Triangle "Trick" Sparklers
2½ in. high.
2811-U-276
Pk./9 $1.09

Wavy "Trick" Sparklers
2½ in. high.
2811-U-270
Pk./10 $2.19

Party Thins
8 in. high.
2811-U-237
Pk./20
$1.09

SOFT COLORS

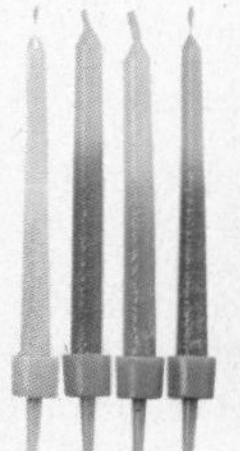

Shimmer
2½ in. high.
2811-U-3664
Pk./10 $2.19

Lattice
2½ in. high.
2811-U-3657
Pk./10 $2.19

Tricolor
2½ in. high.
2811-U-782
Pk./10 $2.19

Wavy "Trick" Sparklers
2½ in. high.
2811-U-289
Pk./10 $2.19

Crayons
3¼ in. high.
2811-U-292
Pk./8 $1.69

Triangle "Trick" Sparklers
2½ in. high.
2811-U-288
Pk./9 $1.09

Rounds
2½ in. high.
2811-U-291
Pk./24
$0.79

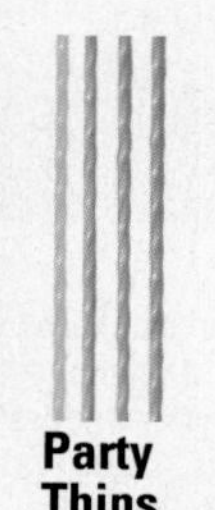

Party Thins
8 in. high.
2811-U-255
Pk./20
$1.09

Musical Candle
Plays "Happy Birthday To You".
4¾ in. high.
2811-U-1231 $4.09

Cake Toppers and Stands

With Wilton toppers, a decorated cake is just minutes away! The excellent detail you expect from Wilton is evident in every design.

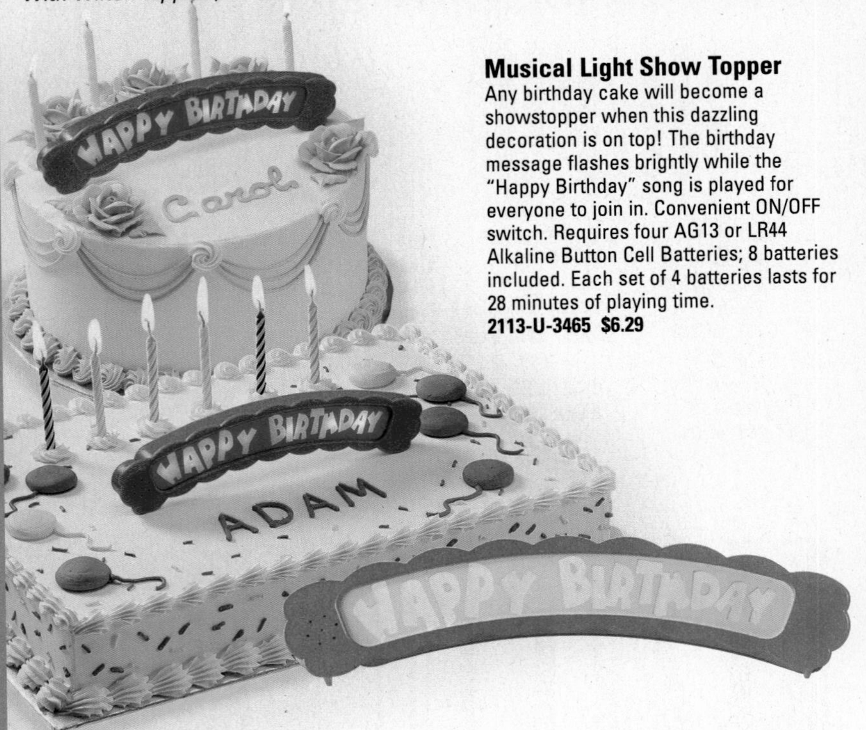

Musical Light Show Topper
Any birthday cake will become a showstopper when this dazzling decoration is on top! The birthday message flashes brightly while the "Happy Birthday" song is played for everyone to join in. Convenient ON/OFF switch. Requires four AG13 or LR44 Alkaline Button Cell Batteries; 8 batteries included. Each set of 4 batteries lasts for 28 minutes of playing time.
2113-U-3465 $6.29

DOLL PICKS

Teen Doll Pick
Her hair and face are prettier than ever—she'll give your Wonder Mold cakes a realism and sophistication unlike anything you've seen. 7¾ in. high with pick. **$3.19**
Brunette 2815-U-101
Blond 2815-U-102
Ethnic 2815-U-103

Mini Doll Pick Set
4¼ in. high with pick.
1511-U-1019
Set/4 $6.29

Circus Animals Set*
Handpainted performers, 2.5 to 3 in. high.
2113-U-9422 Set/4 $4.19

Dinosaur Party Set*
Reptile revelry! 1.75 to 2.5 in. high.
2113-U-9420 Set/4 $4.19

Tumbling Bears Set*
Adorable acrobats, 2 to 2.5 in. high.
2113-U-9421 Set/4 $4.19

Small Derby Clowns Set*
2 in. high with pick.
2113-U-2759
Set/6 $2.09

Circus Balloons Set
12 in a bunch, 3 bunches per set, 6.5 in. high.
2113-U-2366 Set/36 $3.19

*CAUTION: Contains small parts. Not recommended for use by children 3 years and under

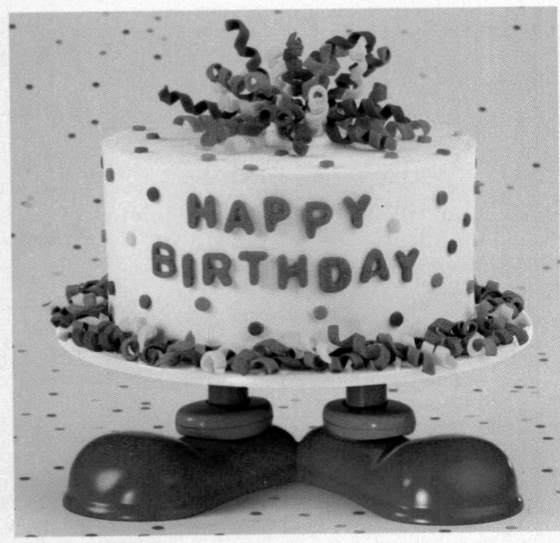

Silly-Feet! Cake Stand
Everyone will get a kick out of your cake when it's served on this fun, footed stand. Just insert the plate onto the foot support, add your decorated cake, cupcakes or other desserts. Then, watch your friends make tracks to your treats! Take the fun a step further—bake and serve cupcakes in Silly-Feet! Silicone Baking Cups (p. 147). 10 in. cake plate holds an 8 in. or 9 in. round cake.
307-U-878 $14.99

RELIGIOUS

Inspiring decorations add a beautiful touch to spiritual events —Christening, Communion, Confirmation, La Quinceañera and more!

La Quinceañera
Honor her on her 15th birthday celebration. Use as cake top decoration or as a favor. Height: 4.5 in. Base: 2.75 in. diameter. Plastic.
203-U-305 $3.99

Inspirational Cross
Polished resin with finely sculpted scroll and bead highlighting. 5.5 in. high.
202-U-398 $14.99

Faith Cross Cake Pick
Sparkling cross decoration looks beautiful in cake tops, centerpieces, floral arrangements. Accented with rhinestones, crafted of painted resin. 4 in. high cross with 2 in. pick.
1006-U-4475 $14.99

Communion Boy†
3.5 in. high.
2113-U-7886
$3.69

Communion Girl†
3.5 in. high.
2113-U-7878
$3.69

† Designed by Ellen Williams

Entertaining

Every big event needs a main attraction—Wilton Fountains will be the most popular stop at the party! Each great-looking design will complement your celebration décor.

CELEBRATE!® PARTY FOUNTAIN

The fountain that's filled with design possibilities!

- Easy to assemble—no tools needed!
- Quiet, no-splash design
- Precision spouts for a neat, even flow
- Contoured rim is the perfect fill line
- Illuminated base adds a dramatic glow
- Holds up to 3 gallons

The Celebrate! Party Fountain is the most versatile beverage fountain you can buy. It's made to be customized to your celebration! Add drama and sparkle with its illuminated base, or display unlit and accented with favorite flowers, holiday decorations and more. Tailor the light color to match your décor. Top off the fountain 2 ways—use the included ornamental plate to show off favorite figurines, floral bouquets and holiday accents. Or use the graceful tulip top to create a simple, elegant silhouette. No tools needed—just assemble pieces using numbers as guides, then add up to 3 gallons of your favorite beverage. Not designed to heat or cool beverages or for use with beverages containing pulp. 120V; UL listed.

2104-U-9009 $149.99

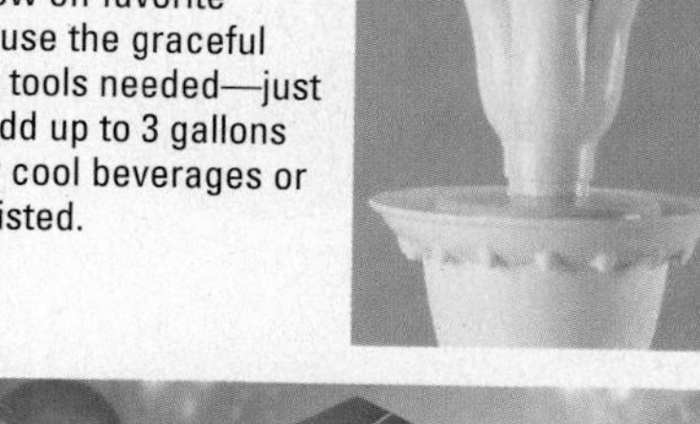

CHOCOLATE PRO® CHOCOLATE FOUNTAIN

- Holds 4 lbs. of melted chocolate
- Tiers come apart for easy cleaning
- Three adjustable feet, plus bubble level, allow perfect leveling from all angles

Bring the excitement of chocolate dipping to your next party! The Chocolate Pro® Chocolate Fountain makes it easy to enjoy delicious hand-dipped desserts any time! The graceful canopy style creates an elegant flow from all 3 levels; the bowl is designed to keep chocolate melted and flowing.

With the Chocolate Pro®, any celebration becomes more special. Let your guests dip cake and cookies for a flavorful finishing touch. Great for fruit, or try a sweet and salty combination by dipping potato chips and pretzels. 120V; UL listed.

2104-U-9008 $109.99

CHOCOLATE PRO® FOUNTAIN AND FONDUE CHOCOLATE

The best real melting chocolate for fountains and fondues is here! Made from premium ingredients for superior melting and a delicious chocolate taste. Ideal texture and rich flavor for making dipped desserts. No tempering needed! 2 lbs.

2104-U-2618 $15.79

ENTERTAINING

Seasonal

Wilton makes every time of year worth celebrating! With so many fun ways to serve cakes, cookies and other treats, it's easy to let everyone taste the excitement of each season.

HALLOWEEN

Bakeware

NEW!

Non-Stick Jack-O-Lantern Mini Cakes Pan

Bake fun single-size cakes, brownies and more. Non-stick steel releases treats easily. One mix makes 24 - 28 jack-o-lanterns, each 3.75 x 1.25 in. deep.
2105-U-1541
$11.99

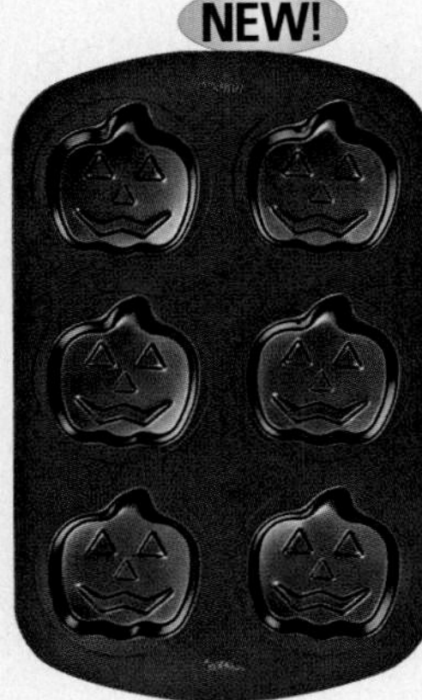

Spooky Ghost Pan

A welcome vision at all your Halloween happenings—from costume parties at home to celebrations at school. Great for easy-to-decorate cakes and gelatin desserts. One-mix pan is 11.5 x 11.5 x 2 in. deep. Aluminum.
2105-U-2090 $9.99

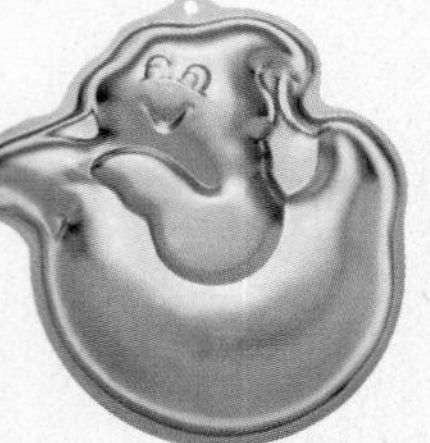

NEW!

SILICONE MOLDS

Discover the convenience and easy release of flexible silicone bakeware! Freezer, refrigerator, microwave and dishwasher safe—oven safe to 500°F. **$9.99**

Mini Spiders & Webs Mold

One mix makes 20 - 24 spiders and webs. 6 cavities, each 2.5 x 1.5 in. deep.
2105-U-4904

Mini Ghost Mold

One mix makes 20-24 ghosts. 6 cavities, each 2.5 x 1.5 in. deep.
2105-U-4877

Mini Jack-O-Lantern Mold

One mix makes 20-24 jack-o-lanterns. 6 cavities, each 2.5 x 1.5 in. deep.
2105-U-4815

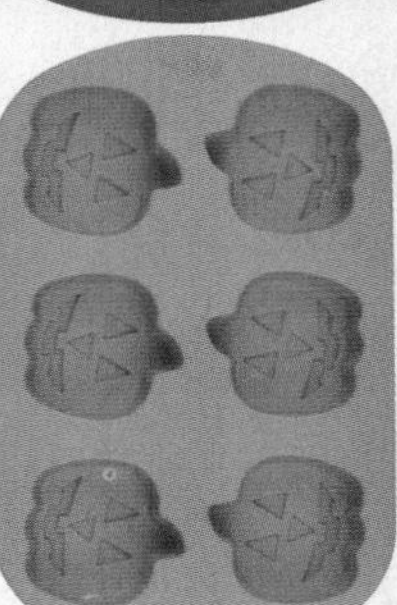

Non-Stick Mini Pumpkin and Ghost Pan

Perfect size for trick-or-treaters! Non-stick steel releases treats easily. One mix makes 24-28 treats. 6 cavities, each 2.75 x 1.25 in. deep.
2105-U-1540 $8.99

Iridescents! Jack-O-Lantern Pan

This bright, colorful shape is as much fun for serving party treats as it is for baking! Designed for quick, easy cake decorating. Also ideal for crisped rice cereal treats, molded gelatin, bread dough and more. One-mix pan is 11.75 x 11.2 x 2 in. deep. Aluminum.
2105-U-2059 $7.49

Petite Jack-O-Lantern Pan

Make personal petite smiling pumpkins. One mix makes 9-13 dozen jack-o-lanterns. 12 cavities, each 2 x 1.2 in. deep. Aluminum.
2105-U-8462 $11.99

Mini Ghost Pan

Create gobs of goblins at one time! One mix makes 9-15 ghosts ready for decorating. 6 cavities, each 4 x 4.9 x 1.4 in. deep. Aluminum.
2105-U-3845 $12.99

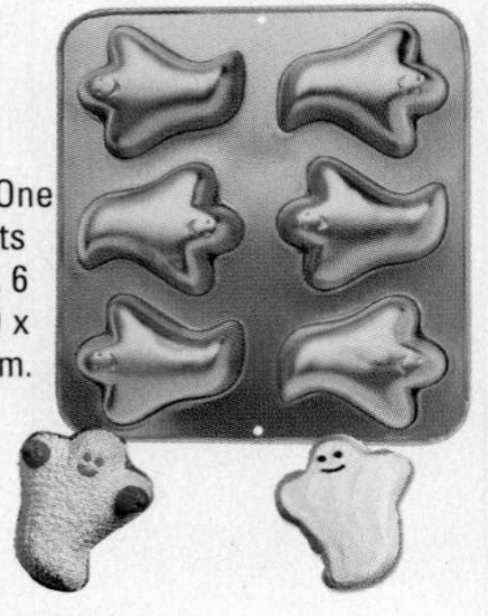

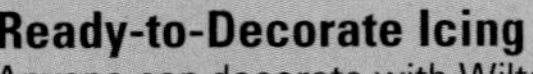

Icings

See Color Guide at right.

Ready-to-Decorate Icing

Anyone can decorate with Wilton Ready-to-Decorate Icing! Our brilliant colors and 4 decorating tips make it a breeze to add an exciting finishing touch to treats—without mixing or mess. 6.4 oz. Certified Kosher. **$4.29**

Orange	**710-U-4410**
Black	**710-U-4404**
Violet	**710-U-4408**
White	**710-U-4402**

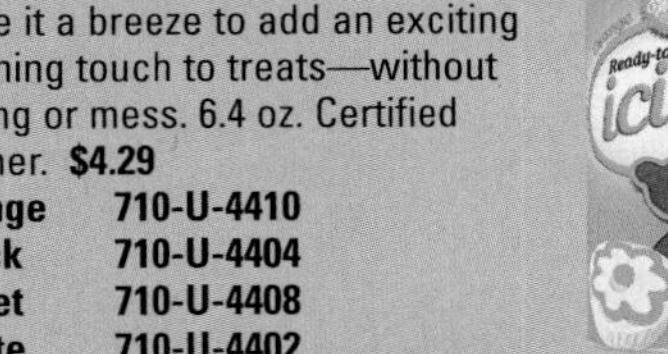

Tube Decorating Gel

Transparent gels are great for writing messages and decorating cakes and cookies. Colors match Wilton Icing Colors (p. 134). .75 oz. Certified Kosher. **$1.49**

Orange	**704-U-312**
Black	**704-U-306**
Violet	**704-U-342**
White	**704-U-302**

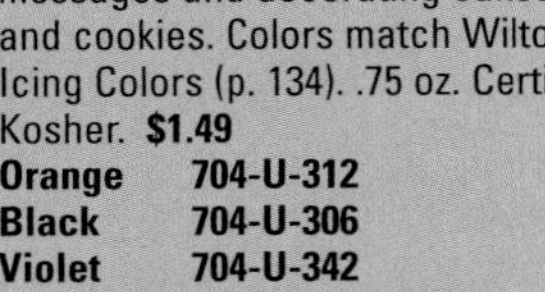

White Cookie Icing

Easy to use—just heat and squeeze onto cookies using the convenient cap. Sets smooth in just 45 minutes. 10 oz. bottle covers approximately 12 cookies, 3 in. each; 20 oz. bottle covers approx. 24. Certified Kosher.

10 oz. Bottle	**704-U-481**	**$4.49**
20 oz. Bottle	**704-U-492**	**$7.99**

Tube Decorating Icing

Tubes can be used with our Tip and Nail Set or Coupler Ring Set (p. 134) and any standard size Wilton metal tip. Colors match Wilton Icing Colors (p. 134). 4.25 oz. Certified Kosher. **$1.99**

Orange	**704-U-212**
Black	**704-U-206**
Violet	**704-U-242**
White	**704-U-200**

Party

Baking Cups
Microwave-safe paper. Standard size, 2 in. diameter; Mini size, 1.25 in. diameter.
Standard Pk./75 $2.09
Mini Pk./100 $2.09

NEW!

Boo! Scary!
Standard 415-U-1709
Mini 415-U-1710

Happy Haunters
Standard 415-U-961
Mini 415-U-962

Spooky Ghosts
Standard 415-U-1601
Mini 415-U-2027

Silicone Baking Cups
No muffin pan needed! Bake and serve in these reusable oven-safe cups. 6 violet, 6 orange.
Standard 415-U-9408 Pk./12 $9.99

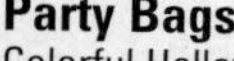

Party Bags
Colorful Halloween designs for candy and cookie treats. Unless otherwise noted, 20 plastic bags, 20 ties included. 4 x 9.5 in.
Pk./20 $2.09

NEW!

Boo! Scary!
1912-U-1225

Happy Haunters
1912-U-2389

Spooky Ghosts
1912-U-1040

NEW!

Boo! Scary! Shaped Bags with Drawstring
Large bags are 6 x 9 in.
1912-U-1222
Pk./15 $2.09

Icing Decorations
Perfect for topping cakes, cupcakes and cookies. Certified Kosher. **$2.29**

Smiling Pumpkins
710-U-7200 Pk./12

NEW!

Spiders & Bats
710-U-187 Pk./10

Petite Ghosts
710-U-3030 Pk./12

NEW!

Fun Pix®
Add a spooky touch to cakes, cupcakes, ice cream and more. Approx. 3½ in. high.
$2.09

Boo! Scary!
Plastic.
2113-U-1307
Pk./12

Happy Haunters
Paper.
2113-U-9216
Pk./12

Halloween Cupcake and Cookie Stencils
Just place one of the fun designs over your baked treat, then sprinkle with Wilton Cake Sparkles™ or Colored Sugars (p. 196) or spray with Color Mist™ Food Color Spray (sold below). 8 designs.
417-U-499 $2.19

Happy Haunters Cupcake Box
Brightly-patterned window boxes are the perfect way to hold and display your cupcakes! Each box includes an insert with recessed space to hold standard cupcakes safely in place. Easy to fold assembly; great for gifts and favors! Holds 4 standard cupcakes. 6.25 x 6.25 x 3 in.
415-U-3220 Pk./3 $5.29

Colors

Halloween Icing Colors Set
.5 oz. jars of Black and Orange. Certified Kosher.
601-U-3010 Set/2 $2.99

FoodWriter™ Edible Color Markers

Use like ink markers to add fun, dazzling color to foods. Decorate on fondant, color flow, royal icing designs and cookie icing. Includes Black and Orange markers (.07 oz. each). Certified Kosher.
609-U-101 Set/2 $4.19

HALLOWEEN COLOR GUIDE

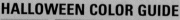

Orange	Black	Violet	White

Color Mist™ Food Color Spray
Gives decorators the versatility and dazzling effects of an airbrush in a convenient can! Use it to add sensational color to iced cookies and cupcakes. No mess, taste-free formula. 1.5 oz. Certified Kosher.
$3.29

Orange	**710-U-5507**
Black	**710-U-5506**
Violet	**710-U-5504**

NEW!

Halloween Cupcakes 'N More® Dessert Stand
Cupcakes are the perfect way to add a personal touch to your Halloween party! Great for caramel apples and party favor bags, too! 9.25 in. high x 9 in. wide. Holds 13 standard cupcakes.
307-U-828 $13.69

Candy

NEW!

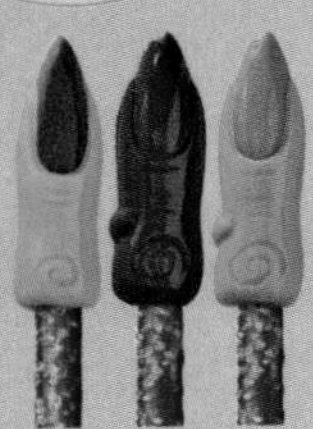

Witch Fingers Pretzel Mold
2 designs, 6 cavities.
2115-U-1616 $1.99

NEW!

Haunted Halloween Pretzel Mold
2 designs, 6 cavities.
2115-U-1417 $1.99

NEW!

Mummies Pretzel Mold
1 design, 6 cavities.
2115-U-1783 $1.99

Halloween Pretzel Mold
1 design, 6 cavities.
2115-U-1500 $1.99

NEW!

Creepy Tombstone Candy Mold
Makes 3 creepy tombstones with interchangeable bases.
2115-U-1415 $1.99

Happy Haunters Candy Mold
4 designs, 4 cavities.
2115-U-1436 $1.99

Monsters Candy Mold
4 designs, 4 cavities.
2115-U-1752 $1.99

Smiling Pumpkins Lollipop Mold
1 design, 7 cavities.
2115-U-1750 $1.99

NEW!

Halloween Candy Making MEGA PACK

Everything you need to make dozens of tasty lollipops and candies for your trick-or-treaters and ghoulish guests. It's easy and fun, with lots of fun shapes and colorful Candy Melts®! Kit includes: 3 molds: Monster Large Lollipop Mold (4 designs, 4 cavities), Spiders and Bats Candy Mold (2 designs, 8 cavities), Ghosts and Jack-O-Lantern Lollipop Mold (2 designs, 6 cavities); 16 oz. Candy Melts brand confectionery coating (4 oz. each light cocoa, white, orange and green); 20 lollipop sticks (6 in.); 4 disposable decorating bags; decorating brush and 20 party bags/ties.
2104-U-3219 $9.99

Candy Melts®*

Ideal for molding, dipping or coating. Artificially vanilla flavored unless otherwise indicated. 14 oz. bag. Certified Kosher Dairy. **$2.79**

Orange	**1911-U-1631**
Yellow	**1911-U-463**
Dark Green	**1911-U-405**
Dark Cocoa	**1911-U-358**
Light Cocoa	**1911-U-544**
Dark Cocoa Mint	**1911-U-1920**
White	**1911-U-498**
Lavender	**1911-U-403**

*Brand confectionery coating.

Halloween Candy Necklace Kit

It's the perfect party activity—kit makes 8 tasty necklaces! Give each kid their own candy necklace pack and watch them have a ball stringing their own treats to wear and share. They'll love the cool colors and great flavors—and stringing the candy beads and charm is a breeze. Includes 8 necklace packs; each pack contains over 50 candy beads (artificial orange and grape flavors), 1 candy pumpkin charm (artificial orange flavor) and 17.5 in. elastic string.
2104-U-1274 $3.19

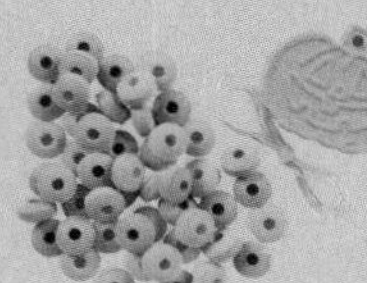

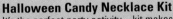

See pages 166-169 for more Wilton candy items.

Sprinkles

INDIVIDUAL BOTTLES

Shake up your Halloween treats with fun colors and designs. Try our Jumbo Sprinkles—big bold toppers perfect for brownies, cookies and more. Plastic bottles for convenient pouring and storing. Certified Kosher.

Hallow Pumpkin Mix
2.5 oz. bottle.
710-U-182 $2.29

Jumbo Ghost
3 oz. bottle.
710-U-567 $4.09

Halloween Confetti
2 oz. bottle.
710-U-184 $2.29

Ghost Mix
2.5 oz. bottle.
710-U-767 $2.29

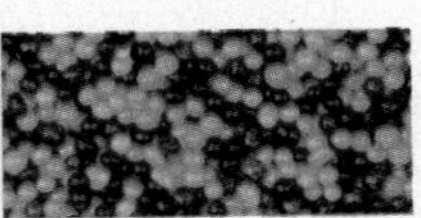

Halloween Nonpareils
3 oz. bottle.
710-U-584 $2.29
5.25 oz. bottle.
710-U-183 $3.29

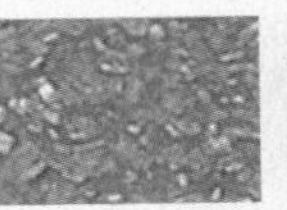

Orange Sugar
3.25 oz. bottle.
710-U-759
$2.29

Black Sugar
3.25 oz. bottle.
710-U-762
$2.29

Lavender Sugar
3.25 oz. bottle.
710-U-758
$2.29

Sparkling Sugars

Coarse texture; brilliant sparkle. 8 oz. Certified Kosher. **$4.49**

Orange/Black
710-U-307

Orange/White
710-U-572

Cake Sparkles™

Edible glitter, .25 oz. bottle. Certified Kosher. **$3.19**

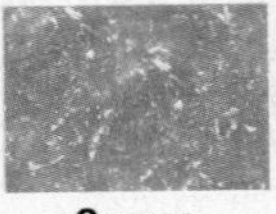

Orange
703-U-1308

Black
703-U-1302

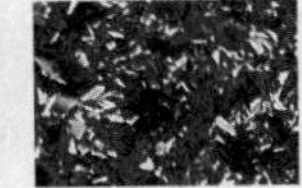

Purple
703-U-1266

ASSORTMENTS

4-Mix Halloween

Includes Hallow Pumpkin Mix, Halloween Nonpareils, Black and Orange Sugars. 4.4 oz. Certified Kosher.
710-U-728 $4.99

6-Mix Halloween Pumpkin

Includes Black and Orange Nonpareils, Halloween Confetti, Hallow Pumpkin Mix, Black, Orange and Purple Sugars. 7.1 oz. Certified Kosher.
710-U-185 $5.99

Cookie Cutters

Halloween Push 'N Print™ Cutter Set

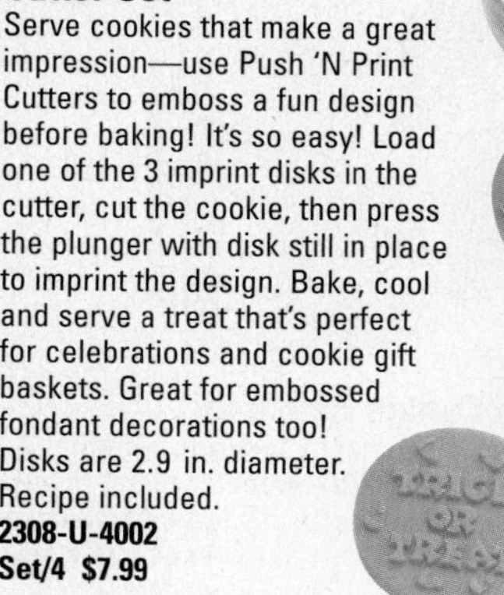

Serve cookies that make a great impression—use Push 'N Print Cutters to emboss a fun design before baking! It's so easy! Load one of the 3 imprint disks in the cutter, cut the cookie, then press the plunger with disk still in place to imprint the design. Bake, cool and serve a treat that's perfect for celebrations and cookie gift baskets. Great for embossed fondant decorations too! Disks are 2.9 in. diameter. Recipe included.
2308-U-4002
Set/4 $7.99

COMFORT GRIP™ CUTTERS

These easy-grip cutters with extra-deep sides are perfect for cutting so many favorite foods into spectacular shapes. The cushion grip gives you comfortable control even when cutting thick desserts. Recipe included.
Stainless steel sides, 4.5 x 4.5 x 1.5 in. deep.
$3.19

Pumpkin
2310-U-600

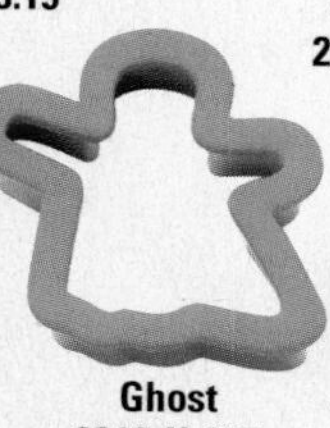

Witch's Hat
2310-U-630

Ghost
2310-U-607

4 PC. GRIPPY™ CUTTER SET

Safe, easy cutting, with a comfortable grip and deep plastic sides. Four shapes include ghost, cat, pumpkin and bat, approx. 3.5 in.
2311-U-257
Set/4 $4.49

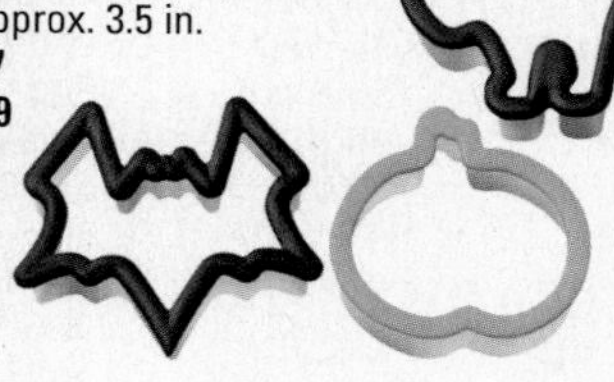

COOKIE TREAT PAN

Jack-O-Lantern

Create cookie blossoms, rice cereal treats and candy pops. Recipe included. Six-cavity pan, each cavity measures 3.25 x .25 in. deep. Aluminum.
2105-U-8100 $9.99

Cookie Treat Sticks

6 in. 1912-U-9319
Pk./20 $1.99
8 in. 1912-U-9318
Pk./20 $2.99

METAL CUTTERS

Put variety in your cookie making with fun Halloween multi-shape sets. There are styles to please everyone. Recipe included.

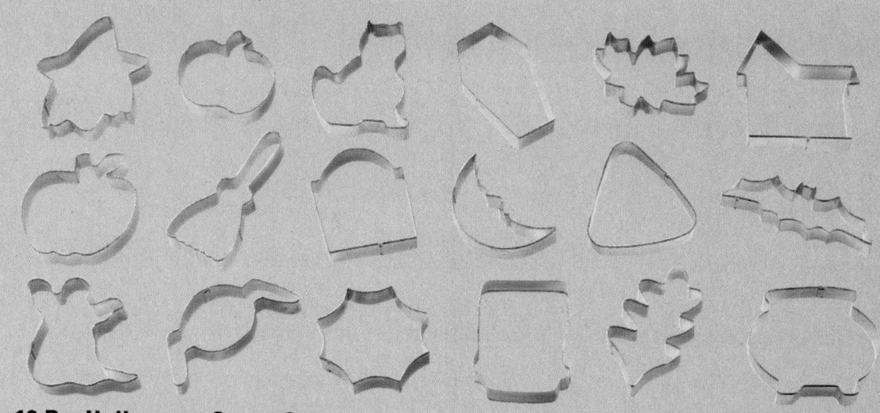

18 Pc. Halloween Cutter Set

Set of 18 includes witch, pumpkin, cat, coffin, maple leaf, house, apple, witch's broom, tombstone, moon, candy corn, bat, ghost, spider, spider web, Frankenstein, oak leaf and cauldron, each approx. 3 in.
2308-U-1131 Set/18 $10.49

3 Pc. Halloween Cutter Set

Set of 3 includes pumpkin, ghost and cat. Each approx. 3 in. Coated metal.
2308-U-1265
Set/3 $3.69

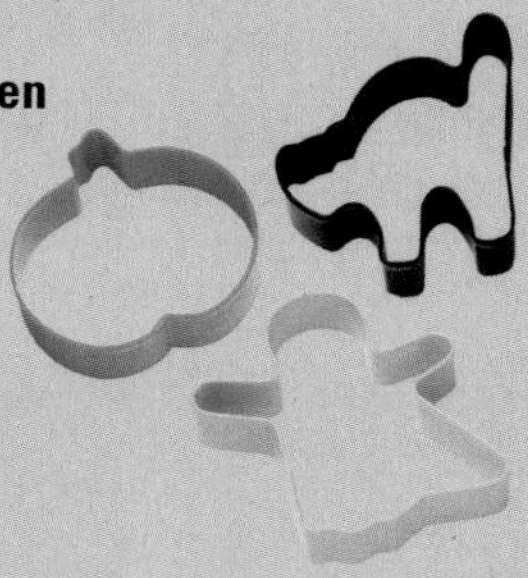

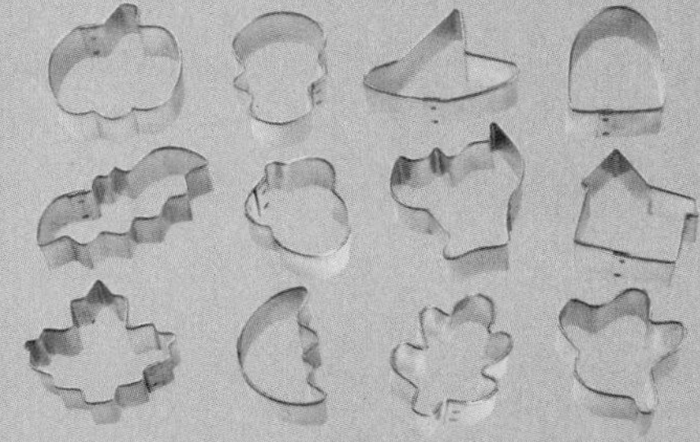

12 Pc. Halloween Mini Cutter Set

Set includes pumpkin, skull, witch's hat, tombstone, bat, acorn, cat, house, maple leaf, moon, oak leaf and ghost, each approx. 1.5 to 2.25 in.
2308-U-1246 Set/12 $5.29

6 Pc. Halloween Mini Cutter Set

Set includes cat, pumpkin, bat, skull, ghost and moon, each approx. 1.5 in.
2308-U-1211
Set/6 $3.19

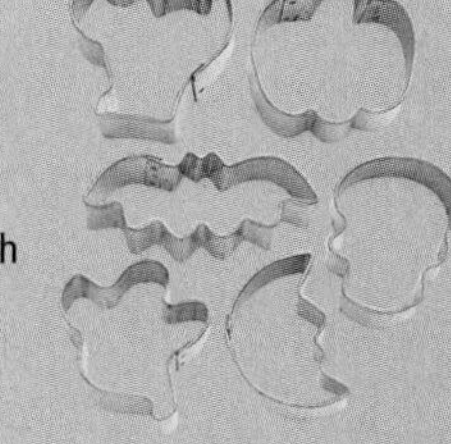

9 Pc. Halloween Cutter Set

Set includes bat, ghost, cat, witch, moon, witch's broom, tombstone, house and pumpkin, each approx. 3 to 3.75 in. Colored aluminum.
2308-U-2501 Set/9 $10.49

4 Pc. Spooky Shapes Cutter Set

Set includes moon, pumpkin, witch and ghost, each approx. 3 in. Coated metal.
2308-U-1200 Set/4 $4.79

4 Pc. Nesting Cutter Sets

Create boo-tiful Halloween treats in 4 sizes. Each cuts neatly and is easy to handle. Sizes from 2.25 to 4.5 in.
Set/4 $4.79

Ghosts
2308-U-1238

Pumpkins
2308-U-1210

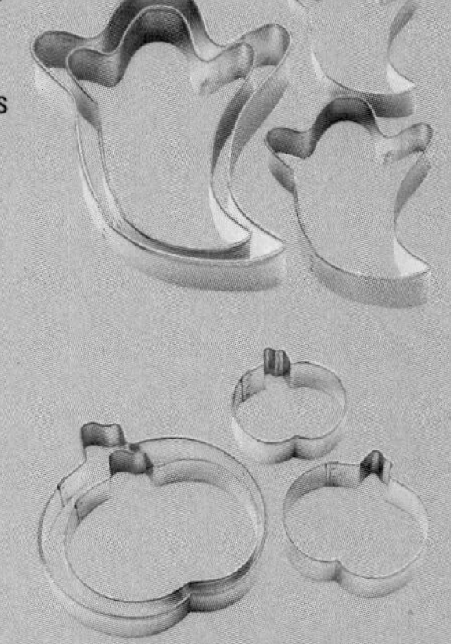

Pre-Baked Cookie Kits

No baking, just fun! Everything you need is included to make great haunted designs.

Pre-Baked Halloween Cookie Kit

Decorate 8 spooky pumpkin-shaped cookies! It's easy and fun for the whole family. Includes 8 pre-baked cookies (approximately 4 in. high), creamy orange icing mix, colorful candies (large sugared gum drops, Halloween mini round candies and green leaves) and decorating instructions.
2104-U-4320 $10.99

Pre-Baked and Pre-Assembled Halloween Cookie House Kit

Everyone will have a howling good time decorating this spooky house! It's the perfect centerpiece for home, school or office celebrations—so easy and fun to make. Includes pre-baked, pre-assembled cookie house (measures 7 x 4 x 8 in. high), orange and black decorating icing mixes, colorful candy (Halloween mini round candies, orange, yellow and black jelly beans, purple round candies), 1 ghost icing decoration, 2 round decorating tips, 2 disposable decorating bags, cardboard base and complete decorating instructions.
2104-U-4319 $13.99

Pre-Baked Halloween Cookie House Kit

Easy to assemble and fun to decorate—it's the ideal family activity for Halloween. Includes 10 pre-baked gingerbread house pieces (assembled house measures 7.75 x 4 x 8.5 in. high), orange and black decorating icing mixes, 1 ghost icing decoration, colorful candy (Halloween mini round candies, jelly beans and candy corn), 2 decorating tips, 2 disposable decorating bags, cardboard base, complete assembly and decorating instructions.
2104-U-4318 $13.99

AUTUMN

Bakeware

Silicone Mini Leaf and Pumpkin Mold

Freezer, refrigerator, microwave and dishwasher safe; oven safe to 500°F. One mix makes 20-24 cakes. 6 cavities, each 2.6 x 2.5 x 1.5 in. deep.
2105-U-4874 $9.99

Pumpkin Pie Pan

Holds one 15 oz. can of pumpkin pie filling. Use for apple, peach and cherry pies, too! Ideal for ready-to-bake pie crusts. 9 x 1.5 in. deep. Aluminum.
2105-U-3970 $8.49

DIMENSIONS® DECORATIVE BAKEWARE

With Dimensions Non-Stick Cast Aluminum Bakeware, anyone can create desserts with elegant shapes and spectacular detail. Heavyweight cast aluminum conducts heat extremely evenly. Premium non-stick surface for easy release and cleanup. Aluminum.

Pumpkin NEW!

Finished cake 6.75 x 6 in. 10 cup total capacity.
2105-U-1184
$30.99

Multi-Cavity Pumpkin NEW!

Finished cakes 3.4 x 3.4 in. 5 cup total capacity.
2105-U-1183
$30.99

Party

Baking Cups

Microwave-safe paper. Standard size, 2 in. diameter; Mini size, 1.25 in. diameter.
Standard Pk./75
Mini Pk./100
$2.09

Autumn Leaves
Standard
415-U-431
Mini
415-U-433

Harvest
Standard
415-U-2160
Mini
415-U-417

Autumn Icing Colors Set

Golden Yellow and Orange in .5 oz. jars. Certified Kosher.
601-U-5583
Set/2 $2.99

Party Bags

Colorful Autumn designs for candy and cookie treats. 20 plastic bags, 20 ties included. 4 x 9.5 in.
Pk./20 $2.09

Autumn Leaves
1912-U-1430

Harvest
1912-U-1288

Scarecrow Fun Pix®

Add an Autumn touch to cakes, cupcakes, ice cream and more. Approx. 3½ in. high. Paper.
2113-U-9217
Pk./12 $2.09

Icing Decorations

Wilton Icing Decorations are perfect for topping cakes, cupcakes and cookies. Certified Kosher.
$2.29

Petite Leaves
710-U-230 Pk./12

Mini Pumpkins
710-U-538 Pk./18

Candy

NEW!

Pumpkin Harvest Pretzel Mold
2 designs, 6 cavities.
2115-U-1420 $1.99

NEW!

Scarecrows Lollipop Mold
2 designs, 4 cavities.
2115-U-1613 $1.99

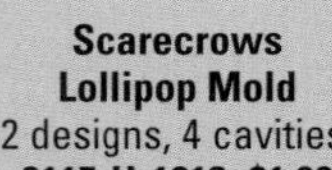

Candy Melts®*

Ideal for all your candy making—molding, dipping or coating. Artificially vanilla flavored unless otherwise indicated. 14 oz. bag. Certified Kosher Dairy. **$2.79**

Red	1911-U-499
Light Cocoa	1911-U-544
Orange	1911-U-1631
Yellow	1911-U-463
Dark Green	1911-U-405
Dark Cocoa	1911-U-358
Dark Cocoa Mint	1911-U-1920
White	1911-U-498
Peanut Butter	1911-U-481

*Brand confectionery coating.

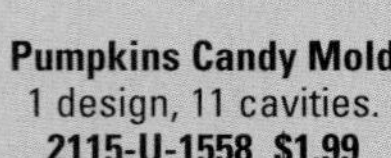

Pumpkins Candy Mold
1 design, 11 cavities.
2115-U-1558 $1.99

See pages 166-169 for more Wilton candy items.

Sprinkles

Individual Bottles

Plastic bottles for convenient pouring and storing. Certified Kosher.

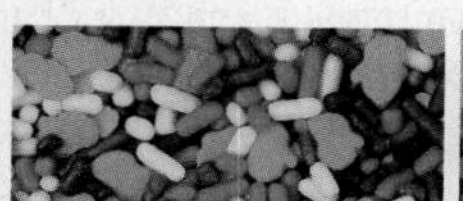

Autumn Pumpkin Mix
2.5 oz. bottle.
710-U-7206 $2.29

Jumbo Leaves Mix
3.25 oz. bottle.
710-U-565 $4.09

Leaves Mix
2.5 oz. bottle.
710-U-787 $2.29

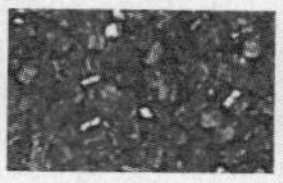

Red Sugar
3.25 oz. bottle.
710-U-766 $2.29

Dark Green Sugar
3.25 oz. bottle.
710-U-764 $2.29

Cake Sparkles™

Edible glitter in .25 oz. bottle. Certified Kosher. **$3.19**

Red	Dark Green	Orange	Yellow
703-U-1284	703-U-1278	703-U-1308	703-U-1272

6-Mix Assortment

Includes Yellow, Red, Orange and Light Green Sugar, Leaves Mix and Chocolate Jimmies. 7.2 oz. Certified Kosher.
710-U-751 $5.99

Cookie

Comfort Grip™ Cutters

Cushion grip cutters have extra-deep stainless steel sides. Great for cutting, cushion grip gives comfortable control. Recipe included. Approx. 4.5 x 1.5 in. deep. **$3.19**

Maple Leaf
2310-U-632

Oak Leaf
2310-U-633

Autumn Cupcake & Cookie Stencils

Just place one of the fun designs over your baked treat, then sprinkle with Wilton Cake Sparkles™ or Colored Sugars (shown at left) or spray with Color Mist™ Food Color Spray (p. 134). 8 designs.
417-U-495 $2.19

METAL CUTTERS

Sure-to-please shapes. Recipe included.

3 Pc. Harvest Cutter Set

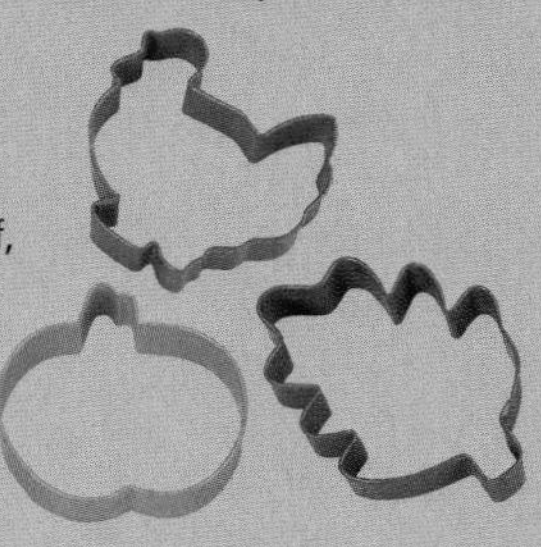

Includes turkey, pumpkin and leaf, each approx. 3 to 3.5 in. Coated metal.
2308-U-1264
Set/3 $3.69

9 Pc. Leaves and Acorns Nesting Cutter Set

Graduated acorns, oak and maple leaves, (3 each). 1.75 to 3.75 in.
2308-U-2000 Set/9 $6.29

Turkey Cutter

Quality metal cuts neatly and is easy to handle. 3 in. Brown coated metal.
2308-U-1319 $0.79

6 Pc. Harvest Mini Cutter Set

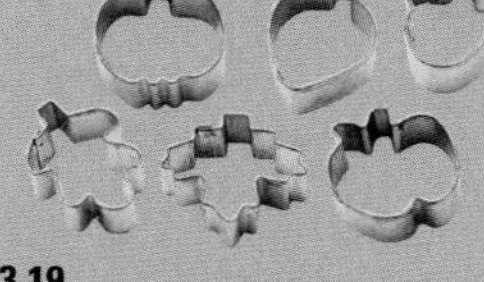

Oak leaf, maple leaf, apple, pumpkin, elm leaf and acorn, approx. 1.5 in.
2308-U-1217 Set/6 $3.19

HANUKKAH

4 Pc. Hanukkah Cookie Cutter Set

Includes Torah, menorah, 6-point star and dreidel, each approx. 3 in. Coated metal.
2308-U-1262
Set/4 $4.79

Colored Sugar

Plastic bottle for pouring and storing. 3.25 oz. Certified Kosher.
$2.29

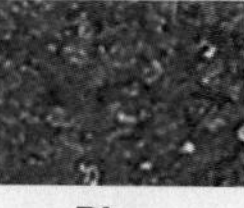

Blue	Yellow
710-U-750	710-U-754

Cake Sparkles™

Edible glitter, .25 oz. bottle. Certified Kosher. **$3.19**

Blue	Yellow	White
703-U-1314	703-U-1272	703-U-1290

Hanukkah Lollipop Mold

5 designs, 10 cavities.
2115-U-1405 $1.99

Candy Melts®*

Ideal for all your candy making—molding, dipping or coating. Artificially vanilla flavored unless otherwise indicated. 14 oz. bag. Certified Kosher Dairy. **$2.79**

Blue	**1911-U-448**	**Light Cocoa**	**1911-U-544**
Yellow	**1911-U-463**	**Dark Cocoa**	**1911-U-358**
White	**1911-U-498**	**Dark Cocoa Mint**	**1911-U-1920**

*Brand confectionery coating.

See pages 166-169 for more Wilton candy items.

Colors & Icings

HANUKKAH COLOR GUIDE

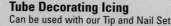

Blue Yellow White

Color Mist™ Food Color Spray

The dazzling effects of an airbrush in a convenient can! Use it to add sensational color to iced cakes, cookies and cupcakes. No mess, taste-free formula. 1.5 oz. Certified Kosher. **$3.29**

Blue	**710-U-5501**
Yellow	**710-U-5502**

Ready-to-Decorate Icing

Anyone can decorate with Wilton Ready-to-Decorate Icing! Our brilliant colors and 4 decorating tips make it a breeze to add an exciting finishing touch to treats without mixing or mess. 6.4 oz. Certified Kosher. **$4.29**

Blue	**710-U-4407**
Yellow	**710-U-4409**
White	**710-U-4402**

Tube Decorating Icing

Can be used with our Tip and Nail Set or Coupler Ring Set (p. 134) and any standard size Wilton metal tip. Colors match Wilton Icing Colors (p. 134). 4.25 oz. Certified Kosher. **$1.99**

Blue 704-U-248 White 704-U-200
Yellow 704-U-236

Tube Decorating Gel

Transparent gels are great for writing messages and decorating cakes and cookies. Colors match Wilton Icing Colors (p. 134). .75 oz. Certified Kosher. **$1.49**

Blue 704-U-348 White 704-U-302
Yellow 704-U-336

Sparkle Gel

Squeeze on sparkling color effects with our ready-to-use gel. Great for dots, messages, water effects and fondant accents. Try it on cookies, cupcakes, ice cream and more! Resealable 3.5 oz. tube. Certified Kosher.
$2.99

Yellow	**704-U-108**
Blue	**704-U-110**

CHRISTMAS

Bakeware

Step-By-Step Snowman Pan

Just bake, ice and decorate. He's also perfect for molding gelatin and ice cream, salads, baking bread and more. One-mix pan is 12 x 9.25 x 2 in. deep. Aluminum.
2105-U-2083
$7.49

Iridescents! Tree Pan

This bright, colorful shape is as much fun for serving party treats as it is for baking! Designed for quick, easy decorating. Also ideal for crisped rice cereal treats, molded gelatin, bread dough and more. One-mix pan is 14 x 10 x 2 in. deep. Aluminum.
2105-U-2081 $7.49

NON-STICK MINI PANS

Perfect size for holiday gift basket treats! Use for your single-serving holiday cakes and molded desserts. Non-stick steel releases treats easily and delivers great detail.

NEW!

Gingerbread Boys and Trees

One mix makes 24-28 gingerbread boys and trees. 6 cavities, each approximately 2.8 x 3.7 x 1.3 in. deep.
2105-U-1515 $11.99

Snowman and Mitten

One mix makes 24-28 snowmen and mittens. 6 cavities, each 2.75 x 1.25 in. deep.
2105-U-3513 $8.99

SILICONE MOLDS

Discover the convenience and easy release of flexible silicone bakeware! Freezer, refrigerator, microwave and dishwasher safe—oven safe to 500°F.

Petite Tree Mold

One mix makes 40-48 trees. 12 cavities, each 2 x 1 in. deep.
2105-U-4898
$9.99

Mini Tree Mold

One mix makes 20-24 trees. 6 cavities, each 2.5 x 1 in. deep.
2105-U-4830 $9.99

Mini Snowflake Mold

One mix makes 20-24 snowflakes. 6 cavities, each 2.5 x 1.5 in. deep.
2105-U-4831 $9.99

Mini Snowman Pan

Bake a blizzard of snowmen! One mix makes 12-18 snowmen. 6 cavities, each 2.9 x 4.6 x 1.9 in. deep. Aluminum.
2105-U-472 $12.99

Bite-Size Gingerbread Boy Pan

Bake plenty of fun little guys for everyone. One mix makes 24-36 boys. 9 cavities, each 2.75 x 3.4 x .75 in. deep. Aluminum.
2105-U-926 $12.99

DIMENSIONS® DECORATIVE BAKEWARE

With Dimensions Non-Stick Cast Aluminum Bakeware, anyone can create Christmas desserts with elegant shapes and spectacular detail. Heavyweight cast aluminum conducts heat extremely evenly. Premium non-stick surface for easy release and cleanup. Aluminum.

Snowflake

Finished cake 12 x 10.5 x 2.75 in.; 11 cup total capacity.
2105-U-5030 $30.99

4-Cavity Mini Snowflakes

Finished cakes 5 x 2.25 in.; 7 cup total capacity.
2105-U-5028 $30.99

Icings

See Color Guide at right.

Ready-to-Decorate Icing

Anyone can decorate with Wilton Ready-to-Decorate Icing! Our brilliant colors and four decorating tips make it a breeze to add an exciting finishing touch to treats—without mixing or mess. 6.4 oz. Certified Kosher.
$4.29

Red 710-U-4400
Green 710-U-4401
White 710-U-4402

Cookie Icing

Easy to use—just heat and squeeze onto cookies using the convenient cap. Sets smooth in just 45 minutes. 10 oz. bottle covers approximately 12 cookies, 3 in. each; 20 oz. bottle covers approx. 24. Certified Kosher.

10 oz. White	**704-U-481**	**$4.49**
20 oz. White	**704-U-492**	**$7.99**
NEW! 10 oz. Red	**704-U-488**	**$4.49**
10 oz. Green	**704-U-493**	**$4.49**

Sparkle Gel

Squeeze on sparkling color effects with our ready-to-use gel. Great for dots, messages, water effects and fondant accents. Resealable 3.5 oz. tube. Certified Kosher.
$2.99
Red 704-U-112
Green 704-U-111

Tube Decorating Icing

Can be used with our Tip and Nail Set or Coupler Ring Set (p. 134) and any standard size Wilton metal tip. Colors match Wilton Icing Colors (p. 134). 4.25 oz. Certified Kosher. **$1.99**

Red	**704-U-218**
Kelly Green	**704-U-227**
Leaf Green	**704-U-224**
White	**704-U-200**

Tube Decorating Gel

Transparent gels are great for writing messages and decorating cakes and cookies. Colors match Wilton Icing Colors (p. 134). .75 oz. Certified Kosher.
$1.49

Red	**704-U-318**
Leaf Green	**704-U-324**
White	**704-U-302**

Party

Baking Cups

Microwave-safe paper. Standard size, 2 in. diameter; Mini size, 1.25 in. diameter.
Standard
Pk./75 $2.09
Mini
Pk./100 $2.09

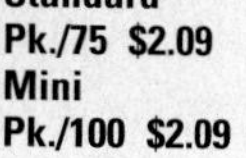

NEW!

Winter Splendor Standard 415-U-443 Mini 415-U-444

Shiver Me Snowman Standard 415-U-5766 Mini 415-U-5765

Santa Standard 415-U-5295 Mini 415-U-5405

Silicone Baking Cups

No muffin pan needed! Bake and serve in these reusable oven-safe cups.
Standard 415-U-9405 Pk./12 $9.99
Mini 415-U-9412 Pk./12 $7.99

Party Bags

Colorful Christmas designs for candy and cookie treats. 20 plastic bags, 20 ties included. 4 x 9.5 in.
Pk./20 $2.09

NEW!

Winter Splendor 1912-U-1229

Shiver Me Snowman 1912-U-9140

Santa 1912-U-1325

Candy Cups

Perfect for holiday sweets! 1 in. dia.
Pk./75 $1.59
Red Foil 415-U-314
Silver Foil 415-U-307
Gold Foil 415-U-306

Red/Green Mini Cups

Mixed, glassine paper. 1 in.
1912-U-1247
Pk./72 $1.59

Icing Decorations

Perfect for topping cakes, cupcakes and cookies Certified Kosher.
$2.29

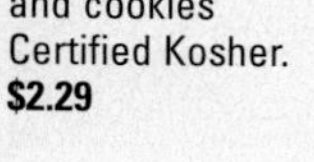

NEW!

Petite Winter Splendor 710-U-543 Pk./12

Snowman 710-U-349 Pk./9

Santa 710-U-697 Pk./12

Petite Loaf Baking Cups

For gift breads. White paper. Fits Petite Loaf Pan (p.154).
415-U-450 Pk./50 $1.59

Fun Pix®

Add a fun holiday touch to cakes, cupcakes, ice cream and more. Approx. 4 in. high.
Pk./24 $2.09

NEW!

Winter Splendor Foil/paper. **2113-U-708**

Shiver Me Snowman Paper. **2113-U-720**

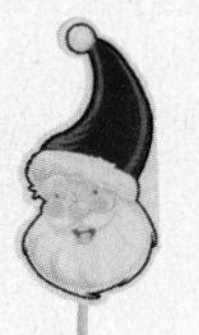

Santa Paper. **2113-U-7610**

Christmas Cupcake and Cookie Stencils

Turn plain treats into holiday visions. Just place 1 of the 8 fun designs over your baked treat, then sprinkle with Wilton Cake Sparkles™ or Colored Sugars (p. 202) or use FoodWriter™ Edible Color Markers or Color Mist™ Food Color Spray (below). 8 designs.
417-U-510 $2.19

Shaped Bags with Drawstring

Large bags are 6.75 x 9.5 in.
Pk./15 $2.09

Shaped Shiver Me Snowman 1912-U-9142

Shaped Santa 1912-U-1328

Colors

Holiday Icing Colors Set

Red-Red and Kelly Green in .5 oz. jars. Certified Kosher.
601-U-3011
Set/2 $2.99

CHRISTMAS COLOR GUIDE

Red **Kelly Green** **Leaf Green** **White**

FoodWriter™ Edible Color Markers

Use like ink markers to add fun, dazzling color to countless foods. Kids love 'em! Decorate on fondant, color flow, royal icing designs and cookie icing. Includes Green and Red markers (.07 oz. each). Certified Kosher.
609-U-102 Set/2 $4.19

Color Mist™ Food Color Spray

The dazzling effects of an airbrush in a convenient can! Use it to add sensational color to iced cakes, cookies and cupcakes. No mess, taste-free formula. 1.5 oz. Certified Kosher. **$3.29**
Green 710-U-5503
Red 710-U-5500

Candy

Pretzel Molds

Easy to mold, fun to eat. Position pretzel rod, spoon in your favorite melted Candy Melts®* and refrigerate to set. Use with lollipop sticks, too.

Christmas Trees Pretzel Mold
1 design, 6 cavities.
2115-U-1747 $1.99

Santa Pretzel Mold
1 design, 6 cavities.
2115-U-1501 $1.99

Shiver Me Snowman Lollipop Mold
3 designs, 6 cavities.
2115-U-1748 $1.99

Santa Lollipop Mold
1 design, 9 cavities.
2115-U-1706 $1.99

Christmas Character Lollipop Mold
3 designs, 6 cavities.
2115-U-1567 $1.99

Christmas Candy Making MEGA PACK

Everything you need to make dozens of festive lollipops and candies for holiday giving. It's easy and fun, with lots of fun shapes and colorful Candy Melts®*! Kit includes: 3 molds: Snowflake Candy (1 design, 9 cavities), Christmas Characters Lollipop (3 designs, 6 cavities), Decorated Trees Large Lollipop (3 designs, 3 cavities); 16 oz. Candy Melts brand confectionery coating (4 oz. each white, light cocoa, red and green); 20 lollipop sticks (6 in.); 4 disposable decorating bags; decorating brush and 20 party bags/ties.
2104-U-3221 $9.99

Candy Melts®*

Ideal for molding, dipping or coating. Artificially vanilla flavored unless otherwise indicated. 14 oz. bag. Certified Kosher Dairy.
$2.79

Red	1911-U-499	**Dark Cocoa**	1911-U-358
White	1911-U-498	**Dark Cocoa Mint**	1911-U-1920
Dark Green	1911-U-405	**Yellow**	1911-U-463
Light Cocoa	1911-U-544		

*Brand confectionery coating.

See pages 166-169 for more Wilton candy items.

Holiday Cookie Set

Four merry cutter shapes and six kinds of colorful sprinkles in one exciting set! An easy way to add variety to your holiday cookie gifts. Includes angel, tree, star and boy metal cutters, each approximately 1.5 x 1.5 in.; 2 oz. each Green and Red Sugar, White Sparkling Sugar, Christmas Nonpareils, 1.5 oz. each Christmas Jimmies and Twinkling Trees Mix.
2109-U-5392 $12.99

Christmas Cookie Gift Bag Set

Wrap up a festive holiday cookie gift with colorful bags, ribbons and tags. Includes 3 each 16 x 20 inch bags, tags and 18 in. ribbon.
415-U-1302 Set/3 $4.19

Sprinkles

Jumbo Sprinkles

Try our Jumbo Sprinkles—big bold toppers perfect for cookies, brownies and more. Plastic bottles for convenient pouring and storing. Certified Kosher. **$4.09**

Trees
2.8 oz. bottle.
710-U-568

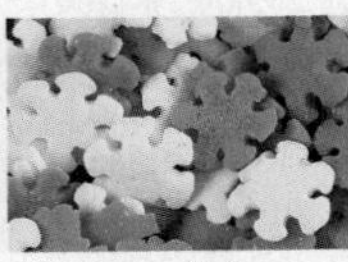

Snowflakes
2.6 oz. bottle.
710-U-569

Gingerbread Boys
2.75 oz. bottle.
710-U-586

Individual Bottles

Shake up your holiday treats with fun colors and designs. Plastic bottles for convenient pouring and storing. Certified Kosher.

Twinkling Trees Mix
2.5 oz. bottle.
710-U-696 $2.29

Christmas Confetti
2 oz. bottle.
710-U-172 $2.29

Snowflake Mix
2.5 oz. bottle.
710-U-797 $2.29

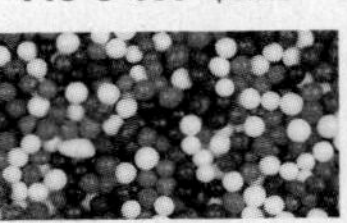

Christmas Nonpareils
3 oz. **710-U-585 $2.29**
5.25 oz. **710-U-173 $3.29**

Cinnamon Drops
3 oz. bottle.
710-U-769 $2.29

Chocolate Jimmies
2.5 oz. bottle.
710-U-774 $2.29

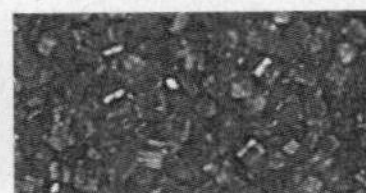

Red Sugar
3.25 oz. bottle.
710-U-766 $2.29

Dark Green Sugar
3.25 oz. bottle.
710-U-764 $2.29

Sparkling Sugars

Easy-pour sugars have a coarse texture and brilliant sparkle. 8 oz. bottle. Certified Kosher. **$4.49**

Holiday Mix
710-U-308

Red/White
710-U-998

Green/White
710-U-997

Cake Sparkles™

Edible glitter in .25 oz. bottle. Certified Kosher.
$3.19

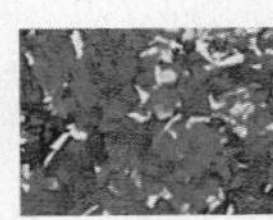

Red
703-U-1284

Green
703-U-1278

White
703-U-1290

ASSORTMENTS

4-Mix
Includes Christmas Trees Mix, Christmas Nonpareils, Dark Green and Red Sugars. 3.95 oz. Certified Kosher.
710-U-729 $4.99

3-Mix Sparkling Sugars
Includes Red/White, Green/White and White. 8.4 oz. Certified Kosher.
710-U-374 $5.99

6-Mix
Includes Christmas Nonpareils, Confetti, Twinkling Trees Mix, Green and Red Sugar and Christmas Jimmies. 6.8 oz. Certified Kosher.
710-U-755 $5.99

Gingerbread Kits

Pre-Baked Gingerbread Boy Cookie Decorating Kit

Decorate 8 fun cookies! Great for gifts or special treats. Includes cookies, icing mix, colorful candies, decorating bag, tip and complete instructions.
2104-U-1090 $10.99

Pre-Baked Gingerbread House Kit

Includes pre-baked house pieces, icing mix, assorted candies, decorating bag and tip, cardboard base, complete instructions and decorating ideas. House measures 5.25 x 5.5 x 4.75 in. high.
2104-U-1537 $10.99

Pre-Baked/ Pre-Assembled Gingerbread House Kit

Includes assembled house with cardboard base, icing mix, candies, decorating bag and tip, complete instructions and decorating ideas. House measures 5.5 x 5.5 x 4.5 in. high.
2104-U-1516 $13.99

Pre-Baked Gingerbread House Kit

Includes pre-baked gingerbread pieces, icing mix, assorted candies, decorating bag and tip, cardboard base, complete instructions and decorating ideas. House measures 8 x 7 x 6.5 in. high.
2104-U-1509 $13.99

Pre-Baked Gingerbread Tree Kit

Just stack pre-baked star cookies, decorate with icing and candy and add the star icing decoration tree top! Includes cookies, white and green icing mix, icing decorations, candies, 2 decorating tips, 2 decorating bags and complete instructions. Tree measures 5.5 x 8.25 in. high.
2104-U-2621 $10.99

Christmas Cookie Tree Cutter Kit

Create a beautiful Yule tree as a perfect holiday centerpiece. . . it's easy and fun! Just bake, stack and decorate. Kit includes 10 plastic star cookie cutters in graduated sizes, 3 disposable decorating bags, round decorating tip, cookie and icing recipes, baking and decorating instructions for 4 great designs. Tree measures approx. 8 x 11 in. high.
2104-U-1555 $7.99

Plastic Cutters

Great shapes for end-of-year celebrations! 3 x 4 in. high.
$0.69

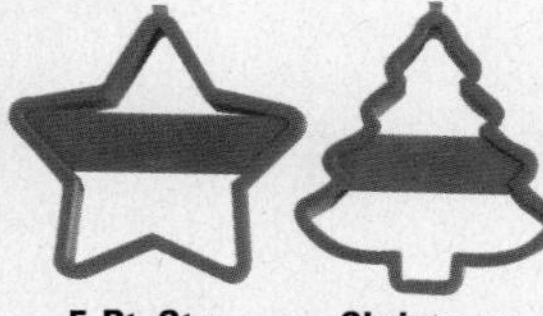

5-Pt. Star
2303-U-135

Christmas Tree
2303-U-132

Holiday Red Cookie Scoop

Festive color and convenient design make holiday baking more fun! Scoops and releases approx. 1 tablespoon of dough with ease. Dishwasher safe plastic.
417-U-320 $2.79

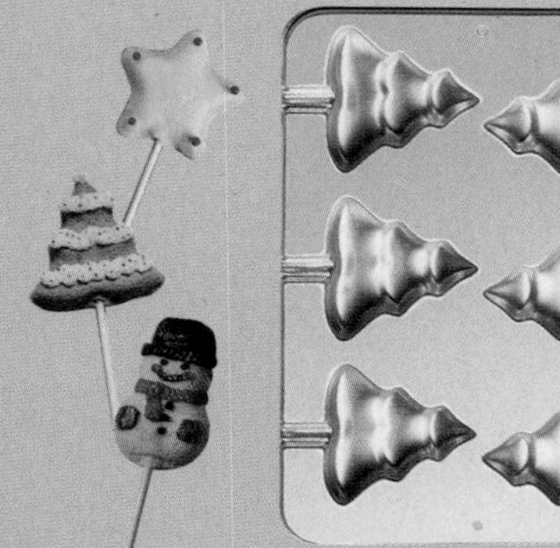

Christmas Tree
2105-U-8101

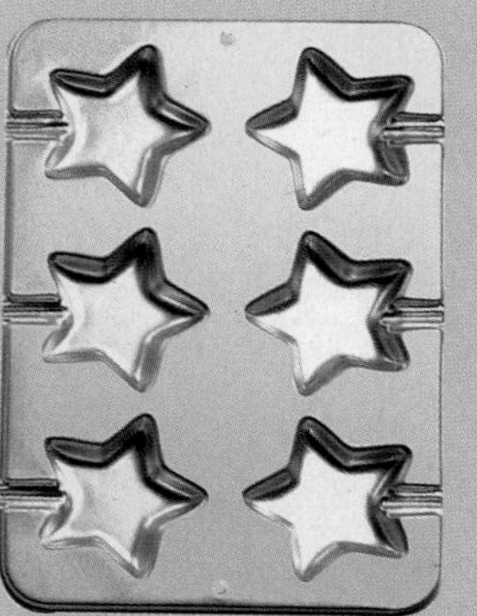

Snowman
2105-U-8107

Star
2105-U-8102

Cookie Treat Pans

Treats on a stick are so easy; just press dough or rice cereal treat mixture into the pan, insert a cookie stick, then bake, cool and decorate. Each pan makes six individual treats, approx. 4 x .5 in. deep. Recipe included. Aluminum.
$9.99

Cookie Treat Sticks

6 in. 1912-U-9319 Pk./20 $1.99 **8 in. 1912-U-9318 Pk./20 $2.99**

NEW!

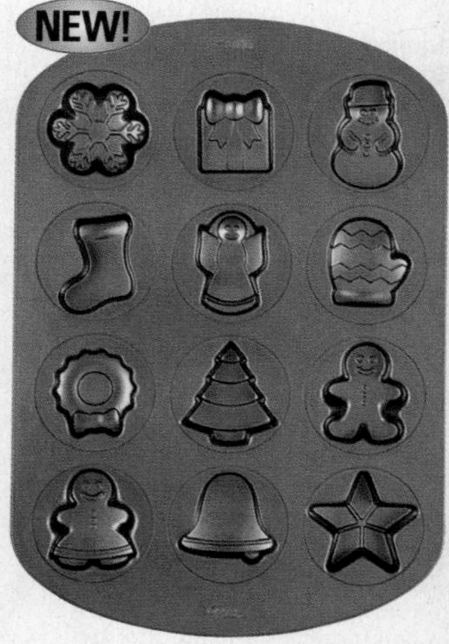

Holiday Cookie Shapes Pan

Includes 12 classic shapes for your single-serving holiday cookies and molded desserts. 12 cavities, each approximately 2.75 x 2.25 x .25 in. deep.
2105-U-8122 $11.99

Cookie Cutters

Christmas Push 'N Print™ Cutter Set

Serve cookies that make a great impression—use Push 'N Print Cutters to emboss a fun design before baking! It's so easy! Load one of the 3 imprint disks in the cutter, cut the cookie, then press the plunger with disk still in place to imprint the design. Bake, cool and serve a treat that's perfect for celebrations and cookie gift baskets. Great for embossed fondant decorations too! Disks are 2.9 in. diameter. Recipe included.
2308-U-4003
Set/4 $7.99

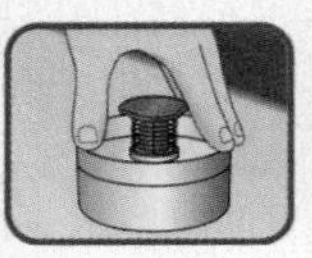
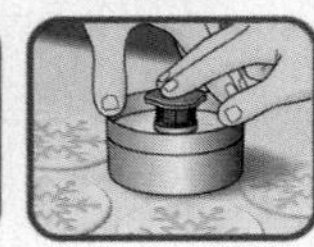

COMFORT GRIP™ CUTTERS

These easy-grip cutters with extra-deep sides are perfect for cutting so many favorite foods into spectacular shapes. The cushion grip gives you comfortable control even when cutting thick desserts. Recipe included. Stainless steel sides, 4.5 x 4.5 x 1.5 in. deep.
$3.19

Candy Cane
2310-U-644

Santa Hat
2310-U-640

Christmas Tree
2310-U-604

Gingerbread Boy
2310-U-602

Mitten
2310-U-639

Snowman
2310-U-634

Star
2310-U-631

4-PC. GRIPPY™ CUTTER SET

Safe, easy cutting, with a comfortable grip and deep plastic sides. Four shapes include stocking, tree, star and gingerbread boy, each approx. 3.5 in.
2311-U-260
Set/4 $4.49

METAL CUTTERS

Put variety in your cookie-making with fun Christmas multi-shape sets. There are styles to please everyone. Recipe included.

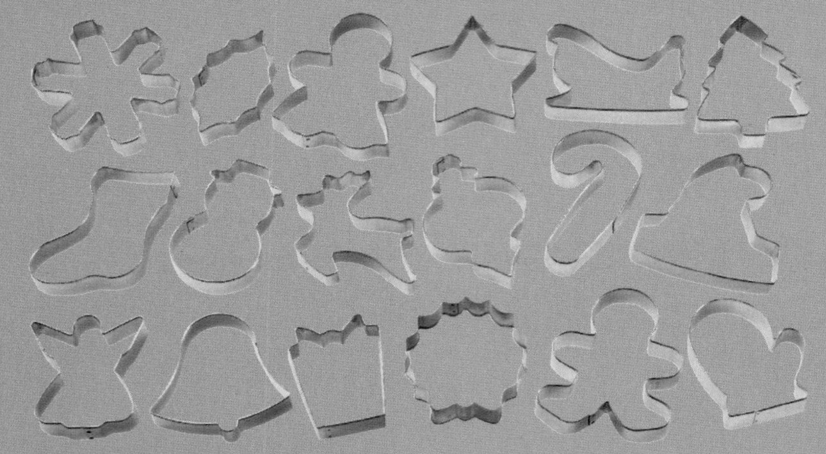

18 Pc. Holiday Cutter Set

Snowflake, holly leaf, gingerbread girl, star, sleigh, tree, stocking, snowman, reindeer, ornament, candy cane, Santa hat, angel, bell, gift, wreath, gingerbread boy and mitten. Each approx. 3 in.
2308-U-1132 Set/18 $10.49

3 Pc. Christmas Cutter Set

Set of 3 includes snowflake, gingerbread boy and tree, each approx. 3 to 3.75 in. Coated metal.
2308-U-1266 Set/3 $3.69

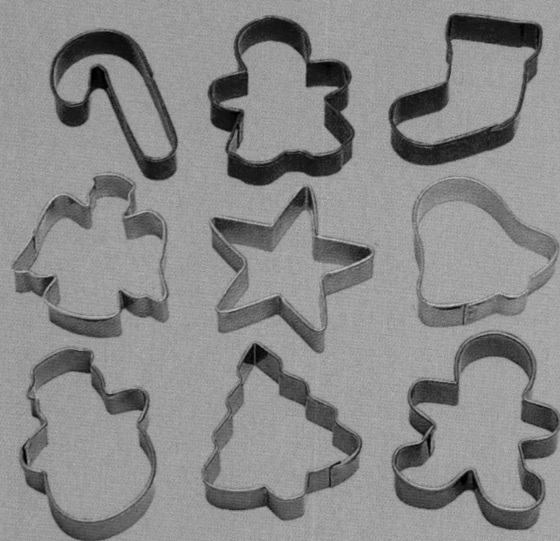

9 Pc. Holiday Cutter Set

Candy cane, gingerbread girl, stocking, angel, star, bell, snowman, tree and gingerbread boy, each approx. 3 to 3.75 in. Colored aluminum.
2308-U-2500 Set/9 $10.49

4 Pc. Jolly Shapes Cutter Set

Stocking, star, tree and candy cane, each approx. 3 in. Coated metal.
2308-U-1201 Set/4 $4.79

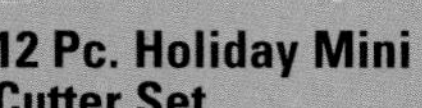

12 Pc. Holiday Mini Cutter Set

Star, angel, gingerbread girl, stocking, candy cane, teddy bear, bell, holly leaf, tree, gingerbread boy, ornament, and sleigh. Each approx. 1.5 in.
2308-U-1250 Set/12 $5.29

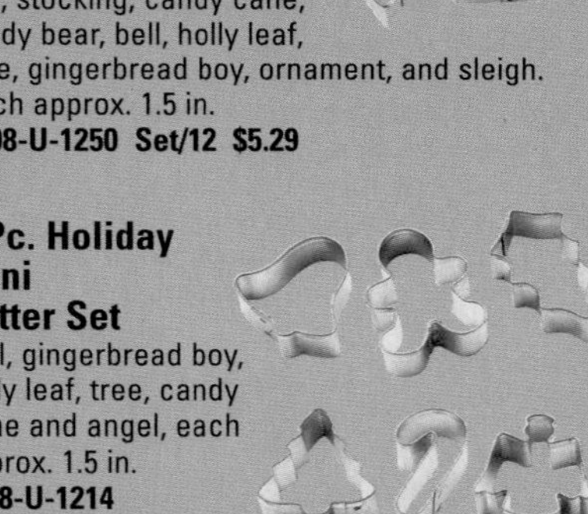

6 Pc. Holiday Mini Cutter Set

Bell, gingerbread boy, holly leaf, tree, candy cane and angel, each approx. 1.5 in.
2308-U-1214
Set/6 $3.19

4 Pc. Nesting Cutter Sets

Bake your favorite holiday shapes in four fun sizes! Quality metal cuts neatly and is easy to handle. Sizes from 5 to 2.5 in.
Set/4 $4.79

Snowflakes
2308-U-1244

Gingerbread Boys
2308-U-1239

Cookie Presses

Making traditional spritz cookies has never been so easy! Cookie Pro Ultra II is designed to be the easiest to fill, most comfortable press you've ever used. And, with 12 terrific shapes, plus 4 fun mini cookie designs, your holiday cookie baskets will be more festive than ever! Includes complete instructions and delicious recipes.
2104-U-4018 Set/17 $24.99

Twelve Disks in Festive Shapes

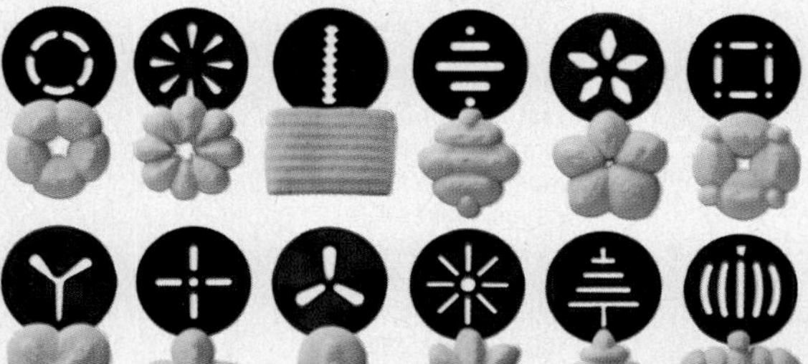

Plus 4 BONUS Disks For Mini Cookies!

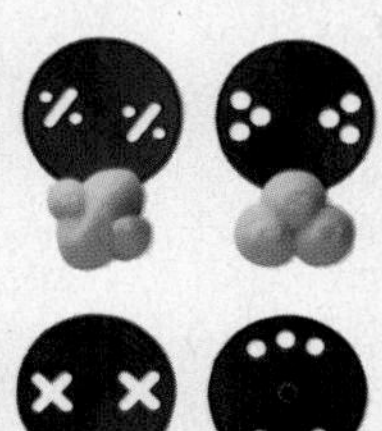

COOKIE MASTER™ Plus
Cordless Cookie Press

Our cordless cookie press is so powerful and easy to operate, you'll use it all year to create cookies, appetizers, desserts and more. Exclusive patented reverse action means there's no need to take press apart for refilling. Ergonomic design is shaped to fit in your hand for excellent comfort.

Includes 12 aluminum disks in classic and seasonal shapes, 4 accent tips for decorating and filling and 2 bonus recipe booklets—sweet and savory. Uses 4 AA batteries, not included.
2104-U-4008 Set/19 $39.99

12 Disk Designs

4 Accent Tips

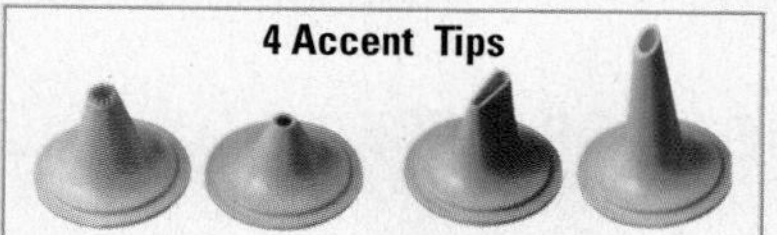

COMFORT GRIP™ Cookie Press

Experience a classic press that is truly comfortable. Its ergonomic handle feels great in your hand and the easy-squeeze action releases perfectly shaped dough. Clear barrel takes the guesswork out of refilling. Fluted bottom raises press off the cookie sheet for better-defined shapes. Includes 12 cookie disks in a variety of shapes and our classic spritz recipe.
2104-U-4011 Set/13 $12.99

12 Disk Designs

Bakeware

Recipe Right® Non-Stick

Built with all the right qualities for better baking results. Pan dimensions are embossed on handles for easy reference. Heavy-gauge construction means pans spread heat evenly and won't warp. Non-stick coating provides exceptionally quick release and easy cleanup.
5-year warranty. Aluminum.

15 x 10 in. Cookie Sheet
2105-U-967 $5.49

12 Cup Muffin Pan
2105-U-954 $6.99

24 Cup Mini Muffin Pan
2105-U-914 $10.99

Bake Easy!™ Non-Stick Spray

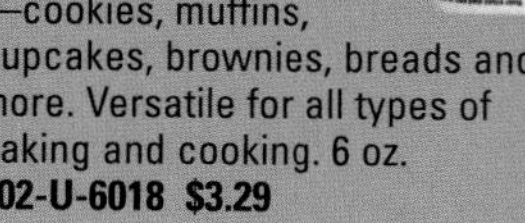

This convenient non-stick spray helps your baked goods release perfectly. Just a light, even coating does the job. Use Bake Easy! for all mixes and recipes—cookies, muffins, cupcakes, brownies, breads and more. Versatile for all types of baking and cooking. 6 oz.
702-U-6018 $3.29

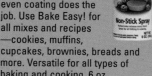

VALENTINE

Bakeware

DIMENSIONS® DECORATIVE BAKEWARE

With Dimensions Non-Stick Cast Aluminum Bakeware everyone can create Valentine desserts with elegant shapes and spectacular detail. Heavyweight cast aluminum conducts heat extremely evenly. Premium non-stick surface for easy release and cleanup. Aluminum.

Mini Heart
Each heart is 4 x 2 in. deep. Six 1 cup cavities.
2105-U-5012
$30.99

Queen Of Hearts
9 x 3.25 in. deep. 10 cup total capacity.
2105-U-5001 $30.99

Crown Of Hearts
11 x 2.5 in. deep. 10 cup total capacity.
2105-U-5011
$30.99

9 in.Non-Stick Heart Pan
Your classic heart cake will release perfectly. Cleanup is easy too. 9 x 2.25 in. deep. Non-stick steel.
2105-U-410 $13.99

Heart Tart Pan
Create luscious desserts and entrees with classic fluted edges. Removable bottom. 10 x 1 in. deep. Non-stick steel.
2105-U-452 $11.99

NEW!

Silicone Heart Molds
Discover the convenience and easy release of flexible silicone bakeware! Freezer, refrigerator, microwave and dishwasher safe—oven safe to 500°F. One mix makes 40-48 petite hearts; 20-24 mini hearts. 12 petite hearts, each 1.5 x 1.5 x 1 in. deep; 6 mini hearts, each 2.6 x 2.5 x 1.5 in. deep.

6-Cavity Ruffled Heart Mold
2105-U-4861 $9.99

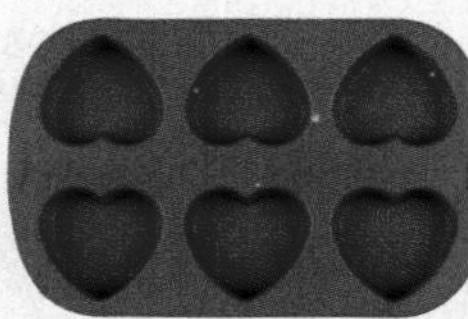

6-Cavity Mini Heart Mold
2105-U-4012 $9.99

12-Cavity Petite Heart Mold
2105-U-4860
$9.99

SweetHeart Pan
Its gently curving shape gives the classic heart a more romantic flair. One-mix pan is 10.25 x 2 in. deep. Aluminum.
2105-U-1197 $12.99

Heart Pans
For graceful expressions of love on Valentine's Day or anytime, in just the size you need. 2 in. deep. Aluminum.
6 in. 2105-U-600 $7.49
9 in. 2105-U-5176 $8.99
12 in. 2105-U-607 $12.99

Non-Stick Mini Heart Pan
Perfect size for party petits fours, molded salads and more. Non-stick steel releases treats easily. One mix makes 20-24 hearts; 6 cavities, each 2.25 x 2.4 x 1.25 in. deep.
2105-U-1539 $8.99

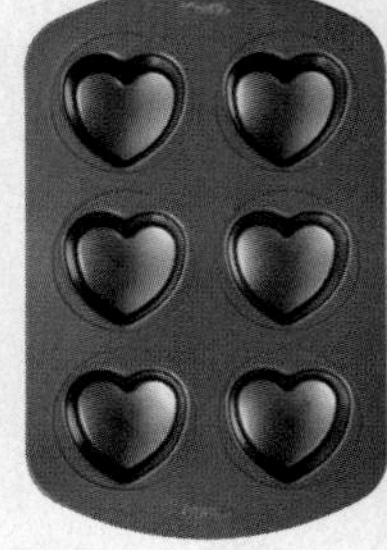

Mini Heart Pan
Great size for petits fours, individual brownies and more. One mix makes 12-18 hearts. 6 cavities, each 3.5 x 1 in. deep. Aluminum.
2105-U-11044 $12.99

Petite Heart Pan
Bite-size muffins, brownies and cookies will win hearts. One mix makes 10-15 dozen hearts. 12 cavities, each 1.75 x 1.6 x .5 in. deep. Aluminum.
2105-U-2432 $11.99

Heart Springform Pans
Create elegant Valentine cheesecakes with these easy-releasing non-stick pans. Springlock sides, removable bottom for easy serving. Non-stick steel.

9 x 2.75 in. Standard
2105-U-419
$21.49

4 x 1.75 in. Mini
2105-U-457
$9.99

Icings

VALENTINE COLOR GUIDE

Red | Pink | Violet | White

Ready-to-Decorate Icing
Anyone can decorate with Wilton Ready-to-Decorate Icing! Our brilliant colors and 4 decorator tips make it a breeze to add an exciting finishing touch to treats without mixing or mess. 6.4 oz. Certified Kosher.
$4.29

Red	**710-U-4400**
Pink	**710-U-4406**
Violet	**710-U-4408**
White	**710-U-4402**

NEW!

Cookie Icing
Just heat and squeeze onto cookies using the convenient cap. Sets smooth in just 45 minutes. 10 oz. bottle covers approximately 12 cookies, 3 in. each; 20 oz. bottle covers approx. 24. Certified Kosher.

10 oz. White	**704-U-481**	**$4.49**
20 oz. White	**704-U-492**	**$7.99**
10 oz. Red	**704-U-488**	**$4.49**
10 oz. Pink	**704-U-486**	**$4.49**

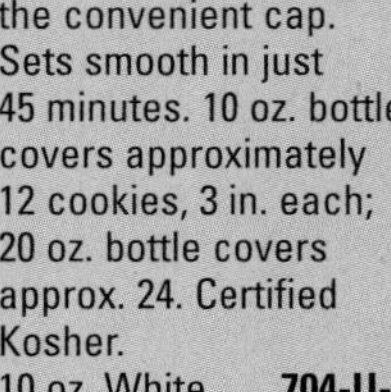

Sparkle Gel
Squeeze on sparkling color effects with our ready-to-use gel. Great for dots, messages, water effects and fondant accents. Resealable 3.5 oz. tubes. Certified Kosher. **$2.99**
Red 704-U-112
Pink 704-U-356

Tube Decorating Icing
Tubes can be used with our Tip and Nail Set or Coupler Ring Set (p. 134) and any standard size Wilton metal tip. Colors match Wilton Icing Colors (p. 134). 4.25 oz. Certified Kosher. **$1.99**
Red 704-U-218 Violet 704-U-242
Pink 704-U-230 White 704-U-200

Tube Decorating Gel
Transparent gels are great for writing messages and decorating cakes and cookies. Colors match Wilton Icing Colors (p. 134). .75 oz. Certified Kosher.
$1.49
Red 704-U-318 Violet 704-U-342
Pink 704-U-330 White 704-U-302

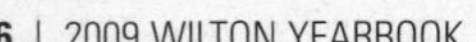

Party

Baking Cups

Microwave-safe paper. Standard size, 2 in. diameter, Mini size, 1.25 in. diameter.
Standard Pk/75 $2.09
Mini Pk/100 $2.09

Hearts
Standard 415-U-517
Mini 415-U-414

Hearts Remembered
Standard 415-U-518
Mini 415-U-519

Party Bags

Colorful solid red and Valentine designs for candy and cookie treats. 20 plastic bags, 20 ties included. 4 x 9.5 in.
Pk./20 $2.09

Red Party Bags
1912-U-2357

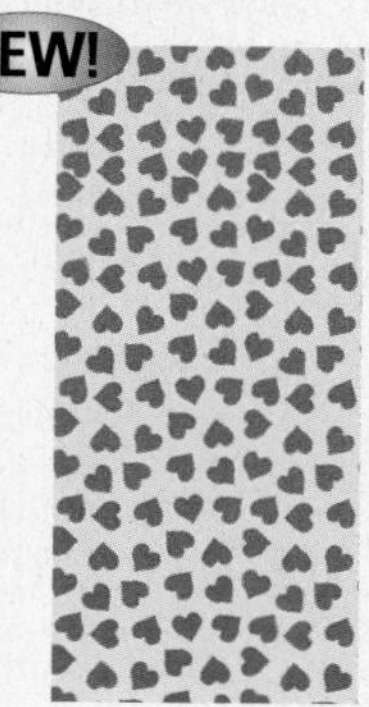

Hearts
1912-U-1269

Hearts Remembered
1912-U-1292

Icing Decorations

Perfect for topping cakes, cupcakes and cookies. Certified Kosher. **$2.29**

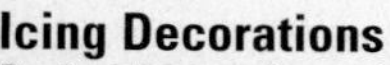

Hearts Remembered
710-U-824 Pk./18

HEART DOILIES

Serve Valentine treats on heart doilies with pretty lace-look edges. **$1.99**

Red:

3.5 in. **Pk./12 2104-U-90703**
6 in. **Pk./12 2104-U-90706**
10 in. **Pk./9 2104-U-90710**

White:

3.5 in. **Pk./12 2104-U-90603**
6 in. **Pk./12 2104-U-90606**
10 in. **Pk./9 2104-U-90610**

Sweetheart Cupcake and Cookie Stencils

Just place 1 of the 8 fun designs over your baked treat, then sprinkle with Wilton Cake Sparkles™ or Colored Sugars or spray with Color Mist™ Food Color Spray. 8 designs.
417-U-494 $2.19

Colors

See Color Guide at left.

Valentine Icing Colors Set

Red-Red and Pink in .5 oz. jars. Certified Kosher.
601-U-5570 Set/2 $2.99

Color Mist™ Food Color Spray

Gives decorators the versatility and dazzling effects of an airbrush in a convenient can! Use it to add sensational color to cakes, iced cookies and cupcakes. No mess, taste-free formula. 1.5 oz. Certified Kosher. **$3.29**
Red 710-U-5500 Pink 710-U-5505 Violet 710-U-5504

Heart Silicone Baking Cups

No muffin pan needed! Bake and serve in these reusable oven-safe cups. 6 red, 6 pink.
Standard 415-U-9409 Pk./12 $9.99
Mini 415-U-9425 Pk./12 $7.99

Valentine Shaped Bags with Drawstring
Large bags are 6 x 9.25 in.
1912-U-9348
Pk./15 $2.09

Candy Cups

Wax-laminated paper on red foil. 1 in. diameter
415-U-314 Pk./75 $1.59

Valentine Cupcakes 'N More® Dessert Stand

Cupcakes are the perfect way to add a personal touch to your Valentine celebration. Optional heart finial adds a festive touch. 9.25 in. high x 9 in. wide. Holds 13 standard cupcakes.
307-U-858 $13.69

Pre-Baked Sweet Heart Cookie Kit

It's the perfect treat for someone sweet any time of year. Includes 8 pre-baked cookies, (approx. 4 in. high); creamy white and pink icing mixes, 2 types of colorful candy, decorating bag and tip, easy instructions.
2104-U-2626 $10.99

Sprinkles

Individual Bottles

Shake up your Valentine treats with fun colors and designs. Try our bold Jumbo Hearts. Plastic bottles for convenient pouring and storing. Certified Kosher.

Jumbo Hearts
3.25 oz. bottle.
710-U-032 $4.09

Chocolate Hearts Mix
Naturally and artificially flavored.
2.5 oz. bottle.
710-U-622 $2.29
3.75 oz. bottle.
710-U-6315 $3.29

Valentine Nonpareils
3 oz. bottle.
710-U-625 $2.29
5.25 oz. bottle.
710-U-558 $3.29

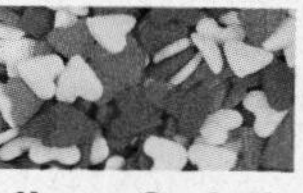

Hearts Confetti
2.0 oz. bottle.
710-U-968 $2.29

Hearts Mix
2.5 oz. bottle.
710-U-854 $2.29

Sugars

3.25 oz. bottle. Certified Kosher. **$2.29**

Red
710-U-766

Pink
710-U-756

Lavender
710-U-758

Sparkling Sugars

Easy-pour sugars have a coarse texture and brilliant sparkle. 8 oz. bottle. Certified Kosher. **$4.49**

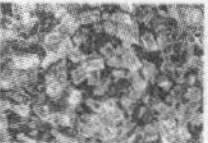

Red/White
710-U-367

Pink/White
710-U-366

Lavender/ White
710-U-371

Cake Sparkles™

Edible glitter, .25 oz. bottle. Certified Kosher. **$3.19**

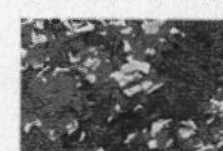

Red
703-U-1284

Pink
703-U-1260

Purple
703-U-1266

ASSORTMENTS

3-Mix

Includes Red/White, Pink/White and White Sparkling Sugars. 8.4 oz. Certified Kosher.
710-U-372 $5.99

6-Mix

Includes 2 Heart Mixes, Sweetheart Nonpareils, Pink, Red and Lavender Sugars. 7.2 oz. Certified Kosher.
710-U-738 $5.99

Candy

NEW!

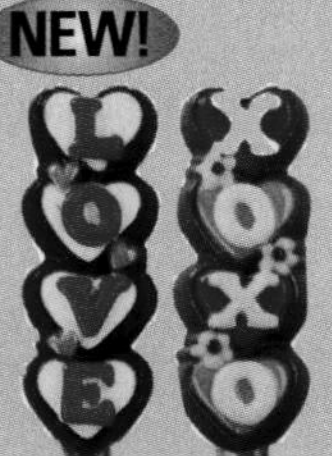

Love Pretzel Mold
2 designs, 6 cavities.
2115-U-1451 $1.99

Heart Pretzel Mold
1 design, 6 cavities.
2115-U-3025 $1.99

NEW!

Kissy Lips Candy Mold
1 design, 8 cavities.
2115-U-1450 $1.99

NEW!

Love Tiles Candy Mold
5 designs, 8 cavities.
2115-U-1456 $1.99

NEW!

Valentine Candy Making MEGA PACK
Lots of fun shapes and colorful Candy Melts®*! Kit includes: Bearing Love Large Lollipop Mold (3 designs, 3 cavities), Valentine Lollipop Mold (3 designs, 6 cavities), Hugs & Kisses Candy Mold (3 designs, 10 cavities); 16 oz. Candy Melts brand confectionery coating (4 oz. each light cocoa, white, red and pink); 20 lollipop sticks (6 in.); 4 disposable decorating bags; decorating brush and 20 party bags/ties.
2104-U-1651 $9.99

Double Heart Large Lollipop Mold
2 designs, 4 cavities.
2115-U-4440 $1.99

Roses and Buds Lollipop Mold
3 designs, 9 cavities.
2115-U-1708 $1.99

Hearts Candy Mold
1 design, 15 cavities.
2115-U-1712 $1.99

Heart Lollipop Mold
2 designs, 8 cavities.
2115-U-1709 $1.99

Candy Melts®*
Ideal for molding, dipping or coating. Artificially vanilla flavored unless otherwise indicated. 14 oz. bag. Certified Kosher Dairy. **$2.79**

Red	**1911-U-499**
Pink	**1911-U-447**
White	**1911-U-498**
Light Cocoa	**1911-U-544**
Dark Cocoa	**1911-U-358**

*Brand confectionery coating.

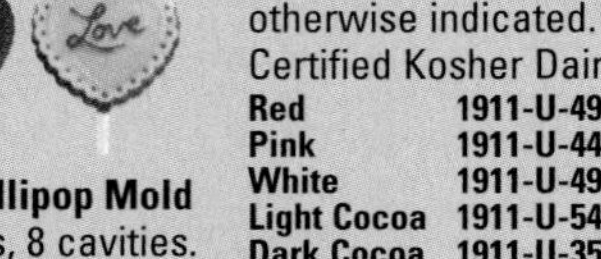

See pages 166-169 for more Wilton candy items.

Cookie

Heart Giant Cookie Pan
Create a giant-sized pan cookie or brownie in a heart shape. Ideal for refrigerated dough and brownie mix. Recipe included. Pan is 11.5 x 10.5 x .5 in. deep. Aluminum.
2105-U-6203 $7.49

Heart Cookie Treat Pan
Just press cookie dough into pan, insert a cookie stick, then bake, cool and decorate. Also great for adding fun shapes to other goodies like rice cereal treats and candy pops. Each treat is 3.5 in. x .25 in. deep. Aluminum.
2105-U-8104 $9.99

Cookie Treat Sticks
6 in. 1912-U-9319 Pk./20 $1.99
8 in. 1912-U-9318 Pk./20 $2.99

Valentine Push 'N Print™ Cutter Set

NEW!

Emboss a fun design in cookies before baking! Load one of the 3 imprint disks in the cutter, cut the cookie, then press the plunger with disk still in place to imprint the design. Disks are 2.9 in. wide. Recipe included.
2308-U-4000
Set/4 $7.99

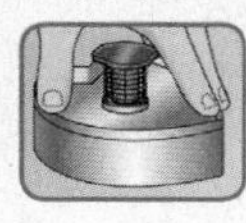

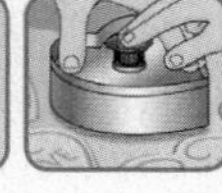

Comfort Grip™ Cutters
Cushion-grip cutters with extra-deep stainless steel sides. The cushion grip gives you comfortable control even when cutting into thick desserts. Recipe included. 4.5 x 4.5 x 1.5 in. deep.
$3.19

Heart
2310-U-616

Lips
2310-U-646

Double Heart
2310-U-647

PLASTIC COOKIE CUTTERS

6 Pc. Nesting Hearts Cutter Set
Great for cookies, imprinting patterns in icing, cutting bread shapes and more. Plastic in sizes from 2.25 to 4.2 in.
2304-U-115 Set/6 $2.99

Heart Cutter
Plastic, 3 x 4 in.
2303-U-100 $0.69

METAL CUTTERS

Put variety in your cookie-making with fun Valentine multi-shape sets. Recipe included.

9 Pc. Valentine Cutter Collection
Great variety of hearts, hugs and kisses designs from 1 to 5 in. Colored aluminum.
2308-U-2502
Set/9 $10.49

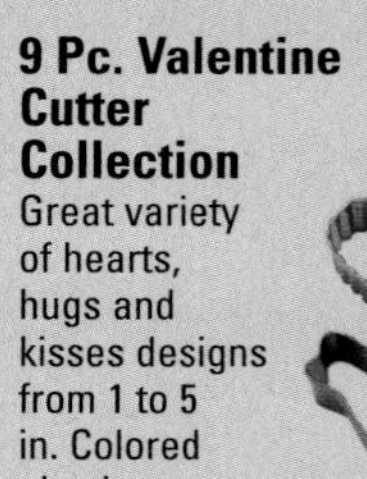

4 Pc. From The Heart Nesting Cutter Set
Includes 2 crinkled shapes. Largest cutter is approx. 5 in. Metal and coated metal.
2308-U-1203 Set/4 $4.79

Heart Cutters

NEW!

Quality metal cuts neatly. 3 in. wide.
Red Metal
2308-U-1322 $0.79
Metal
2308-U-1003 $0.69

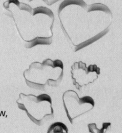

7 Pc. Hearts Cutter Set
7 different heart cutter designs from stylized to traditional. Sizes range from 1.5 to 3 in.
2308-U-1237
Set/7 $5.29

6 Pc. Valentine Mini Cutter Set
Double heart, crinkle heart, heart with arrow, heart, O and X, each approx. 1.5 in.
2308-U-1255 Set/6 $3.19

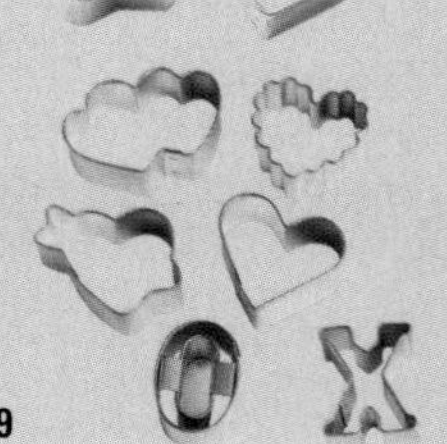

Bakeware

Step-By-Step Bunny Pan

Get springtime celebrations hopping—just bake, ice and decorate! He's also perfect for molding gelatin, ice cream, salads and more. One-mix pan is 9.75 x 14 x 2 in. deep. Aluminum.
2105-U-2074 $7.49

3-D Bunny Pan

Instructions for 5 different decorating ideas included. Two-piece pan bakes bunny approx. 7.25 x 4.75 x 7 in. high. Pan takes 4½ cups of pound cake batter. No heating core needed. Aluminum.
2105-U-2042
Set/2 $14.49

Stand-Up Lamb Pan

This 3-D lamb will charm everyone at your Easter table. Two-piece pan makes lamb 10 x 4.5 x 7 in. high; takes 6 cups of pound cake batter. Instructions included. Aluminum.
2105-U-2010
Set/2 $14.49

3-D Egg Pan

Hatch a great Easter centerpiece! Two-piece pan takes just one cake mix. Includes 2 ring bases for level baking of each half. Each half is 9 x 6 x 2.75 in. Aluminum.
2105-U-4793
Set/4 $14.49

NEW!

6-Cavity Non-Stick Mini Cake Pans

Mini cakes are fun to serve at Easter brunch or wrap them up and add to baskets. Easy-release, easy-clean non-stick steel bakes cakes with great detail. Also excellent for brownies, ice cream molds, muffins and more.

Flower
Each cavity 4 x 4 x 1.5 in. deep. One mix makes about 14 cakes.
2105-U-5490 $11.99

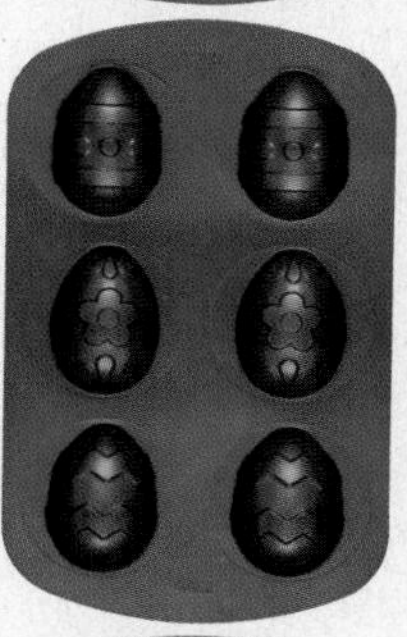

Decorated Egg
Each cavity 4.2 x 2.9 x 1.5 in. deep. One mix makes about 14 cakes.
2105-U-1550 $11.99

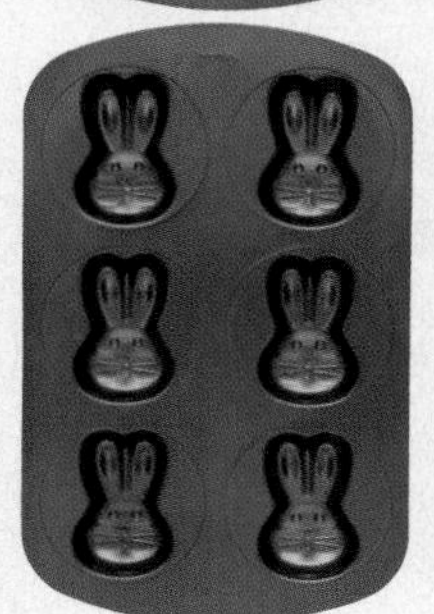

Bunny
Each cavity 4 x 2.6 x 1.2 in. deep. One mix makes about 18 cakes.
2105-U-1551 $11.99

Cross Pan

Truly inspiring for holidays, Christenings and other religious occasions. Bevel design is excellent with rolled fondant. One-mix pan is 14.5 x 11.2 x 2 in. deep. Instructions included. Aluminum.
2105-U-2509 $9.99

Silicone Molds

Discover the convenience and easy release of flexible silicone bakeware! Freezer, refrigerator, microwave and dishwasher safe; oven safe to 500°F.

NEW!

Mini Decorated Egg
Six cavities, each 3.5 x 1.5 in. deep. One mix makes 20-24 eggs.
2105-U-4847
$9.99

NEW!

Mini Tulip/Daisy
Six cavities, each 2.5 x 1.5 in. deep. One mix makes 20-24 flowers.
2105-U-4865
$9.99

NEW!

Petite Easter Egg
Twelve cavities, each 1.75 x 1.5 in. deep. One mix makes 20-24 eggs.
2105-U-4864
$9.99

Mini Egg Pan

Make colorful place markers for the holiday table. One mix makes about 24-36 eggs. 8 cavities, each 3.25 x 2.5 x 1 in. deep. Aluminum.
2105-U-2118 $11.99

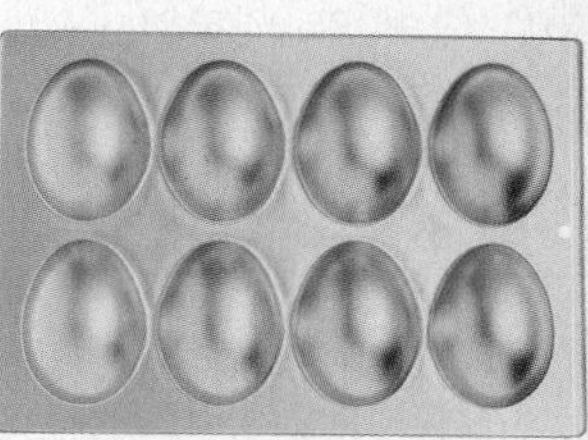

Icings

See Color Guide p. 210.

Ready-to-Decorate Icing

Anyone can decorate with Wilton Ready-to-Decorate Icing! Our brilliant colors and 4 decorating tips make it a breeze to add an exciting finishing touch to treats without mixing or mess. 6.4 oz. Certified Kosher. **$4.29**

Pink 710-U-4406 White 710-U-4402
Violet 710-U-4408
Yellow 710-U-4409
Green 710-U-4401

NEW!

Cookie Icing

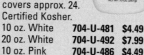

Just heat and squeeze onto cookies using the convenient cap. Sets smooth in just 45 minutes. 10 oz. bottle covers approximately 12 cookies, 3 in. each; 20 oz. bottle covers approx. 24. Certified Kosher.

10 oz. White	**704-U-481**	**$4.49**
20 oz. White	**704-U-492**	**$7.99**
10 oz. Pink	**704-U-486**	**$4.49**
10 oz. Yellow	**704-U-487**	**$4.49**

Sparkle Gel

Squeeze on sparkling color effects with our ready-to-use gel. Great for dots, messages, water effects and fondant accents. Resealable 3.5 oz. tubes. Certified Kosher.
$2.99
Red 704-U-112
Pink 704-U-356
Green 704-U-111

Tube Decorating Icing

Tubes can be used with our Tip and Nail Set or Coupler Ring Set (p. 134) and any standard size Wilton metal tip. Colors match Wilton Icing Colors (p. 134). 4.25 oz. Certified Kosher. **$1.99**

Pink 704-U-230 Yellow 704-U-236
Violet 704-U-242 White 704-U-200
Leaf Green 704-U-224

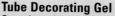

Tube Decorating Gel

Great for writing messages and decorating cakes and cookies. Colors match Wilton Icing Colors (p. 134). .75 oz. Certified Kosher. **$1.49**

Pink 704-U-330 Green 704-U-324
Violet 704-U-342 White 704-U-302
Yellow 704-U-336

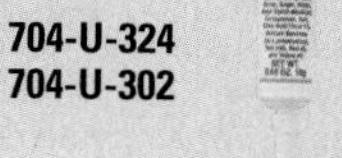

EASTER

Party

Baking Cups

Microwave-safe paper. Standard size, 2 in. diameter; Mini size, 1.25 in. diameter,
Standard
Pk./75 $2.09
Mini
Pk./100 $2.09

NEW!

Fuzzy Bunny
Standard 415-U-163
Mini 415-U-164

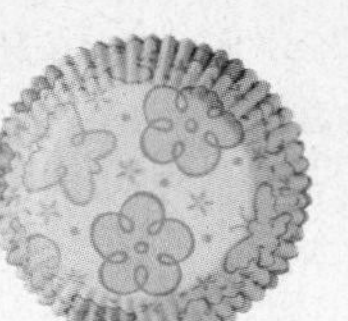

Spring Party
Standard 415-U-4761
Mini 415-U-4762

Party Bags

Colorful Easter designs for candy and cookie treats. 20 plastic bags, 20 ties included. 4 x 9.5 in.
Pk./20 $2.09

NEW!

Fuzzy Bunny
1912-U-9168

Spring Party
1912-U-1204

Icing Decorations

Perfect for topping cakes, cupcakes and cookies. Certified Kosher. **$2.29**

NEW!

Fuzzy Bunny
710-U-3085 Pk./9

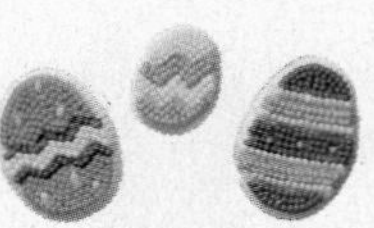

Petite Eggs
710-U-528 Pk./12

Shaped Bags with Drawstring

Large bags are 6 x 9.25 in.
Pk./15 $2.09

NEW!

Fuzzy Bunny
1912-U-1450

NEW!

Egg
1912-U-9169

Fuzzy Bunny Fun Pix®

Add a fun touch to cakes, cupcakes, ice cream and more. Approx. 3.5 in. high. Plastic.
2113-U-1499 Pk./12 $2.09

NEW!

Sprinkles

Individual Bottles

Shake up your Easter treats! Plastic bottles for convenient pouring and storing. Certified Kosher.

NEW!

Spring Nonpareils
5.25 oz. bottle.
710-U-935 $3.29

Bunny/Ducks Mix
2.5 oz. bottle.
710-U-870 $2.29

Spring Confetti
2 oz. bottle.
710-U-1278 $2.29
3 oz. bottle.
710-U-970 $3.29

Colorful Egg Mix
2.5 oz. bottle.
710-U-7486 $2.29
3.75 oz. bottle.
710-U-716 $3.29

Sparkling Sugars

Easy-pour sugars have a coarse texture and brilliant sparkle. 8 oz. Certified Kosher. **$4.49**

Pink/White
710-U-369

Lavender/White
710-U-371

Yellow/White
710-U-370

6-Mix

Includes Bunny/Ducks Sprinkle Mix, Colorful Egg Mix, Spring Confetti, Lavender, Pink and Green Sugars. 6.9 oz. Certified Kosher.
710-U-740 $5.99

DOILIES

Serve springtime treats on sweet pastel doilies in 4 in., 8 in. and 10 in. sizes. Pretty lace-look edges. Includes 4 doilies in each size. **$2.99**
Pink 2104-U-5560 Pk./12 **Yellow 2104-U-5559 Pk./12**

Pastel Silicone Baking Cups

No muffin pan needed! Bake and serve in reusable oven-safe cups in pretty pastels. 3 each pink, yellow, green, blue. Standard size, 2 in. diameter.
415-U-9413 Set/12 $9.99

Assorted Pastel Paper Baking Cups
25 each pink, yellow, blue.
Microwave-safe paper. **$1.59**
Standard 415-U-9396 Pk./75
Mini 415-U-9397 Pk./100

Colors

Easter Icing Colors Set

Lemon Yellow and Violet in .5 oz. jars. Certified Kosher.
601-U-5571 Set/2 $2.99

EASTER COLOR GUIDE

Pink | Violet | Yellow | Green/Leaf Green | White

FoodWriter™ Edible Color Markers

Use like ink markers to add fun and dazzling color to countless foods. Kids love 'em! Decorate on fondant, color flow, royal icing designs and cookie icing. Includes Pink and Purple markers (.07 oz. each). Certified Kosher.
609-U-104 Set/2 $4.19

Color Mist™ Food Color Spray

Gives decorators the versatility and dazzling effects of an airbrush in a convenient can! Use it to add sensational color to cakes, iced cookies and cupcakes. No mess, taste-free formula. 1.5 oz. Certified Kosher. **$3.29**
Pink 710-U-5505 **Yellow 710-U-5502**
Violet 710-U-5504 **Green 710-U-5503**

Candy

NEW!

Hatching Chick Pretzel Mold
2 designs, 6 cavities.
2115-U-1495 $1.99

NEW!

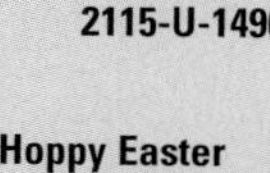

Fuzzy Bunny Lollipop Mold
4 designs, 4 cavities.
2115-U-1496 $1.99

NEW!

Decorated Eggs Lollipop Mold
3 designs, 3 cavities.
2115-U-1497 $1.99

NEW!

Easter Candy Making MEGA PACK

It's easy and fun, with lots of fun shapes and colorful Candy Melts®*! Kit includes: Spring Flowers Large Lollipop Mold (3 designs, 3 cavities), Easter Treats Lollipop Mold (6 designs, 12 cavities), Just Hatched Candy Mold (1 design, 8 cavities); 16 oz. Candy Melts®* (4 oz. each light cocoa, white, pink and yellow); 20 lollipop sticks (6 in.); 4 disposable decorating bags; decorating brush and 20 party bags/ties.
2104-U-1652 $9.99

See pages 166-169 for more Wilton candy items.

Hoppy Easter Lollipop Mold
8 designs, 9 cavities.
2115-U-1718 $1.99

Candy Melts®*

Ideal for molding, dipping or coating. Artificially vanilla flavored unless otherwise indicated. 14 oz. bag. Certified Kosher Dairy. **$2.79**

Pink	**1911-U-447**	**White**	**1911-U-498**
Lavender	**1911-U-403**	**Dark Cocoa Mint**	**1911-U-1920**
Yellow	**1911-U-463**	**Light Cocoa**	**1911-U-544**
Blue	**1911-U-448**	**Dark Cocoa**	**1911-U-358**

*Brand confectionery coating.

Cookie

NEW!

Easter Push 'N Print™ Cutter Set

Emboss a fun design before baking! It's so easy! Load one of the 3 imprint disks in the cutter, cut the cookie, then press the plunger with disk still in place to imprint the design. Disks are 2.9 in. diameter. Recipe included.
2308-U-4001 Set/4 $7.99

COMFORT GRIP™ CUTTERS

Cushion-grip cutters with extra-deep stainless steel sides. Recipe included. Approx. 4.5 x 1.5 in. deep.
$3.19

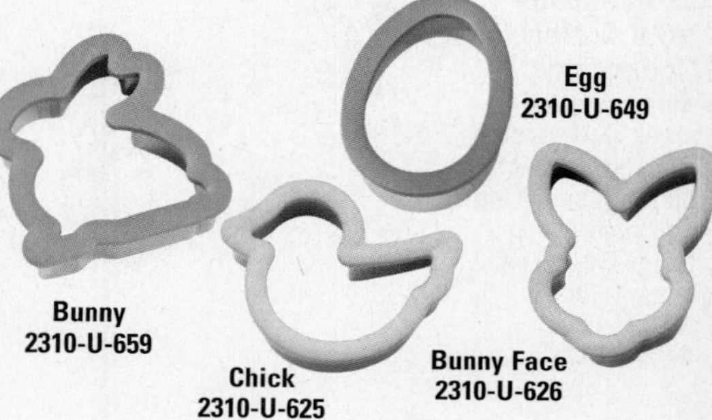

Bunny
2310-U-659

Chick
2310-U-625

Bunny Face
2310-U-626

Egg
2310-U-649

4 PC. GRIPPY™ CUTTER SET

Includes bunny, flower, egg, and butterfly, approx. 3.5 in.
2311-U-258 Set/4 $4.49

NEW!

Pre-Baked Easter Egg Cookie Kit

It's the perfect treat for Easter baskets or brunches. Includes 8 pre-baked cookies, (approx. 4 in. high); creamy white icing mix, 2 types of colorful candy, decorating bag and tip, easy instructions.
2104-U-4118 $10.99

Pre-Baked and Pre-Assembled Bunny Hutch Cookie House Kit

Everything is included: a pre-baked, pre-built hutch, yellow and pink decorating icing mixes, candies, icing decorations, 2 cookie bunny ears, 2 decorating bags and tips, cardboard base and complete instructions. Hutch 5.25 x 5.25 x 6 in. high.
2104-U-1594 $13.99

Easter Cupcake & Cookie Stencils

Place 1 of the 8 designs over treat, then decorate with Wilton Cake Sparkles™, Colored Sugars or Color Mist™ Food Color Spray. 8 designs.
417-U-496 Set/8 $2.19

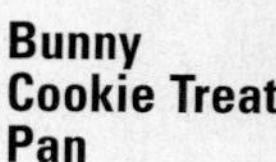

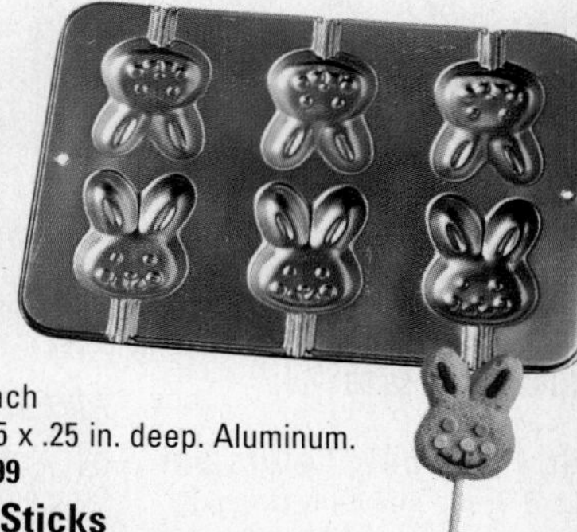

Bunny Cookie Treat Pan

Just press cookie dough into pan, insert a cookie stick, then bake, cool and decorate. Each treat is 3.5 x 2.75 x .25 in. deep. Aluminum.
2105-U-8106 $9.99

Cookie Treat Sticks
6 in. 1912-U-9319 Pk./20 $1.99
8 in. 1912-U-9318 Pk./20 $2.99

PLASTIC CUTTERS

Child-safe design means kids can have a great time helping. And remember all the fun ways to use our cutters—for bread shapes, stencils, sun catchers and so much more.

10 Pc. Easter Egg Canister Cutter Set

A fun and convenient egg canister holds 10 cutters, each approx. 3.5 in.
2304-U-95
Set/10 $5.99

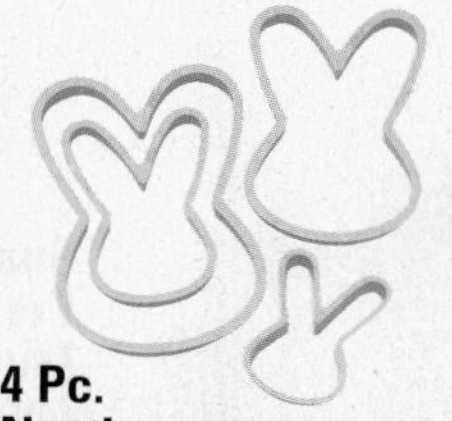

5 Pc. Easter Bite-Size Cutter Set

Bunny, tulip, chick, egg and bunny face shapes. Each approx. 1.5 in.
2303-U-9319
Set/5 $2.49

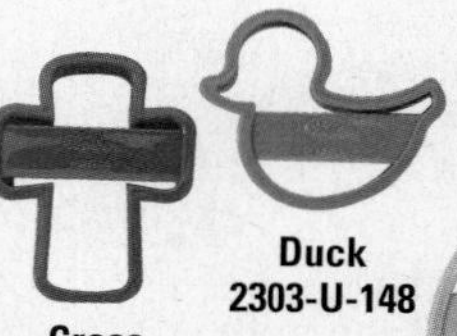

4 Pc. Nesting Bunnies Cutter Set

Sizes from 1.25 to 4.2 in.
2303-U-9270 Set/4 $2.99

Cross
2303-U-141

Duck
2303-U-148

Individual Cutters

Each approx. 3 x 4 in.
$0.69

Egg
2303-U-119

Cookie Cutters

METAL CUTTERS

Put variety in your cookie-making with fun Easter multi-shape sets. There are styles to please everyone. Recipe included.

18 Pc. Easter Cutter Collection
Cross, butterfly, chick, bunny, jelly bean, sun, egg, carrot, basket, leaping bunny, bunny face, daisy, sprinkling can, tulip, umbrella, lamb, rabbit and flower cutters are approx. 3 in.
2308-U-1134
Set/18 $10.49

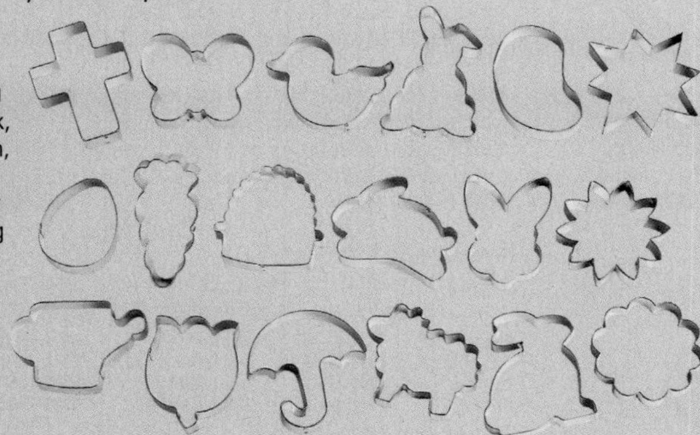

12 Pc. Easter Mini Cutter Collection
Bunny face, egg, cross, flower, tulip, sun, carrot, chick, butterfly, sprinkling can, umbrella and bunny cutters are approx. 1.5 in.
2308-U-1254
Set/12 $5.29

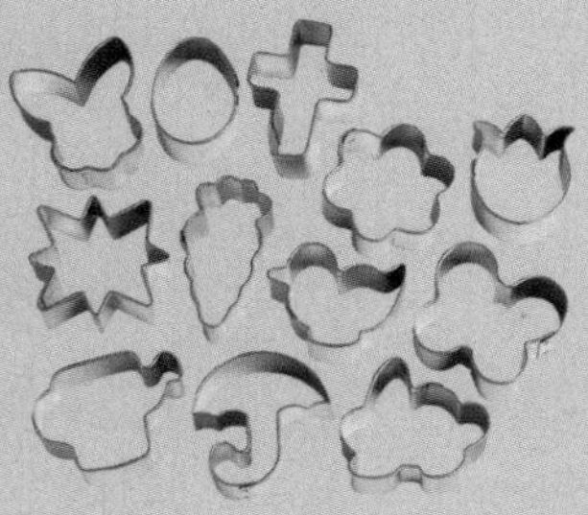

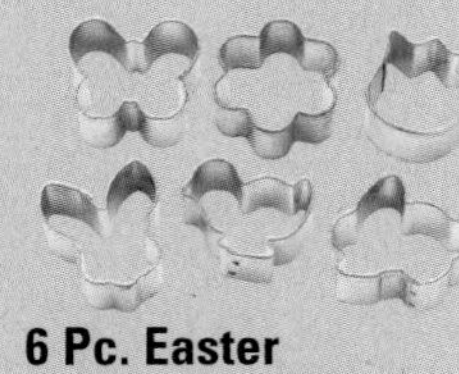

6 Pc. Easter Mini Cutter Set
Butterfly, daisy, tulip, bunny face, chick and bunny, each approx. 1.5 in.
2308-U-1209 Set/6 $3.19

Colorful Cutter Sets

Our metal cutters look great with their bright colors and fun shapes. Perfect for hanging until your next cookie-baking bash.

3 Pc. Easter Cutter Set
Set of 3 includes bunny, tulip and butterfly, each approx. 3 to 3.5 in. Coated metal.
2308-U-1216 Set/3 $3.69

4 Pc. Hoppy Easter Cutter Set
Springtime favorites in pastels of the season. Tulip, egg, butterfly and bunny. Coated metal. Each approx. 3.5 in.
2308-U-1207 Set/4 $4.79

9 Pc. Easter Cutter Collection
Lamb, tulip, flower, bunny, chick, egg, butterfly, bunny face, and carrot cutters are approx. 3 in. Colored aluminum.
2308-U-2503
Set/9 $10.49

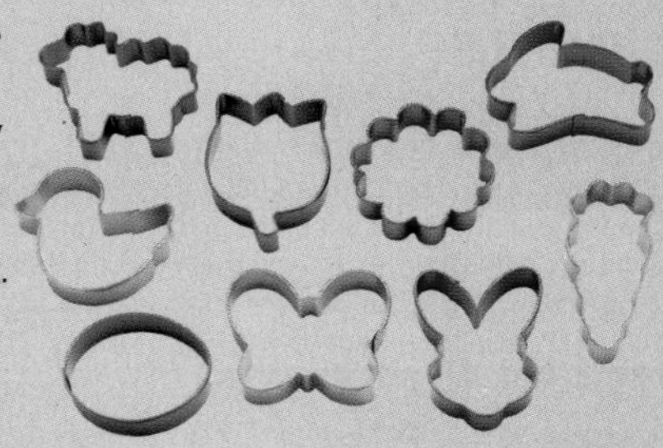

ST. PATRICK'S DAY

Shamrock Pan
Celebrate St. Patrick's Day with this fun symbol of joy and celebration. Also great for school parties, birthdays, sports celebrations and much more. One-mix pan is 11.75 x 2 in. deep. Aluminum.
2105-U-185 $9.99

St. Pat's Icing Colors Set
Leaf Green and Kelly Green in .5 oz. jars. Certified Kosher.
601-U-5571 Set/2 $2.99

Shamrock Icing Decorations
Sugar-flavored. Certified Kosher.
710-U-286 Pk./9 $2.29

Shamrock Shaped Bags with Drawstring
Large bags are 6.75 x 9 in.
1912-U-1052 Pk./15 $2.09

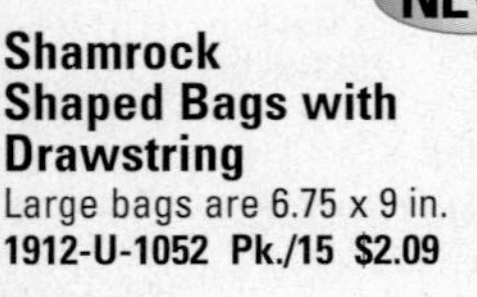

Sparkle Gel
Squeeze on sparkling color effects with our ready-to-use gel. Great for dots, messages, water effects and fondant accents. Resealable 3.5 oz. tubes. Certified Kosher.
Green 704-U-111 $2.99

Shamrock Foil Fun Pix®
Add a shimmering, lucky touch to cakes, cupcakes, ice cream and more. Approx. 3½ in. high. Foil.
2113-U-1347
Pk./12 $2.09

NEW!

Shamrock Pretzel Mold
2 designs, 6 cavities.
2115-U-1499
$1.99

Shamrock Baking Cups
Microwave-safe paper. Standard size, 2 in. diameter; Mini size, 1.25 in. diameter. **$2.09**
Standard 415-U-1410 Pk./75
Mini 415-U-1411 Pk./100

Shamrock Party Bags
20 plastic bags, 20 ties included.
4 x 9.5 in.
1912-U-2233
Pk./20 $2.09

Shamrock Lollipop Mold
1 design, 5 cavities.
2115-U-1545 $1.99

Shamrock Sprinkle Mix
Shake up your St. Patrick's Day treats! Plastic 2.5 oz. bottle for convenient pouring and storing. Certified Kosher.
710-U-7485 $2.29

Shamrock Comfort Grip™ Cutter
Cushion-grip with extra-deep stainless steel sides gives you comfortable control even when cutting into thick desserts. Recipe included. 4.5 x 1.5 in. deep.
2310-U-648
$3.19

Shamrock Green Metal Cookie Cutter
Quality metal cuts neatly. Approx. 3 in.
2308-U-1320
$0.79

4-Leaf Clover Cookie Cutter
Cut cookies, sandwiches and use in crafts. Plastic; 3 in. wide.
2303-U-134 $0.69

PATRIOTIC

Bakeware

Stars and Stripes Pan
Decorate a grand old flag cake perfect for that July 4th cookout. Accent Old Glory with Piping Gel and fresh summer fruit. One-mix pan is 13 x 9 x 2 in. Aluminum.
2105-U-183 $9.99

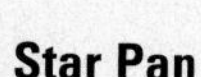

Star Pan
Your colorful star cake will set off sparks on the 4th and brighten parties all year long. One-mix pan is 12.75 x 1.9 in. deep. Aluminum.
2105-U-2512
$12.99

Mini Star Pan
One mix makes 12-16 stars. 6 cavities, 4.75 x 1 in. deep. Aluminum.
2105-U-1235
$14.49

Silicone Mini Star Mold
Microwave freezer, refrigerator, and dishwasher safe oven safe to 500°F. One mix makes 20-24 stars. 6 cavities, each 2.6 x 2.5 x 1.5 in. deep.
2105-U-4819 $9.99

Cookie

NEW!

3 Pc. Red, White and Blue Cutter Set
Bake a star studded salute to the USA with colorful cutters in sizes from 3.25 to 5 in. Coated metal.
2308-U-1240 Set/3 $4.19

Star Metal Cookie Cutter
Quality metal is clean-cutting and easy to handle. 3in.
2308-U-1008 $0.69

Comfort Grip™ Cutters
Cushion-grip cutters with extra-deep stainless steel sides perfect for cutting so many favorite foods into patriotic shapes. The cushion grip gives you comfortable control even when cutting into thick desserts. Recipe included. 4.5 x 1.5 in. deep. **$3.19**

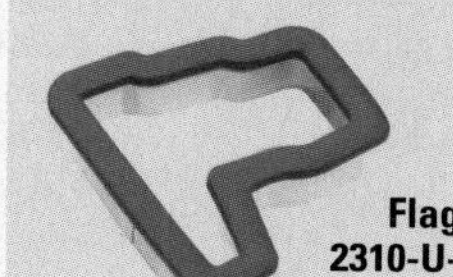

Flag
2310-U-651

Star
2310-U-605

4 Pc. Patriotic Cutter Set
Bold colors add to the fun! Set of 4 favorite shapes includes star, USA, flag and shooting star. Sizes from 3 to 3.5 in. Coated metal.
2308-U-1257
Set/4 $4.79

4 Pc. Nesting Stars Metal Cutter Set
A parade of small to large stars to create fun cookies for the 4th or all year long. Sizes from 5 to 2.5 in.
2308-U-1215 Set/4 $4.79

6 Pc. Nesting Stars Cutter Set
Plastic.
1.6 to 4.6 in.
2304-U-704
Set/6 $2.99

Patriotic Cupcake & Cookie Stencils
Just place one of the fun designs over your baked treat, then sprinkle with Wilton Cake Sparkles™ or Colored Sugars or spray with Color Mist™ Food Color Spray (p. 214). 8 designs.
417-U-498 $2.19

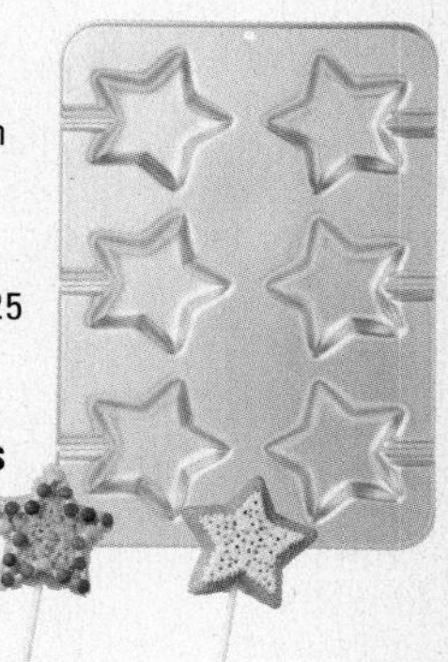

Star Cookie Treat Pan
Just press cookie dough into pan, insert a cookie stick, then bake, cool and decorate. Makes 6 individual treats, 3.5 x .25 in. deep. Aluminum.
2105-U-8102 $9.99

Cookie Treat Sticks
6 in. 1912-U-9319
Pk./20 $1.99
8 in. 1912-U-9318
Pk./20 $2.99

Icings

PATRIOTIC COLOR GUIDE

Red White Blue

Ready-to-Decorate Icing
Anyone can decorate with Wilton Ready-to-Decorate Icing! Our brilliant colors and 4 decorating tips make it a breeze to add an exciting finishing touch to treats without mixing or mess. 6.4 oz. Certified Kosher. **$4.29**

Red	**710-U-4400**
White	**710-U-4402**
Blue	**710-U-4407**

NEW!

Cookie Icing
Just heat and squeeze onto cookies using the convenient cap. Sets smooth in just 45 minutes. 10 oz. bottle covers approx. 12 cookies 3 in. each; 20 oz. bottle covers approximately 24. Certified Kosher.

10 oz. White	**704-U-481**	**$4.49**
20 oz. White	**704-U-492**	**$7.99**
10 oz. Red	**704-U-488**	**$4.49**

Sparkle Gel
Squeeze on sparkling color effects with our ready-to-use gel. Great for dots, messages, water effects and fondant accents. Resealable 3.5 oz. tubes. Certified Kosher.
$2.99

Red	**704-U-112**
Blue	**704-U-110**

Tube Decorating Icing
Tubes can be used with our Tip and Nail Set or Coupler Ring Set (p. 134) and any standard size Wilton metal tip. Colors match Wilton Icing Colors (p. 134). 4.25 oz. Certified Kosher.
$1.99

Red	**704-U-218**
White	**704-U-200**
Royal Blue	**704-U-248**

Tube Decorating Gel
Transparent gels are great for writing messages and decorating cakes and cookies. Colors match Wilton Icing Colors (p. 134). .75 oz. Certified Kosher. **$1.49**

Red	**704-U-318**
White	**704-U-302**
Royal Blue	**704-U-348**

Party

Baking Cups

Microwave-safe paper. Standard size, 2 in. diameter.
Pk./75 $2.09

Old Glory
415-U-2236

Patriotic Stars
415-U-2235

Party Bags

Colorful Patriotic designs for candy and cookie treats. 20 plastic bags, 20 ties included. 4 x 9.5 in.
Pk./20 $2.09

Old Glory
1912-U-3056

Patriotic Stars
1912-U-1254

Icing Decorations

Perfect for topping cakes, cupcakes, cookies. Certified Kosher.
$2.29

Patriotic Flags
710-U-726 Pk./9

Patriotic Stars
710-U-942 Pk./21

CANDLES

Patriotic

Feature bold textured spirals and a fun handcarved star on top. 3¼ in. high.
2811-U-1122
Pk./4 $3.89

Beer Cans
1¾ in. high.
2811-U-9326
Set/6 $3.89

Red and Blue Sparklers
6½ in. high.
2811-U-704
Pk./18 $1.09

Sprinkles

Individual Bottles

Plastic bottles for easy pouring and storing. Certified Kosher. **$2.29**

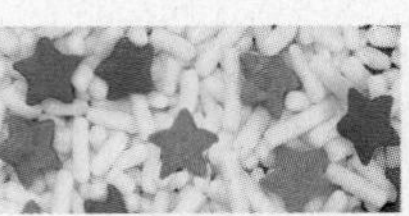

Patriotic Mix
2.5 oz. bottle.
710-U-786

Patriotic Nonpareils
3 oz. bottle.
710-U-1123

Red Sugar
3.25 oz. bottle.
710-U-766

Blue Sugar
3.25 oz. bottle.
710-U-750

Cake Sparkles™

Edible glitter, .25 oz. bottle. Certified Kosher. **$3.19**

Red
703-U-1284

Blue
703-U-1314

6-Mix Assortment

Includes Red and Blue Jimmies, Patriotic Mix, Red and Blue Sugar and Patriotic Sprinkle Sparks. 6.45 oz. Certified Kosher.
710-U-656 $5.99

Stars and Stripes Party Picks

3 in. high mini flags. Paper.
2113-U-704 Pk./40 $1.49

Patriotic Foil Pix

Looks like a dazzling fireworks display on your holiday treats! Great for cakes, cupcakes. 4 in. high. Foil.
2113-U-712 Pk./12 $2.09

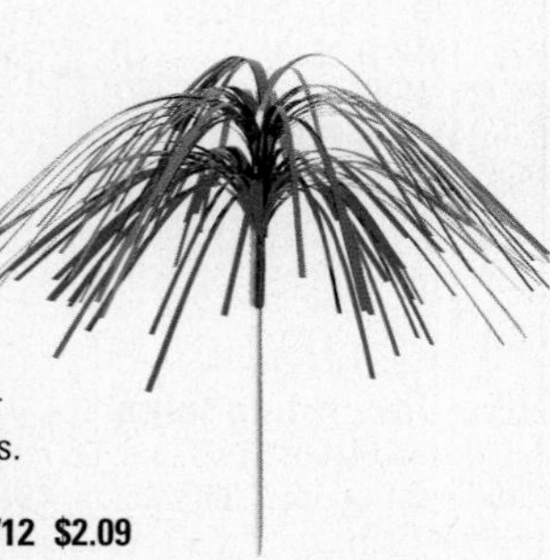

Cupcakes 'N More® Dessert Stands

Individually decorated cupcakes are the perfect way to add a personal touch to celebrations. Now, with Cupcakes 'N More, you have the perfect way to serve them, featuring coated wire spirals to securely hold each cupcake.

38 Count Standard
15 x 18 in. wide. Holds 38 cupcakes
307-U-651 $41.99

23 Count Standard
12 x 13 in. wide. Holds 23 standard cupcakes.
307-U-826 $31.49

13 Count Standard (shown)
9.25 x 9 in. wide. Holds 13 standard cupcakes.
307-U-831 $13.69

24 Count Mini
10.5 x 9 in. wide. Holds 24 mini cupcakes.
307-U-250 $15.79

Colors

See Color Guide p. 213.

Color Mist™ Food Color Spray

Dazzling effects of an airbrush in a convenient can! Add sensational color, to iced cakes, cookies and cupcakes. No mess, taste-free formula. 1.5 oz. Certified Kosher.
$3.29

Red	**710-U-5500**
Blue	**710-U-5501**

Candy

Stars Candy Mold
1 design, 12 cavities,
2115-U-1554 $1.99

Patriotic Pretzel Mold
3 designs, 6 cavities.
2115-U-4439 $1.99

Candy Melts®*

Ideal for molding, dipping or coating. Artificially vanilla flavored unless otherwise indicated.
14 oz. bag. Certified Kosher Dairy. **$2.79**

Red	**1911-U-499**	**Dark Cocoa Mint**	**1911-U-1920**
White	**1911-U-498**	**Light Cocoa**	**1911-U-544**
Blue	**1911-U-448**	**Dark Cocoa**	**1911-U-358**

*Brand confectionery coating.

See pages 166-169 for more Wilton candy items.

COMMUNION

Cross Pan
Beveled design is excellent with rolled fondant. One-mix pan is 14.5 x 11.2 x 2 in. deep. Instructions included. Aluminum.
2105-U-2509 $9.99

TOPPERS

Inspirational Cross
Beautifully designed in sculpted resin. 5½ in. high.
202-U-398 $14.99

Communion Girl†
3½ in. high.
2113-U-7878 $3.69

Communion Boy†
3½ in. high.
2113-U-7886 $3.69

†Designed by Ellen Williams.

FAITH CROSS ACCESSORIES

Stationery
Beautifully designed in white 80 lb. card stock with white pearlized trim. Professionally print at home at **www.wiltonprint.com**.

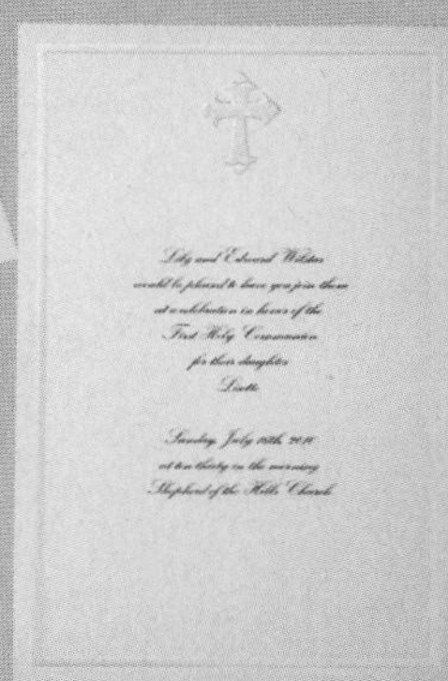

Invitations
Border and cross accent. Invitation: 5.5 x 8.5 in.; envelope: 5.75 x 8.75 in. **1008-U-775 Pk./12 $4.99**

Thank You Cards
Folded cards with script and cross on front. Card: 5.5 x 4.25 in.; envelope: 5.75 x approx. 4.5 in. **1008-U-776 Pk./12 $4.99**

Seals
Self adhesive, silver tone, 1 in. dia.
1008-U-779 Pk./24 $1.99

Centerpiece
Stunning silver and white design, crafted in heavy card stock with honeycomb paper base. Assembled measures 7¾ x 9¾ in. high.
1006-U-7148 $2.99

Cake Pick
Perfect for religious celebrations. Painted resin. Food-safe. 5 in. high.
1006-U-4475 $14.99

Garland
Silver printed crosses on white paper garland make a beautiful, inspirational decoration for your celebration. 6 ft. long, accordion folded. Unfold and use tape or ribbon to hang.
1006-U-498 $5.99

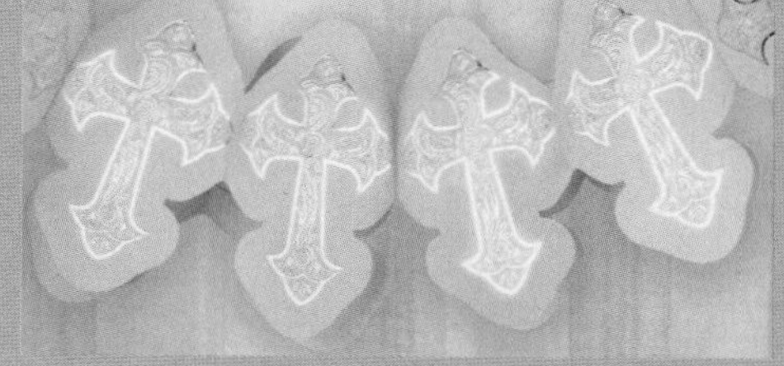

GRADUATION

Smiley Grad Pan
A smart choice to honor any student who's made the grade—boy or girl, kindergartner to collegian. One-mix pan is 10.25 x 12 x 2 in. deep. Aluminum.
2105-U-2073 $9.99

Topping Off Success Pan
Decorate in your grad's school colors. One-mix pan is 14.75 x 11.75 x 2 in. deep. Aluminum.
2105-U-2038 $9.99

Two-Mix Book Pan
Detail any of life's important chapters, including graduation. 11.5 x 15 x 2.75 in. deep. Serves up to 30. Aluminum.
2105-U-2521 $17.99

Graduation Cap Black Metal Cookie Cutter
Quality metal cuts neatly and is easy to handle. Coated metal. Approx. 3.5 in.
509-U-319 $0.79

Party

Baking Cups

Microwave-safe paper. Standard size, 2 in. diameter.
Pk./75 $2.09

Congrats
415-U-1349

Smiley Grad
415-U-4592

Party Bags

Colorful grad designs for candy and cookie treats. 20 plastic bags, 20 ties included.
4 x 9.5 in.
Pk./20 $2.09

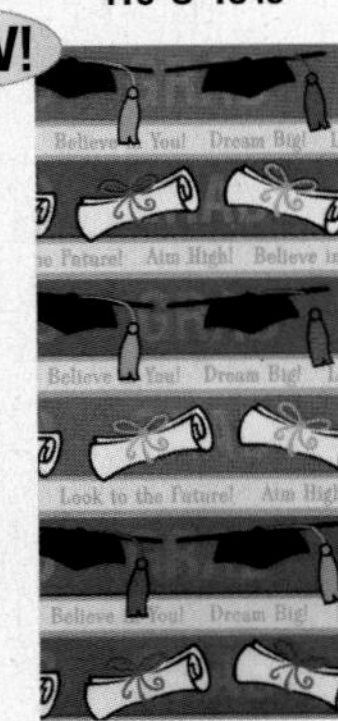

Congrats
1912-U-1349

Smiley Grad
1912-U-1130

Icing Decorations

Perfect on cakes, cupcakes, cookies. Mint-flavored. Certified Kosher. **$2.29**

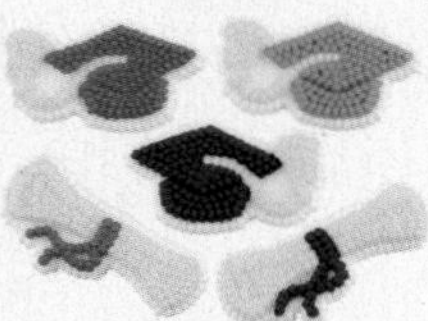

Graduation
710-U-1125 Pk./12

Petite Smiley Grad
710-U-503 Pk./12

Grad Fun Pix®

Add a fun touch to cakes, cupcakes, ice cream and more. Approx. 3½ in. high. Paper.
2113-U-717
Pk./24 $2.09

Autograph Mat

A party memento to be filled with greetings from every guest for the grad to treasure forever. Includes black pen. Fits into your 11 x 14 in. frame, holds 5 x 7 in. photo.
1009-U-241 $5.99

Sprinkles

INDIVIDUAL BOTTLES

Plastic bottles for easy pouring and storing. Certified Kosher. **$2.29**

NEW!

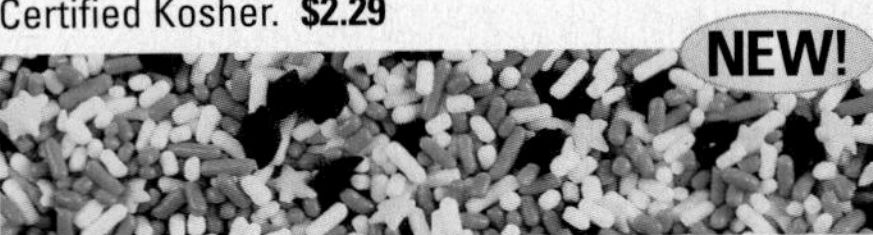

Mortar Board Mix
Contains black mortar boards, blue and white jimmies and yellow stars. 3.25 oz. bottle.
710-U-040

TOPPERS

Graduation Toppers

Capture the day's excitement with our beautifully-detailed plastic toppers on your special cake. Approx. 4¼ in. high.

Female Graduate
2113-U-1821 $2.09

Male Graduate
2113-U-1823 $2.09

Glowing Graduate
2113-U-1833 $2.09

Successful Graduate
2113-U-4549 $2.09

Graduation Caps Set

Great party favors or cake toppers. 2 in. high. Plastic.
Set/2 $2.09
White 2113-U-1800
Black 2113-U-1801

Candle Set

3 caps, 3 diplomas, ½ to 2 in. high.
2811-U-1800 Set/6 $3.89

Champagne Bottle Candles

2 in. high.
2811-U-163 Set/6 $3.89

Candy

Graduation Pretzel Mold
3 designs, 6 cavities.
2115-U-1445 $1.99

Graduation Lollipop Mold
6 designs, 8 cavities,
2115-U-1729 $1.99

Candy Melts®*

Ideal for all your candy molding, dipping or coating. Artificially vanilla flavored unless otherwise indicated. 14 oz. bag. Certified Kosher Dairy. **$2.79**

Yellow	**1911-U-463**
White	**1911-U-498**
Blue	**1911-U-448**
Dark Cocoa Mint	**1911-U-1920**
Light Cocoa	**1911-U-544**
Dark Cocoa	**1911-U-358**

*Brand confectionery coating.

See pages 166-169 for more Wilton candy items.

Print Your Own Stationery

Create your own distinctive invitations and more with professional results right at home. It's easy to do—simply go to www.wiltonprint.com and see how!

Complete Kits

Kits are ready to personalize, print and mail! All are crafted in 80 lb. card stock, feature distinctive accents and include 3 test sheets. Invitations—5.5 x 8.5 in., Reply Cards—5.5 x 4.25 in., Programs—3.75 x 8.5 in.

NEW!

Glitz and Glamour
White/Pearlized White/Glittered Vellum Wrap.
Set of 25 Includes:
- 25 Invitations and Mailing Envelopes
- 25 Reply Cards and Envelopes
- 25 Vellum Wraps
- 25 Ribbon and Flower Embellishments, Adhesives

1008-U-314 Set/25 $24.99

NEW!

Pressed Floral
Ivory with Natural Paper Wrap.
Set of 50 Includes:
- 50 Invitations and Mailing Envelopes
- 50 Reply Cards and Envelopes
- 50 Ribbon and Pre-tied Bows, Adhesives

1008-U-662 Set/50 $34.99

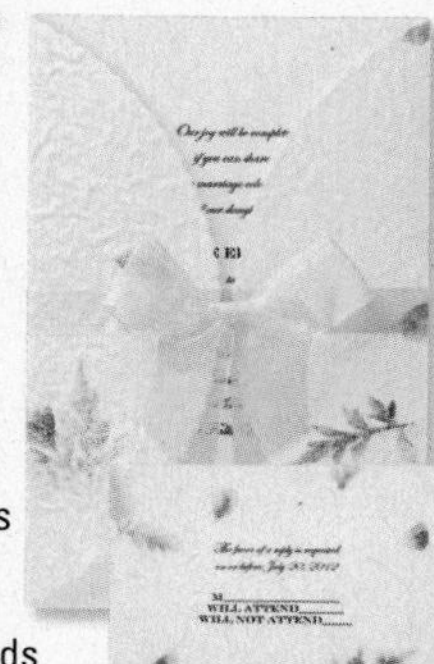

NEW!

Sweet Hearts
White/Silver.
Set of 50 Includes:
- 50 Invitations and Mailing Envelopes
- 50 Reply Cards and Envelopes

1008-U-668
Set/50 $24.99
Also available in Ivory with Gold.
1008-U-110 Set/50 $24.99

NEW!

Sweet Hearts Trifold Programs
White/Silver.
Set of 50 Includes:
- 50 Programs

1008-U-656
Set/50 $14.99

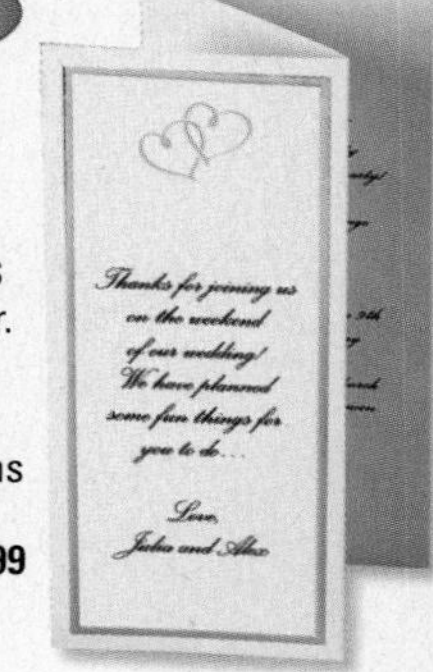

STATIONERY

NEW!

Doves
White.
Set of 50 Includes:
- 50 Invitations and Mailing Envelopes
- 50 Reply Cards and Envelopes

1008-U-972
Set/50 $24.99

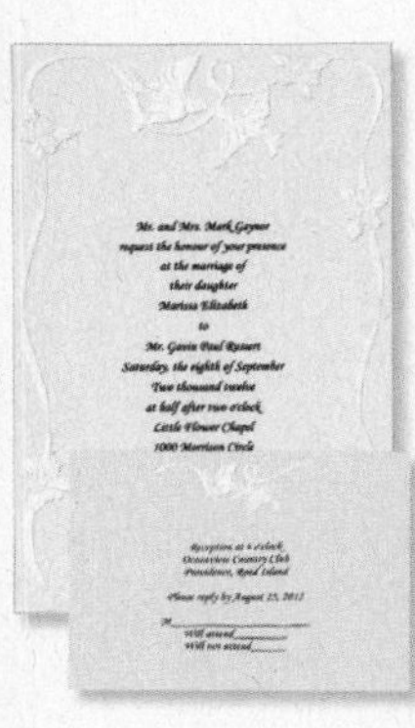

The Two of Us
White.
Set of 25 Includes:
- 25 Invitations and Mailing Envelopes
- 25 Reply Cards and Envelopes
- 25 Pre-tied Bows with Adhesives

Holds 4 x 6 in. image.
1008-U-709 Set/25 $24.99

Simple Yet Elegant
White.
Set of 25 Includes:
- 25 Invitations and Mailing Envelopes
- 25 Reply Cards and Envelopes
- 25 Pre-tied Bows with Adhesives, Circle Tags and Ball Chains

1008-U-530 Set/25 $24.99
Also available in Ivory.
1008-U-531 Set/25 $24.99

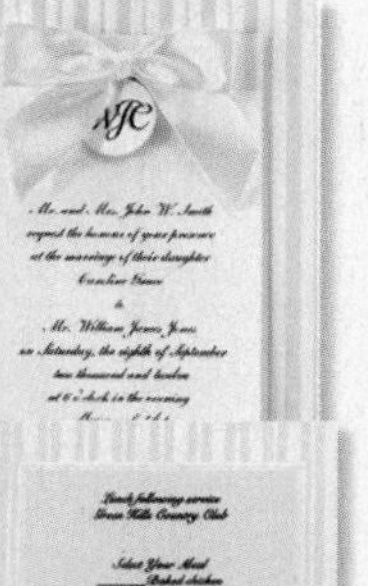

Happy Day
White with White/Glittered Vellum Pocket.
Set of 25 Includes:
- 25 Invitations and Mailing Envelopes
- 25 Reply Cards and Envelopes
- 25 Pre-tied Bows with Faux Rhinestone Trim, Adhesives

1008-U-711 Set/25 $24.99

Soirée
White with Vellum Overlay.
Set of 25 Includes:
- 25 Invitations and Mailing Envelopes
- 25 Reply Cards and Envelopes
- 25 Vellum Overlays
- 25 Rhinestone Buckles with Ribbons

1008-U-710 Set/25 $24.99

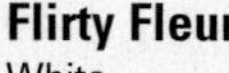

Flirty Fleur
White.
Set of 50 Includes:
- 50 Invitations and Mailing Envelopes
- 50 Reply Cards and Envelopes

1008-U-525
Set/50 $24.99

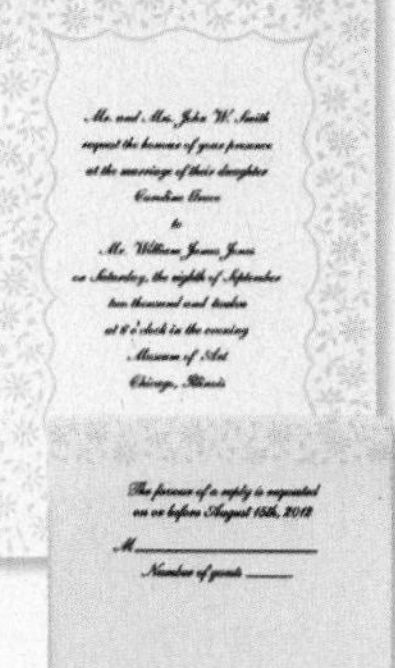

NEW!

Bride
White/Blue.
Set of 12 Includes:
- 12 Invitations and Mailing Envelopes
- 12 Tulle and Pre-tied Bow Embellishments

1008-U-789 Set/12 $9.99

NEW!

Magnets

Engagement Ring
Printable magnets are perfect for Save the Date notices and special announcements. Includes Magnets and Mailing Envelopes, 3 Test Sheets. Printed magnets measure 5.1 x 7.3 in. White/Pink.
3302-U-5511 Set/12 $9.99

Also available in quantities of 6.
3302-U-5502 Set/6 $4.99

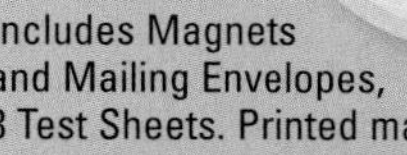

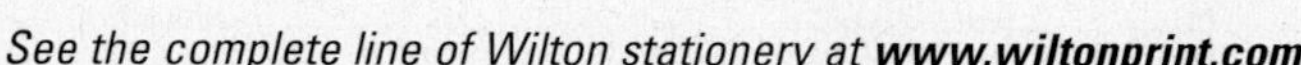

*See the complete line of Wilton stationery at **www.wiltonprint.com**.*

Wedding Style

Wilton has a beautiful selection of products for today's bride. From toasting glasses to garters to favors, we'll help you design the wedding day of your dreams!

Wedding Ensembles

Fulfill your wedding day dreams with the finest coordinated wedding accessories. Nicely presented, a complete collection makes a beautiful gift. Or enjoy the flexibility of choosing individual accessories that personalize the wedding day!

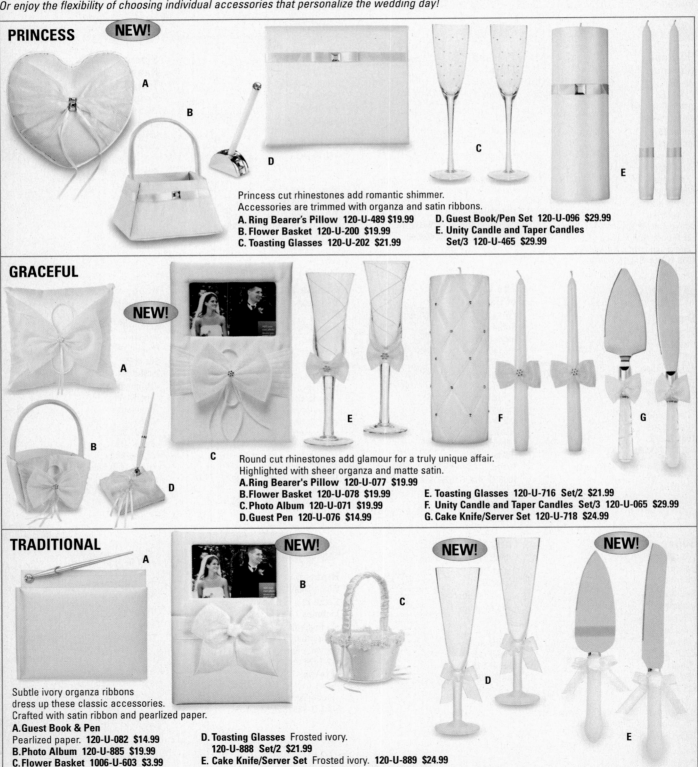

PRINCESS

NEW!

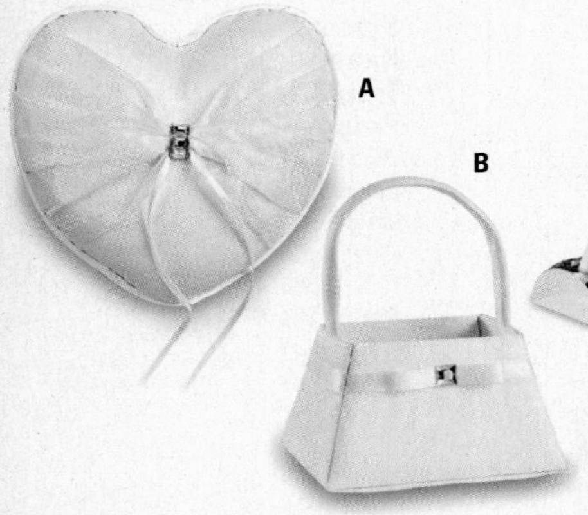

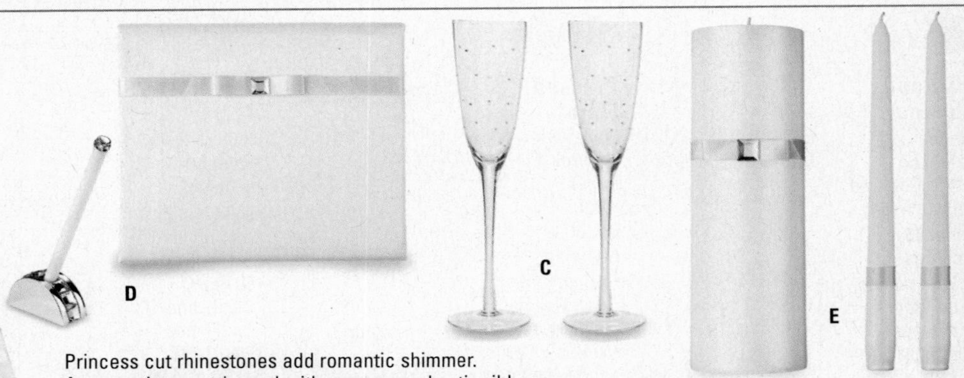

A B C D E

Princess cut rhinestones add romantic shimmer.
Accessories are trimmed with organza and satin ribbons.

A. Ring Bearer's Pillow 120-U-489 $19.99
B. Flower Basket 120-U-200 $19.99
C. Toasting Glasses 120-U-202 $21.99
D. Guest Book/Pen Set 120-U-096 $29.99
E. Unity Candle and Taper Candles Set/3 120-U-465 $29.99

GRACEFUL

NEW!

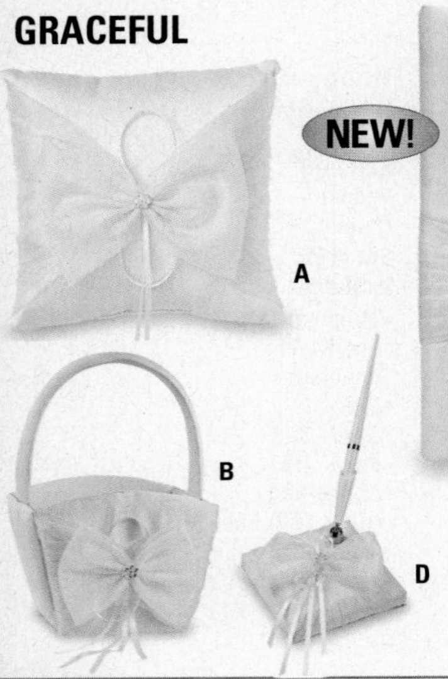

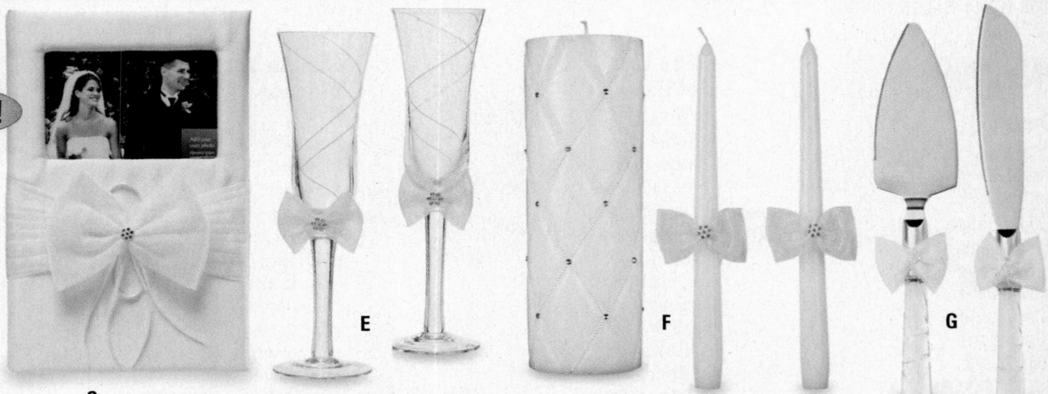

A B C D E F G

Round cut rhinestones add glamour for a truly unique affair.
Highlighted with sheer organza and matte satin.

A. Ring Bearer's Pillow 120-U-077 $19.99
B. Flower Basket 120-U-078 $19.99
C. Photo Album 120-U-071 $19.99
D. Guest Pen 120-U-076 $14.99
E. Toasting Glasses 120-U-716 Set/2 $21.99
F. Unity Candle and Taper Candles Set/3 120-U-065 $29.99
G. Cake Knife/Server Set 120-U-718 $24.99

TRADITIONAL

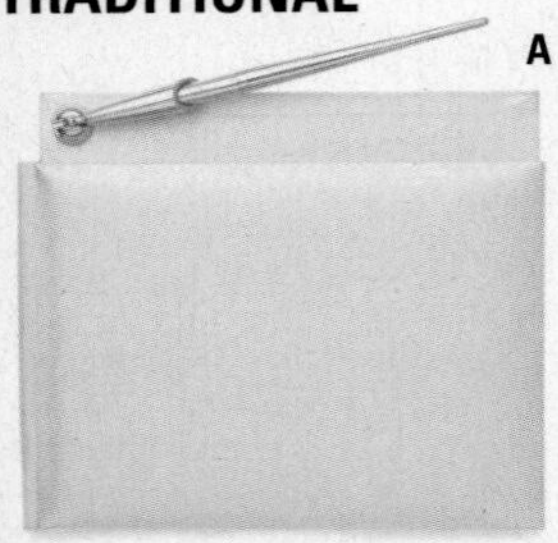

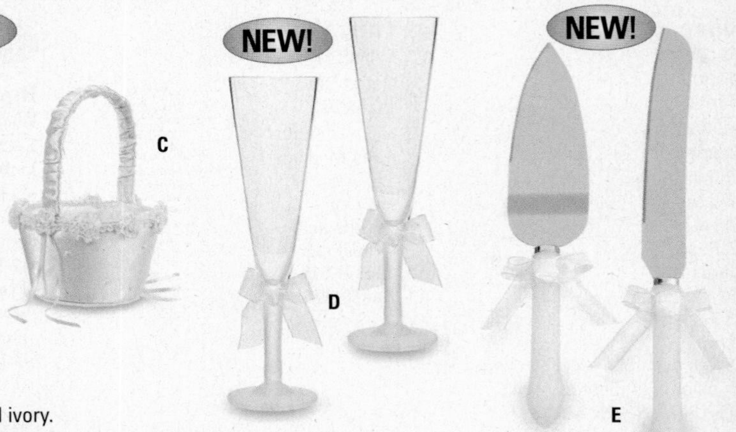

NEW! NEW! NEW!

A B C D E

Subtle ivory organza ribbons dress up these classic accessories. Crafted with satin ribbon and pearlized paper.

A. Guest Book & Pen
Pearlized paper. **120-U-082 $14.99**
B. Photo Album 120-U-885 $19.99
C. Flower Basket 1006-U-603 $3.99
D. Toasting Glasses Frosted ivory. **120-U-888 Set/2 $21.99**
E. Cake Knife/Server Set Frosted ivory. **120-U-889 $24.99**

TIMELESS

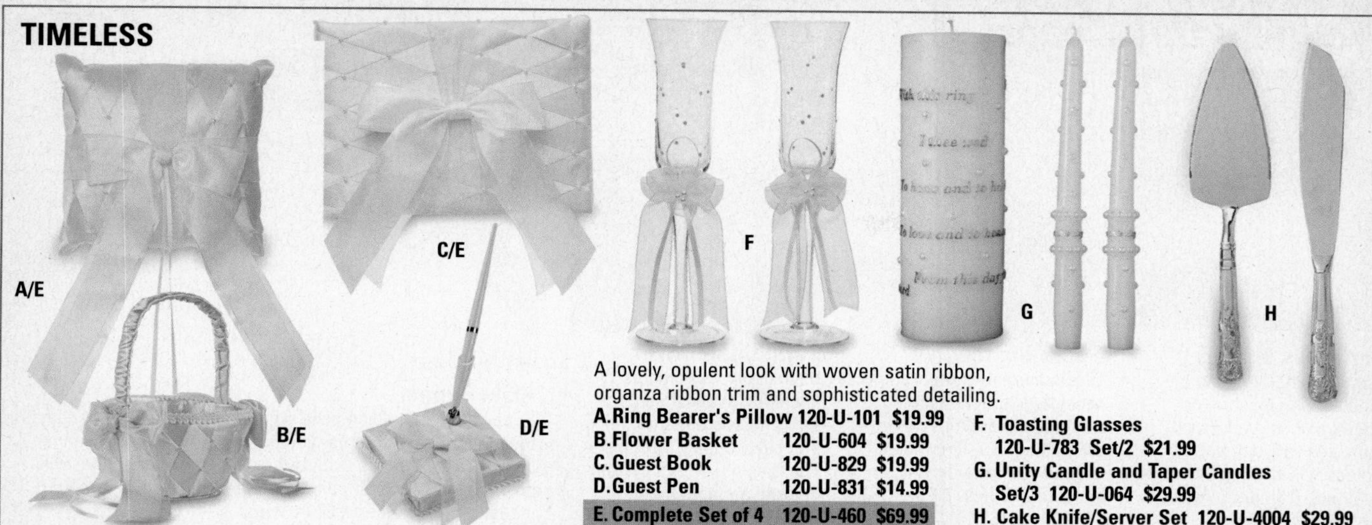

A lovely, opulent look with woven satin ribbon, organza ribbon trim and sophisticated detailing.

A. Ring Bearer's Pillow 120-U-101 $19.99
B. Flower Basket 120-U-604 $19.99
C. Guest Book 120-U-829 $19.99
D. Guest Pen 120-U-831 $14.99
E. Complete Set of 4 120-U-460 $69.99
F. Toasting Glasses 120-U-783 Set/2 $21.99
G. Unity Candle and Taper Candles Set/3 120-U-064 $29.99
H. Cake Knife/Server Set 120-U-4004 $29.99

HEART SILVER

Heart Silver Toasting Glasses and Serving Ensemble
Bring the ultimate look of romance to your celebration. Silver-plated. **120-U-232 Set/4 $49.99**

TOASTING GLASSES

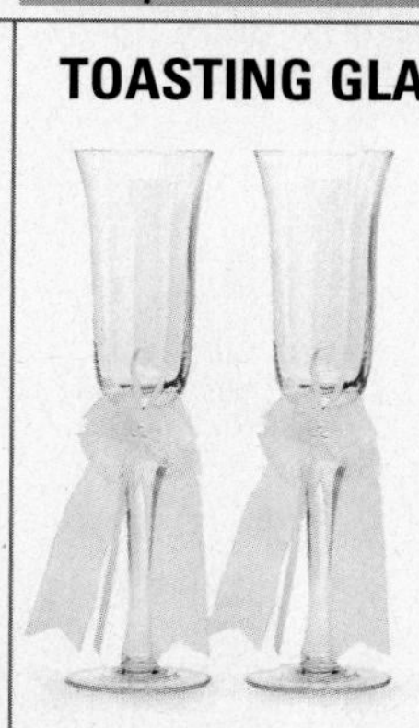

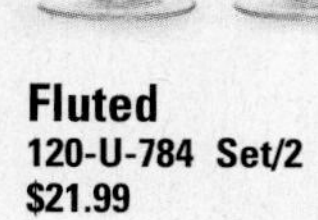

Fluted
120-U-784 Set/2
$21.99

Bride and Groom
120-U-708 Set/2
$21.99

GUEST PENS

Silver-tone
120-U-152
$5.99

White
120-U-814
$5.99

Wedding Day Accessories

French Rose Wedding Bouquet
Perfect, beautiful blooms to keep or to use during the bouquet toss. Hand-crafted, fine faux flowers. Bouquet measures approx. 9.5 in. diameter x 7.5 in.
120-U-1013 $24.99

White Rose Boutonniere
Perfect for weddings, prom, special occasions
1006-U-694 $4.99

Glass Candleholder Set
Bring the beauty and shimmer of crystal-look glass to your candle lighting ceremony. Ribbon trim. Unity candleholder is 5.75 in. high; holds a pillar candle up to 3.75 in. diameter. Each taper candleholder is 4.25 in. high; holds a standard size taper. Candles not included.
120-U-088 Set/3 $34.99

Fresh Look Bouquet Holder
Make bouquets for the wedding party!
It's easy to do, using your favorite silk or fabric flowers.
1006-U-611
$7.99

Silver Bouquet Holder
Arrange the bride's favorite flowers in this keepsake holder. Silver-plated. 7.5 in. long.
120-U-651 $12.99

Flower-Shaped Petals
Fill the flower girl's basket, scatter on the cake table, decorate favors. Lifelike 2.5 in. diameter flower petals. Approx. 300 petals.
$9.99

White Rose
1006-U-698

Red Rose
1006-U-695

Lavender Hydrangea
1006-U-879

WEDDING STYLE

Wedding Day Décor

Flameless Votives
Add the romantic glow of candlelight with safe, no flame candles. Includes: 8 flameless votives (with 8 replaceable CR2032 batteries included), 8 holders. Average battery life: 24 hours.
1006-U-7137 Set/8 $15.99

Sparkling Ice
Distinctive table decoration resembles cracked ice and adds beautiful sparkle when placed with candles, around the cake display, on reception tables. 7.1 oz.
1006-U-342 $9.99

Satin Chair Cover
Distinguish wedding party and special guest seating —fits most standard folding and party chairs. Fabric dye changes cover into perfect-colored accents for your wedding day!
1006-U-131 $9.99

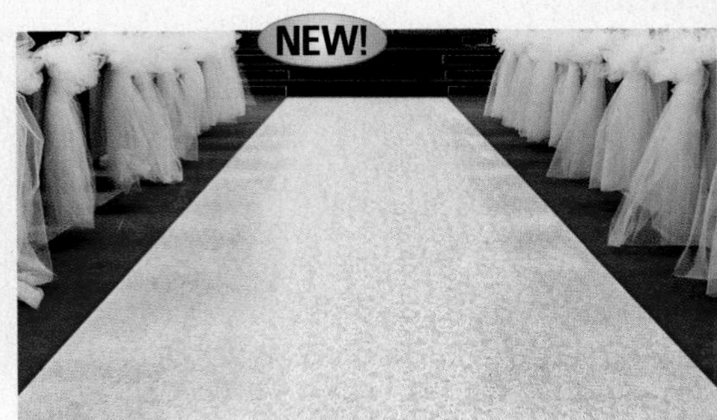

Aisle Runner
Decorate the wedding aisle with a floral runner that adds a touch of elegance to the wedding ceremony. Aisle Runner also ensures that the bride's dress stays clean on the walk down the aisle! With pull cord for even unrolling; runner measures 100 ft. long x 36 in. wide.
1006-U-996 $29.99

BRIDAL GARLANDS
Romantic garland adds a soft glow to your wedding ambiance! You'll find so many uses for the ceremony and reception. Drape on pews and line the aisles, place along table edges and around the cake, wrap around pillars. Lighted garlands are battery operated (uses 2 D Batteries, not included).

Lighted Organza Rose
6 Ft. Length 1006-U-584 $23.99

Lighted White Rose
6 Ft. Length 1006-U-350 $23.99

Rose Garland
Life-like roses strung together by organza ribbon. 6 foot length. Non-lighting.
1006-U-917 $9.99

Car Decorating Kit
Eye-catching decorations trim the bride and groom's getaway vehicle with style! Includes: Magnetic "Just Married" sign, window clings, pre-fluffed pom-poms, streamers, balloons. Crafted of weather-resistant materials, reusable (except balloons).
1006-U-483 $15.79

Celebration Tree
Use it as a party decoration, on the gift table, and as a centerpiece. Easy to assemble. Metal construction. Assembled tree approx. 14 in. high x 11 in. wide. (Favors and decorations shown not included.)
1006-U-571 $9.99

RECEPTION GIFT CARD HOLDERS
Attractively keep the wedding gift cards together at the reception. Tulle, ribbon, flowers and cards not included.

Gift Shape
Whimsical gift box design of sturdy metal construction with faux gem trim, extra long slot for envelopes, box opens from the top, heart-shaped lock and key. 10.75 in. high x 8 in. long x 8 in. deep
120-U-220 $24.99

Bird Cage
After the reception, use as a display for flowers or photos. 12 in. high x 10 in. long x 7 in. deep. White painted wire.
120-U-875 $24.99

Mailbox
Personalize the flag with a photo or saying at www.wiltonprint.com. Includes easy to assemble mailbox, 2 printable labels, 1 test sheet. White printed corrugated cardboard. 12 in. high x 15.25 in. wide x 10.25 in. deep.
1006-U-396 $14.99

Wishing Well
A charming display for any shower, wedding, or anniversary celebration. White printed corrugated cardboard, easy to assemble. 30.5 in. high x 16 in. wide x 14 in. deep.
1006-U-395 $14.99

Favors

Fan Kit

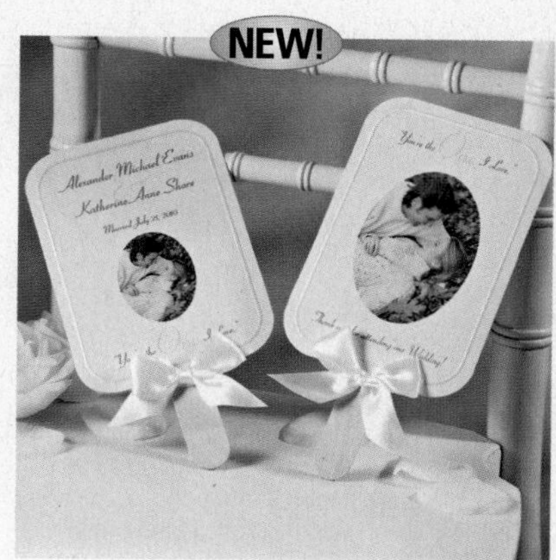

Create a distinctive favor for your special day! Wedding fans not only keep guests comfortable, but let guests wave their approval of the bride and groom! Personalize the fan front and back with photos, special messages, and wedding day details online at www.wiltonprint.com, then print at home. Assembled fan measures approximately 10 in. long. Includes 24 fans, 24 ribbon bows, 24 fan handles, 24 adhesive strips.
120-U-516 Pkg./24 $9.99

Pop Out Streamers

Great for weddings, graduations, birthdays, New Year's celebrations, surprise parties. Just aim and press lever. Each contains ten silver foil streamers that stay attached to tube for easy disposal. Streamers are over 10 feet long. Spring loaded, the streamers do not contain gunpowder or other explosives.
1006-U-932 Pkg./14 $24.99

Large Bling Ring

Makes a big impression as a package tie-on, party favor, napkin ring. Plastic. Measures 3 x 4 in.
1006-U-282 $1.49

Notepad Favors

Perfect as favors and thank you gifts! Matchbook style pads measure 2.75 in. and have 40 sheets.
1006-U-1135 Pk./10 $5.29

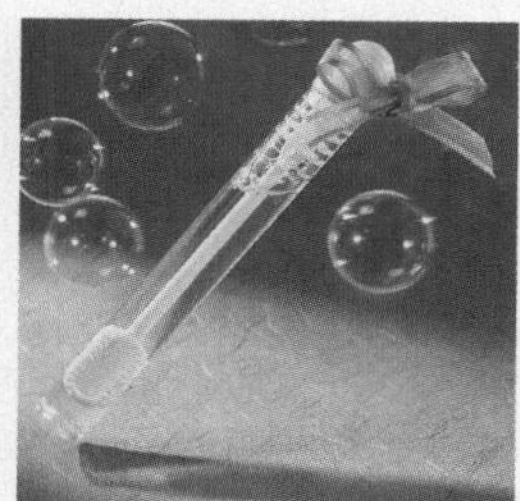

Love Knot Wands

Use after the ceremony or at the reception. 36 wands are packed in a convenient tray for reception table use. Each wand contains .16 fl. oz. bubble solution. Ribbon not included.
1007-U-8017 Pk./36 $9.99

Celebration Bells

Ring for a special kiss after the ceremony and at the reception. Hand to guests exiting the church, and place one at each setting at the reception. Contains 24 metal bells, poem tags and ties. Bell measures 1.25 in. tall.

Silver-tone
1007-U-8012 Pk./24 $6.49
White
1007-U-8013 Pk./24 $6.49

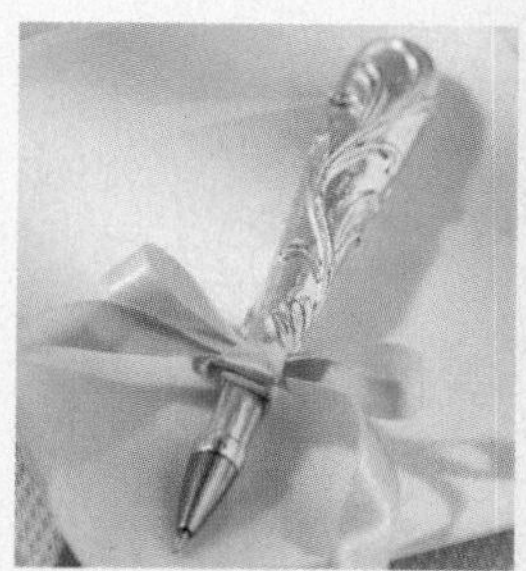

Silver-tone Pens

Perfect as shower, reception, and anniversary favors. Convenient to have on hand for games at showers and parties. Plastic pen. Black ink. Ribbon not included.
1006-U-1008 Pk./6 $9.99

WEDDING STYLE

Favor Accents

Romantic accents add sparkling beauty and elegance to favors, table decorations!

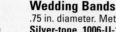

Thank You Tags

Send a message of gratitude —tie to favor boxes or bags. Stamped tin. Measures 1.75 in. diameter.
1006-U-987 Pk./12 $1.99

Sweetheart Charms

Shows the sweet, sentimental sign of love. Stamped tin. Measures 1.25 x .75 in.
1006-U-411 Pk./12 $1.99

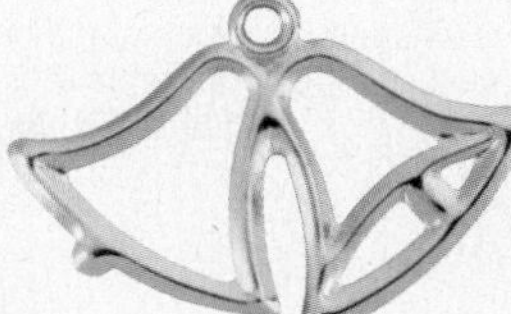

Double Bell Charms

Ring the good news of the bride and groom! Stamped tin. Measures 1.4 x 1 in.
1006-U-1132 Pk./12 $1.99

Love Charms

Spell it out for all to see. Stamped tin. Measures 1.5 in. long.
1006-U-573 Pk./12 $1.99

Glittered Doves

Coated with non-edible glitter. Do not place directly on cake. 2 x 1.5 in.
1006-U-166 Pk./12 $1.99

Engagement Rings

Sparkling favor accents to add beauty to favors, table decorations, centerpieces. "Diamond" measures .25 in. diameter. Metal.
1006-U-115 Pk./12 $1.99

Wedding Bands

.75 in. diameter. Metal.
Silver-tone 1006-U-101 Pk./48 $1.99

Bling Rings

Use these sparkling favor accents to add beauty to favors, table decorations. "Diamond" measures 1 in. diameter. Plastic.
1006-U-919 Pk./12 $5.29

Thank You Tags

Clear oval tags, imprinted in silver are threaded on 11.75 in. organza ribbon lengths. Tie onto favors, wine glass stems, napkins and more.
1006-U-927 Pk./20 $5.29

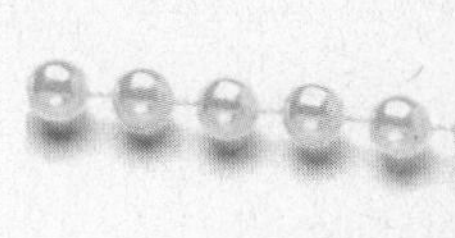

White Pearl Beading

Molded on one continuous 5-yard strand. Plastic.
Large (6 mm)
211-U-1990 $3.99

Favor-Making Kits

Fun and festive kits make it easy to personalize your favors online, at www.wiltonprint.com. Just download the template and print out the tags or labels. Each kit includes instructions and 2 test sheets. Candy not included.

Martini Glass Favor Kit
Create a favor that toasts your guests with a treat and a personalized message. Martini glasses measure 3.5 in. tall. Includes 24 each favor containers, satin ribbons, tulle circles, printable tags.
120-U-518 Pk./24 $24.99

Champagne Bottle Favor Kit
Create a shower or reception favor that toasts your guests with a treat and a personalized message. Bottles measure 4 in. tall. Includes 24 each favor containers, satin ribbons, printable labels.
120-U-519 Pk./24 $24.99

Umbrella Favor Kit
Shower your guests with a favor that carries a personalized message. Use as a place card, add an announcement or a thank you. Umbrellas measure 4 in. tall. Includes 24 each favor containers, satin ribbons, printable tags.
120-U-520 Pk./24 $24.99

Purse Favor Kit
Accessorize the shower or reception with in-fashion purse favors. Fill with your favorite candy, add a personalized tag and place one at each guest's place setting. Purses measure 3 in. long. Includes 24 each favor containers, satin ribbons, printable tags.
120-U-521 Pk./24 $24.99

Flower Favor Kit
Fill these flowers with your favorite candy, add a personalized tag, and plant one at each guest's place setting. Flowers measure 3.3 in. wide. Includes 24 each favor containers, satin ribbons, printable tags.
120-U-522 Pk./24 $24.99

Goblet Favor Kit
Raise the goblet favors and toast the bride and groom! Add a tulle circle, fill with your favorite candy, add a personalized tag and place one at each guest's place setting. Goblets measure 2.75 in. tall. Includes 24 each favor containers, satin ribbons, tulle circles, printable tags.
1006-U-923 Pk./24 $24.99

Heart Favor Kit
Fill with your favorite candy, wrap in the tulle, add a personalized tag to make beautiful favors for bridal shower and wedding reception. Hearts measure 2.5 in. wide x 1 in. deep. Includes 24 each favor containers, satin ribbons, tulle circles, printable tags.
1006-U-924 Pk./24 $24.99

Love Potion Favor Kit
Fill to match your celebration theme and surprise your guests. Bottles measure 2.75 in. high. Kit includes 24 glass bottles with slotted corks. 24 (12 in.) satin ribbon lengths, funnel for easy filling, 24 printable labels. Candy not included.
1006-U-1009 Pk./24 $24.99

Silver-tone Bell Favor Kit
Set a bell at each place setting, guests will ring for the newlyweds to kiss. Bells measure 2.25 in. high. Includes 20 metal favor bells, 20 (12 in.) satin ribbon lengths, 20 printable place cards.
1006-U-1136 Pk./20 $24.99

Favor Tin Kit
Create personalized favor tins for your celebration using your computer, or hand design. Includes 25 tins, 25 adhesive labels and strips. Tins measure 2 in. diameter.
1006-U-8038 Pk./25 $19.99

Favor Containers & Frame

These beautiful containers hold favors for shower, wedding and anniversary celebrations. Perfect for mints, almonds, potpourri and small gifts.

Flirty Fleur Favor Boxes
2.25 in. high x 2.25 in. wide. Paper.
1006-U-936
Pk./10 $4.99

Sweet Heart Ribbon Favor Bags
6 in. high x 3.25 wide x 1.75 in. deep. Includes sheer white ribbon. Paper.
1006-U-940 Pk./10 $4.99

Flirty Fleur Ribbon Favor Bags
6 in. high x 3.25 wide x 1.75 in. deep. Includes sheer white ribbon. Paper.
1006-U-941 Pk./10 $4.99

Simple Yet Elegant Ribbon Favor Bags
6 in. high x 3.25 wide x 1.75 in. deep.Includes sheer white ribbon. Paper.
1006-U-939 Pk./10 $4.99

Tulle Drawstring Sachet Bags
Perfect for favors, rose petals, rice, treats, gifts. Sheer organza fabric pouch closes with a pull of the ribbons. 3.75 x 4 in.
Pk./12 $5.99
White 1006-U-173
Ivory 1006-U-176

Fleur-De-Lis Favor Frames
Insert a favorite photo or use as a place card holder by adding your guest's name. 2.5 in. high x 3.5 in. wide. Silver-tone plastic.
1006-U-376 Pk./5 $5.99

Candy Bar Molds

Create a sweet memory for your guests, a candy bar featuring a special message.

Molding is easy using Wilton Candy Melts® (p. 166). Present them beautifully in Candy Bar Boxes. Each bar measures 3.25 in. wide x 1.75 in. tall x .25 in. deep. 1 design, 4 cavities.
Add-A-Message 2115-U-1356 $1.99

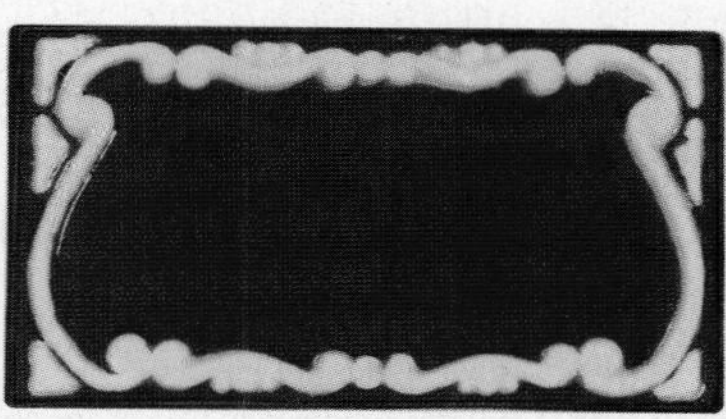

Candy Bar Boxes
The window displays your special message.
Pk./10 $4.19
White 1904-U-1157
Silver 1904-U-1159

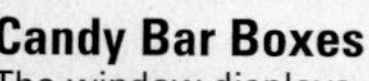

CAKE SLICE BOXES

Favor Cake Boxes
Shaped and decorated like a slice of wedding cake. 20 boxes fit together to form a round cake tier. 4.25 in. long x 2.75 in. high.
1006-U-629 Pk./20 $6.99

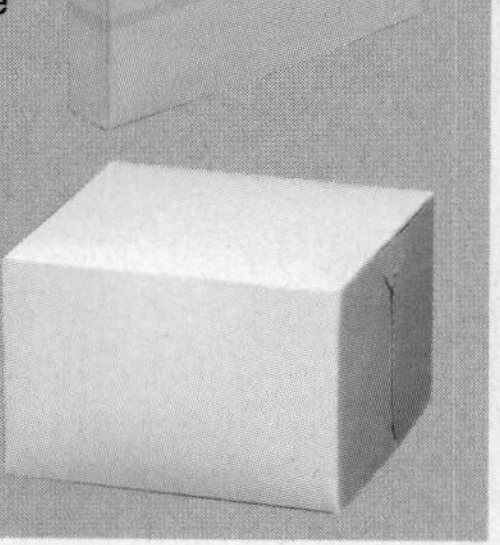

Cake Slice Boxes
Bakery style boxes measure 5 in. square x 3.5 in. high.
415-U-955 Pk./5 $3.89

Favor Candy

Trendy and traditional candies make great fillers for favors and candy dishes at showers, weddings, and celebrations!

NEW!

Classic Doves
Sweet/tart flavored.
12 oz. bag.
1006-U-9052 $6.29

NEW!

Hearts
Sweet/tart strawberry flavored. 12 oz. bag.
1006-U-9053 $6.29

NEW!

Tuxedo Jelly Beans
Fruit flavored.
12 oz. bag.
1006-U-9056 $4.19

NEW!

Pastel Jelly Beans
Fruit flavored.
12 oz. bag.
1006-U-9050 $4.19

NEW!

Peppermint Pearls
10 oz. bag.
1006-U-9401 $4.19

Bling Rings
30 pieces per package. Sweet/tart fruit flavored. Each measures 1.12 in. high x 1 wide.
1006-U-6170 $4.19

Pastel Pearls
Fruit flavored.
10 oz. bag.
Certified Kosher.
1006-U-904 $4.19

Wedding Bells
Sweet/tart flavored.
12 oz. bag.
1006-U-1140 $6.29

Mint Drops
Pastel.
14 oz. bag.
Certified Kosher.
1006-U-788 $6.29

Wedding Message Hearts
Mint flavored.
10 oz. bag.
1006-U-371 $4.19

Jordan Almonds
Certified Kosher.
16 oz. bag. Pastel.
1006-U-779 $7.99
16 oz. bag. White.
1006-U-778 $7.99
44 oz. bag. Pastel.
1006-U-1133 $21.99
44 oz. bag. White.
1006-U-1134 $21.99

Pillow Mints
Pastel.
10 oz. bag.
1006-U-858 $4.19
48 oz. bag.
1006-U-379 $20.99

WEDDING STYLE

Wedding Cakes

From the keepsake figurine on top to the impressive stand below, Wilton has something special just for your wedding cake!

Wedding Toppers

More brides choose Wilton figurines to top their wedding cakes. The rich, sculpted crafting, realistic detailing and romantic designs make these figurines perfect wedding day keepsakes.

NEW!

First Kiss
Height: 6.75 in.
Base: 3 in. diameter.
Bonded Marble.
202-U-258 $24.99

Sweet Couple
Sits on the edge of the cake—perfect when you want a distinctive cake decoration.
Height: 4.25 in.
Base: 1.75 in. Resin.
1006-U-7145 $14.99

Always and Forever Petite Embrace
Height: 3.75 in.
Base: 2.5 in. diameter. Resin.
202-U-311 $21.99

Always and Forever
Height: 6.5 in. Base: 7 x 5 in.
Resin, plastic, fabric.
118-U-200 $37.99

Clear Bianca
Height: 5.5 in. Base: 3.75 x 3.5 in. Acrylic.
Perfect on Lighted Revolving Base.
202-U-424 $24.99

IT LIGHTS!

Lighted Revolving Base
Select just light, just rotate or both at the same time. Uses 3 AA batteries (not included). Height: 2 in. Diameter: 5 in.
201-U-453 $24.99

Elegance
Height: 5.5 in.
Base: 5 x 3 in. Resin.
110-U-863 $34.99

Our Day
Height: 4.75 in.
Base: 2 x 1.75 in. Poly resin.
Blonde/White Gown
202-U-409 $6.99

Threshold of Happiness
Height: 5 in.
Base: 3.25 x 2 in. Resin.
202-U-202 $24.99

With This Ring
Height: 4.5 in.
Base: 3.5 diameter. Resin.
202-U-313 $24.99

Lasting Love
Height: 4.5 in.
Base: 2.25 x 1.75 in. Poly resin.
202-U-302 $6.99

NEW!

MIX & MATCH SINGLE FIGURINES

Decorate your wedding cake top with figurines that reflect your look as a couple.
4.5 in. high. Resin.
$5.99

White Bride
202-U-251

White Groom
202-U-252

Ethnic Bride
202-U-255

Ethnic Groom
202-U-256

Reflections
Porcelain couple. Height: 8 in. Base: 4.75 in. diameter. Plastic, fabric flowers, tulle.
117-U-268 $25.99

Expression of Love
Height: 7.75 in.
Base: 4.5 in. diameter.
Poly resin, plastic, fabric.
101-U-931 $35.99

Simple Joys
Height: 8 in.
Base: 4.5 in. diameter.
Plastic, fabric flowers, fabric.
103-U-150 $24.99

Petite Spring Song
Height: 7 in.
Base: 3.25 in. diameter.
Plastic, fabric flowers.
106-U-159 $12.99

Spring Song
Height: 9.5 in. Base: 4.6 in. diameter. Plastic, fabric flowers.
111-U-2802 $19.99

NEW!

Photo Frame
Holds 5 x 7 in. photo
Height: 7.5 in.
Base: 5.75 in. x 2 in. diameter.
Poly resin, plastic, metal.
120-U-149 $29.99

NEW!

Wedding Gown & Tuxedo
Height: 8 in.
Base: 3 in. diameter.
Metal, fabric.
120-U-491 $24.99

NEW!

Rhinestone Heart Ornament
Height: 8.5 in.
Width 6 in.
Base: 3.75 in. diameter.
Poly resin, metal, fabric.
120-U-204 $24.99

IT LIGHTS!

Castle
Lights from within using 2 D batteries (not included).
Height: 7.5 in.
Base: 4.5 in. Resin.
111-U-2804 $59.99

Inspirational Cross
Height: 5.5 in.
Base: 2 x 1.5 in. Resin.
202-U-398 $14.99

Two Rings
Height: 5.5 in. Base: 3.75 in. diameter. Plastic, resin.
1006-U-1121 $34.99

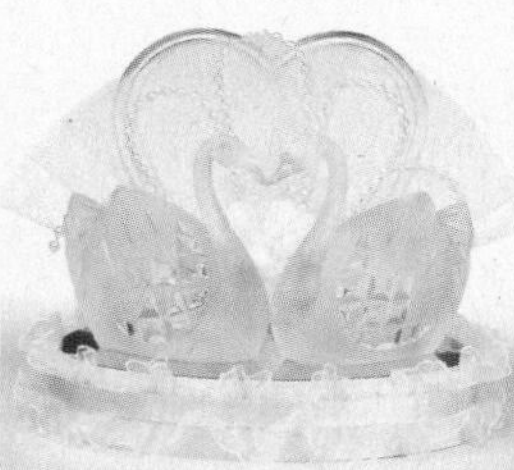

Enduring Love
Height: 5 in. Base: 7 x 5 in. oval. Plastic, tulle.
103-U-235 $35.99

Specialty Toppers

Petite 50th Anniversary
Height: 5.75 in. Base: 3.25 in. diameter. Plastic.
105-U-4273 $9.99

La Quinceañera
Honor her on her 15th birthday celebration. Use as cake top decoration or as a favor. Height: 4.5 in. Base: 2.75 in. diameter. Plastic.
203-U-305 $3.99

HUMOROUS WEDDING FIGURINES

Add a lighthearted touch to the celebration. Sure to bring a smile to the face of anyone who has ever planned a wedding!

Ball and Chain
Height: 2.25 in.
Base: 3.5 in. Resin.
1006-U-7143 $19.99

Oh No You Don't
Height: 4.25 in. Base: 6 x 3 in. Resin.
115-U-102 $19.99 Ethnic 115-U-104 $19.99

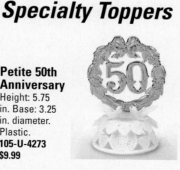

Runaway Bride
Height: 4 in. Base: 3.25 in. Resin.
1006-U-7142 $19.99

Now I Have You
Height: 4.25 in. Base: 4.25 x 3.75 in. Resin.
115-U-101 $19.99

CAKE PICKS

The new look—stunning picks draw attention to your celebration—perfect for cake tops, floral arrangements, bouquets and centerpieces. Beautifully appointed with rhinestones, crafted of painted resin. Approximately 5-5.25 in. high overall, except as noted.

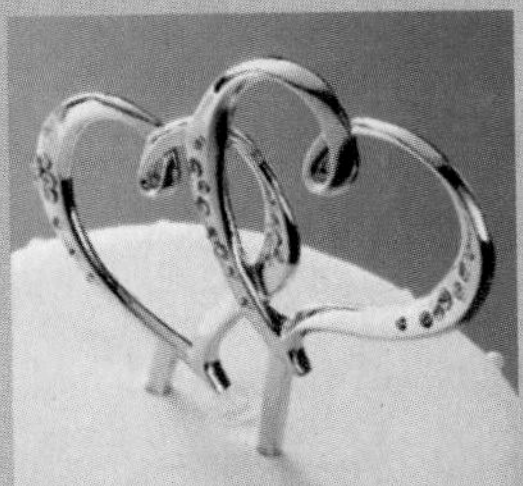

Decorative

Perfect for wedding and anniversary celebrations.

Just Married
2 in. high, 4.25 in. wide.
120-U-025 $14.99

Faith Cross
1006-U-4475 $14.99

Infinity Rings
1008-U-805 $14.99

Double Hearts
1006-U-985 $14.99

Anniversary

Silver 25th
1008-U-758 $14.99

Gold 50th
1008-U-762 $14.99

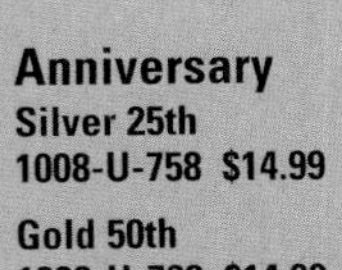

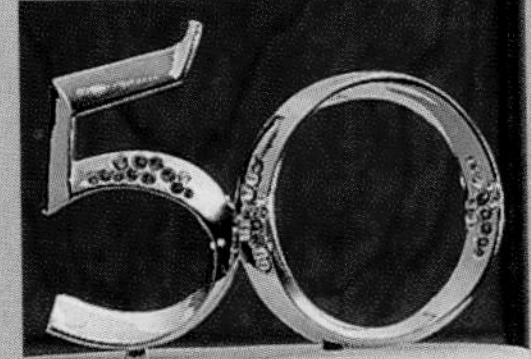

Cake Displays

Stunning Wilton Cake Displays are the perfect way to show off your special wedding cake. Take a look—there's one perfectly suited to your wedding cake size and design.

Fancy Scrolls Cake Stand

The perfect way to display your party cakes or fancy desserts. Slide the two scrolled base pieces together to form the base and place the 12 in. plate on top for a secure cake presentation. After the party, the base pieces easily disassemble and lock into the plate for compact storage.
307-U-854 $14.99

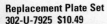

Graceful Tiers Cake Stand

Ideal for garden-themed wedding cakes, but also perfect to display cupcakes, muffins, candies, fruit and more. The three-tiered, scrollwork stand features crystal-clear plates which nest securely in each section. Set includes cream-colored powder-coated metal stand, 14.5 in. wide x 29.5 in. high; 3 clear separator plates, 8, 10 and 12 in. diameter; 1 wrench, all hardware; assembly instructions.
307-U-841 $54.99

Replacement Plate Set
302-U-7925 $10.49

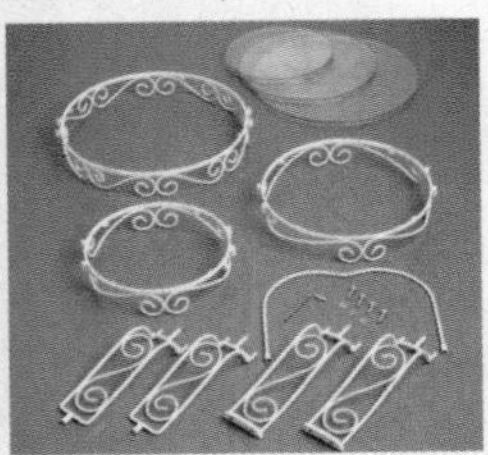

Candlelight Cake Stand

Elegant scrollwork and soft candlelight show off your cake design. Flameless votives are convenient and safe. Stand supports 40 lbs., use with 14 in. smooth or scallop edge separator plate (not included). Set includes 21.5 in. diameter x 5 in. high stand, 4 flameless votives (with 4 replaceable CR2032 batteries included), 4 glass holders. Average battery life: 24 hours.
307-U-351 $44.99

Ceramic Pedestal Cake Stand

Present your cake with elegance on this classic ceramic stand. The white pillar design features a gracefully sculpted base and 12 in. plate. Also use it to serve pies, brownies, cookies, candies and other special desserts. Stand is 4 in. high.
307-U-873 $32.99

Cakes 'N More™ 3-Tier Party Stand

Contemporary stairstep stand with crystal-clear plates puts the focus where it belongs—on your stunning cake and desserts! Constructed in metal with chrome-plated finish, stand holds 3 different size cake plates—8, 10 and 12 in. (included).
307-U-859 $31.49
Replacement Plates Set 302-U-7925 $10.49

FLOATING TIERS CAKE STANDS

The beautiful illusion of floating tiers makes a grand display for your cakes.

Round (Collapsible)

Includes tier support rings, ring support bars, connector bar, 8, 12, and 16 in. separator plates. Assembly required. Instructions and all hardware included. Disassembles for easy storage.
307-U-710 $77.99

Heart (Stationary)

Includes 17 in. high enamel coated white metal stand, 8, 12, and 16 in. Decorator Preferred® Heart Separator Plates and instructions. This is a stationary stand and does not disassemble.
307-U-872 $77.99

Replacement Plates are available at www.wilton.com

NEW!

4-Tier Stacked Dessert Tower

Great way to display cupcakes, appetizers, brownies and other party treats! Four stacking sections with angled tiers for the best view of decorated desserts. Sections easily disassemble and nest for storage; assembled tower is 16.25 in. high x 12 in. wide. Holds 36 standard cupcakes.
307-U-856 $19.99

Collapsible for easy storage

Romantic Castle Cake Set

Create a fairy tale for your wedding. Everything you need to transform your tiered cake into a fantasy castle is included: three sizes of detailed turret towers with removable peak pieces, lattice windows, a paneled door and roof pieces. Complete assembly and decorating ideas included. For design ideas visit **www.wilton.com**!
301-U-910 Set/32 $20.99

CUPCAKES 'N MORE® DESSERT STANDS

Individually decorated cupcakes are the perfect way to add a personal touch to celebrations. Now, with Cupcakes 'N More, you have the perfect way to serve them, featuring wire spirals to securely hold each cupcake.

38 Count Standard
15 in. high x 18 in. wide. Holds 38 cupcakes (shown). **307-U-651 $41.99**

23 Count Standard
12 in. high x 13 in. wide. Holds 23 cupcakes.
307-U-826 $31.49

13 Count Standard
9.25 in. high x 9 in. wide. Holds 13 cupcakes.
307-U-831 $13.69

24 Count Mini
10.5 in. high x 9 in. wide. Holds 24 mini cupcakes.
307-U-250 $15.79

WEDDING CAKES

Cake Assembly Sets

Fluted Bowl Separator Set

Simply fill it with fresh or silk flowers, tulle or patterned fabric, or use it on its own. Setup could not be simpler—spiked separator plates fit inside the top and bottom openings of the bowl for a secure presentation. Set includes 4 in. high fluted bowl and 2 smooth-edge separator plates (6 and 10 in. diameter).
303-U-823 Set/3 $20.99

Globe Pillar and Base Sets

Sophisticated pearl-look globes separate tiered cakes for a dramatic contemporary look. The 2 and 2.5 in. Pillar Sets are positioned between tiers, as globes fit over hidden pillars to provide strong support. The 3 in. Base Set features a reinforced center channel which fits over separator plate feet to hold your base cake. Sets include four globes and four 9 in. pillars. Globe Base Set includes 4 Pillar globe bases.

2 in. Globe Pillar Set 303-U-822 Set/8 $8.39
2.5 in. Globe Pillar Set
303-U-824 Set/8 $10.49
3 in. Globe Base Set
303-U-825 Set/4 $10.49
9 in. Replacement Pillars Set
303-U-4005 Set/4 $4.19

Spiral Separator Sets

Add an elegant touch to your special occasion cakes with these beautifully scrolled separators. The curling, openwork design in white coated metal gives cakes a light, garden style design. Setup could not be simpler—the smooth-edge plates are spiked to fit inside the top and bottom rings for a secure presentation.

10 in. Set
Includes 7 x 4.25 in. high wire separator ring, 2 smooth-edge separator plates, 8 and 10 in. diameter.
303-U-8176 Set/3 $20.99

14 in. Set
Includes 10.5 x 4.25 in. high wire separator ring, 2 smooth-edge separator plates, 10 and 14 in. diameter.
303-U-8175 Set/3 $31.49

Tailored Tiers Cake Display Set

The elegant patterned fabric which covers the foam separators will complement most wedding, shower and anniversary designs and looks wonderful with floral arrangements. As an added bonus, use the included acetate photo wraps to customize the separators with treasured family photos, wrapping paper or an alternate fabric. Set includes 2 satin brocade wrapped craft foam separators (4.25 and 7.25 in. diameter x 2 in. high), 4 smooth-edge separator plates (one 6 in., two 8 in., one 12 in. diameter) and 2 acetate photo wraps.
304-U-8174 Set/8 $31.49

Crystal-Clear Cake Divider Set

Sparkling twist legs push through the cake, rest on plate below and beautifully accent your cake design. (Dowel rods not needed). Includes 6, 8, 10, 12, 14 and 16 in. separator plates, and 24 7.5 in. twist legs.
301-U-9450
Set/30 $52.49

Additional Plates

6 in.
302-U-9730 $3.19
8 in.
302-U-9749 $4.19
10 in.
302-U-9757 $5.29
12 in.
302-U-9765 $7.39
14 in.
302-U-9773 $9.49
16 in.
302-U-9780 $11.59

7.5 in. Twist Legs

303-U-9794
Pk./4 $4.19

9 in. Twist Legs

303-U-977 Pk./4 $5.29

Grecian Pillar and Plate Set

A deluxe money-saving collection for the serious cake decorator. Decorator Preferred® scalloped-edge separator plates and 5 in. pillars. Includes 54 pieces: two each 6 in., 8 in., 10 in., 12 in. and 14 in. plates; 20 Grecian pillars and 24 pegs.
SAVE 27% on set
301-U-8380
Set/54 $52.49

Roman Column Tier Set

Stately Roman pillars and scalloped-edge plates create beautiful settings for all tiered cakes. Includes 8 pieces: six 13.75 in. Roman columns and two 18 in. round Decorator Preferred® separator plates.
301-U-1981
Set/8 $41.99

Arched Tier Set

Includes 14 pieces: Six 13 in. arched columns, two 18 in. round Decorator Preferred® separator plates and six angelic cherubs to attach to columns with royal icing or glue.
301-U-1982
Set/14 $48.29

Tall Tier Cake Stand

Display your multi-tiered cakes up to 6 tiers high with this majestic stand. Lace-look plates enhance every cake design and hold tiers from 6 to 16 in. diameter. The twist-together center columns and strong, interchangeable plates provide stability.

Basic Set

Includes: 5 columns, 6.5 in. high; top nut and bottom bolt; 18 in. footed base plate; 8, 10, 12, 14 and 16 in. separator plates.
304-U-7915 Set/13 $49.99

Replacement Parts

Top Column Cap Nut **304-U-7923 $0.89**
Bottom Column Bolt **304-U-7941 $1.09**

Additional Plates

8 in. **302-U-7894 $4.19**
10 in. **302-U-7908 $5.29**
12 in. **302-U-7924 $6.29**
14 in. **302-U-7940 $9.49**
16 in. **302-U-7967 $12.59**
18 in. **302-U-7983 $15.79**

Additional Columns

6.5 in. **303-U-7910 $2.09**
7.75 in. **304-U-5009 $3.19**
13.5 in. **303-U-703 $5.29**

Glue-On Plate Legs

Convert 14 or 16 in. separator plate to a footed base plate. Order 6 legs for each plate.
304-U-7930 $0.69

Lady Windemere-Look 4-Arm Base

(For Use With Tall-Tier Stand)

Easily adds 4 base cakes to your tall tier cake. The 4-arm base can be used with any plate from the basic set, except the 18 in. footed base plate. Up to 3 graduated tiers can be added to the center columns. Includes 20 in. diameter 4-arm base with 4 stability pegs and base bolt. Use with 13.5 in. column, bottom column bolt and four 12 in. plates, sold above.
304-U-8245 $12.99
Additional Base Bolt
304-U-8253 $0.69

Cake Corer Tube

Essential tool easily and neatly removes center from cake tiers when tall tier stand columns are used. Ice cake before using. Serrated edge removes cake center with one push. Cleans easily.
304-U-8172 $2.19

WEDDING CAKES

Separator Plates and Pillars

Decorator Preferred® Smooth Edge Plates

A fresh, clean edge puts the focus on your cake. Built for unmatched stability, with patented Circles of Strength™ design. Plate feet fit securely on Wilton pillars, available in many styles (p. 229).

6 in.	**302-U-4101**	**$2.39**	14 in.	**302-U-4105**	**$6.29**
8 in.	**302-U-4102**	**$3.19**	16 in.	**302-U-4106**	**$9.49**
10 in.	**302-U-4103**	**$4.19**	18 in.	**302-U-4107**	**$12.59**
12 in.	**302-U-4104**	**$5.29**			

Decorator Preferred® Scalloped Plates

Built for unmatched stability, with patented Circles of Strength™ design.

6 in.	**302-U-6**	**$2.39**	12 in.	**302-U-12**	**$5.29**
7 in.	**302-U-7**	**$2.59**	13 in.	**302-U-13**	**$5.79**
8 in.	**302-U-8**	**$3.19**	14 in.	**302-U-14**	**$6.29**
9 in.	**302-U-9**	**$3.69**	15 in.	**302-U-15**	**$7.39**
10 in.	**302-U-10**	**$4.19**	16 in.	**302-U-16**	**$9.49**
11 in.	**302-U-11**	**$4.79**	18 in.	**302-U-18**	**$12.59**

Decorator Preferred® Heart Plates

Perfectly sized to fit Wilton heart pans, for a stunning tiered heart creation.

8 in.	**302-U-60**	**$3.19**	14 in.	**302-U-63**	**$6.29**
10 in.	**302-U-61**	**$4.19**	16 in.	**302-U-64**	**$9.49**
12 in.	**302-U-62**	**$5.29**	18 in.	**302-U-65**	**$12.59**

Decorator Preferred® Square Plates

Clean lines, smooth edges, unmatched strength. Crafted for today's popular cake designs. Perfectly sized to fit Wilton Square pans.

6 in.	**302-U-1801**	**$3.19**
8 in.	**302-U-1802**	**$4.19**
10 in.	**302-U-1803**	**$5.29**
12 in.	**302-U-1804**	**$6.29**
14 in.	**302-U-1805**	**$7.39**
16 in.	**302-U-1806**	**$10.49**
18 in.	**302-U-1807**	**$13.69**

Crystal-Look Plates

Wilton Crystal-Look plates have an elegance like no other, with ridged sides that look like cut crystal. Use with Crystal-Look pillars (sold below).

7 in.	**302-U-2013**	**$4.19**	13 in.	**302-U-2078**	**$8.39**
9 in.	**302-U-2035**	**$5.29**	* 17 in.	**302-U-1810**	**$15.79**
11 in.	**302-U-2051**	**$6.29**			

*Use only with 13.75 in. Crystal-Look pillars (sold below).

17 in. Crystal-Look Plate and Pillar Set

Contains four 13.75 in. pillars and two 17 in. plates. (not shown)

301-U-1387 $48.29

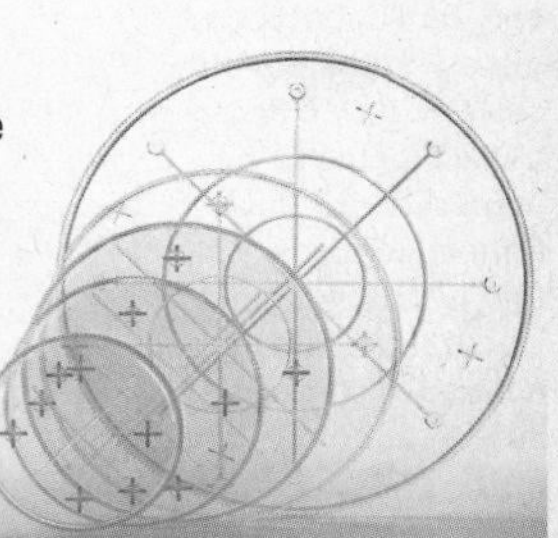

Curved Pillars

Modern, pearlized pillars bring a contemporary look to any classic tiered cake design.

2½ in. **303-U-658 Pk./4 $5.29**
5 in. **303-U-659 Pk./4 $7.39**

"Hidden" Pillars

Separate cake tiers and create a floating illusion. Pushed into tiers as dowel rods, they fit onto all Decorator Preferred® separator plates. Trimmable, hollow plastic. 6 in. high.

303-U-8 Pk./4 $3.19

Grecian Pillars

Elegantly scrolled and ribbed.

3 in. **303-U-3606 Pk./4 $3.19**
5 in. **303-U-3703 Pk./4 $4.19**
7 in. **303-U-3705 Pk./4 $5.29**

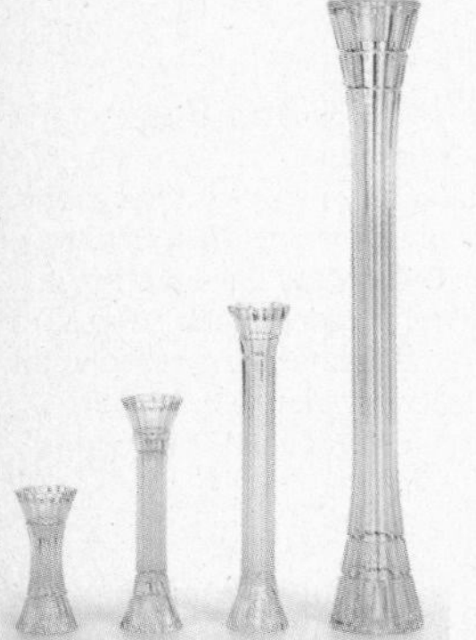

Crystal-Look Pillars

Contemporary cut crystal look.

3 in. **303-U-2171 Pk./4 $3.69**
5 in. **303-U-2196 Pk./4 $4.79**
7 in. **303-U-2197 Pk./4 $5.29**
*13.75 in. **303-U-2242 $4.19**

*Sold singly. Use only with 17 in. Crystal-Look plate (sold above).

Arched Pillars

Grecian-inspired with arched support.

4.5 in. **303-U-452 Pk./4 $4.19**
6.5 in. **303-U-657 Pk./4 $5.29**
13 in. **303-U-9720 Pk./2 $8.39**

Roman Columns

Handsome pillars may be used with 16 and 18 in. plates.

10.25 in. **303-U-8136 Pk./2 $6.29**
13.75 in. **303-U-2130 Pk./2 $7.39**

Baker's Best® Disposable Pillars with Rings

For single plate cake construction.

7 in. **303-U-4000 Pk./4 $3.19**
9 in. **303-U-4001 Pk./4 $3.69**

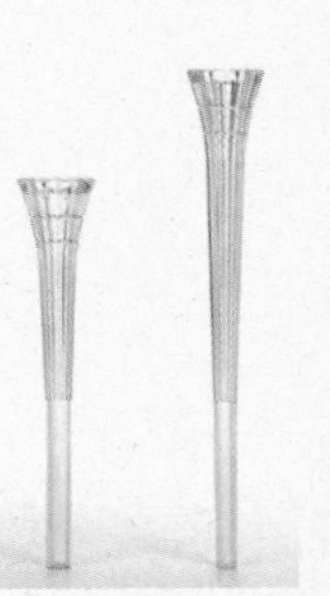

Crystal-Look Spiked Pillars

For single plate cake construction.

7 in. **303-U-2322 Pk./4 $4.79**
9 in. **303-U-2324 Pk./4 $5.79**

Grecian Spiked Pillars

For single plate cake construction. Wide base for increased stability.

5 in. **303-U-3708 Pk./4 $2.59**
7 in. **303-U-3710 Pk./4 $3.69**
9 in. **303-U-3712 Pk./4 $4.79**

Stairways and Bridges

Bridge the gap between lavish tiers.

Crystal Bridge and Graceful Stairway Set
Includes two stairways (16.75 in. long) and one platform (4.75 x 5 in.). Plastic.
205-U-2311
Set/3 $16.49

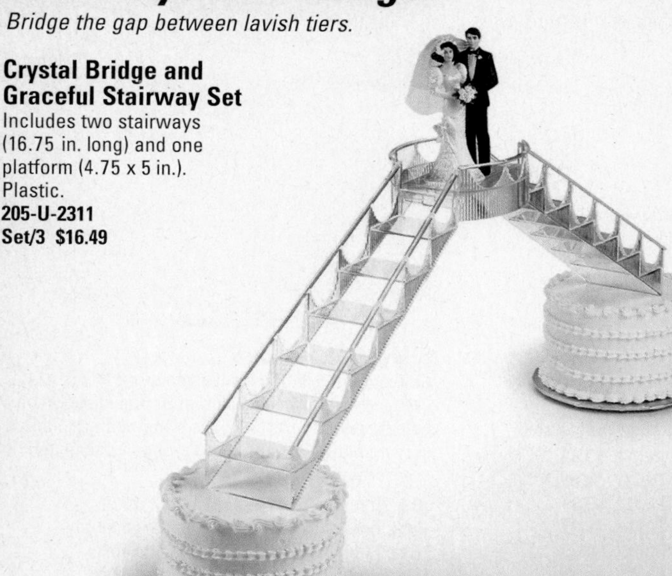

Filigree Bridge and Stairway Set
Includes two stairways (16.25 in. long) and one platform (4.75 x 5 in.). Plastic.
205-U-2109
Set/3 $12.99

Cake Fountains and Accessories

Fanci Fountain
Add the drama of flowing water to your wedding cake design. The crystal-clear design enhances any tiered cake. Adjustable, smooth water flow. Use with 16 or 18 in. scalloped edge plates; or 18 in. smooth edge plate (p. 223). Set-up instructions included. Height: 12 in. Diameter: 10 in.
306-U-2000 $73.49

Replacement Parts for Fanci Fountain are available at www.wilton.com.

Fresh Flower Accessories

Crystal-Look Bowl
4.5 in. diameter. 1.5 in. deep.
205-U-1404 $3.29

Flower Spikes
Fill with water, push into cake, add flowers. Makes cakes safe for insertion of stems or wires. 3 in. high.
1008-U-408
Pk./12 $2.79

Fresh Flower Holders
Insert easily under cake tiers to hold blooms, greenery, pearl sprays, tulle puffs and more. Use with floral oasis to keep flowers fresh.
205-U-8500
Pk./2 $3.29

Flower Holder Ring
Use at the base of Fanci Fountain. 12.5 in. diameter x 2 in. high. 1.75 in. wide opening; inside ring diameter is 8.5 in. Plastic.
305-U-435 $5.49

Dowel Rods and Pegs

Wooden Dowel Rods
Cut and sharpen with strong shears or serrated knife. Length: 12 in. Diam.: .25 in.
399-U-1009 Pk./12 $3.19

Plastic Dowel Rods
Heavy-duty hollow plastic provides strong, stable support. Cut with serrated knife or strong shears to desired length. Length: 12.75 in. Diam.: .75 in.
399-U-801 Pk./4 $2.59

Plastic Pegs
Insure that cake layers and separator plates atop cakes stay in place. Pegs do not add support; dowel rod cake properly before using. Length: 4 in.
399-U-762 Pk./12 $1.49

Cake Boards and Accents

Your cake will look its best when presented with quality Wilton boards, doilies and ruffled trims.

Cake Boards

Shaped cakes look best on boards cut to fit! Strong corrugated cardboard, generously-sized in rectangular shapes. Perfect for sheet and square cakes. For shaped cakes, use the pan as a pattern and cut out board to fit cake.

10 x 14 in. **2104-U-554 Pk./6 $5.29**
13 x 19 in. **2104-U-552 Pk./6 $5.89**

Cake Circles

Corrugated cardboard for strength and stability.

6 in. diameter	**2104-U-64**	**Pk./10**	**$3.59**
8 in. diameter	**2104-U-80**	**Pk./12**	**$4.69**
10 in. diameter	**2104-U-102**	**Pk./12**	**$5.89**
12 in. diameter	**2104-U-129**	**Pk./8**	**$5.89**
14 in. diameter	**2104-U-145**	**Pk./6**	**$6.29**
16 in. diameter	**2104-U-160**	**Pk./6**	**$6.89**

Silver Cake Bases

Convenient .5 in. thick silver-covered bases are grease-resistant, food-safe and reusable. Strong to hold heavy decorated cakes without an additional serving plate. Perfect for all types of cakes and craft creations.

10 in. Round	**2104-U-1187**	**Pk./2**	**$7.99**
12 in. Round	**2104-U-1188**	**Pk./2**	**$8.99**
14 in. Round	**2104-U-1189**	**Pk./2**	**$10.99**
16 in. Round	**2104-U-1190**	**Pk./2**	**$12.99**

Show 'N Serve™ Cake Boards

Scalloped edge has the look of intricate lace. Food-safe, grease-resistant coating.

10 in. diameter	**2104-U-1168**	**Pk./10**	**$4.99**
12 in. diameter	**2104-U-1176**	**Pk./8**	**$5.49**
14 in. diameter	**2104-U-1184**	**Pk./6**	**$5.99**
14 x 20 in. Rectangle	**2104-U-1230**	**Pk./6**	**$6.99**

Ruffle Boards®

Ready-to-use cake board and ruffle in one. Bleached white board and all-white ruffling complement any cake.

8 in. (for 6 in. round cake)	**415-U-950**	**$2.79**
10 in. (for 8 in. round cake)	**415-U-960**	**$3.29**
12 in. (for 10 in. round cake)	**415-U-970**	**$4.49**
14 in. (for 12 in. round cake)	**415-U-980**	**$4.99**
16 in. (for 14 in. round cake)	**415-U-990**	**$5.99**
18 in. (for 16 in. round cake)	**415-U-1000**	**$8.49**

Tuk-'N-Ruffle®

A pretty touch that attaches to edge of your serving tray or board with royal icing or tape.

60 ft. bolt per box.
White **802-U-1008 $16.49**
6 ft. pkg. White
802-U-1991 $3.29

Fanci-Foil

Serving side has a non-toxic grease-resistant surface. FDA-approved for use with food.

Continuous roll:
20 in. x 15 ft.
White **804-U-191 $8.99**
Gold **804-U-183 $8.99**
Silver **804-U-167 $8.99**

Cake Doilies

Add instant elegance to cake plates, dessert trays, entrée and sandwich servings. Use under table centerpieces and plants, for decorations and crafts, too.

Silver Foil

4 in. Round
2104-U-90404 Pk./12 $2.49
6 in. Round
2104-U-90116 Pk./18 $2.49
8 in. Round
2104-U-90006 Pk./12 $2.49
10 in. Round
2104-U-90007 Pk./6 $2.49
12 in. Round
2104-U-90412 Pk./4 $2.49

Gold Foil

4 in. Round
2104-U-90304 Pk./12 $2.49
6 in. Round
2104-U-90306 Pk./18 $2.49
8 in. Round
2104-U-90308 Pk./12 $2.49
10 in. Round
2104-U-90310 Pk./6 $2.49
12 in. Round
2104-U-90312 Pk./4 $2.49

Grease-Proof White

4 in. Round	**2104-U-90204**	**Pk./30**	**$1.99**
6 in. Round	**2104-U-90206**	**Pk./20**	**$1.99**
8 in. Round	**2104-U-90208**	**Pk./16**	**$1.99**
10 in. Round	**2104-U-90210**	**Pk./10**	**$1.99**
12 in. Round	**2104-U-90212**	**Pk./6**	**$1.99**
14 in. Round	**2104-U-90214**	**Pk./4**	**$1.99**
10 x 14 in. Rectangle	**2104-U-90224**	**Pk./6**	**$1.99**

Cake Accents

Romantic accents add a sparkling beauty and elegance to cakes.

White Pearl Beading

Molded on one continuous 5-yard strand. Remove before cutting and serving cake.

Large (6 mm) **211-U-1990 $3.99**

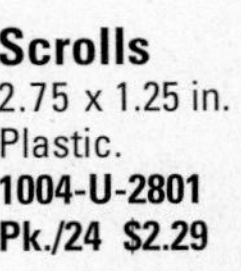

Scrolls

2.75 x 1.25 in.
Plastic.
1004-U-2801
Pk./24 $2.29

Baby

Start planning the party! From pink to blue, and themes in between, this dazzling array of Wilton products will inspire you to make the cutest things for your baby celebration.

Theme Party Products

Give your party personality! See how easy it is to pull your look together with the great selection of Wilton theme products. Find party bags, baking cups, candy molds, cake pans and more—all with the Wilton touch of fun design and detail.

BABY FEET

Waiting for the pitter-patter of little feet was never more colorful or fun!

Invitations
Beautifully designed in white 80 lb. card stock with pastel and white pearlized baby feet embossed trim. Professionally print at home at **www.wiltonprint.com**. 5.5 x 8.5 in. invitations; 5.75 x 8.75 in. envelopes.
1008-U-8135 Pk./12 $4.99

Accents*
Tie on favors and treat bags. Stamped tin, coated in assorted pastel colors. .75 in. diameter.
1003-U-2147
Pk./12 $1.99

Basket
Cutout baby feet decorate the sides of this 4 in. high basket. Coated metal. Candy not included.
1003-U-1042 $1.29

Standard 415-U-113
Mini 415-U-112

Baking Cups
Microwave-safe paper. Standard size, 2 in. diameter, pack 75; mini size, 1.25 in. diameter, pack 100. **$2.09**

Party Bags
Fill with candy, cookies and other goodies. 20 plastic bags, 20 ties included. 4 x 9.5 in.
1912-U-1100
Pk./20 $2.09

Ribbon Favor Bags
Paper bags hold treats and small gifts. Thread the ribbon through the holes at top of bag to close. 2.75 x 4.5 x 1.4 in. Includes 12 ribbon lengths.
1003-U-1053
Pk./12 $5.99

BABY ICONS

From bottles to blocks, adorable baby icons make the party!

Baby Bottle Pan
Here's the formula for a great shower or baby naming celebration—serve a delightful dessert made in this adorable Baby Bottle Pan! Its outstanding detail creates exciting cakes along with molded mousse, gelatin and ice cream. One-mix pan is 13.75 x 7.25 x 2.5 in. deep. Aluminum.
2105-U-1026 $12.99

Cake Server
Whimsical stacked blocks spell out B-A-B-Y on the handle. Crafted in plastic with serrated edge. 10 in. long
1006-U-1312
$5.99

Baby Bottle Garland
The perfect accent for baby showers and celebrations. 8 ft. long. Paper.
1006-U-426 $3.99

Favor Tote Bags
Fill with your favorite baby shower candy or a small gift. Paper bags measure 3 x 2.25 x 5.5 in. Candy not included.
1003-U-1055
Pk./12 $5.99

Favor Boxes
Each box has 2 acetate windows. 2 in. x 2 in. x 2 in. square paper boxes are easy to assemble. Candy not included.
1003-U-1017
Pk./12 $5.99

Baby Blocks Containers*
Removable lids for easy filling. Each 1.25 in. high.
2113-U-419
Set/4 $2.99

Centerpiece
Cute centerpiece is easy to assemble. Paper with ribbon pull. Assembled centerpiece measures 8 x 5 x 14.5 in. high.
1006-U-427 $3.99

Lighted Lantern
Hang for a spectacular effect, or use as table decorations. Uses two AAA batteries, not included. Constructed of paper, plastic, metal. Easy to assemble. 8 x 9 in. wide.
1006-U-423 $4.99

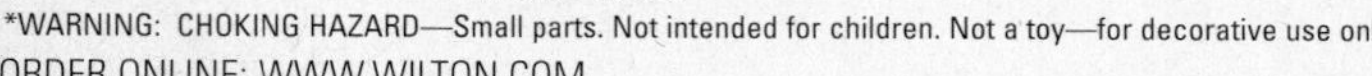

*WARNING: CHOKING HAZARD—Small parts. Not intended for children. Not a toy—for decorative use only.

RUBBER DUCKY

3-D Cake Pan

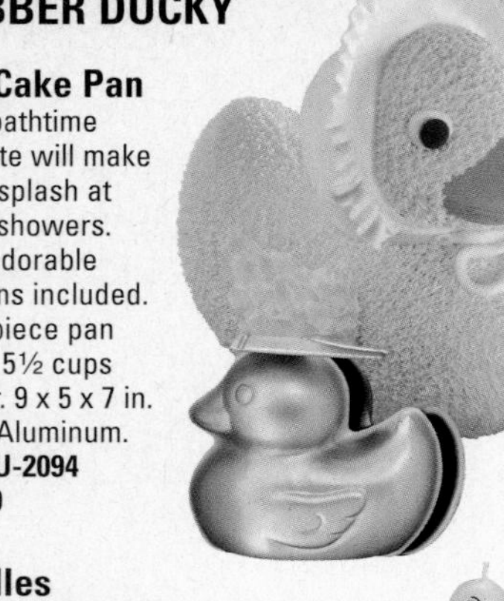

This bathtime favorite will make a big splash at baby showers. Five adorable designs included. Two-piece pan takes 5½ cups batter. 9 x 5 x 7 in. high. Aluminum.
2105-U-2094
$16.49

Candles

Handpainted details, clean-burning design. 1.5 in. high.
2811-U-9337 Set/6 $3.89

Icing Decorations

Mint-flavored edible sugar shapes to decorate cupcakes, cookies, ice cream and cake. Certified Kosher.
710-U-293 Pk./12 $2.29

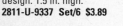

Baking Cups

NEW!

Microwave-safe paper. Standard size, 2 in. diameter, mini size, 1.25 in. diameter.

Ducky Standard
415-U-1016
Pk./75 $2.09
Mini 415-U-1017
Pk./100 $2.09

Rubber Ducky Standard
415-U-378
Pk./50 $1.59

Party Bags

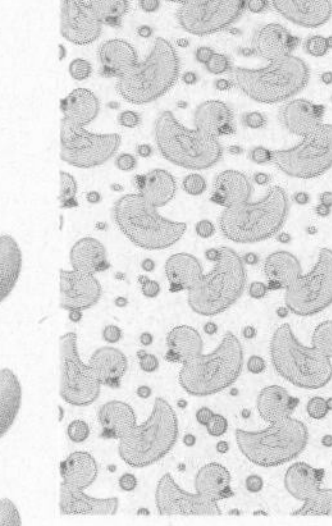

Fill with candy, cookies and other goodies; great for gifts and surprises, too! 20 plastic bags, 20 ties included. 4 x 9.5 in.
1912-U-1275 Pk./20 $2.09

Candy Mold

Complete directions are included. Reusable. Use Wilton Candy Melts®† shown on p. 235. 1 design, 6 cavities.
2115-U-1565 $1.99

†Brand confectionery coating.

NEW!

Guest Book

60 printed pages record guests' names, gifts received and good wishes. Perfect keepsake of the baby shower. 7.6 in x 5.75 in. x 0.3 in.
1003-U-1074 $5.99

FAITH CROSS

Inspiring designs add a beautiful touch to spiritual events.

Stationery

Beautifully designed in white 80 lb. card stock with white pearlized trim. Professionally print at home at **www.wiltonprint.com**.

Thank You Cards
Folded cards with script and cross on front. Card: 5.5 x 4.25 in.; envelope: 5.75 x approx. 4.5 in.
1008-U-776 Pk./12 $4.99

Seals
Self adhesive, silver tone, 1 in. diameter.
1008-U-779 Pk./24 $1.99

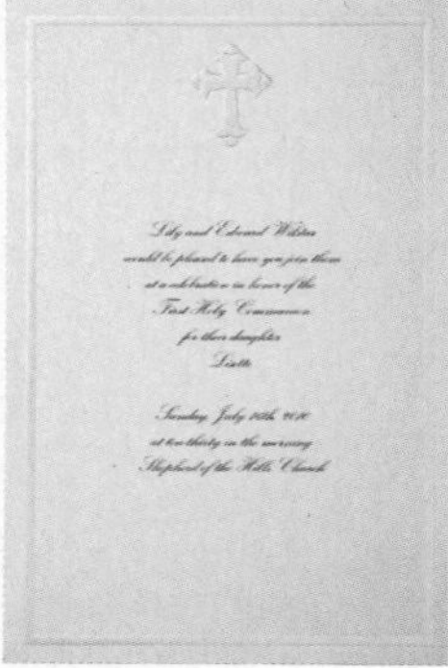

Invitations
White with white border and cross accent. Invitation: 5.5 x 8.5 in.; envelope: 5.75 x 8.75 in.
1008-U-775 Pk./12 $4.99

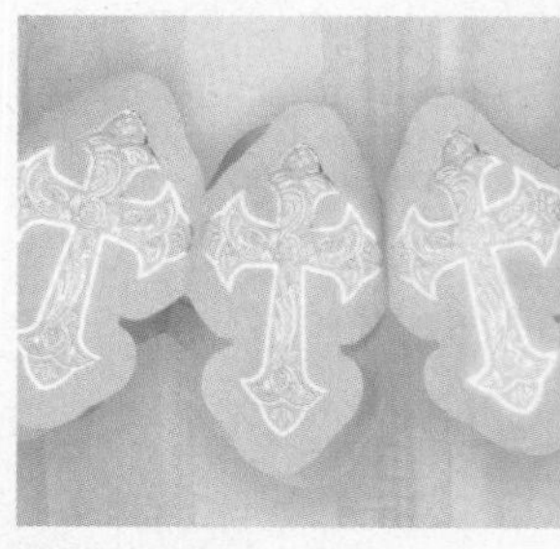

Party Garland

Silver printed crosses on white paper garland. 6 ft. long, accordion folded. Unfold and use tape or ribbon to hang.
1006-U-498 $5.99

Centerpiece

Heavy card stock with honeycomb paper base. Assembled measures 7.75 x 9.75 in. high.
1006-U-7148 $2.99

Announcement Magnets

NEW!

Create a magnetic message to send to family and friends–perfect for baby's special announcements and invitations! Easy to create online at ***www.wiltonprint.com****. Simply print the magnetic sheets, remove the perforated magnetic shapes and send. Includes magnets, mailing envelopes and 3 test sheets.*

Ducky
Printed magnets measure 7.25 x 5.25 in.
3302-U-5523 Set/12 $9.99

Boy Heart
Printed magnets measure 7 x 5 in.
3302-U-5512 Set/12 $9.99

Girl Heart
Printed magnets measure 7 x 5 in.
3302-U-5501 Set/12 $9.99

Shower Accessories

Shower Buttons
Wear a button to let everyone know who's who at the baby shower! 2.5 in. diameter; crafted in metal and paper.
1003-U-1002 Pk./6 $4.99

NEW!

Trivia Coasters
Fun baby shower game—20 clever baby-related trivia questions printed on drink coasters. Play the game and see which guest table has the most correct answers.
1003-U-2501 Pk./20 $5.99

Autograph Mat
Holds a 5 x 7 in. photo, with room for autographs and good wishes from friends and family. Few gifts touch so many like this one! For use in an 11 x 14 in. frame. Pen included.
1009-U-1106 $5.99

Cake Toppers

Baby Face
Oh-so-cute baby tops the baby shower or first birthday cake. 4 in. high; crafted in resin.
1006-U-257 $7.99

Oops!
Designed to top the baby shower cake or decorate the table, this whimsical topper also makes a great keepsake for the mother-to-be! 4.75 in. high; crafted in resin.
1006-U-1331 $7.99

Super Mom-To-Be
Cute cake topper tells it like it is—mom does it all! 4.75 in. high; crafted in resin.
1006-U-259 $7.99

Bakeware

Stork Express
Brings a bundle of joy to showers and baby welcome celebrations as a colorful cake, mousse or glittering gelatin mold. One-mix pan is 13 x 9.5 x 2 in. deep. Aluminum.
2105-U-1191 $12.99

#1
Add the #1 cake to all the important first celebrations. One-mix pan is 12.75 x 8.5 x 2 in. deep. Aluminum.
2105-U-1194 $12.99

Baby Buggy
It's a precious carriage design for shower and christening, for cakes or elegant salads and gelatins. One-mix pan is 11.25 x 11.25 x 2 in. Aluminum.
2105-U-3319 $12.99

Candy Molds

Fun-shaped, reusable molds celebrate baby over and over again. Making candy is easy to do, complete directions are included! Use with Wilton Candy Melts® brand confectionery coating.

Baby Treats
5 designs, 5 cavities.
2115-U-4447 $1.99

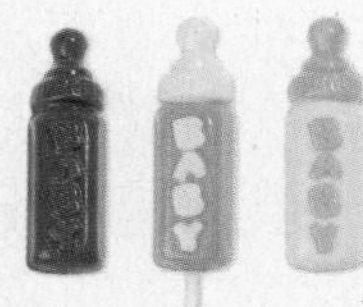

Baby Bottles Lollipop
1 design, 6 cavities.
2115-U-1560 $1.99

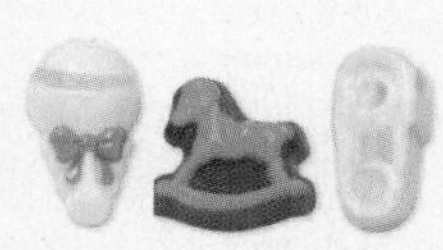

Baby Shower
4 designs, 11 cavities.
2115-U-1710 $1.99

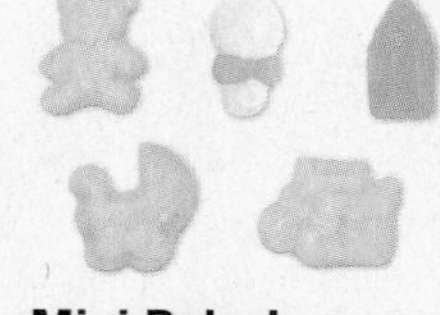

Mini Baby Icons
5 designs, 20 cavities.
2115-U-1537 $1.99

Candy Melts®*
Ideal for molding, dipping or coating. Artificially vanilla flavored unless otherwise indicated. 14 oz. bag. Certified Kosher Dairy. **$2.79**

Orange	**1911-U-1631**	**Yellow**	**1911-U-463**
Dark Green	**1911-U-405**	**Dark Cocoa**	**1911-U-358**
Light Cocoa	**1911-U-544**	**Dark Cocoa Mint**	**1911-U-1920**
White	**1911-U-498**	**Lavender**	**1911-U-403**
Pink	**1911-U-447**	**Blue**	**1911-U-448**

See pages 166-169 for more Wilton candy items.

*Brand confectionery coating.

Favor-Making Kits

Oh-so-cute baby shower favors add so much to the celebration. Conveniently packaged in larger quantities to complete your favor making in no time at all. Personalize the tags at ***www. wiltonprint.com****; it's easy to do, just download the template and print! Use as a place card, add an announcement or a thank you note. All favor containers are food safe. Add your favorite candy (not included), and your favors are ready for the party!*

NEW!

Pacifier Favor Kit
Perfect for fun baby celebrations! Pacifiers measure 2.5 in. long. Multicolor pastel assortment includes: 20 favor containers, 20 ribbons, 20 print-your-own tags, 2 test sheets.
1003-U-1062 Pk./20 $24.99

Rattle Favor Kit
Baby rattles look so sweet at each place setting. Rattles measure 4 in. long. Multicolor pastel assortment includes: 20 favor containers, 20 ribbons, 20 print-your-own tags, 2 test sheets.
1006-U-572 Pk./20 $24.99

NEW!

Umbrella Favor Kit
Shower mom-to-be and your guests with a classic baby shower favor that carries a personalized message. Umbrellas measure 4 in. long. Multicolor pastel assortment includes: 20 favor containers, 20 ribbons, 20 print-your-own tags, 2 test sheets.
1003-U-3134 Pk./20 $24.99

Pail Favor Kit
Perfect for the baby shower, birthday celebration, or garden party. Pails measure 2 in. high with 1.25 in. high handle and are all white. Includes: 18 favor containers, 18 ribbons, 18 print-your-own tags, 2 test sheets. Tulle and safety pin accent not included.
1006-U-916 Pk./18 $24.99
Pail Only 1006-U-915 $1.29 each

Baby Bottle Favor Kit
Mom-to-be will love these adorable favor containers. Bottles measure 4 in. high. Multicolor pastel assortment includes: 24 favor containers, 24 ribbons, 24 print-your-own tags, 2 test sheets. Bear accent not included.
1006-U-577 Pk./24 $24.99
Bottles Only 1006-U-696 Pk./6 $5.99

Baby Block Favor Kit
Favorite baby icon celebrates the big occasion. Blocks measure 1.75 in. square. Multicolor pastel assortment includes: 20 favor containers, 20 ribbons, 20 print-your-own tags, 2 test sheets. Tulle not included.
1006-U-284 Pk./20 $24.99

Favor Finishes

Extras add the finishing touches to baby shower favors.

Drawstring Sachets
Ready to fill with Jordan Almonds, Pillow Mints, small gifts. 3.25 x 3.75 in. high. **Pk./12 $5.99**
Pink 1006-U-179
Blue 1006-U-180

Drawstring Wrappers
They're pre-assembled! Just fill, tie ribbons, and add favor tag. Candy not included. **Pk./12 $12.99**
Pink 1006-U-218
Blue 1006-U-219
White 1006-U-340

Tulle Circles
Sheer tulle circles come in an assortment of pretty pastel shades, perfect for all baby celebrations. Make cute favors, use in centerpieces, decorations and floral arrangements. Contains 5 each pink, lavender, blue, yellow, mint green. 9 in. diameter.
1006-U-288
Pk./25 $2.99

Baby Party Bags
Colorful designs for candy and cookie treats. 20 plastic bags, 20 ties included. 4 x 9.5 in.
1912-U-2365
Pk./20 $2.09

Favor Accents

Add special touches to your baby favors, gift tie-ons and table decorations.

Baby Bracelets*
Pink, blue, yellow, mint green.
1.25 in. high.
1103-U-56
Pk./6 $2.29

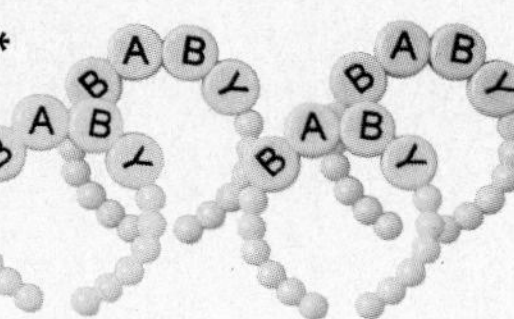

Mini Clothes Pins*
Pink, lavender, blue, yellow, mint green.
1.3 in. high.
1103-U-27
Pk./20 $1.99

Small Safety Pins*
1.5 in. long.
Pk./20 $1.99
Pink 1103-U-21
Blue 1103-U-26
Multicolor
Pink, blue, yellow, mint green.
1103-U-42

Mini Baby Bottles*
Pink, lavender, blue, yellow, mint green. 1.25 in. high.
1103-U-16 Pk./20 $1.99

NEW!

Pacifiers*
Pink, lavender, blue, yellow, mint green.
.75 in. high.
1003-U-1086
Pk./6 $2.99

Baby Bears*
Pink, lavender, blue, yellow, mint green.
1 in. high.
1103-U-46
Pk./6 $2.99

Ethnic Newborn Baby Figurines*
1 in. high.
1103-U-30 Pk./6 $1.99

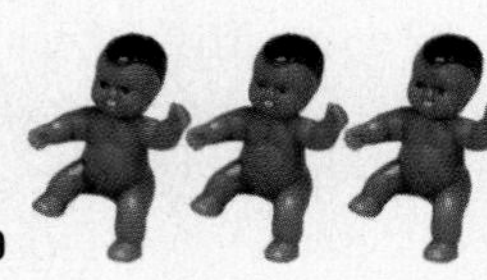

Newborn Baby Figurines*
1 in. high.
1103-U-62 Pk./6 $1.99

Shower Rattles*
Pink, lavender, blue, yellow, mint green.
3.75 in. high.
1103-U-29
Pk./6
$2.99

Mini Rocking Horses*
Pink, lavender, blue, yellow, mint green.
1.25 in. high.
1103-U-52 Pk./6 $1.99

Sleeping Angels Set
A precious pose, one pink and one blue. 2 in. high x 3 in. long.
2113-U-2325
Set/2 $1.99

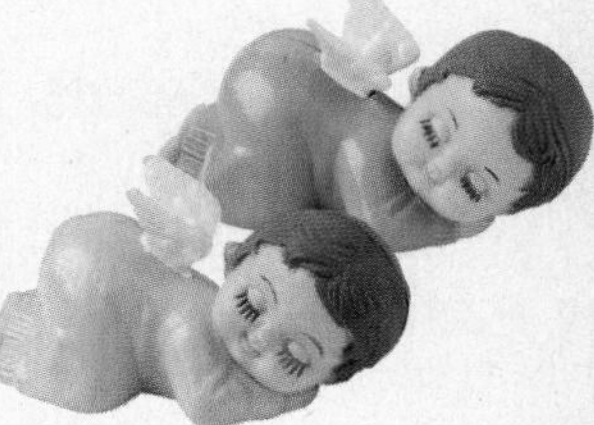

FAVOR TIES

Instant decoration for favors and gifts. Slip one on to close filled bags and tulle favor puffs, or use to decorate any baby favor.

Baby Bottle
Accented with a cute baby bottle.
Pk./6 $2.49
Pink 1006-U-509
Blue 1006-U-508
Multicolor
Pink, lavender, blue, yellow, mint green. **1006-U-575**

Baby Pacifier
Accented with a mini pacifier.
Pk./6 $2.49
Pink 1006-U-566
Blue 1006-U-567
Multicolor
Pink, lavender, blue, yellow, mint green. **1006-U-361**

Favor Candy

Fun shapes, beautiful colors, great flavors! Wilton candy makes the perfect filler for favors, treat bags, candy dishes.

Jordan Almonds
Certified Kosher.
16 oz. bag. Pastel.
1006-U-779 $7.99
16 oz. bag. White.
1006-U-778 $7.99
44 oz. bag. Pastel.
1006-U-1133 $21.99
44 oz. bag. White.
1006-U-1134 $21.99

NEW!

Baby Pins
Sweet/tart flavored.
12 oz. bag.
1006-U-6171 $6.29

NEW!

Pastel Jelly Beans
Fruit flavored.
12 oz. bag.
1006-U-9050 $4.19

NEW!

Baby Buttons
Sweet/tart flavored.
12 oz. bag.
1006-U-9055 $6.29

Mini Pacifiers
Sweet/tart fruit flavored.
12 oz. bag.
1006-U-540 $6.29

Baby Talk
Fruit flavored.
10 oz. bag.
1006-U-1115 $4.19

Mint Drops
Pastel. 14 oz. bag.
Certified Kosher.
1006-U-788 $6.29

Pastel Pearls
Fruit flavored.
10 oz. bag.
Certified Kosher.
1006-U-904 $4.19

Pillow Mints
Pastel.
10 oz. bag.
1006-U-858 $4.19
48 oz. bag.
1006-U-379 $20.99

*WARNING: CHOKING HAZARD—Small parts. Not intended for children. Not a toy—for decorative use only.

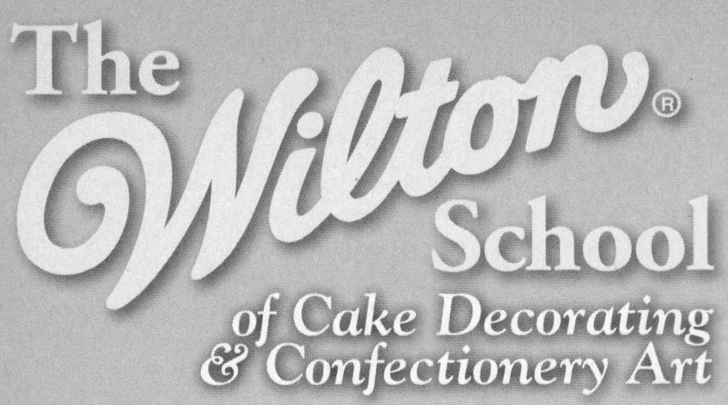

in Darien, Illinois

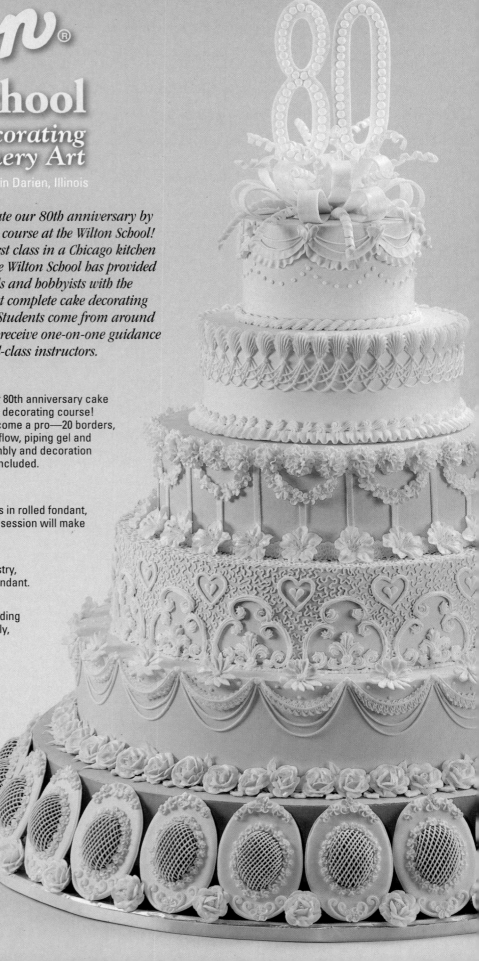

Help celebrate our 80th anniversary by attending a course at the Wilton School! From the first class in a Chicago kitchen in 1929, The Wilton School has provided professionals and hobbyists with the world's most complete cake decorating education. Students come from around the globe to receive one-on-one guidance from world-class instructors.

THE MASTER COURSE
Learn all the beautiful techniques displayed on our 80th anniversary cake and more at the world's most comprehensive cake decorating course! In 2 exciting weeks, students learn the skills to become a pro—20 borders, 15 flowers including The Wilton Rose. Learn color flow, piping gel and figure piping. All of these lead to the design, assembly and decoration of a 3-tiered wedding cake. Virtually all materials included.

SUPPLEMENTARY CLASSES
(available during the Master Course)
Expand your skills with individual specialty courses in rolled fondant, candy making, sugar art and Isomalt design! Each session will make you a more versatile decorator.

EXPLORE OTHER GREAT CLASSES!
Real Tiered Cakes, Lambeth, Advanced Sugar Artistry, Chocolate Inspirations, Advanced Gum Paste & Fondant.

1-DAY WORKSHOPS
Art of Sweet Tables, Floral Arranging for Your Wedding Cakes, Advanced Borders, Wedding Cake Assembly, Cupcakes Galore and more!

CHECK OUT OUR WEEKEND AND BILINGUAL CLASSES!

For class schedules, details and enrollment, visit **www.school.wilton.com**
Or call 630-810-2888 or
800-772-7111, ext. 2888.

Certificate of Approval to operate issued by the Illinois State Board of Education, 100 N. First Street, Springfield, IL 62777.

Celebrating 80 Years!

INDEX

BE SURE TO SEE...

You'll find dozens of new products and designs in the 2009 Wilton Yearbook. Here are a few we think you'll find particularly exciting!

PRODUCT SHOPS

GENERAL PRODUCT

Cake Decorating Supplies

Candy Making Supplies

Cookie Making Supplies

Fondant and Gum Paste Supplies

Icing Supplies

Instructional

Toppers, Figurines & Sets

Party Favors & Accessories

Stands

Wedding, Tiered Cake Supplies

BAKEWARE

Numbers in parentheses indicate pages for designs using these pans.

Classic Bakeware

Mini Pans

Also see Seasonal and Stand-Up/3-D Pans.

Novelty Pans

Seasonal Pans

Silicone Bakeware, Molds, Tools

Stand-Up/3-D Pans

Tiered Pan Sets

LICENSED PANS & THEMES

PARTY THEMES

*Brand confectionery coating.

NEW!

The tools you need